Brains Confounded by the Ode of Abū Shādūf Expounded

Letter from the General Editor

The Library of Arabic Literature series offers Arabic editions and English translations of significant works of Arabic literature, with an emphasis on the seventh to nineteenth centuries. The Library of Arabic Literature thus includes texts from the pre-Islamic era to the cusp of the modern period, and encompasses a wide range of genres, including poetry, poetics, fiction, religion, philosophy, law, science, history, and historiography.

Books in the series are edited and translated by internationally recognized scholars and are published in parallel-text format with Arabic and English on facing pages, and are also made available as English-only paperbacks.

The Library encourages scholars to produce authoritative, though not necessarily critical, Arabic editions, accompanied by modern, lucid English translations. Its ultimate goal is to introduce the rich, largely untapped Arabic literary heritage to both a general audience of readers as well as to scholars and students.

The Library of Arabic Literature is supported by a grant from the New York University Abu Dhabi Institute and is published by NYU Press.

Philip F. Kennedy
General Editor, Library of Arabic Literature

هزّ القحوف

بشرح قصيد أبي شادوف

يوسف الشربينيّ

المجلّد الأوّل

Brains Confounded by the Ode of Abū Shādūf Expounded

Yūsuf al-Shirbīnī

Volume One

Edited and translated by
Humphrey Davies

Volume editors
James E. Montgomery
Geert Jan van Gelder

NEW YORK UNIVERSITY PRESS
New York

NEW YORK UNIVERSITY PRESS
New York

Library of Congress Cataloging-in-Publication Data
Names: Shirbini, Yusuf ibn Muhammad, active 1665-1687, author. | Davies, Humphrey T. (Humphrey Taman), editor translator. | Shirbini, Yusuf ibn Muhammad, active 1665-1687. Hazz al-quhuf fi sharh qasid Abi Shaduf. English. | Shirbini, Yusuf ibn Muhammad, active 1665-1687. Hazz al-quhuf fi sharh qasid Abi Shaduf.
Title: Brains confounded by the ode of Abu Shaduf expounded / Yusuf Ibn Muhammad Ibn Abd al-Jawad Ibn Khidr al-Shirbini; edited and translated by Humphrey Davies.
Description: New York : New York Univeristy Press, 2016. | In English with orginal Arabic text. | Includes bibliographical references and index.
Identifiers: LCCN 2016006848 (print) | LCCN 2016008844 (ebook) | ISBN 9781479882342 (cl : alk. paper) | ISBN 9781479838905 (cl : alk. paper) | ISBN 9781479822362 (e-book) | ISBN 9781479888252 (e-book) | ISBN 9781479809721 (e-book) | ISBN 9781479892389 (e-book)
Subjects: LCSH: Villages--Egypt--Early works to 1800. | Egypt--Rural conditions--Early works to 1800. | Social problems in literature--Early works to 1800. | Satire, Arabic--Egypt--Early works to 1800. | Arabic literature--Egypt--Early works to 1800.
Classification: LCC HN786.A8 .S5513 2016 (print) | LCC HN786.A8 (ebook) | DDC 307.760932--dc23
LC record available at http://lccn.loc.gov/2016006848

New York University Press books are printed on acid-free paper, and their binding materials are chosen for strength and durability.

Series design by Titus Nemeth.

Typeset in Tasmeem, using DecoType Naskh and Emiri.

Typesetting and digitization by Stuart Brown.

Manufactured in the United States of America
c10 9 8 7 6 5 4 3 2 1

Table of Contents

Letter from the General Editor iii

Introduction xi

Note on the Text xlvii

Notes to the Introduction lii

Part One 1

The Author Describes the Ode of Abū Shādūf 4

The Author Embarks on a Description of the Common Country Folk 16

- An Account of a Few of Their Names, Nicknames, and *Kunyah*s 22
- Their Children 28
- Their Women during Intercourse 30
- Their Weddings 30

An Account of Their Escapades 38

- Anecdotes Showing that a Man Cannot Escape His Inborn Nature 38
- Anecdotes Showing the Stupidity of Country People 46
- Accounts of What Happened to Peasants Who Went to the City 68
- The Peasant Who Attended the Friday Prayer in a Village by the River 74
- The Tale of the Three Whores of Cairo 78
- Anecdotes Concerning Country People Who Went to the City and Were Overtaken by the Need to Relieve Themselves, Etc. 86
- The Tale of the Champions of Discourtesy of Cairo and Damascus 92
- The Tale of the Boors of Cairo and Damascus 96
- More Anecdotes Illustrating the Stupidity of Country People 98
- Anecdotes about Country People Who Voided Their Prayers 104

An Account of Their Pastors and of the Compounded Ignorance, Imbecility, and Injuries to Religion and the Like of Which They Are Guilty 112

- The Tale of the Persian Scholar 114

Sermons by Country Pastors 120
Further Anecdotes Showing the Ignorance of Country Pastors 122
Funayn's Letter and Another Missive 138
An Account of Their Poets and of Their Idiocies and Inanities 148
The First of Their Verses: "My shirt kept trailing behind the plow" 148
The Second of Their Verses: "And I said to her, 'Piss on me and spray!'" 166
The Verse of Shaykh Barakāt: "Barakāt was passin' by" 182
The Third of Their Verses: "By God, by God, the Moighty, the Omnipotent" 188
The Fourth of Their Verses: "The soot of my paternal cousin's oven is as black as your kohl marks" 196
The Fifth of Their Verses: "I asked after the beloved. They said, 'He skedaddled from the shack!'" 214
The Sixth of Their Verses: "The rattle staff of our mill makes a sound like your anklets" 230
The Seventh of Their Verses: "I saw my beloved with a plaited whip driving oxen" 244
It Now Behooves Us to Offer a Small Selection of the Verse of Those Who Lay Claim to the Status of Poets but Are in Practice Poltroons, and Who Make Up Rhymes but Are Really Looney Tunes 262
Verses by al-Amīn 262
Verses by Murjān al-Ḥabashī 264
Verses by a Turkish Judge 274
Verses by Shaykh Muḥammad al-Rāziqī 274
Elegy by a Certain Dim-Witted Poet to the Emir Ibn al-Khawājā Muṣṭafā 276
A Chronogram 282
An Account of Their Ignorant Dervishes and of Their Ignorant and Misguided Practices 286
The Practices of the Khawāmis Sect 286
Anecdotes Showing the Ignorance of Country Dervishes 304
More Anecdotes Showing the Beliefs and Practices of Heretical Dervishes 308
Urjūzah Summarizing Part One 344

Notes 371
Index 414
About the NYU Abu Dhabi Institute 426
About the Typefaces 427
Titles Published by the Library of Arabic Literature 428
About the Editor–Translator 430

To Kristina Nelson and Clare and James Davies

Introduction

The Author

Yūsuf ibn Muḥammad ibn ʿAbd al-Jawād ibn Khiḍr al-Shirbīnī was either unknown to or ignored by the biographers of his generation, and no trace of his presence has yet been discovered in Egyptian archives. Our knowledge of him is therefore dependent on what can be gleaned from his literary works, for which we have three titles. The first is that of the work for which he is best known and which is presented in this volume, namely, *Brains Confounded by the Ode of Abū Shādūf Expounded* (*Hazz al-quḥūf bi-sharḥ qaṣīd Abī Shādūf*), hereafter *Brains Confounded.* The second and third titles are *The Pearls* (*Al-La'ālī' wa-l-durar*) and *The Casting Aside of the Clods for the Unstringing of the Pearls* (*Ṭarḥ al-madar li-ḥall al-la'ālī' wa-l-durar*). The second and third titles, however, both appear to refer to the same work: a short homiletic tract, whose most notable feature is that it was written using only undotted letters.

The author refers to Shirbīn as "my town" (vol. 2, §§11.7.9 and 11.37.7) and "our village" (vol. 2, §11.9.2), and it can be assumed that he was born there, in what was, at the time, a significant rural center on the eastern branch of the Nile, in the province of al-Gharbiyyah.[1]

The earliest date in *Brains Confounded* is 1066/1655–56, al-Shirbīnī stating that, at that time, he was living in Dimyāṭ (Damietta), a port on the estuary of the eastern branch of the Nile, some thirty miles northeast of Shirbīn; Dimyāṭ was Egypt's second city during the Ottoman period (§7.32). His reference to his having witnessed certain public events in that city implies that al-Shirbīnī lived there as an adult, say, over the age of twenty. He was thus probably born no later than (and possibly well before) 1046/1636–37.

In 1069/1659, the noted scholar Aḥmad Shihāb al-Dīn ibn Salāmah al-Qalyūbī, whom al-Shirbīnī refers to as "our shaykh" (§4.3), that is, his teacher, died. In all likelihood, therefore, al-Shirbīnī had moved to Cairo before that date and become a student at the mosque-university of al-Azhar.[2] According to al-Muḥibbī, al-Qalyūbī was "a compendium of the religious sciences and thoroughly at home with the rational sciences"; he was also skilled at and practiced in medicine.[3] In *Brains Confounded,* al-Shirbīnī demonstrates acquaintance with medical literature (e.g., vol. 2, §§11.15.7, 11.20.9, 11.23.6) and at least passing acquaintance with other rational sciences, such as physics (vol. 2, §11.7.38) and time-keeping (§5.9.24).

Five years later, in 1074/1664, al-Shirbīnī made the pilgrimage to Mecca (vol. 2, §11.1.3), and he did the same the following year (vol. 2, §11.13.2). These trips may have been made possible by the income derived from a new profession: in 1077/1666–67 the author received a letter sent to him at the book market that speaks of him as a bookseller (§4.38.1). Elsewhere, al-Shirbīnī makes use of an anecdote apparently current in the book trade (§4.15).

Al-Shirbīnī also mentions that, when on pilgrimage and waiting for a ship in al-Quṣayr, on the Red Sea coast, he "stayed for a few days at a hostel on the sea, preaching to the people" (vol. 2, §11.1.3), though he does not indicate that he did so for money or that this was an occupation he followed on a regular basis.

Al-Shirbīnī states that, on one occasion, a heretical dervish failed to recognize that he was a man of knowledge because he was, at the time, "occupied in the craft of weaving and so on" (§7.8). Weaving was a craft that was held in low esteem,[4] and weavers were proverbial for their stupidity;[5] thus the contrast would have struck his readers as funny. This does not, however, mean that al-Shirbīnī made this claim simply for the sake of a somewhat arbitrary joke.

The date of greatest relevance to *Brains Confounded,* and that which establishes the *non ante quem* for its completion, is 1 Jumādā al-Ūlā 1097/26 March 1686, the death date of Aḥmad ibn ʿAlī l-Sandūbī. The author refers to the latter early in the book without naming him, referring to him only as the commissioner of the work and as "one whom I cannot disobey and with whose commands I have no choice but to comply" (§1.1).[6] In the poem that closes the book, al-Shirbīnī makes this reference explicit but speaks of al-Sandūbī in the past tense and includes prayers for his soul (vol. 2, §13.2). One deduces that al-Sandūbī died between the commissioning of the work and its completion. That al-Shirbīnī was still in Cairo at this time is evident from his comment in *Brains Confounded* that "there is no place like Cairo . . . and praise be to God that here I reside" (§§8.44–45).

Prayers in the prologue to *The Pearls* for Ḥamzah Bāshā, viceroy of Egypt from 1094/1682 to 1098/1686, show that it was at this period that al-Shirbīnī also wrote this, his likely only other extant, work.

Finally, a note added by the copyist of one manuscript of *Brains Confounded* states that the author "perished" in 1111/1699–1700[7] (at an age of not less than fifty-four, if our calculations are correct). However, this claim is undocumented and the manuscript itself is described as being "quite new."[8]

Shirbīn appears to have been, in al-Shirbīnī's day as now, a rural center serving the administrative and economic needs of the surrounding villages. Al-Shirbīnī makes it clear, however, that he is not of peasant stock, stating that "we thank God that he has relieved us of farming and its woes; it was never our father's or our grandfathers' occupation" (vol. 2, §11.10.6). When he mentions in passing (and somewhat jocularly) that he married a peasant woman (vol. 2, §11.2.16), he both confirms his closeness to the world of the peasants and his distance from it.

In keeping with its status as a town of some standing, Shirbīn was also a recognized contributor to the literary and religious culture of the day, with biographers recording at least three noted scholars or Sufis from the town in the generations before Yūsuf was born.[9] Al-Shirbīnī boasts that it is "a town of pride in rank / And brains, whose fame all men do hymn" (vol. 2, §11.37.7) and elsewhere refers to it as being "great among cities." He also refers in passing to the fact that Shirbīn was, in his day, sufficiently sophisticated to support *udabāʾ* ("men of letters") who wrote witty verse (vol. 2, §11.31.16). Among these was al-Shirbīnī's own father, to whom he attributes verses replete with "elegant simile and orthographic wordplay" (§7.40). Even after moving to Dimyāṭ and then Cairo, he probably kept up contacts with Shirbīn: he narrates, for example, an (undated) adventure that befell him while traveling up the Nile, from Shirbīn to Cairo (vol. 2, §11.7.9).

While al-Shirbīnī apparently failed to attract the attention of his contemporaries for his learning or, apparently, to attain any post in a teaching or other religious institution, the acquaintance with Qurʾanic exegesis (*tafsīr*), prophetic Traditions (*ḥadīth*), jurisprudence (*fiqh*), literature, philology, medicine, and other sciences that he displays throughout *Brains Confounded* demonstrates that he was a man of broad culture, familiar with both the religious and secular sciences of his time. This familiarity was no doubt due partly to his education (and in particular to his contact with al-Qalyūbī) and partly to his profession as a bookseller. On this evidence, he must have qualified, if not as a full-blown scholar (*ʿālim*), then at least as one of the "men of culture" (*ahl al-adab*) who, while not attached to any institution of learning, had a recognized place within such critical cultural institutions as the *majlis* ("literary gathering or salon").[10]

There he would have hobnobbed with scholars and other members of the religious and intellectual establishment—a point al-Shirbīnī seems to be at pains to make when he mentions that he once heard an anecdote from "a noble *sharīf* [descendant of the Prophet Muḥammad] in al-Maḥallah al-Kubrā, at the house of the Learned Shaykh ʿAbd al-Ḥaqq al-ʿAbdillāwī" (§7.29). It would, no doubt, have been for this milieu that he produced other work that he either quotes from in *Brains Confounded*, such as his occasional verse (see, e.g., §5.3.16) and a short comic sermon on edibles (vol. 2, §11.25.7–13), or that he refers to there in passing, such as the treatise entitled *Riyāḍ al-uns fī-mā jarā bayn al-zubb wa-l-kuss* (*Meadows of Intimate Vim concerning What Transpired ʻtwixt the Prick and the Quim*) (vol. 2, §11.4.10) and another, untitled, on peasant nuptials (§2.26.2).

Baer believes that al-Shirbīnī earned his living as a moneylender (*muʿāmil*) "or at least this was the occupation of the family or social group to which he belonged."[11] There are indeed references in *Brains Confounded* to moneylenders and their trade, usually in the form of complaints about their mistreatment by peasants (e.g., §8.5 and vol. 2, §11.6.5). The text, however, contains no positive statement that moneylending was, in fact, al-Shirbīnī's profession, while explicit references, noted above, refer to other occupations.

Early in the work, a note of disillusionment is struck, the author identifying himself with plaints attributed to al-Būṣīrī, al-Maʿarrī, and others against the neglect of the talented and eloquent in favor of "billy goats" and "pimps and clowns" (§1.4). The result, according to the author, is that "in this age of ours, none survive but those possessed of a measure of buffoonery and profligacy and frivolity and effrontery" (*idem*) and that he "who cannot pen a line is blessed with a living fine, while the master of wit sees of victuals not a whit" (*idem*).[12] A similarly bitter note is sounded in the closing passages of the book (vol. 2, §§12.18–19). Such statements may be to some degree conventional and are also self-serving in that they preempt, with an implied plea of poverty, objections to the author's undertaking of an exercise that, by his own admission, is not without "license and buffoonery" (§1.4). Nevertheless, they appear also to carry conviction.

Despite, or perhaps because of, his low scholarly profile, al-Shirbīnī reveals a lively sense of his right and duty, as a "man of knowledge," to intervene when necessary in defense of true religion. As already noted, al-Shirbīnī recounts how once a heretical dervish who had been filling the head of "one of the eminent" with blasphemies "had no idea that I was a man of knowledge because, at the time, I was occupied in the craft of weaving." Undeterred, or perhaps even galvanized, by this failure to recognize his status, al-Shirbīnī then approaches the dervish, knife in hand, striking terror into him; subsequently he explains to the heretic's victim "how things were and showed him what was truth and what a slur" (§7.8). Elsewhere, al-Shirbīnī mentions that a man whose performance of the prayer was blasphemous "repented at my hand and the Almighty rescued him from error and brought him to right guidance" (§7.36). Similarly, al-Shirbīnī takes pride in putting in their place those who lay false claim to an understanding of grammar, as when he corrects someone whose ignorance of basic semantics was such that he "couldn't tell the name from the thing cited," with the result that "after all the pretension and bluster, he followed me as a sheep its master and submitted in his comings and goings to my sway" (vol. 2, §11.1.3).

The ambiguities inherent in al-Shirbīnī's status as an educated man with no clear position in the scholarly establishment and a declared grievance against his lack of recognition may have made him eager to accept a prominent scholar's request for a book praising the educated elite and mocking the pretensions of outsiders.

The Work

Brains Confounded hails from an underdocumented and understudied period of Egypt's history. The work thus derives part of its importance from its status as a rare witness to an obscure period. This importance is increased by the even greater scarcity of material on its primary topic, the countryside.[13] Indeed, the author's preoccupation with the latter as a cultural, social, economic, and religious site in its own right is probably unique in pre-twentieth-century Arabic literature (and unusual in any pre-twentieth-century scholarly literature).[14] Furthermore, as passages placed in the mouths of peasants are largely in colloquial, the Arabic text provides a rich source for the history of the Egyptian dialect. Last, but by no means least, the book merits attention as an unconventional work of literature, full of mordant wit, cantankerous verve, and elegant displays of satirical and parodic talent.

Part One of *Brains Confounded* consists of an extensive and highly critical survey of rural society, organized into three groups: the peasant (and above all the poor peasant) cultivator (*fallāḥ*); the rural man of religion (*faqīh*); and the mendicant rural dervish (*faqīr*). Other sections in Part One present and critique verses that are ascribed to rural poets or, more generally, to "poltroons" who, while not of rural origin, apparently demonstrate a similar capacity to write bad verse. In Part One, the author seeks to demonstrate, and deride, the ignorance, dirtiness, stupidity, and moral turpitude of the people of the countryside and associate these with the inability to write acceptable poetry.

Part Two is constructed around a forty-seven-line "ode" (*qaṣīd*) supposedly written by a peasant named Abū Shādūf, the ode itself being preceded by an account of the poet's birth and fortunes, as described in the work of other poets of his milieu. Each line of the ode is subjected to extensive commentary (which often digresses to matters felt by the author to be relevant) and the ode closes with "miscellaneous anecdotes," many of which are at the expense of grammarians.

This carefully constructed work depends for its comic impact on two conceits. The first is that the "Ode" and other verses ascribed by the author to peasants are indeed of rural origin and represent actual rural literary production. However, the assertion that the "Ode of Abū Shādūf" and its like are the work of real rural poets is untenable in view of the patently satirical nature of the work as a whole and of the indignities and crimes that "Abū Shādūf" and his peers attribute to themselves in the poems. It is difficult to imagine, for example, that a genuine peasant poet would describe himself as lice- or nit-ridden (vol. 2, §11.2), as defecating upon himself from fear (vol. 2, §11.6), as farting like a loud drum (vol. 2, §11.7), or as stealing slippers from mosques (vol. 2, §11.38). This is the stuff of satire, not self-description. Rejection of the attribution of such verses to real rural poets requires, in turn, the recognition that they were in fact written with the express purpose of being satirized, a supposition that may gain strength from the recent discovery of Muḥammad ibn Maḥfūẓ al-Sanhūrī's *Risible Rhymes* (*Muḍḥik dhawī l-dhawq wa-l-niẓām fī ḥall shadharatin min kalām ahl al-rīf al-ʿawāmm*), a title more literally translated as *Book to Bring a Smile to the Lips of Devotees of Taste and Proper Style through the Decoding of a Sampling of the Verse of the Rural Rank and File*,[15] a work written some forty years before *Brains Confounded* that contains a treatment of some of the same material.

The second conceit is that the "Ode of Abū Shādūf" and its like merit the use of the tools of etymological, grammatical, rhetorical, and historical analysis developed by Arab philologists for the elucidation of the fundamental texts of their culture, such as the Qur'an and classical verse, even while the author takes pains to stress that the material that is the object of these critical attentions is innately ridiculous and unworthy of consideration as literature by virtue both of its "rural" language and of the low social status, and concomitant vices, of its creators. This allows al-Shirbīnī to explore the humorous potential of certain tendencies innate in the conventional philological methodology by taking them to their logical extremes. How subversive may be this parody of contemporary critical scholarship—directed against the very culture with which the author himself identifies—is discussed below.

The work thus consists of both a *satire* ("the use of irony, sarcasm, ridicule, or the like, in exposing, denouncing, or deriding vice, folly, etc.")[16] directed against "the people of the countryside" and a *parody* ("a humorous or satirical imitation")[17] of contemporary literary culture with a focus on the text-and-commentary genre, and it derives much of its dynamism from the interplay between these two elements.

Context and Sources

The Salon, Polite Letters, and the Oral Factor

Brains Confounded is the product of a critical cultural institution of Ottoman Egypt, the *majlis* ("cultural salon"); as al-Shirbīnī says in the work's opening passage, "among the rural verse to come my way . . . and which has become the subject of comment in certain salons, was the 'Ode of Abū Shādūf' . . . ." (§1.1). Nelly Hanna describes the *majlis* as a setting in which "people discussed specific issues of concern; they debated literary or religious questions, they read and composed verse, they listened to an improvisation in verse or prose, and so on . . . . The people who attended these gatherings [were] scholars, shaykhs from al-Azhar or from other towns than Cairo, Sufi shaykhs, government administrators and other men of learning and culture."[18] As such, it was typical of the "kind of informal cultural and educational activity, independent of institutions, and centered around individual residences"[19] that flourished under the Ottomans.

Much of the literature read by those who attended such salons was of the genre known as *adab* (which we translate here as "polite letters") to which *Brains Confounded* belongs.

Like any other author in this tradition, al-Shirbīnī mines a range of sources from the literary canon for anecdotes with which to buttress his argument. We meet with such stock figures of *adab* literature as exemplary caliphs (e.g., ʿUmar ibn al-Khaṭṭāb, ʿAbd al-Malik, and, repeatedly, Hārūn al-Rashīd), as well as the poet Abū Nuwās and the philologist al-Aṣmaʿī. Quotations from or references to well-known authors such as al-Maqrīzī, al-Suyūṭī, Ibn Khallikān, and al-Shirbīnī's near contemporary, the biographer al-Munāwī (952–1031/1545–1621), are also deployed. In addition, prophetic Traditions (albeit many of which are "weak," i.e., of dubious authority) are quoted, as are passages from the Qur'an. The text is liberally interspersed with verses that confirm or summarize a point made in prose. Much of the material in *Brains Confounded*, however, is unattributed and cannot easily be traced. This is particularly true of the verse, much of which probably belongs to the underdocumented Mamluk and Ottoman periods.

Some of the stories of which peasants are the protagonists in *Brains Confounded* are probably adapted from material originally directed against other social groups. A story comparable to that of the passerby who is called upon to solve a dispute over the wording of the Qur'an (§4.18) was apparently also recounted by al-Aṣmaʿī with unidentified actors.[20] In *The Thousand and One Nights* and other works, Bedouin are sometimes the butts of stories reminiscent of those told by al-Shirbīnī of peasants.[21] Many of the stories are to be found in varying forms in older Arab writings. To give but two examples, that of the Persian scholar and his debate with the scholars of al-Azhar (§4.5) occurs as early as the tenth century, in al-Tanūkhī's *Al-Faraj baʿd al-shiddah*,[22] while that of the talking owls (vol. 2, §11.12.17) goes back at least to Abbasid times. Some stories indeed belong to a global tradition of orally transmitted stories and jokes: that of the Persian and the Azharis, for example, is found, with appropriate variations, in Europe, India, Argentina, Japan, the United States, and Turkey,[23] while that of the talking owls is known from Mughal India.[24]

Brains Confounded is, however, distinguished from most works in the genre of polite letters by its frequent recourse to an apparently contemporary tradition of jokes and other oral material about rural life, a tradition that is also part of modern oral culture.[25] Al-Shirbīnī typically introduces anecdotes with the words "[And] it is said" (§3.7) or "And another story is told" (§3.8), etc., and may end an anecdote with "in another version it says that . . ." (§3.39). Further evidence of orality is provided by the formulaic expressions with which several anecdotes end (compare, for example, "the people of his village then went for three years without going to Cairo, for fear of the corvée" (§3.28) with "I'll never go back to the villages on the river so long as I live" (§3.31) and "he never went to the city again as long as he lived" (§3.39)). This oral dimension may even have influenced the transmission of the text itself, since, over the entirety of certain anecdotes, the wording differs constantly in detail among the different manuscripts without diverging significantly in substance, a phenomenon perhaps attributable to a freedom that copyists may have felt in dealing with material that was both informal in idiom and already familiar to them. Sometimes the same joke or device is used in unrelated material. A joke about "a pair of slippers as red as your face," for example, is used twice, the first time in a peasant monologue (§3.17), the second, much later in the text, in an anecdote about the Mamluk poet al-Būṣīrī (vol. 2, §11.38.8). The story of the man who is tricked by a woman into taking off his clothes and descending into a well to recover some bracelets that the woman pretends to have dropped occurs twice in *Brains Confounded*, once as the second episode of the tale of "the three whores of Cairo" (§3.34), in which the humor is turned against a gullible peasant, and a second time with an old woman as the trickster and an unnamed narrator as the victim (§5.4.9); in its second occurrence, the story is adduced to show not the stupidity of the victim but "the wiles of old women and their cunning" (*idem*).

A further distinguishing feature is the personalization of anecdotes. Al-Shirbīnī states that he has himself witnessed much of what he describes, using phrases such as "We have observed many of their weddings and all the futile nonsense that goes on at them" (§2.5) and "I saw a peasant talking to a friend of his and asking him . . ." (§3.61). He even says, in the context of an anecdote explaining why a girl was given a bizarre name, that he "actually saw this Khuraywah and asked her father why he had chosen that word for her name" (§2.17). Similarly, he relates lengthy anecdotes in whose events he is a participant (e.g., §§7.8–10). The credibility of such reports is undermined, however, by the recurrence elsewhere in the book of some of these tales with a different protagonist. For example, the tale, embroidered with much circumstantial and personal detail, of how al-Shirbīnī was inveigled into attending a meeting of heretical Sufis in Cairo and of his subsequent escape (§7.11) is prefigured elsewhere with different actors (§7.2), and the elaborate story of the dervishes who rob houses by night is followed immediately by al-Shirbīnī's assertion that a similar incident occurred while he was living in Dimyāṭ (§§7.31–32). It seems probable, therefore, that even when al-Shirbīnī claims to have personal knowledge of alleged events, he is in fact drawing on a corpus of popular lore about the countryside or even on material not originally dealing with the countryside that could nevertheless be adapted to his purposes. Robert Irwin has discussed the need of medieval Arabic authors to attribute the anecdotes they relate to known figures in order to indicate their truth and thus usefulness, noting that stories "were not supposed to be made up; rather they were transmitted by their compiler."[26]

Techniques: Marshaling, Association, and Disassociation

Authors of works in the tradition of polite letters address a given topic or topics by selecting relevant passages from the literary canon, which the author links together using his own observations, marshaling the whole into a coherent narrative with the goal of instructing, enlightening, and entertaining. While this method can give an impression of randomness, with apparent digressions, the successful author manipulates his material to advance an argument that gains cogency from the examples adduced.

The primary argument of the satirical dimension of *Brains Confounded*—that the "people of the countryside" are possessed of characteristics and guilty of practices that exclude them from consideration as civilized beings—is made using four main strategies: establishment of a framework of values against which to judge the accused; direct demonstration of guilt through the description of the uncivilized qualities of the accused; insinuation of guilt by association of the accused with other exemplars of uncivilized behavior; and disassociation of the accuser (the author) from the accused by demonstrating the latter's qualifications as a member of civilized society.

The first lines of *Brains Confounded* establish the framework, which is that of a moral economy defined by the opposition of refinement (*laṭāfah*) to coarseness (*kathāfah*). This moral economy is explored further below.

The direct attack is delivered largely through the series of anecdotes in Part One that purport to describe the people of the countryside. Here we learn that they are ignorant of religion and elementary sanitary habits, have bizarre names, possess unappealing physical attributes, commit crimes, and so on.

The associative technique appears in the form of passages such as the two tales of "The Champions of Discourtesy of Cairo and Damascus" and "The Boors of Cairo and Damascus," which occur in the middle of the section "An Account of Their [the Peasants'] Escapades." These may appear to be irrelevant to the topic: their setting is explicitly urban, and they contain no mention of "the people of the countryside." Nevertheless, al-Shirbīnī explicitly links them to his main theme by introducing the first with the words "Apropos of this peasant and his discourtesy, I am reminded of how it fell out that the Champion of Discourtesy of Damascus came to Cairo . . ." (§3.46). This linkage to further, nonrural, examples of discourtesy (*ʿadam dhawq*) and boorishness (*thaqālah*) appears to be made in order to situate the country dweller, in whom such characteristics supposedly are innate, in a broader moral context. Once his status as a specific case within an established behavioral pathology is established, the peasant's presence within that universe of obnoxiousness appears the more natural. Similarly, the section on rural poetry in Part One is followed by another ridiculing urban doggerel ("It Now Behooves Us to Offer a Small Selection of the Verse of Those Who Lay Claim to the Status of Poets but Are in Practice Poltroons," etc., §6), thus again associating the peasant with further nonrural examples of barbarous behavior, this time in the form of demonstrably ridiculous pretensions to high literary culture by the unqualified.

Some of the most seemingly irrelevant "digressions" in *Brains Confounded* may be understood as examples of the final tactic in al-Shirbīnī's strategy of satire, namely, the disassociation of the author from his subject. Witty passages replete with quotations from the literary canon on farting (vol. 2, §§11.7.17–40), the different categories of amorous pursuit (§§5.3.2–8), the virtues of white hair (vol. 2, §§11.5.4–9), fish (vol. 2, §§11.35.3–6), the rarity of sincere friendship among men (vol. 2, §§12.18–19), and other topics too numerous to count appear to have no relevance to the topic at hand. Such passages do, however, demonstrate the author's mastery of an accepted cultural discourse and thus confirm his credentials as someone with the authority to criticize the "people of the countryside." They may also serve the function of siting the work, despite its unaccustomed topic, within a larger, already familiar and accepted, worldview, thus lending it credibility.[27]

While contemporary polite letters in general, and *Brains Confounded* in particular, are indisputably products of the salon, Mohamed-Salah Omri makes the corrective point that "*adab* is the work of individual writers. It appropriates other genres by writing them from the author's particular point of view . . . . Focus on the act of writing allows us to shift attention from a writer's sources . . . to the manner of incorporation . . . . *Adab* . . . is the creative writing of the Arabs, not the compiled erudition of their *majlis* discussions."[28]

Al-Shirbīnī's manipulation of the material at hand, recycled as this may be from earlier writings and from a living repertoire of jokes and anecdotes, results not only in accurate targeting of the subject of the satire, but also in the production of a distinctive individual voice; a voice that is cantankerous, witty, and unassuageably partisan. It is precisely this voice, and the window that it opens onto one mid-Ottoman Egyptian writer's personal universe, that makes *Brains Confounded* a work of art capable of being enjoyed today as literature and not merely a text containing material relevant to the needs of historians and other scholars.

Models and Precursors

Examples of an interest, satirical or otherwise, in rural life and of related literary practices are to be found in earlier literature.

Qiṣṣat al-Miṣrī wa-l-rīfī A fragment of an anonymous seventeenth-century colloquial *Rangstreit* (debate over the virtues of two categories) entitled *The Story of the Cairene and the Countryman* (*Qiṣṣat al-Miṣrī wa-l-rīfī*), in which a townsman and a peasant debate the merits of their respective environments, proves that polemical confrontations between the city and the country were of interest to consumers of popular literature of the time. However, the *Story* differs from *Brains Confounded* in that the peasant apologist is not portrayed as intrinsically inferior to his urban opponent; in the pages that survive neither seems to be set up as the obvious victor in the argument.

Ibn Sūdūn The only author acknowledged by al-Shirbīnī as a model is the Mamluk writer ʿAlī ibn Sūdūn al-Bashbughāwī. Al-Shirbīnī indicates at the beginning of *Brains Confounded* that he will provide the reader with "license and buffoonery, with just a touch of Ibn Sūdūn-ery" (§1.4). Al-Shirbīnī quotes twice from Ibn Sūdūn's works. The first quotation is of Funayn's Letter (§§4.36–4.37.6), a long, comically inane missive sent by a certain Funayn from Upper Egypt to his parents in some other, unspecified, part of Egypt, and probably appealed to al-Shirbīnī because of its epistolary form (it initiates a short section on silly letters) and its fit with the naturalistic colloquial prose used in his own peasant monologues. The second quotation from Ibn Sūdūn may have provided direct inspiration for *Brains Confounded*, in that it consists of a commentary on four lines of colloquial verse ("Abū Qurdān / sowed a feddan . . .") followed by a zany explanation of the etymology of the word *mulūkhiyyā* ("Jew's mallow") (vol. 2, §11.12.8). Al-Shirbīnī does not, however, make this connection himself and the passage, which is short, is buried in a larger discussion.

Al-Ṣafadī's *Ikhtirāʿ al-khurāʿ* *The Concoction of Craziness* (*Ikhtirāʿ al-khurāʿ*) of Khalīl ibn Aybak al-Ṣafadī (d. 764/1363) consists of a humorous commentary on two lines of nonsense verse that has many points in common with al-Shirbīnī's work, the most obvious being the exploitation of the comic potential inherent in the text-and-commentary genre and the targeting of unjustified pretensions to participation in the literary culture. The two works also share a mise-en-scène (the verses in question are brought to the attention of a gathering of litterateurs, one of whose members is commissioned to write a commentary "to be strung to fit their strange string") and certain (but by no means all) comic devices, such as false etymologies, incorrect meters, freewheeling word association, and the straight-faced assertion of the patently false, and these impart a sense of kinship to the two texts.

An essential difference between al-Ṣafadī and al-Shirbīnī, however, lies in the fact that al-Ṣafadī's parody lacks any reference to the countryside and that the verses that are its target are more or less pure nonsense, in contrast to the highly meaning-laden odes and *mawāliyā*s (two-line poems of four rhyming hemistichs in *basīṭ* meter, often with colloquial features) of al-Shirbīnī's country people. Their author, likewise, is a cipher, without an identifiable human face, and as such, in contrast to al-Shirbīnī's countryman, represents no particular social group. It follows that al-Ṣafadī's humor is more abstract and, perhaps because it has no flesh-and-blood victim, less malicious than al-Shirbīnī's. By the same token, *The Concoction of Craziness* contains none of the description and critique of social behavior that enriches *Brains Confounded.*

Al-Sanhūrī's *Muḍḥik dhawī l-dhawq*: Inspiration or Genre? Muḥammad ibn Maḥfūẓ al-Sanhūrī's recently discovered work *Risible Rhymes* (*Muḍḥik dhawī l-dhawq wa-l-niẓām fī ḥall shadharatin min kalām ahl al-rīf al-ʿawāmm*) contains six of the ten verses occurring in the section in *Brains Confounded* headed "An Account of Their Poets and of Their Idiocies and Inanities" (§5) and, presented within the same sequence as the latter, four that do not.[29] What might be the relationship between these two works, and what conclusion should we draw from the appearance of *Brains Confounded* some forty years after *Risible Rhymes*?

One possible conclusion is that al-Shirbīnī read al-Sanhūrī's book, found the concept appealing, added some verses (presumably of his own composition), discarded others, and used the whole as a foundation for his more ambitious project, adopting from al-Sanhūrī, in addition, certain comic devices, such as the absurd metrical mnemonics. According to such a scenario, the writing of commentaries on mock-rural verse would be a phenomenon that started with *Risible Rhymes* and ended with *Brains Confounded*, and this may indeed have been the case. However, the occurrence in each work of verses not found in the other suggests another possibility, namely, that each writer drew on a common stock of mock-rural verse that was in circulation at the time, and that the two works thus constitute what has survived, or what we know so far to have survived, of a genre.

Elements in both works imply the existence of such a common stock. Al-Sanhūrī says that he was asked to "decode a sampling of what the rural rank and file have said in verse," while al-Shirbīnī describes the "Ode of Abū Shādūf" as being "among the rural verse to come my way . . . and which has become the subject of comment in certain salons"; such references are not in and of themselves humorous, and it is not obvious why the writer should have made them if they were not true. In addition, the greater number and more elaborated form of such verses in *Brains Confounded* may point to the existence of a larger body of such work. Thus the stanzaic ode (*qaṣīd*) of Abū ʿAfr (*Brains Confounded* §§3.18.1–15), which is more or less equal in length to that of Abū Shādūf, and the "Ode of Abū Shādūf" itself and its associated poems, all far exceed in length the earlier material that is partially shared with *Risible Rhymes* and abandon the couplet in favor of other poetic forms of which al-Sanhūrī's book contains no examples. It may be argued that the presence of certain comic devices—specifically the use of absurd metrical mnemonics and formulas (referring to couplets) of the pattern "its width is from [place A] to [place B], its breadth from [place C] to [place D]"—indicate direct borrowing by al-Shirbīnī from al-Sanhūrī, but that is not necessarily the case. The comic mnemonic, at least, has its forerunners in the work of al-Ṣafadī (see above), who also uses other comic devices (the false etymology, the straight-faced assertion of the patently false) to be found in *Brains Confounded*. Finally, we may wonder whether al-Sanhūrī was a writer of a caliber to have written such mock-rural verses or, as the rest of his book implies, a writer who seized on ready-made materials to fulfil the task he had been given, oblivious, in the case of the mock-rural verse, to the opportunities for satire that these provided and capable of offering only the mundane grammatical and rhetorical critique that he in fact provides.

None of the above arguments for the existence of a genre of commentaries on mock-rural verse is conclusive. Unless further texts of this sort emerge (as *Risible Rhymes* recently has), we shall never know whether al-Shirbīnī was directly and solely inspired by al-Sanhūrī, but should the existence of such a genre be proven, al-Shirbīnī will have to be reassessed, as less an eccentric outlier in the history of Arabic literature and more a writer of talent who saw the potential of an existing genre and exploited it in the service of a particular discourse.

Publication, Reception, and Scholarly Attention

Ten manuscript copies of *Brains Confounded* exist today, indicating at least a modest popularity of the work in the days before printing was introduced to Egypt in the early nineteenth century. An unpublished manuscript entitled *Mukhtaṣar al-Īḍāḥ fī ʿilm al-nikāḥ* (*The Synopsis of The Work of Clarification concerning the Science of Copulation*), which, like *Al-Īḍāḥ fī ʿilm al-nikāḥ* itself, is falsely attributed to Jalāl al-Dīn al-Suyūṭī and which was copied in 1247/1832 (Ms Cantab. Add. 335, folios 8b–9a), contains a brief passage on pimping that the author attributes to *Brains Confounded*, though it does not in fact occur there. Thus, at this time, al-Shirbini was apparently well enough known to be cited as an authority on socio-sexual issues.[30]

Brains Confounded was first printed, at private expense, at the government press at Bulaq in 1274/1857–58, and was reprinted or lithographed thereafter at least five times during the nineteenth century. However, Jean Le Cerf's comment in the 1930s that "les plus anciens journalistes du Caire se souvient d'un *Kitab Abu Shaduf* que nous n'avons pu retrouver, et qui date du temps du Khédive Ismail [*sic*]" indicates that the work was hard to find by the first half of the twentieth century. It was published once again, in a bowdlerized and generally unreliable edition, in 1963.[31]

Western scholars were the first to draw attention to the literary and linguistic importance of the work. The first study, by Mehren, appeared in 1872, twelve years after its first printing.[32] Spitta incorporated material derived from it into his grammar of Egyptian Arabic of 1880,[33] in 1887 Vollers made extensive use of it in a major article on Egyptian Arabic,[34] and in 1906 Kern included mention of it in his review of new [*sic*] humorous writers.[35] None of the above attempted a comprehensive study of the text, and some, if not all, appear to have been under the misapprehension that it dated from the nineteenth century.

Egyptian scholarly interest in *Brains Confounded* begins with Jurji Zaydān's brief notice in 1931.[36] Thereafter, a considerable body of work has been devoted to it by Egyptian writers, much of their attention being devoted to the issue of al-Shirbīnī's attitudes towards his subject and his motives for writing the book. Most have taken the literalist approach (i.e., assumed that the "Ode of Abū Shādūf" is the product of a genuine rural poet), an approach that is rejected here.[37]

The single most important contribution to the understanding of *Brains Confounded* to date is Gabriel Baer's article "Shirbīnī's *Hazz al-quḥūf* and Its

Significance" in *Fellah and Townsman in the Middle East: Studies in Social History* (London 1982).[38] Baer was the first to direct attention to the value of the text for an understanding of the social history of Egypt rather than concentrating on its linguistic and literary aspects. Baer's many valuable insights, which focus on the "relations between the fellah and the city and between urban and rural *ʿulamāʾ*,"[39] remain, for the most part, unchallenged. However, his conclusion that al-Shirbīnī's "attacks against the fellahs are to be understood as a defense against the contempt and derision on the part of the *ʿulamāʾ* from urban families, from which he and his like suffered" and for which he posits as background "the penetration of a rural element into the urban class of *ʿulamāʾ*"[40] is questionable. Baer himself mentions that "throughout the centuries *ʿulamāʾ* of village origin lived, taught and wrote books in the cities," and that "as to the eleventh/seventeenth century . . . one quarter of Cairo's *ʿulamāʾ* whose biographies have been recorded by al-Muḥibbī were of rural origin."[41] Against this, the few examples that Baer provides of *ʿulamāʾ* being mocked for their rural origins[42] all relate either to Syria or to Egypt in the sixteenth century and seem insufficient to justify such a passionate, complex, and extended diatribe as al-Shirbīnī's.

Al-Shirbīnī's Countryside

Because *Brains Confounded* is, in part, a satire, its depiction of the countryside must be treated with caution; as Omri points out, the book is "not an encyclopaedia of information . . . pertaining to peasants."[43] Nevertheless, the object of a satire must be recognizable if it is to be appreciated by its readers, and we may therefore assume that the basic information about the countryside that it provides is accurate.

A Hierarchy of Settlements

The Egypt of *Brains Confounded* extends from Cairo to Dimyāṭ along the eastern branch of the Nile, on which the villages mentioned in the book (Hurbayṭ, Dundayṭ, Shanashah, Samannūd, etc.) are or were situated. The western Delta, Upper Egypt, and other parts of the country are mentioned only in passing. The settlements along this axis are of three types, which form a hierarchy.

In the heading to the first section of the work devoted specifically to the peasant, al-Shirbīnī limits his attention to "the commoners of *certain* of the people of the countryside" (§2.1). References in the material that follows make it clear that this subset of rural society is that living in "the hamlets and the small villages" (vol. 2, §11.21.7), and these, as we shall see below, were generally situated at a distance from the river or, as al-Shirbīnī puts it, "in the margins of the lands" (§7.1); as such, they probably received less water, like "tail-enders" in irrigation systems the world over.[44] Al-Shirbīnī also uses the doublet "the hamlets and the villages of the swamp lands" (*al-kufūr wa-bilād al-malaq*) (vol. 2, §11.10.8), the latter being low-lying areas that remained, post-flood, too swampy and salty for cultivation. In other words, the hamlets whose inhabitants are the butt of the satire were the poorest.

The hamlets lack Friday mosques[45] and have a mill that the villager must operate with his own oxen, in contrast to the villages on the river, which have mills operated by horsepower (vol. 2, §11.21.7). These hamlets are placed by al-Shirbīnī at the bottom of a tripartite hierarchy of settlements that moves upward from the hamlets, through the villages on the river, to the city. According to this hierarchy, the inhabitants of the hamlets are the most ignorant and isolated, those of the city are paragons of sophistication, and those of the villages by the river occupy a middle position.

This hierarchy is made most explicit in the repeated and pointed descriptions of the different recipes according to which various foods are prepared in the three different settings, for, as al-Shirbīnī states at the beginning of his discussion of stewed fava beans, "things are ennobled . . . by virtue of place" (vol. 2, §11.11.2). In dietary terms, this hierarchy is keyed largely to the amount of fat used. Thus, of mallow (*khubbayzah*), he says: "The people of the countryside take the leaves, chop them . . . and eat them . . . . The people of the villages on the river cook it with goose and chicken and so on, and the people of the cities cook it with fatty meats . . . and they add fats, clarified cow's butter, greens, spices, and similar things, and this is the only way it should be eaten . . . . The way the country people do it . . . is worthless, and the same goes for the people of the villages on the river, for these . . . add no clarified butter or fat . . . . The latter is, nevertheless, more refined than the recipe of the country people referred to above. The best place to eat it, however, is in the cities . . . ." (vol. 2, §11.19.3). Similar comments are made in the case of slow-cooked fava beans, fava beans mashed with Jew's mallow (*bīsār*), lentils, and rice pudding. In the latter case, al-Shirbīnī adds that "people of Turkish descent make it with milk alone, without water, and add just a little rice . . . this kind is the best tasting and most appetizing" (vol. 2, §11.25.2), thus placing the latter in a kind of supra-urban category.

The Three Estates of al-Shirbīnī's Rural Society

The terms most frequently used in *Brains Confounded* to designate its subjects collectively are *ahl al-rīf* and *al-rayyāfah*, both meaning "the people of the countryside." The presence in Part One of *Brains Confounded* of three sections devoted to anecdotes about, respectively, "the commoners of certain of the people of the countryside" (*ʿawāmm baʿḍ ahl al-rīf*) (§§2.9–3.76), their "men of religion" (*fuqahāʾ*) (§§4.1–4.41), and their "dervishes" (*fuqarāʾ*, i.e., mendicant Sufis) (§§7.1–7.41) indicates that al-Shirbīnī saw the people of the countryside as being divided into three estates, of roughly similar social, if not numerical, importance. Al-Shirbīnī attacks each of these estates separately, leveling against each specific charges of physical grossness and moral and cultural turpitude.

The Peasant Cultivator As noted above, by "the commoners of certain of the people of the countryside" al-Shirbīnī means the peasant cultivators (*fallāḥūn*), especially those living in the hamlets and small villages away from the river. These are the people who "spend all their time with the plow and the shovel-sledge and shaking their caps around the threshing floors, or rushing about in the swamps and the fields, or bustling around after the crops, or jumping about harvesting and reaping," etc. (§2.3). They are stigmatized by association; for example, al-Shirbīnī notes of the plowman (who, according to him, belongs to a particularly benighted subgroup of peasants) that "his companions by day are oxen and by night are women; consequently his mental capacities never become completely formed" (§5.2.6). They are also mocked for unprepossessing physical attributes: "Their pubic hair's so long it twists as it grows" (§8.8); "The back of his neck had turned black from the heat, his feet were chapped from walking barefoot and from the cold" (§3.1); "His ass, from wear and tear, shows many a scar" (§8.8). The peasant is also taken to task for specific cultural practices: the making of a public spectacle of the bride at the ceremony called "the Showing" is described as "one of their foulest deeds and most wretched ways" (§2.24). Further charges leveled against the peasant include internecine fighting ("war and stubborn confrontation arise among them and villages are ruined at their hands" (§2.3)), with frequent references to the feuding clans of Saʿd (or Jud(h)ām) and Ḥarām (e.g., §2.3) and the village's own foot soliders (*mushāh*) and apparently associated "brave lads" (*jidʿān*) (e.g., §2.23), bad management of land and livestock (vol. 2, §11.6.6), indebtedness (*idem*), flight from the land (*idem*), and even the residual use of Christian religious formulae after conversion to Islam (§3.64). Furthermore, their women are "hyenas" (§2.22) and their children "apes" (§2.21) and "lunatics" (§2.7). In general, "the natures of the people of the countryside . . . are revolting and seek only what is revolting" (vol. 2, §11.17.2), or, as the author puts it even more pithily elsewhere, they are "shit born of shit" (§5.7.7).

The fundamental accusation against the peasants, however, and that which underlies and gives rise to all their other faults, is "their lack of intelligence and overwhelming ignorance" (§2.4)). This means, in its most basic form, that they are ignorant of everything but their immediate environment: "the only things a countryman knows are belts and cudgels, cows and plow-shaft pins, water-wheels and drover's whips," etc. (§2.3). From this follow more specific areas of ignorance—of refined foods (§3.8), of appropriate dress (*idem*), of the appropriate language to use in poetry (§5), of personal hygiene (§8.15), and of such urban institutions as the bathhouse (§3.11) and the latrine (§§3.40–41). Above all, they are ignorant of and indifferent to religion: "They gather in the mosques to calculate their taxes, but not one of them makes a prostration or says a prayer" (§2.7). Al-Shirbīnī illustrates this trait with no fewer than thirteen separate anecdotes describing peasants voiding their prayers through ignorance (§§3.63–76).

Significantly too, al-Shirbīnī points, in his summary of the peasant's characteristics, not only to the former's general turpitude but also to a specific animus against members of the author's own class: "They have no mercy on a scholar / Only on those who practice evil and the oppressor" (§8.18).

The Rural Men of Religion "Rural *fuqahā'*" make up the second estate. These men are acknowledged as religious authorities by the peasants (§§4.22–23). The anecdotes give the impression that every village has one. Rural *fuqahā'* claim expertise in the fields of the Qur'an (§4.18, §4.29, §4.30), jurisprudence (*fiqh*) (e.g., §4.20), and Tradition (*ḥadīth*) (§4.19, §4.24) and also provide services as judges (§4.31), preachers (§§4.10–12), and teachers of the Qur'an to children (§4.15).

Rural *fuqahā'* are subjected to many of the criticisms that are directed against the peasant cultivator. Their associations, for example, render them stupid: "Similar [to the plowman, see §5.2.6] in terms of reduced intellect is the teacher of small children, for they are his companions all day long while all night long he is with women" (§5.2.7). Likewise, they are mocked for their uncouth appearance (one is described as "a man tall of stature, thick of leg, wearing a belt over a woolen wrap, with no shirt and no shoes on his feet, and on his head a huge turban of patent filthiness" (§4.3)).

The most important charge against the rural *faqīh*, however, is that he leads his flock into error through his flawed *ʿilm*, or knowledge of the religious and philological sciences and their methodology. The rural *faqīh*'s ignorance can, for example, result in his giving false interpretations of the Qur'an (§4.1) and even in his making up new words for it (§4.18). It may result in his asking a bookseller for an "abridged version" of the Qur'an for the use of his students (§4.15), and, through his misreading of a text, in leading his congregation in prayer while standing on one leg (§4.34). There is no indication of where the rural *fuqahā'* may have acquired this spurious learning.

Following one of these anecdotes, al-Shirbīnī comments, "I would add that it is because of such cases that they say, 'Learning is a sacred trust' and that a person should be allowed to speak only on the basis of thorough knowledge and wide reading, extreme caution with regard to what is fundamental in a question and what is secondary, and subjection of the process of transmission to critical examination; and that no attention should be paid to what the ignorant among the scholars may come up with" (§4.25). The rural *faqīh*, in other words, is a caricature of the true *ʿālim*. Highlighting the competition between "the ignorant among the scholars" and their properly trained urban counterparts, much of this section consists of anecdotes in which scholars, and especially Azhari scholars, best their rural rivals in contests of knowledge (§§4.3–33). In the conduct of this struggle, the *ʿālim* may have recourse to the authorities, as when an *ʿālim* "exerted himself to have this ignorant pastor leave the village . . . and they expelled him, on the authority of the emir of the village" (§4.33).

The Rural Dervishes (*al-Khawāmis*) Rural dervishes constitute the third estate of al-Shirbīnī's rural society. Passages amounting to more than five thousand words devoted to the rural *fuqarā'* were omitted from the Bulaq and subsequent printed editions, reducing their presence in the work to a shadow of that in the original.[46] The inclusion of this material in the present edition and translation reveals the magnitude of the importance al-Shirbīnī attributed to rural dervishes and the vehemence of his animosity towards them. As in the section on rural men of religion, tales of conflict between scholar and rural dervish constitute the greater part of al-Shirbīnī's exposition.

One of the most striking features of al-Shirbīnī's description of the "rural *fuqarā'*" is the prominence among them of a group he refers to as *al-Khawāmis* ("the Khawāmis").

The term *Khawāmis* (literally, "fifths," referring to ordinals, not fractions) appears to be unique to al-Shirbīnī and does not conform to the pattern of the names normally used to designate Sufi orders (al-Shādhiliyyah, etc.). Nevertheless, the description of the Khawāmis as "a sect that has been raised in the margins of the lands" (§7.1), an allusion earlier in the same passage to "the shaking of their caps" (*hazz quḥūfihim*), and the overall similarity of the language used to describe them to that used of the peasants (e.g., "they are like dumb animals" (§7.1)), place them squarely in the same geographical and social category as al-Shirbīnī's country people, and it is clear that they were central to his picture of the countryside.

In addition to their wearing distinctive headwear, al-Shirbīnī's country *fuqarā'* are distinguished by certain appurtenances, namely their "prayer beads and pitcher . . . their cockerel and fodder" (§7.1); they also carry crutches (§7.33) and wear a bonnet (*zunṭ*) (§8.24). They are described on occasion as shaving their beards (§7.38), they include women (§7.6), and they are accused of claiming that they have been relieved of the requirement to obey God's commands (§7.3, §7.4, §7.7). Al-Shirbīnī holds them guilty of a variety of heretical beliefs (e.g., materialism (§7.34), reincarnation, the transmigration of souls (*idem*), and pantheism (§7.9)) and practices (sexual intercourse with women and boys during their ceremonies (*dhikr*) (§7.7) and prayers (§7.22) and a general propensity for fornication (§7.2), especially the seduction of young male novices (§7.21, §7.30, §7.38)). They practice charlatanism (§7.38), theft (§7.16), burglary (§7.31), murder (§7.7), and even cannibalism (§7.7). They roam the countryside, either with a single disciple (§7.16) or in groups (§7.38), and actively seek to recruit others, including the well-to-do, to their beliefs (§7.8). The tone of al-Shirbīnī's treatment may be illustrated by his lines on a certain dervish who came to a bad end, to the effect that "He lived in vomit and foulness / And he died in shame and shite" (§7.10).

The reprehensible behavior of al-Shirbīnī's rural dervishes parallels many of the practices mentioned in descriptions of various contemporary antinomian Sufi groups.[47] The Muṭāwiʿah and the Malāmatiyyah were accused of pederasty and fornication,[48] and the former also carried pitchers (see n. 435). The solitary retreat (*khalwah*), exploited by al-Shirbīnī's shaykhs for nefarious purposes, was characteristic of the Khalwatiyyah order.[49] There was also said to be a group in Upper Egypt who held pantheistic beliefs and acknowledged no recognized religion.[50]

However, the comprehensive nature of al-Shirbīnī's attack on "rural *fuqarā'*" indicates that he was not concerned simply with their beliefs and practices; indeed, he sometimes accepts similar practices by individual Sufis with equanimity, as when he reports that a certain Shaykh Muḥammad al-Silsilī was "one of the saints who have attained esoteric knowledge, even though licentiousness and enjoyment of women appeared as his predominant characteristics," adding the conventional justification for such behavior, namely, that it was "to disguise his mystical states" (§6.6). It is also noteworthy that, in al-Shirbīnī's day, individuals whose behavior was either extremely eccentric (such as Shaykh Barakāt al-Khayyāṭ, whose tailor's shop was filled with dead dogs, cats, and sheep[51]) or who flouted the most basic tenets of Islam (such as ʿAbd al-Wahhāb al-Shaʿrānī's mentor Ibrāhīm al-Matbūlī, whose conduct "gave much cause for criticism on both religious and moral grounds" and who was suspected of pederasty[52]) were tolerated as "natural saints" (*majādhīb*) or "men of divine states" (*arbāb aḥwāl*). As such, they were patronized and consulted by members of the ruling elite and regarded with (wary) respect by leading religious figures.

The difference between these licensed saints and the dervishes against whom al-Shirbīnī rails may have lain essentially in the latter's strong organization, their hierarchies of leadership—al-Shirbīnī mentions that their leaders hold the power of life and death over their followers (§7.7)—and their apparently nomadic lifestyle. They appear, in these respects, to have differed from Sufis such as al-Matbūlī or al-Khayyāṭ, who lived on their own in cities; from those, such as the followers of al-Shaʿrānī, who lived in a *zāwiyah* (Sufi hostel); and indeed from the many, often educated, members of the recognized Sufi orders.[53] As al-Shirbīnī has a dervish say in the poem (*urjūzah*) at the end of Part One, "No other Way (*ṭarīqah*) than this do I heed, / And my school's either Saʿd or Ḥarām," implying the dervishes' rejection of the recognized Sufi orders in favor of clan-based social allegiances. The rural *fuqarā'* may thus have represented popular mass movements that were not susceptible to control and were therefore threatening.[54]

The hold of Sufism was particularly strong in the countryside: "In the later Middle Ages, the influence of normative Islam, as represented by the *ulama*, on the Egyptian countryside was practically nil. While, in the cities, the Sufis vied with the *ulama* in influencing the Muslim community, in the countryside they replaced them."[55] At the same time, "[the 'new renunciation'] was not restricted in either social origin or appeal to 'lower' social strata . . . . There is certainly sufficient evidence to establish that these movements frequently recruited from the middle and higher social strata . . . . Socially deviant renunciation exercised a strong attraction on the hearts and minds of many Muslim intellectuals."[56] This appeal must have made them even more of a threat to the religious elite.

The Satire on Rural Life

Constructing a Moral Economy

Al-Shirbīnī takes pains from the outset of *Brains Confounded* to provide a moral framework to support his construction of the "people of the countryside." It is by linking his subjects to the elements of that framework that he generates the authority needed to judge and condemn them.

The Refined and the Coarse

The moral economy invoked in *Brains Confounded* is defined by the opposition between refinement (or subtlety or grace) (*laṭāfah* or *luṭf*) and coarseness (or grossness or crudeness) (*kathāfah*), terms that are linked to the inhabitants of the book from the opening statement of themes. There, al-Shirbīnī proclaims the requirement to praise God because He "has distinguished the man of sound taste with refinement of form and sweetness of tongue, while bestowing on his opposites—the likes of the common people of the countryside . . . —wickedness of disposition and coarseness of nature" (§0.1).

This opposition between what is refined (*laṭīf*) and what is coarse (*kathīf*) continues throughout the book. In a chapter heading, the author promises to tell of things that befell certain common people of the countryside and give a description of "their vulgarity" (*ṭabʿuhum al-kathīf*) (§2.1). A simile used by a rural poet is condemned as a "coarse comparison" (*tashbīh kathīf*) (§5.8.3). Peasant names are grotesque, for it is a fact that "names point to the refinement (*laṭāfah*) or coarseness (*kathāfah*) of those who bear them . . ." (§2.13), and so on.

This moral polarity is reflected in geographical and social terms in the contrast between the countryside and its people on the one hand and Cairo and its people on the other. Cairo is both the city par excellence—as already noted, when peasants refer to "the city," they mean Cairo (vol. 2, §11.37.2)—and the font of all that is refined. From al-Shirbīnī's perspective, there is "no place like Cairo, / And no people like its people" (§8.44). He prays that God may protect it because it is "the city of conviviality and amusement, of pleasure and fulfillment, whose women God has distinguished by making them comely and handsome, full of loveliness and perfection, sweet in their social relations, refined in their conversations" (vol. 2, §11.37.2). The contrast is, of course, in Cairo's favor: "God reward [the men of Cairo] for their doughtiness, granting them everlasting pleasure in their womenfolk and seasoning to perfection their togetherness, and God protect us from the countryside and its stupidities, the coarseness of its food and of its people's proclivities!" (vol. 2, §11.12.6). In terms of literature, a "despicable comparison" made by a rural peasant (§5.6.12) is contrasted with "a witty simile referring to a refined beloved" penned by al-Shirbīnī himself (§5.6.13). In the first passage in the book in which he directly contrasts the urban and rural forms of an item of physical culture (in this case, the *jubbah*, a garment), al-Shirbīnī also explicitly links the urban religious and secular educated elites by remarking on their shared taste for the refined: "The urban sort is the one used by the people of the cities, especially scholars and sophisticates" (vol. 2, §11.2.16).

The fundamental nature of these associations is perhaps most clearly emphasized by the way in which they bridge the moral and physical universes. Thus, above, al-Shirbīnī speaks of the man who is distinguished by God with "sound taste . . . and sweetness of tongue" as being endowed also with "grace of person." In contrast, of course, the peasant is distinguished not only by his "coarseness of nature" but also by his coarseness of form, as in the examples given. The full set of associations, as built up over the course of the book, consists of, on the "refined" side, religious knowledge, adherence to the norms of polite culture, eloquence (especially mastery of the techniques of formal poetry), good taste, physical beauty, and affective and mental refinement, and, on the "coarse" side, ignorance of true religion and heresy, deviance from the norms of polite culture, an inability to master the rules of versification, grotesque naming practices, grossness of physical form, and general boorishness and obnoxiousness.

The Immutability of Man's Inborn Nature

Al-Shirbīnī makes it plain that the categories "coarse" and "refined" are not only a result of one's circumstances but determine them too, and as such are immutable.

Several axioms reinforce, explain, and rationalize the determinative nature of the dichotomy. One of these is the assertion that "like attracts like," which occurs as a leitmotiv at various points in the book (§3.56, §5.2.16, §5.6.2). It is because like attracts like that coarseness of nature accompanies coarseness of behavior (and thus in turn coarseness of appearance, dress, food, etc.). Thus, for example, after dissecting the risible vulgarity of a peasant eulogy, al-Shirbīnī points out that "the peasant's panegyric accords with his condition and is limited by it, and 'like attracts like'" (§3.56).

Secondly, if the world is divided between the refined and the coarse and each must act accordingly, it is also the case, as al-Shirbīnī makes clear by prefacing his main topic with a series of anecdotes to this effect, that these God-given characteristics are immutable. A wolf cub, for example, rescued by a Bedouin and suckled by a ewe, turns on its foster mother one day and rips out her stomach, leading the Bedouin to ask a rhetorical question to which he has his own ready answer: "You were fed with her milk and raised among us, / So who told you that your father was a wolf? / When an inborn nature's disposed to evil, / No teaching and no teacher is of use!" (§3.2). Similarly, on the human plane, the despicable behavior of a man "of low birth" (not specified as rural) is explained by his origins: his mother is "Murjānah, a black slave" (§3.5). Of direct relevance, a peasant taken from the fields by a king and provided with the finest education acquires great skill in divination by letters and by sand; however, when the king hides his ring in his hand and asks the peasant what it is, the man opines that, since it is round and has a hole, it must be a millstone. As the king's vizier complacently notes, "his original nature won out," for "Apples will never sprout from the twig / Of one whose roots are a sycamore fig" (§3.1).

Indeed, by a circular (and hence irrefutable) argument, only those who are "refined" by nature have the right of access to education and knowledge, while the coarse, such as the peasants, are incapable of rising above the condition into which they were born and hence have no right to higher things. Indeed, encouraging them to think otherwise is both pointless and dangerous: "And among the sayings of the Imam ʿAlī, God be pleased with him, we find, 'Do not instruct the children of the rabble in knowledge, for if they learn, they will seek high office, and if they attain that, they will devote themselves to the humiliation of the noble.' And the Imam al-Shāfiʿī, God be pleased with him, has said: 'To bestow knowledge on the ignorant is to waste it / While to deny it to the deserving is unjust'" (§3.4). This philosophy is, of course, self-serving: things must be so if the inferior status of the people of the countryside, and thus their exploitation, is to be justified. "Appropriateness" or "consistency" thus becomes not simply a fact of life but also a principle to which appeal is often made ("if it be asked . . . where is the appropriateness of the comparison . . . we would say" (§5.8.3)). In the final analysis, "appropriateness is required" (§5.5.13).

The Transformational Power of Immutability

The transformational power of the principle that man's character is determined at birth and immutable is so great that it can determine the nature, and thus the acceptability of, any behavior. Al-Shirbīnī devotes considerable space, for example, to farting as a characteristic behavior of country people and one that confirms their coarseness. On the other hand, in one anecdote, a fart delivered by a refined person turns out to be a veritable social coup: a youth, who is "comely of person, refined of personality" puts to flight, with an inadvertent fart, "a bunch of those whose persons are coarse and natures gross." Al-Shirbīnī assuages the youth's embarrassment with a verse to the effect that the boy has cleverly saved the situation by showing his disdain for the "people of coarseness and disagreeableness" with a "delicate sound (*laṭīf lafẓ*), like honey." In other words, it is not what is done that matters but who does it: from the refined all things are refined and to the refined all things are forgiven. The converse is equally true: a peasant praised by a poet for his beauty cannot be truly beautiful, for "the actions of a peasant, however beautiful he may be, are well known to be devoid of any refinement" (§5.8.6).

The People of the Countryside as Surrogates for the Coarse in General

While al-Shirbīnī's satire of "the people of the countryside" may be read as simply that—an attack on one social group—another reading is suggested here. According to this, "the people of the countryside," whether peasants, men of religion, or dervishes, while undeniably the proximate target of al-Shirbīnī's satire, ultimately play the role of surrogates for all that al-Shirbīnī perceived as "coarse (*kathīf*)" in the Egypt of his day. The coarse, in al-Shirbīnī's worldview, are the coarse in general, the masses, the great unwashed, the opposite of all that is refined in terms of disposition, aptitude, behavior, appearance, linguistic competence, dress, and food. This reading rests on a contradiction between some of the evidence used by the author to demonstrate the rural nature of those people and the objective character of that evidence.

In the opening lines of the work, al-Shirbīnī promises to "embellish it with an explanation of the linguistic peculiarities of the countryside" (§1.1). In his actual analysis of those rural "linguistic peculiarities," however, al-Shirbīnī routinely characterizes as "rural" linguistic phenomena that are not so. For example, despite the fact that the shift from interdental fricative consonants to dental consonants is attested in urban speech from at least as early as the thirteenth century,[57] al-Shirbīnī states that "the word *t(a)bāt* originally has a *thā'*, but, being a rural word, just as they say *mīrāt* ('legacy') with *tā'* (for *mīrāth*), so also they say *tabāt* (for *thabāt*)" (§5.2.20), a claim that he also makes in connection with the shift from *ẓ* to *ḍ* (§5.5.2, vol. 2, §11.15.8, etc.) and *dh* to *d* (vol. 2, §11.36.16). Similarly, assimilation of *f* in *niṣf* ("half"), resulting in the standard colloquial form *nuṣṣ*, is described as being "in accordance with the rural language" (vol. 2, §11.11.10). At the lexical level, the relative pronoun *illī* ("who") (vol. 2, §11.27.5), the phrase *yā raytanī* ("would that I") (§5.6.12), and numerous other items commonly used in modern urban Egyptian Arabic are characterized by the author as being "rural forms."

For al-Shirbīnī, "rural speech" thus consists of forms that deviate from the literary norm, or, to put it differently, "rural speech" as he describes it is simply the standard colloquial language of his day, as spoken in the cities as well as in the countryside.[58] Intrinsically rural lexical items (such as certain types of vessel) aside, no rural-urban isoglosses can be discerned in the language of al-Shirbīnī's country people. At the same time, colloquial forms used in verse are typically explained by al-Shirbīnī as being adaptations of literary forms made "for the meter." Examples—among almost two dozen such cases—are *naḥīf* for *naḥīfan* (vol. 2, §11.1.21), *la-jat* for *la-jā'at* (vol. 2, §11.3.19), and *la-minnū* for *minhu* (vol. 2, §11.4.3). Any language that deviates from standard literary norms is thus denied autonomy. In fact, whenever al-Shirbīnī describes a nonstandard form as "rural" or being "for the meter," this information may safely be ignored.

The slipperiness of the designation "rural" is also conspicuous outside the field of language. The heretical dervishes who play such an important role in the work are, on the one hand, explicitly described as rural: they are "a sect that has been raised in the margins of the lands" (§7.1). On the other hand, the anecdotes describing them in Part One include little rural circumstantiality, with only three out of a score containing references to the countryside. Moreover, in several stories the events recounted are explicitly described as taking place in urban settings such as Alexandria (§7.12), al-Maḥallah al-Kubrā (§7.29), Cairo (§7.31), or Dimyāṭ (§7.32). The sophistication of the philosophical and religious concepts attributed to these Sufis also moves the reader far from al-Shirbīnī's stereotypical peasant who "knows only belts and cudgels, palm switches and plow-shaft pins, waterwheels and drover's whips."

Similarly, the section on rural poetry in Part One is followed by another ridiculing the pretensions of *nonrural* poetasters ("It Now Behooves Us to Offer a

Small Selection of the Verse of Those Who Lay Claim to the Status of Poets but Are in Practice Poltroons") (§6), thus leading the reader again towards broader vistas of "coarseness." The inclusion there of long quotations (§§6.2–4) from verses written by "the Amīr Murjān al-Ḥabashī," a black African, reinforces the identification of "coarseness" with a broader marginality (just as we have seen earlier, a man's base behavior is explained by the fact that his mother—Murjānah—is a black slave (§3.5)).

It seems, therefore, that in *Brains Confounded* "rurality" is equated with the broader deviance of the "coarse," wherever they may be found, from the linguistic, religious, and social norms defined by the "refined." Al-Shirbīnī's argument seems to be that, without regard to geographical location, the common people—or at least those of them who are guilty of the charges of ignorance, spurious pretensions to participation in elite culture, and perversion of religion that he brings against "the people of the countryside"—pose a threat to the elite.

The Threat and the Response

Summing up at the end of his section on bad rural poetry, al-Shirbīnī asserts that "all this [bad verse] stems from lack of intelligence and perspicacity, an excess of ignorance, and a paucity of instruction. A man of sound taste, in contrast, would never allow such poor language to pass his lips" (§6.8). This objective lack of learning, however, does not prevent members of the commons from *claiming* to be possessed of knowledge, or learning, (*ʻilm*), and the book is full of anecdotes in which these pretensions are manifested, only to be deflated, by Azharis, other scholars, or "sophisticates." Al-Shirbīnī clearly felt that access to education by those who had no innate right to it was an issue that needed addressing in the Egypt of his day. As he says of rural men of religion, "The condition of such people is well known, the likes of them are everywhere, and their goings-on are beyond numbering" (§3.76).

It has been hypothesized that the relegation of Cairo from the status of imperial capital under the Mamluks to provincial capital under the Ottomans resulted in a decentralization of cultural control and education, which spread to encompass larger numbers, drawn from previously excluded classes: "When the state is decentralized . . . and the structures at the top are weaker, the cultural forms and patterns from below are more likely to emerge";[59] this tendency would have been aided by the fact that "the policy of the Ottomans towards their provinces was one of restrained intervention in matters that were not of immediate interest to them. The Ottomans, for instance, did not have a policy of ottomanizing culture."[60]

According to this theory, evidence of this decentralization is to be seen in the spread of the *kuttāb*, a school in which young children memorized the Qur'an and achieved basic literacy and numeracy, as a result of which "many more people knew how to read and write beyond those who were attached to institutions of higher education"[61] and literacy spread, especially among artisans and tradesmen.[62] In other words, the scholars ". . . cannot be said to have had a complete monopoly on knowledge, since the kind of knowledge associated with the *ʿulamāʾ* was not the only kind of socially accepted knowledge."[63] Al-Shirbīnī's bugbear, popular Sufism, may have played an important role in spreading literacy.

At the same time, for reasons that are yet to be convincingly explained and are, on the face of it, in contradiction to the above, it was during the Ottoman period that a single dominant institution, the mosque-university of al-Azhar, emerged to promote religious orthodoxy in Egypt and foster the influence of the scholars.[64] A contemporary traveler from Morocco, Abū Sālim al-ʿAyyāshī, impressed by its obvious dynamism, describes how he "spent the night at the al-Azhar mosque, it being the twenty-seventh night [of Ramadan]; but in fact, every night in that mosque is like the Night of Power because it is alive with *dhikr*, recitation of the Qur'an, and teaching throughout the night and the day, while worship there never ceases, night or day, summer or winter, for it is without peer among the mosques of the entire world."[65]

Thus the scene would seem to have been set for a clash between the burgeoning energy of a hegemonistic al-Azhar and the decentralized, multi-faceted forces released by the spread of education. In this struggle, al-Shirbīnī identifies with al-Azhar heart and soul. When its scholars are mentioned, he prays God to "send them victorious and let them lead the Muslims unto the Day of Judgment!" (§4.5) and he champions them consistently through a series of anecdotes that exude a palpable sense of competition between urban scholars (*ʿulamāʾ*) and rural men of religion (*fuqahāʾ*) (§4.14ff).

Brains Confounded may thus represent a counterattack on behalf of the Azharites—and, more broadly, the representatives of "refined" culture—against the threat to their hegemony from the "coarse." With larger numbers of people being educated and with independent and self-confident Sufis playing an important role in the intellectual and cultural leadership of the newly literate, it is perhaps not surprising to find al-Shirbīnī, the bookseller and marginal scholar, defending the rights of the flagship institution of the mainstream cultural elite by associating its enemies with the despised world of the countryside.

Al-Shirbīnī's Condemnations of Abuses

It remains to address a seeming anomaly—those rare, albeit eloquent, passages in which al-Shirbīnī takes the side of the peasant against the tyranny and injustices of the government. These passages target specific practices. One is the extortion of the *wajbah* (a levy in the form of food for visiting officials and their animals), of which al-Shirbīnī says, "It is a form of injustice, and eating such food is forbidden by religion so long as the peasants do not give it of their own free will and cheerfully" (vol. 2, §11.3.10). Other practices condemned by the author are the corvée, the related "fine on the landless," and various fiscal imposts, all of which were unofficial levies that were imposed for the first time during the seventeenth century and were, as Raymond notes, "incessantly denounced, periodically abolished, but almost always re-instated."[66]

Al-Shirbīnī's argument against these practices rests on their characterization as *bidʿah*, that is, innovations unsanctioned by religion, for, as he says when considering the question of whether a tax farmer (*multazim*) has the right to continue "the fine on the landless" when he takes over a village where it was imposed by his predecessor, "the answer is to be found in the Tradition of the Prophet, upon whom blessings and peace, that says, 'He who introduces into this affair of ours that which is not in it is rejected' . . . such things being called 'innovation'" (vol. 2, §11.3.11). These innovations al-Shirbīnī contrasts with an earlier, utopian, state of affairs, which he identifies with "the first [tax-collection] apparatus in Egypt [which] was created at the direction of Our Master ʿAmr ibn al-ʿĀṣ when he conquered Egypt, though it was not organized in a uniform manner" (vol. 2, §11.6.7). Not only was this early, sanctioned, system productive of "enormous wealth" (*idem*), it was also, according to al-Shirbīnī, better for farming, for "in earlier times . . . a person would farm the land and the tax calculated on it would be light, and the levy in kind in support of the tax farmer and his lieutenants (*wajbah*) and the fine on the landless and the rest were quite unknown. Blessing was unconfined, all the land was under cultivation, and the people enjoyed the greatest good fortune, affluence, and profit" (vol. 2, §11.8.7).

Despite his condemnation of later practice, however, al-Shirbīnī clearly supports the status quo. He does not see the abuses he condemns as providing excuses for the peasant to avoid his duties, for "there is no escape, in any case, from paying the tax, even if that results in affliction and woe" and if the peasant is "put in prison to be beaten and punished," it is "so that the ordinances of the Almighty may be implemented against him" (vol. 2, §11.6.3). His discussion of the troublesome area of tax collection, where the legitimate right of the state to collect revenue and the oppression that may result from the way in which that right is applied are inextricably intertwined, ends with a telling disquisition on the differences between the good peasant and the bad (vol. 2, §11.6.5), in which al-Shirbīnī makes it plain that one of the most important distinguishing characteristics of the former is that he pays both his taxes and his debts (*idem*), while the latter pays neither (*idem*). The fact that this passage contains the only positive description of a peasant in the entire work indicates that al-Shirbīnī may have felt that "the good peasant" was more a logically necessary residual category than a living reality.

In the end, it would seem that al-Shirbīnī wanted to have it both ways: to condemn the "people of the countryside" and all they represented while criticizing the secular authorities for their violations of religious law. This must have been a comfortable position for a scholar (or would-be scholar) concerned to maintain for his like, as society's best representatives of refinement, a distance between the challenge from the coarse on the one hand and the arrogance of the ruling elite on the other.[67] At the same time, it would be anachronistic to assume that this position implies sympathy for the country dweller or objection to his treatment by the authorities, outside of the narrow area of practice identified by the author. Nowhere in *Brains Confounded* is there a declaration of sympathy for, or defense of, "the people of the countryside" equal in size or scope to the condemnation and vilification to which they are subjected throughout most of the work.

The Parody of Literary Culture

Brains Confounded is not only a satire directed against the "people of the countryside" but also a parody of textual commentary (*sharḥ*), a culturally central and highly elaborated genre that aimed to extract from a text, whether in the field of grammar and philology, poetry, religious sciences (in which context it was often called *tafsīr*), or philosophy,[68] the maximum value for the literate community. While the parody consists, in essence, of abusing the venerable conventions of *sharḥ* by applying these to material that is, in the author's view, unworthy, the process is not without danger to the satire itself, for by pushing these conventions to their logical extremes, the author risks exposing them to ridicule, thus undermining the assumptions of contemporary literary discourse to which they bear witness and on which the satire depends.

It seems likely, however, that in choosing the *sharḥ* genre as a vehicle for his satire, al-Shirbīnī was inspired, in the first instance at least, by the authority, and thus the advantage over his adversary, that these assumptions granted him. As Rippin remarks, "As an implement for asserting the scholar's status and authority, arguments over grammar have no rival."[69] Any subversion of the genre itself may have been an unavoidable result of the momentum of the parody rather than its deliberate purpose, and ultimately the author's attitude to his own parody appears ambiguous.

The Conventions Parodied

The commentators' preoccupations most prominently parodied by al-Shirbīnī are meter, etymology, conventions for the identification of verbal paradigms and morphological patterns, and the use of lexical authorities in support of the latter, as well as probative verse quotations and the rhetorical debate as a heuristic tool.

In his commentary on the first example of rural verse in the "Account of Their Poets and of Their Idiocies and Inanities" (§5.2), al-Shirbīnī plunges immediately into an analysis of the meter, which he claims belongs to *baḥr al-kharā al-wāfir*, or "the 'abundant' ocean of shite" (§5.2.1) playing on the dual sense of *baḥr* as "ocean" and as "meter," as well as on the name of one of the commoner meters, *al-wāfir*, literally "the abundant." In this context, a conventional commentator might be expected to provide the standard mnemonic for this meter, using forms of the root *f-ʿ-l* ("to do"), to represent the pattern of long (L) and short (S) syllables for a hemistich, namely, *mufāʿalatun mufāʿalatun faʿūlun* (i.e., SLSSL|SLSSL|SLL). Al-Shirbīnī does provide a mnemonic but uses the root *kh-b-ṭ*, claiming that the meter is to be parsed as *mutakhabbiṭun khābiṭun mutakhabbiṭun khubāṭ* (i.e., SSLSL|LSL|SSLSL|SL). Not only does this bear no relation to *al-wāfir*, but the author, by using this root, which includes within its semantic range the concepts of "striking," "trampling," "dust," "diabolical madness," and "sheep bloat," is able to bring the verse, and hence its author and audience, into linguistic and cultural areas that are both opprobrious in and of themselves and ridiculously inappropriate for a prestigious undertaking such as textual commentary. This joke is repeated throughout. Roots employed for such mnemonics include *h-b-l* ("foolishness," "raving"), *kh-l-b-ṭ* ("causing malicious trouble; confusing"), *th-q-l* ("heaviness; boorishness"), and many others.

Al-Shirbīnī also follows the grammarians' habit of using words of a given pattern or measure of long and short syllables (*wazn*) to disambiguate that of the word under discussion. Again, for comic effect, he employs the technique of using as disambiguators words of mundane or undignified connotation. Thus "*kūz* ('mug for water') is of the pattern of *būz* ('muzzle') because its wide mouth resembles the muzzle of a cow or a calf" (vol. 2, §11.3.4) and "*jubnah* ('piece of cheese') [is] of the measure of *ubnah* ('passive sodomy')" (vol. 2, §11.26.3), and so on.

Al-Shirbīnī also provides spurious etymologies for many words. For example, he claims that *ma-ḍāl* ("he ceased not to" or "he kept on" (doing something)) derives from *ḍall* ("error") or *ḍalāl* ("delusion") or *ḍa'īlah* ("slender snake, viper"). Not only are these etymons incorrect (*ḍall* and *ḍalāl* derive from the root *ḍ-l-l, ḍa'īlah* from *ḍ-'-l*; *ḍāl*, a strictly colloquial form, might be considered to derive from *ḍ-w-l* or *ḍ-y-l* but historically derives from *z-w-l* with conflation of this root with *ẓ-l-l*), they also exploit the technique of ridicule by association used with regard to the meters. On occasion, these false etymologies are elaborated into lengthy flights of whimsicality, as when al-Shirbīnī provides four possible etymons, all entirely spurious, for the word *qarrūfih* (a sort of vessel) (vol. 2, §11.3.5). In support of such etymologies al-Shirbīnī often invokes the authority of the nonexistent dictionary *Al-Qāmūs al-azraq wa-l-nāmūs al-ablaq* (*The Blue Ocean and Piebald Canon*), a title reminiscent of al-Fīrūzābādhī's famous *Al-Qāmūs al-muḥīṭ* (*The Encompassing Ocean*) and perhaps other lexica (see n. 128).

Similar are the "paradigms" (*maṣādir*, singular *maṣdar*)[70] with which al-Shirbīnī sometimes completes his analysis of a given word, mimicking the lexicographers' habit of using these to establish the base forms of the conjugation. Thus, according to the author, the *maṣdar* of *ḍāl* is "*ḍalla*, *yaḍillu*, *ḍalālan*, and *ḍāllun* and *maḍlūlun*" (§5.2.2); in reality, however, this paradigm is that of the verb *ḍalla* ("to go astray"), which bears no etymological relationship to the word under discussion. Other paradigms contain made-up, humorous, or eccentric forms that may contain coded references (see, e.g., n. 243) or serve to introduce further vulgar, obscene, or inappropriate words to bolster the comic impact (see, e.g., vol. 2, §11.2.8).

Probative quotations (*shawāhid*) are also used, as is standard in *sharḥ*, to lend authority to the commentator's statements. Not all of these are themselves opprobrious or ridiculous. The use of a well-known quotation such as that attributed dubiously by al-Shirbīnī to Maʿn ibn Zāʾidah—"We are a tribe whom the wide-eyed pupil / Melts . . ." (§5.2.13)—for instance, relies for its comic effect simply on the incongruity of its occurrence in the context of a verse in the course of which the beloved declares "I'm off for a crap." Others, albeit obscene or playful, may be quotations from contemporary poets whose wit the author admires and may be used for their congruity with the matter at hand (as, e.g., "I saw a leper deep down in a well" (§5.2.16)). Still others, however, seem to be invented simply to make fun of the implied tendency of some commentators to use *shawāhid* to say in verse what they have just said in prose, e.g., (following discussion of the etymology of the words in question (§5.5.4)):

> *Khabṭ* from *khubāṭ* derives
> And *ḍarṭ* from *ḍurāṭ* likewise.

Perhaps the weightiest of the conventions of commentary that al-Shirbīnī puts to comic use is the heuristic rhetorical debate in which the author first poses and then responds to and dismisses an objection to an argument he has put forward earlier. Al-Shirbīnī usually refers to such a passage as a "debate" (*masʾalah*), which he generally characterizes as "silly" (*habāliyyah*), though he sometimes uses the opening "If it be said . . ." (*fa-in qīla . . .*) or a variant, a wording that led to the technique being named *fanqalah*. A typical "silly debate" occurs in the author's discussion of a metaphorical usage of the phrase "cutting out" as used to refer to the action of the lover's fingers in removing (figuratively) his heart from his breast: "Why does he talk of 'cutting out' with the fingers, rather than with a knife or a razor, given that it is of the nature of cutting that it should be done with a sharp instrument and, the heart being flesh, cutting it with the fingers or the fingernails would not work?" We reply: "The fatuous response is . . ." (§5.5.14); for an example of *fanqalah*, see §5.5.12.

The Logical Absurdities of Grammar

The notion that the relationship between the real world and grammar was not arbitrary seems to have been commonplace in al-Shirbīnī's time. There is no reason to think that he is being humorous when he says that a certain Sufi shaykh (of whom he approves) is "by nature attracted to the feminine, to the extent that he would eat only from a *zubdiyyah* ('bowl') [and] drink only from a *qullah* ('water pitcher')" (§6.6) (these words being grammatically feminine), or that a man would describe his wife as being "so modest that she covers her face from the moon [*qamar*, grammatically masculine] and from everything else [grammatically] masculine" (§7.31).

This is taken to an extreme, however, when al-Shirbīnī first contends, for example, that all lice are female because the word *qamlah* ("louse") is grammatically feminine and then uses this argument to explain that the louse cannot jump because "the louse . . . is . . . female, and the female is weaker than the male" (vol. 2, §11.2.3). Similarly, he implies elsewhere that, because the word *liḥḥīs* (a sort of vermin) is related through their common root to the word *laḥīs*, and because the latter may be coupled with the word *taʿīs* ("miserable") in the phrase *taʿīs laḥīs* (for which al-Shirbīnī gives various meanings, all unpleasant), the creatures known as *liḥḥīs* are themselves rendered more harmful (vol. 2, §11.2.2). Likewise, al-Shirbīnī contends that there is "a certain appropriateness" to the fact that the written word *kishk* ("groats formed into balls") reads as a palindrome in Arabic because "their bottoms are just like their tops, and the beginning of each piece of *kishk* is the same as its end" (vol. 2, §11.10.11).

In such absurd applications of grammar to life, al-Shirbīnī probes the limits of linguistic logic in pursuit of comic effect, propelling himself into a world where grammar is fundamental and life incidental; that is, where life imitates grammar. While the reader may laugh, he can also hardly fail to notice the intrinsic absurdity of such arguments, which may, in turn, lead him to question the sanity of the discipline in whose name they are produced.

Subversion versus Affirmation

The tendency of the techniques described above to make textual commentary itself appear comic raises the possibility that al-Shirbīnī actually intended to subvert the genre and the literary culture from which it grew. Other elements in the work also point in that direction.

On occasion, for instance, al-Shirbīnī seems nonchalant toward the very process of commentary. Thus, *baṭṭāṭ* ("to pat out") is derived "from *baṭbaṭa* . . . or from *biṭaṭ* . . . or, quite possibly, from sheer stuff and nonsense" (vol. 2, §11.21.5). It may also be significant that three of the "miscellaneous anecdotes" that make up the penultimate section of the book concern the absurdities into which pedantry can lead grammarians (vol. 2, §§12.7, 12.8, 12.12).

At the same time, however, al-Shirbīnī appears to disclaim any subversive intent by applying to his commentary descriptors such as "silly" (*habālī*) (as noted above), "facetious" (*fashrawī*) (§5.8.20, vol. 2, §11.4.8, etc.), or "lame" (*fushkulī*) (§5.3.10).

Al-Shirbīnī's attitude to the implications of his parody of textual commentary thus appears ambiguous, though affirmation of its validity as a genre, and of the validity of the assumptions that underpin it, predominate.

It remains for me to acknowledge the help that I have received in preparing this revised edition and translation of al-Shirbīnī's *Brains Confounded*, and the edition and translation of al-Sanhūrī's *Muḍḥik dhawī l-dhawq*, which will be published separately. Without the goodwill of the executive editors of the Library of Arabic Literature, headed by General Editor Philip F. Kennedy, the enterprise would never have gotten off the ground. It was kept in that position by the generous help and input of, first and foremost, Geert Jan van Gelder, who read the work in both languages and made numerous corrections, suggestions, and improvements; further invaluable assistance was provided by James Montgomery. I was also fortunate to have the input of my Cairo colleague Ahmed Seddik, who helped me to unravel many of the complexities of *Risible Rhymes*, of Noah Gardiner, who made an assessment of the manuscript of the latter, and of Adam Talib. Last, but by no means least, I benefited from the unfailing support of Stuart Brown, Gemma Juan-Simó, and, above all, Chip Rossetti, all of the New York office of the Library of Arabic Literature.

Note on the Text

The present edition of the Arabic text is a revised version of that published in 2005, which was based on a stemma developed from a review of eight manuscripts and the first printed edition (Bulaq 1274/1858).[71]

The 2005 edition established a text that differed significantly from that of the then-available printed editions. Most importantly, from the perspective of content, it restored several passages found in all the manuscripts but missing from the Bulaq edition. The longest of these, in the section on rural dervishes, or *fuqarāʾ*, (§§7.1–29 and §§7.31–32 in the present edition), is over five thousand words; without the passage, this section is notably shorter in the Bulaq edition than the sections on peasant cultivators (*fallāḥūn*), and rural pastors/teachers (*fuqahāʾ*). The restoration of these passages redresses this imbalance and allows us to see more clearly the importance that al-Shirbīnī attributed to the role of dervishes on the rural stage and the vehemence of his animosity towards them. Also restored in the 2005 edition are the last twenty-nine lines of the poem, in *rajaz* meter, with which Part One ends.

The 2005 edition also omits several passages found only in the Bulaq edition and consisting largely of quotations taken from the mainstream jurisprudential, historical, polite-letters (*adab*), and classical-verse traditions; these appear to have been inserted in a pietistic or didactic spirit and often have little relevance to their context.

Finally, at the level of language, the 2005 edition appears more rough-hewn than the Bulaq edition. Many "Middle Arabic" features that occur, inconsistently, in the manuscripts and were "corrected," inconsistently, in the Bulaq edition are maintained there.

All the above features have been retained in the present edition, which does, however, differ from its predecessor in one important area: in this edition a less laissez-faire approach has been taken to the meter of verse in the standard (i.e., non-"rural") language. Major violations of meter have been corrected, often by reference to citations in other works. In practice, this has often meant returning to the readings of the Bulaq edition, whose editors no doubt went through the same process. In making these changes, we have been guided by the maxim that most poets would rather commit errors of grammar than of meter and that the solecisms that have been removed probably represent the slips of unschooled copyists rather than admissible variants to what are, in many cases, well-known lines of verse. Without these metrical faux pas the verse is often, naturally, less hurtful to the ear.

"Rural" verse poses particular metrical problems. The verses that al-Shirbīnī so characterizes exhibit both colloquial and literary features. Taking the "Ode of Abū Shādūf" as an example, it may be seen that readings imposed by the meter (*al-ṭawīl*) sometimes contradict colloquial norms by including both short word-final vowels that conform to literary rules (e.g., *yaqūlu*, vol. 2, §11.1) and short word-final vowels that conform to neither colloquial nor literary rules (e.g., *Abū Shādūfi*, vol. 2, §11.1). In the latter case, one cannot be certain how these would have been pronounced; here we treat them as remnants of an underlying literary form (*Abū Shādūfin* → *Abū Shādūfi*), though we might, with equal validity, have assigned to them any other character to represent this unknown vowel (e.g., *Abū Shādūfo*). Examples of *tanwīn* also occur (e.g., *lawʿatun*, vol. 2, §11.5). As van Gelder has pointed out, "it would seem that one is supposed to read as many classical forms as possible . . . to the extent of producing hybrid forms."[72] Indeed, such verses might be described as belonging, as a whole, to a hybrid colloquial/literary language variety. Nonfinal short vowels in colloquial words, in prose or in verse, are given literary values (e.g., *miḥrāt*, "plow," rather than *muḥrāt*). This convention is employed simply to avoid having to justify the voweling for every transcribed colloquial word, it being assumed that that voweling was not always the same in the seventeenth century as it is now. Occasional exceptions are made, either because the author makes a colloquial spelling explicit (e.g., *libbih* for *libbah* (vol. 2, §11.23.9) and *yiʿiffu* for *yaʿiffu* (vol. 2, §11.36.14)) or because the meter demands colloquial forms (e.g., *wa-yitʿanṭaz . . . wa-yijjaʿmaṣ* (vol. 2, §10.11.3).

In the case of the "Ode of Abū Shādūf" itself, we have found it necessary, in this edition, to revise our understanding of the acceptable parameters of the meter in question. Thus, while the only possible endings of a line in standard *ṭawīl* meter are SLLL, SLSL, and SLL,[73] the frequent occurrence of SLX SL or SLL L in the "Ode" have convinced us that this unconventional form is intentional. New vocalizations have therefore been given in this edition. Thus we read, for example, *yaḍāl naḥīf* (vol. 2, §11.1) and *khulbat līf* (vol. 2, §11.4).

This adjustment also allows us to avoid such bizarre forms, required by the standard meter, as *takhawīf* and *tajarīf* in favor of *takhwīf* (vol. 2, §11.6) and *tajrīf* (vol. 2, §11.14).

The footnotes to the 2005 edition, which contain all variants that are viable according to the stemma (family tree of the manuscripts), have been omitted from this edition. Here, with rare exceptions, only corrections to the 2005 edition, whether of the metrical solecisms mentioned above or of misprints, are included, though only where these affect the consonantal skeleton. In such cases, the original form is preceded by بي, standing for "Peeters: *OLA 141*." When the new form is not to be found among the variants listed in the apparatus of the 2005 edition, that is, does not occur in any of the witnesses, all readings are noted.[74] The exceptions concern one passage present in the 2005 text that has been excluded from the present edition, based on a reexamination of the stemma (see §1.4), and the replacement, in the verse and commentary, of طحونتنا ("our mill") (§5.8) with طاحونتنا since, though the former is supported stemmatically for *Brains Confounded*, it does not fit the meter, and the latter, which does fit the meter, is the form found in *Risible Rhymes*.

In this edition, verses that are the subject of commentary are indented; other verses are right-aligned. Reiterations in the body of the text of verses that are the subject of commentary are enclosed in parentheses, following the example of the first Bulaq edition (in the manuscripts, such verses and their pericopes are generally distinguished by marks such as a triangle of dots, or overlining, or rubrication, or a combination of these).

The present translation is a revised version of that published in 2007.[75] In revising the translation, I have sought to correct errors in its predecessor. I have also shortened the notes in keeping with the guidelines of the Library of Arabic Literature; areas that have been systematically cut in the interests of reducing the academic apparatus are the two particularly complex areas of the sourcing of prophetic traditions and the tracing of sources for prose stories and topoi. I have, however, been able to increase the number of identifications of poets cited anonymously or erroneously by al-Shirbīnī (though, again in the interest of reducing the academic apparatus, ambiguous and disputed attributions have largely been omitted); this has been possible due only to the efforts of Geert Jan van Gelder, to whom I am greatly indebted, for this as for much else.

In addition, I have removed from the endnotes most references related to the lexicology of Egyptian words. Interested readers are referred to a lexicon that I have compiled dealing with words not found in Martin Hinds and El-Said Badawi's *A Dictionary of Egyptian Arabic*.[76] Those who wish to study in greater depth what *Brains Confounded* can tell us about Egyptian Arabic in al-Shirbīnī's day are referred to my dissertation on the topic.[77]

The difficulties of rendering poetry into another language are well known; I have tried, at least, to use rhyme and rhythm in these passages, though without seeking to produce anything that imitates, for example, Arabic meter, but because Arabic hemistichs often appear as a single line in the translation, verse consisting of a single line in Arabic (two in English) is not usually rhymed. The reader should also bear in mind that much of the poetry, whether a quotation or made up by the author, was deliberately chosen or written to be bad. If such verse reads as doggerel, the translation has achieved its purpose.

Rhymed prose—phrases, usually short, that rhyme but are not metered—poses a special problem, as English has no equivalent category. Its role in the structure of the work is, however, important, because it is used at moments of heightened emotional or rhetorical tension or to lend authority to and drive home an argument elaborated in immediately preceding unrhymed prose. I have used rhyme, indeed, but also assonance, alliteration, and rhythm, to distinguish many of these passages. I have also been influenced, however, by Newmark's theories of "importance," according to which "the more important the language of the text, the more closely it should be translated" (Newmark, *Translation*, 1)—"important" language being defined, in this context, as "language that denotes what is exceptionally valuable, significant, necessary, or permanent" (*idem*, 2). I have therefore sacrificed, on occasion, the aesthetic demands of the text to the need for literalism. This is the case with passages that convey facts or opinions whose significance I believe to be too great, from the author's standpoint, to permit the massaging that inevitably occurs in the search for aesthetic equivalence. An example of such a passage is that beginning "Indeed, they never escape their condition of uncouthness because . . . ," in which the author provides an initial description, in rhymed prose, of the countryman that is critical for an understanding of his attitude towards him (§2.3); this and equivalent passages I have rendered in unrhymed prose. I have made no attempt to rhyme the "Ode of Abū Shādūf" itself for the same reasons.

English is the metalanguage of this series. In the translation, technical terms, such as those referring to rural officials and rhetorical devices, have been rendered by English equivalents (and their meanings explained in greater detail in the Glossary). Similarly, the titles of books are given in English first, and the use of transliterated Arabic has been reduced to a minimum. Nevertheless, *Brains Confounded* contains passages of textual commentary (*sharḥ*) that are central to its purpose. In our translation we have borne in mind that these commentaries on specific verses are commentaries on Arabic and not on English texts and that it is Arabic words and not English words that are at issue. When the commentator discusses *ʿadīm* (colloquial for *ʿaẓīm*), he is not discussing the English word "mighty"; in such cases, the English translation is an approximation whose lexical boundaries differ, in all likelihood, from those of its Arabic "equivalent." In these passages, therefore, Arabic has been privileged, in the sense that the verses in question are reproduced in transcription in the English text and precede their English translations, both when they first occur and in the commentary. The reader who does not know Arabic may well allow his eye to skip these transcriptions; they are, however, essential to the logic of the text.

Notes to the Introduction

1 According to Awliyā' Shalabī (Evliya Çelebi), who visited Egypt during al-Shirbīnī's lifetime, Shirbīn boasted 1,700 houses, a Friday mosque, fifty other mosques, and one *madrasah* (Baer, "Significance," 38 n. 8; Baer does, however, point out that Shalabī was given to exaggeration). Shirbīn now falls within the more recently created governorate of al-Daqahliyyah.

2 Al-Muḥibbī, *Khulāṣat al-athar*, 1:175. Though al-Muḥibbī does not say so explicitly, it is highly likely that a scholar as prominent as al-Qalyūbī (whom al-Muḥibbī describes as "one of the leading *'ulamā'*") was an Azhari; this is supported by the fact that he was also a teacher of Aḥmad al-Sandūbī, whom al-Muḥibbī describes as such.

3 Al-Muḥibbī, *Khulāṣat al-athar*, 1:175.

4 See, e.g., M. A. J. Beg, "Ḥā'ik," in *EI2*.

5 "It is said, 'stupidity is of ten parts, nine of which are to be found in weavers'" (al-Rāghib al-Iṣfahānī, *Muḥāḍarāt*, 1:284).

6 Al-Sandūbī was "one of the leading teachers of al-Azhar" and, like al-Shirbīnī, studied under al-Qalyūbī (al-Muḥibbī, *Khulāṣat al-athar*, 1:156). He wrote several works, including a commentary on the *Alfiyyah* of Ibn Mālik, and "much verse" (al-Muḥibbī, *Khulāṣat al-athar*, 1:256–57). The relationship may have been based, in part, on the fact that the two men came from the same region (Minyat Sandūb lies on the eastern branch of the Nile about thirty miles south of al-Manṣūrah).

7 MS Gotha (A) 2346 (see *OLA 141*), at the top of p. 2[b] according to the "Arabic" numbering and following mention of the author's name in the colophon at the end of Part Two: *fa-halaka fī sanati iḥdā 'ashrata wa-mi'atin ba'd al-alfi l-hijriyyah.*

8 Pertsch, *Katalog*, 4:329.

9 Mubārak, *al-Khiṭaṭ*, 1:127–28.

10 On the cultural importance of the *majlis*, see Hanna, "Culture," 99.

11 Baer defines *mu'āmil* as "merchant or moneylender" (Baer, *Fellah and Townsman in the Middle East*, 6), but the references to *mu'āmils* in *Brains Confounded* concern moneylending only (see Davies, *Lexicon*, 78–79).

12 *Ṭarḥ al-madar* opens with a similar, though more explicitly personal, complaint: "I am, however, of good fortune and recognition deprived . . . and rare it is in these times for a master of eloquence to triumph" (p. 1).

13 Winter notes that he was unable to devote a chapter of his *Egyptian Society under Ottoman Rule 1517–1798* "to that social class which formed the majority of the Egyptian population in the Ottoman period, namely the fellahin. To do the subject any measure of justice would have required much more information than is available to me at present" (p. xv).

14 It is difficult to find other than incidental mention of peasants in the histories that extensively chronicle Egypt's political life. Al-Jabartī (1167–1241/1753–1825) devotes a few lines to peasants in connection with Muḥammad ʿAlī's abolition of the tax-farming system (where he speaks of them in terms remarkably similar to those used by al-Shirbīnī; *ʿAjāʾib*, 4:64). In the modern period, according to a study of the peasant in Arabic literature, the first mention of the peasant in a literary prose context was made by ʿAbd Allāh al-Nadīm in the 1880s (see his recently republished play "Al-Waṭan" (*Akhbār al-adab* 217, Sept. 2003)), the first in poetry occurs in 1908 (see Ḥasan, *Al-Fallāḥ*, 24), and the first in "literary journalism" in 1933 (*ibid.*, 121). Two early Egyptian novels, Maḥmūd Haqqī's *Dīnshiwāy* (1906) and Muḥammad Ḥusayn Haykal's *Zaynab* (1913), have rural settings.

15 An edition and translation of al-Sanhūrī's work is being published by the Library of Arabic Literature under the title *Risible Rhymes*.

16 Jess Stern (ed.), *The Random House Dictionary of the English Language* (New York: Random House, 1979). Van Gelder argues that, because Arabic lacks an exact equivalent for the term "satire," it may be dangerous to apply the term to "a tradition that had its own system of modes and genres" (van Gelder, "Satire, medieval," in *EAL*). However, the presence in *Brains Confounded* of precisely the "moral dimension which is the hallmark of true satire" (*idem*) and of the "wit and sparkle usually associated with satire" (*idem*) seem to justify its use.

17 *Random House Dictionary*. Van Gelder has previously noted this double nature of the work (van Gelder, "Satire, medieval," in *EAL*), but, while he sees these two sides to the work as mutually exclusive, I see them as complementary.

18 Hanna, "Chronicles," 243.

19 Hanna, "Culture," 98.

20 Ṣabrī, *Riḥlah*, 24.

21 For the *Thousand and One Nights*, see, e.g., Irwin, *Companion*, 122; similar is al-Ibshīhī, *Al-Mustaṭraf*, 1:266.

22 Al-Tanūkhī, *Al-Faraj*, 144–53.

23 In a version recorded in three different forms between 1959 and 1963 in Los Angeles, the protagonists are the pope and a rabbi; in a Turkish version, the protagonists are Nasrettin Hoca and, once more, a Persian scholar (see Greene, "Trickster").

24 In the Indian version, which has Sanskrit roots, the actors are Akbar and his vizier Birbal (Marzolph, *Arabia Ridens*, 1:145); for older Arabic versions, see al-Ṭurṭūshī, *Sirāj*, 370 (where the story is told to the caliph al-Ma'mūn), al-Ibshīhī, *Al-Mustaṭraf*, 1:108, and al-Damīrī, *Ḥayawān*, 1:160.

25 See Baer, "Significance," 24–25, for examples of stories said still to be current. An anonymous pamphlet entitled *Tamaddun al-fallāḥīn* (*The Civilization of the Peasants*), undated but probably mid-twentieth-century, contains "pleasant stories and curious and comic anecdotes about the contentious peasants," most of which are in colloquial Arabic and several of which recall those in *Brains Confounded*.

26 Irwin, *Companion*, 54.

27 Not every digression can be attached without strain to the main frame of the work. The long passage narrating the death of al-Ḥusayn, introduced on the excuse that the word *ṭafīf* ("brimming"), which occurs in the "Ode of Abū Shādūf," may derive from al-Ṭaff, the place where the Prophet's grandson met his end, is more difficult to reconcile with the overall purpose of the book. It may be a particularly extreme example of al-Shirbīnī seeking to assert his credentials as a member of the erudite classes, in this instance going so far as to introduce material that cannot, by its nature, be treated humorously, or it may be that the reference to a dispute among Sufis over the final resting place of the martyr's head (vol. 2, §11.31.14) points, in a coded way, to some allegiance of al-Shirbīnī's.

28 Omri, "Adab," 174.

29 Al-Shirbīnī lists seven poems under this heading (§§5.1–5.9.27). To these may be added three that occur as probative verses in the commentary on the first of the numbered poems. These extra poems are those starting *shaḥṭiṭ ṣuḥaybak wa-rukhkhuh alfa farqillah* (§5.2.4), *taḍāl innak yā miḥrāt tāʾib jamāʿatak* (the verse has no clear meter and the voweling is tentative), and *qūmī mʿakī yā Khuṭayṭah shiʿratik bi-l-khayṭ* (§5.2.15). Verses occurring (with minor variants) in both works are those beginning *wa-llāhi wa-llāhi l-ʿaḍīmi l-qādirī* (§5.5), *hibabu furni-bni ʿammī* (§5.6), *saʾaltu ʿani l-ḥibb* (§5.7), *wa-qultu lahā būlī ʿalayya wa-sharshirī* (§5.3), *raqqāṣu ṭāḥūninā* (§5.8), and *raʾayt ḥarīfī bi-farqillah* (§5.9). Verses occurring in al-Shirbīnī only are *mā ḍāl qamīṣī yushaḥṭaṭ* (§5.2) and the three "extra" poems mentioned above.

30 I am indebted to Mark Muehlhaeusler for bringing this to my attention. The sentence reads "We learn, among other things, from *Hazz al-quḥūf ʿalā sharḥ Abī Shādūf* [*sic*] that pimping is of various kinds, styles, and types. One of these is called 'turning a blind

eye' (*al-taṭnīsh*), when the man is not gainfully employed and the woman is well-off and feeds and clothes him. Thus if he notices anything about her, he can say nothing to her and all he can do is pretend not to know what is going on and behave as though he has seen and heard nothing."

31 Muḥammad Qindīl al-Baqlī (ed.), under the title *Our Egyptian Village before the Revolution – 1* (*Qaryatunā l-Miṣriyyah qabla l-thawrah – 1*). The retitling underlines the ideological impetus behind the work's republication during the Nasserist era.

32 Mehren's article is devoted mainly to the historical and literary background and a summary of the contents, and it has a limited Arabic-French glossary of words occurring in the work and "little used in the literary language" (Mehren, "Et Par Bildrag Bedømmelse").

33 Spitta, *Grammatik*, Texts VIII and X. Spitta's two texts combine three stories from *Brains Confounded* in an order different from that of the original and with passages originally in literary Arabic translated into colloquial. Spitta probably transcribed the stories as they were read to him by an informant from the book (Spitta, *Grammatik*; see, further, Davies, *Profile*, 34–35).

34 Vollers's article is the most systematic and penetrating of the three but is limited largely to linguistic analysis (Vollers, "Beiträge").

35 Kern, "Neuere ägyptische Humoristen."

36 Zaydān, *Ta'rīkh adab*, 3:276–77.

37 The issue of whether or not the "Ode" is "genuine" is inextricably bound up with question of al-Shirbīnī's motives in writing *Brains Confounded* and his attitude towards its subjects. Arguments in support of a literalist reading are comprehensively presented and analyzed by Baer ("Significance," 25–35), according to whom, in the light of the renewed interest in and empathy for the peasant that came with the Egyptian Revolution of 1952, "Shirbīnī's book confronted [Egyptian scholars] with a difficult problem. How should they explain that a native Egyptian writer born himself in an Egyptian village mocked and despised the fellah as if he expressed the views of the fellah's Turkish and Mamluk oppressors?" (p. 28). Baer detects two responses to this problem. The first is to see al-Shirbīnī in a favorable light. Scholars taking this approach believe that al-Shirbīnī intended to condemn the exploitation and oppression of Egyptians by the Ottomans "by describing the poverty of the people and their oppression by the foreign *kāshif*s and *multazims*" (*idem*); he also intended to condemn the *fallāḥ*'s cultural backwardness in order to "arouse the *'ulamā'* . . . and remind them of their responsibility to educate society properly" (p. 29). Most writers who espouse these ideas explain al-Shirbīnī's apparent hostility to the peasant as camouflage to protect the author from a putative (but, in

fact, nonexistent) Ottoman censorship. A second group holds that, while al-Shirbīnī was hostile to the peasant and the book "clearly reflects the social struggle between fellahs and townsmen, their derision by them and the townsmen's arrogance in their treatment of the peasants" (p. 32), the author expressed these negative sentiments either because he did not write the book of his own free will or because he did so to ingratiate himself with the Ottoman authorities; an extension of the latter theory would have it that al-Shirbīnī was an agent of the same authorities, who employed him to deride the poem by "the unknown popular poet Abū Shādūf, the voice of the silent oppressed," as one scholar of this persuasion characterizes him (p. 34).

38 A shorter version of the article (lacking the discussion of the debate over attitudes and motives) appeared as "Fellah and Townsman in Ottoman Egypt: A Study of Shirbīnī's Hazz al-Quḥūf," *Asian and African Studies* [Jerusalem] 8 (1972): 221–56. Muhsin al-Musawi, *The Medieval Islamic Republic of Letters*, devotes a chapter to *Brains Confounded*, describing it as a "contribution to contrafaction" of critical importance to the literature of the period; unfortunately, it appeared too recently to allow a consideration of his arguments.

39 Baer, "Significance," 3.

40 Baer, "Significance," 35.

41 Baer, "Significance," 35.

42 Baer, "Significance," 36.

43 Omri, "Adab," 187.

44 "The documents are full of numerous examples of the neglect of the dykes or their cutting before the irrigation of distant areas, leading to the non-irrigation of thousands of feddons in those areas" (Ibrāhīm, *Al-Azamāt*, 109).

45 Baer quotes Aḥmad al-Jazzār Bāshā, "Behind some of the villages there are small villages without minarets. The people of Egypt call them *kafr*" (Baer, "Significance," 8). Numerous anecdotes in *Brains Confounded* attest, however, to the existence of mosques, albeit of a primitive sort, in the *kufūr*.

46 Restored passages are §§7.1–29 and §§7.31–32. On possible reasons for this omission, see Note on the Text.

47 A new wave of Sufi thought, based on what Ahmet Karamustafa calls "socially deviant renunciation," arose in Iran and Anatolia in the thirteenth century and soon spread to Syria and Egypt (Karamustafa, *Friends*, 10). According to the same source, "ethnically . . . the leaders—and one suspects the rank and file—of the movement at this stage were not Arabs but mostly Iranians" (*ibid.*, 55). However, Sabra has pointed out that, "while there is not much doubt that the leaders were Iranians, the composition of the

rank and file is less clear. It is not out of the question that locals joined these groups" (Sabra, *Poverty*, 29). There is nothing in *Brains Confounded* to suggest that the dervishes referred to there were anything but Egyptians.

48 Winter, *Society and Religion*, 104, 114; al-Ṭawīl, *Al-Taṣawwuf*, 1:116.

49 Winter, *Society and Religion*, 106.

50 Winter, *Society and Religion*, 106.

51 Winter, *Society and Religion*, 116.

52 Winter, *Society and Religion*, 115.

53 Membership in one or several Sufi orders was usual among the *ʿulamāʾ* of al-Shirbīnī's day, including shaykhs of al-Azhar.

54 Al-Shirbīnī's attitude to rural *fuqarāʾ* does not imply hostility on his part to Sufism per se; on the contrary, the text is peppered with approving references to Sufis such as al-Shaʿrānī and other "initiates of God." Rather, as Karamustafa points out, "to the 'enlightened' cultural elite . . . the antinomian dervish was the symbol *par excellence* of the religion of the vulgar" (Karamustafa, *Friends*, 8).

55 Winter, *Egyptian Society*, 51.

56 Karamustafa, *Friends*, 10.

57 Davies, *Profile*, 66–67.

58 On the persistence of a conceptual distance between the medium of expression of the educated and that of the uneducated, whereby only the latter—in disregard of the facts—speak the colloquial language, see Armbrust, who writes that "sometimes when colloquial is retained in written language it is to confirm the ideology of social separation by emphasizing a class difference" (Armbrust, *Culture*, 54).

59 Hanna, "Culture," 87.

60 Hanna, "Culture," 88.

61 Hanna, "Culture," 103.

62 Hanna, "Culture," 102.

63 Hanna, "Culture," 95.

64 Winter, *Egyptian Society*, 118–19: "While Al-Azhar had acquired a special prestige under Ayyubid and Mamluke rule, it was only in the 17th and 18th centuries that it eclipsed the other madrasas (religious teaching establishments) of Cairo to become completely identified with the ulama establishment."

65 Al-ʿAyyāshī, *Al-Riḥlah*, 1:126.

66 Raymond, *Artisans*, 2:614.

67 Raymond makes the point that "il y avait une contradiction latente entre les liens matériels et sociaux qui unissaient les cheikhs à la caste dirigeante et le rôle de porte-parole

qu'étaient censés pour les *'ulamā'* vis-à-vis de la population égyptienne puisque ses difficultés et les abus dont elle soufrait avaient précisément pour causes principales le mauvais gouvernement ou la tyrannie des Mamelouks et de leurs gens. Aussi les *'ulamā'* eurent-ils parfois une attitude ambiguë à l'égard des mouvements populaires et il leur arriva de ne les soutenir qu'avec une évidente réserve" (Raymond, *Artisans*, 2:431). It would be equally true that, despite their links to the ruling elite, the obligation of the *'ulamā'* to support the sharia may have made them, on occasion, sympathetic (albeit always with that "certain reserve") to the complaints of the masses.

68 Despite its importance, *sharḥ* appears to be little studied as a genre. For an orientation to the various subgenres, see Gilliot, "Sharḥ" and Rippin, "Tafsīr," in *EI2*.

69 Rippin, "Tafsīr," in *EI2*: 84.

70 Al-Shirbīnī's use of *maṣdar*, which more correctly means "verbal noun," for this purpose is idiosyncratic.

71 *OLA 141*, where the interested reader will find a full description of the witnesses and a statement of the general orthographic conventions followed.

72 Van Gelder, *Noddles*, 53.

73 In this notation, S stands for a short syllable, such as *da*, L for a long syllable (*dā* or *dal*) or—in colloquial verse—also an overlong syllable (*dāll*), and X for a position in the meter that may be filled by a short or a long syllable, at the poet's discretion.

74 Sigla for the other witnesses used in the 2005 edition, and hence also occasionally referred to in the apparatus to the Arabic text that follows, are: ب = Bulaq (Dār al-Ṭibā'ah al-'Āmirah, 1274/1858); ك = Cambridge (Cambridge University Library, Or. 1420 (Part I) and Or. 1421 (Part II)); با = Paris (Bibliothèque Nationale, MS Arabe 3267 (Part I) and 3268 (Part II); م = Mingana (Birmingham, Selly Oaks Colleges Library: Mingana Collection, Islamic 1564–65).

75 Humphrey Davies. *Yūsuf al-Shirbīnī's Brains Confounded*, Vol. 2, *English Translation*. Only short passages of *Brains Confounded* have been translated elsewhere (in any language, to my knowledge). The story of the "Persian Savant" (§§4.5–9) was rendered into English by Herbert Howarth and Ibrahim Shukrallah sixty years ago (Howarth and Shukrallah, *Images*, 21–23) and again recently by Geert Jan van Gelder, along with the story of the peasants who visit a bathhouse (§§3.25–27) (van Gelder, *Anthology*, 339–44 and notes on 422–24). J. Finkel includes a translation of a brief passage from al-Shirbīnī's mock sermon on foods (vol. 2, §11.25.7) in his essay on a Mamluk work of the same type (Finkel, "King Mutton," 132–36).

76 Davies, *Lexicon*.

77 Davies, *Profile*.

هزّ القحوف

بشرح قصيد أبي شادوف

Brains Confounded by the Ode of Abū Shādūf Expounded

المجلّد الأوّل

Part One

بسم الله الرحمن الرحيم

وبه العون

(الحمد لله) الذي شرّف نوع الإنسان * بنطق اللسان * وخصّه بعموم مزيد الفضل ١،٠
والامتنان * وهيّأه لإدراك حقائق المعرفة والبيان * وتوّجه بتاج الكرامة والبراعة والإتقان * وجعل الطبائع مختلفة والأخلاق متباينة على ممرّ الأزمان * وميّز صاحب الذوق السليم بلطافة الذات وحلاوة اللسان * وخصّ أضداده بسوء الخُلُق وكثافة الطبع كعوام الريف أراذل الجُدْران * والصلاة والسلام على سيّدنا محمّد المبعوث من أفضل جرثوم[١] العرب من عدنان * المخصوص بجوامع الكَلِم ولوامع التِبْيان * وعلى آله وأصحابه الذين جعلهم الله لاقتطاف جواهر العلم أفنان * صلاةً وسلاماً دائمَيْن متلازمَيْن في كلّ وقت وأوان

١ بي: جرتوم.

In the Name of God
The Merciful, the Compassionate
To Whom We Turn for Help

Praise be to God,[1] Who has honored Man with the gift of speech and singled him out for bounty and blessings of every kind, Who has equipped him to grasp the verities of knowledge and persuasive argument, Who has crowned his brow with dignity, prowess, and virtuosity, Who has made his constitutions diverse and tempers disparate as long as time shall last, and Who has distinguished the man of sound taste with refinement of person and sweetness of tongue while bestowing on his opposites—the likes of the common people of the countryside, the base loafers by the walls—wickedness of disposition and coarseness of nature! And blessings and peace upon our Lord Muḥammad, sent forth from the noblest stock of the Arabs of ʿAdnān, endowed with pithiness in speech and brilliance in exposition, and upon his kin and Companions, whom God made adept at gathering wisdom's pearls[2]—for ever and ever, in every age and time! 0.1

(وبعد) فيقول العبد الفقير إلى الله تعالى يوسف بن محمّد بن عبد الجواد بن خِضَر ١٠١
الشِرْبينيّ كان الله له ورحم الله سلفه إنّ ممّا مرّ عليّ من نظم شعر الأرياف * الموصوف بكثافة اللفظ بلا خلاف * المشابه في رصّه لطين الجوالس * وجرى ذكره في بعض المجالس * قصيد أبي شادوف * المحاكي لبعر الخروف * أو طين الجروف * فوجدته قصيداً يا له من قصيد * كأنّه عُمِلَ من حديد * أو رُصَّ من قحوف الجريد * فالتمس منّي من لا يَسَعُني مخالفته * ولا يمكنني إلّا طاعته * أن أضع عليه شرحاً كريش الفراش * أو غبار العفاش * وزوابع السباخ * يحلّ ألفاظه السخيمه * ويبيّن معانيه الذميمه * ويكشف القناع عن وجه لغاته الفشرويّه * ومصادره الفُشْكُليّه * ومعانيه الركيكه * ومبانيه الدكيكه * ومقاصده العبيطه * وألفاظه الحويطه * وأن أُنْتِجَه بحكايات غريبة ومسائل هباليّة عجيبه * وأن أُتْحِفَه بشرح لغات الأرياف * التي هي في معنى ضراط النمل بلا خلاف * وأشعارهم المغترَفة من بحر التخابيط * واشتقاق بعض كلماتها التي هي في الصفات تشبه الشراميط * ووقائع وقعت لبعضهم باتّفاق * في مصر وثغر بولاق * وذكر فقهائهم الجهّال * وعلمهم الذي شبيه ماء النُخال * وفقرائهم الأجلاف * وأحوال الأوباش منهم والأطراف * وذكر نسائهم عند الهراش * وملاعبتهنّ في الفِراش * التي هي شبيه نطّ القرود * أو بربرة الهنود * وأن أُورد جَوْل كلام المتن بمعنًى إذا ذُقْتَه أيّها السامع يحكي طعم البول * وإذا اقتطفت من يانع ثمار لفظه أيّها الناظر فكأنّك قطفت زبل الغول * وإذا نظرت إلى أشعاره فكأنّها رَصُّ القُلْقَيْل * وإذا تأمّلت عفاشة كلامه فكأنّك تلوك زبل الخَيل * وأن أصرّح ببعض فُكاهيّات هَزْليّه *

The Author Describes the Ode of Abū Shādūf

To proceed. The humble slave of the Almighty, Yūsuf ibn Muḥammad ibn ʿAbd al-Jawād ibn Khiḍr al-Shirbīnī, may God be his support and have mercy on his ancestors, declares: among the rural verse to come my way—verse characterized by a coarseness of expression that cannot be gainsaid, with lines set out like blocks of mud for making walls—and which has become the subject of comment in certain salons, was the "Ode of Abū Shādūf," a thing redolent of sheep's droppings or shoveled mud. And what an ode I found it to be—as though made out of iron or by stacking the thick ends of palm fronds![3] Then one whom I cannot disobey and with whose commands I have no choice but to comply[4] besought me to stick on it a commentary, like butterfly feathers, or clouds of dust and whirlwinds of manure, that would unravel its tepid turns of phrase, make plain its uncommendable motifs, and strip the mask from the face of its tongue-in-cheek dialectalisms and lame paradigms, its banal motifs and battered constructions, its silly senses and tendentious terms; to round it out with strange tales and amazing nonsensical discussions; and to embellish it with an explanation of the linguistic peculiarities of the countryside, which are on a par, without a doubt, with the farting of ants, of their poetry, ladled out from the ocean of chaos, and of the etymologies of some of the words resembling old clouts in shape and form that occur therein, as well as of the misadventures that befell certain among them, by chance, in al-Qāhirah, Miṣr, and the port of Bulaq;[5] to include an account of their ignorant dervishes, whose learning is to knowledge as gruel is to porridge, of their uncouth village pastors, and of the condition of both the riffraff among them and the elite; to mention their women when slapping and tickling and at their sport in bed, which resembles the gamboling of apes or the jabbering of Indians; and to make available the eddying dust devils of the original text, which, should you taste it, Dear Listener, would put you in mind of urine, and whose ripe lexical fruits, should you pluck them, Dear Reader, would make you think of ghoul droppings, while the contemplation of its verses would remind you of clods of mud stacked in courses and the scrutiny of its slovenly language would convince 1.1

وحِكَم هِباليّه * على سبيل المُجون والخَلاعه * والدَيْدَنة والسقاعه * حتّى يشتهر شرح هذا القصيد من دُمْياط إلى الصعيد * وأرجو أن لا يخلو منه إقليم أيْ ولا بلد من بلاد العبيد * وقلّ أن يخلو سامعه من تواتر الألفاظ التي كالوَلاش * وربما اعترى قارئه ضرب من الطُراش * فهو إن مرّ على المسامع يمرّ كالريح * وإن مجّه الطبع كان الفرض الصحيح * كما قال فيه الشاعر الفصيح * الملتقط شعره من الدُرّ الوضيح [وافر]

إِذَا حَقَّقْتَ أَنَّ ٱللَّفْظَ صَوْتٌ وَأَنَّ ٱلصَّوْتَ مَعْنًى يَا فَصِيحُ
فَحَقِّقْ أَنَّ تَأْلِيفِي كَلَامٌ تَلَذُّ بِهِ ٱلْمَسَامِعُ وَهْوَ رِيحُ

وفي المثل في البحر سمك يفسي نار قالوا كان الماء يطفيه قال هذا كلام اسمعه والّا خلّيه

٢،١ ولا بأس بوصف هذا الشرح بأبيات * كأنّها بول البنات * فأقول [وافر]

كِتَابٌ قَد حَوَى فَنَّ الوَلَاشِ كِتَابٌ قَد حَوَى رِيشَ الفَرَاشِ
كِتَابٌ فِيهِ أوراقٌ وحِبْرٌ وقَولٌ صادِقٌ مَعَ قَولِ لاشِ
وفِيهِ يا أخي مِن كُلِّ مَعنًى إذا ما ذُقْتَهُ طَعمُ العَفاشِ
وألفاظٌ بِهِ تحكي لِبَولٍ عَليها رَونَقٌ مثلُ العَماشِ
وفيهِ مَسائِلٌ حازَتْ هُبالًا عَليها سابِلٌ مثلُ القُماشِ[1]
وفيهِ النَّظمُ شِبْهُ الطوبِ رَصًّا وفِيهِ مَسائِلٌ جاءَتْ بِلاشِ
إذا طالَعْتَهُ حقًّا وصِدْقًا فَلا تَأْمَنْ سَرِيعًا من طُراشِ

وكل هذا لمناسبة ألفاظ القصيد * وحلّ معانيه التي تحكي قحوف الجريد * فالشارح لا يخرج عن كلام الماتن * كما هو عادة القاطن في هذا الفنّ والظاعن *

١ بي: كالقُماشِ.

you you were chewing on horse dung; and that I include within it some comic quips and moronic maxims, by way of something obscene and lewd, and frivolous and rude, so that knowledge of my commentary on the ode be guaranteed from Dimyāṭ to the Ṣaʿīd. And indeed, I pray that not one clime, nay, nor any of the countries of mankind, be without it, since rare is he who, having once heard this ode, can put the droning of its worthless phrases from his mind, or, having once read it, is not taken with an urge to vomit, for when it passes by the ear, it does so like wind, and, should the body reject it, that's only to be expected. As the poet of chaste speech has said, in these verses gleaned from *The Glowing Pearls*:[6]

> Grant but that utterance[7] is sound,
> And sound meaning, O you of eloquence undimmed,
> And you will grant that what I write are words
> That charm the ear, and also wind.

And, as the proverb has it, "Said one, 'There's a fish farts fire in the seas.' 'The water,' said others, 'would put it out!' 'It's all talk,' returned the first, 'Take it or leave it as you please!'"

Likewise, there being no harm in depicting this commentary in verses fragrant as maidens' pee, I declare it to be: 1.2

> A book full of the art of naught, a book full of the feathers of butterflies!
> A book with pages, ink, and words—some true, some lies!
> Within, my friend, are examples foul-tasting of every topos,
> And phrases like piss that glisten with eye pus.
> Within it are debates[8] infantile
> Draped over it all like a mantle,
> While the verses it contains are like bricks in their stacking,
> And there are learned discussions free for the taking.
> Gaze on it well and peruse it truly
> And very soon you'll find your stomach's unruly!

All of this has been done to match the phrasing of the ode itself and to unravel its meanings that resemble the butt ends of palm branches, for the commentator from the author's text should never depart, according to the custom of those, be they experts or dabblers, who practice this art.

٣،١ فيا له من شرح لو وُضِعَ على أعلى الجبل لتدكدك * ولو نُقِشَ على عامود الصواري لتحرّك * ولو مسَخ حجرًا لتشطّر * ولو أُلْقِيَ في اليمّ لتكدّر * فهو جدير بأن يُرْقَمَ ببول الجحوش على جدران الكنائس * وحقيق بأن يُسَطَّرَ على بيوت الأخلية ببول العرائس * وأَوْلى بأن يُلْقَى على رؤوس المزابل * وأحقر بأن يرقم على جدران المكاسل * فهو شرح عديم النظير في الكثافه * لكونه في معنى أوصاف الريّافه * وليس له شبيه في الثقاله * لكونه في وصف ذوي الرذاله *

٤،١ واعلم أنّ كلّ شرح لا بدّ له من اسم يناسبه * وعَلَمٍ عليه يقاربه * وقد سمّيتُ هذا الشرح (هزّ القحوف * بشرح قصيد أبي شادوف) وأطلب من القريحة الفاسده * والفكرة الكاسده * الإعانة على كلام أغرفه من بنات الأفكار * وأسطّره في الأوراق فُشار في فشار * وأن يكون من بحر الخرافات * والأمور الهباليّات * والخلاعة والمجون * وشيء يحاكي كلام ابن سُودُون * فقد يلتذّ السامع بكلام فيه الضحك والخلاعه * ولا يميل إلى قول فيه البلاغة والبراعه * لأنّ النفوس الآن متشوّقة إلى شيء يسلّيها الهموم * ويزيل عنها وارد الغموم * وفي هذا المعنى أقول [طويل]

فَفي مَذهَبي أنَّ الخَلاعَةَ راحَةٌ تُسَلّي هُمومَ الشَّخصِ عِندَ انقِباضِهِ

وزماننا هذا لا يعيش فيه إلّا من عنده طرف من التمسخر والخلاعه * والدَيْدَنة والسقاعه * ولهذا قال الشاعر [خفيف]

ماتَ من عاشَ بالفَصاحةِ جُوعا وحَظِي مَن يَقودُ أو يَتَمَسخَرْ

وقد تساق الأرزاق * لمن لا يُدرِكُ الخطّ في الأوراق * ويُحَرَّمُ صاحب البلاغه * ولا يجد من القوت بلاغه * ولهذا قال الشاعر [كامل]

And what a commentary it has turned out to be! Set it on the highest mountain, and the mountain would tumble! Engrave it on the Pillar of the Columns,[9] and the Pillar would crumble! Were a rock but to touch it, the latter would shatter, and were it thrown in the ocean, it would churn in commotion! Meet it is to be inscribed in donkey foals' piss on the walls of a church, and to be written out in the urine of brides, outhouse walls to besmirch; yet more that it be thrown on top of a midden, being so despicable that it should on the walls where the loafers sit be written, for it is a commentary in coarseness without peer, on the characteristics of the people of the countryside brought to bear, and in boorishness without rival, being devoted to describing the ignoble. 1.3

Now, you must know that every commentary should have a title that's right and a name that's apposite. This, then, I have entitled *Brains Confounded by the Ode of Abū Shādūf Expounded*, calling on a talent that's turned and a wit that's spurned for help with words I've dredged up that are brainchildren of mine, and with setting them down, line after empty, vaunting line, hoping they will take their place in the ocean of nonsensicality and farcicality, and of license and buffoonery, with just a touch of Ibn Sūdūn-ery; for the listener will often take pleasure in laughter and license and show no interest in eloquence and excellence, because, in these times, it's for distractions that the soul yearns, and for whatever may sweep aside its worries and concerns. I have composed a verse to this effect that says: 1.4

To my mind, licentiousness is rest—
It dispels one's worries when depressed.

In this age of ours, none survive but those possessed of a measure of profligacy and buffoonery, and frivolity and effrontery, which is why the poet says:

Dead of hunger is he who lived by eloquence,
While Fortune smiles on pimps and clowns.

He who cannot pen a line is blessed with a living fine, while the master of wit sees of victuals not a whit, leading the poet to say:

تُعْطِي التُّيُوسَ الرِّزْقَ بِسُهُولَةٍ   وَذَوُو الفَصاحةِ رِزْقُها مَسْجُونُ
إنْ كانَ حِرْماني لِأَجْلِ فَصاحَتي   أُمْنُنْ عَلَيَّ مِنَ التُّيُوسِ أَكُونُ

وقال الأبي صيري الأديب رحمه الله تعالى مَوالِيا [بسيط]

رَبُّ الفَصاحةْ عَظِيمُ الذَّوْقِ يَقِفُ أَشْلَمْ   وَالأَبْلَمُ التَّيْسُ مُصَدَّرْ ومُتْعَظِّمْ
يا رَبِّ إنْ كانَ حِرْماني كَما تَعْلَمْ   أُمْنُنْ عَلَيَّ أَكُونْ تَيْسَ ٱبْنَ تَيْسْ أَبْلَمْ

وقال ابن الراونديّ عفى الله عنه[1] [بسيط]

يا قاسِمَ الرِّزْقِ كَمْ ضاقَتْ بِيَ القِسَمُ   ما أَنْتَ مُتَّهَمٌ قُلْ لي مَنِ اتَّهَمُ
تُعْطِي اليَهودَ قَناطيراً مُقَنْطَرَةً   مِنَ اللُّجَيْنِ ورِجْلي ما لها قَدَمُ
أَعْطَيْتَني حِكَماً لِمْ تُعْطِني وَرَقاً   قُلْ لي بِلا وَرِقٍ ما تَنْفَعُ الحِكَمُ

٥،١ فالشخص يكون مع زمانه بحسب حاله * ويداري وقته بما يناسب لأحواله * ويكون حذراً من دهره وصَوْلته * ويرقص للقِرْد في دَوْلته * ويعاشر الناس على قدر أحوالهم * ويدور معهم بحسب أدوارهم * ويندرج فى مدراج خلاعاتهم * ويظهر في مظاهر براعاتهم * قال بعضهم [سريع]

ودارِهِمْ ما دُمْتَ في دارِهِمْ   وحَيِّهِمْ ما دُمْتَ في حَيِّهِمْ
وأَحْسِنِ العِشْرةَ مَعْ بَعْضِهِمْ   يُعِينُكَ البَعْضُ عَلى كُلِّهِمْ

وفي الحديث أُمِرْتُ بمداراة الناس

١ في بي يين (عنه) و(يا قاسم): كَمْ عالِمٍ عالِمٍ أَعْيَتْ مذاهِبُهُ * وجاهِلٍ جاهِلٍ تلقاه مرزوقا // هذا الذي ترك الأوهامَ حائرةً وصيّرَ العالِمَ النِحْرِيرَ زِنْديقا ولبعضهم قال.

Billy goats get given their livelihood with ease
While that of the eloquent is refused;
If my eloquence be the cause of my privation,
Let me with the billy goats be confused!

And the leading man of letters al-Būṣīrī, may the Almighty have mercy on his soul, said in a *mawāliyā*:

The man of great taste stands puzzled and at a loss,
While the billy goat advances and puts on airs.
Lord, let me be a billy goat, son of a dumb billy goat,
If you intend no relief for my cares!

And Ibn al-Rāwandī, God excuse his sins, said:

Allocator of our Daily Bread, how Fate has straitened me!
If You are not to blame, pray tell me, who might be?
You give silver in bushels brimming[10] to the Jews
When I don't have enough to even buy shoes.
You gave me wisdom, but not lucre.
Tell me, without the one, what use is the other?

It follows that one should stay in tune with one's days, humor the age by acting in keeping with its ways, be on guard against whatever assaults Fate may bring, and "dance for the ape when he is king." One should get along with people as best he may, perform any role he may be asked to play, implicate himself in men's excesses, and number himself among them in their successes. As a poet has said: 1.5

Humor them in their homes,
Greet them courteously while their guest.
Make friends with some
That those may help you against the rest.

And in a Tradition it says, "I have been commanded to deal circumspectly with others."

(وقيل إنّ بعض الملوك مات إمامه) فقال لوزرائه وخواصّ دولته انظروا لنا إماماً يكون ورعاً زاهداً فيه لِين الجانب وهداوة النفس فاجتمع رأيهم على رجل بالمدينة فيه هذه الأوصاف إلّا أنّه فقير الحال فقال الملك عليّ به فلمّا حضر بين يديه أكرمه وعظّمه وأعلى منزلته وصيّره أرقى من وزرائه وأجرى عليه النعم فلمّا رأى نفسه فى هذه الحالة تعاظم على أبناء جنسه واحتقرهم وترك مداراة الناس ولم يعتبرهم واحتقر أرباب الدولة فاتّفق رأيهم على مكيدة يهلكونه بها فلمّا كان يوم الجمعة وأراد الملك أن يصلّي فى بعض المساجد أرسل السجّادة ففُرِشَتْ له في ذلك المسجد ودخل وجلس عليها هو وذلك الإمام وكان اتّفاقهم في ذلك على أنّهم صنعوا صورة صليب صغير من الذهب والجوهر وأعطوه لرجل من خواصّ الملك ممّن يكتم السرّ وجعلوا له جعلاً وقالوا له تضعه تحت السجّادة تحت جبهة الإمام بحيث أنّه لا يشعر بك أحد ففعل ذلك فلمّا فرغ الناس من صلاة الجمعة وأراد الملك الانصراف أخذ الفرّاش السجّادة فرأى الصليب فأعرضه على الملك فأنكره وقال لأرباب دولته ما هذا الأمر فإنّه قد رؤي هذا الصليب تحت جبهة الإمام فقالوا له هذا كافر ومستتر علينا فغضب الملك وأمر بقتله فلمّا مرّت جنازته أنشد بعضهم يقول [رمل] ٦٫١

كانَ واللهِ تَقِيّاً صالِحا مُنْصِفاً عَدْلاً وَما قَطُّ اتُّهِمْ

فأجابه آخر يقول [رمل]

كانَ لا يَدري مُداراةَ الوَرَى وَمُداراةُ الوَرَى أمرٌ مُهِمْ

فالسلامة في مداراة الناس * وحسن الانطباع معهم بلطف الإيناس * وأن يكون الشخص متنقّلاً في أطوارهم * دائرًا تحت فَلَك أدوارهم * كما صرّحت بذلك في بعض المقامات بهذه الأبيات [طويل]

The tale is told that a certain king's imam died. The king said to his ministers and the privy councilors of the realm, "Find me an imam who is God-fearing and ascetic, gentle in nature and unassuming." Their choice fell on a man of the city who answered to that description but was poor. "Bring him to me," said the king. When the man appeared, the king honored and made much of him, raising him in rank till he was more exalted than his ministers and showering him with favors. Finding himself in this state, the man started to lord it over his own kind and to treat them with contempt; he ceased to humor people or pay them due respect, and he treated the great men of the realm with contempt. These then agreed to set a trap to destroy him. Now, it was the king's custom, when it was Friday and he wished to pray in a certain mosque, to send his prayer rug on ahead. There it would be spread out for him, and he would enter and sit on it with this imam beside him. What they agreed to do was to have a small cross of gold and jewels made and to give it, with a gift, to a certain intimate of the king's who could be trusted to keep a secret, telling him, "Place this under the prayer rug where the imam's forehead touches it, in such a fashion that no one sees you." This he did. When the people dispersed following the prayer and the king was about to depart, the mosque attendant picked up the rug and saw the cross. He presented it to the king, who denied all knowledge of it and said to the great men of the realm, "What's this? This cross has been found under the place where the imam's forehead touches the rug!" "He must be an infidel," they replied, "who has been hiding his true nature from us!" At this the king grew angry and ordered the man killed. As his funeral procession passed by, a poet declaimed: 1.6

> Pious he was, God knows—righteous,
> Fair and just, and ne'er before accused.

To which another replied:

> He had no sense of how to humor men,
> And that's a sin too great to be excused.

Thus safety lies in humoring others, and using winning ways to get along with one's brothers. One should adapt himself to their different manners and march under their changing banners, as I make clear in the following lines from a *maqāmah* of mine:

فطَوْرًا تَراني عالِمًا ومُـدَرِّسا   وطَوْرًا تَراني فاسِـقًا فَلَفوسا
وطَوْرًا تَراني ع المَزامِرِ[١] عاكِفا   وطَوْرًا تَراني سـيِّدًا و رئيسا
مَظاهِرُ أُنسٍ إنْ تحقَّقْتَ سِرَّها   تُرِيكَ بُدُورًا أقبَلَتْ وشُموسا

١ بي: على المزامر.

One day you'll find me a scholar and a teacher,
 The next a sinner and freethinker.
One day you'll find me buried in the crowd,
 The next a lord and master proud.
A pleasant manner, once you have the knack,
 Will bring you pendant gems and money by the sack.

(ولنشرع الآن فيما وعدنا * وما زمرنا به ورقصنا)

١،٢ والشخص يغلب عليه علمه وفنّه * والزامر لا يخبّي ذقنه * وقبل الخَوْض في بحر هذا الكلام * والمشابهة له من جنس النظام * (نذكر ما وقع لعوامّ بعض أهل الريف) * ووصف طبعهم الكثيف * وأخلاقهم الرذيله * وذواتهم الهبيله * وأسمائهم المقلّبه * وقحوفهم المُشَقْلَبه * وقمصانهم المُشَرْمَطه * وأشعارهم المُخَلْبَطه * ونسائهم المُزَنْجات * وما لهم من الدواهي والبليّات *

٢،٢ فنقول أمّا سوء أخلاقهم وقلّة لطافتهم فمن كثرة معاشرتهم للبهائم والأبقار * وملازمتهم لشيل الطين والعَفار * وعدم اكتراثهم بأهل اللطافه * وامتزاجهم بأهل الكثافه * كأنّهم خُلِقُوا من طينة البهائم * كما قال في ذلك الناظم [سريع]

لا تَصْحَبِ الفلّاح لَوْ أَنَّهُ   نَاَفِجَةٌ أَرْيَاحُها صاعِدَهْ
ثِيرانُهم قَدْ أَخْبَرَتْ عَنْهُمُ   بِأَنَّهُمْ مِنْ طِينَةٍ واحِدَهْ

٣،٢ فهم لا يخرجون عن طَوْر القحافه * لملازمتهم المحراث والجرّافه * وهزّ قحوفهم حول الأجران * وطردهم في المَلَق والغيطان * ودورانهم حول الزرع * ونطّهم في الحصيدة والقلع * وغطوسهم في الجِلّة والطين * وعدم اكتراثهم بالصلاة والدين * إذ الواحد منهم لا يعرف غير الحزام والنَبُّوت * والبقرة والأَنْتُوت * والساقية والفَرْقلّه * وشيل الطين والجِلّه * والعياط والغاره * والطبلة والزُمّاره * والحِدْوة خلف قفاه * ومزراقه وهزّ رِداه * وحزامه الليف * والتبن والشليف * وخَلَقَته المشرمطة وصورته المخلبطه * وقاووقه الدَنِس * وكرّه الغَلِس * وطرده للغارات * والدواهي والبليّات * ومشيه حافي * في الحرّ والحلافي * وعياطه في الظلام *

The Author Embarks on a Description of the Common Country Folk

Let us now then embark on what we promised in advance and the occasion for all this song and dance—for a man's knowledge and craft must make themselves heard, and "the piper doesn't hide his beard."[11] Before wading, however, into the ocean of this verse, and others like it or even worse, we will tell of things that befell the commoners of certain of the people of the countryside, with a description of their vulgarity, scurrility, and personal puerility, of their names that are arsy-varsy and their hats that are topsy-turvy, of their shifts all frayed and their verses disarrayed, and of their disquieting womenfolk with the calamities and disasters they provoke. 2.1

Thus we declare: the baseness of their morals and their lack of refinement are the result of spending so much time in the company of beasts and cattle and of constantly hauling mud and dust, not to mention their lack of contact with the refined and their frequent intercourse with the coarse. They and the beasts are as though created from the same raw material, leading the poet to say: 2.2

Befriend not the peasant, be he a musk pot of fragrant bouquet!
Their oxen have let out the secret, that they're both of one clay.

Indeed, they never escape their condition of uncouthness, because they spend all their time with the plow and the shovel-sledge and shaking their caps around the threshing floors, or rushing about in the swamps[12] and the fields, or bustling around after the crops, or jumping about harvesting and reaping, or plunging into dung and mud, while devoting little time to prayer or religion. For the only things a countryman knows are belts and cudgels, cows and plow-shaft pins, waterwheels and drover's whips, hauling mud and dung, shouting and screaming, drums and pipes, his leather sandals slung behind his neck, his lance and the shaking of his robe, his palm-fiber belt, straw and net sacks, his tattered garment and tatterdemalion form, his grubby cap and filthy turban, rushing off on raids, disasters and calamities, walking barefoot in the heat and through the esparto grass, and crying out loud in the dark, "Clan of Ḥarām!" 2.3

بالصوت يا لَحَرام * فتجتمع عليه اللموم * ويهجموا بلاد القوم * وهم سعد وحرام * ويخرجوا إليهم بالتمام * فيقع بينهم الحرب والعناد * وتَخْرُبُ بسببهم البلاد * ويقطعوا الطريق * على العدوّ والصديق * ويترتّب من ذلك المفاسد * وتمتنع عن بلادهم الفوائد *

٤،٢ وكلّ هذا من قلّة عقلهم * وكثرة جهلهم * وسوء أخلاقهم * وعدم اتّفاقهم * إذ كلّهم في الظاهر مسلمون * والقتل عندهم حُكْمَ الديون * وأيضاً عندهم قلّة الوفاء * وعدم الأنس والصفاء * لا يؤدّوا القرض * ولا يعرفوا السُنّة والفرض * إن عاملتهم أكلوك * وإن نصحتهم بغضوك * وإن أقمت لهم الشرع رفضوك * وإن ألنت لهم الجانب مقتوك * العالم عندهم حقير * والظالم عندهم كبير * أمورهم معانده * وليس عندهم فائده * عندهم قابض المال * أعزّ من العمّ والخال * سود الوجوه * إذا رأوا معروفاً أنكروه * قال الشاعر [بسيط]

أَهْلُ الفِلاحةِ لا تُكْرِمْهُمُ[١] أَبَدًا   فَإِنَّ[٢] إِكْرامَهُمُ في عَقْبِهِ نَدَمُ
يُبْدوا الصِّياحَ بِلا ضَرْبٍ وَلا أَلَمٍ   سُودُ الوُجوهِ إِذا لَمْ يُظْلَمُوا ظَلَمُوا

٥،٢ إذا أقاموا أفراح * لا تكون إلّا بالعياط والصياح * والطرد والكرب * وربّما وقع فيها البطح والضرب * وقد شاهدنا كثيراً من أفراحهم * وما يقع فيها من عدم نجاحهم * وسيأتي كيفيّة أفراحهم وأعراسهم * وعدم ذوقهم مع جلاسهم * وأمّا إكرامهم للضيوف * فهو هزّ الأردية و القحوف * والجلوس على المصاطب * ونفش اللحى والشوارب * وإن حصل منهم الكرَم بإضرار * يكون العدس والبيسار * أو الكِشك الحامض بالفول * أو نوع من المدمّس والبقول *

٦،٢ ولو مكث الشخص منهم مدّة في مصر ودمياط * لا يكتسب من اللطافة قيراط * وبعض أكابرهم المشار إليه * والمعوّل في الأمور إليه * إذا طلع مصر لمقابلة

---

١ بي: تكرِمَنّهُمْ. ٢ بي وجميع النسخ: كان.

At this the war bands gather around him and attack the villages of their enemies, be they Saʿd[13] or Ḥarām, and turn out against them to the last man. Thus war and stubborn confrontation arise among them, and villages are ruined at their hands. They block the roads against friend and foe, leading to evil consequences and depriving their villages of benefits.

All this is due to their lack of intelligence and overwhelming ignorance, the baseness of their morals and their contentiousness—for while all of them in outward show are Muslims, murder to them is no different from debt. Furthermore, they cannot be trusted to keep their word and have no sociability and good cheer. They will not repay a loan and cannot tell what the Law demands from what one is free to decide on his own.[14] If you do business with them, they devour you. If you offer them advice, they hate you. If you try to enforce the Divine Law with them, they will have nothing to do with you, and if you show them kindness, they repay you with malice. To them a scholar is nothing, while a tyrant is a hero. Their ways are contrary, and they are of use to none. To them the tax collector is dearer than an uncle.[15] Their faces are black; if done a good turn they don't pay it back. As the poet states: 2.4

Be not generous to the peasant, ever,
For that brings repentance in its wake!
They yell when neither beaten nor hurt;
Black of face, if not oppressed, others their victims they make!

When they put on a wedding, it has to be with shouting and screaming, with commotion and calamity, and often enough with breaking of pates and brawling. We have observed many of their weddings and all the futile nonsense that goes on at them, and a description of their nuptials and of their unseemly behavior towards their guests will follow. As for the entertainment they show their guests, it consists of shaking their robes and hats and sitting on benches while preening their beards and moustaches. If they are compelled to provide a meal, it is of lentils and *bīsār* and sour wheat groats with fava beans, or other kinds of stewed beans and herbs. 2.5

Even were one of them to reside a while in Cairo and Dimyāṭ, he would not acquire an ounce of refinement, and should one of their great men, the cynosure and patron of all, go to Cairo to meet with the emir or to settle some business with the vizier, he will be seen wearing fine clothes but, for all that, 2.6

الأمير * أو قضاء حاجة من الوزير * ترى عليه لبس محبوب * ومع ذلك يمشي حافي بلا مركوب * وأمورهم ليس لها انضباط * وأحوالهم خُباط وعِياط * ووِرْدهم عند الأسحار * التفكّر في الغنم والأبقار * وتسبيحهم في الظلام * هات النبُّوت والحزام * وحُطّ العَلَف * وهات الكَلَف * قال الشاعر [كامل]

لا تَسْكُنِ الأَرْيافَ إِنْ رُمْتَ العُلا   إِنَّ المَذَلَّةَ فِي القُرى مِيراثُ
تَسْبِيحُهم هاتِ العَلَفْ حُطِّ الكَلَفْ   عَلِّقْ لِثَوْرِكَ جاءَكَ المِحْراثُ

٧،٢ لا يرحموا صغيرا * ولا يوقّروا كبيرا * عورتهم عند الاستنجاء على الفساقي مكشوفه * وثيابهم بالنجاسة محفوفه * يجتمعوا لحساب المال في المساجد * وليس فيهم راكع ولا ساجد * أولادهم دائماً عريانين * وتراهم في صورة المجانين * الرحمة فيهم قليله * والرأفة منهم ذليله * كما أنّه يُكتَب لطرد النمل بلا مِرا * ارحل أيّها النمل كما رحلت الرحمة من قلوب شيوخ القرى *

٨،٢ ومن وصايا الإمام مالك للإمام الشافعيّ رضي الله عنهما لا تسكن الأرياف فيضيع علمُك وجاهُك * وقال سيّدنا عبد الوهّاب الشَعْرانيّ نفعنا الله به لبعض تلامذته عليك بسُكنى المدن فإنّ المقت إذا نزل في بلاد الريف طوفان يكون في المدينة كخُلخال الرِجْل قلت وإذا صحّفْتَ لفظة ريف مع قلب حروفها كانت قبر فالساكن في الريف معدوم اللذّات لأنّه دائماً في انقباض وطرّ * وجَرْي وكرّ وفرّ * وحبس وضرب * ولعن وسبّ * وهَوان وسَخْر * وشيل أبيار وحَفْر * وسروح للعَوْنه * وتعب من جهة المُونه * وإن كان ذو فضل ضاع فضله * أو ذو عقل ذهب عقله * أو ذو مال أغْرَوا عليه الحُكّام * أو ذو تجارة نهبوه في الظلام * فالحقّ عندهم مضاع * والباطل عندهم مذاع * وحُكْم الله ليس له اندفاع

walking barefoot, innocent of shoes; there is no order to their affairs, and they exist in a state of hubbub and hullabaloo. Their devotion before dawn is to meditate on the cattle and sheep, and their magnificat in the dark is "Fetch me my belt and staff!" and "Put out the fodder and bring in the feed!" As the poet says:

> Don't live in the country if you seek higher things,
> For abjection in the villages is something bequeathed.
> Their Gloria is "Fetch the fodder, put out the feed!
> Hitch up your ox, the plow's arrived!"

They have no compassion for the young and no respect for the old. They expose their privates when they wash at the waterspouts after defecating, and their garments are rimmed with filth. They gather in the mosques to calculate their taxes, but not one of them makes a prostration or says a prayer. Their children go naked; if you saw them, you'd think them lunatics. Mercy among them is scarcely to be found and any kindness they show is paltry—as it is written in charms for the efficacious expulsion of ants, "Be gone, ye ants, as mercy is gone from the hearts of the village shaykhs!"[16] 2.7

The Imam Mālik advised the Imam al-Shāfiʿī, may the Almighty have mercy on them both, as follows: "Do not dwell in the villages, for if you do, you will lose both your learning and your dignity!" And My Master ʿAbd al-Wahhāb al-Shaʿrānī, may the Almighty have mercy on him, said to one of his pupils, "You should live in the city, for, while hatred descends like a deluge in a village, in the city it is no more than the shaking of anklets!"[17] I might add that, if one changes the dots in the word ريف (*rīf*; "countryside") and reverses the order of the letters, it becomes قبر (*qabr*; "grave")[18]—and certainly the country-dweller is deprived of all joys, as he is always dejected and harried, scurrying hither and hurrying thither, imprisoned and beaten, cursed and abused, degraded and upbraided, clearing wells and digging, setting off to work on the corvée, and exhausted by the search for provisions. If he be a man of virtue, his virtue is destroyed, if a man of intelligence, his intelligence will vanish, if a man of wealth, the others will incite the authorities against him, and if he be engaged in trade, they will rob him in the dark; for they are lost to the Truth, and falsehood is everywhere amongst them—but God's law cannot be denied! 2.8

(ذكر طرف يسير من أسمائهم وألقابهم وما يُكَنَّوا به)

٩.٢ (أمّا أسماؤهم) فإنّها كأسماء العفاريت * أو رُقَع الشلاتيت * فيُسَمَّوا جُنَيْجِل وجُلَيْجِل * وعَفْر ودعموم وزُعَيْط ومُعَيْط وقُسَيْط * وشلاطه ولهاطه * وشقليط ومقليط * وصفّار وبهوار وجعمار * وعِمْران وشعوان * وشمضوت وبرغوت * والعفش والنتش وكسبر وقفندر * وحنين وبنين * ودقيرى وفنديشه * وشُحَيْبَر وبُعَيْبَر ومحمّد بكسر الميم والحاء ومحمّدين والأسماء وإن كانت لا تُعلَّل * فإنّ أسمائهم هذه تشبه العِلَل *

١٠.٢ وقد يسمّوا بالفال كما اتّفق أنّ رجلاً وُلِدَ له غلام فسمع رجلاً يقول لآخر يا أعمش العين فقال نسمّيه عَمّوش فسُمّي بذلك واتّفق أنّ رجلاً ولدت زوجته أنثى فسمع رجلاً يقول لآخر هات الزبل فقال لأمّها سمّيها زُبَيْله فسُمّيت بذلك وزبيلة تصغير زبلة وزبلة فيها معنيان كونها واحدة الزبل وكونها مشتقّة من الزبالة والزبلة على وزن عجلة أو فجلة أو نملة أو قملة وقال الشاعر [وافر]

وزِبْلَهْ وَزنُها عِجْلَهْ وفِجْلَهْ وَنَمْلَةُ ثُمَّ رَمْلَهْ ثُمَّ قَمْلَهْ

١١.٢ (وقد ذكرتُ بتسمية هذا الفال ما يقرب من هذا المعنى) وهو ما حكى بعضهم أنّ زوجته ولدت غلاماً فسمع رجلاً يقول لآخر دم الحس قفاك فسمّاه بذلك ثمّ ولد له ثاني فسمع رجلاً يقول لآخر شاربك في الخرا فسمّاه بذلك ثمّ إنّ دم الحس قفاك كبر وانتشأ وكذلك شاربك في الخرا بلغ من العمر عشر سنين فأرسلهما للكُتّاب فقرأ دم الحس قفاك القرآن وبرع فيه وكذلك شاربك في الخرا إلى يوم من بعض الأيّام قال دم الحس قفاك لأخيه شاربك في الخرا قصدنا يا أخي الذهاب لبحر النيل نسبح فيه فقال شاربك في الخرا السمع والطاعه فتوجّه دم الحس قفاك هو وأخوه شاربك في

An Account of a Few of Their Names, Nicknames, and *Kunyahs*[19]

Their names are like those of demons or like patches on tatters. They are called Junayjil ("Little Bell") and Julayjil (ditto), ʿAfr ("Dust") and Duʿmūm, Zuʿayṭ, Muʿayṭ, and Qusayṭ ("Little Milk Can"), Shallāṭah ("Mattock") and Lahhāṭah,[20] Shuqlayṭ and Muqlayṭ,[21] Ṣaffār ("Whistler"), Bahwār ("Braggart") and Jaʿmār, ʿImrān and Shaʿwān, Shamḍūt and Burghūt ("Fleas"), al-ʿAfsh ("Field Trash") and al-Natsh ("Snatching, Swiping"), Kusbur[22] and Qafandar, Ḥunayn and Bunayn, Duqmayrī and Fandīshah, Shuḥaybir[23] and Buʿaybir, Miḥimmad with "i" after both the "m" and the "ḥ," and Miḥimmadayn. Though it's true that names can't be "diagnosed," theirs are certainly sick! 2.9

Sometimes they give names to commemorate an auspicious event. For example, it happened that a boy was born to a man who heard another say to someone, "You there, bleary eyes!" and the father said, "We'll call him Little Bleary Eyes," and so he was named. Similarly, it happened that a man's wife gave birth to a female and the father heard one man saying to another, "Fetch the droppings (*zibl*)!" and he said to the mother, "We'll call her Little Dropping (Zubaylah)," and so she was named. Zubaylah is the diminutive of *ziblah*[24] and *ziblah* has two meanings, being both the unit noun[25] of *zibl* ("dung") and derived from *zubālah* ("garbage").[26] *Ziblah* is of the measure[27] of *ʿijlah* ("calf"), *fijlah* ("radish"), *namlah* ("ant"), or *qamlah* ("louse"). As the poet has it: 2.10

The measure of *ziblah*, they say, is *ʿijlah* and *fijlah*,
And *namlah*, plus *ramlah* ("patch of sand") and *qamlah*.

Such naming techniques remind me of a somewhat similar story, which is that a man once said that his wife gave birth to a boy and he heard one man say to another, "Blood slap the back of your neck!"[28] so he made that the boy's name. Then another son was born to him and he heard another man say to someone, "Your moustache in the shit!" so he called him the same. Now, Blood-Slap-the-Back-of-Your-Neck grew up and became a big boy and Your-Moustache-in-the-Shit likewise reached the age of ten, so their father sent them to school, where Blood-Slap-the-Back-of-Your-Neck learned the Qur'an and Your-Moustache-in-the-Shit did likewise. One day, Blood-Slap-the-Back-of-Your-Neck said to his brother Your-Moustache-in-the-Shit, "Verily, we have determined, O my brother, to hie us unto the river Nile, therein to bathe!" To which Your-Moustache-in-the-Shit replied, "We hear 2.11

الخرا إلى أن أشرفا على بحر النيل ونزلا فيه وكان دم الحس قفاك ماهرًا في العوم وشاربك في الخرا عومه قليل فسبق دم الحس قفاك أخوه شاربك في الخرا فتضايق شاربك في الخرا واشتدّ به الأمر وأشرف على الغرق فالتفت إليه دم الحس قفاك فرأى شاربك في الخرا في شدّة عظيمة فأقبل عليه ووضع يده تحت إبطه وأسنده على ظهره ولم يزل يتلطّف به حتّى أوصله إلى البرّ فلولا أن دم الحس قفاك لبق وإلّا كان شاربك في الخرا غرق

١٢،٢ (ومرّ رجل بغلام يضرب أباه) ويَسْخَرُ به ويَسُبُّه فقال له يا غلام إن لأبيك عليك حق أن لا تَنْهَرَه ولا تُؤْذِيَه وأن تُحْسِنَ الأدب معه ولوكان كافرا فقال له يا سيدي وأنا الآخر لي عليه حق فقال وما حقّك عليه فقال أن يحسن اسمي ويعلّمني القرآن وأن يرشدني إلى أحسن الصنائع وهذا سمّاني دَبّوس * وعلّمني لسان المَجُوس * وصيّرني بين الناس خَلْبوص * أفلا أضربه فقال بل صُكّه بالنعال * فإنّه مستحق لأقبح الفعال *

١٣،٢ (ومرّ رجل على سيّدنا عمر بن الخطّاب رضي الله عنه) فقال له ما اسمك قال تُنُور قال وأمّك قال شَرارة قال وأبوك قال لَهَب قال وفي أيّ واد أنت قال في وادي النار فقال له عمر رضي الله عنه اذهب إلى واديك فإنّ أهلك قد احترقوا قال فمضى الرجل فرأى الأمر كما ذكره سيّدنا عمر رضي الله عنه والأسماء تدلّ على لطافة المسمّى أو على كثافته وفي كلام أهل العلم والتدريب * كلّ أحد له من اسمه نصيب *

١٤،٢ (ويُكَنّوا) أبو شعره وأبو معره وأبو متارد وأبو شوالي وأبو جاموس وأبو قادوس وأبو عفره وأبو دعموم وأبو شادوف وأبو جاروف وأبو مشكاح وأبو رمّاح وأبو

and obey!" So Blood-Slap-the-Back-of-Your-Neck and his brother Your-Moustache-in-the-Shit proceeded to the edge of the river Nile and went in. Now Blood-Slap-the-Back-of-Your-Neck was a skilled swimmer, while his brother Your-Moustache-in-the-Shit hardly knew how to swim, so Blood-Slap-the-Back-of-Your-Neck overtook Your-Moustache-in-the-Shit. At this Your-Moustache-in-the-Shit grew angry, got into difficulties, and would have drowned had not Blood-Slap-the-Back-of-Your-Neck turned and seen that Your-Moustache-in-the-Shit was in a desperate plight. Going to him, he put his hands under his brother's arms, turned him on his back, and drew him gently along until he brought him to shore. Thus, had Blood-Slap-the-Back-of-Your-Neck not got there first, Your-Moustache-in-the-Shit would have drowned![29]

Similarly, a man once came upon a boy beating his father and mocking and abusing him the while. The man said to him, "Young man, it is your duty not to speak harshly to your father or do him harm! Be he an infidel, you must treat him politely!" to which the boy replied, "Sir, I too have the right to demand certain things of him," "And what might those be?" said the man. "To give me a decent name, teach me the Qur'an, and direct me towards a worthy profession. But this man named me Skewer, taught me the language of the Magians,[30] and sent me out in public as a buffoon![31] Why then should I not beat him?" The first replied, "On the contrary, you should thrash him with a shoe, for he deserves the very worst that you can do!" 2.12

And once a man passed Our Master ʿUmar ibn al-Khaṭṭāb, may the Almighty be pleased with him, and the latter asked him, "What is your name?" "Oven," he replied. "And your mother's?" "Spark." "And your father's?" "Flame." "And in what valley do you dwell?" "In Fire Valley."[32] Then said Our Master ʿUmar, may the Almighty be pleased with him, "Go back to your valley, for your family has all burned!" When the man got home, he found it to be as Our Master ʿUmar, may the Almighty be pleased with him, had said.[33] It is a fact that names point to the refinement or coarseness of those who bear them, and, as men of learning and experience relate, "Each man's name determines his fate." 2.13

Their *kunyah*s are Abū Shiʿrah ("Father of Pubic Hair") and Abū Miʿrah,[34] Abū Matārid ("Father of Crocks"), Abū Shawālī ("Father of Bowls"), Abū Jāmūs ("Father of a Buffalo"), and Abū Qādūs ("Father of a Waterwheel Scoop/Jar"), Abū ʿAfrah ("Father of Dust"), Abū Duʿmūm, Abū Shādūf ("Father of the Shadoof"[35]), and Abū Jārūf ("Father of a Shovel"), Abū Mishkāḥ and Abū Rammāḥ ("Father of a Lancer") and Abū Naṭṭāḥ ("Father of a Head-Butter"), Abū Baqar 2.14

نطّاح وأبو بقر وأبو مطر وأبو هودج وأبو خرق النورج وأبو ضلام وأبو شقرير وأبو قشقوش وأبو قسيم وأبو جريده وأبو طعيمه وأبو بليله وأبو زغلول وأبو سيسي وأبو جاهل وأبو قصاله وأبو زباله وأبو بعبوص وأبو نموص وأبو لبده وأبو غده وأبو زعيط وأبو معيط وأبو بريطع وأبو زعيزع وأبو تعيتع وأبو شعيشع وأبو صابر وأبو خنافر وأبو هوير وأبو طرطر وأبو عوكل وأبو حوقل وأبو هبول وأبو عسقول وأبو ربابه وأبو زغابه وأبو طريف وأبو قحيف وأبو عريش وأبو كريش وأبو فتيشه وأبو دشيشه وأبو قَزَق وأبو قلّوط وأبو جلاط وأبو جيص وأبو كانون وأبو مقلد وأبو جعباظ

١٥،٢ (ويُلَقَّبوا) عِمْران القَلَط * وعُمَيْر الضَرْط * وعنطوز الباب * وشلاطه محلاب * ومحمّد القلّاب * وكُسْبُر العُقْله وبَرْبور الهَشْله ولهّاطة الزِبْله * ومشالي العجله * ونحو ذلك كثير لا غاية له

١٦،٢ (ويجيبوا السائل) بلفظ هاه وهيه وايشمالك واي مالك وايه هاه ممّا هو مشهور بينهم

١٧،٢ (وأمّا أسماء نسائهم) من معنى أسمائهم فيُسَمّوا زعره وبعره * وهيطله وميكله * وخطيطه وحويطه * ومعيكه وركيكه * وشَباره وزراره * وعلاره وعباره * وشلبايه وعطايه * وعليوه وحليوه * وهديه وبليه * ولبده وغده * وشمة وبلمه *

("Father of Cows") and Abū Maṭar ("Father of Rain"), Abū Hawdaj ("Father of a Camel Litter") and Abū Kharq al-Nawraj ("Father of the Hole in the Threshing Sled"), Abū Ḍalām ("Father of Darkness"), Abū Shuqrayr, Abū Qashqūsh,[36] Abū Qusaym ("Father of a Little Yoke Peg"), Abū Jarīdah ("Father of a Palm Frond"), Abū Ṭaʿīmah, and Abū Balīlah ("Father of Boiled Wheat"), Abū Zughlūl ("Father of a Squab"), Abū Sīsī ("Father of a Pony"), Abū Jāhil ("Father of an Ignorant One"), Abū Qaṣālah ("Father of Knotty Wheat Stalks"),[37] and Abū Zubālah ("Father of Garbage"), Abū Baʿbūṣ ("Father of a Poke in the Ass") and Abū Nāmūs ("Father of Mosquitoes"), Abū Libdah ("Father of a Felt Cap") and Abū Ghuddah ("Father of a Gland"), Abū Zuʿayṭ and Abū Muʿayṭ, Abū Burayṭaʿ[38] and Abū Zuʿayzaʿ ("Father of a Little Sugarcane Spike"), Abū Tuʿaytaʿ[39] and Abū Shuʿayshaʿ ("Father of a Little Pigeon Perch"),[40] Abū Ṣābir ("Father of a Donkey"),[41] Abū Khanāfir,[42] Abū Huwayr ("Father of a Little Yoke Rope"), Abū Ṭarṭar,[43] Abū ʿAwkal, and Abū Ḥawkal, Abū Habūl[44] and Abū ʿAsqūl ("Father of a Heel Tendon"), Abū Rabābah ("Father of a Rebab") and Abū Zughābah,[45] Abū Ṭurayf and Abū Quḥayf ("Father of a Little Peasant Hat"), Abū ʿUraysh[46] and Abū Kuraysh ("Father of a Little Belly"), Abū Fatīshah[47] and Abū Dashīshah ("Father of Coarse Porridge"), Abū Qazaq ("Father of a Trolley"), Abū Qallūṭ ("Father of a Large Turd"), Abū Jaḥlāṭ and Abū Jīṣ ("Father of a Loud Fart"), Abū Kānūn ("Father of a Brazier"), Abū Muqallad[48] and Abū Jaʿbāẓ.

Their nicknames[49] are ʿImrān the Big Shitter (ʿImran al-Qalṭ), ʿUmayr the Fart (ʿUmayr al-Ḍarṭ), ʿAnṭūz[50] the Door (ʿAnṭūz al-Bab), Shallāṭāh Milk Crock (Shallāṭāh Miḥlāb), Muḥammad the Flap (Muḥammad al-Qallāb), Kusbur the Knuckle-Bone (Kusbur al-ʿUqlah), Porridge-Snot (Barbūr al-Hashlah), Shit-Gobbler (Laḥḥāṭat al-Ziblah), Mashālī[51] the Dung Cakes (Mashālī al-Jillah) and many, many more. 2.15

When asked a question, they answer "*hāh*?" and "*hīh*?" and "*Aysh mālak*" or "*Ay mālak*" ("What's up with you?") and "*ayh hāh*?" and other expressions well known among them. 2.16

The names of their women are as bad as their own. They are called Zaʿrah ("Bobtail") and Baʿrah ("Dung Pellet"), Hayṭalah and Maykalah, Khuṭayṭah ("Little Furrow") and Ḥuwayṭah ("Little Wall"), Muʿaykah ("Little Rub") and Rukaykah, Shabārah ("Nile Perch") and Zarārah ("Gherkin"),[52] ʿAlārah and ʿAbārah, Shilbāyah ("Catfish") and ʿAṭāyah ("Gift"), ʿUlaywah ("Little Heap of Garbage") and Ḥulaywah ("Little Sweetie"), Hadiyyah ("Present") and Baliyyah ("Calamity"), Libdah ("Cap") and Ghuddah ("Gland"), Shammah 2.17

وسروه وبلاوه * وفسيوه وخريوه * ولقد رأيت خريوه هذه وسألت والدها عن سبب تسميتها بهذا اللفظ فذكر لي أنّها كانت في صغرها كثيرة الخرا وأي نقرة وجدتها تخرا فيها فاشْتُقَّ لها هذا الاسم من هذا اللفظ

١٨،٢ (ويُكنّوا) أم جعيص وأم عميص * وأم شليح وأم رميح * وأم عرّام وأم زوّام * وأم شقيره وأم صقيره * وأم شواهي وأم دواهي *

١٩،٢ (ويُلَقَّبوا) بجِلّايه وكِرْسايه * وغاسوله * وفاره وفرفاره * وغاره وغايره * فهذه أسماء وألقاب وكُنًى وجودها كالعدم إنّما هي ألفاظ يضعوها مناسبة لذواتهم ليطابق الاسم المسمّى

٢٠،٢ (وبعضهم إذا نادى لزوجته يقول لها) يا داهيه يا داهيه تقول له تجيلك من الحيط كما اتّفق أنّ رجلاً منهم دخل منزله فرأى زوجته عند الجيران فناداها يا داهيه يا داهيه فقالت له تجيك من الحيط فقال لها تعالي اتعشّي فقالت له ابنك يخرى كلْ انت وقال شخص منهم لزوجته يا قطيعه قالت له تجيك يا ابو عنطوز

٢١،٢ (وأمّا أولادهم) فإنّهم مثل أولاد الهنود * أو أولاد القرود * دائماً في شلاتيت وشراميط * ترى الواحد منهم دائماً مكشوف الرأس * غارق في الجلّة والساس * مهده المَدْوِد * وشربه من المَتْرِد * وأكله من الجله * ولعبه حول العجله * يشخّ ويخرى في ثيابه * دائماً في سخامة وهبابه * عمره في دناسه * وأمّه في نجاسه * وإذا درج في الحاره * لا يعرف غير الطبلة والزُمّاره * والطرد وراء الثور والعجل * وسخامة في الجلّة والوحل * لا يلبس له قميص * وعيشته في تنغيص * خالي من التنظيف * قحف من قحوف الريف

("Sniff") and Balmah ("Stupid"), Sarwah ("Cypress") and Balāwah,[53] Fusaywah ("Little Silent Fart") and Khuraywah ("Little Piece of Shit"). I actually saw this Khuraywah and asked her father why he had chosen that word for her name. He told me that, when she was a little girl, she was always shitting and would shit in any hole she came across, so he coined a name for her from that same word.

Their *kunyah*s are Umm Juʿayṣ[54] and Umm ʿUmayṣ,[55] Umm Shulayḥ[56] and Umm Rumayḥ ("Mother of a Little Lance"), Umm ʿArrām[57] and Umm Zawwām, Umm Shuqayrah ("Mother of a Little Blond Girl") and Umm Ṣuqayrah ("Mother of a Little Hawk"), Umm Shawāhī ("Mother of Appetites") and Umm Dawāhī ("Mother of Disasters"). **2.18**

Their nicknames are "Dung Cake" and "Dung Slab," "Potash," "Rat" and Farfārah,[58] "Raid" and "Sunken-Eye." **2.19**

These names, nicknames, and *kunyah*s are utterly without value. They are nothing but words that they make up to match their persons, so that the name fits its bearer.

When one of them calls to his wife, he says, "Calamity! Calamity!"[59] and she replies, "She's a-coming to you from the wall!"[60] Thus it happened that a peasant entered his dwelling and found that his wife was at the neighbors'. "Calamity! Calamity!" he called to her. "She's a-coming to you from the wall!" she answered. Then he said, "Come and have dinner!" to which she replied, "Your son's taking a crap! Do eat!" Another said, "Drat!" to his wife, and she replied, "She's a-coming to you, Abū ʿAnṭūz!" **2.20**

Their Children

Their children are like the children of Indians or of apes, always in rags and tatters. You will never find one that is not caked in dung and straw, sleeping in the feeding trough and drinking from the kneading bowl. His food is dung cakes and he plays among the calves. He pisses and shits in his clothes and is always covered in filth and grime. His life is spent in befoulment, and his mother's in defilement. As he scuttles around his quarter, all he knows how to do is blow the pipes and beat the drums, chase around after the ox and the bull, and make a mess of himself in the dung and the mire. He never puts on a shift, and his life is spent in vexation. Of all cleanliness free, naught but a country clod is he. **2.21**

(وأمّا نساؤهم عند الجماع) * فإنّهن في حكم الضباع * يدخلن الأفران * ويُضْرِموا ٢٢،٢
فيها النيران * ويَعْبَقُ عليهم الدخان * وتظهر لهم روائح الدِمَس * حتّى يصيروا
كأنّهم في قَلَس * ثمّ ينضجعوا إلى شيء من القَشّ * وما يتيسّر من القصالة
والعَفَش * بعد أكلهم المدمّس والبيسار * حتّى يصير الشخص منهم كأنّه حمار *
ثمّ يضمّ زوجته إليه * وهي تتشقلب عليه * فيظهر من بين الاثنين * روائح الجلّة
والطين * وتعطيه رجليها * وينظر إلى عَمْشة عينيها * ويطرحها على جنبها *
فتستغيث بربّها * وتقول أحَيّه جتك داهيه أحَيّه جتك مصيبه أحَيّه جتك غاره
فعنجها بليّه * وجماعها رزيّه * وربما جامع الشخص منهم زوجته في مدود الحماره *
أو في الغيط جنب العبّاره * وقد تمكث المرأة منهنّ الجمعه * لا تغسل من الجنابة
لمعه * وكذلك الرجل بتحقيق * في أعظم الدناسة وعدم التوفيق *

(وأمّا أعراسهم) فإنّها مثل قيام الغارات * أو تعفير الكلاب في الحارات * ٢٣،٢
يدوروا بالعريس دَوْره * وهم في غارة أو غَوْره * وعائط وصرخات * ودواهي
وبليّات * وزعيق وعفره * وصياح وغبره * والكلاب تنبح * والشعراء تمدح *
والطبل يضرب * والمشاة حوله تلعب * والجدعان تخبط بالنبابيت * والأولاد
تنطّ بالشراميط * وربما كانوا في هزل صاروا في جدّ وربما هشموا بعضهم البعض
وقد يموت الواحد منهم والاثنين * ويحصل من ذلك الفرح الهمّ والشَيْن * وتخرب
من فعلهم البلد * ويزيد الهمّ والنكد *

ثمّ بعد هذه الدوره * يفرشوا للعريس جنب الجوره * ويُجْلِسوه على نَخّ أو حصير * ٢٤،٢
أو تُرْس من أتراس البير * ويأتوا له بالعروس * كأنّها فحل جاموس * منقّشة
بالحِبْر والهِباب * وقدّامها الشاعر بالرَباب * وخلفها الصبايا بالزغاريط تصيح *
والجدعان تمشي بالمصابيح * ويَرُشّوا عليها الملح خَوْفَ النَظْره * وقد خلبطوا وجهها

Their Women during Intercourse

Their women during intercourse are like hyenas. They go into the ovens and set the fires burning, so that the smoke clings to them and the odors of the ashes on them cannot be ignored, till they are as though steeped in vomit. Then the two of them lie down on a bit of straw and some shucks and sweepings, after eating stewed fava beans and *bīsār*, till both are indistinguishable from donkeys. The man now clasps his wife to his breast and she flips over onto his chest, and from between them emerge odors of dung and earth. She gives him her legs and he gazes into her rheumy eyes and throws her on her side, while she calls on her Lord for aid, saying, "*Aḥḥēḥ*![61] Disaster befall you! *Aḥḥēḥ*! Calamity strike you! *Aḥḥēḥ*! A raiding party take you!" Thus her cries when in heat are a pain, and coition with her is a bane. Sometimes a man will have intercourse with his wife in the donkey's trough or in the field next the path and the woman may go for a week without washing off the traces of her impurity,[62] while the man likewise assuredly persists in the worst possible state of filth and futility. 2.22

Their Weddings

Their weddings are like raiding parties at their setting off or dogs fighting and kicking up dust in the lanes. They make a circuit of the village with the groom, making a hubbub and a hullaballoo, shouting and screaming, creating disasters and calamities, shrieking and kicking up the dust and yelling and making a mess, while the dogs bark, the bards sing the praises of the Prophet, the drums beat, the foot soldiers play around the groom, the brave lads bash one another with their staves, and the children leap around in their rags. Often what started in jest ends in earnest, with the breaking of one another's bones and one or two of them maybe dying, so that the celebration ends in woe and shame, the village is ruined by their doings, and woe and misery increase. 2.23

After this parade, they make up a bed for the groom next to the fire chamber of the oven and seat him on a straw mat or pallet, or on a cog from the waterwheel, and bring him the bride looking like a buffalo bull, her face all daubed with ink and soot.[63] Before her goes the bard with his rebab, while behind her the girls shriek their ululations and the brave lads walk with lanterns, scattering salt over her for fear of the Evil Eye. Before this they have disfigured her face with black and red and unveiled it at the Showing,[64] by which evil custom 2.24

بالسواد والحُمْره * وكشفوا وجهها عند الجَلا * وصارت بهذه الفَعلة مُثْلة بين المَلا * وهذا من أقبح أفعالهم * وأتعس أحوالهم * إذ لا يجوز هذا في الشرع * ولا يقول به أصل ولا فرع * ثمّ إنهم يُجْلِسوها على شيء عالي * ويأتي إليها الكبالي * ويُنْشِدوها الأشعار * ممّا هو مناسب لها باعتبار [رمل]

يَا عَـرُوسَـهْ يَا ٱمَّ غَـالِي   اِنْجَـلِي وَلَا تُبَـالِي
اِنْجَـلِي يَا وَجْـهَ بُومَـهْ   زَاعِـقَهْ وَسْطَ ٱللَّيَالِي
وَجْـهُكِي بِالنَّقْشِ يُشْـبِهْ   وَجْهَ ضَبْعَهْ فِي ٱلرِّمَالِ
لِكْ مَسِيحَةْ شَعْرِ مَرْبُوطْ   فَوْقَ رَاسِكْ لَا مُحَالِ
تُشْـبِهِي بُو أَمَّ مُجْبِـرْ   دَايِرَهْ وَسْـطَ ٱلتِّلَالِ
يَا عَـرِيسْ قُمْ خُذْ عَرُوسَكْ   وَٱطْلَعِ ٱلْيَوْمَ فِي ٱلْعَلَالِي
وَٱفْـرِشُوا ٱلْقُـبَّهْ وَنَامُوا   فَوْقَهَـا جُـنْحَ ٱللَّيَالِي
وَٱسْخَرِي لُو وَٱغْـنِجَي لُو   بِٱلدَّوَاهِي وَٱلْهِبَالِ
تَصْـلَحِي لُو يَا عَـرُوسَهْ   تَمَّ أَمْرُكْ بِٱلْكَمَالِ

ثمّ إنّهم يجتمعوا حول العروس * وينادي بينهم رجل فلفوس * بيده شُعْلة من ٢٥،٢
شرموط * هاتوا النُقوط * صاحب العرس تقي وأمان * هاتوا يا مشاه يا جدعان * فيعطيه الشخص منهم الدرهم والدرهمين * والبرمكي يرمي نصف أو نصفين * وبعد هذا يقبلوا على العروس * بوجوه كأنّها وجوه التيوس * وينادوا قمح والّا شعير * والّا سمسم مقشور غزير * فإن كانت مليحة قالوا قمح زَرّيع أو سمسم مقشور * وإن كانت قبيحة قالوا شعير نبت فوق الجسور * ثمّ إنهم يُدْخِلوهما إلى الفرن أو البيت * ويُسْرِجوا لهم بشيء من عُكارة الزيت * ويفرشوا لهم شيء من التبن أو القَصَل * ويضعوا لهم وسائد محشيّة من قشر البَصَل * ويُغْلِقوا عليهما الباب * ويدقّوا لهم بالحجارة على الأعتاب * فإن أخذ وجهها هنّوه * وإلّا جرّسوه وهتكوه * وقالوا

she is turned into a spectacle for the public gaze—and this is one of their foulest deeds and most wretched ways, for it is a practice the Divine Law does not permit and that neither the Law's theory nor its practice admit. Then they seat her on something high and the dressing women come and serenade her with songs appropriate to her state:

O bride! O Umm Ghālī![65]
 Show yourself and feel no fright!
Show yourself, with your face like an owl
 Screeching in the night!
Your face all daubed looks like
 A hyena's among the dunes!
The hairpiece tied atop your head, no doubt about it,
 Makes you look like Umm Mujbir,[66] prowling among the tombs!
Groom! Arise and take your bride,
 And mount today to the topmost rooms!
Make your bed on the stove and lie
 There, whiling the night away!
Snort and whimper to him
 Whatever calamities and foolishness you may,
And then you'll suit him fine, my dear—
 May your future all be fair!

After this, they gather round the groom, while some reprobate, rag-torch in hand, calls out, "Cough up your money![67] The host is God-fearing and trustworthy! Hand it over, you foot soldiers, you brave lads!" At this, each of them gives him a dirham or two, and the master of ceremonies throws down a silver piece or two. Then they approach the bride, with faces like billygoats, and cry, "Wheat, or barley, or husked sesame aplenty?" If she's pretty, they say, "Sprouting wheat!" or "Husked sesame!" But if she's ugly they say, "Barley sprung wild atop the dikes!" Then they take the couple into the bake-oven or the house, light the lamp with a few dregs of oil, put down a little straw or shucks for them, lay out pillows stuffed with onion skins, shut the door on them, and beat stones for them[68] on the threshold. If he takes her maidenhood, they give him their congratulations. If he fails, they hold him up to public ridicule and put him to shame, telling him, "You have brought disaster down on 2.25

له شرقت البلاد * وهتكتنا بين الأولاد * فعرسهم هَتيكه * وفرحهم مُصيبه *

٢٦،٢ (ووليمتهم) الكِشْك والفول * ونوع من البقول * والأرز بالعسل يشبه الطين * والأرز باللبن يشبه طعام المجانين * وقد ذكر هذه الأوصاف صاحب الدُهُكس حيث قال في القصيد [طويل]

١،٢٦،٢ وَيَوْمَ عَمِلْنَا ٱلْعُرْسَ يَامَا رَقَصْنَا وَيَامَا حَرَقْنَا قَشّ جُوَّا ٱلْمَسَاطِحْ
وَنَصَّصْتُهَا بِالزُّنْطِ مِنْ فَوْقِ قِمَّتِي وَكَانْ ٱنْهَدَمْ يَامَا قَشَعْنَا فَضَايِحْ
وَأَخْرَجْتُهَا لِلضَّوْءِ بَرَّا ٱلزَّرِيبَهْ بَقَا شَيْ يَقُولْ مُشْعِرْ وَشَيْ يَقُولْ قَامِحْ
وَلِلْفُرْنِ جِينَا نَلْتَقِيهِ مُدَمَّسْ بَقَى دِمْسُهُ يَا نَاسْ لِلْجَوِّ فَايِحْ
وَلَا قَشْتُهَا بِالطَّبْلِ قَالَتْ مُصِيبَهْ وَعِدُّ دَوَاهِي وَأَنْتَ مَبْهُوتُ كَالِحْ
٢،٢٦،٢ وَجَلَتْ خَفَايَهْ دِي ٱلصَّبِيَّهْ بِغُنْجِهَا وَعَادْ شُخَاخِي فِي ٱلشَّلَاتِيتِ سَايِحْ
وَصِبِحَتْ تُهَنِّينَا أَكَابِرْ بَلَدْنَا عَلَيَّ تِقَالُ ٱلْعَيْشِ مَسْبُولْ سَايِحْ
هَدَادِيهُ تَخْبِطْ عَلَى قِفْلِ رُكْبَتِي وَأَنَا بِلَا لِبْدَهْ قَلِيلُ ٱلْمَلَايِحْ
وَجَلَسْ بِجَنْبِي إِبْنُ جَرْوٍ وَكُلْ خَرَا وَإِبْنُ ٱلْغَفِيرِ وَأَنَا أُرَوِّحْ رَوَايِحْ

أي جلس بجانب مشايخ الكَفْر وهم هؤلاء المذكورون فلا يحتاج إلى إعادتهم لأنّ الإعادة في ذكرهم ليس فيها إفادة وقد أفردتُ عرسهم بمؤلّف فراجعه

٢٧،٢ ثمّ إنّهم عند الصباحيّه * يجتمعوا المشاة في الظُهريّه * ويجعلوا بينهم وبين العريس حكومه * لا قدر لها ولا قيمه * ويجتمعوا مع بعضهم البعض * ويرمحوا بالطول والعرض * ويقولوا حَكَمْنا عليك يا فلان * قوم هات العيش والمِشّ ورطل دخان * ويأكلوا وينطّوا * ويشيلوا ويحطّوا * ويأتوا بحجارة للدخان مثل أرباع الكيل * ويصيروا في عياط وشياط إلى الليل * وسمّوا هذا اليوم يوم الهُروبه * وأمورهم كلّها مقلوبه * وبعد ثلاثة أيّام * يُخرجوا العروسة بالتمام * ويكشفوا وجهها

the villages and dishonored us among the boys!" Thus, their nuptials are a scandal and their weddings a disgrace.

Their banquets are of wheat groats and fava beans, with some kind of greens, and rice with honey, like mud, and rice with milk, like lunatics' grub. The Master of The Drover's Whip Handle[69] refers to these traits when he says in the ode: 2.26

The day we did the wedding, how we danced, 2.26.1
And how much straw we burned on the drying-grounds![70]
I displayed her wearing the bonnet[71] from off my head,
Which was all stove in, and what scandals we saw!
I brought her out to the light outside the byre,
And some said, "Barley-colored!" and some said, "Wheaten!"
To the oven we came and found it stoked,
The ashes, good people, exuding odors to the air.
I whispered sweet nothings to her to the sound of the drums. She said,
"A disaster,
And so many[72] calamities, and you're gobsmacked and scowling!"
And this maid revealed secrets in her groans of pleasure, 2.26.2
And my piss started to soak through my rags.
In the morning the big men of the village came to wish us well,
While the flour cloth[73] was draped over me, flowing,
Its fringes knocking the joints of my knees,
And I was capless and far from elegant
And by me sat Son-of-Puppy and Eat-Shit,
And Son-of-the-Constable, while I exuded odors.

—in other words, he sat next to the shaykhs of the village, that is to say, those already mentioned; there is nothing to be gained by repeating their names. I have devoted a work to their nuptials, so consult that.

On the morning after the marriage, the foot soldiers gather around noon and hold a sort of trial—null and void—with the groom. They gather all together and gallivant hither and thither and say, "So-and-so, our sentence is pronounced! Go fetch the bread and *mishsh* and a pound of tobacco!"[74] Then they eat and they leap and they hurry and they scurry and they bring pipe bowls as big as cups for measuring grain, and the uproar goes on until night. This they call the Day of Escape—but all their doings are out of shape. 2.27

ثاني مرّه * ويجعلوها للناس شُهره * ويأخذوا أيضاً النُقوط من الناس * وأحوالهم في أعكاس

Then, three days later, they bring the bride out and uncover her face a second time, making a public spectacle of her and taking money from people too—their affairs are indeed perverse, through and through.

‹ذكر وقائعهم›

١،٣ ‹حُكِيَ أنّ بعض الملوك خرج هو ووزيره قاصدًا لتنزُّه› فمرّ على رجل فلاح يحرث وعلى رأسه لبدة مشرمطة ولابس خلقة مقطّعة ترى عورته منها وقد حصره البول فبال عليها حتّى غرقها ولم يبال بالنجاسة وقد اسودّ قفاه من الحرّ وتشقّقت قدماه من الحفا وشدّة البرد وهو في حالة مُكْرِبة فقال الملك لوزيره ما حال هذا الرجل فقال له يا ملك هذا من فلّاحين الريف ينشأ الشخص منهم على التعب والنصب والهمّ والغمّ والطرد والجري وقلّة الدين والجهل ولا يجد من يرشده للعبادة والصلاة فيصير في هذه الحالة كما ترى فهم هَمَج الهَمَج لا يعرفون غير الثور والمحراث فحُكمهم حُكم البهائم والكلاب قال الشاعر [طويل]

مَنْ فاتَهُ العِلْمُ وأَخْطاهُ الغِنَى فَذاكَ وَالكَلْبُ عَلَى حَدٍّ سَوَا

فقال الملك لوزيره ألا ترى إذا أخذناه وعلّمناه القرآن وأشغلناه بالعلم وألبسناه ملابس النُعَم يتغيّر طبعه ويرقّ قلبه وتخفّ ذاته وينتقل من طَوْر الكثافة إلى طَوْر اللطافة فقال الوزير أيّد الله الملك وأدام بقاه أما سمعت قول الشاعر [سريع]

لا يَخْرُجُ الإِنْسانُ مِنْ طَبْعِهِ حَتَّى يَعُودَ الدَرُّ في ضَرْعِهِ
مَنْ كان مِنْ جُمَّيْزةٍ أَصلُهُ لا يَنْبُتُ التُفّاحُ في فَرْعِهِ

وقال آخر [بسيط]

An Account of Their Escapades

Anecdotes Showing that a Man Cannot Escape His Inborn Nature

The story is told that a certain king went out with his minister to take the air 3.1
and came upon a peasant plowing. On his head was a tattered cap, and he wore a single torn garment through which his privates could be seen. He had been overtaken by a sudden need to relieve himself and had urinated on this garment till it was soaked but paid no heed to this defilement. The back of his neck had turned black from the heat, his feet were chapped from walking barefoot and from the cold, and he was altogether in a pitiful state. "What ails the man?" the king asked his minister, who replied, "King, this is a peasant of the countryside, one of those who are raised to hardship and sickness, woe and worry, hurry and scurry, ignorance and neglect of religion, and who find no one to direct them towards worship and prayer. Thus, they turn out as you see, the most savage of savages, ignorant of everything but the ox and the plow, and indistinguishable from beasts and dogs. As the poet[75] says:

Whom knowledge has passed by and riches shunned,
He and the dogs are on a par."

The king said to the minister, "Don't you think that, if we took him and taught him the Qur'an and set him to studying and dressed him in fine clothes, his nature would change, his heart soften, and his personal appearance become more agreeable, so that he would be translated from the domain of coarseness to that of refinement?" "God save the king," the minister responded, "and send him long life! Have you not heard the words of the poet:

Man will not escape his nature
Till the milk returns to the udder.
Apples will never sprout from the twig
Of one whose roots are a sycamore fig?

"And another has said:

الطَّبْعُ وَالرُّوحُ مَخْلوقانِ[1] في جَسَدٍ لا يَنْفَدُ الطَّبْعُ حَتَّى تَنْفَدُ الرُّوحُ

وقال بعضهم يحول عن وَكْرِه ولا يحول عن طبعه وفي الحديث إذا حُدِّثْتُمْ أنّ جبلاً زال عن مكانه فصدّقوا وإذا حُدِّثْتُمْ أنّ رجلاً زال عن طبعه فلا تصدّقوا

٢،٣ وحكي أنّ رجلاً أعرابيّاً مرّ بقارعة الطريق فرأى جَرْو ذئب صغيراً فرحمه وأخذه إلى منزله وكان عنده شاة تُرْضِع فربّاه عليها إلى أن كبر فعدا يوماً على الشاة فبَقَرَ بطنها ووَلَغَ في لحمها ودمها فلمّا رجع الأعرابيّ ورأى ما فعل أنشد يقول [وافر]

غُذِيتَ بِدَرِّها وَنَشَأْتَ فِينا فَمَنْ أَنْباكَ أَنَّ أَباكَ ذِيبُ
إِذا كانَ الطِّباعُ طِباعَ سُوءٍ فَلا أَدَبٌ يُفِيدُ وَلا أَدِيبُ

٣،٣ ومن ذلك ما حكي أنّ جماعة قصدوا صيد ضبعة فالتجأت إلى أعرابيّ ودخلت منزله فخرج الأعرابيّ إليهم وبيده السيف مصلّتاً وقال لهم لا تعرّضوا لضيفي فإنّه قد استجار بي فقالوا يا هذا لا تَحُلْ بيننا وبين صيدنا فقال هذا لا يكون أبداً ولا أسلّمها لكم أبداً وجعل يغذّيها اللبن فتجرّد الأعرابيّ يوماً ليغتسل فلمّا بصرته عرياناً عَدَتْ عليه فشقّت بطنه وولغت في لحمه ودمه فقيل لابن الأعرابيّ فأنشد [طويل]

وَمَنْ يَفْعَلِ المَعْرُوفَ مَعْ غَيْرِ أَهْلِهِ يُجازَى كَما جُوزِيَ مُجِيرُ أُمِّ عامِرِ
أَعَدَّ لَها لَمّا اِسْتَجارَتْ بِقُرْبِهِ مِنَ الدَّرِّ أَلْبانَ اللِّقاحِ الدَّواسِرِ
وَأَشْبَعَها حَتَّى إِذا ما تَمَكَّنَتْ فَرَتْهُ بِأَنْيابٍ لَها وَأَظافِرِ
فَقُلْ لِذَوِي المَعْرُوفِ هٰذا جَزاءُ مَنْ يُوَجِّهُ مَعْرُوفاً إِلى غَيْرِ شاكِرِ

[1] بي: قد خُلِقا في جسد؛ ب: في جسم قد خلقا؛ ك: قد خلقات (كذا) في جسد؛ ب وم: قد خلقان (كذا) في جسد.

Man's nature and spirit in one body were made;
As long as the soul lasts, his nature won't fade.

"And another has said, 'The bird will abandon its nest before it abandons its nature' and a Tradition has it, 'If you are told that a mountain has moved from its place believe it, but if you are told that a man has changed his nature, do not believe it!'

"The story is told that a Bedouin was travelling down the road when he found a small wolf cub and took pity on it and brought it home, where he had a ewe in milk, which he used to raise the cub till it was grown. One day the wolf attacked the ewe, ripped open her belly, and gorged itself on her flesh and blood. When the Bedouin came back and saw what it had done, he spoke the following verses: 3.2

You were fed with her milk and raised among us,
So who told you that your father was a wolf?
When an inborn nature's disposed to evil,
No teaching and no teacher is of use!

"Similarly, it is related that a company set forth to hunt a hyena, which took refuge with a Bedouin in his tent. The Bedouin went out towards the hunters, sword in hand, and told them, 'Do not meddle with my guest, for it has sought my protection!' 'Fellow,' they replied, 'do not come between us and our quarry!' to which the Bedouin responded, 'That cannot be, and never will I hand it over to you!' and thereafter he nourished it with milk. One day the Bedouin stripped himself to wash. When the hyena saw him naked, it leapt on him, rent his belly, and gorged itself on his flesh and blood. When his son was told, he declared: 3.3

He who does kindness to one not of his kind
The hyena's protector's reward will find:
He prepared for it, when it sought to use him as a shield,
Milk from the balky milch-camels' yield.
He fed it well, till, when its chance it saw,
It ripped him apart with fang and with claw.
So say to do-gooders, 'Such is the reward
Of those who to the ingrate would be kind!'

ومن كلام الإمام عليّ رضي الله عنه لا تعلّموا أولاد السَفَلة العلم فإنّهم إذا تعلّموا طلبوا معالي الأمور فإذا نالوها اعتنوا بمذلّة الأشراف وقال الإمام الشافعيّ رضي الله عنه [طويل] ٤،٣

فَمَنْ مَنَحَ الجُهّالَ عِلْماً أَضاعَهُ   وَمَنْ كَتَمَ المُسْتَوْجِبِينَ فَقَدْ ظَلَمْ

وهذا الرجل لو علّمت[١] فيه الحكمة وقيّدت له من يعلّمه العلم والقرآن لا يخرج عن طبعه ويرجع إلى عادته الأولى خصوصاً طباع جَهَلة الريف وعوامّهم فإنّهم أجلاف قحوف كأنّهم خُلِقوا من صخر قال الشاعر [كامل]

إِنَّ اللَّطافَةَ لَمْ تَزَلْ   بَيْنَ الأَكابِرِ فاشِيَهْ
فَهَلْ رَأَيْتُمُ فِي الوَرَى   قُحْفاً رَقِيقَ الحاشِيَهْ

فاللطافة لا تخرج عن طور الأكابر ولا تتعدّى لعوامّ الريف الأراذل خصوصاً دنيء الأصل إذا ادّعى العلم والفضل كما اتّفق أنّ امرأة ذات حسن وجمال * وقدّ واعتدال * كانت متزوّجة بابن عمّ لها وهي متضجّرة منه وراغبة في فراقه فأرسلت للعلماء في تدبير حيلة للفراق فلم تتمكّن من ذلك حتّى وصلت إلى وضيع دنيء الأصل تعلّم العلم فدبّرها أنّها تُظْهِرُ أنّها تدّعي أنّها ارتدّت عن دين الإسلام والعياذ بالله تعالى وتختفي إلى أن تنقضي عِدّتها فتصل إلى الحاكم الشرعيّ وتعترف بصدور ذلك منها وأنّها تابت ورجعت إلى الإسلام وأخذ على ذلك جعلاً ففعلت ما أمرها به فاستغرب الناس ذلك وجزموا أن لا يصدر هذا التعليم إلّا من ذلك الشخص فتفقّدوه فلم يجدوه وفي هذا المعنى قول الإمام الشافعيّ رضي الله عنه فمن منح الجهّال إلى آخره

---

١ بي: عملت.

"And among the sayings of the Imam ʿAlī, God be pleased with him, we find, 'Do not instruct the children of the rabble in knowledge, for if they learn, they will seek high office, and if they attain that, they will devote themselves to the humiliation of the noble.' And the Imam al-Shāfiʿī,[76] God be pleased with him, has said: 3.4

> To bestow knowledge on the ignorant is to waste it,
> And to deny it to the deserving is unjust.

"So," continued the minister, "even if you teach this man wisdom and engage someone to instruct him in the sciences and the Qur'an, he will never escape his nature and will always revert to his former ways. This is especially true of the inborn nature of the ignorant people of the countryside and their common folk, for they are such louts and clods you would think they had been created out of rock. The poet[77] has said:

> Refinement among the great ever spreads its rays,
> But when did you last see a clod with polished ways?

"For refinement never spreads beyond the realm of great men, nor does it extend to the base commons of the countryside, and especially not to those persons of low birth who lay false claim to knowledge and virtue. For example, it happened that a woman of great beauty, endowed with a graceful and well-proportioned form, was married to a cousin of hers. However, becoming estranged from him and wanting to leave him, she sent to the scholars of religion to devise a stratagem by which she might do so.[78] She had no success, however, until she applied to a base wretch of low birth who had acquired learning. What he came up with was that she should pretend that she had abandoned the religion of Islam[79]—we seek refuge with the Almighty!—and to hide herself until her waiting period[80] was over. Then she was to go to the legal authorities, confess what she had done, and claim that she had repented and returned to Islam. The man took money from her for this advice. When the woman did as he had advised, the people were amazed and asserted that such instructions could only have come from that individual, and they looked for him but they could not find him. This is the point that the Imam al-Shāfiʿī, may God be pleased with him, was making when he said, 'To bestow knowledge . . .' and so on.

٣،٥ وعلى هذا يا ملك الحكاية المشهورة وهو أنّ رجلاً دنيء الأصل سافر إلى مدينة فاشتدّ به الجوع فرأى رجلاً يبيع الزَلابِيَة فوقف قبالة دُكّانه حائرًا فرق له صاحب الزلابية ورحمه وقال له ادخل أغدّيك صَدَقَةً عنّي فدخل فقدّم له ما يكفيه من الزلابية والعسل فأكل حتّى شبع وإذا بمحتسب المدينة مارًا ينادي على السوقة ويوزن ويحذّرهم نقص الموازين وكذلك صنّاع الزلابية أن يُنْضِجوها ولا يبيعوها طريّة فقام هذا الرجل وأخذ حلقة من الزلابية وعجنها بيده وقال للمحتسب نصرك الله في هذا الرجل بيّاع الزلابية انظر ما يفعله للناس من الغِشّ قال فأخذ المحتسب صانع الزلابية وضربه ضربًا مؤلمًا فالتفت إلى هذا الرجل وقال له ما ذنبي معك وأنا شفقت عليك وأطعمتك حتّى شبعت صدقة عنّي فسكت وقال له ما اسمك قال فلان قال وأبوك قال فلان قال وأمّك قال مرجانة جارية سوداء فقال صانع الزلابية لا ألومك أبدًا جاءك الطبع الخبيث من جهة أمّك ثمّ إنّه أخرجه من دكّانه ومضى إلى سبيله * وفي هذه الحكاية يا ملك مواعظ واعتبار

٣،٦ فقال الملك لا بدّ من أخذه وتعليمه ولا أركن إلى ما تقول فقال له الوزير افعل ما بدا لك فأخذ الفلّاح وأنعم عليه وألبسه الثياب الحسنة الفاخرة وقيّد له من يعلّمه القرآن والعلم فحفظ القرآن وبرع في علم الرمل والحرف حتّى صار يُخْرِج الضمير ويبيّن الضائع قال فتذكّر الملك مقالة الوزير في حقّ الفلّاح ونصحه الملك في عدم أخذه وتعليمه فأرسل إليه فلمّا حضر قال له يا وزير خابت فراستك في الفلّاح فإنّه الآن بقي على غاية من العلوم وصار له براعة في علم الرمل والحرف ويخرج الضمير ويبيّن الضائع فقال الوزير يا ملك اختبره وانظر طبعه وخُلُقه فأرسل إليه فحضر فقال له الملك بلغني أنّه صار لك قوّة في إخراج الضمير وبيان الضائع فقال له نعم بسعادة الملك إن شاء الله فقال له مرادي أن أُضْمِرَ على شيء وتبيّنه لي فقال افعل فتوارى الملك وقلع خاتمه وأطبق عليه يده وقال له انظر ما في يدي قال فأقام

“There is another well-known story to the same effect, King, that tells how a man of low birth made a journey to a certain city. There, hard-pressed by hunger, he saw a man selling fritters and, at wit’s end, he stopped in front of his shop till the fritter maker felt sorry for him and took pity on him and said, ‘Come in and I will feed you, for charity’s sake.’ The man went in, and the fritter maker gave him as many fritters with honey as he could eat and he ate till he was full. At that moment, the city’s Inspector of Markets happened to pass by, summoning the merchants, testing their weights, and warning them against selling short; and summoning likewise the fritter makers, warning them to cook their fritters thoroughly and not sell them underdone. Now, this man stood up and, taking a fritter, kneaded it in his hand and said to the inspector, ‘God aid you against this fritter maker! See how he cheats the people!’ and the inspector took the fritter maker and gave him a painful beating. Afterwards, the fritter maker turned to the man and asked him, ‘What harm did I ever do you? Did I not take pity on you and feed you till you were satisfied, for charity’s sake?’ The man, however, said nothing. The fritter maker then asked him, ‘What is your name?’ He answered, ‘So and so.’ ‘And your father’s?’ ‘So and so.’ ‘And your mother’s?’ ‘Murjānah, a black slave.’ ‘I no longer blame you at all then,’ said the fritter maker. ‘You got your despicable nature from your mother’s side.’ Then he expelled him from his shop, and the man went on his way. In this story, King, are words that are wise and lessons to prize.” 3.5

But the king said, “He must be taken and educated! I will not take what you say on trust!” “As you think best,” said the minister. So the king took the peasant and lavished gifts upon him and clothed him in luxurious, handsome garments and engaged someone to instruct him in the Qur’an and the sciences, and the man memorized the Qur’an and became a master of the sciences of divination by sand and by letters,[81] to the point that he could read men’s minds and find things that were lost. Then the king, remembering what his minister had said to him against the peasant and how he had advised him against taking him and educating him, sent for him, saying to him when he appeared, “Minister, your reading of the peasant’s character has proven false. He has now become most learned in the sciences, is a master of divination by sand and by letters, and he reads men’s minds and finds what is lost.” To this the minister responded, “Test him, King, and observe his true nature and disposition.” So the king sent for the man and he came and the king said to him, “It has reached me that you have become skilled in reading men’s minds and finding what is lost.” The man replied, “Indeed it 3.6

الأشكال وقال في يدك شيء مدوّر قال نعم قال وهو خالي الوَسَط قال صدّقت ولكن ما هو فسكت ساعة ثمّ قال أظنّ والله أعلم أنّه حجر طاحون قال فضحك الوزير وقال ردّ عليه طبعه الأوّل يا ملك قال فاغتاظ الملك منه وسلب نعمته وردّه إلى حالته الأولى

(وقيل التزم بعض الأمراء بقرية من قرى الريف) فسافر إليها لينظر أحوالها كما هو عادة الملتزمين فلمّا دخلها ونزل في دار الحكم وتسمّى عندهم دار الشَدّ فأقبلت إليه الفلّاحون ﴿وَهُم مِّن كُلِّ حَدَبٍ يَنسِلُونَ﴾ وأمامهم شيخ كبير قد طعن في السنّ وبيده عصا يتوكّأ عليها قال فلمّا رآه الملتزم قام إليه وأكرمه لكبر سنّه وقال في نفسه لعلّه من أهل الصلاح لأنّ ما في هذه القرية أكبر منه ثمّ إنّ الأمير صار يحثّهم على الزرع والقلع وعلى سداد مال السلطان والغرامة وأنّهم يجتهدوا ويفيقوا لأنفسهم ويكونوا مع بعضهم البعض قال فعند ذلك قام هذا الشيخ الكبير ووقف بين يدي الأمير وقال له إنّي أريد أن أنصحك أيّها الأمير وأرشدك على شيء تفعله فإنْ أنت فعلته فاقوا لأنفسهم وسدّوا المال فقال له الأمير تكلّم يا شيخ فإنّ ما فيهم من هو أكبر منك سنّاً وأعلى قدراً فقال إن كان مرادك النصيحة اهدم دا الجامع الّي في وسط البلد فإنّهم كلّ يوم يجتمعوا فيه للصلاة الّي يقولوا عليها الناس ويتركوا مصالحهم فإذا انهدم فاقوا للزرع والقلع وسدّوا المال ولو انّي طاوعتهم يا أمير وصرت كلّ يوم أدخل دا الجامع كان انكسر عليّ مال السلطان وما نفعني إلّا طول عمري ما اعرف دي الصلاة الّي يقول عليها الناس ولا دخلت الجامع أبداً فتعجّب الأمير من طول عمره وقلّة دينه وشدّة جهله وقال له أنت رجل طال عمرك وساء عملك ثمّ إنّه علق ٧.٣

is so, Your Majesty, if God wills." "I intend to hide something," said the king, "and you must tell me what it is." "By all means," said the man. The king then hid himself and, having removed his ring and concealed it in his hand, said to him, "Look and see what is in my hand!" The peasant set up his figures and said, "In your hand is something round." "Correct!" said the king. "And it has a hole in the middle." "True," said the king, "but what is it?" The peasant was silent for a while. Then he said, "I think (though God knows best!) it must be a millstone." The minister laughed and said, "His first nature got the better of him in the end, King!" The king, however, was furious with the man and stripped him of the favors he had bestowed on him and returned him to his former state.

Anecdotes Showing the Stupidity of Country People

It is said that an emir who had obtained the tax farm of a village in the country 3.7
went to inspect it, as is the custom of tax farmers. After he had entered the village and set himself up at the place of authority, which the peasants call the House of Binding, the peasants came to meet him, «swarming in from every hillside»[82] and led by an aged shaykh leaning on a staff. When the tax farmer saw the old man, he stood up to honor him and sat him down beside him out of respect for his age, saying to himself, "He may well be a righteous man, for there is none in the village older than he." Then the emir set about urging them to sow and to reap and to pay the sultan's taxes and the fine on the landless[83] and to work hard and look lively and help one another. When he was done, the aged shaykh arose and, placing himself in front of the emir, said, "I would like to give you some advice and guidance, Emir, about something that you should do and which, if you do it, will make them look lively and pay the tax." "Speak, Shaykh," the emir told him, "for there is none among them of greater age or higher standing than yourself." "If you want my advice then," said the shaykh, "knock down that there mosque in the middle of the village, for every day they gather there for that prayer business that people go on about and drop what they ought to be doing. If it's knocked down, they'll get on with the sowing and reaping and pay the tax. If I'd listened to them, Emir, and taken to going to the mosque every day, I would have fallen behind on the sultan's taxes and gotten nothing out of it in return, but all my life I've refused to have anything to do with this prayer business that people go on about, and I've never even been inside the mosque!" The emir marveled at the man's great age, lack of religion,

في رقبته الأوطية وأركبه حماراً معكوساً ونادى عليه حول البلد بعد أن ضربه ضرباً موجعاً وأخرجه من القرية على أسوأ حال

٨،٣ (ويحكى أنّ أبا نواس جلس يوماً هو والخليفة هارون الرشيد في محلّ المنادمة والملاطفة) فأحضر بين يدي أبي نواس صحناً من الخُشْتَنانَك المحشوّ بالسكر وصار يأكل هو وإيّاه فقال الخليفة يا أبا نواس يمكن أنّ أحداً من الناس لا يعرف هذا فقال نعم يا ملك عوامّ الريف وفلّاحين القرى وأضرابهم فإنّهم أناس نشأوا في أكل الدُخْن والذرة فضلاً عن الحِنْطة ولا يعرفوا هذا ولا غيره من المأكولات إلّا العدس والبيسار فقال له الخليفة لا بدّ أن تُحْضِرَ لي رجلاً منهم في هذه الساعة وإلّا قتلتك قال فقام أبو نواس من عند الخليفة متحيّراً يمشي في شوارع بغداد فرأى رجلاً يحاكي سارية الجبل من طوله وعليه جُبّة من صوف إلى ركبته وقد اتّسخت وتمزّقت من سائر الجوانب وكلّما حكّ جلده من الوسخ تمزّقت من تقادم العهد بها وطول الزمن وإذا أراد أن يتحزّم عليها بان أيره وانكشفت عورته وإذا بال بال عليها من غير مانع لكونه لا يعرف الطهارة من النجاسة وعلى رأسه لِبْدة من الصوف طويلة مثل القحف دائر من غير سقف وقد ربط وطاه في حبل ولفعه خلف قفاه وبيده رغيف ذرة يأكل فيه وهو ينظر إلى الحوانيت مثل المرتاب وهو في حيرة لا يدري أين يذهب ويأكل وينظر إلى الناس مثل المجانين وقد طارت عيناه

٩،٣ قال فلمّا رآه أبو نواس في هذه الحالة عرف أنّه قحف من قحوف الريف فسلّم عليه فلم يردّ عليه السلام وتحيّر في نفسه ولم يعرف سلام ولا كلام بل ظنّ أنّه يريد أن يأخذ منه الرغيف فحطّه في عُبّه وقال له يا جندي أنا ما معي شي تاكله غير هذا الرغيف وانا إن اعطيته لك قتلني الجوع فاعتقني وخلّي رغيفي أنا سايق عليك ابو زعطوط واعلم يا جندي اني عمري ما طلعت هذا الكفر وانا بانظر فيه جنادي كتير مثلك ودور مثل دورنا وخايف من الجنادي لا يقطعوا راسي فقال أبو نواس في

and extreme ignorance, and he told him, "You are a man whose life has been long and whose deeds have been evil!" Then he hung his sandals round his neck, mounted him backwards on a donkey, and had him paraded around the village while his crimes were proclaimed, after first having severely beaten him, and he expelled him from the village in a most parlous state.

And another story is told, that Abū Nuwās was sitting one day with the caliph 3.8
Hārūn al-Rashīd in the apartments set aside for conviviality and elegant intercourse when the caliph had a dish of *khushtanānak* filled with sugar set before Abū Nuwās and the two started eating. The caliph asked, "Abū Nuwās, could it be that there is a soul alive who does not know what this is?" "Certainly, Your Majesty," he replied. "The common people of the countryside, the peasants and their like, for they are a people raised on millet and maize and know nothing of wheat, and they are ignorant of *khushtanānak* or any food other than lentils and *bīsār*." Said the caliph, "Bring me one this second, or it's off with your head!" So Abū Nuwās left the caliph's presence and wandered at his wit's end in the streets of Baghdad, until he noticed a man tall as a flagpole on a mountaintop, wearing a dirty woolen *jubbah* that was ripped all over and came down to his knees. It was so worn out and old that every time he scratched at the dirt on his hide, he made a fresh rip in it and, when he tried to hitch it up with his belt, his penis appeared and his privates were exposed, and when he urinated he urinated on his coat without caring, since he couldn't tell purity from pollution. On his head was a woolen hat, as tall as a peasant's cap, round, with no top to it. He had tied his slippers to a rope and slung them over his shoulders behind his neck and in his hand he held a loaf of maize bread that he munched on while he gazed wide-eyed at the shops. The man was at his wit's end, not knowing where to go, and eating and gawping at people like a lunatic, his eyes popping.

When Abū Nuwās saw him in this state, he knew him for a clod from the 3.9
countryside, and so he greeted him—but the other did not return his greeting and was quite at a loss, knowing nothing of salutations and such. Indeed, he thought that Abū Nuwās wanted to take his loaf from him, so he tucked it into the breast of his robe and said, "Trooper, I have nothing for you to eat but this loaf and if I give it you I'll die of hunger, so please let me go and leave me my loaf, in the name of Abū Zuʿṭūṭ![84] You should know, Trooper, that I've never been to this hamlet before, but I see that there are lots of troopers like you and houses just like ours, and I'm afraid that the troopers will cut off my head!"

نفسه الحمد لله الذي أوقعني في هذا هو المطلوب الذي لم يعرف الكفر من المدينة ثمّ إنّه لاطفه بالكلام وقال له لا تخف ولا تَفْزَعْ فما لي حاجة برغيفك ولا أنا جيعان وأنا مرادي أغدّيك غدوة عظيمة فقال له حياك الله يا جندي وانا الآخر لما تغدّيني وتبيّض وجهك معي ازورك باربع بيضات وان فقست وزّتنا اجيب لك وزّه خضرا واجعلك صاحبي ولا تخلّي احد يقطع راسي لانّي خايف اروّح الكفر بلا راس قال فضحك عليه أبو نواس وقال له امضي معي في هذه الساعة أغدّيك وأصافيك قال

١٠،٣ فسار معه وهو لا يدري أين يذهب حتّى أقبل على ديوان أمير المؤمنين هارون الرشيد قال فلمّا رأى الديوان وكثرة العسكر بهت وحار في أمره واندهش وقال الله أكبر القيامة قامت ودا المَحْشَر لا كلام ثمّ إنّه أراد الهروب فقبض عليه أبو نواس وقال له لا تخف ولا تخشى من شيء وضمانك عليّ فقال له يا جندي أخاف العرض على ربّي والحساب لا يحاسبني على ضرب البهائم ونيك الحمير في الغيط لأنّي ما خلّيت حماره في الغيط بلا نيك من خوف لا أهجم على نسوان الكفر يمسكني المَشَدّ يقطع راسي وباسمع الناس وهم يقولوا كلّ من نكح دابّة يجي يوم القيامه وهو حاملها وانا نكحت دوابّ كتير حتّى الكلبه والقطه لا أقدر أحملهم في هذا اليوم وانت تشفع لي عند ربّي يسامحني في هذا اليوم ممّا فعلت فقال له أبو نواس لا تظنّ أنّ هذا يوم القيامة هذا ديوان الخليفة هارون الرشيد فقال له يا جندي أنا ما رايت متل هذا المحل أبداً ولكن ما يكون الخليفه قال له السلطان فصرخ الفلّاح وقال له يا جندي السلطان يقطع روس الفلّاحين ولا يخلّي فلّاح من غير قطع راس وأراد الهروب

١١،٣ فلمّا سمع الخليفة كلامه سأل عن القضيّة فأخبروه بها فضحك وأرسل يطلبه قال فأخذه أبو نواس وأقبل به على هارون الرشيد وهو مغمى عليه من شدّة الدهشة والحيرة ممّا رأى من كثرة الجند والعسكر حتّى وقف بين يدي الخليفة فقال أنا في

Said Abū Nuwās to himself, "Praise be to God who threw him in my path! Here's just the person I need: someone who can't tell the hamlet from the city!" Then he spoke to him kindly and said, "Fear not and do not be alarmed! I don't need your loaf, and I'm not hungry. All I want is to give you a huge lunch." "God save you, Trooper!" replied the peasant, "and as for me, once you've given me lunch and used me to make yourself a good reputation, I'll come see you with four eggs, and if our goose has hatched her clutch, I'll bring you a gosling, and we'll be friends and you won't let anyone cut off my head because I'm afraid to go back to the village without one!" Abū Nuwās laughed and said, "Come along with me right now and I'll give you lunch and make good my promise."

So the peasant went with him, not knowing where he was headed, till he 3.10
grew close to the audience chamber of the Commander of the Faithful, Hārūn al-Rashīd. When he saw the chamber with all its soldiers, however, he turned pale with perplexity and amazement and cried, "God is Greater! The Last Day is upon us, and this is the congregation of souls for Judgment, for sure!" and he tried to flee, but Abū Nuwās grabbed him and told him, "Fear not and do not be alarmed! I guarantee your safety." The peasant replied, "Trooper, I'm afraid of coming before my Lord for judgment lest He hold me to account for beating the animals and fucking the donkeys in the field, for there isn't a she-donkey in the field that I haven't fucked, because I was afraid that otherwise I'd assault the women of the village and the bailiff would arrest me and cut off my head. And I hear people say, 'Anyone who has intercourse with an animal, come the Day of Resurrection will find himself carrying it,' and I've fucked so many animals, even bitches and she-cats, that I won't be able to carry them all on that day, so you intercede for me with the Lord so that He'll forgive me this day for what I've done!" Said Abū Nuwās, "Don't imagine that this is the Day of Resurrection—this is the audience chamber of the Caliph Hārūn al-Rashīd!" "Never, Trooper, have I seen such a place!" said the peasant. "But what's a caliph?" "The sultan," replied Abū Nuwās, "who collects the taxes from the villages and hamlets of the countryside." At this the peasant let out a shriek and said, "Trooper, the sultan cuts off peasants' heads and doesn't leave a single peasant with his head in place!" and he tried to run away.

When the caliph heard him talking, he asked what was going on and they 3.11
told him, so he laughed and sent for the peasant. Abū Nuwās took him and approached Hārūn al-Rashīd with him, the peasant swooning from wonder

جيرتك يا رسول الله انا في جيرة ابو عفر وابو دعموم أنا في جيرتك يا ابو زعبل يا الله يا مشايخ الكفر خلّصوني قال فأمر الملك أن يلاطفوه بالكلام فلاطفوه حتّى سكن رُعْبه ورَوْعه ثمّ إنّه نظر فرأى الخليفة جالساً على الكرسي وعلى رأسه التاج الكِسْرَوِيّ فقال له أنا في جيرتك يا خطيب المسلمين قال فضحك الخليفة وقال له يا فلّاح من أي البلاد أنت فقال له أنا من كفر ابو زعبل وانا شيخ الكفر وعندي بيت ملان تبن وقصل وعندي عنز ومركوب احمر واحيات راس السامعين وعندي فرختين وديكهم واشتوان عضم وقحف طويل مثل قحفك دا يا خطيب فضحك عليه الخليفة وقال له من أحضرك إلى عندي قال دا الجندي صبيّك لا جزاه الله خير كان مراده ياكل رغيفي دا ثمّ إنّه أخرج الرغيف من عبّه وأوراه للخليفة فقال له الخليفة أنت جيعان فقال يا خطيب صبيّك أوعدني بغدوة مليحة فقال له الخليفة ما تشتهي قال العدس والبيسار هات لي مترد عدس ومترد بيسار ورغيفين دره وانا اخلّي امّ خطيطه تدعي لك فقال له الخليفة اجلس يا فلّاح قال فقعد ومدّ رجليه بحضرة الخليفة وحطّ النَبُّوت بجانبه والمركوب خلف قفاه وقد ربطه في حزامه خوفاً عليه لا يقع وراء ظهره فأمر الخليفة أن يقدّموا له الصحن الخشتنانك فقدّموه إليه فلمّا رأى الصحن قال يا خطيب المسلمين أعطني من دا المتردكوره العب بها في الكفر أنا وابو دعموم واولاد الكفر فضحك عليه الخليفة وقال له كل منهم كوره فقال يا خطيب الكوره تتاكل فقال له كل على بركة الله تعالى قال فأخذ الفلّاح واحدة ووضعها في فمه ومضغها فلمّا استقرّت حلاوتها في جوفه صار يأخذ كلّ أربع حبّات سوا ويحنهم في يده ويقطع منهم ويبلع وتارة يسفّ وتارة يمضغ وهو في حالة المجانين فضحك عليه الخليفة وقال له يا فلّاح ما يكون هذا الذي تأكله وما اسمه فقال يا خطيب المسلمين عمري آكل العدس والبيسار والكِشْك بالفول والمدمّس ما ريت مثل دا أبداً إلّا إنّي سمعت عن امّ معيكه جدّتي تقول نعيم الدنيا الحمّام والله أعلم إن دا هو الحمّام الّي يقولوا عليه الناس فضحك عليه الخليفة وقال له مرحباً بك يا فلّاح كلْ واشبع فقال له يا

and confusion at the huge numbers of cavalrymen and infantrymen that he beheld, till he stood before the caliph, at which point he said, "Messenger of God, protect me! Abū ʿAfr[85] and Abū Daʿmūm, protect me! Abū Zaʿbal protect me! O God, O shaykhs of the village, save me!" So the king ordered them to talk soothingly to him, and they did so till his terror and awe abated. Then he looked and saw the caliph sitting on the throne, with the crown of Chosroes on his head, and he said to him, "Preacher of the Muslims, protect me!" The caliph laughed and asked, "Where are you from, peasant?" He replied, "I am from the hamlet of Abū Zaʿbal. I am its shaykh and I have a house full of straw and cornstalks and a goat and a pair of red shoes, I swear by the life of all who hear! And I have two hens and a cock and an *ishtiwān* of bone[86] and a tall hat just like yours, Preacher!" The caliph laughed and said, "Who brought you here?" "This trooper lad of yours—may God not reward him well!" he said. "He wanted to eat this loaf of mine!" And he drew the loaf from the breast of his robe and showed it to the caliph. "Are you hungry?" asked the caliph. "Your boy promised me a nice lunch, preacher," he replied. "What would you like?" asked the caliph. "Lentils and *bīsār*," he said. "Get me a crock of lentils and a crock of *bīsār* with two loaves of corn bread and I'll have Umm Khuṭayṭah[87] call down blessings on your head!" So the caliph said to him, "Sit, peasant," and he sat, stretching his legs out in front of him in the caliph's presence,[88] placing his cudgel beside him, and putting his slippers, which he had tied to his belt as he was afraid that they might fall behind his back, round his neck. Then the caliph ordered them to serve him the dish of *khushtanānak*, which they did. When the peasant saw the dish he said, "Preacher of the Muslims, give me a ball from that crock to play with in the hamlet, me and Abū Duʿmūm and the boys of the hamlet!" The caliph laughed at him and said, "Take one and eat it!" to which the peasant replied, "Preacher of the Muslims, how can you eat a ball?" "Eat," he replied, "and trust in the Almighty!" So the peasant took one and put it in his mouth and munched on it. As its sweetness spread through his belly, he started eating them four at a time, mashing them in his hand and breaking off a piece and swallowing, sometimes gulping them down whole and sometimes munching on them, as though he had gone crazy. The caliph laughed at the sight and said, "Peasant, what do you think it is that you're eating and what might its name be?" The peasant replied, "Preacher of the Muslims, all my life long I've eaten lentils and *bīsār*, wheat groats with fava beans, and stewed fava beans, and I've never seen the likes of this at all. However, I did hear my grandmother

خطيب المسلمين واحيات وجهك لمّا اروّح الكفر ازورك بِجمل جِلّة ومحلاب لبن من بقرتنا الحمرا وخمس بيضات وانت الآخر لا تحرمني من نعيم الدنيا دا لمّا احضر بالهدية فضحك الخليفة من كلامه وأنعم عليه وأذن له في الانصراف ومضى إلى حال سبيله

١٢،٣ (ولقي بعض أهل الأرياف صديقاً له) وقد اشترى بُرْدة من الصوف فقال له دي بردتك فقال جاريتك وعبداتك فقال له بكم اشتريتها فقال له بداهيه كبيره فقال له تلفك وتلفّ وليداتك في الشتا

١٣،٣ (وجلس بعض أهل الأرياف بين أصحابه) فدخل عليه ولده وهو يبكي وقال له يابويه فحل الفراخ مات فقال لا حول ولا قوّة إلّا بالله العام الماضي عتيقه والعام دا ديك إحنا يا ولدي اصحاب الرزايا والمصايب ربّنا يعوّض علينا ثمّ إنّ أصحابه عزّوه وصار كأنّه مات له ميت

١٤،٣ (وولدت لشخص منهم حمارة) فلقي صديق له فقال حمارتك ولدت فقال له وسبّعت فقال له ما جاب الله فقال له جحيش كيفك سوا بسوا فقال له الله يخلّيه لك ويجعله جحش الحياة

١٥،٣ (وعطس رجل من الأرياف) فقال له آخر يرحمك الله فقال له حيّاك الله بارك الله فيك لاقيني على الغيط اعطيك حلابة البقره

١٦،٣ (وعطس رجل منهم أيضاً) فقال له رجل من أهل الذوق يرحمك الّي عطّسك ولو شاء لفطّسك وأخرج العطسه من قبر قراقير الّي خلفك فقال له الفلّاح يا فقي لا عدت تنسانا من قراءة دي السوره تقراها علينا في المسا والصباح وان شاء الله اعطيك ايّام المقات اربع بطّيخات وتقرا السوره كلّ يوم لامّ معيكه وتهديها لابو زعبل فإنّه مات من مدّة شهرين قال فضحك عليه الرجل ومضى إلى حال سبيله

Umm Muʿaykah say, 'Heaven on Earth is the bathhouse!'[89] so God knows, maybe this is the bathhouse that people go on about!" The caliph laughed again and said, "Welcome, peasant! Eat your fill!" Answered the peasant, "Preacher of the Muslims, by the life of your face, after I've been back to the hamlet, I'll come and visit you with a camel load of dung, a jug of milk from our red cow, and five eggs! But you, for your part, mustn't deny me this Heaven on Earth when I bring my present!" The caliph laughed at what he said and bestowed gifts on him and gave him permission to depart, and the man went his way.

And once a countryman ran into a friend of his who had bought a woolen mantle. "Is that your mantle?" he asked. "Ever at your service!" replied his friend. "How much did you pay for it?" the man asked. "A mighty disaster!" said the friend. "May it consume you and your children in the winter!" said the man.[90] 3.12

And a countryman was sitting among his friends when his son came in crying and said to him, "Daddy, the rooster's dead!" "There is no power or strength but in God!" said the man. "Last year an old hen and this year a rooster! Son, we have been singled out for calamity and affliction. May the Lord recompense us!" Then his friends paid him their condolences, and it was as though one of his family had died. 3.13

And one of them had an ass that foaled, and he met a friend of his who asked him, "Has your ass foaled?" "And had her *subūʿ* too!" he said. "And what did God send?" his friend asked. "A little baby jackass, the spitting image of yourself!" he replied. "God preserve him for you and make him the jackass of your life!" said the friend. 3.14

And a countryman sneezed, and another one said to him, "Bless you!" The first replied, "God grant you life and benison! Meet me in the field and I'll give you the milk from the cow!" 3.15

And another one sneezed, and a man of discernment said to him, "May He who made you sneeze have mercy on you! And were He to wish it, He could choke you to death and extract the sneeze from the grave of Qarāqīr who begat you!"[91] Said the peasant, "Pastor, from now on make sure we're around whenever you recite this chapter of the Qur'an,[92] and if you recite it for us evening and morning, God willing, come the squash season, I'll give you four watermelons! And recite the same chapter every day to Umm Muʿaykah with a dedication to Abū Zaʿbal, because he died two months ago!" At this, the man mocked him and went his way. 3.16

١٧،٣ (وجلس جماعة من أهل الأرياف يتحادثون في أحوال الزمان وإقباله وإدباره) فقام رجل منهم يقال له أبو عَفَر وسحب رداه واتّكأ على عصاه ثمّ ضرب بها الأرض وقال لهم يا شيوخ الكفر زمن الفرح ولّى وراح ولا بقى في الدنيا خير ولا عاد يجي زمن مثل زماننا الّي كنّا فيه ومخصّا ايّام الاعياد والمواسم فقالوا له الله عليك يا بو عفر إحكي لنا على زمن الفرح الّي شفته فقال لهم رحت يوم عيد الله الكبير أنا وابو معيكه وابو دعموم وكان معي ابني فرقع الليل ولد صغير واحنا بنجري متل الكلاب السعاره وانا نافش وعليّ ردا من محر الكتّان شريته بنصّ فلوس جدد الدراع وجبّه صوف خدتها بخمسة جدد الدراع ولِبّده خدتها بعتماني وانا مزوّق على العيد كيف عنز الضحيه واتحزمت بِسَيْر وسِكّين خدتهم من سوق هُرَيْط باربعة انصاص فلوس جدد وعلى راسي كرّ مِشَنْيَر خدته من سوق شَنَشَه بنصّين فلوس جدد ونَبُّوت كنت سرقته من زمان الشطاره ومركوب احمر كيف وجوهكم يا شيوخ الكفر كانت سرقته ام زعبل من واحد حضري دخل دارنا الّي على البِرَكه بالاماره يشتري بيض ورحت انا والجماعه نشتري مصالح العيد نمشي على الطريق الّي تطلع على الكفر بتاع ابو عنطوز نجري عليها كيف كلاب الغنم وكنّا نلقى واحد دبح جدي يجي خمسة ارطال لحم فوقفت انا واصحابي على راس صاحبه وهو عمّال يسلخ فيه فقال لي ما تطلب يا شيخ الكفر أنت واصحابك فقلت له اسمع يا عرص يا راس الدُقّاق واحيات امّ زعبل إن كنت ما تكارمني اليوم وتتوصّا بي والّا ما عدت اخلّيك تدبح جدي ولا كلب فقال لي يا شيخ الكفر تطلب من اللحم والا السَقَط فقلت له أطلب السقط أقسمه بيني وبين اصحابي كلّ واحد ياخذ تلته فأخذت منه السقط بعد عياط وشياط وضراط واحيات الحاكم يا اولاد كفرنا بنصّ فلوس جدد ولولا عيّنت له الضرب وقلت له يا عرص يا تيس أنا تورّد عليّ الجدعان اليوم أطبخ واغرف وانا معمود في الكفر والّا ما كان اعطاني السقط

And a group of countrymen were sitting talking of past times good and bad, when one of them named Abū ʿAfr got up, drew his robe about him, and stood leaning on his stick. Then he struck the ground with it and said, "Shaykhs of the hamlet, the good old days are gone forever, and there's nothing good left in this world! Times like the ones we saw will never come again, specially the feasts and the holidays!" "Good for you, Abū ʿAfr!" they responded, "Tell us about the good times you saw!" So he went on: "On the day of God's Big Feast,[93] I took off, me, Abū Muʿaykah, and Abū Daʿmūm, and my son Night-Cracker, who was just a little lad, was with me too, and we went running about like mad dogs! I was all got up, wearing a robe of combed linen I bought for one silver-piece-worth of coppers a cubit with a woolen jubbah I got for five silver-pieces-worth of coppers a cubit and a cap I got for one silver piece of Istanbul—I was all decked out for the feast like a goat for the sacrifice. I had belted myself with a strap and a knife that I got at the Hurbayṭ market for four silver-pieces-worth of coppers, and on my head I had a fringed turban that I got at the Shanashah market for two silver-pieces-worth of coppers, plus I had a cudgel I stole in the days when I was a sharp lad and a pair of slippers as red as your faces, shaykhs of the hamlet, that Umm Zaʿbal[94] stole from a city type who came to our house, which is by the pond[95]—to buy eggs, if you don't believe me. Me and the gang had taken off down the road that takes you to the hamlet of Abū ʿAnṭūz to buy the makings for the feast, running like sheepdogs, when we came across a man who'd slaughtered a kid with maybe five pounds of meat on it. So me and my friends went and stood over the man, who was busily skinning away at it, and he said to me, 'What do you want, Shaykh of the hamlet, you and your friends?' So I told him, 'Listen, you pimp you, you mallet-head! By the life of Umm Zaʿbal, if you don't treat me handsome today and do me proud, I'll never let you slaughter kid, or dog, again!' So he said to me, 'Shaykh of the hamlet, do you want from the meat or the offal?' I told him, 'I want the offal. I'll divide it up between myself and my friends and each of us can take a third.' So after a lot of hubbub, hullabaloo, and farting about, I swear by the life of your beards, sons of our hamlet, I got the offal from him for one silver-piece-worth of coppers, but if I hadn't threatened him with a beating and said to him, 'You pimp, you billy goat!' and 'The brave lads will be bringing in their taxes today so I'll be cooking and dishing out!' and 'I'm the one in charge at the hamlet!' he would never have given it me. 3.17

وقسمناه إحنا التلاته كلّ واحد خد بجديدين لكن واحد من شركاتي غار عليّ وخد ١٨،٣ رجل زايده وانا سرقت ودن من اودان الجدي وطلبت اسرق سنّه من اسنانه اعلّقها على راس ابني عفر تمنع عنه النضره اشتلقوا عليّ شركاتي وقالوا لي يا ابو عفر لا تخون الامانه إن جات الاسنان في حصّتك خد ما تريد فتركت الامرده وخدت حصّتي في طرف ردايه وكلّ واحد من شركاتي خد حصّته ولفعت نبّوتي على كتفي وبقينا كيف الكلاب السعرانه وانا اعفر بين الكيمان والكلاب تجري ورايه على ريحة اللحم وكان حزقني شخاخي واحيات الحاكم ومن خوفي من الكلاب لا ياخدوا مني السقط وكنت اشخّ على ردايه حتّى غرقتها شخاخ ولمّا دخلت البيت شفت امّ عفر حشا العيب قاعده في جنب مدود الحماره كيف كلبة المشدّ تعمل الجلّه عليها قميص من قطن مخطّط كنت شريته لها من زمن الفرح بعشرة انصاص فلوس جدد وفوق راسها طرحه كبيره متل الردا خدتها باربعة انصاص فلوس جدد وسركوج اخضر واحمر مصبوغ بحنّا وبرسيم سابل للخوران وفي رجليها حجل نحاس مطلي بقزدير وفي يديها نبايل نحاس اصفر وفي اودانها حلق طارات فدخلت عليها مشنغر بدقن كيف دقن التيس وشوارب مطرطره كلّ من شافهم شخّ من الجزعه فقامت امّ عفر ومسحت ايديها من الجلّه ولاقتني بالحضن لا تقول الّا بقينا كيف الكلاب الجياع وبعدما لاقشتها ولاقشتني ولاطعتها ولاطعتني وعملت معها ما تعمل الرجال مع النسوان يعني ديك الحكايه وانا بتعرفوا انّي حدق وشاطر وما يطلع من حنكي عيب وما انتم شفتم ايه من الفرح وبعد دا ودا وعمري اغنّي ورا البهايم والمحرات واتعلّمت الغنا من ابويه وجدّي وانا فصيح قوي فقلت لها يا امّ عفر ربّنا يخلّي لي شلشولك وقامتك وانا بانضر حلقك بيشتم الناس وهو مايل على اودانك وانا رايح اغنّي عليه فقالت لي يا ابو عفر واحيات شاربك الّي كيف شارب الكلب الزَغبي أوحشنا غناك وقصدنا تسمّعنا قصيدك فنشدت لها قصيد ومن صلّى على النبي يستفيد [هزج]

3.18 "So the three of us divided it up among ourselves and each of us took two copper-pieces-worth, except that one of my partners jumped me and took an extra foot and I stole one of the kid's ears and I tried to steal one of its teeth to hang on the head of my son ʿAfr to keep off the Eye, but my partners saw what I was up to and said, 'Fair's fair, Abū ʿAfr! If the teeth come out in your share, you can take what you want!' so I dropped that and took my share in the skirt of my robe and each of my partners took his share and I shouldered my stick and we set off like mad dogs. I was kicking up the dust among the mounds with the dogs chasing me after the smell of the meat and by the life of your beards I couldn't keep from pissing I was so afraid the dogs would take the offal from me and I kept on pissing on my robe till I was drenched with piss. When I went into the house, I saw Umm ʿAfr (excuse the mention!) sitting by the donkey's trough just like the bailiff's bitch, making dung cakes. She had on a striped cotton shift that I bought her for ten silver-pieces-worth of coppers when we got married, and on her head she had a headscarf big as a cloak that I bought for four silver-pieces-worth of coppers and a green and red *sarkūj* dyed with henna and clover that fell all the way to her ass. On her feet were copper anklets plated with tin, on her wrists brass bracelets, and in her ears hoop earrings. I went in to her bristling, my beard like a billy goat's and my moustaches standing straight up fit to make anyone who saw them piss in terror! Umm ʿAfr got up and wiped the dung off her hands and met me with open arms—you'd have thought we'd turned into ravening dogs! After I'd whispered a few sweet nothings to her and she to me and I'd pasted a kiss on her and she on me and I'd done with her what men do with women—meaning that business that you wot of but you know I'm too downy a bird to let a rude word pass my lips—my, you never saw people have such fun! Anyway, after a bit of this and a bit of the other, well, you know, I've always been one to sing when walking behind the animals and the plow, because I learned to sing from my father and my grandfather, and I've got a real way with words, so I said to Umm ʿAfr, 'The Lord keep you for me, tresses and trunk! I see that your earrings say saucy things to people as they rest against your ears, and I'm going to sing a song about them!' Said she to me, 'Do sing, Abū ʿAfr! By the life of your shaggy-dog moustache, we've missed your singing, and we've been meaning to make you sing us your ode!' So, I performed for her an ode, and all who bless the Prophet get reward:

أَلا يَابُو حَلَقْ طَارَاتْ   تْبِيعُ ٱلْوَرْدَ بِٱرْطَالَاتْ   ١،١٨،٣
تَبِيعُ ٱلْوَرْدَ فِي ٱلصُّبْحَهْ   قَمِيصُكْ زَيِّنَ ٱلطَّرْحَهْ
عَسَى ٱللهْ أَنْضُرَكْ لَمْحَهْ   تُجَمِّعْ عِنْدَنَا ٱلْجِلاَّتْ

أَلا يَابُو حَلَقْ طَارَاتْ   تْبِيعُ ٱلْوَرْدَ بِٱرْطَالَاتْ   ٢،١٨،٣
أَلا يَابُو قَمِيصْ هُرَيْبِطْ   عَسَى ٱللهْ أَنْضُرَكْ فِي ٱلْغَيْطْ
وَأَدِّي لَكْ قَدَحْ مُخَيَّطْ   وَأَدِّي لَكْ شِمَالْ كُرَّاتْ

أَلا يَابُو حَلَقْ طَارَاتْ   تْبِيعُ ٱلْوَرْدَ بِٱرْطَالَاتْ   ٣،١٨،٣
وَأُعْطِي لَكْ كَمَانْ خُبَيِّزْ   وَأُعْطِي لَكْ قَدَحْ جُمَّيْزْ
وَأَجْعَلْ لَكْ عَلَيَّ مِيزْ   فَطِيرَةْ دُخْنِ فِي ٱلصُّبْحَاتْ

أَلا يَابُو حَلَقْ طَارَاتْ   تْبِيعُ ٱلْوَرْدَ بِٱرْطَالَاتْ   ٤،١٨،٣
أَنَا حُبَّكْ كَمَا ٱلْعِجْلَهْ   وَيَا زَيْنَكْ حِدَا ٱلْجِلَّهْ
تَعَالَى ٱلْغَيْطْ بِلَا مُهْلَهْ   وَتِتْفَرَّجْ عَلَى ٱلْعِجْلَاتْ

أَلا يَابُو حَلَقْ طَارَاتْ   تْبِيعُ ٱلْوَرْدَ بِٱرْطَالَاتْ   ٥،١٨،٣
تَعَا عِنْدِي وَكُلْ جُعْضَيْضْ   وَٱجِيبْ لَكْ يَا مَلِيحْ حُمَّيْضْ
وَأَقْلِي لَكْ كَمَانِي بَيْضْ   بِزَيْتْ حَارْ مِنْ حِدَا ٱلزَّيَّاتْ

Hey, you with the earrings round, 3.18.1
Selling roses by the pound,
Selling roses at early morn,
How your shift your headscarf does adorn!
God grant I get a glimpse of you,
Gathering dung-cakes here around!

Hey, you with the earrings round, 3.18.2
Selling roses by the pound,
Hey, you with the Hurbayṭ shift,
God grant I see you in't field
To give you a punnet of sebesten,
And I'll give you leeks tied and bound!

Hey, you with the earrings round, 3.18.3
Selling roses by the pound,
I'll give you mallows, what's more,
And I'll give you a punnet of sycamore,
And I'll make for your sake
Each morn a millet cake!

Hey, you with the earrings round, 3.18.4
Selling roses by the pound,
I love you like a calf,
And next the dung cakes how lovely you are!
Come to the field right now,
And take a look at the calves!

Hey, you with the earrings round, 3.18.5
Selling roses by the pound,
Come over to my place and eat sow thistle,
And I'll bring you, my lovely, sorrel
And I'll fry you eggs as well
In linseed from the oilman's barrel!

٣،١٨،٦ أَلَا يَابُو حَلَقْ طَارَاتْ   تِبِيعْ ٱلْوَرْدْ بِٱرْطَالَاتْ
أَنَا حِينْتِنْ أَقُولْ تَعَالْ   تُطَاوِعْنِي عَلَى دِي ٱلْحَالْ
تَعَا ٱتْمَشَّى وَضَالْ عَمَّالْ   أَرُوحْ بِكْ دَارْنَا وَتْبَاتْ

٣،١٨،٧ أَلَا يَابُو حَلَقْ طَارَاتْ   تِبِيعْ ٱلْوَرْدْ بِٱرْطَالَاتْ
وَٱدَمِّسْ لَكْ أَنَا ٱلْقُبَّهْ   وَٱجِيبْ لَكْ فُولْ مِنَ ٱلْقَضْبَهْ
وَكُلْ وَٱشْرِبْ كَمَانْ شَرْبَهْ   تُخَلِّيكْ تُشْبِهُ ٱلْعَنْزَاتْ

٣،١٨،٨ أَلَا يَابُو حَلَقْ طَارَاتْ   تِبِيعْ ٱلْوَرْدْ بِٱرْطَالَاتْ
وَٱحُطَّكْ جَنْبَ مِدْوَدْنَا   وَإِلَّا جَنْبَ جِلَّتْنَا
وَوَرِّيكْ بُوزَ بَقْرِتْنَا   وَهِيَ تَقْرِشْ مِنَ ٱلْقَصَلَاتْ

٣،١٨،٩ أَلَا يَابُو حَلَقْ طَارَاتْ   تِبِيعْ ٱلْوَرْدْ بِٱرْطَالَاتْ
وَٱجِيبْ لَكْ عَدَسْ مَعْ بِيسَارْ   وَكِسْرَةْ عَيْشْ مَعْ فُولْ حَارْ
وَٱجِيبْ لَكْ مِسْرَجَةْ زَيْتْ حَارْ   تُنَوِّرْ لَكْ كَمَا ٱلْقَمَرَاتْ

٣،١٨،١٠ أَلَا يَابُو حَلَقْ طَارَاتْ   تِبِيعْ ٱلْوَرْدْ بِٱرْطَالَاتْ
وَإِنْ شَا ٱللّٰهْ أَرُوحْ طَلْخَهْ   وَٱجِيبْ لَكْ يَا مَلِيحْ فَرْخَهْ
وَفِي ٱلدَّارْ إِنْ تُرِيدْ شَخَّهْ   عَلَيْهَا صُبْ مِنَ ٱلْبَوْلَاتْ

Hey, you with the earrings round, 3.18.6
Selling roses by the pound,
When I say, 'Come!'
Obey me right away!
Come on and walk, and keep on going,
And I'll take you to our house to spend the night!

Hey, you with the earrings round, 3.18.7
Selling roses by the pound,
I'll get the oven[96] glowing
And bring you fresh beans to eat,
So eat, and drink another draught,
That'll make you look like a nanny goat!

Hey, you with the earrings round, 3.18.8
Selling roses by the pound,
I'll put you next to our manger
Or next to our pile of dung
And I'll show you our cow's muzzle
Munching on straw and stalks!

Hey, you with the earrings round, 3.18.9
Selling roses by the pound,
I'll bring you lentils and *bīsār* as well
And a crust with beans in linseed oil,
And I'll bring you a linseed lamp,
To light you like the moon!

Hey, you with the earrings round, 3.18.10
Selling roses by the pound,
God willing, I'll go to Ṭalkhah
And bring you, you pretty, a chicken
And at home if you want to pee,
Spread it all around in streams!

١١،١٨،٣ أَلَا يَابُو حَلَقْ طَارَاتْ   تِبِيعُ ٱلْوَرْدْ بِٱرْطَالَاتْ
وَٱخَلِّيكْ كِيفْ أَبُو بُرْبُورْ   وَتِتْمَلْقِشْ وِتِتْشَخْتَرْ
وَتِتْشَقْلِبْ وِتِتْبَسْتَرْ   وَتِبْقَى لِي كَمَا ٱلْكَلْبَاتْ

١٢،١٨،٣ أَلَا يَابُو حَلَقْ طَارَاتْ   تِبِيعُ ٱلْوَرْدْ بِٱرْطَالَاتْ
وَتُعْطِيهْ لِي وَتِتْبَكَّهْ[1]   وَٱحُطُّهْ فِيكْ وَٱتْكَّهْ
وَٱنَا بُو عَفْرْ أَبُو دَكَّهْ   أَبِيعُ ٱلْمِشّ فِي ٱلْحَارَاتْ

١٣،١٨،٣ أَلَا يَابُو حَلَقْ طَارَاتْ   تِبِيعُ ٱلْوَرْدْ بِٱرْطَالَاتْ
وَٱنَا شَاعِرْ وَشَيْخُ ٱلْكَفْرْ   نَشَدتُّ قَصِيدْ كِيفْ الزَّمْرْ
وَقُومِي أَرْقُصِي أَبِنِي عَفْرْ   وَدَا يَوْمْ عِيدْ لَهُ طَنَّاتْ

١٤،١٨،٣ أَلَا يَابُو حَلَقْ طَارَاتْ   تِبِيعُ ٱلْوَرْدْ بِٱرْطَالَاتْ
وَحُطِّي ٱللَّحْمْ وَالْفِشَّهْ   عَلَى ٱلْكَانُونْ وَٱلْكِرْشَهْ
وَنِتْغَدَّا وَنِتْعَشَّهْ   وَنَعْزِمْ دَارْ أَبُو كُرَّاتْ

١٥،١٨،٣ أَلَا يَابُو حَلَقْ طَارَاتْ   تِبِيعُ ٱلْوَرْدْ بِٱرْطَالَاتْ
وَنَخْتِمْ قَوْلَنَا لَا بَاسْ   نُصَلِّي عَلَى ٱلنَّبِي يَا نَاسْ
وَٱنَا بُو عَفْرْ أَبُو تِرْبَاسْ   وَأُنْشِدْ فِي ٱلْمَلِيحْ أَبْيَاتْ
أَلَا يَابُو حَلَقْ طَارَاتْ   تِبِيعُ ٱلْوَرْدْ بِٱرْطَالَاتْ

١ بي: وتشبكه.

Hey, you with the earrings round, 3.18.11
Selling roses by the pound,
I'll make you wet as a runny nose,
And you'll giggle and you'll snort,
And you'll roll over and waggle your ass,
And make for me like a bitch!

Hey, you with the earrings round, 3.18.12
Selling roses by the pound,
You'll give it to me and you'll whimper,
And I'll stick it in you and press down,
For I'm Abū ʿAfr the Rammer,
Who sells *mishsh* among the lanes!

Hey, you with the earrings round, 3.18.13
Selling roses by the pound,
I'm a poet and shaykh of the hamlet
And I've said an ode like a squeal on the pipes,
So up with you and dance, my little boy ʿAfr,
For today's a feast, with bells on!

Hey, you with the earrings round, 3.18.14
Selling roses by the pound,
Put the meat and the lungs
On the stove, plus the tripes,
And we'll lunch and dine
And invite over the house of Abū Kurrāt!

Hey, you with the earrings round, 3.18.15
Selling roses by the pound,
To close these words, why not,
Let's praise the Prophet, you lot,
And I'm Abū ʿAfr, the Bolter,[97]
And I make up my poems for my lovely!
Hey, you with the earrings round,
Selling roses by the pound!

١٩،٣ فقامت أمّ عفر من الفرح ورقصت هي وابنها عفر واخوه فَرْقَعْ الليل حتّى وقعت الطرحه من على راسها وسمعوا الجيران فجونا وقالوا يابو عفر سمّعنا القصيد فسمّعتهم أوّل وتاني وقالوا غداً يسمع بك نصراني البلد ويقرّبك وتبقى تجلس حداه ركبه بركبه ويقول لك يا عرص تقول له يا سيدي وان شا الله يعطيك كيلة شعير وقدح قمح فقلت لهم إن اعطاني شي انعمت عليكم

٢٠،٣ ولمّا تمّت الفرحه بنشد القصيد قامت امّ عفر للسقط تطبخه وقالت لي يابو عفر بقا عليك البخور فقلت لها واحيات شلشولك ما بقى معي فلوس وانا قشلان فقالت لي من خلّى شي لعقب الزمان نفعه أنا خلّيت في الصومعه اربع بيضات خدهم ولا تقول لحدّ فإنّ الناس تحسد الناس وخصّا يوم العيد وانت اليوم يابو عفر في نعمه كبيره هات لنا ببيضه مَرْسِين وببيضه مَحْلَب وببيضه نعناع وبالبيضه الرابعه عُصْفُر نزعفر به ثوب ابنك عفر واخوه فرقع الليل حتّى يبانوا بين اولاد الكفر ويبقى لهم الكلام والحمد لله عندنا شويّت زيت حارّ أدهن بها شعر راسي وتدهن بها دقنك وشواربك وتنطّ بين الجدعان وتنبسط على شلشول كيف شلشول العنز السمينه

٢١،٣ فخدت الاربع بيضات وجبت لها ما طلبته ولقينا في كِرْش الجِدْي شويّة فول صحيح خدته امّ عفر وفركته بالمفراك حتّى بقى متل البيسار وقلّت للطعام بتوم وزيت حارّ وصبّته عليه حتّى بقى متل طعام المشدّ وجوني المشاه والجدعان يغنّوا حربي ويخبطوا بالنبابيت ففرّقت لهم امّ عفر لقّان طعام فأكلوا وفرحوا ولعبوا ورقصوا المُرْد بينهم وكان يوم ما عاد يجي متله فقالوا له أصحابه زمانك يابو عفر ولّى وراح ولا بقي فرح وماتت الناس وجارت الظالمين

"At this Umm ʿAfr leaped to her feet with joy and danced with her son ʿAfr and his brother Night-Cracker till the headscarf fell off her head, and the neighbors heard and came over and said, 'Abū ʿAfr, recite us the ode too!' so I recited it for them once and again, and they said, 'Any day now the Christian of the village will hear about you, and he'll make you his intimate, and you'll sit next to him knee to knee, and he'll say, "Pimp!" and you'll answer, "Master!" and, God willing, he'll give you a bushel of barley and a peck of wheat!' I told them, 'If he gives me anything, I'll treat you all!' 3.19

"After the recitation of the ode had made our joy complete, Umm ʿAfr set about cooking the offal and told me, 'Abū ʿAfr, the perfume's[98] on you!' 'By the life of your tresses,' I told her, 'I don't have a penny left. I'm flat broke.' Said she, 'As they say, "He who puts something aside for a rainy day will find it serves him well." I left four eggs in the grain store. Take them but don't tell a soul, for people get jealous of others, specially on a feast, and you are having such a lucky day, Abū ʿAfr! Buy us an egg's worth of myrtle, an egg's worth of mahaleb kernels, and an egg's worth of mint, and with the fourth get some safflower so that we can stain your son ʿAfr's and his brother Night-Cracker's clothes yellow so they stand out among the village boys and can boss them around. Praise God, we have a little linseed oil left I can grease my hair with, and you can grease your beard and moustache with what's left over and leap about among the brave lads and smack your lips over tresses as thick as a fat nanny goat's tail!' 3.20

"So I took the four eggs and brought her what she asked for and we found a few whole beans left in the kid's tripes, and Umm ʿAfr took these and stirred them up fine with the stirrer till they were like *bīsār*. Then she fried up some garlic and linseed oil and poured them over the beans till it was just the sort of food the bailiff eats. The foot soldiers and the brave lads came to me to sing war songs and joust with their sticks and Umm ʿAfr shared out a pot of food among them. They ate and were happy and played and danced, the beardless boys in their midst, and it was a day the like of which will never be seen again!" Abū ʿAfr's friends told him, "Your days are over and done with, Abū ʿAfr, and there are no more good times to be had. The real men[99] have died, and the tyrants oppress us!" 3.21

(وقيل طلع رجل فلّاح يُورِد لأستاذه المال) فأنزله في محل فيه طاقة مفتوحة تشرف على حريم الأمير فلمّا جاء الليل قال الفلّاح في نفسه يا ترى يابو معيكه الاماره لمّا تختلي بنسوانهم كيف يفعلوا ولكن انضر كيف ما يفعل استادك مع امراته ولمّا تروّح الكفر احكى لامّ معيكه تعمل لك ديك العمله متل ما تعمل الاماره وتحظّك امّ معيكه بديك العمله ولا بدّ ما يرطنوا على بعضهم البعض بالتركي وانت تنضر طريقة ما يفعلوا لحريمهم وتبقى تقول للجدعان انا بقيت متل الاماره وبقت امّ معيكه متل امراة الامير استاد البلد ثمّ إنّه صبر حتّى أقبل الليل ودخل الأمير إلى منزله فقام الفلّاح ونظر من الطاقة فرأى الأمير جالس على سرير من العاج وعليه أنواع الفرش وجلست زوجته على سرير مثله ثمّ إنّ الأمير صار يلاطفها وينادمها برقيق الكلام تارة بالتركيّ وتارة بالعربيّ إلى أن اشتهى منها قضاء الحاجه فأخذ من جانبه وردة ورماها بها فأتت إليه وتملّى بحسنها وجمالها على أحسن حال وأتمّ سرور وحبور ومنوال ثمّ إنّه كلّ واحد منهما انضجع على سريره ونام ٢٢،٣

قال فلمّا أصبح الصباح أخذ الفلّاح خاطر أستاذه وتوجّه إلى بلده فلمّا طلع الكفر لاقته زوجته أمّ معيكه وسلّمت عليه وجلست هي وإيّاه في منادمة مثل منادمة القرود أو بربرة الهنود إلى أن سألته عن المدينة وعن أستاذ البلد فقال لها يا امّ معيكه المدينة مليحه ولا صعب غير الشخاخ فيها ولا مليح كاني الّا امراة استادنا تشنّ وترنّ وعليها خُلْقان مليحه كيف نوّار ابو النوم اصفر واحمر وعلى راسها قحف متل قحفي الّي البسه نهار العيد الّي شريته ايّام الفرح بنصّ فضّه وجديد وفي ايديها اساور صفر الله أعلم أنّهم من اسباط النخل ولابسه قميص احمر مخيّط متل الزكيبه الّي نعبّي فيها الفول الاخضر وفي سيقانها حجل متل حجل امّ دعموم الّي شريته لها بخمسة انصاف فلوس جدد ولابسه شايه خضره الله أعلم أنّها صبغتها بيرسيم ويا مَحْسَنْها في وقت ديك العمله الّي يعملوها الناس مع النسوان وخاطري يا امّ معيكه تعملي لي ٢٣،٣

Accounts of What Happened to Peasants Who Went to the City

And it is said that a peasant came and brought his master his taxes and the latter put him up in a room that had an aperture overlooking the private quarters of the emir. When night came the peasant said to himself, "I wonder, Abū Muʿaykah, what the emirs do with their women when they're by themselves. Just watch what your master does with his wife and when you go back to the hamlet you can tell Umm Muʿaykah to do it like the emirs and she'll pleasure you the very same way. I bet they spout gibberish to one another in Turkish.[100] Just you watch the way they do it with their women, and you'll be able to tell the brave lads, 'Now I'm just like the emirs and Umm Muʿaykah's like the wife of the emir, the master of the village!'" So he waited patiently until night came and the emir entered his house. Then the peasant got up and, looking through the aperture, saw the emir sitting on a bed of ivory furnished with all kinds of coverings, and his wife came and sat on another just like it. The emir engaged with her in gentle talk and conversation of a refined sort, now in Turkish and now in Arabic, till, desiring to consummate the act with her, he took a rose from his side and tossed it at her, and she came to him and he luxuriated in her comeliness and beauty to his heart's content, and with the most perfect pleasure, satisfaction, and abandonment, after which each one lay down on his own bed and went to sleep. 3.22

Come morning, the peasant took leave of his master and set off for his village. When he reached the hamlet, he was met by his wife, Umm Muʿaykah, and she greeted him and they sat down together for a conversation like the converse of apes or the jabbering of Indians, and so it went until she asked him about the city and about the master of the village, and he told her, "Umm Muʿaykah, the city's a fine place and there's nothing that's hard there except for pissing![101] And there's nothing so fair either as our master's wife—she jingles and jangles and wears clothes pretty as poppy flowers, red and yellow, and on her head she wears a cap just like the one I wear at the Feast that I bought when we got married for a silver piece and a copper piece, and on her wrists she has yellow bracelets made of God only knows what—date stalks or something. She was wearing a red shift sewn like the sacks we pack fresh-picked beans in, and on her legs were anklets like Umm Duʿmūm's[102] that I bought her for five silver-pieces-worth of coppers and she was wearing a green jacket, God only knows what she'd dyed it with—clover or something. 3.23

متلها حتّى يقولوا الناس ومشايخ الكفر ابو معيكه بقا متل الاماره فقالت يابو معيكه إحكي لي يا ابو معيكه على الّي شفته من امراة استادك فقال لها لمّا رحت المدينه وطلعت للاستاد وحطّني في موضع فيه طاقه تطلّ على الحريم وعلى الموضع الّي ينام فيه الامير فصبرت لمّا دخل الليل وبقيت اتخنّس كيف الكلب الزوّام فشفت الامير استادنا قعد على خشبه سوده مربوطه بشراميط بيض لها اربع رِجلَيْن كيف عريشة المَقات الّي نعملها ايّام البطّيخ في الغيط وقعدت امراته على خشبه كيفها متل جرّافة الغيط وبقا يكلّمها بكلام الجنادي يقول لها شلضم بلضم تقول له شقلب مقلب حتّى اشتهى منها ديك العمله فحدفها بنوّاره حمره متل نوّارة ابو النوم فقامت تشنّ وترنّ حتّى جت له وعمل فيها العمله فقالت له أمّ معيكه واحيات شاربك الّي كيف شارب التيس لا اعمل لك متل عمل الاماره وتنفش على مشايخ الكفر اصبر لمّا يجي الليل تبلغ مرادك

قال فصبر الفلّاح حتّى دخل الليل فقال لها اقعدي في مَدْوِد الحماره وانا اقعد في مدود البقره قصادك ففعلت وقعدت في المدود وعليها الشلاتيت والشراميط وآثار الجلّة وفيها الشُخاخ أيضاً قال فلمّا خطر التعيس الناصية قضاء الحاجة بعد أن صار ينادمها بكلام مثل نبيح الكلاب شياط وعياط وضراط وسؤال عن البقرة والعجلة والتور والجلّة وغير ذلك أراد أن يرميها بشيء مثل ما فعل الأمير فخطّ يده في المدود فرأى قالب طوب محروق فأخذه وحدفها به فوقع في وسط رأسها ففلقها وسال الدم فصرخت بأعلى صوتها فأقبلوا الجيران ومشايخ البلد ووصل الخبر إلى حاكم البلد فأقبل هو وطائفته وسأل عن القضيّة فأخبروه بها فأخذه وضربه ضرباً موجعاً وأحضروا للمرأة جرائحي قطب رأسها ومكث يجري عليها شهراً كاملاً حتّى برئت فانظر لهذا النحس التعيس * وقلّة عقله الخسيس * كيف ظهر من ملاعبته لزوجته الهمّ والنكد * وقيام الغارات في البلد * ٢٤.٣

How fine she looked when they did the thing that people do with women, and I want you, Umm Muʻaykah, to do it for me just like she did, so that the people and the shaykhs of the hamlet say, 'Now Abū Muʻaykah's just like the emirs!'" Said she, "Tell me, Abū Muʻaykah, what you saw your master's wife do, Abū Muʻaykah." He told her, "When I went to the city and went to the master's and he put me in a room with an aperture looking down into the private quarters and the room where the emir sleeps, I waited till night came, crouched like a snarling dog. Then I saw our master the emir sit down on a black wooden thing tied together with white rags. It had four legs, just like the squash trellis that we put up in the fields at the watermelon harvest. His wife sat down on a wooden thing of the same sort, like the shovel-sledge they use to flatten the fields. He started talking trooper talk to her, saying, 'Humpety-tumpety!' and she answered, 'Upsy-downsy!' and so it went on till he wanted to do it with her. Then he heaved a red flower like a poppy at her and she got up jingling and jangling and went to him and he did it to her." Said Umm Muʻaykah, "I swear by your billy-goat whiskers, I'll do it for you like the emirs do and then you can preen yourself in front of the shaykhs of the hamlet. Be patient until nightfall and you will attain your desire!"

So the peasant waited till night and then said to her, "You sit in the donkey's 3.24
trough and I'll sit in the cow's in front of you!" So she did as he said and sat down in the trough in her rags and tatters and traces of dung, not to mention the piss that was on her. When the miserable wretch decided to consummate the act—after he'd engaged with her in converse sweet as the barking of dogs, with hubbub and hullabaloo and farting and questions about the cow and the calf and the ox and the dung cakes and so forth—he wanted to toss something at her as the emir had done, so he put his hand into the trough and saw a piece of burnt brick, which he took and heaved at her. The brick hit her in the middle of her head and cracked it open and the blood ran and she screamed at the top of her lungs, and the neighbors and the shaykhs of the village came and the news reached the chief of police of the village, who proceeded to the place with his entourage and enquired into the matter. They told him what had happened and he took the man and beat him severely; and they got the woman a surgeon, who sewed up her head and spent a whole month treating her before she recovered. Observe this wretch with luck ungraced and the stupidity of his mind debased, and how, from his clowning with his wife, sorrow, woe, and mayhem in the village grew!

٢٥،٣ (واتّفق أنّ ثلاثة أنفار من قحوف الريف أرادوا طلوع المدينة) فساروا حتّى قربوا منها فقال كبيرهم وصاحب الرأي فيهم إنّ مدينة مصر كلّها جنادي وعسكر يقطعوا الروس واحنا فلّاحين وانْ لم نعمل متلهم ونرطن عليهم بالتركي وإلّا يقطعوا روسنا فقالوا له أصحابه يابو دعموم إحنا ما نعرف تركي ولا غيره فقال لهم أنا تعلّمت التركي زمان إن كنت اقعد حدا المشدّ والنصراني ركبه بركبه فقالوا له أصحابه علّمنا التركي فقال لهم إذا طلعنا المدينه نروح الحمّام الّي يقولوا عليه نعيم الدنيا نستحمّا فيه ونغسل جلودنا ويقولوا فيه نقره غويطه يشخّوا ويخروا فيها وبعد ما نخرج من نعيم الدنيا ونقف نلتفّ في بردنا ونتمّ امرنا اقول لكم قَرْداش محمّد قولوا لبيّك وهاه نوار أقول لكم معاكم شي بِيز مُنقار يعني جديد قولوا يوق يوق يعني ما معنا شي فيخاف صاحب الحمّام ويقول لعقله دول جنادي غُرُب يقطعوا الروس ويخلينا نخرج بلا فلوس وتهيبنا الناس ونبقى في مصر متل الاماره ويشيع خبرنا في الكفر انّنا بقينا أماره نرطن بالتركي فيخافوا منّا مشايخ الكفر ولا يبقى لهم علينا كلام أبدًا فقالوا له أصحابه دي شوره صواب يابو دعموم

٢٦،٣ قال فساروا حتّى طلعوا مصر وسألوا عن الحمّام فدلّوهم عليه فدخلوا وشلحوا الزعابيط وأرموا البرد والشلاتيت وصاروا عريانين مثل ما يفعلوا في البرك والأبيار فقال لهم صاحب الحمّام استروا أنفسكم فأرادوا أن يأخذوا البرد يستتروا بها فأرموا لهم صنّاع الحمّام فُوَط قُدْم من رجيع الحمّام فربطوها على عوراتهم غصب عنهم وصارت عوراتهم في الغالب مكشوفة وأيورهم مدلية ودخلوا الحمّام مثل فحول الجاموس * أو المعيز أو التيوس *

٢٧،٣ حتّى بقوا داخل الحمّام * وغسلوا ما عليهم من الوسخ والسخام * وغطسوا في الحيضان * مثل الثيران أو الجديان * وخرجوا مع بعضهم البعض * وقد تزلزلت منهم الأرض * وهم في حالة الأثوار * وصور الأبقار * حتّى لبسوا الزعابيط * وتلفّعوا بتلك الشلاتيت * وسحبوا النبابيت * على الأكتاف * وأرادوا الخروج بلا

And it happened once that three clods from the countryside decided to go to the city. When they were almost there, their leader and counselor said, "The city of Cairo is all troopers and foot-soldiers that cut off people's heads, and we are peasants, and if we don't do as they do and gabble at them in Turkish, they'll chop off our heads." "Abū Duʿmūm," said his companions, "we know nothing about Turkish or anything else!" "I learnt Turkish long ago," he answered them, "when I used to sit next to the bailiff and the Christian, knee to knee." So his companions said to him, "Teach us Turkish!" "When we get to the city," he said, "we'll go to the bathhouse, which people call Heaven on Earth, and take a bath and wash our hides—they say it has a deep hole that they shit and piss in! As we're leaving Heaven on Earth and are wrapping ourselves in our cloaks and about to be on our way, I'll say to you, '*Kardeş Mehmet!*' ('Brother Mehmet!') and you say, 'At your command!' and '*Hah! Ne var?*' ('Huh! What's up?'). Then I'll ask you, 'Do you have *bir munqār*?' [103] meaning a copper piece, and you say, '*Yok yok!*' meaning 'No, we don't.' Then the bathhouse keeper will get scared and say to himself, 'These are foreign troopers who chop off people's heads!' and he'll let us leave without paying and everyone will stand in awe of us and we'll be treated in Cairo like emirs. Word will spread in the hamlet that we've become emirs and speak Turkish, and the shaykhs of the hamlet will be afraid of us and they'll have no more authority over us at all!" "Sound thinking, Abū Duʿmūm!" said his companions. 3.25

So they proceeded until they reached Cairo and asked for the bathhouse, and the people directed them to it and they entered, shedding their woolen wraps and throwing their cloaks and the rest of their rags on the ground and leaving themselves naked, just as they do at the ponds and wells. "Make yourselves decent!" the bathhouse keeper told them, and they were about to take their cloaks and cover themselves with those when the bathhouse workers threw them some old, used towels. Like it or not, they had to tie these over their privates, though these remained for the most part exposed, and, penises wagging, they went into the bathhouse, looking like buffalo bulls or billies and bucks. 3.26

Once inside, they washed off the muck and the mire, plunging into the tanks like young oxen or kids, and emerged again all together, the ground shaking beneath them as in a tremor, like oxen in condition and cattle in apparition. Then they donned their cloaks, wrapped themselves in their rags, shouldered 3.27

خلاف * قال فصاح عليهم صاحب الحمّام * هاتوا الأجره يا عرصات يا ليام * فالتفت كبيرهم وقال لأصحابه قرداش محمّد فقالوا له لبّيك وهاه نوار فقال لهم معاكم شي بير منقار يعني جديد فقالوا يوق يوق يعني ما معنا شي فقال لهم صاحب الحمّام في أيّ وقت يا تيوس اتعلّمتم التركي المعكوس وبقيتم أكابر وأمارة وما هذا التركي الذي يشبه الخرا أقسم بالله لا يخرج منكم عرص حتّى يحطّ الأجره بزياده وإلّا حطّوا البرد رهن على الأجره قال ثمّ إنّه أمر أصحابه بصكّهم وضربهم وأخذوا البرد منهم وخرجوا من عنده وتداركوا في الأجرة واقترضوها من أهالي الكفر وخلّصوا بردهم وتوجّهوا إلى حال سبيلهم

٢٨.٣ (وطلع رجل منهم المدينة فصادف الجلاد) ينادي في الأسواق على رجل استحقّ القتل يقول يا معاشر الناس فظنّ أنه ينادي العونه يا فلّاحين ففرّ هارباً حتّى وصل إلى الكفر فرأى جماعة من بلده يريدوا الذهاب إلى المدينة فقال لهم لا تطلعوا المدينة فإنّهم ينادوا فيها للعونه والسخره قال فمكثوا أهل بلده ثلاث سنين ما يطلعوا مصر خوفاً من السخرة والعونة فانظر إلى قلّة عقولهم وخساسة رأيهم

٢٩.٣ (وطلع رجل منهم قرية على شاطئ النيل نهار الجمعة) فرأى الناس قاصدين إلى صلاة الجمعة فاعتقد أنّهم ذاهبون إلى ضيافة أو إلى هروبة صنعها لهم أمير البلد أو شيخها فذهب مع الناس إلى أن دخلوا المسجد فجلس في بعض الصفوف إلى أن أقبل الخطيب وصعد على المنبر قال فصار الفلّاح ينظر إليه وهو خائف مرتاب متحيّر إلى أن فرغ الخطيب من الخطبة وأقيمت الصلاة فلمّا رأى قيام الناس إلى الصلاة وسمع ضجيجهم بالتكبير فاعتقد أنّها هرجة وقعت بينهم قال فصاح وقال حاس يالسعد يالحرام الله اكبر وسحب النبّوت وخرج هارباً وهو يقول خدوك القوم يابوكتكوت ولم يزل في خوف وكرب حتّى وصل إلى الكفر

their cudgels, and were about to leave without more ado, when the bathhouse keeper shouted after them, "Hand over the money, you pimps, you cheats!" At this the leader turned and said to his companions, "*Kardeş Mehmet!*" to which the others replied, "At your command!" and "*Hah! Ne var?*" and he said, "Do you have *bir munqār*?" meaning "a copper piece" and they answered, "*Yok yok*," meaning "No, we don't." The bathhouse keeper said to them, "When did you bucks learn this Turkish that sucks and become big men and emirs, and what is this Turkish that sounds like shit? I swear to God, not one of you pimps leaves till he hands over the entrance fee and then some, or you leave your cloaks as pledges for it!" Then he ordered his friends to kick them and beat them and they took their cloaks from them and the peasants left and came up with the fee, which they borrowed from the people of the hamlet, and they redeemed their cloaks and went on their way.

And one of these people went to the city and arrived just as the public executioner was crying out "Oyez!" in the marketplaces apropos of a man who had been sentenced to die. The peasant thought that he must be calling, "All peasants to the corvée!" and fled back to the hamlet. There he found a party from his village about to set off for the city, so he said to them, "Don't go up to the city, for they're summoning people to the corvée!" and the people of his village then went three years without going to Cairo, for fear of the corvée. Observe their stupidity and the baseness of their thinking! 3.28

The Peasant Who Attended the Friday Prayer in a Village by the River

And another went to a village on the banks of the Nile on a Friday and saw the people making their way to Friday prayer.[104] He reckoned they must be going to a party or a wedding picnic put on for them by the emir of the village or its shaykh, so he went with them till they entered the mosque, where he sat down in one of the rows. After a while the preacher approached and climbed the pulpit. The peasant gazed at him in fear, amazement, and perplexity until he finished preaching and the prayer commenced. When he saw the people stand for the prayer and heard the clamor of "God is Greater!" and "There is no god but God!"[105] he thought a brawl had broken out among them and yelled out, "Avaunt, Clan of Saʿd! Clan of Ḥarām, God is Greater!" and pulled out his cudgel and fled, saying, "The enemy's got you, Abū Katkūt!" and he remained in fear and trembling until he reached the hamlet. 3.29

٣٠،٣ فلاقوه أصحابه وسلّموا عليه فرأوا حالته متغيّرة فقالوا له ايش اصابك ودهاك يابو كَكوت فقال لهم ياما قاسيت في دي السفره كانوا القوم مرادهم ياخدوني ولولا إنّي سحبت النبّوت وخرجت هارب والّا كانوا قتلوني فقالوا له ايش الخبر يابوكَكوت فقال لهم وقعت هرجه كبيره ولا سلّمني إلّا الله وبركة الشيخ أبو طبل فقالوا له إحكي لنا على ما جرى لك فقال لهم دخلت بلد على البحر الكبير فريت ناس كتير رايحين زي قطايع الغنم فقلت لا بدّ أنّهم رايحين لضيافه أو لهروبه فرحت معاهم حتّى دخلنا دار كبيره فيها حجارة طوال منقامه زي الدعايم بتوع العريشه الّي نعملها في الغيط وعليها بنيان زيّ قناطر الصابوني وفيها احبال مدليّه زيّ احبال التيران في كلّ قنطره حبل وفي جنب حيط من حيطان الدار خشبه عاليه لها سلالم زيّ سلالم القاعه الّي نعملها على البيوت من الكِرْس والطين ونلطخها من الوحل من اوّلها لآخرها والخشبه دي لها راس كبيره زيّ الناطور الّي نعمله في المَقات وقصادها عريشة مربّعه زيّ العريشه الّي نحرص فيها الحمّص والدره في الغيط ولها سلالم كمان فطلع فوقها جماعه وقعدوا ساعه وقام واحد منهم وحطّ ايده على صرصور ودنه وقال كلام ما حدّ يعرفه إلّا وواحد خرج من حاصل في جنب الدار عليه عمامه كبيره الله أعلم أنّه قاضي ومعاه سيف ساحبه وشقّ صفوف القوم بقلب قوي ووجهه كاشر زيّ وجه تيس الوِسِيّه وما ضال طالع على سلالم الخشبه حتّى قعد على آخر سلم منها وبقت القبّه فوق راسه ونضر للناس الّي تحته وبهت فيهم وكشّر على انيابه وهو ساكت غضبان كلّ من شاف شواربه شخّ من الطربه واحيات لِحاكم ولا عمري شفت أقوى قلب منه ولا أشدّ حَيل ولولا انه صبي راس ماكان عمل دي العمل وطلع وحده وسحب السيف على القوم ثمّ واحد من الجماعه الّي على العريشه قصاده قام بقلب قوي وصار يشتمه ويسبّه ويقول له كلام كتير فانحمق الآخر منه وشتمه ولعنه ووقعوا في بعضهم البعض شتم وسبّ ولعن ثمّ أن نزل الراجل الّي على الخشبه ونزل ساحب السيف يعارك في الناس الّي تحته قاعدين فلمّا شافوه نازل لهم بالسيف قاموا على حَيلهم

There his friends met him and greeted him, but when they saw what a state he was in, they asked him, "What has befallen you and afflicted you, Abū Katkūt?" "How I suffered on that journey!" he replied. "The enemy tried to get me and if I hadn't pulled out my cudgel and fled, they would have killed me!" "What was the matter, Abū Katkūt?" they asked and he replied, "A great brawl broke out, and only God and the grace of Shaykh Abū Ṭabl[106] saved me!" "Tell us what happened!" they said and he told them, "I went into a village on the Big River and saw crowds of people moving like flocks of sheep and goats, so I thought, 'They must be on their way to a party or a wedding picnic,' and I went along with them till they went into a big house with tall stones set on end like the posts of the platform we build in the fields, with masonry built over them like the Bridges of al-Ṣābūnī and ropes dangling in them like ox ropes, a rope to each arch.[107] Against one of the walls of the house there was a tall wooden structure with stairs[108] like the stairs to the rooms we build on the tops of houses out of dung and mud and cover over with daub from top to bottom. This wooden thing had a big head like the lookout platform that we set up in the melon patch. Opposite it was a square platform like the one on which we guard the corn and the chickpeas in the field, and with stairs too.[109] Then a bunch of guys climbed the stairs and sat for a while until one of them stood up and cupped his ear in his hand[110] and said stuff such as no one has ever heard. Then all of a sudden someone else popped out from a closet in the side of the house wearing a big turban[111]—God only knows if he was a judge or what—and with a drawn sword[112] in his hand, and hacked his way through the enemy ranks with a stout heart, scowling like the billy goat of the emir's demesne, and mounted the steps of the wooden thing until he sat down on the top one with the dome over his head and gazed out over the people below him, glaring at them and baring his fangs in silent rage. I swear by your beards, anyone who saw his moustache would have pissed with terror, and never in my life did I see a man more stouthearted or doughtier than him—if he hadn't been a tough lad, he would never have done what he did and climbed up on his own and drawn his sword against his enemies! Then one of the guys on the platform in front of him stood up with a stout heart and started insulting him and abusing him and cursing him up and down, so the other got really mad and insulted him back and cursed him and they let fly at one another with insults, abuses, and curses.[113] Next, the man on the wooden thing came down with his sword drawn to do battle with the people sitting beneath him and when they 3.30

وصرخوا وقالوا الله اكبر وقامت العيطه وكنت اسحب نَبُّوتي وخرجت هارب وما سلّمني إلّا الله وبركة الشيخ ابو طبل

٣١،٣ فقالوا له أهل الكفر والله يابوكُنكوت لولا عمرك طويل ما سلمت من القوم وكانوا قتلوك وانت بتعرف انّ بلاد البحر كلّها قوم والقتل عندهم من خطوه فقال لهم يا شيوخ الكفر ما عدت اروح بلاد البحر طول عمري فانظر إلى قلّة عقل هذا الفلّاح ومن جهله وسقاعة ذقنه الذي لم يعرف الصلاة من قيام الهرجة

٣٢،٣ (واتّفق أنّ ثلاث نسوة من عواهر مصر خرجن يتفرّجن في أزقّة المدينة) فلقين رجلاً من قحوف الريف وهو في حالة رذلة وعلى رأسه قَفَص ملآن أفراخ يريد أن يبيعهم ويسدّ بثمنهم مال السلطان فقالت إحداهن للأخرى ما تقولي في الّي ياخد الفراخ من الفلّاح ده فقالت الثانية واناخد تيابه فقالت الثالثة كلّ ده ما هو شطاره الشطاره في الّي تبيعه بيع العبيد أو للمقداف أو الجرّافه

٣٣،٣ قال ثمّ إنّ الأولى التي التزمت بأخذ فراخه أقبلت إليه وأرغبته بزيادة في الثمن وقالت له إمضي معي إلى منزلي خذ الثمن قال فمضى معها إلى أن أقبلت على درب من دروب مصر نافد وقالت له اقعد هنا على الباب فإنّه باب بيتي واصبر حتّى اجي لك بالفلوس ثمّ أخذت القفص الفراخ ومضت إلى حال سبيلها من الباب الثاني

٣٤،٣ ولم يزل الفلّاح جالس إلى أن قرب الظهر لم يأته أحد ورأى الناس داخلين وخارجين من ذلك الدرب فتحيّر في نفسه وقال لا بدّ انّ دي دار كبيره فسأل عن المرأة التي أخذت الفراخ فقالوا له يا سقيع الدقن وقليل العقل الدرب ده نافد وكم ناس رجّاله ونسوان داخلين وخارجين قال فتمشّى الفلّاح فرأى درب كبير فاحتار وصاح ولطم على وجهه وأقام الصراخ فبينما هو في هذه الحالة إذ أقبلت عليه الثانية وقالت له ايش صابك ودهاك يا مسكين وانت راجل غريب وعليك مال السلطان

saw him coming at them with the sword, they jumped up and shouted, 'God is Greater!' and all hell broke loose. I was about to pull out my cudgel and I fled, and only God and the grace of Shaykh Abū Ṭabl saved me!"

The people of the hamlet said to him, "By God, Abū Katkūt, if you weren't 3.31
destined to live a long life, you would never have escaped from the enemy and they would have killed you! You know that the villages on the river are full of enemy folk, and murder is second nature to them!" Replied he, "Shaykhs of the hamlet, I'll never go back to the villages on the river so long as I live!" Observe the stupidity of this peasant, who, out of ignorance and obtuseness, could not tell the prayer from a brawl!

The Tale of the Three Whores of Cairo

It also happened that three of the whores of Cairo went out one day to see 3.32
what was up in the alleyways of the city and came across a clod from the countryside, in a filthy condition and with a coop full of chickens on his head, which he wanted to sell to pay off the sultan's taxes. Said one of them to the others, "What would you say of someone who took the chickens away from that peasant?" The second said, "And I'll take his clothes!" But the third said, "There's nothing clever in any of that! The clever one will be the one who sells him as a slave or to work on the galleys or on the dredging crews."

Then the first, who had taken it upon herself to get the man's chickens, went 3.33
up to him and excited his interest by offering him a high price. "Come along with me to my house," she told him, "and take your money!" So he went with her till she came to one of Cairo's interconnecting side streets, where she told him, "Sit here at this gate, for it is the gate to my house, and wait while I get you the money."[114] Then she took the coop with the chickens and went her way through the gate at the other end.

The peasant sat there till it was almost noon but no one came to him. Seeing 3.34
people entering and leaving the street, he became puzzled and said to himself, "This must certainly be a big house!" and he asked about the woman who had taken his chickens. "Impudent fellow!" said the people. "Dolt! This street goes through to the next and dozens of people, men and women, go in and out all the time." So the peasant walked on a bit and saw a large street. Then he was at his wit's end and he yelled and slapped his cheeks and set up a racket. While he was thus engaged, the second woman approached him and said,

وضحكت عليك دي العاهره وخدت منك الفراخ وتركتك في دي الحاله فقال لها الفلّاح واحيات عيونك يا مليحه ما معي غيرهم فقالت له إمشى معاي إلى بيتي وانا اعطيك شي من الدراهم صدقة عنّي فقال لها الفلّاح الله يجزيك خير وانا الآخر لمّا اروح الكفر ازورك بحزمة لَحلاح وحزمة بصل وشوية قُرُلّه وتبقي صاحبتي وان شا الله اجيب لك كمانه عشرين قرص جله قال فأخذته وسارت إلى أن أقبلت على بيت كبير عالي البنيان فسألت عن صاحبه فقالوا لها هذا بيت الأمير فلان وقد توجّه هو وطائفته إلى بعض المنتزهات قال فدخلت إلى البيت فلم تر فيه أحداً ما عدا رجلاً كبيراً بوّاب ودخل الفلّاح معها إلى وسط البيت فرأت فيه بيراً من الماء يملومنه الحريم قال فوقفت ونظرت في البير ثمّ إنّها ولولت وصرخت وبكت بكاء شديداً فقال لها الفلّاح بتبكي ليه يا مليحه فقالت له يا فلّاح كعبك ميشوم وقعت ساورتي الدهب في البير فقال لها ما تخافيش انا انزل وطلّعهم لكي من البير فقالت له تعرف تغطس في الما فقال لها دي صنعتي وطول عمري في الهمّ والغمّ وخصّا دي السنه الّي خرى فيها القوي والضعيف ثمّ إنّه قال لها اربطيني في حبل البَكَره ودلّيني في البير ثمّ إنّه قلع ثيابه التي كانت عليه ودلته في البير إلى أن وصل إلى الماء فأرخت الحبل عليه وأخذت ثيابه وتوجّهت إلى حال سبيلها

٣٥،٣ هذا ماكان منها وأمّا ماكان من تعريص الفلّاح فإنّه لم يزل يغوص في الماء ويفتّش في قعر البير حتّى كلّ وملّ واسودّ جلده من برد الماء وكان في زمن الشتاء فلم ير شيئاً قال فلمّا اشتدّ به الأمرصار يصيح في البير وينادي المرأة فلم يجبه أحد فبينما هو في هذه الحالة إذ أقبل الأمير وطائفته فسمعوا الفلّاح يصيح في البير وينادي طلّعيني يا صبيّه طلّعيني يا مليحه دا ماهوش مليح منك ودا عيب عليكي وانا متّ من السقيع والبرد فقالوا له الخدام أنت إنسي أم جنّي فقال لهم انا ابو زعبل بن جنيجل بن كلب المشّ فقالوا دا عفريت لا كلام فقال لهم والله يا وجوه الخير مانا عفريت أنا راجل

"What calamity has befallen you, poor soul, and you a stranger with the sultan's taxes to pay, and that wicked whore pulling a trick on you and taking your chickens and leaving you in this pitiful state?" "By the life of your eyes, pretty one," replied the peasant, "they're all I have!" "Come with me to my house," she told him, "and I'll give you a little money for charity's sake!" "God bless you!" replied the peasant, "And for my part, after I've been back to the hamlet, I'll come and see you with a bunch of thistles, a bunch of onions, and a little corn mustard, and you can be my girlfriend and, God willing, I'll bring you twenty dung cakes too!" So she took him and proceeded until they came to the house of a great emir, with high walls. There she asked after the owner, and they told her, "This is the house of Emir So-and-so," who, it turned out, had gone off with his entourage to a pleasure garden. She entered the house and found no one there except an old man, a doorkeeper. The peasant went with her into the courtyard of the house, where she spied a well from which the women of the house took their water. After standing and looking down into the well, she set up a wailing and a shrieking and a prodigious weeping. "Why are you crying, pretty one?" asked the peasant. "You have brought me bad luck, Peasant!" she replied. "My gold bracelets have fallen into the well!" "Don't worry," he responded, "I'll go down and fetch them up for you." "Do you know how to swim under water?" she asked. "That's my job," he replied, "and all my life has been spent in toil and trouble, especially this year, when the weak and the strong alike have shat bricks!" Then he told her, "Tie me to the pulley rope and lower me into the well!" and he took off the clothes he was wearing and she lowered him into the well until he reached the water. Then she let the rope fall on top of him, took his clothes, and went her way.

So it was with her. As for that wretch of a peasant, he went on swimming 3.35
around in the water and searching the bottom of the well till he became weary and fed up and his skin turned blue from the chill of the water (for it was winter) but he found nothing. When he found himself at the end of his strength, he started shouting in the well and calling to the woman but no one answered, and, while he was thus engaged, the emir and his entourage suddenly returned and heard the peasant shouting inside the well, and calling out, "Get me out, young lady! Get me out, pretty one! This isn't nice of you! Shame on you! I'm dying of the icy cold!" The servants said to him, "Are you man or jinn?" He replied, "I'm Abū Zaʿbal son of Junayjil son of Curd-Dog." "It's an afreet, no doubt about it!" they said. "I swear, good people," he said, "I'm not an afreet,

فلّاح وأحكى لهم قصّته قال فدلّوا له الحبل فتعلّق فيه فلمّا رأوه الخدم وعلموا أنّه إنس قالوا دا حرامي وقع في البير فنزلوا عليه بالضرب والصكّ وطردوه فمضى يجري وهو عريان بردان جيعان سقعان وهو لا يعرف أين يذهب

٣٦،٣ قال فأقبلت إليه الثالثة وهو في هذه الحالة وقد صارت الأولاد تضربه ويقولوا مجنون فوضعت يدها على ظهره ومسحت وجهه بمنديل كان معها وسترته بفوطة وقالت له أمرك إلى الله يا مسكين يا حزين ضحكت عليك نسوان مصر العواهر وخلّوك في دي الحاله وانت راجل غريب وعليك مال السلطان قال فبكى الفلّاح وشكى وقال لها يا مليحه واحيات شلشولك خدوا فراخي وتيابي وحزامي الليف وكَرِّي ومركوبي وما عدت اصدّق كلام نسوان أبدًا فقالت له لا تظنّ أنّي من عواهر مصر أنا عمري ما خرجت من بيتي غير النهار ده ولمّا رأيتك في دي الحاله شفقت عليك ومرادي افعل معك الخير واخدك إلى بيتي والبّسك لبس مليح واخلّيك شَلَبي ظريف واعملك مملوك وحطّ لك خنجر في حزامك واعلّمك التركي وتبقى تقول شندي بندي على فلاص جعاص[1] فقال لها الفلّاح أنا في جيرتك يا مليحه تعلّميني جندي وعلّميني التركي وانا عليّ الحلال من امّ شحيبر كلّ من عاد يقول لي كاني ماني في زماني قطعت راسه ولوكان ابو عوكل شيخ الكفر فقالت له سر بنا يا فلّاح على بركة الله تعالى

٣٧،٣ قال فسار هو وإيّاها إلى أن أقبلت على منزلها فأدخلته محلّها ووضعت بين يديه الطعام فأكل وشرب وارتاح في نفسه ثمّ إنّها أتته بماء ساخن وغسلته بالليفة والصابون وألبسته قميص رفيع وزبون[2] جوخ وشُخْشَيْر وقاووق قطيفة وشاش قَصَب وحزّمته بِحِياصة وخنجر في حزامه وحلقت ذقنه وشواربه وجعلته في صفة مملوك حليق وأعطته بابوج جديد ومِحْرَمة في حزامه وقالت له إذا كلّمك حدّ فلا تردّ عليه جواب بَسّ هزّ راسك فإذا ألحّ عليك في الكلام وشدّد عليك قول له كَِتَه هَريف بوك

---

[1] بي: جلاص. [2] بي: وزربون.

I'm a peasant," and he told them his story. Then they lowered him the rope, and he caught hold of it, but when the servants saw him and discovered that he was indeed human, they said, "It must be a thief who has fallen in the well," and they rained blows and kicks upon him and threw him out. Naked, cold, hungry, and shivering, he set off at a run, not knowing where he was going.

While he was in this state, with the children hitting him and shouting 3.36
"Madman!" the third woman approached and laid her hand on his back and wiped his face with a kerchief she had on her and covered his nakedness with a towel and said, "God have pity on you, you poor sorrowing soul! The whorish women of Cairo have tricked you and left you in this pitiful state, and you a stranger with the sultan's taxes to pay!" The peasant wept and complained, telling her, "By the life of your tresses, they took my chickens and my clothes and my palm-fiber belt and my turban and my slippers, and I'll never again believe a word a woman says!" "Don't think for a moment," said she, "that I am one of the whores of Cairo! I have never left my house before today, but when I saw you in this state, I was overcome with pity for you. I would like to do something good for you and take you to my house and dress you in nice clothes and turn you into a fine dandy. I'll make you a mamluk and put a dagger in your belt and teach you Turkish, so you can say '*Shindi bindi with a falāṣ ja'āṣ!*'"[115] Said the peasant, "I implore you, pretty one, teach me trooper-talk and teach me Turkish! I swear to divorce Umm Shuḥaybar if I don't chop off the head of anyone who gives me any lip again, even if it's Abū 'Awkal, shaykh of the hamlet!" "Off with us then, peasant," said the woman, "and may the Almighty bless our enterprise!"

So he went with her until she came to her house, where she took him inside 3.37
and placed food before him, and he ate and drank and was comforted. Then she brought him hot water and scrubbed him with a loofah and soap and dressed him in a shirt of fine cloth, with a broadcloth waistcoat, hose, a tall velvet cap, and a brocaded shawl. She wrapped a richly worked belt around his waist and put a dagger in it, and she shaved off his beard and moustache and turned him into a clean-shaven mamluk. She also gave him a new pair of slippers and put a handkerchief in his belt.[116] Then she told him, "If anyone speaks to you, say nothing in reply. Just shake your head.[117] If he should press you rudely to speak and is rough with you, say '*Kerata herif, bok yeme!*' ('Rascally cuckold, eat shit!') and leave it at that, for these words are the very essence of

يَمَه ولا تزيد عليه غير ذلك فإنّ الكلمه دي أصل التركي إذا عرفتها ما يمضي عليك شهر زمان إلّا وانت صنجق ويبقى لك طبل وزَمْر

٣٨،٣ فقال لها الفلّاح أنا في جيرتك يا مليحه تخلّيني ابقى صنجق ويصير لي سَطْوَه في الكفر وكلّ من قال لي كل خره اقطع راسه وابقى ان شاء الله ازورك بِرُبْع كِشْك وعشر طور كَعْك من الّي تعمله امّ شحيبر واعمل لك قاعه والبّسها لك بالوحل والجله وافرشها لك بالتبن والقَصَل وتبقي تنامي فيها ويبقوا يقولوا الجدعان أبو شحيبر طلع المدينه فلّاح وعاد صنجق يقول شندي بندي ويقطع الروس قال ثمّ إنّها أخذته ونزلت من منزلها تمشي وهو يمشي خلفها إلى أن أقبلت على سوق الشَرْب وجلست على دكان رجل من التجّار عنده أنواع الأقمشة من الخزّ والديباج والأطالس والشاشات وغير ذلك فقالت له أريد كذا وكذا ما يساوي مائتين دينار فأحضر لها ما قالت عليه وربطه في محرمة كانت معها وقالت له يا سيدي يكون المملوك ده عندك حتّى أذهب إلى بيت الأمير وأعرض على حريمه الحوائج وآتيك بالدراهم فقال لها التاجر توجّهي على بركة الله تعالى قال فأخذت الحوايج وتركت عنده الفلّاح جالس

٣٩،٣ هذا ما كان منها وأمّا ما كان من التاجر فإنّه مضى نصف النهار ولم تأته المرأة فتضايق والتفت إلى الفلّاح وهو في هذه الحالة وقال له ستّك أبطأت علينا فهزّ رأسه حُكْم ما أوصته فكرّر عليه التاجر الكلام فهزّ رأسه أوّل وثاني ولم يتكلّم فتضايق التاجر من عدم كلامه وقال لجيرانه من التجّار ما هذه البليّة في هذا المملوك كلّما أكلّمه يهزّ رأسه كأنّه ما يعرف إلّا بالتركي قال فبينما التاجر على هذه الحالة إذ أقبل رجل عسكريّ فقال له التاجر بالله عليك يا سيدي كلّم لنا هذا المملوك بالتركي وعرّفنا عن حاله قال فكلّمه الجندي بالتركي فهزّ رأسه فاغتاظ منه وسلّ عليه الخنجر وأراد ضربه فلمّا رآه يريد ذلك واشتدّ عليه الأمر صرخ وقال له كرته هريف بوك يمه قال فلمّا سمع منه ذلك نزل عليه بالضرب فصار يصيح ويتكلّم بكلام الفلّاحين ويقول أنا في جيرتك يابو زعبل فضحك عليه الجندي وبقيّة التجّار فاستخبروه فحكى لهم على

Turkish—once you know them, not a month will pass before you become a sanjak, with drums and pipes."[118]

The peasant replied, "I beseech you, pretty one, let me become a sanjak, so that I can have power in the hamlet and cut off the head of anyone who tells me 'Eat shit!' And afterwards, God willing, I'll visit you with a quartern of wheat groats and forty pieces of the short pastry that Umm Shuḥaybar makes, and I'll build you a winter room daubed with mud and dung and spread straw and corn stalks for you on the floor so that you can sleep there. And the brave lads will say, 'Abū Shuḥaybar went to the city a peasant and came back a trooper, saying *shindi bindi* and chopping off heads.'" So the woman took him and left her house and walked with him behind her until she reached the market of al-Sharb, where she took a seat in the shop of a merchant who had all kinds of cloth—cotton-silk, brocades, satins, muslins, and more—and she told him, "I want such-and-such from you," to a value of two hundred dinars. He brought her what she asked for and she tied it up in a wrapper she had with her. Then she said to him, "Sir, let this mamluk stay with you while I go to the emir's house and show the cloth to his women, and then come back to you with the money."[119] "Good fortune go with you!" said the merchant. So she took the goods and left the peasant sitting there. 3.38

So it was with her. As for the merchant, half the day passed and the woman did not come back. Eventually he got annoyed and, turning to the peasant, who was as we have described, said to him, "Your mistress is taking her time!" But the peasant just shook his head, as she had instructed him. The merchant repeated what he had said and the peasant shook his head a second and a third time, but did not say a word. Then the merchant grew angry at his silence and said to the neighboring merchants, "What affliction have we here in the form of this mamluk? Every time I speak to him, he shakes his head, as though he understood only Turkish!" While the merchant was speaking thus, a soldier happened by, so the merchant said to him, "In God's name, sir, speak to this mamluk for us in Turkish and find out for us what's up with him!" So the trooper spoke to him in Turkish and the peasant shook his head. At this, the soldier got angry and drew his dagger and was about to strike him when the peasant, seeing what was up and that things were looking grim, cried out, "*Kerata herif, bok yeme!*" Hearing this, the soldier showered him with blows and the peasant started talking in the language of the peasants and screaming, "Protect me, Abū Zaʿbal!" The trooper and the rest of the merchants laughed 3.39

قضيّته فعرفوا أنّها حيلة عملت على التاجر والفلّاح قال فقام التاجر وأخذ جميع ما عليه وأراد بيعه للمقداف فشفعوا فيه فتركه ومضى إلى حال سبيله عريان محلوق الذقن وهو في أيشم حال حتّى وصل الكفر ومكث مدة حتّى طلعت ذقنه ولم يطلع المدينة بقية عمره وفي رواية أنّ التاجر باعه للمقداف بعشرين دينارًا ومكث فيه سنة وخلّص منه بالهروب ليلاً

٤٠،٣ (وطلع رجل من الأرياف إلى المدينة فحصره البول والغائط) فسأل عن عطفة يخرأ فيها فدلّوه على المطهرة فدخل يريد بيت الخلاء وقد دخل وقت الصلاة فرأى الناس مزدحمين على بيوت الأخلية فوقف على باب كنيف يشيل رجل ويضع أخرى من شدّة ما هو فيه من الحصر فطال عليه الوقوف واشتدّ به الأمر فهجم على الرجل الذي في الكنيف وقبض على أطواقه ورفع ثيابه وجلس بجانبه وقال له دي نقره غويطه طويله أخرا انا وايّاك فيها كلّ واحد من جنب ولم يزل قابضاً على الرجل حتّى قضى حاجته على عجل وقام يجري من غير استنجاء والناس يضحكون عليه حتّى غاب عن أعينهم

٤١،٣ (وطلع رجل آخر المدينة فأدركه الغائط) فتحيّر ولم يعرف له عطفة يخرأ فيها فلمّا اشتدّ به الأمر شكى إلى بعض أبناء مصر حرّسها الله تعالى وقال له قد تضايقت من البول والخره وكلّما أردت أن أشخّ قدّام دكان يمنعوني الناس ويشتموني فقال له الرجل يا فلّاح المدينة ما يخرا فيها أحد إلّا بفلوس إن كان معك فلوس دلّيتك على عطفه أو نقره تخرا فيها وإلّا تخرا على روحك فقال له واحيات لحيتك ما معايا إلّا نصّين فلوس جدد بعت بهم بيض خدهم ودلّني على محلّ الخره وان شا الله ازورك بعشرين

and questioned him, and he told them what had happened to him. Then they realized that it was a trick that had been played on both the merchant and the peasant, and the merchant arose and stripped him and took everything that was on him and would have sold him to the galleys had not others interceded for him, so he let him go, and the man went his way, naked, shaven, and in the most wretched state, till he reached the hamlet. It was a while before his beard grew back, and he never went to the city again as long as he lived. In another version, it says that the merchant sold him to the galleys for twenty gold pieces and he stayed there a year before escaping at night.

Anecdotes Concerning Country People Who Went to the City and Were Overtaken by the Need to Relieve Themselves, Etc.

And once a man from the country went to the city, where he was overtaken by the need to urinate and defecate, so he inquired about an alley in which he might take a shit. The people directed him to the ablution courtyard of a mosque and he entered, looking for the lavatories. The prayer time was at hand, and, seeing the people crowding around the lavatories, he took up a position by the door of a latrine, hopping from foot to foot he was in such a hurry to go. However, the wait seemed interminable and, finding himself in dire straits, he threw himself on the man inside the latrine, grabbed him by the front of his robe, pulled up his own clothes, and sat down next to him. "The hole is long and deep," said he. "You and I can shit in it together, each one from his own side!" And he held on to the man until he had relieved himself in a hurry and then ran off without cleaning himself, the people mocking him till he disappeared from their sight. 3.40

And another man from the countryside went up to the city and was overtaken by the need to defecate, but found himself at a loss, not knowing of an alley in which he could take a shit. When things became unbearable he complained to a citizen of Cairo, may the Almighty protect it, and told him, "I can't go any longer without taking a leak and a crap, but whenever I try to piss in front of a shop, the people stop me and abuse me!" Said the man, "Peasant, in the city no one shits without paying. If you have money on you, I'll show you an alley or a hole where you can shit. If not, you can shit on yourself." "By the life of your beard," said the peasant, "all I have with me is the two silver-pieces-worth of coppers I got for my eggs! Take them and show me where people shit, and 3.41

بيضه وزالوع كَبَر قال فأخذ الرجل منه النصفين وأتى به إلى المطهرة وأوقفه على بيت الخلاء وقال له إذا خرج الرجل ادخل أنت تجد شقّ طويل ونقرة غويطة شُخّ واخرا فيها قال فوقف الفلّاح على باب الكنيف فسمع الرجل من داخل يخرأ ويقول قطن قطن ويكرّر هذه الكلمة قال فلمّا سمع الفلّاح مقالته ظنّ في نفسه أنّ الشخص في مصر لا يسهُل عليه خروج الخارج إلّا أن قال هذه الكلمة ويكرّرها مع الحزق الشديد وكان السبب في ذلك وذكر هذا الرجل هذا الكلمة وتكريرها أنّ زوجته لمّا خرج من عندها قالت له اشتري لنا قطن وكان كثير النِسيان فصار يكرّر اسم القطن حتّى لا ينساه ودخل بيت الخلاء وهو يكرّر اسمه حتّى وقف عليه الفلّاح وسمع كلامه قال فلمّا قضى حاجته وخرج من الكنيف دخل الفلّاح وجلس على كرسيّ بيت الخلاء وصار يقول مثل الرجل قطن قطن فبينما هو في هذه الحالة إذا أقبل رجل عسكريّ وطرق الباب على الفلّاح فقال الفلّاح قطن قطن فتضايق الجندي وهجم عليه وصار يضربه وهو يصيح والجندي يقول له يا أنجس الفلّاحين ايش معنى قطن قطن وانت في بيت الخلاء ولم يزل يضربه حتّى أقبل عليه الناس وخلّصوه منه ولم يزل يجري حتّى خرج من المدينة ودخل بلده فلاقاه أهل البلد وسلّموا عليه وقالوا له كيف حال المدينة يا ابو دعموم فقال لهم المدينة مليحه إلّا انك تاكل فيها بجديد وتخرى فيها بنصّين وان قلت قطن قطنوا عينيك من الضرب

(وطلع آخر المدينة فصادف رجلاً من غلمان أستاذه) فعزمه إلى منزله وأحضر له سمكًا صغيرًا مقليًا يسمّوه أهل مصر بِساريه له لذّة في الطعم قال فصار الفلّاح يسفّ منه ولا يعرف ما هو ثمّ قال في نفسه دا شيء عمرك ما أكلته ولا رأيته ولا بدّ يابو قريطم ما هو الكنافه الّي يقولوا عليها تطلع في المدينة وتاكلها الاماره وغدًا تطلع الكفر ويلاقوك المشاه والجدعان ويسلّموا عليك وتقعد انت وايّاهم على كوم ابو عنطوز تغزلوا فلّ وصوف كيف الكلاب الكواشر وتبقى بينهم تجعّمص كيف تيس الوسيه ويقولوا لك يابو قريطم قل لنا ايش اكلت في المدينة من الطعام الّي ياكلوه الاماره تقول لهم ٤٢،٣

later on I'll come and see you with twenty eggs and a jar of capers." So the man took the two silver pieces from him and took him into the ablutions courtyard of a mosque and, setting him in front of the lavatory, told him, "When the man comes out, you go in. You'll find a long crack and a deep hole. Piss and shit in them." So the peasant stood by the door of the latrine. Inside he heard the man shitting and saying, "Cotton, cotton," over and over. Hearing this, the peasant made up his mind that no one could relieve himself comfortably in Cairo without saying that particular word and repeating it, to the accompaniment of much straining. In fact, the real reason for this and for the man repeating the word was that his wife had told him before he left her, "Buy us some cotton!" and, because he was extremely forgetful, he kept saying "cotton" so that he wouldn't forget; thus it was that he came to enter the latrine repeating the word and then the peasant came and stood by it and heard him. When he had finished, the man left the latrine and the peasant went in, sat down on the lavatory seat and started saying, "Cotton, cotton," like the man. While he was thus engaged, a soldier came up and knocked at the door where the peasant was. "Cotton, cotton!" said the peasant. The trooper got annoyed and attacked him, the peasant screaming the while and the trooper saying, "Filthiest of peasants, what's this 'cotton, cotton' while you're in the lavatory?" and he went on beating him till people came and freed the peasant, who ran without stopping until he left the city and got to his village. There the people of the village met him and greeted him and said, "How's the city, Abū Daʿmūm?" to which he replied, "The city's fine, except that it costs you a copper piece to eat there and two silver pieces to shit, and if you say 'cotton,' they 'cotton out' your eyes with beating!"

And another went to the city, where he ran into one of his master's servants, 3.42
who invited him to his house and set in front of him the small fried fish that the people of Cairo call *bisāriyah*, which have the most delicious taste. The peasant started gulping it down but, having no idea what it was, he said to himself, "This is something you've never eaten or seen before, but I do believe, Abū Qurayṭim,[120] that it must be the *kunāfah* that they say grows in the city and that the emirs eat. Tomorrow you'll go to the hamlet, and the foot soldiers and the brave lads will meet you and greet you and you'll sit down with them on the mound of Abū ʿAnṭūz spinning jute and wool, like snarling dogs, and you'll lounge among them like the billy goat of the emir's demesne, and they'll say to you, 'Abū Qurayṭim, tell us which of the dishes of the emirs you ate in the city!' and you'll tell them, 'I ate *kunāfah*,' but they'll never believe you and they'll

اكلت الكنافه فما يصدّقوا قولك ويقولوا لك تكدب يا عرص والصواب انك تاخد لك عضمتين من عضامها وتحطّهم في قحفك ولمّا يكابروك تقلع بالعضم عينيهم قال

٤٣،٣ ثمّ إنّه حطّ في قحفه من السمك شيئًا يسيرًا وسافر حتّى طلع الكفر فأقبل عليه مشايخ الكفر مثل الكلاب السعارة وهم دندوف وشخيبر وزعيبر وبعيبر وأتت إليه المشاة مثل تروفر وقنافد ولقالق وزرّاره ونيّاك الحماره وسلّموا عليه وقالوا له يابو قريطم اطلع بنا الكوم وقل لنا على المدينه وما اكلت فيها فقال لهم المدينه مليحه قوي وفيها جنادي كتير وفيها الخيار الاصفر خدت منه بجديد وخدت بجديد مقلي وخدت من الّي يقولوا عليه الحضر كرشه الّي يبيعوها على خشبه عاليه عريضه كيف الجرّافه وتكلت واتنعمت واشبرقت حتّى خدت كمان واحيات لحاكم بجديد ترمس مملّح وتكلت الفول الحارّ فقالوا له يابو قريطم كسرت عليك مال السلطان وعمايلك دي ما تخلّي رزق وانت عمرك تبعزق ولا تحسب حساب الزمان فقال لهم الرزق على الله يا شيوخ الكفر واقول لكم كمانه اكلت الكنافه الّي بتاكلها الاماره قال فلمّا سمعوا كلامه قاموا عليه وكذّبوه فقلع قحفه من على رأسه وأوراهم السمك فلما رأوه صدّقوا كلامه وفرحوا وانشرحوا ورقصوا وغنّوا حربي وزغرطوا النسوان وقالوا له يابو قريطم بقيت زيّ الاماره وغدًا أستاد الكفر يشوّش عليك ويقول بقى ابو قريطم سعيد وياكل ما تاكل الاماره ومتى بلغه الخبر شيّعك المقداف أو الجرافه وأنت تكتم سرّك ولا تقول لا لقريب ولا لغريب اكلت الكنافه أبدًا فقال لهم وانتم يا شيوخ الكفر تكتموا الخبر وتحلفوا لي على الشيخ ابو طبل فحلفوا كلّهم انّ لا حد يبيح بدي القضيّه فانظر إلى قلّة عقولهم وشدّة جهلهم

٤٤،٣ (وطلع رجل منهم المدينة يبيع بيض) فاشتراه منه رجل جنديّ وقال له امضي معي إلى المنزل خذ الدراهم فمضى معه فحصر الجنديّ البول فرأى في طريقه كنيف فدخله ليقضي الحاجة فوقف الفلّاح ينتظره فأبطأ عليه فدقّ عليه الباب فتنحنح الجنديّ

say to you, 'You're lying, you pimp!' So the thing to do is to take a couple of bones with you and put them in your cap and when they try to lord it over you, you can poke out their eyes with the bones!"

So he put a little of the fish in his cap and journeyed until he reached the hamlet and the shaykhs of the hamlet—Dundūf, Shukhaybir, Zuʿaybir, and Buʿaybir[121] by name—came out like mad dogs to meet him, and the foot soldiers came to him—among them Turawfar, Qanāfid ("Hedgehogs"), Laqāliq ("Storks"), Zarāra, and Donkey-Fucker—and they greeted him and said, "Abū Qurayṭim, come up to the mound with us and tell us about the city and what you ate there." "The city's very fine," he said. "It has lots of troopers in it and yellow cucumbers, which I got a copper-piece-worth of, and I got a copper-piece-worth of fried bean sprouts, and I got some of what the city folk call 'tripes,' which they sell from a tall, wide wooden thing like a shovel-sledge,[122] and I ate and had a good time and treated myself and, by the life of your beards, I even bought a copper-piece-worth of salted lupine too and ate fava beans in linseed oil!" Said the others, "Abū Qurayṭim, you have put yourself behind on the sultan's taxes, and these goings-on of yours will be the ruin of you! All your life you've thrown your money around and not given a thought to the future!" He replied, "Shaykhs of the hamlet, God will provide! And let me tell you something else: I ate the *kunāfah* that the emirs eat!" When they heard this, they attacked him and called him a liar, so he pulled his hat off his head and showed them the fish bones. Seeing these, they believed what he said, and their happiness knew no bounds, and they danced and sang war songs, and the women let out trills of joy. They said to him, "Abū Qurayṭam, now you've become like an emir, and tomorrow the master of the hamlet will spread rumors about you and say, 'Abū Qurayṭim has gotten rich and eats what the emirs eat,' and as soon as he gets the news he'll send you off to the galleys or the dredging crews. So keep quiet about it and don't tell anyone, family or stranger, that you ate *kunāfah*!" He replied, "And you, shaykhs of the hamlet, keep the lid on it too and swear to me by Shaykh Abū Ṭabl that you'll do so!" So they all swore that nobody would reveal the matter. Observe their stupidity and the depths of their ignorance! 3.43

And one of them went to the city to sell eggs, and a trooper bought them from him and said to him, "Come with me to the house, and take your money!" So the peasant went with him. The trooper, however, was taken short and, seeing a latrine on his way, went in to relieve himself. The peasant stood waiting 3.44

فصاح الفلّاح أعطيني حقّي يا جنديّ ما يحلّ لك من الله تاخد بيضي وتخلّيني واقف على باب بيتك كلّما اكلمك تنخخ وأقام الفلّاح الغارات والصياح قال فأقبلت إليه الناس فخرج الجنديّ وهو قابض على سراويله ومسك أطواق الفلّاح وصار يضربه بالمحرمة التي فيها البيض حتّى كسره على رأسه وسال على لحيته وشواربه والناس تضحك عليه ثمّ خلّصوه منه وفرّ هاربًا

٤٥،٣ (وطلع آخر المدينة يبيع تبن) فاشتراه رجل منه وأعطاه الدراهم فأتى إلى رجل ينقُدها له فقال له امضي بهم إلى الصيرفي فسأل عنه فدلّوه على دكّانه فأتى إليه فلم يجده فسأل عنه فقال له ولد صغير إنّه ذهب لقضاء الحاجة فقال للولد بالله دلّني عليه فأخذ الولد الفلّاح وتوجه به حتّى أوقفه على بيت الخلاء والصيرفي من داخله يقضي الحاجة قال فهجم الفلّاح على الصيرفي وفي يده الدراهم وقال له خد دي الفلوس وبيّن لي منها النحاس والمقصوص أنا راجل فلّاح وعليّ مال السلطان ودلّوني على بيتك ده قال فاندهش الصيرفي وقام على حيله وهو قابض على سراويله يضرب الفلّاح والناس تضحك عليه وصار لهم هجّة وضجّة عظيمة فانظر إلى عدم ذوق هذا الفلّاح وجهله وكونه لا يعرف بيت الخلاء من غيره

٤٦،٣ (وبذكر هذا الفلّاح وعدم ذوقه ذكرت ما اتّفق أن قيِّم الشام في عدم الذوق جاء إلى مصر) يزور قيّمها في عدم الذوق ويفتخر معه بملعوب حكم ما تفعل أرباب الملاعيب قال فسافر حتّى وصل إلى مصر واجتمع بقيّمها في عدم الذوق فسلّم عليه فقال له قيّم مصر ما تريد يا قيّم الشام قال أريد أن ألعب معك في عدم الذوق وكلّ من كان أَعْدَم ذوق من صاحبه وشهدت له الناس بذلك يكون قيّم مصر والشام فقال له

for him, but the trooper took his time, so in the end the peasant knocked on the door. The trooper cleared his throat, and the peasant shouted, "Give me my money, trooper! You have no right to take my eggs and leave me standing at the door of your house, clearing your throat whenever I speak to you!" The peasant created a great ruckus and commotion, and people came over, and the trooper emerged, holding on to his drawers, and grabbed the peasant by the front of his robe and started beating him with the napkin containing the eggs till he broke them over his head and they ran down his beard and moustache, while the people mocked him. Then they released him and he fled.

And another went to the city to sell straw, and a man bought it from him 3.45
and gave him some silver coins. The peasant then went up to a man and asked him to change these for him into smaller coin. The man told him, "Take them to the money changer's." So he made enquiries, and they gave him directions to the money changer's shop. When he got there, however, he did not find him, so he asked after him, and a small boy told him that he had gone to relieve himself. "In God's name," he said to the boy, "show me where he is!" so the boy went with the peasant and left him before the lavatory inside which the money changer was relieving himself, and the peasant set upon the money changer with the silver coins in his hand and told him, "Take this money and sort out for me the copper coins from the clipped ones! I'm a peasant with the sultan's taxes to pay, and they showed me to your house here!" The money changer was astonished and stood up, holding on to his drawers and beating the peasant, while the people mocked him and there was great hubbub and hullabaloo. Observe the peasant's ill manners and ignorance and his inability to tell the difference between a lavatory and any other building!

The Tale of the Champions of Discourtesy of Cairo and Damascus

Apropos of this peasant and his discourtesy, I am reminded of how it fell out 3.46
that the Champion of Discourtesy of Damascus came to Cairo to visit the latter's own Champion of Discourtesy and show off to him his tricks, as street entertainers do. He traveled until he reached Cairo, where he met with the Champion of Discourtesy of that city and made his salutations. "What desire you, Champion of Damascus?" asked the Champion of Cairo. The former replied, "It is my earnest desire to engage you in a contest of discourtesy, and let him whose manners are worse than his fellow's, as attested by the people, be

حباً وكرامة في غداة غد إن شاء الله تعالى نجمع أصحابنا عديمين الذوق ونلعب وتبيّن شطارتك

٤٧،٣ قال فلما أصبح الصباح جمع قيّم مصر طائفته في عدم الذوق وحضر قيّم الشام وقالوا له العب واجتهد في عدم الذوق قال فذهب قيم الشام واحتطب حزمة حطب كلّها شوك وسَنْط وحملها على الأكتاف وشقّ بها بين الناس في الزحام فصار الشوك والسنط يشتبك في ثياب الناس وهم يستعدموا ذوقه ويسبّوه ويلعنوه إلى أن تمّ ملعوبه وأتى إلى قيّم مصر وطائفته وهم ينظرون ما فعل فقال له قيّم مصر بقاشي عندك من عدم الذوق غير دا تفعله قال لا فقال له دي ما هي شطارة لأنّ الناس استعدموا ذوقك لكونك جيتهم بشي أذاهم وشوّش عليهم وأنا أفعل أعجب من ده وهو إني أخلّي الناس يستعدموا ذوقي بالورد والنِسْرِين والرَيحان ونحو ذلك فقال قيّم الشام هذا شي له ريحه طيّبه وزيّ ما تعمل فقال له بكره تشوف ما أعمل

٤٨،٣ فلمّا أصبح الصباح قال قيّم مصر لقيّم الشام امضي معي انضر ما أخبرتك عنه البارحة قال فمضوا جميعاً حتّى أقبلوا على بيّاع الزهور فأخذ قيّم مصر منه شيئاً يسيراً من الورد والنسرين والريحان ومضى هو وقيّم الشام والطائفه حتّى أقبلوا على ميضة المسجد والناس في ازدحام وقت الصلاة على بيوت الأخلية فصار قيّم مصر يدخل على الرجل وهو جالس في بيت الخلاء وبيده الورد والنسرين والريحان ويقول له خد يا سيدي شمّ هذا الورد وغيره يبقى نهارك مبارك واعطيني ما يتيّسر فيتضايق الرجل منه ويسبّه ويلعنه ويقول له ما أعدم ذوقك انضر أنا في أي محلّ وصار يدخل على هذا وعلى هذا والناس تسبّه وتلعنه ويستعدموا ذوقه بهذه الفعلة قال فعند ذلك أذعن له قيّم الشام وصار تحت حكمه وأمره وأخذ خاطره وتوجّه إلى بلده

champion of both Cairo and Damascus!" "A pleasure and an honor!" declared the other. "Tomorrow morning early, the Almighty willing, we shall gather our fellow practitioners of discourtesy, you and I shall compete, and you shall demonstrate your skill."

When the morning came, the Champion of Cairo gathered his fellows, the Champion of Damascus presented himself, and they told him, "Perform your tricks and do your rudest!" So the Champion of Damascus went and gathered a bundle of kindling that was all thorns and acacia and lifted it onto his shoulders and forced his way through the crowds with it, the thorns and the acacia twigs catching in people's clothes while they deplored his discourtesy and reviled and cursed him. When the performance was over, he came to the Champion of Cairo and his fellows, who had been watching what he did. "Is that the worst you can come up with by way of discourtesy?" asked the Champion of Cairo. "Yes," the first replied. Then said the other, "There's no skill in that, for the people deplored your discourtesy because you exposed them to something that bothered and annoyed them. I can do something more wonderful than that, which is to make people deplore my discourtesy using only roses, myrtle, sweet basil, and the like." "Those are sweet-smelling things," said the Champion of Damascus, "so how will you manage it?" "Tomorrow," said the other, "you will see what I shall do." 3.47

When the morning came, the Champion of Cairo said to the Champion of Damascus, "Come with me and observe what I told you of yesterday!" So they proceeded until they came to a flower seller, from whom the Champion of Cairo bought a few roses and some myrtle and sweet basil. Then he proceeded with the Champion of Damascus and their companions until they came to the ablutions courtyard of a mosque at prayer time, where the people were crowded about the lavatories, and the Champion of Cairo set about bursting in on people as they sat in the lavatory, roses, myrtle, and sweet basil in hand, saying, "Here, sir, sniff these roses, etc., and may your day be blessed, and spare me a little something!" The man would get annoyed and revile and curse him and say, "How ill-mannered you are! Can't you see where I am?" The Champion continued forcing his way in on this man and that while all abused him, cursed him, and deplored his discourtesy for so behaving. At this, the Champion of Damascus acknowledged defeat and submitted himself to the tutelage and command of the Champion of Cairo, and he took his leave of him and set off for his own country. 3.48

(ونظير ذلك ما اتّفق أن ثقيل مصر قصد زيارة ثقيل الشام) والمسامرة معه واللعب ٤٩،٣
والانبساط فتوجّه إليه حتّى بلغ دمشق الشام واجتمع به وسلّم عليه فأخذه إلى منزله ووضع بين يديه المأكل والمشرب ثمّ إنّه سأله عن سبب مجيئه فسكت ولم يتكلّم مدّة ثلاثة أيّام حتّى أكل جميع ما كان عند ثقيل الشام ممّا جمعه من الثقالة والرذالة وبعد الثلاثة أيّام قال له يا أخي أخبرك ما حصل لي في الطريق وما ذاك إلّا أنّي سافرت مع القَفَل ففقدنا الماء في بعض المراحل فتوجّهت نحو جبل بالقرب منّا فرأيت في جانبه بيرًا مهجورًا وفيه ماء كثير فقلعت ثيابي ونزلت إليه ولم أزل نازل نازل وصار يكرّر لفظة نازل على ثقيل الشام وهو نازل في الأكل والشرب مدّة ثلاثين يومًا فقال له ثقيل الشام يا هذا ما بقي عندى شيء تأكله وآخر نزولك يا أخي ما فعلت في البير فقال له فلمّا انتهيت إلى قاع البير وجدت فيه حجر طاحون فوضعته على كتفي ولم أزل طالع طالع وصار يكرّرها فقال له ثقيل الشام امسك ما معك أنت مكثت مدّة ثلاثين يومًا نازل في البير من غير شيء فكيف طلوعك وأنت حامل حجر طاحون أشهد على أنّك قيّم الثقلاء في مصر والشام وأنا من تحت يدك انصرف عنّي قال فأخذ خاطره ومضى بعد أن كتب له مَحْضَر بذلك أنّه قيّم مصر والشام في الثقالة والرذالة وعدم الذوق

واعلم أن أهل الثقالة على أنواع فمنهم من يكون ثقيل الذات خفيف الصفات ٥٠،٣
وبالعكس ومنهم من يكون ثقيل الذات والصفات قال الشاعر [رمل]

وَثَقِيلٍ قالَ صِفْني   قُلْتُ أَيْش فِيكَ أَصِفْ
كلّ ما فيكَ ثقيلٌ   حِلَّ عنّي وٱنْصَرِفْ

The Tale of the Boors of Cairo and Damascus

Similarly, it happened that the Boor of Cairo[123] decided to visit the Boor of Damascus to pass with him a few evenings of pleasant conversation, recreation, and good cheer. So he proceeded until he reached Damascus, where he met him and made his salutations, and the Boor of Damascus took him to his house and set food and drink before him. Then he asked him the reason for his coming. The other, however, kept silent and said nothing for three days, during which time he ate everything the Boor of Damascus had acquired by his boorishness and insolence. After the three days, he said, "Brother, let me tell you what happened on the road. I was traveling with the caravan and we ran out of water on one of the stages, so I made my way towards a nearby hill, where I saw that a deep well, full of water, had been dug at its foot. I took off my clothes and descended into its depths, and I kept going down down . . ." and he went on saying "down" to the Boor of Damascus over and over while continuing to plunge on down through his stocks of food and drink for a further thirty days. Then the Boor of Damascus said to him, "Hey, you! I've got nothing left for you to eat! When you got all the way down, brother, what did you do in the well?" He answered, "When I got to the bottom of the well, I saw a millstone there, so I put it on my shoulder and I kept going up up . . ." and he started saying it over and over again, but the Boor of Damascus said to him, "Pick up your things! You took thirty days to go down into the well empty-handed, so how long will it take you to come up carrying a millstone? I bear witness that you are the Champion of Boors of both Cairo and Damascus and I am under your command. Now get out of my sight!" So the man took his leave and went off, after the other had written him an affidavit to the effect that he was the Champion of both Cairo and Damascus in boorishness, insolence, and discourtesy. 3.49

Note that boors are of different kinds. There are those who are obnoxious of person and delightful of personality, or vice versa, and there are those who are obnoxious of both person and personality. The poet says: 3.50

And once a boor said, "Describe me!"
 Said I, "What's there to say?
Everything about you's obnoxious.
 Leave me alone and get on your way!"

وقال آخر [خفيف] ٥١،٣

وثقيلٍ تبسّما[1] أصبحَ الكونُ مُظلما
حطّ في الشرقِ رِجلَه مالتِ الأرضُ والسّما

فمن كان فيه هذه الثقالة وحوى هذه الرذالة ينبغي الرحلة عنه والفرار منه قال الشاعر [وافر] ٥٢،٣

سَأَرحَلُ عَنْ بِلادِكَ أَلْفَ عَامٍ مَسيرَةُ كُلّ عامٍ أَلْفُ ميلِ
وَلَوْ كانَتْ بِلادُكَ[2] أَلْفَ مِصْرٍ وَيَرْوِي كُلّ مِصْرٍ أَلْفُ نيلِ
تَكَدَّرَتِ الخَواطِرُ مِنكَ حَتَّى قَنِعْنا مِنْ دِيارِكَ بِالرَّحيلِ
وأُنْشِدُ في فِراقِكَ بَيْتَ شِعْرٍ تَلَقّاهُ فَضِيلٌ عَنْ فَضِيلِ
إذا حَلَّ الثَّقيلُ بِأَرْضِ قَوْمٍ فَما لِلسّاكِنينَ سِوى الرَّحيلِ

٥٣،٣ (واشتكى بعض الفلاّحين رجلاً إلى القاضي) وادّعى عليه أنّه نزل غيطه بغير إذنه وحشّ منه برسيماً لدابّته فأحضر القاضي الرجل المدّعى عليه وسأله فقال نعم نزلت غيطه إلّا أنّه ضربني وشوّش علي فقال القاضي للفلاّح وإذا نزل غيطك تضربه فقال الفلاّح أتابيك يا قاضي تور ونزلت غيطي يا هل ترى اضربك اكسر قرنك والّا اخلّيك تطلع سالم والّا ترعى غيطي فقال له القاضي اخرج قبّح الله الأبعد ما أجهلك وما أقبح هذا المثل الذي شبّهتني به ثمّ إنّه طرده ولم يسمع له كلاماً

٥٤،٣ (ويقرب من هذا المعنى أنّ رجلاً فلاّحاً دخل على الأمير حمّار بن بقر) وأنشد يقول [وزن غير معروف]

---

١ بي: وثقيلٍ إذا تبسّما. ٢ بي: عطاياك.

And another says: 3.51

> And once a boor did smile—
> The universe grew dim.
> He placed his foot in the east—
> Earth and sky were bent out of trim!

One must abandon and flee from any possessed of such obnoxiousness and imbued with such insolence. As the poet says: 3.52

> I'll flee your country for a thousand years,
> Traveling each year a thousand miles,
> And were your country a thousand Egypts,
> Each watered by a thousand Niles,
> Our hearts would be so sick at you,
> Your lands we'd gladly for good eschew,
> And, taking leave, this lay,
> Passed down by noble hands, I'd say:
> "When a boor alights at their tents,
> It's time for the tribe to go thence!"

More Anecdotes Illustrating the Stupidity of Country People

And a peasant brought a complaint against a man to the judge, claiming that the former had entered his field without permission and cut clover from it for his animal. The judge had the accused brought and questioned him. The man responded, "It's true I went into his field, but it's also true that he beat me and used me ill." So the judge said to the peasant, "You beat him, just for going into your field?" The peasant responded, "Imagine, Your Honor, that you were an ox! If you entered my field, which do you think I'd do—beat you till your horns broke or let you leave unharmed or let you to graze in my field?" The judge said, "Get out, God disfigure you! What an ignoramus you are, and how ugly the image to which you liken me!" Then he threw him out and would not hear another word from him. 3.53

Similarly, a peasant visited the emir Ḥammār ibn Baqar[124] and recited before him: 3.54

يا ابن بقر ما انت الا تور   والناس حداك عجاجيل
لما تعمل بقرونك هاش   يولّوا الكل جفافيل

٥٥،٣ ومعنى هذا الكلام أنت أيّها الأمير في هيبتك وجلالتك وعظم قدرتك مثل الثور العظيم المهاب والناس حولك مثل العجاجيل أي مثل العجول الصغار فإذا التفتّ إليهم ولّوا من هيبتك مثل ما أنّ الثور إذا التفت بقرونه وهاش في العجول ولّت من بين يديه فأنشده هذا الفلّاح على حسب ما اقتضاه حاله وما ناسب جهله وهباله

٥٦،٣ أقول وعجاجيل على وزن هبابيل كما هو في القاموس الأزرق والناموس الأبلق واستعمالها من هذا المعنى كما قال بعض جهلة الريف مواليا [بسيط مع كسر]

رأيتُ أمّ زغابه في المعازيلِ   تطحنْ وتعجنْ وتغزلْ بالمغازيلِ
وحولها شفتُ سربهْ من عجاجيلِ   وهمْ ينطّوا وهيّ تلعبْ حناجيلِ

والعجاجيل[١] جمع عجل كما أنّ الحناجيل جمع حَنجُول على وزن هِبوّل وهو مشتقّ من التحنجل وهي لغة ريفيّة فإنّهم يقولوا فلان بيتحنجل أي يجري جريًا خفيفًا وينطّ نطًّا عنيفًا ومعنى هذا الكلام أنّي رأيت محبوبتي هذه وهي أمّ زغابه في معزل من المعازل تتعاطى فيه الطحن والعجن وتغزل فيه أيضًا وحولها العجول يلعبوا وينطّوا وهي الأخرى تتحنجل بينهم وتلاعبهم فناسب مدح هذا الفلّاح له وعليه وشِبْهُ الشيء منجذب إليه

٥٧،٣ (وطلع رجل منهم المدينة لقضاء حاجة من أستاذه) فلمّا قضاها ورجع إلى بلده لاقوه أصحابه وسلّموا عليه وقالوا له كيف حال المدينه فقال لهم المدينه مليحه فقالوا له يابو عوكل اشّربقت فيها فقال لهم اشبرقت شبرقه مليحه واكلت الزلوبيه الّي

١ بي: قوله المغازيل جمع مغزل كما أن المنازل جمع منزل.

Ibn Baqar, you are indeed an ox
  And those about you but calflings!
When you go "Whoosh!" with your horns,
  They shy away like panicky camelings!

The meaning of these words is as follows:[125] "You, O emir, in your dignity, majesty, and high estate are like the mighty, awe-inspiring ox, and the people around you are like caflings, that is, like small calves. When you turn towards them, they shy away from your awesomeness, just as, when the ox turns with its horns and lunges at the calves, they shy away from him." Thus the peasant recited verse of a sort to fit his condition and in keeping with his ignorance and imbecility. 3.55

I declare that *ʿajājīl* ("calflings") is of the measure of *habābīl* ("simpletons"),[126] as stated in *The Blue Ocean and Piebald Canon*.[127] An example of its use in that sense occurs in the following *mawāliyā* by a certain ignoramus of the countryside: 3.56

I beheld Umm Zaghābah, off in a quiet spot,
  Grinding and kneading and with spindles spinning.
Around her I saw a herd of calflings (*ʿajājīl*);
  They were leaping, while she was playing at hopping and skipping (*ḥanājīl*).

The word *ʿajājīl* is the plural of *ʿijl* ("calf"),[128] just as *ḥanājīl* ("hopping and skipping") is the plural of *ḥanjūl*, of the measure *hibbawl* ("simpleton"), and is derived from *taḥanjul*, which is a rural word.[129] They say, "So and so *biyitḥanjil*," that is, "he runs a few steps and makes a mighty leap." The verse thus means, "I saw this beloved of mine, namely Umm Zaghābah, in a secluded place, engaged in grinding and kneading there, and, likewise, indeed, in spinning; about her the calves were playing and leaping, while she too was skipping among them and playing with them." Thus, the peasant's panegyric accords with his condition and is limited by it, and "like attracts like."

And one of them went to the city to see to some business with his master. When he was done and had returned to his village, his friends met him, greeted him, and asked him, "How was the city?" "The city was fine," he replied. "Did you treat yourself to a blowout there, Abū ʿAwkal?" they asked. He answered, "I gave myself lots of lovely treats there and I ate those 3.57

يقولوا عليها الحضور خدت منها بجديد وسمعت واحد ينادي في المدينه ويقول حلو بارد يا تين بناموسه يا تين فخدت منه عشرين جميّزه باط بجديد وحطّيتهم في مَتْرِد وعفصتهم بايدي وشربت عليهم جَرّة مويه من البحر فقالوا له هنيئاً لك يابو عوكل عمرك تضيّع وتبعزق ولا تخلّي فلوس واحنا خايفين لا ينكسر عليك مال السلطان فقال لهم يا وجوه الخير الدنيا زايله ياما ضيّعنا واصرفنا فضاضي وجدايد

(وقال رجل فلاح لصديق له) يا فلان عملت السنه كعك في العيد فقال له عملت رُبَعين كبيره فقال له حطّيت فيهم ايدام كتير فقال له حطيت فيهم بجديدين سيرج فقال له أفقرت نفسك وكسرت عليك مال السلطان بقى منهم عندك شي قال بقى عندي فِرَد واحده انخس بها الحماره من كفر دُنْضَيط إلى كفر هُرَبيْط ٥٨،٣

(وأرسل بعض الأمراء غلاماً له فلاّحاً بنصف فضّة) وقال له اشتري لنا به كعك بسمسم وهات عليه زعتر نفطر به فأخذ النصف واشترى بأربعة جدد كعك وأربعة جدد زعتر من غير دَقّ ووضع الجميع بين يدي الأمير فلمّا رأوه الحاضرون ضحكوا عليه فاغتاظ الأمير وطرده فتوجّه إلى بلاده ٥٩،٣

(وأرسل أيضاً بعض الأمراء غلاماً له فلاّحاً وقال له خد دي الدراهم واشتري لنا دُبّة) أيْ بطّة جلد يضعوا فيها السمن أو العسل فتوجّه الغلام إلى الرُمَيْلة وسأل عن بياع الدبب فدلوه على القريداتي فأتاه فرآه يلعب بالقرد والدبّة والكلب فصبر عليه حتّى فرغ من لعبه وتقدّم إليه هذا الغلام الفلاّح وقال له مرادي للأمير دبّه مليحه فقال له القريداتي عندي واحده مليحه امضي بنا نفرّج عليها الأمير قال فمضى الغلام هو والقريداتي ومعهما القرد والكلب والدبّة حتّى دخلوا البيت وكان الأمير في ذلك الوقت عنده جماعة من الأكابر جالسين فلمّا رآهم القريداتي قام يده في الطار وسحب القرد والدبّة والكلب يرقّصهم ويلعّبهم فقال الأمير له أيش ده فقال له القريداتي إنّ ٦٠،٣

'frotters'[130] that the city folk go on about, which I got a copper-piece-worth of. And I heard a man in the city crying, 'Sweet, cool figs! Figs with the gnats still on them!' so I got twenty sour sycamore figs from him for a copper piece and put them in a crock and squashed them up with my hands and washed them down with a jug of water from the river." "Good health to you, Abū 'Awkal!" they said. "You're always squandering your money and throwing it around and ending up with none, and we're afraid you'll fall behind on the sultan's taxes." "Good folks," he replied, "life is short! How often we've thrown our money around and spent silver and copper pieces!"

And a peasant said to a friend of his, "So-and-so, did you make short pastry 3.58
this year at the feast?" The other answered, "I made two quarterns by the big measure!" "And did you put in much shortening?" he asked. "Two copper-pieces-worth of sesame oil!" he said. "You've ruined yourself and you'll fall behind on the sultan's taxes!" said the first. "Do you have any left?" The man replied, "A few, one of which I'll use to goad the donkey from Kafr Dundayṭ to Kafr Hurbayṭ!"

And an emir sent off one of his pages, who was a peasant, with a silver piece 3.59
and told him "Buy us some short pastry with sesame and some thyme to go with it for breakfast!" So the man took the silver piece and bought four copper-pieces-worth of short pastry and four copper-pieces-worth of unground thyme and put the lot in front of the emir. When those present saw it, they laughed at him, but the emir was furious and threw him out, and the man set off back to his village.

And another emir also sent off a page of his who was a peasant, telling him, 3.60
"Take these coins and buy us a 'bear,'" by which he meant a leather bottle of the sort they put drawn butter and honey in. So the page set off for al-Rumaylah and asked who sold bears, and the people directed him to a monkey trainer, whom he found putting an ape, a bear, and a dog through their tricks. Waiting till the man had finished his performance, the peasant page approached him and said, "I want a nice bear for the emir." "I have a beauty," said the monkey trainer. "Let's go show it to the emir!" So the page and the monkey trainer set off together with the ape, the dog, and the bear till they entered the house. The emir was at home at the time, sitting with a group of grandees. Seeing the latter, the monkey trainer set his hand to the tambourine and pulled the ape, the bear, and the dog forward to make them dance and do their tricks. "What's all this?" asked the emir. The monkey trainer replied, "This servant

خدّامك ده جانى وأخبرني أن مرادك تشتري دبّه فجيتك بها وبالقرد والكلب تنضر لعبهم وتشتري منهم ما تريد قال فضحكوا عليه الأمارة فأمر بضربه وحبسه ثمّ إنّهم شفعوا فيه فأطلقه وطرده من عنده فتوجّه إلى بلاده وأحسن الأمير بالقريداتي وأمره بالانصراف

٦١،٣ (ورأيت رجلا فلّاحا يتكلّم مع صديق له فقال له يا فلان انت تعرف تقرا) قال ايوه فقال له ايش هجاك ابريق[١] فقال له بربق واو فقال له ايش عرّفك انّ فيها واو فقال دلّتني عليها النقطه الّي فوق الواو فقال له إن عشت تبقى فصيح لا خوالك

٦٢،٣ (وقال رجل فلّاح لآخر اسمع ما قالوا العشّاق) فقال له وما قالوا فقال شعر [لعلّ الوزن المقصود البسيط]

ولقد اقولـــ له جـيش خـلوت به انست منزلنا يا طلعة القمر وشن

فقال له دا كلام مون فقال له دا كلام هارين الرشاد الّي وقع في الجبّ لقفه التمساح الّي نزل عليه الوحل في جامع طيلون الّي النار برّد وسلام فقال له يا نعم يا نعم كذلك عيسى ابن مريم ابن ابو طالوب جرى له زيّ ما جرى

٦٣،٣ (وصلّى رجل فلّاح) فلمّا نوى وقرأ الفاتحة حطّ يده على راسه وقال آه يا راسي فقال له رجل عارف بطلت صلاتك فقال له أنا ما باشكي لك أنا باشكي لربّي وجع راسي ثمّ إنّه ركع وصلّى وأتمّ صلاته ولم يبال بالكلام ولا اعتبر بقول هذا العارف

٦٤،٣ (وصلّى رجل آخر من الفلّاحين) فأحرم بالصلاة وقال يا ربّ خلّي لنا بهايمنا

---

١ بي: بربق.

of yours came to me and informed me that you wanted to buy a bear, so I've brought you one, along with the ape and the dog, so that you can see them do their tricks and buy whichever you want." The other emirs laughed, but the emir ordered his page to be beaten and imprisoned. Those sitting with him interceded on his behalf, however, and he released him and threw him out of his house. The peasant set off for his village, and the emir ordered the monkey trainer to leave, after rewarding him well.

And I saw a peasant talking to a friend of his and asking him, "So-and-so, do you know how to read?" "Yes," he replied. "So how do you spell *ibrīq* ('water pitcher')?" he asked him. "*B*, *r*, *b*, *q*, plus *w*," replied the other. "How do you know that there's a *w* in it?" he asked. He said, "The dot over the *w* led me to that conclusion."[131] Said the first, "If you live, you'll be a credit to your maternal uncles with your mastery of Arabic!" 3.61

And one peasant said to another, "Hear what the lovers[132] have said!" "What have they said?" asked the second. Then the first recited: 3.62

Verily I say to him an army alone I was happy,
With him, our abode, you with the face like the moon,
tiddely-pom![133]

"Whose woids are those?"[134] the other asked him. He said, "Those are the words of Hārīn al-Rashād, who fell into the pit. He was gobbled up by the crocodile upon whom the mud descended in the mosque of al-Ṭaylūn, who made the fire to be cold and safe." "How true! How true!" said the other. "Likewise ʿĪsā son of Maryam son of Abū Ṭālūb—the very same happened to him."

Anecdotes about Country People Who Voided Their Prayers

And a peasant performed the prayer,[135] but after making the declaration of intent and reading the *Fātiḥah*, he put his hand to his head and exclaimed, "Oh my head!" A man well instructed in religion told him, "You have voided your prayer!" to which the peasant replied, "I wasn't complaining to you, I was complaining to my Lord of the pain in my head." Then he performed a prostration and prayed and completed his orisons, paying no heed to what had been said to him and ignoring the words of that well-instructed man. 3.63

And another peasant performed the prayer. After entering into the consecrated state he said, "O Lord, preserve us our farm animals and our dogs and 3.64

وكلابنا وقططنا وحميرنا وطلّع لنا زرعنا وخلّي لي وليدي عنطوز هذا كيف وليدك يا ربّ فقال له رجل عارف كفرت يا فلّاح الله تعالى مُنَزَّه عن الصاحبة والولد فقال له الفلّاح أنا سمعت هذا الكلام من ابويه وجدّي قبل موتهم فقال له الرجل كلّكم كفرة أولاد كفرة

(وصلّى آخر) فلمّا ركع بان أيره لقصر ثوبه وانكشفت عورته فقبض عليه رجل آخر من خلفه فصرخ الفلّاح بقوله أطلقني فضحك وأطلقه ثمّ إنّه أتمّ الصلاة على هذه الحالة ولم يعرف الصحّة من الفساد ٣،٦٥

(وصلّى آخر) فلمّا جلس للتشهّد الأخير جاء ولده وقال يا ابويه البقره روّحت من الغيط فقال له وهو متلبّس بالصلاة خد شحيبر يحلبها في محلاب ثمّ سلّم بعد ذلك من الصلاة ٣،٦٦

(وصلّى آخر) فلمّا جلس للتشهّد جاء ولده وركب على أكتافه وصكّه في قفاه ومسك لحيته بيده وفيها الوحل والجلّة فقال له يا ولدي انزل عني حتّى أتمّ صلاتي ثمّ إنّه تشهّد وسلّم فقال له رجل عارف صلاتك باطلة فقال له الفلّاح سمعت ابويه وجدّي يقولوا حديث عن امّ زغابه جدّتنا القديمه من لا يسقع دقنه ما يربّي ابنه والاولاد الصغار متل اولاد المعزه وابوهم كيف التيس ينطوا عليه فقال له الرجل قبّح الله الأبعد وحديثه وأمثاله ثمّ إنّه تركه ومضى ٣،٦٧

(وصلّى رجل منهم) فلمّا كبر رفع يديه وقال والتين والزيتون والنارنج والليمون وقبر معيكه المجنون جيتك يا ربّي بلحيتي وجلّتي وقفاي ومركوبي لا تردّني يا ربّي خايب لا من رحمتك ولا من رجاك الله اكبر وركع وتمّ الصلاة الفشرويّة ٣،٦٨

our cats and our donkeys and make our crops grow, and preserve me this little son of mine, ʿAnṭūz, just as you have preserved Your Own Son, O Lord!" A man well instructed in religion told him, "You blaspheme, peasant! The Almighty has neither spouse nor child!" The peasant replied, "I heard these words from my father and my grandfather before they died." Said the other, "You are all infidels and sons of infidels!"

And another performed the prayer, but, when he prostrated himself, his penis popped into view because his garment was too short to hide his privates. Another man then grabbed him from behind, making the peasant yell out "Lemme go!" at which the man laughingly complied. Then the first man concluded his prayer as he was, incapable of telling the difference between the correct and the corrupt. 3.65

And another performed the prayer, but when he sat to make the final profession of faith his son came up to him and said, "Dad, the cow has come home from the field," so he told him, while still in the act of praying, "Go get Shuḥaybar to milk her into the pail!" Then he made the closing salutations. 3.66

And another performed the prayer, and when he sat up to make the closing profession of faith, his son came up to him, climbed on his shoulders, kicked him on the back of his neck, and took his beard in his hand, which was covered with mud and dung. "Get down off me, boy," the man told him, "till I've finished my prayer!" Then he made the profession of faith and finished his prayer. A man well instructed in religion told him, "Your prayer is voided!" The peasant replied, "I heard my father and grandfather tell a Tradition from Umm Zaghābah, our great-grandmother: 'He who doesn't grow a thick skin will never raise his son, and a man's little children are like young goats, and their father is like the billy goat on whom they jump.'" The man said to him, "God disfigure you and your Tradition and all like it!" Then he left him and went away. 3.67

And one of them performed the prayer, and after he had said, "God is most great!" and raised his hands,[136] he said, "By the fig and the olive[137] and the bitter orange and the lime and the grave of Muʿaykah[138] the Madman, I come to you, Lord, with my beard and my dung and my nape and my shoes! Do not send me away disappointed, O Lord, either in your Mercy or in my hopes of You! God is most great!" Then he made a prostration and completed his fatuous orisons. 3.68

٦٩،٣ (وصلّى آخر) فلمّا قرأ الفاتحة أتى لعند قوله تعالى ﴿اهدنا الصراط المستقيم﴾ فأبدل النون ميماً وقال اهدموا الصراط المستقيم فقال له رجل عارف بطّل الصلاة وخلّي الصراط بلا هدم قاتل الله الأبعد وقام عليه حتّى تركها

٧٠،٣ (وصلّى فقيه ريف) بجماعة فلمّا قرأ الفاتحة وأتى إلى آخرها قال ولا الضالّون فقال الرجل من خلفه آمون فالتفت إليه وقال له لحنْت فقال له بل أنت كفرت

٧١،٣ (وحُكي أنّ رجلاً من جهلة العرب صلّى بآخر مثله) فقال الإمام هذا اللفظ شنتير كيف بنتير جماعه راكبين فيل جتهم طير أبابيل خلّتهم متل الفطير ثمّ ركع وركع الآخر خلفه وأتمّا صلاتهما التي لا فَيْش ولا عَلَيْش

٧٢،٣ (وصلّى آخر من الفلّاحين) فلمّا سجد لدغته عقرب فضرط من شدّة اللدغة ثمّ رفع رأسه بسرعة وقال يا ربّ أنت تعلم أنّي ما ضرطت بخاطري إلّا غصب عني سامحني يا ربّ ثمّ إنّه سجد وسلّم

٧٣،٣ (وصلّى آخر) فلمّا سجد رأى تحت جبهته انخفاضاً فأخذ قرص جلّة ووضعه تحت جبهته وأتمّ صلاته عليه

٧٤،٣ (وصلّت امرأة من نساء الأرياف) فلمّا تلبّست بالصلاة جاء الكلب وأخذ من جانبها رغيفاً فمسكته وقبضته على آذانه وشتمته ونهرته وخلّصت الرغيف من فمه وأتمّت صلاتها

٧٥،٣ (وكان بعض الأولاد يقرأ في كُتّاب) فجاءت أمّه واشتكته للفقي وقالت له الولد ده بيئذيني ويشوّش عليّ وانا اصلّي واذا ركعت شلح ثيابه وشخّ وبال عليّ فقال له الفقي أحقّ ما تقول أمّك قال نعم يا سيدي فقال له ما السبب أنّك تؤذيها وهي في الصلاة فقال

And another performed the prayer, and, when he was reciting the *Fātiḥah* and reached the words of the Almighty, «*ihdinā l-ṣirāṭa l-mustaqīm*» ("Guide us to the Straight Path"), he changed the *n* to an *m* and said, "*ihdimū al-ṣirāṭa l-mustaqīm*" ("Demolish the Straight Path"). A well-instructed man said to him, "Have done and leave the Straight Path in one piece, God strike you dead!" and he set upon him, forcing the man to abandon his prayers. 3.69

And a country pastor performed the prayer with a group, and, when he was reciting the *Fātiḥah* and came to the end, he said, "*Wa-lā al-ḍāllūn*" ("Nor those who have gone astray"),[139] so a man behind him said, "*Āmūn*!"[140] The imam turned to him and said, "You pronounced it wrong!" to which the other retorted, "And you blasphemed!"[141] 3.70

And the story is told of an ignorant Arab[142] who performed the prayer with another of the same sort, and the one leading the prayer said the following words, "Shintīr like unto Bintīr! A gang riding on an elephant! They were attacked by birds, which left them like pastry!"[143] Then he made a prostration, and the other man made a prostration behind him, and they completed their worthless prayer! 3.71

And another peasant was performing the prayer, and, when he prostrated himself, a scorpion stung him and he farted with pain. Quickly raising his head, he then said, "O Lord, You know that I did not fart of my own will but in spite of myself. Forgive me, O Lord!" Then he made the profession of faith and the salutations! 3.72

And another was performing the prayer, and when he prostrated himself he saw a depression in the ground under his forehead, so he took a cake of dung and put it beneath his forehead and completed his prayer on that! 3.73

And a countrywoman performed the prayer, and while she was in the midst of it, a dog came up and stole a loaf from her side. The woman caught the dog, grabbed it by the ears, cursed and swore at it, and wrested the loaf from its mouth. Then she went on to complete her prayer! 3.74

And a boy was studying in the *kuttāb* when his mother came and complained to the schoolmaster, telling him, "Sir, this boy annoys me and disturbs me while I pray, and when I make a prostration, he pulls up his clothes and pisses on me!" So the schoolmaster asked him, "Is it true what your mother says?" "Yes, sir," replied the boy. "And what is your reason," he asked, "for molesting her during her prayers?" "Sir," he answered, "I do it because her worship is void and worthless. Ask her yourself what she says and how she recites her prayers." 3.75

له يا سيدي لأنّ عبادتها باطلة لا فَيْش ولا عَلَيْش اسألها ما تقول في الصلاة فقال لها الفقي أنت تحسني الصلاة فقالت وكيف لا أحسنها وانا اعرفها من امّي وجدّتي وجدّة جدّتي فقال لها اقريْ الفاتحة فقالت بسم الله الرحمن الرحيم الحمد لله ربّ العالمين إذا جاك الحجّ نصر الدين افتح له الباب إنّه كان طوّاب فقال لها الفقيه قاتلك الله ما هذا قرآن ما عدا البسملة وأوّل الفاتحة فقال الولد اسألها يا سيدي ما تقول بعد الصلاة فسألها فقالت أقول زيّ ما كانت امّي وجدّتي تقول سبحان الله قبل الله سبحان الله بعد الله قال فصاح الفقيه عليها وقال لها كفرت يا ملعونة ثمّ إنّه التفت إلى الولد وقال له أمرتك أن تخرأ عليها فضلاً عن الشخاخ ثمّ إنّه زجَرها فخرجت من عنده وتوجّهت إلى حال سبيلها

٧٦،٣ (وصلّى رجل فلّاح) ولمّا كبّر وأراد أن يقرأ دعاء الافتتاح قال لحت وجهي للي شرخ السموات والأرض لانّي لا حنيفاً ولا مسلماً ولا من القوم الكافرين فقال له رجل عارف فمن أي مِلّة أنت قاتل الله الأبعد فقال أنا من بني عُقْبه فضحك عليه ثمّ تركه ومضى وأحوالهم مشهورة وأضرابهم كثير وأمورهم لا تنحصر

So the schoolmaster asked her, "Do you know the prayer well?" "How should I not," she replied, "when I learnt it from my mother and my grandmother and my grandmother's grandmother?" So he said to her, "Recite the *Fātiḥah*!" and she said, "In the name of God the Merciful, the Compassionate! Praise be to God, Lord of the Worlds! When al-Ḥājj Naṣr al-Dīn comes to you, open the door to him! Verily, he was once a maker of bricks."[144] The schoolmaster said, "God strike you dead! This has nothing to do with the Qur'an except for the invocation of God's name and the two opening verses!" The boy then said to him, "Ask her, sir, what she says after the prayer!" So he asked her and she said, "I say as my mother and grandmother used to say before me, 'Glory to God before God! Glory to God after God!'" "You blaspheme, accursed woman!" the schoolmaster shouted at her, and turning to the boy he said, "I order you to shit on her, as well as piss!" Then he chided her and expelled her from his presence, and she left and went her way.

And a peasant performed the prayer, and, after he had said "God is most 3.76
great!" and wanted to recite the introductory supplication, he said, "I have flung my face towards Him who cracked the Heavens and the Earth, for I am neither a monotheist nor a Muslim nor an Unbeliever!"[145] A man well instructed in religion said to him, "Of what sect are you then, God strike you dead?" The man replied, "I am of the Banī 'Uqbah!" The well-instructed man mocked him and left him and departed.

The condition of such people is well known, the likes of them are everywhere, and their goings-on are beyond numbering.

(وذكر فقهائهم وما يقع منهم من الجهل المركَّب وقلّة العقل والخبط في الدين ونحو ذلك)

(سئل فقيه ريفيّ عن قوله تعالى) ﴿وَقِيلَ يَا أَرْضُ ابْلَعِي مَاءَكِ وَيَا سَمَاءُ أَقْلِعِي﴾ ما معنى اقلعي فقال أيْ سيري مثل المراكب المقلّعة ١،٤

(وتولّى بعض فقهاء الريف عقد نكاح) فقال للوليّ قل أنكحتُكَ بنتي خطيطه البيضاة اللون الشقراة الشعرالّي عينها اليمين حولا وعينها الشمال بلا حَوَل بشرط أن تكون في طاعتك وتقيّد لدارها وتلزّق الجلّه فيها وتفرش فرشها وتسرج فتيلتها ثمّ قال للخاطب قول قبلت شكاحها ونكاحها وهراشها وفراشها ٢،٤

(وكان شيخنا العلّامة الشيخ شهاب الدين القليوبيّ رحمه الله تعالى) يقول زرنا سنة من السنين سيّدي أحمد البدويّ نفعنا الله به فلمّا رجعنا من الزيارة أدركنا المبيت في قرية من قرى الريف فدخلنا مسجدها فرأيناه حكم زريبة البقر فيه آثار الجلّة والوحل ومفروش بيسير من الحشيش وجانب منه خال فيه بعض عجول وبقر مربطة فجلسنا في الجانب المسقوف منه بعيد عن العجول نتذاكر العلم فدخل علينا جماعة من الفلّاحين ومعهم رجل طويل القامة غليظ الساقين محزّم على بِشْت صوف من غير قميص حافي من غير مركوب وعلى رأسه عمامة كبيرة عليها الدناسة ظاهرة فقال لنا ما تكونوا فقلنا فقهاء من الجامع الأزهر فقال لنا تقروا في القرآن قلنا نعم فقال أسألكم سؤال قُدّام شيوخ بلدي إن قلتولي عليه ورديتم جوابي عشّيتكم وبيّتّكم وإن ما عرفتم الجواب طردتكم من البلد فإنّي فقيه البلد وخطيبها وما عمر حدّ غلبني ولا عرف سؤالي ٣،٤

An Account of Their Pastors and of the Compounded Ignorance, Imbecility, and Injuries to Religion and the Like of Which They Are Guilty

A country pastor was asked concerning the words of the Almighty «*wa-qīla* 4.1
yā arḍu blaʿī māʾaki wa-yā samāʾu qlaʿī» («And it was said, "O earth, swallow thy water and O sky, be cleared of clouds!"»),[146] "What is the meaning of *iqlaʿī* ('be cleared')?" and the ignoramus replied, "It means, 'Proceed like ships with sails (*muqallaʿah*)'"![147]

4.2 And a country pastor was executing a contract of marriage and told the bride's proxy, "Say, 'I give you in marriage my daughter Khuṭayṭah of the fair complexion and the blond hair, whose right eye squints and whose left eye is squintless, with the undertaking that she obey you, be confined to your house, make its dung cakes, spread its furnishings, and light its lamp!'" Then he told the fiancé, "Say, 'I agree to bugger her, fuck her, fondle her, and bed her'!"[148]

4.3 And our shaykh, the learned Shihāb al-Dīn al-Qalyūbī, may the Almighty benefit us through him, said, "One year we went to visit Our Master Aḥmad al-Badawī,[149] God benefit us through him. As we were returning from the visit, night overtook us in a village of the countryside, so we entered its mosque. This we found to resemble a cattle byre, with traces of dung and mud, green plants spread on the floor, one part open to the sky, and a few calves and cows tied up in a corner. We had sat ourselves under the roofed part, at some distance from the calves, to discuss scholarly matters, when in came a group of peasants, one of whom was a man tall of stature, thick of leg, wearing a belt over a woolen wrap, with no shirt and no shoes on his feet, and on his head a huge turban of patent filthiness. 'What are you?' he asked us, and we replied, 'Jurisprudents from the mosque of al-Azhar.' 'Do you know the Qur'an?' he asked. 'Indeed,' we replied. Then he said, 'I'm going to ask you a question in front of the shaykhs of my village. If you give me the right answer, I'll give you supper and a place to sleep, but if you don't answer me right, I'll throw you out of the village, for I'm *its* jurisprudent and its preacher, and no one has ever gotten the better of me or known the answer to my question!' We laughed and said, 'Ask away!' So he said, 'Jurisprudents of al-Azhar! How many elements are there

قال فضحكنا عليه وقلنا له اسأل ما بدا لك فقال يا فقهاء الأزهر الصلاة لها كام عنصر وفين عنصرها الأوّلاني وعنصرها الأخراني قال الشيخ عفا الله عنه فقال رجل من أتباعنا الصلاة لها تلتماية وستّين عنصر الأوّلاني من عناصرها رجليك والتاني ايديك والتالت طيزك والأخراني دقنك قال فسكت واحتار في أمره فقالوا له أهل بلده غلبوك مشايخ الأزهر يابو حنجول فقال لهم طول عمري أسأل الفقها وغيرهم السؤال ده ما شفت حدّ جاوبني عنه إلّا دولي وأنا أقل لكم يا شيوخ البلد الحقّ أنّهم غلبوني قال الشيخ سامحه الله ثمّ إنّه توجّه إلى منزله وأحضر لنا متردين لبن بدشيش وخبز ذرة فأكلنا ونمنا مكاننا إلى أن أصبح الصباح فحضر إلينا ورحّب بنا وأخذنا خاطره وتوجّهنا والحال أنّنا لم نعرف معنى السؤال ولا الجواب ولا عرفنا هذا الكلام غير أن تابعنا لشدّة حِذْقه أجابه من معنى سؤاله وأعطاه كلام قصاد كلام

٤،٤ (وسأل بعض الفلّاحين أخينا في الله تعالى الشيخ عبد العزيز الدُنْجَيْهي) رحمه الله تعالى فقال له فين هي قبلة طيزك فقال له دقنك فخجل الفلّاح وضحك عليه الحاضرون

٥،٤ (قلت ونظير ذلك ما حكاه شيخنا أنّ ممّا اتّفق في بعض السنين أنّه حضر رجل من العجم لمصر المحروسة) واجتمع بوزيرها وأخبره أنّه من علماء العجم ولا أحد يقاومه في العلم ودخل على عقل الوزير بالكلام وغيره حتّى مال إليه وصار عنده في منزلة عظيمة فقال له الوزير هل فيك قوّة لمناظرة علماء الجامع الأزهر فقال نعم أسألهم بحضرتك سؤال فإن أجابوني فأنا من تحت أمرهم وإلّا يصير لي الفَخار عليهم قال فأرسل الوزير إلى علماء الأزهر نصرهم الله وجعلهم أئمّة المسلمين إلى يوم الدين فلمّا حضروا بين يديه وغَصّ المجلس بأهله أعرض عليهم الأمر فقالوا يسأل العجميّ ما بدا له فقام العجميّ بين أيديهم وسألهم بالإشارة من غير كلام يتلفّظ به فقالوا له يا وزير الإشارة لا تكون إلّا للأخرس ولا نعرف مقصوده فقال لهم لا بدّ أن تجيبوه

in the prayer, and what are its first and its last elements?'" The Shaykh, God excuse him, continued, "One of our party answered him, 'The prayer has three hundred and sixty elements. The first is your feet, the second is your hands, the third is your bum, and the last is your beard.' At this the man fell silent, at a loss for words, and the villagers said to him, 'The shaykhs of al-Azhar have got you, Abū Ḥanjūl!' He replied, 'All my life I've asked jurisprudents and others this question, but I never heard anyone answer it but these. I tell you, shaykhs of the village, they've got me, and that's a fact!'" The Shaykh, may God forgive him, went on, "Then he went home and had two crocks of milk with husked fava beans and maize bread brought to us, and we ate and slept where we were till morning, when he came to us and made us welcome and we took our leave and departed. But the fact is that we didn't know the meaning of either the question or the answer and had no idea what he was talking about. Our companion was just so quick-witted that he was able to answer his question in the same coin and give him empty words for empty words."

And a peasant asked our brother in God Almighty Shaykh ʿAbd al-ʿAzīz al-Dunjayhī, may the Almighty have mercy on him, "What is the point with which you should align your bum when praying?" He told him, "Your beard." The peasant was abashed, and those present mocked him. 4.4

The Tale of the Persian Scholar

A similar story, I might add, is that told by our shaykh of how one year a Persian came to Divinely Protected Cairo and obtained an audience with its vizier, telling him that he was a Persian scholar whose knowledge of religion no one could rival. With talk of this sort, and other things, he wormed his way into the vizier's confidence, until the latter came to hold him in the highest esteem. One day the vizier asked him, "Are you strong enough to debate with the scholars of al-Azhar?" "Indeed I am!" he replied. "I will put a question to them in your presence. If they answer correctly, I shall be theirs to command. If not, it will be I who lords it over them!" So the vizier sent for the scholars of al-Azhar—God send them victorious and let them lead the Muslims unto the Day of Judgment!—and, when they presented themselves before him and the vizier's salon had filled with his cronies, he explained the situation to them. "Let the Persian ask whatever he likes," they said. Then the Persian rose and stood before them and asked them a question in sign language, without uttering a word. "Vizier," replied the Azharis, "sign language is for the dumb. We have no idea what he 4.5

على سؤاله وألزمهم بذلك لميله للعجميّ ومحبّته له فقالوا له أمهلنا ثلاثة أيّام حتّى ننظر بقيّة مشايخنا فأمهلهم الوزير

فتوجّهوا العلماء حفظهم الله من عنده فقالوا لبعضهم كيف الرأي في دفع هذا العجميّ وردّه إلى بلاده مقهوراً فقال رجل منهم الرأي عندي أنّا ننظر لنا رجلاً من أجلاف الريف وقحوفهم لا يعرف السماء من الأرض ولا الطول من العرض ونجعله شيخنا ونلبسه لبس العلماء ونمشي خلفه ونطلع به إلى الوزير ونقول له هذا شيخنا وهو الذي يجيب العجميّ ونعامله بما يناسب مقامه ونسلّط الكلب على الخنزير قال فذهب هو وجماعة منهم يفتّشوا على هذه الصفة فرأوا رجلاً من أجلاف الريف طويل القامة عريض القفا غليظ الساقين كبير اللحية على رأسه قحف طويل وجبّة من الصوف لركبته وهو جالس في حانوت يأكل بيض مصلوق فدخلوا عليه وكان قد فضل معه بيضة واحدة فلمّا رآهم ظن أنّهم يريدوا أخذ البيضة منه فأخذها ووضعها في قحفه من داخله وأراد الهروب منهم فقبضوا عليه فقال لهم أنا في جيرتك يا شعرا فقالوا له لا تخف يا فلّاح ولا تخش من شيء فقال أنا خايف تخدوني لاستادي يقطع راسي وانا عمري ما طلعت مصر غير السنه دي واناكنت جيعان فضل معايه اربع بيضات شويتهم أكلت تلاته وفضلت معايه واحده فخفت منكم وشلتها في قحفي وانا مكسور عليّ مال السلطان قرشين فقالوا له إحنا مرادنا نفعل معك خير وإن طاوعتنا أعطيناك القرشين وغدّيناك وبسطناك فقال لهم وانا الآخر إن كان معكم فحت بير أو هدم حيط أو شيل طين أو جلّه عملته لكم في ساعه واحده وان كنتم رايحين في عركه هاتوا لي نَبُّوت وانا اضرب لكم القوم ولوكانوا ألف راجل أبطحهم فقالوا له ما مرادنا ذلك وما مرادنا إلّا نعملك شيخنا ونطلع بك لواحد عجميّ يسألك سؤال تجيبه عنه وتغلبه ولكن هذا العجميّ يتكلّم بالإشارة فتكلّمه مثل ما يكلّمك فقال لهم خدوني للمعرّص ده وان طلبتم ضربه ضربته بلكّاميّتي قتلته ولو ٦.٤

means." But the vizier told them, "Answer his question you must!" and he gave them no choice in the matter because of his partiality for and affection towards the Persian. So the scholars said to him, "Give us three days' grace in which to consult the rest of our shaykhs!" and the vizier granted them this reprieve.

Once the scholars, God preserve them, had left his presence, they asked each other, "How can we drive this Persian away and send him back to his country with his tail between his legs?" "In my opinion," said one of them, "we should find ourselves some clod or bumpkin from the countryside who can't tell ground from sky or short from high and make him our shaykh and dress him as an scholar and, walking behind him, go to the vizier and tell him, 'This is our shaykh, and he's the one who will answer the Persian.' That way we can deal with him as he deserves and sic the dog on the pig!" So he and a group of them went searching for someone of this description and came across a country bumpkin, tall of stature, broad of nape, thick of thigh, and large of beard. He was wearing a tall peasant hat and a woolen coat that came down to his knees, and he was sitting in a shop eating boiled eggs. When they went up to him, he had one egg left and, supposing when he saw them that they wanted to take it from him, he took it and put it inside his cap and tried to run. When they caught him, he said, "I throw myself on your protection, bards!"[150] but they told him, "Fear nothing, peasant!" He replied, "I fear you'll take me to my master and he'll chop off my head. I've never been to Cairo before this year, and I was hungry and I had four eggs left, so I roasted them and I've eaten three and there's one left, but I was afraid of you so I hid it in my cap, and I'm a couple of piasters behind on the sultan's taxes." "We'd like to do you a good turn," they told him. "If you do as we say, we'll give you the piasters, plus we'll give you lunch and show you a good time." Said the peasant, "And me, if you have a well to dig, a wall to knock down, or mud and dung to haul around, I'll have it done for you in an hour! And if you're on your way to a dustup, get me a quarter staff and I'll thrash their men for you. Be they a thousand, I'll smash them to pieces!" "Such is not our desire," they said. "All we want is to make you our shaykh and take you with us to meet a certain Persian, who will ask you a question. You must answer his question and get the better of him, but this Persian speaks in sign language, and you must speak to him in the same." "Just take me to that pimp," said the peasant, "and if you want, I'll give him a punch that'll kill him, be he in the presence of the sultan or the vizier! 4.6

كان حدا السلطان أو الوزير وانا ياما قتلت وياما سرقت وانا عليّ مال السلطان وعليّ إنّي اردّ العجميّ ده مغلوب

٧،٤ قال فأخذوه وألبسوه لبس الفقهاء وعمّموه على قحفه عمامة مدوّرة وحطّ البيضة من داخل عُبّه فقالوا له خلّيها هنا لمّا ترجع فقال لهم وحياتكم لم اخلّيها لانّها بيضة فرختي واوّل بيضها ولمّا اجوع آكلها فقالوا له خلّيها معك ومضوا به على حالهم حتّى أقبلوا به على الوزير والعجميّ بين يديه جالس فقام إليهم وأعظم منزلتهم فقالوا له هذا شيخنا وهو الذي يجيب العجميّ على سؤاله قال فجلس العجميّ متأدّبًا جلوس طلبة العلم وجلس الفلاّح ومدّ رجليه ولم يعتبر بالمجلس كأنّه في زريبة بقر فلمّا رآه العجميّ على هذه الحالة استعظمه وقال في نفسه لولا أنّه من العلماء الأجلاّء ما احتقر هذا المجلس ومدّ رجليه بحضرة الوزير ثمّ إنّ العجميّ أشار إليه بالسؤال يريد منه الجواب وأقام له إصبعاً من أصابعه قال فأقام الفلاّح له اصبعين اثنين قال ثمّ إنّ العجميّ رفع يده إلى السماء قال فوضع الفلاّح يديه على الأرض قال ثمّ إنّ العجميّ أخرج من جانبه علبة وفتحها وأخرج منها فرّوجاً صغيرًا وأرماه إلى الفلاّح قال فتذكر الفلاّح البيضة التي في قحفه فأخذها من رأسه وألقاها إلى العجميّ قال فعند ذلك هزّ العجميّ رأسه وتعجّب منه وقال للوزير ولبقيّة العلماء قد أجابني عن سؤالي الذي أشرت له به وأشهدكم أنّي صرت من بعض تلامذته وأتباعه قال ثمّ إنّ الوزير أكرم الفلاّح والعلماء وانصرفوا مؤيَّدين منصورين

٨،٤ ثمّ إنّهم قالوا للفلاّح بعد انصرافهم نحن ما عرفنا حقيقة السؤال ولا الجواب فأخبرنا عنه فقال لهم الفلاّح يا خساره عليكم انتم فقها ولكن ما تعرفوا شي تردّوا للناس جواباتهم أنا لمّا قعدت قبال وجهه رايت عينيه عينين خاين وهم حمر وهو في غضب وشاورلي بصباعه يقول لي اصحى لنفسك والاّ خرقت عينك بصباعي ده فأشرت إليه أنا لآخر وقلت له إن خرقت عيني بصباعك أخرق عينيك الاثنين بصباعيني دول وأقتهم في وجهه ثمّ إنّه شال ايده في السقف يشير لي اني إذ لم

How often I've murdered and how often I've robbed! I've got to pay my taxes, and I've got to send this Persian away in defeat!"

So they took him and dressed him as a jurisprudent and tied a round turban around his cap. The peasant put his egg inside the breast of his robe, and when they said, "Leave it here until you come back," he told them, "By your lives, I never will not, for it's from my own hen and it's the first she laid, and when I get hungry, I'm going to eat it!" So they said, "Keep it with you," and they proceeded with him as they were till they came to the vizier, where they found the Persian seated before him. The vizier rose to greet them and treated them with the utmost respect, and they told him, "This is our shaykh, and he will answer the Persian concerning his question." The Persian was seated politely, in the posture of a student seeking knowledge, and the peasant sat down and stretched his legs out in front of him, paying no heed to those present, just as though he were sitting in a cow pen. When the Persian saw him behave thus, he was greatly impressed and said to himself, "Were he not a most illustrious scholar, he would not dare to treat the assembly with contempt and stretch his legs out in front of the vizier!" Then the Persian signaled to him the question he wanted answered by holding up to the peasant one of his fingers. In return, the peasant held up to him two of his. Then the Persian raised his hand towards the sky, at which the peasant placed his on the ground. Next, the Persian pulled a box from the front of his robe and, opening it, extracted a small chick, which he tossed at the peasant. At this, the peasant remembered the egg that was in his cap and took it out and threw it at the Persian. This made the Persian shake his head in wonder at him and he said to the vizier and to the other scholars, "He has answered the question that I expressed in signs, and, as you are my witnesses, henceforth I number myself among his students and followers!" The vizier showered gifts upon the peasant and the scholars, and they departed, vindicated and victorious. 4.7

After they left, the scholars said to the peasant, "We didn't understand the meaning of either the question or the answer, so enlighten us!" The peasant said, "What washouts! You're called jurisprudents, but you can't answer people's questions! Me, when I sat across from him, I saw that he had the red eyes of a villain and was in a fury, and he wagged his finger at me as though to say, 'Watch it, or I'll poke out your eye with this finger of mine!' So I signaled back to him, 'If you poke out my eye with your finger, I'll poke out both of yours with these two fingers of mine!' and I shoved them in his face. Then he raised 4.8

أطيع والّا صلبني في السقف فوضعت أنا الآخر ايدي على الأرض أشير إليه إن ردت تفعل معي ما بتقول خبطتك في الأرض خبطه طلّعت عفاريتك فلمّا رآني غالبه وظافر عليه أخرج فرّوج دجاج صغير يورّيني أنّه كلّ يوم ياكل فراخ وانّه متنعّم في الاكل والشرب فأخرجت له أنا الآخر البيضه المصلوقه أورّيه أنّي متنعّم في اكل البيضه المصلوقه فغلبته وردّيت سؤاله قال

٩،٤ فلمّا سمعوا كلام الفلاّح وعرفوه قاموا وتوجّه إلى العجميّ واجتمعوا به وسألوه عن الجواب فقال لهم طول عمري أسأل العلماء هذا السؤال وأناظرهم به فما عرفه حدّ إلّا شيخكم هذا فقالوا له أخبرنا عن السؤال وعن حقيقته فقال لهم أقمت له إصبعي أشير له أن الله واحد فأقام لي الأصبعين يشير لي بما أنه ليس له ثاني فرفعت له يدي إلى فوق أشير إليه أنّه رفع السماء بغير عمد فوضع يده إلى الأرض يعني وبسط الأرض على ماء جمد فأخرجت له الفروج أشير له أنه يُخْرِج الحيّ من الميت فأخرج إليّ البيضة يعني ويخرج الميت من الحيّ فأجابني جواباً شافياً فما رأيت أعلم منه فعرفوا أن الفلاّح كان في مقصد والعجميّ في مقصد آخر على حدّ قول القائل [كامل]

صارَتْ مُشرِّقةً وصِرتُ مُغرِّباً　　شَتّانَ بَيْنَ مُشَرِّقٍ وَمُغَرِّبِ

فالإشارات مصادفة والمقاصد مختلفة (كما اتّفق) أنّ رجلاً مسك لحيته فضرط حماره فقال صادفت النكتة

١٠،٤ (وخطب فقيه من فقهاء الريف) فقال أيّها الناس أراكم تلتهوا في الحصيدة وفي الزرع والقلع وغدا يجيكم اللموم * وتحضر لكم القوم * فاستعدّوا لقتالهم بالمزاريق * فما لكم عند الله عذر ولا تعويق * واعلموا يا اهل بلدنا الّي وراه عدوّ * ما وراه

his hand towards the roof as if to tell me that if I didn't obey him, he'd pin me spread-eagled to the ceiling. So I put my hand on the ground to tell him, 'Just try, and I'll knock you down so hard you'll lose your marbles!' When he saw that I'd got the better of him and was the winner, he pulled out a little chick to show me that he eats chicken every day and that he's living the high life as far as food and drink go, so I pulled the boiled egg out to show him that I was living the high life and eating boiled eggs. Thus I beat him and answered his question."

When they had heard the peasant's account and understood it, the scholars took themselves off to the Persian and asked him about the answer. He told them, "All my life I've been asking scholars this question and putting them to the test, but no one has known the answer until that shaykh of yours." So they said to him, "Tell us about the question and what the answer should really be." "First," he said, "I held up to him one finger to signal that I was saying 'God is one,' and he pointed at me with two fingers to signal 'He has no second.' So I raised my hand, to signal to him that 'He raised the sky without supports,'[151] and he lowered his hand to tell me 'and He spread out the Earth on water that had become firm.'[152] Then I pulled out the chick for him, to signal to him that 'He produces the living from the dead,'[153] and he pulled out the egg for me, to signal 'and He produces the dead from the living.' Thus he gave me an unequivocal answer to my question, and never have I come across anyone more learned than he!" At this they realized that the peasant had had one thing in mind and the Persian another, after the manner of the poet who says: 4.9

She went east and I went west
And how great the gap 'tween eastbound and westbound!

—for the gestures were only coincidentally convergent, while the intentions were divergent, like the man whose donkey farted when he grasped his beard: said he, "She caught the joke on the wing!"

Sermons by Country Pastors

And a country pastor gave a sermon and said, "Good people! I see you disporting yourselves in harvesting, sowing, and reaping. Any day now the war bands will descend and the enemy attend, so make ready your lances for the fray, for you have no excuse before God and no call for delay! Know, good people of 4.10

هدوّ * قوّاكم الله يا جيش جُدام * على جيش حَرام * فأنتم تحترصوا أن يجيكم العدوّ من جنب النُقره * فصلّوا كلكم واطلبوا من الله النُصره * وقولوا يا حنّان يا منّان * انصر شيخ البلد عمران * قولوا آمين فقالوا آمين ثمّ نزل وصلّى بهم صلاة معزاويّة لا فرض ولا نيّة

١١،٤ (وخطب آخر) فلمّا صعد المنبر قال اعلموا يا اهل بلدنا انّ عندكم قمح كتير * وتبن وشعير * وانتم بخير من ربّ العالمين فانتم تفيقوا لزرع الوسيّه * والّا صبحكم الكاشف بداهيه وبليّه * وغداً تسرحوا للعونه والسَخَر * وفيقوا للغنم والبَقَر * وافحتوا ابياركم * وقيموا دولابكم * وأكرموا الخُطّار * بالعدس والبيسار * تنجوا من عذاب النار * قال الله تعالى الذي في سماه احتجب * عَلَيْش يا حبايب تهجرونا بلا سبب * الله الله قولوا لا إله إلّا الله من وحّد الله لا خيّبه الله آمين والحمد لله ربّ العالمين ثمّ نزل وصلّى بهم

١٢،٤ (وخطب آخر) فلمّا شرع في الخطبة أقاموا الفلّاحين الشياط والعياط في حساب المال والزرع والقلع فقال شخص منهم يا جماعه اسمعوا للخطيب وعِدّنُه كلب بينبح

١٣،٤ (وواعد فقيه ريف جماعة على أنّه يسرق هو وإيّاهم فول أخضر من الغيط) فذهبوا معه ليلاً حتّى أتوا إلى غيط رجل من القرية وأخذ كلّ واحد منهم عُمُر كبير من الفول وأخذ الفقيه عمرين قال فلمّا أصبح الصباح وقربت الصلاة وكان يوم الجمعة طلع هذا الفقي يخطب فلمّا انتهى إلى الوعظ قال أيّها الناس فقالوا له أصحابه في السرقة ما للناس كلّ واحد خد عمر وانت خدت عمرين

١٤،٤ (وسأل فقيه ريف بعض العلماء) وقال له مرادي أقرأ الجُرُوميّة على مذهب الإمام الشافعيّ فضحك عليه من جهله وطرده

our village, that he behind whom lies a foe, no peace of mind can know! God strengthen you, army of Judām, against the army of Ḥarām! Beware lest you find the enemy from next the hole[154] attacking, and all of you pray and fast and ask for God's backing! Say, 'O Loving, O Benign, with the shaykh of our village, 'Imrān, Yourself align!' Say, 'Amen'!" So they said, "Amen," and then he came down from the pulpit and performed with them a goatish prayer, which, unprescribed and unpurposed, [155] was neither here nor there.

And another preached a sermon and, after mounting the pulpit, said, 4.11
"Know, good people of our village, that you have much wheat and straw, and barley galore, and are blessed by the Lord of the Worlds! So look you to the sowing of the tax farmer's estate, or you'll awake to find the Inspector's visited on you a horrible fate! Tomorrow you'll set off on the corvée, and the flocks and cattle you must oversee. You must dig your wells, set up your waterwheels, and provide generously for wayfarers with lentils and *bīsār*, thus escaping the agony of the Fire! Says the Almighty, hidden away up in His Heaven, 'Wherefore, best beloveds, do you fly from us without reason?'[156] O God! O God! Say, 'There is no god but God!' Who confesses His Oneness, God will not let down! Amen and praise be to God, Lord of the Worlds!" Then he descended and prayed with them.

And another preached a sermon, but as soon as he started to preach, the 4.12
peasants broke out into a clamor and a hullabaloo about computing the tax and the sowing and reaping. One of them said, "Everyone, listen to the preacher and treat him as you would a barking dog!"[157]

And a country pastor arranged with some people to go with them to steal 4.13
green fava beans from the field, so they went with him at night till they came to the field of a man from the village and everyone took a large armful of beans, except for the pastor, who took two. The next morning, a Friday, as it grew close to the prayer time, the pastor went up to preach. As he reached the homily and pronounced, "Good people!" his companions in theft said, "What have you to tell the people? Each of us took one armful but you took two!"

Further Anecdotes Showing the Ignorance of Country Pastors

And a country pastor asked a question of a scholar, saying to him, "It is my 4.14
wish to read the Jurrūmiyyah[158] according to the school of the Imam al-Shāfi'ī." The man mocked him for his ignorance and threw him out.

(ودخل على العلاّمة الحُمَيديّ رحمه الله تعالى رجل من فقهاء الريف) وقال له عندك مختصر القرآن وكان الحميديّ شيخ الصحّافين بمصر فقال الشيخ رحمه الله نعم اجلس حتّى أنظره لك فجلس عنده وإذا برجل أقبل على الشيخ وقال له عندك يا سيّدي مختصر مسلم فقال له نعم خذ تعريص هذا فإنّه مختصر مسلم لا كلام وطرده من عنده فتعجّب الحاضرون منه غاية العجب ثمّ إنّهم سألوا فقيه الريف عن حاله فقال لهم أنا رجل اقرّي الأولاد في بلدي القرآن وقد ثقل عليهم لطوله فقلت لعل أحداً اختصره فيكون سهل على الأولاد ويحفظوه بالسرعه فضحك عليه الحاضرون ومضى إلى حال سبيله ١٥،٤

(وسعى رجل من الأكابر عند قاضي القضاة بمصر المحروسة ليأخذ لرجل فقيه نيابة في بعض المحاكم) ومدحه عنده فقال ائتني به فلمّا حضر بين يديه قال له القاضي هل تحفظ القرآن قال نعم أيّد الله مولانا القاضي وعندي مصحف مليح بخط المؤلّف قال فتحقّق القاضي جهله وضحك عليه وطرده فمضى إلى حال سبيله ١٦،٤

(ودخل بعض الفقهاء الجهّال على أبي حنيفة النعمان رضي الله عنه) ورجل الإمام ممدودة لوجع أصابها فلمّا رآه الإمام في هيئة حسنة وثياب فاخرة لمّ رجله وكان الإمام يقرّر في مسألة صلاة الصبح ما حكمها إذا طلعت الشمس ونحو ذلك فقال له هذا الجاهل إذا طلعت الشمس قبل الفجر ما حكم الصلاة فقال الإمام آن لأبي حنيفة أن يمدّ رجله ثمّ مدّها في وجهه ومضى على درسه ولم يلتفت إليه ١٧،٤

(واتّفق أنّ اثنين اختصما في آية من كتاب الله تعالى) فقال أحدهما لعلّهم يتفكّرون وقال الآخر لعلّهم يشكرون فبينما هم في المشاجرة إذ طلع عليهم فقيه من فقهاء الريف فسألوه لاعتقادهم أنّه يحفظ القرآن هل يتفكّرون أو يشكرون فقال الأَوّلى أنّنا نأخذ ١٨،٤

And a country pastor visited the learned scholar al-Ḥumaydī, may the Almighty have mercy on him, and asked him, "Do you have an abridged Qur'an?" Shaykh al-Ḥumaydī was Shaykh of the Book Traders in Cairo. The shaykh, God have mercy on him, told him, "Certainly. Sit down while I find it for you." So he sat down. Then another man came to the shaykh and said to him, "Sir, do you have an abridged Muslim?"[159] "Indeed I do," said the shaykh: "Take this wretch, for he's an abridged Muslim, no two ways about it!" and he threw the pastor out. Those present were utterly amazed and asked the pastor about himself and he told them, "I am one who teaches the children in my village to read the Qur'an, but they find it boring because it's so long, so I thought maybe someone had abridged it, which would be easier for the children and allow them to memorize it quickly." Those present mocked him and he went his way. 4.15

And a certain grandee exerted his influence with the chief judge in Divinely Protected Cairo to get a post for a pastor as a deputy judge in one of the courts, singing the man's praises. The judge said, "Send him to me." When the man was before him, the judge asked, "Have you memorized the Qur'an?" and the man replied, "Yes indeed, God aid Your Worship, and I've got a lovely copy in the author's own handwriting!" The judge saw how ignorant he was and mocked him and threw him out, and he went his way. 4.16

And an ignorant country pastor paid a visit to Abū Ḥanīfah al-Nuʿmān, may God be pleased with him, at a moment when the imam had his leg stretched out in front of him because of some pain he was suffering from. When the imam saw that the man was of dignified appearance and dressed in fine clothes, he drew in his leg. At the time, the imam happened to be giving instruction on the question of the morning prayer and what rule applied should the sun rise during the prayer and so on.[160] The ignoramus asked him, "What's the rule for the prayer if the sun rises before dawn?" Said the imam, "It seems it's time for Abū Ḥanīfah to stretch out his leg again!" and he did so in the man's face and went on with his teaching and paid him no further attention. 4.17

And it happened that two men differed over a verse of God's Word, one saying *laʿallahum yatafakkarūn* ("perhaps they will bethink themselves"), the other *laʿallahum yashkurūn* ("perhaps they will be grateful").[161] While they were arguing, a country pastor appeared, and, believing him to have memorized the Qur'an, they asked him, "Is it *yatafakkarūn or yashkurūn*?" That ignoramus told them, "The best thing to do is for us to take a little from 4.18

من كلّ كلمة جانباً ونجعلها لكما لعلّهم يتفشكرون ونبطّل المشاجرة بينكما فقالا قاتل الله الأبعد كفر وغيّر كلام الله

١٩،٤ (ودخل رجل من العلماء قرية من قرى الريف) فرأى رجلاً يدرّس في مسجدها ويخبط خبط عشواء وسمعه يروي حديثاً باطلاً فقال له رأيت هذا الحديث في أيّ كتاب فقال له في كتاب عندي يسمّى الدَلْهَمة والبطّال فقال له أضعفت حين أسندت ثمّ قام عليه وأبطله الدرس ومضى إلى سبيله

٢٠،٤ (وحكى بعض العلماء) قال دخلت قرية من قرى الريف وقت المساء فقلت في نفسي أسأل على فقيه البلد وأنام عنده قال فسألت عنه قال فقالوا لي انضره على كوم عالي وسط البلد مات له حمار وهو يطرد الكلاب عنه لأجل ما يسلخ جلده ويبيعه قال فتوجّهت إليه فرأيته على الكوم وبيده حجارة يضرب بها الكلاب ويمنعهم عن حمار ميّت حكم ما ذكروا وهو في حالة رذلة وثياب دنسة حافي القدم تعيس الناصية فسلّمت عليه فردّ عليّ السلام بتكلّف وهو مشغول بما هو فيه وهو يقول إخصا جرّ روح يا ميشوم ويضرب بالحجارة الكلاب وهو في كرب كأنّه يعارك القوم قال فجلست ساعة أنظر في حاله وإذا برجل أقبل عليه من أهالي قريته وقال له يا فقيه أنا قلت لامراتي أنت طالق ثلاثاً وسألت فما حد ردّها لي وقالوا لي ما عادت تحلّ لك حتّى ينكحها واحد غيرك وانا خاطري تردّها لي وتخلّصني وخد لك كيلة شعير قال فالتفت إليه وقال له إن كان مرادك أخلّصك من اليمين ما آخد إلّا كيلتين شعير فقال له أعطيك ما تطلب فقال له خد امراتك وقت السحر وروح بها بِرْكَة الماء اللّي في المحلّ الفلاني وخلّيها تشلح ثيابها وتخوض في البركه حتّى يبلغ الماء سُرّتها ولا تخلّيها تضمّ رجليها حتّى يدخل الماء فرجها وينكحها فإنّ الماء مَلَك والملك ذكر وصدق عليه أنه نكحها قال الله تعالى وخلق من الماء بشرًا سويًّا قال فلمّا سمعت ما قاله لهذا الرجل أخذتني الغيرة في دين الله تعالى وقمت عليه بالسبّ واللعن وقلت له قاتل الله الأبعد

each word and make it *yatafashkarūn*[162] and put an end to your quarreling." "God strike you dead!" they said to him. "He has blasphemed, and changed the word of God!"

And one of the scholars entered a country village and found a man teaching in its mosque and spouting any nonsense that came into his head. Hearing him transmit a false Tradition, he asked him, "In what book did you find that?" The man replied, "In a book I have at home called *Al-Dalhamah and the Worthless One*."[163] The scholar said, "Your authority adds nothing to its credibility!"[164] Then he set upon him, put an end to his lesson, and went his way. **4.19**

And a certain scholar recounted the following story: "I entered one of the villages of the countryside as evening was falling, thinking to myself, 'I'll ask for the pastor of the place and sleep at his house.' So I asked after him and they told me, 'Look for him on the high mound in the middle of the village. A donkey of his has died and he's keeping the dogs off so that he can strip the skin and sell it.' I made my way there and found him on the mound with a handful of stones, pelting the dogs to keep them off a dead donkey, just as they had told me. He was in a disgusting state, with filthy clothes, bare feet, and wretched mien. I greeted him, and he returned the greeting haughtily, all the while busy with what he was doing and saying, 'Shame on you! Shoo! Away, wretched animal!' and pelting the dogs with the stones, as worked up as though he were doing battle with an enemy band. I had been sitting observing him for a while when a man from his village came up to him and said to him, 'Pastor, I told my wife, "You're divorced, thrice over!"[165] and then I asked around but no one would undo the divorce; they said, "She cannot be your legitimate spouse again until someone else has had intercourse with her." I want you to undo the divorce and release me from my oath, and you can have a bushel of barley for your pains!' The pastor turned to him and said, 'If you want me to release you from your oath, I won't take less than two bushels!' 'I will give you what you ask,' said the man. So the pastor said, 'Take your wife at daybreak and go with her to the pool of water at such and such a place. Have her take off her clothes and wade into the water till it reaches her navel but don't let her close her legs, so that the water can enter her vagina, and have intercourse with her, for water is an angel and an angel is a male and we can say in all truth that he has had intercourse with her. The Almighty has said, "And He hath created a man without fault from water."'[166] When I heard what he was saying to the man, I was filled with zeal for the religion of **4.20**

وعلمه وقريته ونهيت السائل عن هذه الفعلة وقلت له وقع عليك الطلاق الثلاث ولا يجوز لك أن تفعل بما قال لك هذا الجاهل الخبيث وحلفت أنّي لا أقعد في هذه القرية ولا أبات فيها لأجل هذا اللئيم ثمّ مضيت إلى قرية أخرى ونمت بمسجدها إلى أن طلع النهار وتوجّهت إلى حال سبيلي

٢١،٤ (وقال بعض فقهاء الريف لتلامذته) قد ظهر لي في القرآن بحث وهو قوله تعالى (وَقِيلَ يَا أَرْضُ ابْلَعِي مَاءَكِ) أنّه وجه ضعيف لأنّه محكيّ بِقيل

٢٢،٤ (ودخل بعض العلماء قرية من قرى البحر بنواحي الجبل) فرأى محلاً يشبه المسجد وفيه البقر والغنم وقد اشتدّ به الجوع فجلس يقرأ في سورة الكهف فاجتمع عليه جماعة من تلك القرية يسمعوا قراءته إلى أن وصل إلى قوله تعالى ﴿سَيَقُولُونَ ثَلَاثَةٌ رَّابِعُهُمْ كَلْبُهُمْ﴾ فقالوا له يا شيخ نجست القرآن كلام الله ما فيه كلاب وانت تجعل فيه كلاب اخرج من بلدنا والّا قتلناك قال فقام رجل منهم وقال لا تضربوه ولا تقتلوه حتّى نرسل لفقي بلدنا الحاجّ مخالف الله ونسأله فإن قال لنا إنّ القرآن فيه كلاب تركناه والّا قتلناه قال فأرسلوا خلف هذا الرجل فحضر شخص كأنّه سارية الجبل من طوله أو عمود الصواري من غلظه وثقل ذاته ورؤيته تقشعرّ منها الجلود وهو ملفّع بحرام أبيض دنس لا غير فلمّا حضر وجلس أخبروه بالقضيّة فنظر يميناً وشمالاً وقال لهم اصبروا حتّى أبيّن لكم الأمر وأكشف لكم الحال ثمّ إنّه انضجع على قفاه وقال لهم اطرحوا عليّ الحرام فطرحوه عليه فسكت ساعة على هذه الحالة لا يتحرّك ثمّ إنّه قام بسرعة عريان مكشوف الرأس والعورة ووقف ساعة بهذه الحالة ينظر نحو السماء وهو في وجد وكرب ثمّ ادّعى بحرامه فالتفّ فيه وجلس وقال لهم طلعت العشر سماوات الّي خلقها الله فرايت أوّل سما فيها بقر وتاني سما فيها جاموس وتالت سما فيها عجول ورابع سما فيها تيران وخامس سما كذا وسادس سما كذا وصار يعدّ أصناف حيوانات إلى أن

Almighty God and set upon him with abuse and curses and told him, 'God destroy you, your learning, and your village!' and I forbade the questioner to do what the man had said, telling him, 'You are in a state of binding divorce, and you are not permitted to do what this vile ignoramus has told you!' and I swore that I would not stay in that village or spend the night there because of that rascal, and I went on to another village and slept in its mosque till daybreak, when I went on my way."

And a certain pastor of the countryside said to his pupils, "I have done some investigation into the Qur'an and have discovered the following, namely, that the words of the Almighty «and it was said, 'Earth, swallow thy waters!'»[167] are of dubious authority because they are preceded by the words 'it was said.'"[168] 4.21

And a scholar entered one of the villages on the banks of the river close to the desert and saw what looked like a mosque, with cattle and sheep and goats in it. He was extremely hungry, so he sat down and recited from *Sūrat al-Kahf*,[169] and a group of people from the village gathered around to listen. However, when he came to the words of the Almighty «Some will say, "They were three, their dog the fourth"»[170] they said to him, "Shaykh, you have defiled the Qur'an! God's Word has no dogs in it, and you have put dogs in it! Get out of our village before we kill you!" One of them, however, stood up and said, "Don't beat him or kill him till we've sent for the pastor of our village, al-Ḥājj Mukhālif Allāh[171] and asked him. If he tells us that the Qur'an has dogs in it, we'll leave him be. If not, we'll kill him!" So they sent for this man and an individual appeared, tall as a flagpole on a mountain and bulky and heavy in physique as the Pillar of the Columns, so that just looking at him was enough to make the skin crawl. He was enveloped in a filthy white blanket and nothing else. When he came and had sat down, they informed him of the situation. He looked to the right and to the left and then said to them, "Be patient till I reveal to you the truth and discover you the essence of the matter!" Then he lay down on his back and told them, "Throw the blanket over me!" which they did. He remained thus for a while without speaking or moving, then suddenly leapt up, naked, head and privates exposed, and stood thus for a while gazing into the sky in a state of ecstatic agony. Eventually, he called for his blanket and wrapped it about him and sat down. "I have visited the Ten Heavens that the Almighty created," he said, "and I saw that in the First Heaven are cows and in the Second Heaven buffalos and in the Third Heaven calves and in the Fourth Heaven oxen and in the Fifth Heaven such-and-such and in the Sixth Heaven such-and-such," and he 4.22

قال وشفت عاشرسما مليانه غنم وانتم تعرفوا انّ الغنم تعوز الكلاب ولا تفارقها وراعى الغنم لا بدّ له من كلب يحرس غنمه خلّوا الراجل يروح ولا تقتلوه واعطوه رغيفين دره ياكلهم قال فأخذ الرغيفين ومضى وهو يحمد الله الذي خلّصه من هؤلاء الجهلة

٢٣،٤ (وجاء رجل إلى فقيه بلدة) يسأله عن رجل أخذ له ديكًا وذبحه ماذا يلزمه فقال في هذا انظر لك في باب الديّات والقتل

٢٤،٤ (وكان بعض فقهاء الريف يدرّس في قرية من بعض قرى الريف) وكلّما سئل عن مسألة أجاب عنها بسرعة نظمًا ونثرًا ولم يتوقّف في الجواب لشدّة جراءته في الكلام من غير معرفة إلى أن حضر درسه جماعة من العلماء ورأوا سرعة جوابه في المسائل وإتيانه بكلام ليس هو في كتب الفقه إلّا أنّ فيه رائحة المناسبة فقالوا أمر هذا المدرّس عجيب فقال رجل منهم أنا أختبره لكم وأبيّن لكم صدقه من كذبه كلّ شخص منكم يأخذ له حرفًا من حروف الهجاء ونجعلها كلمة واحدة ونسأله عنها فقالوا هذا صواب فأخذوا الأحرف وجمعوها فصارت خُنفِشار ثمّ إنّهم جلسوا حوله وقت الدرس فلمّا فرغ يدرّس ويدردش قالوا له يا مولانا رأينا في بعض الكتب يقول خذ الخنفشار وما عرفنا ما يكون فقال لهم هذا واضح وهو نبات يطلع في أرض اليمن يُعقَد به اللبن قال الشاعر [وافر]

لَقَدْ عَقَدَتْ مَحَبَّتُكُمْ بِقَلْبِي كَمَا عَقَدَ الْحَلِيبَ الْخُنُفِشَارُ

وقال صلّى الله عليه وسلّم وأراد أن يذكر حديثًا باطلًا فقالوا له أمسك ما معك قبّح الله الأبعد أمّا كلامك في حقّ الحكماء والعلماء فقد سلّمنا لك في الكذب عليهم وأمّا الحديث فلا نسلّم لك فيه ثمّ إنّهم قاموا عليه وأبطلوه من الدرس

٢٥،٤ قلت ولهذا ذكروا أنّ العلم أمانة وأنّ الشخص لا يجوز له أن يتكلّم فيه إلّا عن خُبْر

went on enumerating the various types of animals until he said, "and I saw that the Tenth Heaven was full of flocks of sheep and goats, and as you know flocks need dogs, which they are never without, and the shepherd has to have a dog to guard his flocks. Let the man go and do not kill him, and give him two loaves of corn bread to eat!" So the scholar took the two loaves and went away, praising the Almighty for saving him from those ignoramuses.

And a man went to the pastor of a village to ask him what compensation 4.23
was owed by a man who had taken a cockerel of his and slaughtered it. "In such cases," said the pastor, "refer to the chapter on blood money and homicide"!

And there was a country pastor who used to teach in a certain village and 4.24
would answer instantly any question put to him, in verse and prose, and was so bold in speaking of things he knew nothing about that he never hesitated over the answer. One day, a group of scholars attended his class and noted the speed of his responses to knotty problems and how he would quote things that were not to be found in any book of jurisprudence but merely had some smell of pertinence to them. "This teacher's case is amazing!" they said. One of them said, "I'll test him for you and sort out his truths from his lies. Let each one of you pick a letter of the alphabet, and then we'll make them into a single word and ask him about it." "A sound idea!" they agreed. So they took the letters and combined them and it came out as *khunfishār*.[172] Then they seated themselves around the man at class time and, when he had finished teaching and chatting away, said to him, "Your Reverence, in a certain book we found the words 'Take the *khunfishār*!' but we do not know what the word means." He replied, "That's easy! It's a plant that grows in the land of Yemen and is used in the inspissation of milk. Says the poet:

> My love for you has coagulated in my heart,
> Just as *khunfishār* thickens the milk!

"And the Prophet, God bless him and grant him peace, has said . . ." and he was about to utter a spurious Tradition when they said to him, "Spare us what you were about to say, God disfigure you! As for what you falsely attribute to the philosophers and scholars, we will allow you your fabrications against them, but we will not let you get away with it when it comes to falsifying a Tradition!" and they set upon him and barred him from teaching.

I would add that it is because of such cases that they say, "Learning is a 4.25
sacred trust" and that a person should be allowed to speak only on the basis of

واطّلاع وشدّة احتياط بأصول المسائل وفروعها ومراجعة النقول ولا يلتفت لما يقع من جهلة العلماء

٢٦،٤ (فقد سأل بعضهم رجلاً من أهل العلم عن وصف كلب أهل الكهف) فقال لا أعرف وأتى والده وكان من العلماء فقال له إنّي سئلت اليوم عن وصف كلب أهل الكهف فقلت لا أعرف ولم يبلغني في وصفه بشيء ثابت فقال له أبوه لأيّ شيء توقّفت في الجواب كنت تقول لهم وصفه كذا وكذا ولونه كذا ولا تنسب نفسك إلى الجهل قال فاغتاظ منه ولده غيظاً شديداً وأصبح ينادي عليه في الجامع ويقول لا تأخذوا عن والدي العلم فإنّه رجل كذّاب مدلّس وقع منه كذا وكذا وذكر لهم القصّة

٢٧،٤ (وأوصى لُقمان ابنه) فقال له يا بُنَيَّ إذا سألك الناس فقل لهم لا أدري فإنّك إذا قلت لهم لا أدري سألوك حتّى تدري وإن قلت أدري سألوك حتّى لا تدري

٢٨،٤ (وقرأ بعض الفقهاء الجهّال) وإذا بطستم بطستم خبّازين يريد ﴿وَإِذَا بَطَشْتُم بَطَشْتُمْ جَبَّارِينَ﴾

٢٩،٤ (وقرأ آخر) ولله ميزاب السموات والأرض فقيل له ما معنى ميزاب فقال الذي ينـزل منه المطر

٣٠،٤ (وادّعى فقيه حفظ القرآن) فقيل له في أيّ سورة الحمد لله لا شريك له من لم يقلها لنفسه ظلماً فأطرق ساعة ثمّ قال في سورة الدخان

٣١،٤ (واشتكى رجل ولده للقاضي) وقال له أصلح الله القاضي هذا ولدي يشرب الخمر ولا يصلّي فقال له القاضي ما تقول قال إنّه يقول غير الصحيح إنّي أصلّي ولا أشرب الخمر فقال له أبوه هذا يزعم أنّه يقرأ القرآن وأنّه فقيه البلد فقل له يقرأ شيئاً منه قال له القاضي اقرأ يا غلام فقال بسم الله الرحمن الرحيم [رمل]

thorough knowledge and wide reading, extreme caution with regard to what is fundamental in a question and what is secondary, and subjection of the process of transmission to critical examination; and that no attention should be paid to what the ignorant among the scholars may come up with.

And someone once asked a man of learning about the appearance of the dog belonging to the People of the Cave,[173] and he replied, "I do not know." Then he went to his father, who was a scholar, and said to him, "I was asked today about the appearance of the dog belonging to the People of the Cave, and I said, 'I do not know, and nothing reliable has reached me concerning the matter.'" But his father said to him, "Why did you refuse to answer? You should have said, 'His appearance was such and such and his color was thus and so' and not let yourself appear ignorant." This made the son extremely angry at him, and he set about denouncing him in the mosque, saying, "Do not accept instruction from my father, for he is a liar and a charlatan and he did such and such!" and telling them the story. 4.26

And Luqmān counseled his son, "My child, if people ask you a question, say 'I know not,' for if you tell them 'I know not,' they will keep on asking you until you do know, but if you tell them 'I know,' they will keep on at you until they find something you do not know!" 4.27

And an ignorant pastor recited *wa-idhā baṭastum baṭastum khabbāzīn* for «*wa-idhā baṭashtum batashṭum jabbārīn*» («and if ye seize by force, seize ye as tyrants?»)![174] 4.28

And another recited, "and God's is the drain pipe (*mīzāb*) of the heavens and the earth."[175] He was asked, "What is the meaning of *mīzāb*?" and he replied, "The thing that the rain goes down"! 4.29

And a pastor who claimed to have memorized the Qur'an was asked, "In which of its chapters do the words *al-ḥamdu li-llāhi lā sharīka lahu man lam yaqulhā li-nafsihi ẓulman* occur?"[176] The man bowed his head in silence for a while, then said, "In *Sūrat al-Dukhān*!"[177] 4.30

And a man complained against his son to the judge and said to him, "God save the Judge, this boy of mine drinks alcohol and does not pray." So the judge asked the son, "What say you?" He replied, "What he says is untrue, for I do pray and I do not drink alcohol." His father responded, "He claims that he knows the Qur'an and that he is the pastor of the village, so tell him to recite something from it." The judge said, "Recite, young man!" and the youth recited, "In the name of God, the Merciful, the Compassionate: 4.31

عَلِقَ القَلْبُ الرَبابا   بَعْدَ ما شابَتْ وَشابا
إِنَّ دِينَ اللهِ حَقٌّ   لا نُغَيِّرُهُ اِرْتِيابا

فقال أبوه هذه سورة كنت حفظتها من زمان ونسيتها اليوم فقال القاضي وأنا كنت أحفظ فيها آية أخرى وهي [رمل]

فَٱرْحَمي صَبّاً كَئِيبا   قَدْ رَأَى ٱلْبُعْدَ عَذابا

ثمّ قال القاضي خذ ابنك فإنّه ماهر في القرآن عارف فانظر إلى جهل الغلام وأبيه وتعجّب من جهل القاضي الذي لم يفرُق بين الشعر والقرآن

٣٢،٤ (وكان بعض العلماء كلّما سئل عن مسئلة يقول من جهله فيها قولان) فقال له رجل أفي الله شكّ فقال فيه قولان فكفر بحسب عبارته وبعضهم أجاب عنه بأنّ فيها قولان من جهة النحو

٣٣،٤ (ودخل بعض العلماء قرية من قرى الريف يوم الجمعة) فلمّا قربت الصلاة توجّه ليصلّي فرأى أهل القرية جميعاً داخلين المسجد وكلّ واحد منهم معه قُفّة من خوص وفيها مِغْرَفة من خشب وسِكّينة من حديد وفار ميّت معلّق في عنقه فتعجّب من فعلهم وقال لا بدّ أنّي أسأل فقيه القرية عن هذا الأمر فبينما هو متعجّب من فعلهم وإذا بالفقيه داخل المسجد للخطابة وهو أيضاً مثلهم حامل قفّة فيها مغرفة وخشبة وسكّين ومعلّق في عنقه فاراً ميّتاً وراهم كلّهم يصلّون بهذه الحالة قال فتقدّم إلى الخطيب وسأله عن هذا الأمر ومَنْ أَمَرَ أهل القرية بهذه الفعلة فقال له أنا أمرتهم بذلك فقال له هذا أمر باطل والصلاة باطلة وما دليلك في ذلك فقال حديث رأيته عندي

My heart grew fond of Rabāb
After her hair and mine had turned gray.
Verily, God's religion is Truth;
We'll not change it, doubt though we may!"[178]

His father said, "That's a chapter of the Qur'an I used to know by heart long ago, but I'd forgotten it today." And the judge said, "And I used to know another verse from it that goes:

Have mercy on a heartsick lover
Who finds separation a torture!"

Then the judge told the man, "Take your son, for he is skilled at the Qur'an!" Observe, reader, the ignorance of the youth and his father, and wonder at the ignorance of a judge who could not tell the difference between the Qur'an and poetry!

And a certain scholar, whenever asked about an issue in dispute, would say 4.32
out of ignorance, "There are two opinions on the matter." Once a man asked him, "Is there any doubt concerning God's existence?" and he answered, "There are two opinions on the matter," thus making himself an infidel with his pet phrase. Another answered the same question by saying, "There are two opinions on the matter from the grammatical perspective"!

And a scholar once entered a country village on a Friday. When the time for 4.33
the prayer drew near, he set off to pray and found all the villagers going into the mosque, each one of them carrying a palm-leaf basket containing a ladle, a piece of wood, and an iron knife, and each with a dead mouse hanging round his neck. The scholar was amazed at these doings and said to himself, "I must ask the village pastor about the matter." While he was wondering thus at their behavior, the pastor himself came into the mosque to preach, and he too was carrying a basket containing a ladle, a piece of wood, and a knife, and he too had a dead mouse hanging from his neck. The scholar watched them all pray in this state and then went up to the preacher and asked him about the matter and specifically who had ordered the people of the village to do this. "I did," the man replied. So the scholar told him, "Your order is invalid and the prayer is void! What is your authority for it?" The preacher replied, "A Tradition that I saw in a book I have called *Kitāb al-Tashbīh* (*The Book of Anthropomorphization*),[179] whose text reads as follows:[180] 'I was informed by Taḥtī son of Taḥtī on

في كتاب واسمه كتاب التشبيه ولفظه يقول حدّثني تحتي[1] بن تحتي عن شعبان النُوريّ أنّ النبيّ صلّى الله عليه وسلّم قال لا تصحّ جمعة أحدكم إلّا بقفّة ومغرفة وخشبة وسكّينة وفار فقال له ائتني بالكتاب أنظره فأتاه بالكتاب فرآه كتاب التنبيه تصحّفت عليه بالتشبيه أنّ النبيّ صلّى الله عليه وسلّم قال لا تصحّ جمعة أحدكم إلا بعِفّة تصحّفت عليه بقُفّة وسَكِينة تحرّفت عليه بِسكّينة وخَشية تصحّفت بخَشَبَة ومَعْرِفة تصحّفت عليه بمِغْرَفة ووَقار تصحّفت عليه بفار وأمّا سند الحديث فهو حدّثني يحيى بن يحيى عن سُفْيان الثَوْريّ فتصحّفت مثل ما مرّ قال فقام عليه هذا الرجل وعلى أهل القرية وأبطلهم هذا الأمر وسعى في خروج هذا الفقيه الجاهل من القرية لعدم معرفته وقلّة عقله فأخرجوه من البلد بيد أمير البلد وطردوه

(ودخل بعضهم قرية من قرى الشام) فسمع المؤذّن يؤذّن ولم ينطق بالشهادتين بل يقول وأنتم يا أهل هذه القرية تشهّدوا أنّ محمّداً رسول الله قال فتعجّب من ذلك ودخل المسجد فرأى الناس مزدحمين على شيء يباع فيه فنظر فإذا هو خمر قد صبّوه في إناء ورجل يتناول منه للناس ويقبض منهم الثمن فقال وهذه أعجب ثمّ مضى إلى المحراب ليسأل الإمام فوجده قد أقبل يمشي على رجل واحدة ورجله الأخرى مرفوعة وأقيمت الصلاة فصلّى ورجله على حالها فلمّا خرج من صلاته سأله عن القضيّة وعن رفع رجله في الصلاة فقال له اعلم يا سيّدي أنّ المؤذّن الذي سمعته لا ينطق بالشهادتين فإنّه نصرانيّ احتجنا إليه لمرض أصاب مؤذّن الجامع ورأيناه صَيّتاً فأقمناه مقامه حتّى يبرأ من مرضه فهو لا يقدر ينطق بالشهادتين وأمّا الخمر الذي رأيته يباع في المسجد فإنّ المسجد له كرم عنب موقوف عليه وإذا بعناه من غير عصير لا يقوم ثمنه بالمستحقّين فعصرناه وجعلناه خمراً لأجل زيادة الثمن للمستحقّين وأرباب الوظائف وأمّا رفع رجلي التي رأيتها فقد صادفتها نجاسة وأنا داخل المسجد وأدركت الصلاة فقلت أرفعها ٣٤،٤

[1] بي: بختي.

the authority of Shaʿbān al-Nūrī[181] that the Prophet, God bless him and grant him peace, said, "No one's Friday prayer is performed correctly unless it be with a basket, a ladle, a piece of wood, a knife, and a mouse."'" The scholar asked to see the book, and it turned out to be *Kitāb al-Tanbīh* (*The Book of Instruction*)—which the man had misread as *al-Tashbīh*—and that the Prophet had said, "No one's Friday prayer will be performed correctly unless it be with *ʿiffah* ('decency')," which he had misread as *quffah* ("a basket"), *sakīnah* ("serenity"), which he had changed to *sikkīnah* ("a knife"), *khashyah* ("fear"), which he had misread as *kashabah* ("a piece of wood"), *maʿrifah* ("knowledge"), which he had misread as *mighrafah* ("a ladle"), and *waqār* ("gravity"), which he had misread as *bi-fār* ("with a mouse"). As for the chain of transmission, it read, "I was informed by Yaḥyā ibn Yaḥyā[182] on the authority of Sufyān al-Thawrī," which he had misread as given. The scholar set upon the man, and the people of the village and stopped them from doing these things and he exerted himself to have this ignorant pastor leave the village because of his lack of knowledge and his stupidity, and they expelled him on the authority of the emir of the village and threw him out.

And a man entered a village in Syria and heard the muezzin giving the call 4.34
to prayer. However, instead of pronouncing the two professions of faith,[183] he said, "You people of this village bear witness that Muḥammad is the messenger of God!" Wondering at this, the man entered the mosque. There he saw the people crowded around something that was being sold, which turned out to be wine that they had poured into a vessel from which one of them was ladling it out to people, collecting payment. "Stranger still!" he said. Next, he went up to the prayer niche to question the imam, and he found that the man had come forward hopping on one foot, with his other foot raised, and that the prayer had started and he had prayed with his foot in this position. When the imam had finished his prayers, the man asked him what was going on and why he had kept his foot raised during the prayer. "You must know, Good Sir," replied the imam, "that the muezzin whom you heard not pronouncing the two professions of faith is a Christian to whom we had recourse because our regular muezzin is sick. We knew he had a loud voice, so we put him in the other's place till he gets better. This is why he cannot pronounce the two professions of faith. As for the wine that you saw being sold in the mosque, the mosque is endowed with a vineyard; if we sold the grapes unpressed, the price would not suffice for the beneficiaries, so we have pressed it and made it into

وأصلّي على رجل واحدة لأجل صحّة الصلاة لأنّي خشيت من المشي عليها فيحصل التلوّث للمسجد وتبطُل الصلاة قال فتعجّب الرجل من قلّة عقولهم وشدّة جهلهم فأتى القاضي فدخل عليه ليسأله عن هذا الأمر فوجد غلاماً يلوط فيه فاحتار في أمره وقال له ما هذا يا مولانا القاضي فقضيّتك أغرب ممّا رأيت وأعجب فقال له لا تعجب إنّ هذا الغلام يدّعوا أهله أنّه بلغ الحُلُم وجماعة يقولون إنّه قاصر فأخذته لأختبره وقلت إن فعل وأنزل يكون قد بلغ الحلم وإلّا يكون قاصر فرأيته قد أنزل المَنِيّ فتحقّقت بحلمه وبلوغه وهذا من باب التجربة لأجل إقامة الشرع فقال الرجل قبّح الله الأبعد وقريته وحلف أن لا يعود إليها بقيّة عمره

٣٥،٤ (وتولّى بعض فقهاء الريف الجهّال القضاء) فأرسل إلى من ولاه هديّة وأرسل معها مكتوب مضمونه بعد السلام على مولانا الأفندي إنّ الواصل لكم هديّة خروفَيْن وسرموجتَيْن الأفندي خروف وسرموجة والنايب خروف وسرموجة قال فلمّا بلغ القاضي مكتوبه أمر بعزله وحقارته وإخراجه من القرية

٣٦،٤ (قلت ونظير ذلك مكتوب فنين) الذي أرسله لأهله من الصعيد في عنوانه يصل إن شاء الله تعالى إلى دربنا المحروس الذي ضبّته مشط ولعبه يسلَّم ليد أهل البيت بتاع فنين

١،٣٧،٤ وفي داخل المكتوب السلام عليكم عدد ما في نخيل البلد من أوراق سلام لا يسعه طبق ولا طبقين ولا أطباق أطول من مقود زرافه ولوكان طاق أو طاقين أو ثلاثة

wine, to increase the return for the beneficiaries and administrators. And as for the raising of my foot that you observed, it happened to step in some filth as I was entering the mosque and the prayer started, so I thought 'I'll raise it and pray on one foot so that the prayer is valid,' since I was afraid to walk on it and pollute the mosque and so render the prayer void." Wondering at their stupidity and extreme ignorance, the man went to the judge to ask him about the matter and, on entering, found him being sodomized by a young man. Now he was totally at a loss and said to the judge, "What is this, Your Honor? Your case is yet stranger and more amazing than all that I have seen before!" "Wonder not!" said the judge. "This young man's family claims that he has reached puberty, while others say that he is still prepubescent. I took him to try him out, thinking that if he performs and produces semen, he must have reached puberty, and if not, then he is still prepubescent. Now I observe that he has indeed produced semen, and I have thus confirmed that he is pubescent and virile, this falling under the rubric of 'the use of praxis to establish the Divine Law.'" "God disfigure you and your whole village!" said the man, and he swore he would never go back there as long as he lived.

And an ignorant country pastor was appointed as a judge, so he sent presents to the man who had appointed him, along with a letter, which read as follows: "Greetings to Our Lord the Effendi! Accompanying this is a gift of two sheep and two pairs of slippers—the effendi a sheep and a pair of slippers, and his deputy a sheep and pair of slippers."[184] When the letter reached the judge, he ordered the man removed from his position, humiliated, and expelled from the village. 4.35

Funayn's Letter and Another Missive

I would note that somewhat similar is Funayn's Letter, which he sent to his relatives from Upper Egypt:[185] 4.36

> Address: "To be delivered, the Almighty willing, to our protected lane, whose lock is a comb and a toy,[186] and handed over to the folk at Funayn's house."

Inside it says: 4.37.1

> Greetings to you, as many as there are leaves on the palm trees of our village, greetings too broad for one platter or two platters or even more and longer

كان أطول من كلّ بدّ وسبب شعر [طويل مع كسر]

إن كانَ أبي ما مات وأمي كمـاني تعـيش   فودّي لهـم عـنّي يا ريح السـلاماتْ
وروحْ قلْ لهم إنّي مع الناسِ في البلدْ   وقلبي من الأشواق لو لا سلا ماتْ
وأنتـم لفي غفـلهْ كبـيرهْ عن ابنكـم   ويا ما جرى لي بعـدكم من حكاياتْ
أنا إن عشت حتّى لقيتكم اقول لكـم   وانا إن مت فقولوا لا حيله فين ماتْ

٢،٣٧،٤ والذي نعلمكم به إن كنتم لسعا بالحياة طيّبين إنّي أرسلت لكم صُحبة القاصد جوز وزّ فقس بيتي النصف من ذلك وزّه وأيضاً خروف أبلق تربِيه وخروف بلا بلاق ويا سبحان الله تبقوا تتكلّموا أجزاف أرسلتم تطلبوا حبل تنشروا عليه الغسيل وقلتم لنا على طوله وما قلتم لنا على عرضه وأرسلتم تطلبوا كِشْك وانا إن أرسلته لكم من غير طبيخ فضيحه وانا إن طبختُه ما يوصل لكم حتّى يبرد وطلبتم نَيْده وما قلتم لي بعسل أو بلاشي وطلبتم قُلَيْلات والفلّاحين ما يزرعوا إلّا قرع طوال فيكون ذلك في خاطركم من حقّه وبلغني انّ امراتي حبله من بعدي فلا تخلّوها تولد حتّى آجي وإن ولدت قبل ذلك فلا يكون إلّا صبي وسمّوه دار الخطيب فإنّي دخلت دار الخطيب ورأيت فيها طعام كتير أعجبني

٣،٣٧،٤ وجرت لي فيه حكاية ولكن لا تقولوها لحدّ أبداً تبقى فضيحه وذلك أنّي أكلت يوم بطيخ ونمت في بيت الفلّاحين حشاكم فشخّيت في تيابي وانا معذور وبزيادة فإن البطيخ يكتّر الشخاخ فغسلت قميصي وعلّقته في السطوح فقام بالأمر المقدّر ضربة الهوا وقع من فوق لأسفل وارتجفت بسلامتي رجفة وضعفت ضعفه لو ضعفها غيري كان مات وعرفت أنها ما هي بشارة خير وأنّها تدلّ على موت أمّي وأبويه والحمد لله الذي كانوا فدايه وأنّي صلّيت وصمت حتّى الذى ما كنت في القميص وانا لوكنت فيه كنت انكسرت وحوالينا ولا علينا ولكن من الرجفه وجعتني عيني التي تبقى من ناحية المَسِيد وقت أخرج من بيتنا

than a giraffe's tether, be it one length or two or even three, in any case and howsoever! Verse:

If Dad's not dead and Mum's alive too,
Send them from me, O wind, my best!
Go tell them I'm with the folks back home,
And my heart, if not consoled, will die, it's that distress't!
You don't have a clue what's become of your son,
And, since I saw you, with how many adventures I've been blest!
If I live to see you, I'll tell you all about it,
And if I die, just say, "Too bad! Funayn's gone west!"

What I want you to know—if you're still alive and in good health—is that I've 4.37.2
sent you "by kind hand of bearer" a pair of home-hatched geese, one half of which makes a goose, plus a hand-raised piebald sheep and a sheep without pies, and, praise the Lord, how weird you talk now! You sent asking for a clothesline, and you told us how long but didn't say how wide, and you sent asking for wheat groats, but if I sent it to you uncooked, it'd be a disgrace, and if I cooked it, it'd be cold by the time it arrived, and you asked for blancmange, but you didn't tell me with honey or without, and you asked for *qulaylāt,*[187] but the peasants only grow long squash, which you should bear in mind for a fact. You told me too that my wife got pregnant after I left, so don't let her have a baby till I get back, and if she does have a baby before then, it's got to be a boy and you must call him Preacher's-House, because once I went into the preacher's house and I saw lots of food there, which made me feel good.

And something happened to me here but you mustn't tell a soul because 4.37.3
it would be a disgrace, which is that one day I ate a watermelon and I slept at the house of the peasants—excuse the mention!—and I peed in my clothes, but it wasn't really my fault at all because watermelons do make you pee a lot. So I washed my shirt and hung it out on the roof, but a gust of wind—by Providence Ordained!—came along and it fell from up to down, so that, poor me, I shuddered a shudder and turned a turn that would have been the death of anyone else. I knew that it did not bode well and that it meant the death of my father and mother, and praise the Lord that it was them not me! So I prayed and I fasted for thanks that I wasn't in my shirt at the time. If I had been, I would have gotten broken, so "Better around us than upon us!" But the shuddering hurt my eye that's on the mosque side when I leave our house.

٤،٣٧،٤ والذي نعلم به الوالد زوج الوالدة أنّي دخلت يوم البستان أنا والخولي فرأيت فيه نخيل شي طويل وشي قصير وشي ما يشبه شي فقلت وده ايه قال توت ورأيت يا أبي نخله فيها كلّ ورقه قدر الصُّفه الّي تتخنّت أمّي فيها قلت وده فقال لي موز فعجبني قوي وقلت الموز يطلع في البستان فقال لي أَيْوَه قلت والجبن المقلي يطلع فين قال يطلع في طاجن الجبّان واناكلّ يوم آجي واطلّ من الطاقه وعمرى ما شفت في طاجن الجبّان نخلة جبن مقلي فواعدت الخولي وراهنته من امراتي الحبله لا مراته التي بلا حبل بأنّه يعمل امراتي يوم وانا اعمل امراته يوم فلا تخلّوه ياخد امراتي وابقى يتيم وانا افتكرت وكأنّي وودن الشيطان مسدوده أصبحت صاحب فكره أكتب لي محضر واخد خاطر الجيران انهم ما رأوا نخلة في طاجن جبن مقلي

٥،٣٧،٤ والذي نعرّفكم به اني لمّا طلعت البلد ولقيت الصابون غالي فبعت فرسي البيضه واشتريت لي حماره سوده حتّى لا تتوسّخ وكمانه كلام كتير فإنّي لوكتبت لكم الّذي في خاطري لكان الكلام يجي من حدّ عندكم إلى فنين

٦،٣٧،٤ وبعد السلام على أهل الحاره كلّ واحد باسمه كتير كتير بتاريخ صبحة يوم الجمعه الحرام بعد صلاة التراويح من يوم عاشورا السابع والثلاثون من جماد الأوسط سنة ما اعرف شي الّي تقولوا عليه وبالأماره مطرت المطره وأهل البلد يعرفوا ذلك

١،٣٨،٤ ونظاير هذا المكتوب كثيرة لا تحصى (فقد أرسل إلىّ بعض فقهاء الريف مكتوبًا) في سنة سبع وسبعين وألف يقول فيه السلام من الفقي أبو علي الّي اسمه محمّد على حضرة صاحبنا الّي يطالع في القرآن * زيّ ما يطلع الزرع في الغيطان * ويتكلّم بالفهامه * وياما له علينا شهامه * الّي يبيع الكتب المنظومه من الكلام * زيّ قصّة الجارية تَوَدُّد والورد في الأكمام * حاوي الكتابة في السطور * ومن يعرف كتاب الفخ والعصفور * وأنا في شوق واشتياقه * لا يحمله جمل ولا ناقه * ولا حمار ولا حمارين * ولا بغل ولا بغلين *

And I want to inform my father, husband of my mother, that one day I went into the orchard with the surveyor and there I saw palm trees, some tall, some short, and some like nothing else, so I said to him, "What's that?" "Mulberry," said he. And, Father, I saw a palm tree each of whose leaves was as big as the settle my mother gets screwed on. I said, "What's that?" "Bananas," said he. Then I was very happy, and I said, "Do bananas really grow in orchards?" and he told me "Yes." "So where does fried cheese[188] grow?" I asked him, and he said, "It grows in the cheese maker's basin," but I go and look out of the window every day and I've never seen a fried-cheese palm in the cheese maker's basin. So I made an arrangement with the surveyor, and I bet my wife who's pregnant against his that isn't that he could do my wife for one day and I'd do his for one day, if what he said was true. So don't let him win and take my wife and leave me an orphan! And I've done some thinking and come up with an idea of my own, as you might say—Satan's ear be stopped!—which is that I should write myself an affidavit and get the neighbors to say that they've never seen a fried-cheese palm in the cheese maker's basin. 4.37.4

And I have to inform you too that, when I came to the village and found that soap was dear, I sold my white mare and bought myself a black donkey so that it wouldn't show the dirt, and oh, lots of other stuff, but if I wrote down everything that's in my head the words would stretch all the way from you to Funayn! 4.37.5

Greetings to the folk of the quarter, each one on his own by name, lots and lots! Dated early morning on holy Friday after the special Ramadan prayers for ʿĀshūrāʾ, the thirty-seventh of the month of Middle Jamād[189] in the year of what's-its-name. And, by the way, it's been raining and the people in the village are aware of that. 4.37.6

Missives of this type are innumerable. For example, in 1077[190] a country pastor sent me a letter that said: 4.38.1

Greetings from Pastor Abū ʿAlī, Muḥammad by name, to our honored friend who zips through the Qurʾan as fast as the crops shoot up in the fields and talks so clever and who we're all so proud of and who sells books with words in rhymes, like "The Slave Girl Tawaddud,"[191] and "The Unblown Rose,"[192] full of writing in lines, and who knows *The Book of the Snare and the Sparrow*![193] I've got cravings and hankerings for you more than a camel could bear, or a she-camel, or a donkey, or two donkeys, or a mule, or two mules!

شعر [غير موزون] ٢،٣٨،٤

السلام عليك يا سيدي والرحمه   سلام من هو ما بياكل بعدك لقمه
إلا صايمٍ عن الزاد وهو زي الاعمه   وانا قصدي اشوفك ولو في الضلمه

وانا كنت أردت اجيك واحيات راسك ما عوقني الّا سرموجتي مقطّعه وانّي اقول لك تشوف لي كتاب كنت شفته من زمان وسمعت به آه عليه وياما قالوا لي عليه الناس وهو قصّة مدينة النحاس وياما جرى فيها من العجايب والغرايب وانا انبارحه كنت رايح اشيّع لك كلام افتكرته وعاودت نسيته الله يسامحك ويسامحني الله الله لا غالب إلّا الله والسلام عليكم وعلى من هم جيرانك على اليمين والشمال وكتب هذا الكتاب أبو علي واسمه محمّد

٣٩،٤ وكتب عنوانه توصل دي الورقه مع ابو عمّار الّي يبيع في بلدنا الفول الاخضر يوصّلها لبولاق وواحديبقى يوصّلها لسوق الكتب الّي يقولوا فيه حراج حراج فانظر إلى شدّة هذا الجهل وإلى هذا الكلام الّذي يشبه الوحل

٤٠،٤ وأضراب هؤلاء الجهّال كثير ولقد أحسن الإمام حجّة الإسلام أبو حامد الغزاليّ في قوله [طويل]

تَصدَّرَ للتَدْرِيسِ كُلُّ مُهوَّسٍ   بَليدٍ يُسَمَّى بِالْفَقيهِ الْمُدَرِّسِ
فَحُقَّ لِأَهْلِ الْعِلْمِ أَنْ يَتَمَثَّلُوا   بِبَيْتٍ نَفِيسٍ شاعَ فِي كُلِّ مَجْلِسِ
لَقَدْ هُزِلَتْ حَتَّى بَدا مِنْ هُزالِها   كُلاها وحَتَّى سامَها كُلُّ مُفْلِسِ

٤١،٤ وممّا يُنْسَبُ لسيّدي عبد العزيز الديرينيّ نفعنا الله به [مخلع البسيط]

Verse: 4.38.2

Peace, Dear Sir, upon you, and mercy
From one who, after meeting you, couldn't eat a bite
But gave up provisions and is like a blind man—
And I have to see you, even without light!

I wanted to come and see you, I swear, and the only thing that held me up was that my slippers were torn. And I tell you, find me a book that I saw a long time ago and heard so many raving about and that so many have told me about, which is *The Tale of the City of Brass*,[194] where so many wonderful and amazing things happened! Yesterday I was going to send you something I thought of but then I forgot it again, God forgive us both! O God! O God! There is no Victor but God! Peace be upon you and upon your neighbors on the right and on the left. This letter was written by Abū ʿAlī, Muḥammad by name.

And for the address he wrote: 4.39

This piece of paper is to go with Abū ʿAmmār, who sells green fava beans in our village, and *mishsh*, and linseed oil, and he's to deliver it to Bulaq, and from there someone has to deliver it to the book market, where they cry, "For auction! For auction!"[195]

Observe the depths of the man's stupidity and these words that resemble mud and mire in their turbidity!

The likes of such ignoramuses are everywhere. The Imam, Proof of Islam, 4.40
Abū Ḥāmid al-Ghazālī[196] put it well when he said:

Each doltish fool presents himself to teach—
Such should be called "the Teaching Faqīh,"
While scholars should rightly be limned by a precious verse,
In salons everywhere these days well rehearsed:
"She grew so thin her kidneys showed, she was that gaunt,
And by every pauper she was hawked."[197]

The following verses are attributed to My Master ʿAbd al-ʿAzīz al-Dīrīnī, 4.41
God grant us benefit through him:

إنْ شِئْتَ تُدْعَى فَقِيهَ قَوْمٍ فَطَوِّلِ الْكُمَّ ثُمَّ عَمِّمْ
وَاجْعَلْ عَلَى الرَّأْسِ طَيْلَسانًا وَاعْقِدْ عَلَى الْمَنْكِبَيْنِ وَاخْتِمْ
وَاجْلِسْ مَعَ الْقَوْمِ فِي صِياحٍ لا بِالْبُخارِيِّ وَلا بِمُسْلِمْ
إلّا صِياحًا وَنَفْضَ كُمٍّ وَلا وَلِمَ لا وَلا نُسَلِّمْ
وَإنْ رَأَوا الْوَقْفَ يأْكُلُوهُ وَقَدْ نَسُوا الْعِلْمَ وَالْمُعَلِّمْ
ثِيابُهُمْ بُيِّضُوا رِياءً وَقَلْبُهُمْ بِالسَّوادِ مُظْلِمْ
فَإنْ تَرَى فِي الْوَرَى فَقِيهًا فَصِحْ وَقُلْ يا سَلامُ سَلِّمْ

أي إذا رأيت فقيهاً على هذه الحالة فاسأل الله السلامة منه والبعد عنه نسأل الله العفو والعافية في الدين والدنيا والآخرة

If you want to be called the pastor of a people,
    Lengthen your sleeves, then don a turban.[198]
Wrap your head in a shawl,
    Knot it round your shoulders, then rattle off the Qur'an.
Sit with the people in a hubbub—
    Not with al-Bukhārī and not with Muslim
But with din and sleeve-shaking
    And "No!" and "Why not?" and "We'll never give in!"
If they find a *waqf*, they devour it,
    And they've forgotten what's a teacher and what knowledge lies in.
Their clothes are bleached with deceit,
    But their hearts are darkened with blackness,
So, should you see a pastor among the people,
    Cry out and say, "God save us!"

In other words, if you see a pastor of this type, ask God to save you from him and keep you at a distance from him—we pray God for His pardon and for well-being in this world and the next!

(ذكر شعرائهم ورثاهم وفُشارهم)

١،٥ قيل مرّ بعض أهل الأرياف بجماعة من اللطفاء ينشدون الأشعار في معنى العشق فقال لهم زيدوا يا مغنّيين القوم من دي القول المليح فقد ذكّرتوني نشيد مليح قلته وانا احرت في الغيط إكّنّي عشقت ام معيكه وكنت رايح اموت من عشقها وغرامها فقال له هؤلاء الجماعة أنشدنا ما قلت في أم معيكة فأنشد يقول مواليا [بسيط]

٢،٥ مَا ضَالْ قَمِيصِي يُشَحْطَطْ مِنْ وَرَا ٱلْمِحْرَاتْ حَتَّى أَتَتْنِي صَبِيَّهْ رَايِحَهْ بِتْبَاتْ
فَقُلْتُ يَا ٱمَّ مُعَيْكَهْ إِرْحَمِي مَنْ مَاتْ قَالَتْ أَنَا رَايِحَهْ أَخْرَا وَجِيكْ بِتْبَاتْ

١،٢،٥ أقول هذا الكلام من بحر الخرا الوافر * الّذي ليس له أوّل ولا آخر * وقائله من أبلد البشر * أو من أغشم البقر * وتفاعيله باحتباط * متخبّط خابط متخبّط خباط * وطوله بالتوكيد * من إسكندريّة لرشيد * وعرضه باحتياط * من الصعيد لدمياط * ومعناه الذميم * ومبناه السخيم

٢،٢،٥ (مَا ضَالْ) هذه الكلمة يستعملها أهل الأرياف وردت في القاموس الأزرق والناموس الأبلق وأصلها ما زال فيبدّلون الزاي ضاداً لاعوجاج ألسنتهم

An Account of Their Poets and of Their Idiocies and Inanities[199]

It is said that a countryman happened across a group of men of refinement reciting verses on the theme of love. "Give us more of these fine words, you Singers of the People," he said, "for you've put me in mind of a fine poem I made up while plowing in the fields, seeing as how I'd fallen in love with Umm Muʿaykah and was like to die of love and longing for her." So the men said, "Recite us what you said about Umm Muʿaykah," and he recited the following *mawāliyā*. 5.1

The First of Their Verses: "My shirt kept trailing behind the plow"

mā ḍāl qamīṣī yushaḥṭaṭ min warā l-miḥrāt 5.2
ḥattā ʾatatnī ṣabiyyah rāyiḥah bi-tbāt
fa-qultu yā-mma Muʿaykah ʾirḥamī man māt
qālat ʾanā rāyiḥah ʾakhrā wa-jīk bi-tbāt

My shirt kept trailing behind the plow
Till a maid came along, going home for the night.
"Umm Muʿaykah," said I, "take pity on one who's died!"
"I'm off for a crap," said she, "but I'll come to you all right!"

These words, I declare, are drawn from the "abundant" ocean of shite[200] that has no beginning and no end in sight, and the poet is among the stupidest of men, or the dumbest of cattle that live in a pen. The feet, which are bloated, go *mutakhabbiṭun khābiṭun mutakhabbiṭun khubāṭ*,[201] while their length, at the very least, is from Alexandria to Rashīd for sure, their breadth from Upper Egypt to Dimyāṭ or more. As to its meaning base and basis demeaning, they are as follows: 5.2.1

mā ḍāl ("kept on"): this word is used by the people of the countryside and is to be found in *The Blue Ocean and Piebald Canon*. It was originally *mā zāl*,[202] but they change the letter *z* into *ḍ* because of the crookedness of their tongues. 5.2.2

واشتقاقها من الضلّ أو الضلال أو من الضئيلة وهي الحيّة قال الشاعر [طويل]

فَبِتُّ كَأَنِّي سَاوَرَتْنِي ضَئِيلَةٌ   مِنَ الرَّقْشِ فِي أَنْيَابِهَا السَّمُّ نَاقِعُ

ومصدرها الفشرويّ ضلّ يضلّ ضلالاً فهو ضالاً ومضلولاً

٥،٢،٣ (قُمِيصِي) على وزن حريصي أو جعيصي واشتقاقه من القَمْص أي قمص الحمار يقال حمار قمّاص أو من بلد يقال لها مِنْيَة القُمُّص ومصدره قمص يقمص قمصاً فهو قامص ومقموص والقميص ما يُلْبَسُ من الكتّان وغيره

٥،٢،٤ (يُشَحْطَط) مأخوذ من الشحططة أو من الشَحّوطة أي ينسحب وينجرّ على الأرض يقال شحططه إذا جرّه على الأرض وهذه من لغات الأرياف قال بعض شعرائهم مواليا [بسيط]

شَحْطِطْ صُحَيْبَكْ وِرُخْهُ أَلْفَ فَرْقَلَّةْ   وَاكْوِيهِ بِالنَّارِ حَتَّى يَلْتَقِي العِلَّهْ
حَتَّى يَلِينُ وَيَبْقَى قُرْصَ مِنْ جِلَّهْ   قَوْمْ أَطْعِمُو[١] العَدْسَ وَالبِيسَارَ وَبِسِلَّهْ

والشاهد في قوله شحطط صبيحك وشحطط على وزن ضرّط بتشديد الراء وضرّط فيها مناسبة من وجهين الأوّل الوزن والثاني إذا شحطط آخر على الأرض أو في جورة أو في نقرة ربما ضرط فيها من شدّة ما يحصل له من المشقّة وألم الشحططة فكان المعنى ظاهر وقوله

٥،٢،٥ (مِنْ وَرَا المِحْرَات) أي من خلفه ووصفه قميصه بأنّه صار ينجرّ خلف المحرات لأحد أمور إمّا لأنّه غلب عليه الشقاء وكثرة التعب وشدّة النصب والحرّ فخلع كُمَّه من يده حكم ما تفعله الحرّاثون إذا اشتدّ عليهم التعب وزاد عليهم النصب فيفعلوا ذلك

١ بي وجميع النسخ: أطعمه.

It is derived from *ḍall* ("error") or *ḍalāl* ("delusion") or from *ḍaʾīlah* ("slender snake, viper").[203] As the poet[204] says:

I spent the night like one bitten by the maculate
Viper (*ḍaʾīlah*), whose fangs a deadly venom contain.

Its facetious paradigm is *ḍalla, yaḍillu, ḍalālan,* and *ḍāllun* and *maḍlūlun.*[205]

qamīṣī ("my shirt"): of the measure of *ḥarīṣī* ("my rags") or *jaʿīṣī* ("my pompous one") and derived from *qamṣ* ("galloping") as in *qamaṣa l-ḥimār* ("the donkey galloped")—one speaks of a *himār qammāṣ* ("a fast-running donkey")—or from a town called Minyat al-Qummuṣ. The paradigm is *qamaṣa, yaqmuṣu, qamṣan,* and *qāmiṣan* and *maqmūṣan.* A *qamīṣ* ("shirt, shift") is whatever one wears that is made of linen and so on. 5.2.3

yushaḥṭaṭ ("trailing"): derived from *shaḥṭaṭah*[206] or from *shaḥḥūṭah* ("chisel with teeth")[207] and meaning that it was pulled and dragged over the ground. One says *shaḥṭaṭahu* ("he trailed it") if he dragged it over the ground. It is a rural expression. One of their poets says: 5.2.4

Wipe the floor with (*shaḥṭiṭ*) your buddy and give him a thousand
lashes
And brand him with fire till he's struck with disease.
Then, when he goes soft and turns into a cow pat,
Go feed him lentils and *bīsār* and peas!

—the citation here consisting of *shaḥṭiṭ ṣuḥaybak* ("wipe the floor with your buddy"). The word *shaḥṭiṭ* is of the measure of *ḍarriṭ* ("fart audibly") with double *r*, the latter being appropriate from two points of view—the first, that it is of the same measure, and the second, that, if he were trailed around on, and dragged over, the ground, or the heating chamber of an oven or a hole, he might well fart out loud from the hardship and the pain of all that trailing, and the connection would be obvious.

The words *min warā l-miḥrāt* ("behind the plow") mean "at the back of it." He describes the shirt as being dragged behind the plow for several possible reasons. It might be because the hardship, fatigue, exhaustion, and heat had overcome him, so he removed his arms from the sleeves, as plowmen do when their exhaustion reaches the limit and the fatigue is too much for them. They 5.2.5

لترويح أجسادهم وهذا لا يفعله إلّا أكابر الحرّاثين وأمّا غيرهم فإنه في الغالب لا يحرث إلّا وهو عريان أو عليه خَلَقَة مقطّعة لا تستر العورة وإنّني مررت بقرية فرأيت رجل حرّاث عَمّال يحرث وهو عريان فقلت له يا هذا أما علمت أنّ كشف العورة حرام فقال لي إنّي سمعت أبو معيكه يقول سمعت أبو شبيكه يقول سمعت أبو تفال يقول كشف العورة في الحرث مباح لأنها عند الضروريات تُباح المحظورات[1] فهذا يدلّ على أنّه كان من أكابر الحرّاثين أو ربّما كان قميصه مشرمط فصار ينجرّ خلفه وينشبك في الشوك والحلفة أو يقال إنّه قلعه ووضعه على كتفه كعادة الحرّاثين وصار ينجرّ خلفه ويتخبّل من الحرث وكثرة التعب وسوق الأثوار فارتخى وانهلّ من على كتفه وصار ينجرّ خلف المحراث ومن شدّة تعبه من الحرث واعتنائه بما هو فيه لم يلتفت إليه ولم يجد له مروّة يلُمّه من الأرض حتّى جاءته تلك الصبيّة

٦،٢،٥ (وِالمِحْراثْ) آلة معروفة عند الفلاّحين مجموعها خشب وسَلَب وحديد ولهذا صار فيه التعب والمشقّة وسواد الوجه من الحرّ والبرد قال الشاعر [غير موزون]

تضال إنّك يا محراث تاعب جماعتك لما ليوم الحشر ما انت مفارق

فالحرّاث دائماً في تعب شديد وهمّ مزيد وليس في الفلاّحين أتعب منه خصوصاً إذا كان في الجَرَافة السلطانيّة وهو أقلّ عقل من غيره لأنّه بالنهار رفيق الأثوار وبالليل رفيق النساء فلا يكمل له عقل

٧،٢،٥ ومثله في قلّة العقل مؤدّب الأطفال فإنّه طول نهاره رفيق الأطفال وطول ليله مع النساء ويدلّ على قلّة عقل مؤدّب الأطفال قبول شهادة القاصر على البالغ وإن ضرب وشتم ولد ولداً آخر وجّه الشتمة إلى الفقي بقوله بيقول لي الولد ده دم الحس

[1] بي: الحظورات.

do this to bring relief to their bodies, albeit it is only the eminent ones among them who do so, the rest for the most part plowing naked or wearing just a torn rag that doesn't even conceal their privates. Indeed, I once passed a village and seeing a plowman plowing away stark naked I said to him, "Hey, you! Hasn't anyone told you that it's wrong to expose your privates?" to which he replied, "I heard Abū Muʿaykah say:[208] I heard Abū Shubaykah say: I heard Abū Tifāl say: The exposure of the privates while plowing is permitted, since 'In cases of necessity, the forbidden is admitted.'" This would indicate that the poet was a plowman of standing. Or it may be that his shift was already ripped or shredded and so got dragged behind him and caught on the thistles and esparto grass. Or it may be that he had taken it off and put it over his shoulder, as plowmen do, so that it was dragged along behind him and that he became disorientated from the plowing, the fatigue, and the driving of the oxen, with the result that it slipped and fell off his shoulder and was then dragged along behind the plow and that he was so tired out with plowing and so taken up with what he was doing that he failed to notice it and did not have the energy to gather it from off the ground until this girl came along.

The plow (*miḥrāt*) is an implement well known to peasants and consists of wood, rope, and iron, which explains why he suffered from fatigue and travail and why his face had become weathered from the heat and the cold. The poet says: 5.2.6

All your life, plow, you exhaust your people—
Till Resurrection Day you'll not leave us be!

Thus the plowman suffers constantly from great fatigue and excessive distress and there is no peasant worse off than he, especially if he is on one of the crews that work at maintaining the sultan's dikes.[209] He is also less well-endowed mentally than his fellows, as his companions by day are oxen and by night are women; consequently his mental capacities never become completely formed.

Similar in terms of reduced intellect is the teacher of small children, for they are his companions all day long while all night long he is with women. Evidence of the stupidity of such schoolmasters is their habit of accepting the testimony of the immature boy over that of the adult, and the way that, if a boy beats and insults another, the second will turn the insult against the teacher by saying, "Sir, that boy says to me, 'Blood slap the back of your neck!' and 5.2.7

قفاك يا سيدنا ويقول لي يا ابن القحبه يا سيدنا ويقول لي دم اخرق عينك يا سيدنا ونحوذلك من هذه الألفاظ وقد وجد عند مؤدّب أطفال طبلة وزُمّارة وفَرْقَلة فسئل عن ذلك فقال أجمعهم بالطبلة وأفرّقهم بالزمّارة وأضربهم بالفرقلة

٨،٢،٥ ورأيت في بعض الكتب أنّ فقيها كان يعلّم الأطفال القرآن في غرفة له فاتّفق الأولاد على أنّهم يبنوا على باب الغرفة حائطاً ويمنعوه من الدخول إليها ففعلوا ذلك ليلاً ولمّا أصبحوا جاؤا إلى الفقي وقالوا له إنّ الغرفة هربت بالليل قال فشدّ وسطه وغدا في طلبها وما زال في البَرّية يمشي حتّى قارب الليل فلم يجد شيئاً فرأى صومعة فيها راهب فسأله هل رأيت غرفة فيها ألواح وأدوية فقال الراهب في نفسه إنّه أحمق لا عقل له ثمّ قال له نعم إنّها مرّت عليّ الظهر وأنت لا تلحقها ولكن بات عندي إلى السحر وأنت تلقاها فقبل منه ذلك القول وصعد إلى عنده وقد هلك من الجوع والعطش وقد أضرّه التعب فأحضر له الأكل فأكل وشرب حتّى شبع ثمّ أسكره وأنومه وقام إليه وحلق وسط رأسه وقلّعه الثياب التي كانت عليه وألبسه ثياب الرهبان وشدّ له زُنّارا وتركه فلمّا كان وقت السحر نبّهه وقال له ويحك إنّ الغرفة رجعت البلد فقم وادخل البلد تجدها قال فقام ومضى إلى البلد فرحاناً مسروراً فلمّا رآه الناس قالوا له أنت صرت راهب قال لا والله إلّا أنّي بتّ عند راهب وقلت له نبّهني وقت السحر فأيقظ نفسه وتركني قال ثمّ إنّه رجع إلى صومعة الراهب وصار يتذلّل له ويقول بالله عليك يا راهب نبّه نفسي حتّى أروّح البلد وخذ نفسك اجعلها مكانها صدقة عنك بحقّ المسيح قال فصار الراهب يضحك عليه حتّى أيس منه وانصرف فانظر إلى قلّة عقله وشدّة جهله

٩،٢،٥ (وكان أيضاً بعض مؤدّبي الأطفال) إذا وقف يصلّي وركع أخرج رأسه من بين رجليه وقال شفتك يا ابن القحبه رأيتك يا ابن العرص ويشتم الأولاد ثمّ يسجد ويتمّ

sir, he says to me, 'You son of a whore!' and he says to me, 'Blood pierce your eye!'" and other such expressions. One schoolmaster was found in possession of a drum, a pipe, and a whip. When he was asked about them, he replied, "I summon them with the drum, dismiss them with the pipe, and beat them with the whip!"[210]

I saw in a book that there was a schoolmaster who used to teach children 5.2.8
the Qur'an in a room of his. The children agreed together to block the door of the room with a wall and stop him getting in. They did this one night, and the next morning they went to the schoolmaster and told him that the room had run away during the night. The man hitched up his skirts and ran off in search of it and kept going through the desert until it was almost night and he had found nothing. Then he spied a cell harboring a monk, so he asked him, "Have you seen a room with writingboards and inkhorns?" The monk said to himself, "The man's a simpleton, totally brainless!" and replied, "Indeed—it passed me at noon, but you'll never catch up with it now. Just stay here with me till daybreak, and then you'll be able to find it." The teacher accepted the invitation and climbed up to the cell, by this time almost dead from hunger and thirst and quite worn out. The monk prepared food for him, and he ate and drank until he was full. Then the monk got him drunk until he fell asleep, approached him, shaved the middle of his head, stripped him of the clothes he was wearing, dressed him up as a monk, tied a girdle around his waist, and left him. At daybreak, he roused the man and said to him, "Alack for you—the room went back to the village! Get up, go to the village, and you'll find it!" So the man got up and went to the village, quite overcome with joy, but when the people saw him, they said to him, "Have you turned monk?" "No, by God!" he replied, "but I did spend the night with a monk and I told him to rouse me at daybreak. He must have woken himself instead and left me behind!" Then he returned to the cell and started pleading with the monk, saying to him, "I beseech you, monk, wake me up so that I can go back to the village, and take your own self and put it where it belongs, as an act of charity for the sake of the Messiah!" but the monk just kept laughing at him till the man despaired and went his way. Observe the exiguousness of his intellect and the egregiousness of his ignorance!

Also, a certain schoolteacher, when standing at prayer and bending over 5.2.9
to perform a prostration, would stick his head out between his legs and say, "I see you, you son of a whore! I've got you, you son of a pimp!" and curse the

الصلاة فانظر إلى قلّة عقله وعظم جهله وقوله

(حَتَّىٰ أَتَتْنِي صَبِيَّة) أي لم أزل على هذه الحالة السخيمة والعيشة الذميمة والكرب والتعب ومعاشرة إخواني الأبقار في الليل والنهار حتّى مرّت بي هذه الصبيّة وهي ضدّ العجوز وصبيّة على وزن بَليّة أو رَزِيّة مشتقّة من الصَبْوة على وزن اللَبْوة أو من الصابون أو من مصبنة الغُز فشُغِفْتُ بحبّها وقَنِعْتُ بجمالها وسباني هواها لا سيّما وهي من ملاح الريف وخصوصاً إذا كانت في وقت جمع الجلّة وشيل الزبل إذا كان عليها وهي متضمّخة بالنجاسة وتلك الروائح وهي ٥،٢،١٠

(رَايِحَة بِتْبَاتْ) أي والحال أنّها مروّحة من الغيط إلى دارها تبات فيها كما هو عادة الفلّاحين أنّهم يسرحوا للغيط ليشتغلوا فيه بالزرع والقلع وتلقيط الجلّة الناشفة والضمّ ونحو ذلك ثمّ إنّهم يروّحوا بيوتهم آخر النهار أو في نصفه على قدر تمام شغلهم فيجدوا العدس والبيسار أو المدمّس قد طاب أمره وحسن طعمه فيأكلوا ويتنعّموا بنسائهم على الأفران ومداود البقر وشُوَن التبن وغُرَف الجلّة ونحو ذلك ٥،٢،١١

(فَقُلْتُ يَا أُمّ مُعَيكَة) أي إنّه لمّا اشتغل بحبّها عندما أقبلت إليه وهي مروّحة من الغيط كما تقدّم نظرها وحبّها والعين توقّع القلب في أشدّ ما يكون من الحبّ والغرام والوجد والهيام قال القائل [دوبيت] ٥،٢،١٢

عَيْنِي نَظَرَتْ وَآفَتِي مِن عَيْنِي   مَا يَقْتُلُنِي إِلَّا سَوَادُ العَيْنِ

وقال الشاعر [وافر]

children—and then prostrate himself and complete his prayer! Observe the exiguity of his intellect and the enormity of his ignorance!

ḥattā ʾatatnī ṣabiyyah ("till a maid came along"): that is, I continued in this sordid state and ignoble condition and in distress and fatigue, living cheek by jowl with my brethren the cattle by night and by day, until this *ṣabiyyah* ("maid") passed by me, *ṣabiyyah* being the opposite of *ʿajūz* ("old woman"). *Ṣabiyyah* is of the measure of *baliyyah* ("calamity") or *raziyyah* ("disaster") and is derived from *ṣabwah* ("youthful passion"), of the measure of *labwah* ("lioness; sexually voracious woman"), or from *ṣābūn* ("soap") or from Maṣbanat al-Ghuzz ("the Soap Works of the Ghuzz"). The maid then distracted me with love and bewitched me with her beauty, and passion for her took my heart captive, which is hardly surprisingly, given that she was a country cutie, and never so much as when seen gathering cow pats and hauling droppings, if the latter were all over her and she were slathered in the filth and its accompanying odors and she was: 5.2.10

rāyiḥah bi-tbāt ("going home for the night"), that is, the context was that she was returning to her house from the fields to spend the night there, after the custom of the peasants, who set off to the fields in the morning to work there at sowing and reaping and gleaning dry dung cakes and harvesting and so on and then go back to their houses at the end of the day, or in the middle, depending on when they finish their work, at which point they find that the lentils and the *bīsār* or the stewed fava beans have reached perfection and acquired an exquisite taste, so they eat and enjoy themselves with their women on top of the ovens, and in the cattle troughs, the straw stores, the dung sheds, and the like. 5.2.11

fa-qultu yā-mma Muʿaykah ("'Umm Muʿaykah,' said I"): that is, he became distracted by love for her as she came towards him on her way home from the fields as previously mentioned, and looked at her and fell in love, for the eye may entangle the heart in the greatest excesses of love and passion, ardor and infatuation—as the poet says: 5.2.12

> My eye beheld, and by my eye I'm bound.
> Nothing slays me like the black of the eye!

And the poet[211] says:

نَظرْتُكَ نَظرَةً بالخَيْفِ كانَتْ   جِلِيَّ العَيْنِ مِنّي بَلْ ضِياهـا
فـآهٍ كيف تَجْمَعُنا اللَّيـالي   وآهٍ من تَفَـرُّقِنـا وآهـا

١٣،٢،٥ فاحتاج أن يخاطبها ويتذلّل بين يديها كما هو عادة المحبّين أنّهم يتذلّلوا لمن يحبّوه ويبذلون له الأرواح فضلاً عن الأموال ويهيموا بحسنه وجماله لأنّ أحداق الملاح تذيب أجساد العشّاق * وحلاوة الجمال تزيد في الاشتياق * ومحاسن الحبيب * تجذب روح العاشق الكئيب * ولله درّ مَعْن بن زائدة حيث قال [خفيف]

نَحْنُ قَوْمٌ تُذيبُنا الحَدَقُ النُّجْـ   ـلُ عَلَى أَنّنا نُذيبُ الحَديدا
وَتَرانا عِنْدَ الكَرِيهَـةِ أَحْـرا   رًا وَفي السِّلْمِ لِلْغَواني عَبِيدا

١٤،٢،٥ وخطابه لها بالكنية لاشتهارها بها والكنية ما صدرت بأمّ أو بأب كما هو مقرّر ومعيكة تصغير معكة وهي على وزن رَكّة أو حَكّة أو دَكّة أو لَبْكة وغلبت عليها هذه الكنية وصارت عَلَماً عليها لكثرة ما كانت تمعك شِعْرتها أي عانتها على جدران الشجر عند اشتداد أكلان الشعر من طوله وقلّة نتفه وغليان الشهوة لأنّ الشعر إذا كثر وطال ربّما اشتدّ غليانه وزاد أكلانه فلا يبرّده على النساء إلّا النيك خصوصاً في زمان الصيف وبعضهم يستحسن بقاء الشعر على الكُسّ أيّام الشتاء لأنّ الشِعْرتين إذا التقيا تولّد من بينهما الحرارة فيسخن الأير والكس فتحصل اللذّة من الجانبين قال الشاعر [طويل]

At al-Khayf I cast at you a glance
That my whole eye's effulgence did contain, nay, did surpass.
Alas, how will the nights unite us?
Alas for our separation and alas!

Accordingly, he felt the need to speak to her and grovel before her, as is the custom of lovers, who grovel to those whom they love, surrendering to them their lives—to say nothing of their money—and mooning over their comeliness and beauty, for the glances of the gorgeous make the bodies of their lovers deliquesce, while the sweetness of their beauty increases the lover's longing to excess, and the charms of the beloved attract the soul of the lover, no matter how broken-hearted. As Maʿn ibn Zāʾidah[212] put it so well: 5.2.13

We are a tribe whom the wide-eyed pupil
Melts, though we melt iron ourselves.
In war, you'll find us noble men;
In peace, we're slaves to pretty girls.

He addresses her by her *kunyah* because that is how she was generally known, the *kunyah* being anything preceded by the word *Umm* ("mother of . . .") or *Abū* ("father of . . ."), as is well known.[213] Muʿaykah is the diminutive of *maʿkah* ("an (act of) rubbing"), which is of the measure of *rakkah* ("broodiness (of a hen)") or of *ḥakkah* ("an (act of) scratching") or *dakkah* ("(an act of) ramming") or *labkah* ("(an instance of) embarrassment"). This particular *kunyah* stuck to her and became the name by which she was known because of the frequency with which she would rub her bush—that is, her pubes—against the roots of trees when it got too itchy (it being too long and too infrequently plucked) and the consequent ebullition of lust—for if the hair is allowed to grow long and thick, this ebullition may intensify and the itching may increase, in which case the only thing that will soothe it for a woman is a fuck, especially in summer. Some people, however, think it good to leave the hair on the cunt during the winter, because the two sets of pubic hair, on coming into contact with one another, generate warmth and the penis and the cunt generate heat, to the pleasure of both parties. As the poet says: 5.2.14

وَلَمّا كَشَفْتُ الذَّيْلَ عَنْ سَطْحِ كُسِّها   وَجَدْتُ عَلَيْهِ الشَّعْرَ أَسْوَدَ كَالزِنْجِي
فَقُلْتُ لَهَا مَاذا الَّذي قَدْ رَأَيْتُهُ   فَقالَتْ طَواشي كاتِبَ الدَّخْلِ وَالخَرْجِ
وَهذا زَمانُ البَرْدِ وَالشَّعْرُ حارِرٌ[1]   فَاسْفُقْ أَيا[2] هذا بِجُهْدٍ بِلا حَرَجِ

واشتقاقه من المعك وهو الحكّ يقال معك يمعك معكاً فهو ماعك وممعوك ودليل كونه مشتقّ من المعك قول بعض شعراء أهل الريف مواليا [بسيط] ١٥،٢،٥

قُومي ٱمْعَكي يا خُطَيْطَهْ شِعْرَتِكْ بِالخَيْطْ   لَمّا أَجِلِكْ هَدِيَّهْ طُورَتَيْنْ مُخَيَّطْ
وَٱعْطِيكْ وَراسي فِداكْ مركوبَ مِنْ هُرَيْطْ   وَآجي لِعَنْدِكْ وَشِيلْ رِجْلَيكِ جُوّا الغَيْطْ

ومقول القول

(إِرْحَمِي مَنْ مَاتْ) أي تعطّفي بالرحمة والشفقة على من أشرف من حبّك وغرامك على حالة تُشْعِر بالموت أو بالخُناق المستعجل وهذا على حدّ قولهم حزين وواعي لأنّ تعريصه في حالة تعب وارتكاب نصب من الحرث وشدّة الحرّ وتراكم الهموم والقهر فحصل منه هذا العشق الذي يُفْضي إلى الموت فكأنّه يقول أنا يا أمّ معيكة قد أشرفت من حبّك على الهلاك والموت فِرِقّي لحالي وانظري ما أنا فيه من معالجة إخواني الأبقار ومقاساة الحرث بالليل والنهار وأنت صبيّة قصيفة وتكرهي الشعرة المنتوفة فاسمحي لي بسَحْبَتَيْن فيما بين العَلَمَيْن وأزور الشيخ أبو قبّه ولو أخذتِ البِشْت والجُبّة وإلّا يحصل لي من بعدك وغرامك الموت وتنقص المغاربة دَيُّوث فلمّا فهمت من حاله هذه القضيّة وابتلت بهذه البليّة ورأت الذي لها مثل الذي عليه وشبيه الشيء منجذب إليه قال الشاعر [وافر] ١٦،٢،٥

١ بي: حار؛ ب: ساخن؛ ك با: حار؛ م (المصراع): فقالت زمان البرد فيه لذاذة.   ٢ بي: يا.

Raising the skirt from off her cunt
I found the hair thereon as black as any Moor.
"What's this I see?" asked I.
"A eunuch," she said, "who writes down every visitor.[214]
But now the weather's cold, while hair is warm,
So to it, good fellow, without demur, and slam that door!"

Muʿaykah derives from *maʿk* ("(the act of) rubbing"), which is the same as *ḥakk* ("(the act of) abrading"). One says *maʿaka, yamʿaku, maʿkan, māʿikan,* and *mamʿūkan.* The proof that it derives from *maʿk* is the verse of a country poet, who says in a *mawāliyā*: **5.2.15**

Arise, Khuṭayṭah, and polish off (*imʿakī*) your pubic hair with thread[215]
While I bring you eight plums as a gift,
And I'll give you slippers from Hurbayṭ, by my head,
And come to you in the field to give your legs a lift!

ʾirḥamī man māt ("take pity on one who's died"): that is, feel compassion and pity for one who, out of love and passion for you, has reached the point at which he is in a state that makes him feel that he is about to suffer death, or a sudden quinsy, such a one being what they call "suffering and sentient," because the wretch is in a state of fatigue and experiencing exhaustion from the plowing, the fierce heat, and the cumulative effect of his worries and oppression, and has therefore conceived this passion that is leading him to his death. It is therefore as though he were saying, "I, Umm Muʿaykah, as a result of my love for you, have been brought close to perdition and death—so take pity on my condition and behold the state I am in from looking after my brethren the cattle and from the hardship of plowing by night and by day; and you being a smartly turned-out girl who hates a plucked bush, allow me to plow a couple of furrows between the guide posts[216] and pay a visit to the shaykh beneath the dome,[217] though you take my wrap and my coat—or else I'll die of longing and passion for you, and 'the Maghribis will be one wittol the fewer.'"[218] So, when she grasped the issue through observation of his condition and was herself afflicted in like manner and realized that she and he were in the same pass—for "like attracts like" and, as the poet says: **5.2.16**

رَأَيْتُ مُجَذَّماً في قَاعِ بِيرٍ وَآخَرَ أَبْرَصَ يَخْرا عليهِ
فَقُلْتُ تَعَجَّبوا مِن صُنعِ رَبّي شَبيهُ الشَّيءِ مُنْجَذِبٌ إِليهِ

فلهذا أبدت إليه العذر الموجب لذهابها في هذه الحالة الراهنة وعدم تعطّفها عليه وهي في تلك المشقّة العظيمة * والداهية العميمة * وهي حدوث الخراء عليها بلا إنكار * ومكابدة دفعه مع المشقّة والأضرار * لأنّه ثقيل في الصُرْم * خفيف في الكم * إذا أدرك الشخص بين ناسه * خرئ في لباسه *

(فَقَالَتْ) له على سبيل الوفاء بالوصال ولم تَدَعْه يقاسي ألم الحبّ والنكال ١٧،٢،٥

(أَنَا رَايِحَهْ أَخْرَا) وفي رواية (خاطري أخرا) والمعنى في الذوق واحد ولكنّ الرواية ١٨،٢،٥
الأولى أَوْلى لتأكيدها من جهة الخراء كما لا يخفى على صاحب الذوق المستمع للعبارة والقارئ لها أيضاً والمعنى أنّ مرادي أفرّغ نفسي من هذه البليّة في نقرة أخرا فيها مثلاً أو فوق سطح أو جنب شجرة أو في الغيط ونحوه كما هو عادة الأرياف فإنّ المرأة منهنّ تجلس لقضاء الحاجة وسط الزريبة أو فوق الكوم خارج البلد وأيّ نقرة وجدتها بالت وغوّطت فيها لأنّ بيوتهم ليس لها مراحيض يخروا فيها قال الشاعر [طويل]

سَأَلْتُ بَني الأَرْيافِ ما لِبُيوتِكُمْ مَراحيضُ قَالوا لا مَراحيضَ لِلْقَوْمِ
فَقُلْتُ فَماذا تَصنَعوا في نِسائِكُمْ فَقالوا جَميعاً نَحْنُ نَخْرا عَلى الْكَوْمِ

والرجال من باب أَوْلى

ثمّ إنّها أرادت بقولها هذا تفهيمها إيّاه حالها وغرضها كأنّها تقول له إنّي إذا أتيت ١٩،٢،٥
إليك * وصرت بين يديك * ربّما تضايقت من هذا الأمر المشروح * ورائحته عليك تفوح * ولكن عندما أزيل هذه الضرورة * ويفرغوا الأولاد من لعب

I saw a leper deep down in a well
    And another with vitiligo whose shit on him fell.
Said I, "Behold what your Lord hath wrought—
    The like of a thing attracts its own sort!"

—she offered him the excuse that explained her having to move on under the prevailing conditions and her inability to take immediate pity on him while she was in that well-known state of major duress and general distress that consists of the irresistible onset of a shit and the need to resist the urge, with the distress and inconveniences that go along with it, for it is "heavy in the bum, but light in the leg; if it catches you in company, you shit in your drawers,"[219] so

qālat ("said she"): to him, by way of indicating that their union would indeed transpire and not leaving him to suffer the pangs and punishments of love, **5.2.17**

ʾana rāyiḥah akhrā ("I'm off for a crap")—or, in another recension, *khāṭirī akhrā* ("I want to crap"), the meaning being the same from the perspective of taste, though the first recension is preferable because it emphasizes the imminence of the shit, a point that will not be lost on the man of good taste who hears or, equally, reads this expression—meaning "I desire to relieve myself of this catastrophe in a hole (for example) in which I can shit, or on top of a roof, or next to a tree, or in the fields, or in any similar place," as is the custom in the countryside, for their womenfolk squat to defecate in the middle of the animal pen or on top of the dump outside the village, and they will urinate or defecate in any hole they find, since their houses have no latrines for them to shit in; as the poet says: **5.2.18**

I asked the countrymen, "No latrines have your houses?"
    Said they, "Not one!"
"What do you, then," I asked, "with your spouses?"
    Said they, "All of us shit on the dump as one!"

—and the men, a fortiori, do the same.

With these words, she was trying to make him understand the state she was in and her intended course of action, as though she were saying to him, "Were I to come to you and present myself, you might be incommoded by this matter to which I have just alluded, what with the associated odors wafting about you, but the moment I've relieved myself of this need, and the children **5.2.19**

الكورة ❊أوفي بالوعد ولمّ الشتات❊

(وَجِيكْ بِتّبَاتّ) ❊ أي بأمر ثابت محقّق وأجابرك فيه وأصله بالثاء المثلّثة غير أنّ ٢٠،٢،٥
هذه من ألفاظ الأرياف فكما يقولوا في الميراث ميرات بالتاء المثنّاة فوق فكذلك تبات
ووارت أيضاً بالمثناة الفوقيّة ونحو ذلك ووقع في رواية أخرى (اجيك وابات) لكن
يكون فيه الإيطاء وهو معيب في الشعر وإن كان مناسب للمقام إذ هو شعر كلا
شيء فعلى الرواية الأولى يكون المعنى أنا قولي ثابت في المجيء إليك والبيات عندك
والبيات مأخوذ من بيات الفراخ لأنّ نساء الريف يقولوا للفراخ عند المساء بَيْت بَيْت
فلعلّه مشتقّ من هذا المعنى ولا يضرّ إدخال حرف الجرّ على الفعل لأنّه مناسب
لثقل الكلام وركاكته وبين تبات وبيات الجناس المحرّف أو المصحّف على اللغة الأصليّة
ويمكن أن يكون قوله رايحه بتبات أي هذه الليلة وقولها أجي وأبات أي الليلة الثانية
كما لا يخفى فكان البيات الأوّل غير البيات الثاني وإن كان هو عينه في باطن الأمر
فاتّجه الفرق بين تبات الأوّل وتبات الثاني فإنّ الأوّل منسوب لقول الرجل والثاني
لقول المرأة ولعلّها أرادت بتأكيد البيات عنده عدم تعذيبه بالهَجْر وسرعة تعطّفها عليه
كما هو شأن من يريد الوفاء بالوصال ويكافئ العاشق بلذّة القرب والجمال فقالت في
نفسها هذه الصبيّة هذا لا يرضيه منّي إلّا ليلة على كمالها يتملّى بتلك المحاسن ويشمّ
تلك الروائح وهي آثار جلّة الغيط وأرقد أنا وإيّاه في الفرن أو في مدود البقرة أو الحمارة

have finished their game of ball, I will make good my promise and be united with you."

wa-jīk bi-tbāt ("but I'll come to you all right"):[220] that is, certainly and assuredly, and I'll console you. The word *t(a)bāt* originally has a *thā'*, but, being a rural word, just as they say *mīrāt* ("legacy") with *tā'* (for *mīrāth*), so also they say *tabāt* (for *thabāt*) and also *wārit* ("heir") and so on with *tā'*.[221] In another recension, the phrase occurs as *wa-jīk w-abāt* ("and I'll come to you and spend the night"), but this would involve using the same verb twice for the rhyme,[222] which is considered a defect in poetry, though it would be perfectly in keeping with the standard of the totally worthless verse in question. According to the first recension, then, the meaning would be "My word is reliable as regards coming to you and spending the night with you," *bayāt* ("to spend the night") being taken from the *bayāt* of chickens, because the women of the countryside say to the chickens in the evening "*bayt, bayt*" ("Home! Home!"), and it thus perhaps derives from the latter.[223] Attaching the preposition to the verb does no harm, because it is of a piece with the overall boorishness of the words and their feeble style.[224] There is identity of ductus with a difference of diacritical pointing between *bayāt* and *tabāt*, vis-à-vis the original forms.[225] It is possible, too, that the words *rāyiḥah bi-tbāt* ("going home to spend the night") imply that very same night, while her words *ajīk wa-bāt* ("I'll come to you and spend the night") imply the following night, as is plain. In this case, "spending the night" in the first line would be different from "spending the night" in the second, though the two are identical in the deep structure. This resolves the discrepancy between the first *t(i/a)bāt* and the second, for the first forms part of what the man says, while the second forms part of what the woman says. Perhaps by confirming that she would spend the night at his house she wanted to avoid subjecting him to the torture of abandonment and to demonstrate how quickly she had become attached to him, as is the wont of those who wish to bring their union to fruition and reward their lover by bestowing on him the joys of proximity and by availing him of their beauty. In such a case, the maid would have said to herself, "This lover will be satisfied with nothing less from me than an entire night in which to revel in these charms and smell these odors (meaning the traces of dung from the fields). We will lie, he and I, in the oven, or in the cow or donkey trough, or on the threshing floor, or on top of the dry dung cakes. We will do this at night, because his entire day is taken **5.2.20**

أو على الجرن أو فوق الجلّة الناشفة لأنّ نهاره على كامله في الحرت والتعب ولا يتفرّغ لمحبوبته ولا لغيرها لكونه في كدّ المعيشة وتعبها وهوانها ونصبها قال الشاعر [كامل]

قَالَتْ تُسافِرُ يا فَتَى وَتُفارِقُ الوَجْهَ الحَسَنْ
فَأَجَبْتُها بِتَذَلُّلٍ وَالقَلْبُ يَعْلُوهُ الشَّجَنْ
هَمُّ المَعِيشَةِ فُرْقَةٌ بَيْنَ الأَحِبَّةِ وَالوَطَنْ

٥،٢،٢١ وتأكيدها في البيات يُشْعِر أيضاً أنها تريد من هذا العاشق أنّه يتهيّأ لما يناسب من حضرتها تلك الليلة من العدس والبيسار أو الفول المدمّس ونحوه ومصدره بات يبيت بياتاً وقولها السابق (أخرا) لفظة الخراء فيها لغات ذكرها صاحب القاموس الأزرق والناموس الأبلق وقد تقدّم معناه ويطلق عليه الغائط والعَذِرة ونحو ذلك انتهى

(الثاني من أشعارهم)

٥،٣ [طويل]

وَقُلْتُ لَها بُولي عَلَيَّ وَشَرْشِري عَرِيضُ القَفا للنّائِباتِ صَبُورُ

٥،٣،١ هذا الكلام من بحر الخراء الطويل الّذي عرضه من الحسينيّة لبركة الفيل وتفاعيله متهابل متهابل متهابل ومعنى كلامه الثقيل ولفظه الهبيل أنّ هذا القائل لمّا تولّع قلبه بالعشق والغرام بحبّ هذه المليحة واحتاج أن يتذلّل لجمالها وأن يجتمع بمحاسنها وأن يتحمّل منها المشقّات والدواهي والبليّات كما هو عادة المحبّين ومذهب العاشقين خصوصاً إذا كان العاشق به ضرب من الإفلاس فهو في أشدّ المشقّات مع محبوبه بين الناس قال الشاعر مواليا [بسيط]

up with plowing and hard labor and he will never be able to take time off for his beloved, or anyone else, so preoccupied is he with the hardships involved in making a living, and the toil, degradation, and suffering that that involves." As the poet[226] says:

"Wilt thou travel, young man," said she,
  "And leave this lovely face?"
And abjectly I replied,
  My heart o'ercome with grief,
"Life's bane is separation
  From loved ones and birthplace!"

Her confirmation that she will spend the night also implies that she wants her swain to prepare the lentils and *bīsār* or stewed beans and whatnot appropriate to her gracious presence that night. The paradigm is *bāta, yabītu, bayātan*. The word *akhrā* ("to shit") that she uses earlier has several dialectal forms that are mentioned by the author of *The Blue Ocean and Piebald Canon* and has been discussed above;[227] it is also called *al-ghāʾiṭ, al-ʿadhirah*, and so on. The end. 5.2.21

The Second of Their Verses: "And I said to her, 'Piss on me and spray!'"[228]

wa-qultu lahā būlī ʿalayya wa-sharshirī 5.3
  ʿarīḍu l-qafā li-l-nāʾibāti ṣabūr

And I said to her, "Piss on me and spray!
  One whose nape is broad endures the blows of fate!"

This verse is drawn from the "long" river of shit,[229] whose breadth between al-Ḥusayniyyah and Birkat al-Fīl would fit. The feet are *mutahābilun mutahābilun mutahābilun,*[230] and the meaning of its obnoxious words and inane expressions is that the poet, his heart enflamed with desire and passion for this pretty girl, felt the need to debase himself before her beauty, to be united with her charms, and to endure trials, tribulations, and calamities at her hands, as is the wont of lovers and the practice of suitors, especially if the suitor is suffering from an attack of insolvency, for such people suffer worse hardships with their beloved than does anyone else. Thus a poet says in a *mawāliyā*: 5.3.1

عَشِقْتُ ذَلَّيْتُ حَكَّ الجوعُ جِسْمي حَكْ   وصُمْتُ عامينِ لمّا صُمْتُ يومَ الشَكْ
وَحَقِّ مَن لو الجِبالُ الراسِيَهْ تَنْدَكْ   يَسْتَأْهِلُ العاشِقُ المُفْلِسْ طَرِيحَةْ صَكْ

٢،٣،٥ فالعاشق يحتاج إلى ثلاثة أمور أن يكون أجرأ من كلب وأوزن من صيرفيّ وأذلّ من يهوديّ وعشق الفَسَقَة على خمسة أقسام عشق شَفَقَة وعشق نَفَقَة وعشق حَدَقَة وعشق لقلقة وعشق عَلَقَة فهي خمسة أقسام ونحن نوردها لإخواننا المتاعيس على التمام

٣،٣،٥ (فأمّا عشق الشفقة) هو أن يميل العاشق إلى الولد الجميل أو المرأة الجميلة ويكون معه أو مع المرأة على حسب المراد وقضاء الحاجة والمدحة لمحبوبه والشفقة عليه حتّى يصير أحنّ عليه من الوالدة على ولدها ويدفع عنه المَضَرّات ويتحمّل من أجله البليّات ويكون حريصاً على أمواله شفوقاً على حوائجه مسرعاً في قضاء حاجاته حتّى يقضي منه المراد على أتمّ حال قال الشاعر [طويل مع نقص في الشطر الثاني]

لَقَدْ صِرْتُ فرّاشاً لِحُبّي وَسائِساً   زَماناً لحتّى نِلْتُ مُرادِيا

٤،٣،٥ (وعشق نفقة) وهو أن يكون الشخص صاحب يسرة وأموال فهذا لا يحتاج إلى تعب في جلب محبوبه بل كلّ محبوب أظهر له الدراهم حضر إلى عنده وقضى منه المراد على أحسن حال قال الشاعر [رمل]

فَخْرَةُ العُشّاقِ يا مَنْ عَشِقوا   ضَرْبٌ مِنْ ذَهَبٍ أَوْ وَرِقْ
وَإذا ما غَلَقوا[١] بابَ الرِضا   يَفْتَحُ الدِرْهَمُ باباً غَلَقوا
هٰكَذا قَدْ قالَ في تَنْزيلِهِ ﴿لَنْ تَنالُوا الْبِرَّ حَتَّىٰ تُنْفِقُوا﴾

١ بي: قد غُلِقَ؛ ب (المصراع): وإذا باب الرضا قد أغلقوا؛ ك با م: قد غلق.

I loved, I was abased.
Starvation made my body waste.
Two years it seemed to last,
That day my heart made its unlawful fast.[231]
By Him before whom the hills collapse,
The penniless lover deserves a volley of slaps!

The fact is that a suitor needs to be three things: more daring than a dog, 5.3.2
more calculating than a money changer, and more abject than a Jew. Wooing among the reprobate comes in five categories: wooing with tenderness, wooing with money, wooing with glances, wooing with fast talk, and wooing by adhesion—five categories in all, which we shall now set out in full for our unhappy brethren.

"Wooing with tenderness" consists in the lover's being attracted to a beauti- 5.3.3
ful boy or beautiful woman and in his being with him or her as he desires and making love to and singing the praises of the beloved, and feeling tenderness for him until he becomes more affectionate towards him than a mother to her child, protects him from all harm, and endures misfortunes for his sake. He is careful with his beloved's money, solicitous of his belongings, and quick to fulfill his wishes—till he obtains what he desires from him in the most perfect fashion. Thus a poet says:

I became a valet to my love and groom
A while, till I obtained my wish.

Then there is "wooing with money," which is when the person concerned 5.3.4
disposes of wealth and property and therefore does not have to exert himself to win his beloved; on the contrary, any object of his affections to whom he shows a few coins will go to his place and he will get what he wants from him most consummately. As the poet says:

The vaunt of suitors, O you who plead your suits,
Is a shower of gold or silver coin displayed;
And if the door to satisfaction has been shut,
A dirham will open any barricade.
For in His Revelation He's thus declared:
«You'll ne'er attain favor till you've paid . . .»![232]

٥،٣،٥ (وعشق حدقة) وهو أن يكون من إخواننا الفقراء وقلبه يميل إلى الملاح وليس له حيلة إلّا النظر إلى الأمرد الجميل وطرفه يشير إليه أنّه مسكين وعاشق وفقير مفارق وليس معه دنيا إلّا الدعاء لحضرة هذا الجمال ثمّ يتذلّل بين يديه بالدعاء بقوله أطال الله بقاءك أدام الله جمالك أسعد الله أيّامك ونحو ذلك فيعرف الأمرد من دوام نظره إليه ودعائه له أنّ مراده الوصال لما يرى من دوام نظره إليه ومن فقره وإفلاسه قال الشاعر [طويل]

وما نَظَرُ اللّوطِيِّ إلّا فِراسَةً   وما تَحْتَ عَيْنِ العِلْقِ إلّا مُنَجِّمُ

٦،٣،٥ فيعطف عليه ويمكّنه من نفسه ومؤلّف هذا الكتاب من هذا القسم على حدّ قول القائل [رمل]

إنْ أَجِدْ وَجْهاً مَليحًا   أَلْقَ في الفِضّةِ خِفَّهْ
أَو أَجِدْ هذا وهذا   لَمْ أَجِدْ في الحَيِّ غُرْفَهْ
أو أجِدْ هاتيكَ جَمْعًا   أَلْقَ في الحارَةِ زَفَّهْ
فَلِهذا طولَ عُمْري   تائِبٌ مِنْ غَيْرِ عِفَّهْ

٧،٣،٥ (وعشق لقلقة) وهو أن يكون العاشق عنده لسان وشدّة بلاغة ورقّة انبساط وخلاعة ونكتة ونادرة وحكايات ومنادمات فيحتوي بخلاعته وهزله إلى الأمرد أو المرأة فيملك عقله ويَشْبِكُ معه لأجل انشراحه ويصير معه على قدم التمسخر فعند ذلك يمكّنه من نفسه ولا يخالفه قال الشاعر [طويل]

جَعَلْتُ خَلاعي ثُمَّ بَسْطي تَوَصُّلاً   إلى بَدْرِ تَمٍّ كان عِنْدي مُحَجَّبا

٨،٣،٥ (وعشق علقة) وهو أن يكون العاشق عديم الذوق سيّء الطبع كثيف الذات إذا

And there is "wooing with looks," which is when the lover is one of our brethren the paupers and his heart is attracted to cute boys and he can do nothing but look at the beautiful beardless youth, his glances indicating that he is to be pitied as a poor and abandoned suitor with no assets to offer in this world but his supplications to that divine beauty. He grovels at his feet uttering such blessings as "God lengthen your life! God preserve your beauty! God make your days happy!" and so on, and the boy understands from the lover's persistent gazing at him and his prayers on his behalf and his poverty and pennilessness that he wants to make love to him. As the poet says: 5.3.5

The sodomite's gaze is just to read the face
And through each faggot's eye an astrologer peers.

As a result, the boy feels affection for the man and gives himself to him. The author of this book belongs to this category, according to the words of the poet who said: 5.3.6

If I find a pretty face
My silver comes up skimpy.
If I find both this and that,
In the quarter I can't find a cubby.[233]
If all three are there to hand,
A wedding's afoot in the alley —
And so I go through life,
Continent without chastity.

And then there is "wooing with fast talk," which is when the suitor has the gift of the gab and is very persuasive, with a light and cheerful way about him, and given to risqué behavior, jokes, funny stories, anecdotes, and skits. He wins the boy or the woman over with his racy ways and his humor, to the point that the other falls completely under his spell and is ensnared by his bonhomie and takes to going around with him for the laughs, at which point he gives himself to him and denies him nothing. As the poet says: 5.3.7

I made my raciness and cheer a path
To a blazing moon who'd barred himself to me till then.

And finally there is "wooing by adhesion," which is when the suitor is a boor, of evil disposition and coarse appearance. If he sees a beardless boy, he 5.3.8

رأى الأمرد علق معه مثل الدبّور فلا يفارقه ولو ضربه بالمقارع أو صكّه بالنعال لا يرجع عنه ولو عرض له أنواع البلايا وألقاه في أشدّ المصائب لا ينفكّ عنه ولا يخلص منه إلّا بمراده كَرْهاً أو برضا قال أبو نواس [وافر]

إِذا رَقَدَ النَّدامَى خَلِّ عَنِّي ۝ وَعَمَّنْ كانَ يَصْلُحُ لِلدَّبِيبِ
أَلَذُّ النَّيْكِ ما كانَ ٱغْتِصاباً ۝ بِمَنْعِ الحُبِّ أَوخَوْفَ الرَّقِيبِ

٩،٣،٥ ولعلّ الناظم من هذا القسم بدليل قوله الآتي (بُولِي عَلَيَّ وَشَرْشِرِي) أي إنّ محبوبته لمّا رأته عالقاً بها كعُلوق النار في الحطب أو الدبّور في الخشب علمت أنّه لا يفارقها إلّا أن قضي مراده منها لعدم ذوقه وقوّة جهله ولم تقدر تمنعه بصكّ ولا بشيء من أنواع الرذالة فأرادت أن تتناوله بشيء نجس لأجل ما ينزجر عنها ويمتنع عن عشقها ويترك العلوق بها رفعت قميصها وأوهمت أنّها تريد البول عليه أو على لحيته حتّى تملأها ولكنّها في وهم منه وحيرة فأكّد عليها بالقول وأمرها أن تفعل فقال (وَقُلْتُ لَها بولي عَلَيَّ وَشَرْشِري) أي إنّي لم أبالي بما تفعليه معي من النجاسة ولم أتكدّر من الخساسة لأنّي عاشق مَشُوق وقليل الهندام والذوق كقول القائل [وزن غير معروف]

أحبكم واخرا على بابكم من فوق ۝ بالله اعذروا العاشق الخرا عديم الذوق

فلا أبالي بالبول عليّ وعلى لحيتي لأنّي (عَرِيضُ القَفا) وتخينه ومن شأن عريض القفا وتخينه وبليد الطبع أن يكون (لِلنّائِباتِ صَبورُ) وأن لا يَضْجَرَ ولا يقلق من البول وغيره ويصبر على حوادث الدهر ومصائبه لشدّة بلادته وعدم ذوقه وقلّة تدبيره قال الشاعر [طويل]

follows him around like a hornet and won't leave him even if the boy beats him with whips or thrashes him with shoes. He never retreats even if the boy exposes him to every type of calamity and drags him into the worst disasters, and never detaches himself from him until he gets what he wants, with or without his consent. As Abū Nuwās says:[234]

When friends lie down to sleep, leave me alone
With a boy who's ripe for a stealthy poke.
The sweetest of fucks are without consent,
When the beloved says no, or for fear of prying folk.

The author of the verse under discussion may well belong to this last category, because he says to her next "*būlī ʿalayya wa-sharshirī*" ("Piss on me and spray"), meaning that when his beloved saw that he clung to her like fire to the fuel or a hornet to wood, she realized that he was so boorish and ignorant that he would not leave her alone until he had gotten what he wanted from her and that she would not be able to repel him with blows or any other form of humiliation. Consequently, she decided to treat him to something filthy, so to drive him off, stop him pursuing her, and make him quit clinging to her, she lifted her shift and made as though she intended to urinate on him, or on his beard, till she had drenched it. Then, however, she found she had misjudged him and she ended up in a quandary, for with this verse he urged her on and commanded her to go ahead, saying, "I said to her, 'Piss on me and spray,' meaning 'I don't care what filthy things you do to me and I won't get upset at being defiled, for I am a lovelorn suitor, short on smart clothes and short on manners.' As the poet says on the subject: 5.3.9

I adore you and shit on your door from above.
By God, excuse the suitor—beshatten, mannerless, in love!

"Thus I don't care if someone pisses on me and on my beard, for I am 'one whose nape is broad' and thick, and it is the nature of those whose napes are broad and thick and whose temperaments are dull that they 'endure the blows of fate' and are not troubled or bothered by piss or anything else and endure patiently the vicissitudes and calamities of fate because of their extreme slowmindedness and boorishness and their inability to take thought for the morrow. The poet says:

يعرّضْ قفاهُ لِلهُمومِ جَميعِها   وذاكَ لِسوءِ الطَّبعِ فَهوَ بَليدُ

وقوله بولي مشتقّ من المِبْوَلة على وزن المِزْبَلة والمزبلة شيء يُعْمَل من الخُوص أو الحَلْفة يشيلوا عليها الزبل وربّما يكون فيها الجلّة والوحل فسمّيت باسم ما وُضِعَ فيها من تسمية الظرف باسم المظروف أو المحلّ باسم الحالّ فيه ومصدره بال يبول بولاً ومبالاً ومبولة ومبلّة أيضاً وهي ما يُبَلُّ فيها الكتّان فإن قيل إذا كانت لفظة البول فيها هذه المصادر فلأيّ شيء اكتفى الناظم بقوله (بُولِي عَلَيّ) ولم يصرّفها بقوله (بولي عليّ بولاً ومبالة) إلى آخره قلنا يمكن الجواب الفشرويّ عن هذا الإشكال الفشكليّ وهو أنّ قوله بولي فيها التكرار إذا تصرّفت فيها واشْتُقَّ منها المصادر فيلزم من هذا اختلاف الوزن وخروجه عن قاعدة النظم فيكون الكلام ركيكاً وإن كان في حدّ ذاته ثقيلاً فاكتفى الناظم بقوله بولي أو يقال إنّ هذا من باب الاكتفاء وهو ما يدلّ موجوده على محذوفه قال الشاعر [كامل] ١٠،٣،٥

بالَتْ عليّ مبالةً ومَبَلّةً   حتّى اكْتَفَيْتُ بِبَوْلِها وأنا أبولُ

أي وأنا أبول عليها أيضاً ليناسب بولها بولي لأجل اتّفاق المعنى ومناسبة المحبّة وائتلاف العشرة لأنّها لمّا بالت عليّ بلت أنا الآخر عليها بيقين ومن الاكتفاء والاقتباس قول بعضهم [بسيط]

مَليكةَ الحُسْنِ جودي باللِقا كَرَمًا   لِمُغْرَمٍ قَلْبُهُ قد ذابَ فيكِ أَذا
أَفْسَدتِ قلبي فقالت تلك عادَتُنا   قد قالَ سُبحانَه إنَّ المُلُوكَ إِذَا

أي ﴿ إِذَا دَخَلُوا قَرْيَةً أَفْسَدُوهَا ﴾ وقوله

He bares his nape to each distress
Because his nature's vile, and being thus, he's slow."

būlī ("piss") is derived from *mibwalah* ("urinal"), of the measure of *mizbalah*, **5.3.10**
which is a thing made of palm fronds or esparto grass on which they carry droppings, and in which, on occasion, one may also find dung cakes and mud; thus it is named after the thing that is placed in it, according to the rule of naming the container after the thing contained,[235] or the site after the situation. The paradigm is *bāla, yabūlu, bawlan,* and *mabālan* ("place for urinating") and *mibwalatan* ("urinal"), not to mention *miballatan*, which is the place where flax is wetted and soaked.[236] If it be said, "If *miballatan* has all these derived forms, why does the poet limit himself to using *būlī* alone, and why doesn't he parse the whole thing and say, 'Piss on me a pissing and a peeing,' etc.?" we reply, "The facetious response to this lame *problématique* may be framed as follows, namely, that to parse *būlī* and set out all its derived forms would involve repetition, which would, in turn, impose a break in the meter and a departure from the rules of prosody, enfeebling the style (which is tedious enough as is); thus the poet restrained himself from using anything but *būlī*. Alternatively, it may be argued that this is an example of 'restraint' in the rhetorical sense, which is when what is present implies what is omitted.[237] As the poet says:

She pissed upon me a pissing and a peeing
Till I'd had enough of her pissing and I too began to piss

"—meaning, 'and I too began to piss on her, so that my pissing would correspond to hers, for the sake of agreement in sense, correspondence in love, and intimacy of association, since, when she pissed on me, I, for my part, most assuredly pissed on her.'" An example of "restraint" combined with "quotation" are the words of a certain poet:

"O Queen of Beauty, grant a meeting, of your bounty,
To a swain whose heart's dissolved for you in pain—
My heart you've wrecked!" To which she said, "Such is our way:
God, to Whom be glory, said, «Lo! Kings, when . . .»"

that is, «. . . when they enter a village, ruin it.»[238]

(عَلَيَّ) أي بولي على ذاتي جميعاً حتّى يشمل البول شواربه ولحيته وما جاورها حتّى لا يبقى فيه منبت شعرة إلّا وقد عمّها البول ظاهراً وباطناً وقوله ١١،٣،٥

(وَشَرْشِري) معطوف على بولي وهي من لغة الأرياف وقد وردت في القاموس الأزرق والناموس الأبلق وهي مشتقّة من الشراء أو من الشرّ أو من الشرور أو من أولاد أبي شُرَيْشَر وهم جماعة فلاّحون أو من الشرشرة وهي آلة محدوبة تُعْمَل من الحديد يضعها الفلاّح في حزامه إذا سرح في الغيط يحشّ بها الزرع والحشيش للبهائم وشر وشرشر جناس مذيَّل ومصدره شرشر شرشرة فهو مشرشر وأكّد على محبوبته في القول بلفظ شرشري لكونها أنثى ولوكانت ذكرًا لكان الأنسب أن يقول له بول عليّ وطرطر لأنّ المرأة إذا بالت شرشرت بمعنى أنّ بولها ينزل من فَرْجها مُشَرْشِرًا حكم أسنان الشرشرة لطول فرجها واتّساعه بخلاف الرجل فإنّ أيره ضيّق المنفذ فكان المناسب أنّه إذا بال طرطر لأنّ بول الرجل يخرق في الأرض وبول الأنثى يُرَشّ عليها قال الشاعر [طويل] ١٢،٣،٥

إِذا بالَتِ الأُنثَى عَلى الأَرْضِ شَرْشَرَتْ   وإِنْ بالَ شَخصٌ فَهْوَ في الأَرضِ يَخْرِقُ

وفي رواية (رشرشت) بتقديم الراء فيكون فيه جناس مقلوب والمعنى واحد

ويؤكّد ما قلنا إنّ عنترة لمّا رماه بعض الأعداء بسهم ومات به خاف أهل قبيلته وهم بنو عَبْس من العدوّ أن يَدْهَمهم على حين غفلة إن شعروا بموته وكانوا على أُهْبة سفر فاتّفقوا أن يجعلوا ابنة عمّه مكانه ويزيّوها بزِيّ رجل مثله ففعلوا ذلك وركبت الجواد وسارت أمام قومها فنظر العدوّ إليها فلم يشكّوا إلّا أنّها عنترة فتحيّروا في هذا الأمر وكان فيهم رجل صاحب رأي وفراسة فقال لهم أنا أكشف لكم الأمر وهو أنّي أتوقّع نزوله لقضاء الحاجة فإن كان بوله يخرق في الأرض فهو عنترة وإن كان مشرشرًا ١٣،٣،٥

The word *ʿalayya* ("on me") means "piss on my person in its entirety till the piss covers my mustache, my beard, and all adjacent areas, to the point that not one follicle is left that has not been comprehensively covered in piss, externally and internally." **5.3.11**

wa-sharshirī ("and spray") is parallel to *būlī* ("piss"). It is a rural dialecticism and is to be found in *The Blue Ocean and Piebald Canon*. It derives from *shirāʾ* ("purchasing") or from *sharr* ("evil") or from *shurūr* ("evils") or from the Abū Shurayshar Troupe, who are a group of peasants, or from *sharsharah* ("sickle"), a curved implement made of iron that the peasant puts in his belt when he sets off for the fields and with which he cuts plants and grass for his animals.[239] The words *sharr* and *sharshir* are an example of "caudal paronomasia." The paradigm is *sharshara, sharsharatan, musharshir*. By using the word *sharshirī*, the poet also emphasizes the feminine gender of his beloved since, were he a male, it would have been more appropriate to say, "piss on me and hose me down," because a woman, when she urinates, sprays, meaning that her urine descends from her vagina in dentated form, like the teeth of a serrated sickle, because the vagina is long and wide, while the man, on the other hand, having a narrow opening in his penis, is more properly described as "hosing" when he urinates, since the man's urine bores into the ground, while that of the woman is sprinkled upon it. As the poet says: **5.3.12**

> The female, when she pisses, sprays.
> When it's a male, he bores into the ground.

In another recension it says *rashrashat*, with the *r* in front, in which case it would be an example of "inverted paronomasia," though the meaning stays the same.

Proof of our contention is that, when ʿAntarah was shot with an arrow by his enemies and died, his tribe, the Banū ʿAbs, feared that, if the enemy learned of his death, they would attack them unawares and catch them unprepared, because they were on the point of moving camp; so they agreed that they would put his girl-cousin in his place and dress her up as a man like him. They did that, and she mounted his steed and proceeded at the head of her people. Seeing her, the enemy did not doubt that she was ʿAntarah and were puzzled as to how this could be. Among them was a man of keen judgment, who had the power to discern the inner truth from outward appearances. He said to **5.3.13**

فهي عبلة ابنة عمّه ويكون عنترة قد مات فتعقّب الرجل الأمر وكشف عن الحال فوجده عبلة فهجموا عليهم ودهموهم والقصّة مشهورة في محلّها وقد تطلق الشرشرة على فعل الرجل قال الشاعر [طويل]

إِذا المَرْءُ لَم يَنْفَعْكَ والدَّهرُ مُقْبِلٌ   عَليهِ ولم تَخْطِرْ عليهِ ببالِ
فَصَوِّرْهُ في وَسْطِ الكَنيفِ بِفَحْمَةٍ   وشَرْشِرْ عَليهِ عِندَ كلِّ مَبالِ

وقوله (عَرِيض القَفا) على وزن صقيع اللحا وعريض القفا مشتقّ من العروض أو من العرضي وهو ما يُلَفّ على الرأس بلغة الريّافة ويسمّوه أيضاً الكرّ أو من عارضة الباب قلت والأنسب اشتقاقه من العارض وهو الغَمام لأنّ قفاه صار متعرّضاً للبول والصكّ وغيره كتعرّض الغمام في أفق السماء والقفا مشتقّ من القفوة أي قفوة الإنكشاريّة أو من القُفّة أو من القَفْقولة وهي بوشة صغيرة يطبخوا فيها الريّافة طبيخ البيسار وقيل هو من قَفَوْتُ الشيء إذا تبعته لأنّ القفا دائماً تابع للرأس فلا يفارقه أبداً إلّا عند قطعه ومتى سارت سار معها قال الشاعر [بسيط] ١٤،٣،٥

الرَّأسُ يَتْبَعُها في السَيرِ أَرْبَعَةٌ   وَجْهٌ وَذَقْنٌ وآذانٌ وعَرْضُ قَفَا

وقد يطلق القفا على ذات الرجل جميعها ويخاطَب به الإنسان إذا كان بليداً جبان القلب قال الشاعر [بسيط] ١٥،٣،٥

صَادٍ بِبابِكَ يا بحرَ الوَفا وَقَفَا   فَعاقَهُ عَنكَ بَقْفٌ واقِفٌ وَقَفَا

them, "I will get to the bottom of the matter for you as follows. I shall wait until he dismounts to relieve himself. If his urine bores into the ground, then it is ʿAntarah. But if it sprays out, then it is ʿAblah, his cousin, and ʿAntarah is dead." So the man pursued this plan, discovered the facts, and found that it was ʿAblah, and they attacked them and took them unprepared. The story is well known in the places where it is told. It is also possible to apply the word *sharshara* to what the man does, as in the words of the poet:

If someone lets you down while Fortune smiles
　On him, and he's not the sort you'd miss,
Draw him with charcoal in the middle of the loo,
　And spray him each time you piss!

The words *ʿarīḍu l-qafā* ("broad of nape") are of the measure of *saqīʿu l-liḥā* 5.3.14
(literally "cold of beard," i.e., "thick-skinned, brazen, shameless"). The word *ʿarīḍ* is derived from *ʿirḍ* ("armpit") or *ʿarḍī*, meaning, in the language of country people, the thing that is wrapped around the head,[240] which they also call a *karr*, or from the *ʿāriḍah* ("lintel") of a door. I would say, however, that the most appropriate derivation is from *ʿāriḍ*, meaning "clouds," because his nape was presented laterally to the piss and the blows, etc., just as clouds present themselves laterally across the horizon. The word *qafā* is derived from *qafwah*, that is, the *qafwah* ("neck piece") of the Janissaries,[241] or from *quffah* ("basket"), or from *qafqūlah*, meaning a small pot in which the people of the countryside cook *bīsār*. Some say that it is from *qafawtu al-shayʾ*, meaning "I followed something," because the nape always follows the head and is never separated from it (unless it be cut off), and wherever the one goes, the other goes too. The poet says:

Four things go along with the head on its trek—
　A face, beard, ears, and a nice broad back of the neck.

The term *qafā* may also be applied to the whole of a man's person, and it 5.3.15
may be used as a form of address to a person, if he is a dullard and a coward. As the poet says:

Thirsty, O Sea of Fulfillment, he stood at your gate
　But was kept from you by an inert lout, a lily-livered dunderpate.

وفي هذا البيت الجناس التامّ المزيد وقوله

١٦،٣،٥ (للنَّائِباتِ) جمع نائبة ونائبة ما ينوب الإنسان من البلايا والمشاقّ وقد تنتج من خبايا الأيّام وحوادث الدهر وعجائبه على وفق إرادة الله تعالى قال الشاعر [خفيف]

اللَّيالي مِنَ الزَّمانِ حَبالى ... مُثْقَلاتٌ تَلِدْنَ كُلَّ عَجِيبَهْ

ومصدرها ناب ينوب نيابة وقوله

١٧،٣،٥ صبور على وزن عَبور وقيل بمعنى صابر وعلى هذا أيضاً يكون عبور بمعنى عابر وهو مشتقّ من الصبر أو من الصبّارة التي تُعَلَّقُ في البيوت وقد تنبت في بعض المقابر فهي لشدّة مرارتها وحدوثها على حين غفلة وصبر الرجال عليها اشْتُقَّ لها هذا الاسم من هذا المعنى وقد صرحت بما يقرب من معنى ذلك في مطلع قصيدة قلتها في شكوى الدهر وعجائبه وسرعة انقلابه وهي هذه [بسيط]

حَوادِثُ الدَّهْرِ قَدْ تَأْتي عَلى خَطَرٍ ... فَاحْذَرْ عَواقِبَها تَنْجُو من القَدَرِ
واعددْ لها من سِهام الصَّبرِ سابغة[1] ... تقيكَ شدّتها[2] إذ تُرمَ بالشَرَرِ

إلى آخرها وقد أتى لفظ العُبور بمعنى العُبُراية أو عبور الغنم كما تقدّم

وقد وردت لفظة العبراية في نظم الشيخ بركات وسبب قصتّه أنّه كان رحمه الله من البلداء واتّفق أنّه سافر إلى بلاد الروم ووصل إلى مدينة القسطنطينيّة العظمى فصادف صديقاً له مارًّا في بعض شوارعها فسلّم عليه وسأله عن حاله وحال الملك فقال له يا شيخ بركات قد أجازني بكذا وكذا على قصيدة مدحته بها فقال له الشيخ بركات لا بدّ أنا الآخر أمدحه وأُثني عليه وكان صديقه هذا يعرف بلادته وسوء طبعه فمنعه فلم يقدر على منعه عن الملك فطرق الباب وكان من عادة الملوك في قديم الزمان

١ بي: سابقة. ٢ بي: من شرتها.

Note that the verse contains an example of augmentative perfect paronomasia.[242]

li-l-nāʾibāti ("to the blows of fate"): *nāʾibāt* is the plural of *nāʾibah*, meaning any disaster or hardship that may befall a man and that may issue from the unknown things that the days hold in store for us and from the incidents and marvels of Fate, according to the will of the Almighty. As the poet says: **5.3.16**

The nights of time with the future
Are gravid, and give birth to marvel upon marvel.

The paradigm is *nāba, yanūbu, niyābatan*.[243]

The word *ṣabūr* ("capable of bearing") is of the measure of *ʿabūr* ("transient, in passage") and is said to mean the same as *ṣābir* ("patient"), in which case *ʿabūr* should mean the same as *ʿābir* ("crosser, passerby"). It is derived from *ṣabr* ("patience") or from the *ṣabbārah* ("aloe plant"), which is hung up in houses and sometimes grows in cemeteries and which, because of its bitter taste, its habit of suddenly sprouting up, and the fact that people put up with it despite all this, derives its name from this sense. I have expressed a similar sentiment in the opening lines of an ode of mine protesting against Fate, its surprises and sudden upsets, saying: **5.3.17**

The accidents of Fate may be to your peril,
So beware their outcome and escape Fate's ire.
Prepare against them an ample coat of mail from patience,
To protect you from their fierceness when showered with their fire

and so on. The word *ʿubūr* sometimes occurs in the sense of *ʿuburāyah* ("crossing place for flocks") as already mentioned.[244]

The latter term occurs in the verse of Shaykh Barakāt, the story being that the Shaykh, God bless him, was a simpleton. It happened that he traveled to the Land of the Romans[245] and arrived at the city of Great Constantinople, where, walking in one of its streets, he came across a friend of his. He saluted the man and asked him how he was and how the king was. His friend answered, "Shaykh Barakāt, he gave me such and such an amount to reward me for an ode I composed in his praise." Shaykh Barakāt said to him, "I too will compose a eulogy for him and sing his praises!" Now his friend, aware of his stupidity and poor breeding, told him not to, but nothing he could do could stop the shaykh

أنّهم لا يمنعوا أحدًا عن أبوابهم فخرجت إليه امرأة عجوز وقيل جاءت له من خلف دار الملك كما سيأتي في نظمه وقالت له ما تريد فقال أريد الملك فقالت له تأتي إليه في وقت غير هذا وإن كان ولا بدّ تعرّفنا حالك نخبره به قال فأخذ دَواة وورقة وكتب فيها يقول [رمل]

بَرَكَاتُ عُبُرَايَهْ   جا يُسَلِّمْ ما قَدَرْ شي ٤،٥
مِنْ عَجُوزٍ خَلْفَ دارٍ   كَالْأُسُودِ الضَّارِيَاتِ

وطواها وأعطاها للعجوز وجلس ينتظر الجائزة من الملك قال فلمّا وقعت الرقعة في يد الملك وقرأ الأبيات أمر بإحضاره فلمّا مَثَلَ بين يديه ورأى ذاته وبلادته وثقل نظمه وبرودة لحيته فضحك عليه وقال له ما تريد قال الجائزة على هذا النظم قال وكان الملك صاحب ذوق ولطافة فقال له نعم أجيزك جائزة تناسب نظمك هذا ثمّ ألبسه بَرْذَعة حمار وأمر أن يجعلوا في فمه الصريمة وعلى رأسه التَفركادة الحمير ثمّ أمر أن ينادى عليه في المدينة هذا جزاء من يمدح الملوك بمثل هذه الألفاظ ثمّ أنعم عليه بعد ذلك وأمر بإخراجه من المدينة قلتُ ولهذا ذكروا أنّ الشاعر لا يهدي قصيدته لملك أو غيره حتّى ينظر في ألفاظها ويهديها أو يعرضها على أرباب الخبرة من أهل الذكاء والفطنة لئلّا يقع في محظور مثل هذا البليد

ولنرجع إلى شرح أبيات الشيخ بركات قوله

from going to the king. Thus it was that he went and knocked at the gate, for in ancient times it was the custom of kings to turn away no one from their doors. An old woman came out to him—it is said that she came to him from behind the king's abode, as the shaykh's verse will mention—and she asked him, "What do you want?" He replied, "I want the king." She told him, "Come some other time, or, if it must be now, tell us what you want so that we may inform him." So the shaykh took his pen case and a sheet of paper and wrote on it as follows:

The Verse of Shaykh Barakāt: "Barakāt was passin' by"

Barakātun ʿuburāyah 5.4
jā yusallim mā qadar shī
min ʿajūzin khalfa dārin
ka-l-usūdi l-ḍāriyātī

Barakāt was passin' by,
Came to say "Hi!"—but no way,
'Cos of an old crone behind an abode,
"Like unto lions savaging their prey!"

and he folded it and gave it to the old woman and sat and waited for the king's reward. When the note was put into the king's hand and he read the two lines of verse, he ordered that the shaykh be brought before him, and when he was in front of him and he had taken note of his appearance and his slow-wittedness, the obnoxiousness of his verse, and his thick-skinnedness, he laughed and asked, "What do you want?" "The reward for these verses," said the shaykh. The king, being a man of taste and refinement, said, "I shall indeed give you a reward to match these verses of yours!" and he had him saddled with a donkey's saddle and ordered them to put the bit in his mouth and the crupper over his head, just like a donkey. Then he ordered them to proclaim around the city, "This is the reward of them that use such language to praise kings!" Afterwards he gave him presents and ordered him expelled from the city. This, I would point out, is why people have stated that a poet should never dedicate his ode to a king or to anyone else without examining the language carefully before presenting it or showing it to people of intelligence and discernment with experience in such things, lest he commit a faux pas like this dimwit.

Let us now return to the analysis of the verse of Shaykh Barakāt.

١،٤،٥ (بَرَكَاتُ عُبُرَايَهْ) جمع بَرَكة وهو علَمَ عليه مشتق من بِرْكة الفيل بمصر أو من بِرْكة الجمل وقوله عبراية أي يريد العُبور على الملك وتقدّم اشتقاقه وقوله

٢،٤،٥ (جا يُسَلِّمْ ما قَدَرْشي) أي أراد السلام ما قدر والمانع له من السلام

٣،٤،٥ (عجوز) رآها

٤،٤،٥ (خَلْفَ دارٍ) الملك وتقدّم اشتقاق لفظة عجوز لها قوّة وشدّة في منعه

٥،٤،٥ (كَالأُسودِ) أي السباع

٦،٤،٥ (الضَّارِيَاتِ) العاديات التي تقدر على الإنسان وغيره وتفترسه

٧،٤،٥ ولفظ العجوز يطلق على المرأة الكبيرة إذا انحنى ظهرها وشاب رأسها فيصير قربها همّ وجماعها غمّ إلّا على من يميل إلى عشق العجائز ويفضّلهنّ على ذوات النهود البارزات ويمتثل بقول الشاعر [طويل]

تَعَشَّقْتُها شَمْطاءَ شَابَ وَلِيدُها   وللنّاسِ فيما يَعْشَقونَ مَذاهِبُ

ويقرب من هذا المعنى أنه وُصِفَ لأبي نواس رحمه الله رجل حدّاد بمصر يقول الشعر ارتجالاً فسافر إليه متنكّراً يختبر فصاحته حتّى دخل مصر وسأل عليه فدلّوه على حانوته فوقف عليه وسلّم عليه فردّ السلام فأنشد أبو نواس يقول [بسيط]

ماذا تَقولُ رَعاكَ اللهُ في رَجُلٍ   أَضْناهُ حُبُّ عَجوزٍ بِنتِ تِسْعِينِ

Concerning the words *Barakātun ʿuburāyah* ("Barakāt was passin' by"): *barakāt* is the plural of *barakah* ("blessing"), and is a proper name, derived from Birkat al-Fīl[246] in Cairo or from the *birkah* ("manner of kneeling") of camels. By *ʿuburāyah* he means "passing by" (*al-ʿubūr ʿalā*) the king; the etymology is given above. 5.4.1

By the words *jā yusallim mā qadar shī* ("He came to say 'Hi!' but no way") he means "he arrived desiring to make his salutations but was unable to do so," the thing preventing him from doing so being 5.4.2

ʿajūzin ("an old crone") he saw 5.4.3

khalfa dārin ("behind an abode") of the king's. The etymology of *ʿajūz* has already been given.[247] This crone had the strength and fierceness to prevent him 5.4.4

ka-l-usūdi ("like unto lions"), that is, like predators 5.4.5

l-ḍāriyāti ("ravaging their prey"), that is, like the savage beasts that bring down men and other things and take them as their prey. 5.4.6

The word *ʿajūz* is used of an old woman when her back has bent and her hair turned white, rendering proximity to her a woe and intercourse with her a bane—unless one happens to be one of those who are drawn to old women and prefer them to the ones with perky breasts—one of those, that is, referred to by the poet when he says: 5.4.7

> I loved her as a gray-haired hag, whose own son's hair had turned—
> For one man's meat, in love, is by another spurned![248]

which reminds me of something similar, namely, that Abū Nuwās, God have mercy on him, was told of a blacksmith in Cairo who could improvise poetry at the drop of a hat, so he set off in disguise to test his skill. He reached Cairo and asked after him and they directed him to the man's shop, and he stood before him and greeted him, and the man returned his greeting. Then Abū Nuwās[249] recited:

> What say you, God keep you, of a man
> By love of a ninety-year-old worn to a frazzle?

فأجابه الحدّاد بقوله [بسيط]

يُبكى عليهِ فَقدْ أَودى بمُهجتِهِ حُبُّ القِباحِ وتَرْكُ الحورِ والعِينِ

فقال له أبو نواس مثلك لا يكون إلّا نديماً لأمير المؤمنين فقال ما لي وما لأمير المؤمنين أنا صنعتي تكفيني ولا حاجة لي إليه فتركه وانصرف

٨،٤،٥ وقد يطلق العجوز على الخمرة إذا عتُقت وطال زمنها وقيل لبعض الحكماء مَن أشرُّ الناس قال العجائز وقال بعضهم في تفسير قوله تعالى حكاية عن سيّدنا سليمان عليه الصلاة والسلام في حقّ الهُدهُد ﴿لَأُعَذِّبَنَّهُ عَذَاباً شَدِيداً﴾ قيل أراد أن يزوّجه بعجوز وقال سيّدنا عليّ كرّم الله وجهه إيّاك ومجامعة العجوز فإنّها تأخذ منك القوى وتَهُدّ الحيَل وقيل الشابّة من النساء شهوة والعجوز بلوة وذات الولد دعوة وذكروا أنّ أصل حرب البَسُوس من امرأة عجوز كانت تسمّى البسوس وكان لها ناقة ترعاها فضربها كُلَيب بسهم فقتلها فذهبت إلى جسّاس وألقت الفتنة بين الفريقين فاقتتلوا ووقع الحرب بينهم أربعين عاماً وذكر بعضهم أنّ فتنة التتار التي لم يوجد في الإسلام أعظم منها إلّا خروج الدجّال كان سببها امرأة عجوز (وأمّا حِيَلهن) في القيادة وجمع النساء للمفاسيد فإنّها تغلب حيل إبليس قال الشاعر [وافر مع كسر]

عَجوزُ السُوءِ لا يُرحَمْ صِباها ولا يُغفَرْ لها يومَ تموتْ
تَقودُ من السِّياسةِ ألفَ بَغلٍ إذا حَرَنوا بِخَيطِ العَنكَبوتْ

٩،٤،٥ وقال بعضهم مررت بعجوز جالسة خلف بير تبكي وتنوح فقلت لها ما الذي دهاك فقالت لي يا سيّدي وقعت لي إسوِرة من ذهب في هذا البير قال فاعتقدتُ صدقها فنزعت ثيابي ونزلت البير فلمّا رأتني وصلت إلى قاعه أخذت ثيابي وانصرفت وتركتني عرياناً ففتّشت في البير فلم أر شيئاً فطلعت من البير فلم أرها فسرت إلى

The blacksmith replied:

Weep for him, for this will do him in—
Loving the dogs and eschewing the dark-eyed gazelle!

Abū Nuwās said, "Such a one as you has no business to be anything but a companion of the Commander of the Faithful." The man replied, "What have I to do with the Commander of the Faithful? My work provides for my wants, and I have no need of him." So Abū Nuwās left him and departed.

ʿAjūz may also be applied to wine, when it is aged and matured. A certain sage was asked, "Who are the worst of people?" and he said, "Old women." Some commentators on the words of the Almighty placed on the tongue of Our Master Sulaymān, blessings and peace upon him, when he condemned the hoopoe, saying, «Verily I will punish him with a hard punishment»,[250] say that what he meant was that he would marry him to an old woman. And Our Master ʿAlī,[251] God honor his face, said, "Beware of intercourse with old women for they take away your strength and destroy your stamina." And they say, "A young woman excites, an old one blights, and one who has borne a child invites." People say too that the War of al-Basūs was caused by an old woman called al-Basūs who had a she-camel that she used to graze; Kulayb shot the camel with an arrow and killed it, so she went to Jassās and incited dissension between the two groups, who fell to fighting, and the war between them lasted forty years. Others say that the war of the Tartars,[252] than which Islam will know none greater until the appearance of the Antichrist, was caused by an old woman. As for their wiles as panders and in bringing women together for evil purposes, they exceed even those of Satan. Says the poet: 5.4.8

An evil hag—may she find no mercy in her youth
And no forgiveness for her sins when dead!—
By craft could lead a thousand mules,
Though they balk, by a spider's thread.

Someone said,[253] "I passed an old woman sitting behind a well, weeping. 'What ails thee?' I asked her, and she replied, 'Sir, my gold bracelet has fallen into the well.' I believed her and stripped off my clothes and went down into the well. When she saw that I'd reached the bottom, she took my clothes and departed, leaving me naked. I searched in the well but found nothing. Then, 5.4.9

منزلي عرياناً ولبست ثياباً غيرها فكان هذا من حِيَل العجائز ومكرهنّ فحيلهنّ عجيبة * وأمورهنّ غريبة * فينبغي التحرّز منهنّ * والبعد عنهنّ * فهنّ أصحاب العجائب * وأرباب الدواهي والمصائب *

فإن قيل إنّ لفظة (قَدَرْشي) في نظم الشيخ بركات التي تقدّم ذكرها بمعنى قدر فلأيّ ١٠،٤،٥
شيء لم يكتف بها مع أنها أقلّ حروفاً من قدرشي وكان حقّه أن يقول (جا يسلم ما
قدر) وكان هذا أولى وأخصر في اللفظ قلنا هذا من باب قَطَعَ وقَطَّعَ فإنّ زيادة البناء
تدلّ على زيادة المعنى فلفظة قدرشي أبلغ من لفظة قدر وأيضاً ربّما اختلّ النظم فراعى
في ذلك زيادة الحروف لأجل وزن الشعر وأمّا ركاكة المعنى وثقل الكلام واختلاف
القافية فلا تطالبنا به لبلادة قائله وكثافة طبعه انتهى

(الثالث من أشعارهم)

قيل جلس جماعة من الظرفاء يتناشدون الأشعار * وبينهم شيء من الحَلْوى ٥،٥
والثمار * فمرّ بهم رجل فلاّح * الهمّ والخزى على وجهه قد لاح * فلما رآهم في
هذه الحاله * انقضّ عليهم بلا محَاله * وقال لهم ذكّرتموني زمان العشق للملاح *
وقولي فيهم بلا مُزاح * وأراد أن يأكل معهم فحصل منهم انقباض * فقال لهم لا
بدّ ما أرمي عليكم أنقاض * أي ألغاز بلغة شعراء الريف ثمّ إنّه أنشد يقول [الكامل]

وَاللهِ وَاللهِ العَـضيمِ القادِرِ هُوَ عالِمًا بِسَرايِري وَخَبايِطي
إنْ عادَ قَلْبي دا المَشومُ ذِكِرْكُمو لَأُقَطِّعو مِنْ مُهْجَتي بِصَوابِعي

emerging from the well and not finding her, I went to my house naked and put on other clothes." This is an example of the wiles of old women and their cunning. Indeed their wiles are a wonder and their manners a marvel, and one should beware of them and shun them, for they are full of amazements and possessed of calamities and disasters.

If it be said that the expression *qadar shī* ("(No way) he could") in the above-mentioned verse of Shaykh Barakāt has the same meaning as *qadar*, so why was he not content with the latter, given that it has fewer letters than *qadar shī*, and that he should have said *jā yusallim mā qadar*, which would have been more correct and shorter to pronounce, we would answer, "This falls into the category of emphatic usage, as in the contrast between *qaṭaʿa* ('he cut') and *qaṭṭaʿa* ('he cut to pieces'), for augmentation of form indicates augmentation of meaning. On this basis the expression *qadar shī* has greater force than *qadar* alone.[254] Also the verse would have been thrown out of kilter otherwise, so he had resort to the extra letters for the sake of the meter. As for the triteness of the meaning, the obnoxiousness of the words, and the break in the rhyme, don't ask me about them, for the author was too stupid and coarse-natured for his verses to lend themselves to any acceptable explanation! End." 5.4.10

The Third of Their Verses: "By God, by God, the Moighty, the Omnipotent"[255]

It is said that a party of elegants had sat down, verses to compare, a few sweetmeats and a little fruit before them by way of fare, when along came a man, a son of the soil, signs etched on his face of ignominy and toil. Seeing them in this state, he pounced upon them, leaving them no escape, and told them, "You've set me thinking of the days of falling in love with the good-looking and of the poetry I composed about them, no joking!" His idea was to eat with them—which made them quite depressed—so he told them, "I have a few *anqāḍ* (meaning 'riddles' in the language of the country poets)[256] I'd like to test." Then he recited: 5.5

wa-llāhi wa-llāhi l-ʿaḍīmi l-qādirī
huwa ʿāliman bi-sarāyirī wa-khabāyiṭī
in ʿāda qalbī dā l-mashūmu dhikirkamū
la-uqattiʿu min muhjatī bi-ṣawābiʿī

هذا الكلام من بحر الهلفطه * والمعاني المشرمطه * وتفاعيله متخلبِط متخلبِط ١،٥،٥
متخلبِط * وعرضه بيقين * من زِنْجيّة لِشرْبين * وطوله باحتياط * من السِرْو لِدِمّياط *
وأمّا شرح معانيه المسخّمَة * وحلّ مبانيه الملطَّمه * فقوله

(وَاللهِ وَاللهِ العَضيمِ القادِرِ) يريد القَسَم غير أنّه لم يقع الموقع لأنه ذكر الصفة بالضادّ ٢،٥،٥
المُعجَمَة لا بالظاء المشالة جريًا على لغة أمثاله من أهل الريف فأخلّ المعنى في ذكر الصفة
وإن كان الموصوف الذي هو الاسم الكريم باقي على حاله وقوله

(هُوَ عالِمًا) بنصب عالمًا مع أنّه مرفوع ليس على قاعدة النحويّين إلّا أنّ لسانه لم يساعده ٣،٥،٥
على ذلك لأنّ ألسنة أهل الريف تنصب المرفوع وترفع المنصوب كما يقولوا عبد الرحمن
برفع راء الرحمن وهذا من باب عجرفة الكلام المناسبة هؤلاء الأقوام وقوله

(بِسَرايِري وَخَبايِطي) السراير جمع سريرة وهو ما يُسِرّه الإنسان من خير أو شرّ ٤،٥،٥
والخبايط جمع خبيطة على وزن عبيطة وخبايطي على وزن عبايطي مشتقّة
من الخبط يقال فلان خبط فلان إذا ألقاه على الأرض أو من الخُباط على وزن
الضُّراط ولفظة الضراط فيها المناسبة بل هي أولى قال الشاعر [رجز]

الخَـبْطُ مُشْـتَقٌّ من الخُـباطِ كَذاكَ فيهـا الضَّرْطُ كالضُـراطِ

ومصدرها خبط يخبط خبطًا فهو خابط ومخبوط وقوله

By God, by God, the Moighty, the Omnipotent,
He is cognizunt of my secrets and my clangers!
If this unlucky heart of mine should turn again to thoughts of youse
I'll cut it out of my heart with my fangers!

This verse is taken from the ocean of mendacious meters and massacred motifs, and its feet are *mutakhalbiṭun mutakhalbiṭun mutakhalbiṭun.*[257] Its breadth, as may be seen, is from Zinjiyyah to Shirbīn; its length, no doubt about it, from al-Sirw to Dimyāṭ. As for the elucidation of its mucky motifs and the analysis of its contused constructions, we say, 5.5.1

wa-llāhi wa-llāhi l-ʿaḍīmi l-qādirī ("By God, by God, the Moighty, the Omnipotent"): he wants to use the well-known oath, but it doesn't work, as he pronounces the attribute of God with a *ḍād* instead of a *ẓā'*, after the manner of his like among the people of the countryside.[258] As a result, the meaning is distorted with regard to the attribute, even though the referent, namely, the Divine Name, remains unaffected. 5.5.2

His words *huwa ʿāliman* ("He is cognizunt"), with the ending *-an* when it ought to be *-un*, is not according to the rules of the grammarians.[259] However, perhaps he should be excused, as his tongue is of no help to him in this, for the tongues of the people of the countryside change *a* into *u* and vice versa. Thus they say ʿAbd al-Ruḥmān, with *u* after the *r* of al-Raḥmān.[260] This is part and parcel of the uncouthness of speech appropriate to such people. 5.5.3

His words *bi-sarāyirī wa-khabāyiṭī* ("of my secrets and my clangers"): *sarāyir* ("secrets") is the plural of *sarīrah*, which is anything that a man conceals, be it good or evil; and *khabāyiṭ* ("clangers") is the plural of *khabīṭah*, of the measure of *ʿabīṭah* ("a stupidity"); thus *khabāyiṭī* is of the measure of *ʿabāyiṭī* ("my stupidities").[261] It is derived from *khabṭ* ("knocking"); one says, "So-and-so *khabaṭa* so-and-so" if he knocked him to the ground; or from *khubāṭ* ("sheep bloat"), of the measure of *ḍurāṭ* ("audible farting"), which latter would fit the context even better, and indeed would be preferable. As the poet says: 5.5.4

Khabṭ from *khubāṭ* derives
And *ḍarṭ* from *ḍurāṭ* likewise.

The paradigm goes *khabaṭa, yakhbiṭu, khabṭan,* plus *khābiṭun* and *makhbūṭun.*

٥،٥،٥ (إنْ عادَ قَلْبِي دا المَشومُ ذِكْرَكُمو * لَأُقَطِّعو مِنْ مُهْجَتِي بِصَوابِعِي) هذا جواب القسم والقطع هو فصل الشيء وبُعْده يقال فلان قطع فلانًا إذا بعُد عنه والقلب مشتقّ من التقلّب قال الشاعر [طويل]

وما سُمِّيَ الإنسانُ إلّا لِنَسْيِهِ ولا القلبُ إلّا أنه يَتَقَلَّبُ

والمهجة معلومة

٦،٥،٥ والصوابع على وزن الفراقع وهي معلومة أيضاً وأسماؤها الخِنْصِر والبِنْصِر والوُسطَى والشاهد والإبهام فهي خمسة بيقين لا شكّ فيها ومعنى الكلام أنّ هذا البليد أقسم بالله العظيم القادر على كلّ شيء العالم بسرائره وخبائطه أي ما أسرّه من الأفعال القبيحة والنيّات الخبيثة وما يخبطه في الليل من سرقة الغنم والفراخ والنطّ في الدور وقَرْط الزرع وسرقة الجلّة وموالسته على زرع شريكه وأخذه بالليل ونحو ذلك من الخبائط الّتي يفعلها هو وغيره من أراذل الريّافة وقوله

٧،٥،٥ (إنْ عادَ قَلْبِي) أي إن رجع إلى محبّتكم بعد ما قاسى من همومكم وترككم إيّاه وهو يتذلّل لكم بالمحبّة ويسرح لكم الغيط في الحرّ ويصالحكم بالزبل ويسرق لكم الجلّة وترسلوا له القفّة يملأها خراء ناشف وزبل غنم ونحو ذلك ويسرح بالليل يقرط لكم من زرع الناس ويطعمكم وأنتم تشتغلوا بغيره وتهجروه ولا تعرفوا الجميل الذي فعله فأنا الآخر

The words in *ʿāda qalbī dā l-mashūmu dhikirkamū * la-uqattiʿu min muhjatī bi-ṣawābiʿī* ("If this unlucky heart of mine should turn once more to thoughts of youse * I'll cut it out of my heart with my fangers!") are the complement to the oath. *Qaṭʿ* ("cutting") is the severing of a thing and its detachment. One says, "So-and-so 'cut' so-and-so" if he shunned him.[262] The word *qalb* ("heart") is derived from *taqallub* ("inconstancy"). The poet says: 5.5.5

> ***Man*** **(*insān*)** is so called for his **a**mnesia (***nasy***)
> And the **heart** (*qalb*) for its **heart**less inconsistency (*taqallub*).[263]

The *muhjah* ("heart") is too familiar to require discussion.[264]

The word *ṣawābiʿ* ("fingers") is of the measure of *farāqiʿ* ("crackings, e.g., of the joints") and is likewise too familiar too require further explanation. The names of the fingers are *khinṣir* ("little finger, pinkie"), *binṣir* ("fourth finger"), *wusṭā* ("middle finger"), *shāhid* ("index finger"), and *ibhām* ("thumb"); they are five in number—this is quite certain, and there is no doubt about it. As for what the words mean, this dimwit swears by God the Mighty, the Omnipotent over all things, who is cognizant of his secrets and his "clangers," that is, of whatever ugly deeds and base thoughts he has hidden away and whatever he has knocked off (*yakhbiṭuhu*)[265] at night by way of stealing sheep and chickens and gamboling about in people's houses and cutting off the tops of the standing crops and stealing dung cakes and swindling his partner by taking his crops at night, and all the other "clangers" that he and similar rural trash commit. 5.5.6

The words *in ʿāda qalbī* ("if this unlucky heart of mine should turn again") mean: if the poet should start loving you once more after the woes he has suffered because of you and your abandonment of him, despite his groveling with love before you and going off to the fields for you in the heat and giving you droppings as a peace offering and stealing dung cakes for you and, whenever you send him a basket, filling it with dry shit and sheep's droppings and so on, and going off at night for you to cut the tops off the crops from people's fields, and feeding you, when all the time you were occupied with another and had abandoned him and refused to acknowledge the favors he has done you, then he, for his part, [266] 5.5.7

٨،٥،٥ إن عاد قلبي (دا المَشومُ) ووصفه بأنّه مشوم لأنّه وافق على محبّة قليلين الخير ناكرين الجميل وقوله

٩،٥،٥ (ذِكْرَكْمو) بنصب الكاف الثانية جريًا على لغة الأرياف كما تقدّم أي تحرّك بذكركم بعد هذا كله

١٠،٥،٥ (لَأُقَطِّعُو مِنْ مُهْجَتِي) أي أنزعه منها وأقطعه

١١،٥،٥ (بِصوابِعِي) وفي رواية (بضوافري) والمعنى واحد لأنّ الأضافر تابعة للأصابع

١٢،٥،٥ فان قيل إنّ القلب لا يتصوّر قطعه إلّا بعد موت الإنسان لو فرض ولا يمكن الشخص وهو في حالة الحياة نزع قلبه ولا قطعه فما وجه كلام الناظم قلنا الجواب أنّ هذا قطع معنويّ لا حِسّيّ بمعنى أنّه يزجر قلبه عن ذكرهم بحيث أنّه لو صُوِّرَ بين يديه وخالفه لقطعه بصوابعه أو بضوافره كما تقدّم ومن هذا المعنى قول العارف بالله تعالى ابن عروس [مجتثّ]

يا قـلبُ لَأَكْوِيكَ بِالنـارْ وَآن كُنْتَ عاشِقْ لَأَزِيدَكْ
يا قلبُ حَـمَّلتَنِي العـارْ تُـرِيدُ مَنْ لا يُـرِيـدَكْ

١٣،٥،٥ وقوله (مِنْ مُهْجَتِي) وليس القلب في المهجة وإنّما هو في الصدر ممّا يلي الشقّ الأيسر هذا من عدم معرفته وقلّة ذوقه إذ لو كان له أدنى إدراك ومعرفة لم يقل هذا الكلام ولم يجعل القافية على هذا النمط لأنّ قافية البيت الأوّل خبايطي والثاني صوابعي أو ضوافري وهو غير الوضع العروضيّ ولا يساوي قشرة بيضه * وناظمه أثقل من حجارة الميضه * غير أنّ قائله من أرباب القحوف المقلوبه * والمناسبة مطلوبه *

in ʿāda qalbī dā l-mashūmu ("if this unlucky heart of mine should turn again")—he describes it as "unlucky" because it consented to love a good-for-nothing ingrate— 5.5.8

dhikirkamū ("to thoughts of youse")[267] (with an *a* after the second *k* in the manner of the rural dialects as mentioned above), meaning "become active with the thought of you" 5.5.9

la-uqattiʿu min muhjatī ("I'll cut it out of my heart"), that is, I'll wrench it and cut it out from it 5.5.10

bi-ṣawābiʿī ("with my fangers")[268] or, in another recension, *bi-ḍawāfirī* ("with my fingernails"), though the meaning is the same, as the fingernails pertain to the fingers. 5.5.11

If it be said, "It is impossible to imagine cutting out a person's heart, if it is to be done at all, until after his death, and a person while alive would be incapable of wrenching out or cutting out his own heart, so how then are we to interpret the poet's words?" we respond that this is a figurative, not a physical, cutting, meaning that he commands his heart to suppress all mention of his beloved, with the warning that should it appear before him and disobey him, he would cut it out with his fingers or fingernails, as described above. In the same vein, God's Initiate Ibn ʿArūs says: 5.5.12

Heart, I'll brand you with flame—
  And if you love, I'll hurt you yet more.
Heart, you have brought me shame—
  He wants you not, the one you're longing for.

The words *min muhjatī* ("from my heart") demand some explanation, for the heart is not situated in the *muhjah*[269] but in the chest, on the left side. The error results from his ignorance and boorishness, because, had he the slightest awareness and knowledge, he would never have used these words, nor would he have fashioned the rhyme after this pattern, as the rhyme word in the first verse is *khabāyiṭī* ("my clangers"), while in the second it is *ṣawābiʿī* (or *ḍawāfirī*), which violates the rules of prosody[270] and is not worth an eggshell, while the poet himself is "heavier" than the stones of an ablution tank. This is not surprising, however, as he is of the inside-out-caps persuasion, and appropriateness is required, on this and every occasion. 5.5.13

(مسئلة هباليّة) لأيّ شيء ذكر القطع بالأصابع ولم يقل بالسِكّين أو الموسى إذ من شأن القطع أن يكون بآلة محدودة وكون القلب لحمًا فلا يتّجه قطعه بالأصابع ولا بالأضافر قلنا لعلّ الجواب الفشرويّ أن يقال إنّما ذكر القطع بالأصابع لكونه أخفّ في الألم من قطع السكّين أو لأنّ العمل والحركة لا تتأتّى إلّا بالأصابع إذ لا يمكن أن يقطع الشيء إلّا بيده وأصابعه فهو حينئذ لا يستغنى عن الأصابع فيكون الكلام على تقدير حذف المضاف وتقدير الكلام لأقطّعه من مهجتي بسكّينة مقبوض عليها أصابعي ومن هذا المعنى قوله تعالى ولكن لَا يَكَادُونَ يَفْقَهُونَ حَدِيثًا من قولهم لك يا محمّد ﴿مَا أَصَابَكَ مِنْ حَسَنَةٍ فَمِنَ اللهِ﴾ إلى آخره أو أنّ السكّين إذا قطع بها قلبه يمكن أن يقال فلان جرح نفسه بسكّين أو قتل نفسه بها فذكر الأصابع هنا لينفي عنه الريبة أو أنّه من باب خلبطة النظام وعجرفة الكلام ولو قال لا قطعو من مهجتي بصوابعي وسكّينتي لكان أولى للجمع بينهما أيّ الأصابع والسكّين إلّا أنّ الناظم الهبيل *لم يساعده الوزن على هذا المعنى الثقيل * فاتّضح الجواب * وبان الصواب * ١٤،٥،٥

(الرابع من أشعارهم)

مواليا [بسيط] ٦،٥

هِبابُ فُرْنِ ٱبْنِ عَمّي سودُ كُحْلاتِكْ   وَحَبْلُ طَوْرِ ٱبْنِ خالي كَيْفَ مِدَلّاتِكْ
يا مَنْ عَجَنْتي قُلَيْبي ـــفي وُحَيْلاتِكْ   يا رَبَّتَني قُرْصَ جِلَّهْ بَيْنْ أُدَيّاتِكْ

A Silly Debate: "Why does he talk of 'cutting out' with the fingers, rather than with a knife or a razor, given that it is of the nature of cutting that it should be done with a sharp instrument and, the heart being flesh, cutting it with the fingers or fingernails would not work?" We reply: "The fatuous response is to say that he talks of cutting with the fingers because it would be less painful than with a knife, or because the movement and action of cutting have to originate with the fingers, since one can only cut something with one's hand, and thus with one's fingers. Thus, at the moment of cutting, he would not be able to dispense with his fingers, in which case the words should be taken as including a suppressed phrase, the implicit sense being, 'I'll cut it from my heart with *a knife gripped by* my fangers.' Of similar import are the words of the Almighty, 'But they fail to understand a single thing said,'[271] *this being indicated by their words to you, O Muḥammad* «if a good thing befall you, they say, 'This is God's doing,'» etc.[272] Or, the correct answer may be that if he were to say that he cut his heart out with a knife, some people might think, 'So-and-so has wounded himself with a knife' or 'killed himself' with it; therefore he mentions the fingers here in order to dispel any misconceptions. Or it might be simply a case of messy verse and uncouth words; and had he said, 'I'll cut it from my heart with my fingers and my knife,' it would have been more correct, given that this combines the fingers and the knife—but the meter did not allow the idiot poet to express this tedious meaning. The answer is thus and so and now the truth we know!"[273] 5.5.14

The Fourth of Their Verses: "The soot of my paternal cousin's oven is as black as your kohl marks"[274]

hibābu furni-bni ʿammī sūdu kuḥlātik 5.6
wa-ḥablu ṭawri-bni khālī kayf midallātik
yā man ʿajantī qulaybī fī wuḥaylātik
yā raytanī qurṣa jillah bayn ʾudayyātik

The soot of my paternal cousin's oven is as black as your kohl marks,
and my maternal cousin's ox-rope is like the chains on your lovelocks.
O you, who have kneaded my heart into your daubies,
Would I were a dung cake between your handies!

١،٦،٥ هذا القول العكيس * والنظم الخسيس * والمعاني الغلسه * والألفاظ النجسه * من بحر الخرافات الإسرائيليّه * والألفاظ الهباليّه * والتشبيه الخارج عن الأوضاع * والمعاني التي تمجّها النفوس والطباع * وهو إن ثبتت أوزانه * وتخلبطت أركانه * فهو على أربعة أضرب مستخبطن خابطن مستخبطن خبطاً وطوله باتّفاق * من الخانكه لبولاق * وعرضه بيقين * من باب زُوَيْله لسويقة السبّاعين * ومعناه غريب * ومبناه عجيب * فقوله

٢،٦،٥ (هِبابُ فُرْنِ ٱبْنِ عَمّي سُودُ كُحَلاتِكْ) يريد هذا العاشق البليد التشبيه الخارج عن الماهيّة الجارح للقلوب عند سماعه فكأنّه يشبه الرزيّة وهذا من العَجَب العُجاب أنّ هذا البليد الطبع شبّه كحل محبوبته بالهباب لكن هو الأنسب لها ولعشقه إيّاها وشبيه الشيء منجذب إليه والطيور على أجناسها تقع وخصّ الهباب بفرن ابن عمه لكونه لم يكن في بلده أكبر منه ولا أكثر هباباً وأنّ غالب نساء الكفر تخبز فيه العيش وتطبخ فيه الطعام فيتراكم الهباب فيه فلتراكمه يسودّ سواداً شديداً فلهذا أوقع التشبيه لكحلاتها بسوادها وقوله

٣،٦،٥ (ٱبْنِ عَمّي) ولم يقل فرني لكونه كان فقيراً لا فرن له إلّا بالتصحيف

٤،٦،٥ وهذا من قبيل التغزّل الفشرويّ لأنّه لمّا عشق هذه المليحة ورأى الكحل في عينها أراد أن يتغزّل فيه بما يناسبه ويشبّهه بتشبيه لا يكون خارجاً عن الماهيّة فنظر ببلادة طبعه فلم ير شيئاً أسود منه فشبّه كحلاتها بذلك لأنّ الشخص إذا أَلِفَ محلّاً صار يرى كلّ ما فيه حسناً وكذلك إذا ألف شخصاً لا يراه إلّا بعين الكمال ولا يشاهد فيه عيباً إلّا ويلوّح له ما ينفيه عنه ويشفع عنده في قبوله قال الشاعر [كامل]

وإذا المُحِبُّ أَتَى بِذَنْبٍ واحِدٍ   جاءَتْ مَحاسِنُهُ بِأَلْفِ شَفيعِ[١]

---

١ بي: شقيعْ.

These perverse pronouncements and vile verses, these dirty denotations and unclean utterances, belong to the ocean of Israelite confabulations[275] and fatuous phrases, of similes that violate all law, and meanings that stick in mind and body's craw. Once its measures are sorted out, its fundamentals turned inside out, its feet appear as four: *mustakhbiṭun khābiṭan mustakhbiṭun khabṭan.*[276] Its length, for a fact, is from al-Khānkah to Bulaq, and its breadth, as may be seen, from Bāb Zuwaylah to Suwayqat al-Sabbāʿīn. Its meaning astounds, its construction confounds. 5.6.1

hibābu furni-bni ʿammī sūdu kuḥlātik ("The soot of my paternal cousin's oven is as black as your kohl marks"): this doltish lover tries to pull off a simile that has nothing to do with the real nature of the thing described and that it pains the heart to hear; indeed, he might as well be describing a cataclysm. What is extraordinary is that this dimwit should compare his beloved's kohl to soot—though one might say in fact that this is the thing that best fits her and his passion for her, for "like attracts like" and "birds of a feather flock together." He specifies the soot from his paternal cousin's oven because it was the largest and sootiest in his village and because most of the women of the hamlet would bake their bread and cook their food there, with the result that the soot built up inside it so much that it turned an intense black, which gave him the idea of comparing her kohl to its soot. 5.6.2

ibni ʿammī ("my paternal cousin"): he does not say "*my* oven" because he is poor, without an oven to his name (unless one changes the dots).[277] 5.6.3

The words discussed above fall under the rubric of "fatuous amatory lyrics," because, when he fell in love with this cutie-pie and saw the kohl in her eye, he wanted to say something appropriately amatory about it and find a simile that would not be at variance with its essential nature, so he looked around and, with his doltish temperament, could find nothing blacker than that particular soot, so he compared her kohl to that. For just as when someone, having become used to a place, starts to see everything in it as comely, so, if someone becomes used to a person, he can only see the good things in him and, as soon as he notices a defect, something else comes along to cancel out the defect and plead with him to accept it. As the poet says: 5.6.4

If the beloved reveals a single fault,
His charms rush forward with a thousand pleas.

وقال آخر [طويل]

يَقولونَ في البُستانِ لِلعَينِ نُزهَةٌ وَشيءٌ مِنَ الماءِ الَّذي غَيرِ آسنِ
إذا شئتَ أَنْ تَلقى المحاسِنَ كُلَّها فَفي وَجهِ مَنْ تَهوى جَميعُ المحاسِنِ

٥،٦،٥ (وعادة نساء الأرياف) أنّها تهوى الأفران لأجل تدميس الفول وطبخ البيسار وتقمير الخبز وتنفيض الثياب من القمل ونحو ذلك فكانت هذه المحبوبة تحبّ تراكم الهباب عليها لكثرة اشتغالها بالخبز والطبخ فشبّه كحلاتها به لكونها دائماً في هذه الحالة وهذا من باب قولهم سُخام بهباب

٦،٦،٥ ثمّ إنّه لمّا شبّه كحلاتها بسواد هباب فرن ابن عمّه مشيراً إليها أنّها تفهم من ذلك أنّه محبّ لها ومصرّ على عشقها أراد أن يشبّه مدلاتها أيضاً ليحصل لها بذلك غاية المدحة بين نساء الأرياف وأن يكون التشبيه من ماهيّة ما سبق من تشبيه كحلاتها فقال

٧،٦،٥ (وَحَبلُ طَوِرِ ٱبنِ خالي كَيفَ مِدَلّاتِكْ) هذا الكلام فيه تقديم وتأخير وتقديره أنّ مدلاتك في الطول تشبه حبل طور ابن خالي والمدلّات سلاسل من فضّة تعلّق على الاصداغ وترتخي إلى الصدر ويجعلوا في آخرها جلاجل من فضّة وبَرَق ونحو ذلك وتسمّى أيضاً مضنّات كما هو مشهور عند نساء الأرياف

٨،٦،٥ (فإن قيل) إن المدلّات هذه نحو ذراع أو أقلّ منه وحبل الثور ربما يكون أكثر من ذراع أو ذراعين غير ما يكون ملتفّاً على أذنيه فما يكون هذا التشبيه وما حكمه (قلنا) هذا من باب الغلوّ في الشيء والتفنّن فيه لأنّه لمّا عشقها ورأى هذه المدلّات مرخيّة على صدرها ولم ير في بلده أحسن من طور ابن خاله ولا أطول من حبله شبّه مدلّاتها به وأتى بهذه الاستعارة الذميمة والتشبيه الخسيس ليناسب نظمه

And another says:

They say that gardens bring refreshment for the eye
With bodies of water unsullied and pure,
But if you seek the world's charms all together in one place,
It's in the face of the one you love that you'll find every allure.

Country women generally love ovens because these are what they use to stew beans, cook *bīsār*, warm up bread, shake the lice out of their clothes, and so on. This beloved of his used to love the buildup of soot on her person because she did so much baking and cooking there, and this led him to compare her kohl to the soot because she was always in this state. Such a simile belongs to the class of what they call "crud plus soot."[278] **5.6.5**

Next, having compared her kohl to the soot of his paternal cousin's oven, thus indicating to her that she should understand that he was in love with her and determined not to let her escape, he sought a simile for the chains on her lovelocks too, so as to give her the highest praise possible among the women of the countryside and so that the comparison would be of a piece with the preceding simile of the kohl. Thus he said: **5.6.6**

wa-ḥablu ṭawri-bni khālī kayf midallātik ("and my maternal cousin's ox rope is like the chains on your lovelocks [*midallātik*]"): the words constitute an example of "advancement and deferment."[279] The implied meaning is that the chains on your lovelocks resemble in length the ox rope of my maternal cousin. *Midallāt* are silver chains that are suspended from the lovelocks and hang down to the chest, to the ends of which silver bells, sequins, and so on are attached. They are also called *maḍannāt*, as the women of the countryside know well. **5.6.7**

If it be said "These lovelocks are about one cubit or less in length, while an ox rope may be more than one cubit, or even two cubits, not counting the end that's wound round its ears, so what kind of simile is this and under what rule does it fall?" we reply, "This falls under the rubric of 'the attribution of exaggerated value to, and going into great detail about, a thing,' for, when he fell in love with her and saw her *midallāt* hanging down on her breast and could see nothing in his village finer than his maternal cousin's ox and nothing longer than its rope, he used the latter as a comparator for the *midallāt* and came up with this low image and this vile simile to match the miserable nature of **5.6.8**

التعيس وأمّا كونه منع نفسه قبول كلامه عند محبوبته التي خاطبها باستعارته ثور ابن خاله وحبله ولم يذكر شيئاً يدلّ على المِلْك لأجل ما يلين قلب محبوبته فهذا من شدّة فكره وقصر ذيله وشقاوته وظهور حاله أنّه عاشق مفلس فليس له دواء إلّا الصكّ بالنعال كما قال صاحب الموال [بسيط مع كسر]

انّي معه مال لو طلب الثريّا نال   وانّي بلا مال صكّوه الملاح بنعالْ
وإن كان معك مال هاته تبلغ الآمال   ماكان معك مال طردوك الملاح في الحالْ

فاتّضح الحال * وظهر المقال * عن هذا الكلام المشلوق * الوارد من عديم الذوق *

وقوله[1] (وطور ابن خالي) بالطاء المُهْمَلة جرياً على لغة الأرياف لأنّهم يبدلوا الثاء المثلّثة ٩،٦،٥
في الثور بالطاء أو بالتاء المُثنّاة فيقولوا طور وتور وقوله

(يا من عجنتي قلبي في وحيلاتك) هذا البليد الطبع الخسيس العقل لمّا وجد محبوبته تعجن ١٠،٦،٥
الوحل والطين عقب المطر يعني أنّها تلمّه وتدوسه برجليها كما هو عادة نساء الأرياف إذا نزل المطر في الزريبة واختلط بالجلّة والزبل والطين فيجعلوه معجنة كبيرة ويكون فيها الزبل والجلّة والوحل بيقين ويسمّوا مجموع ذلك وحلاً وقد يطلق على فرد من تلك الأفراد عند أهل الريف ثمّ إنّهم يجعلوه جواليس ويليّسوا به بيوتهم وأفرانهم وربّما جعلوا منه مداود للبقر وغير ذلك ممّا يحتاجوا إليه فلمّا رآها في هذه الحالة أخذت قلبه وعجنته برجليها في هذا الوحل خاطبها بياء النداء تنبيهاً لها أنّ هذا لا يجوز من المحبوب أن يتملّك قلب المحبّ ويعجنه ويدوسه في الوحل والجلّة والزبل وغير ذلك بل يترفّق به ويرقّ له ثمّ إنّه استشعر سؤالاً عن جواب مقدّر كأنّ قائلاً يقول له المحبّ

---

١ بي: وقولة طور ابن عمي.

his poetry. As for the fact that he guaranteed that his words would be unacceptable to the beloved whom he addresses, by virtue of the very fact that he refers to his *maternal cousin's* ox and its rope, and likewise to his *paternal cousin's* oven and its soot, and fails to mention any property of his own that might soften his beloved's heart, this may be attributed to his lovesickness, his inadequacy, his rascality, and the undeniable fact that he is a penniless lover whom no remedy will cure short of a good beating with shoes as described by the author of the *mawāliyā* that goes:

> One with money, though he demand the stars, succeeds;
> One without, the chicks'll beat with shoes till he bleeds.
> If you've got it, use it—you'll get what you essay.
> Don't have it?—the chicks'll chuck you, right away."

Thus the situation's rendered clear, the real imports of these ill-bred words, output of a boor, appear.

ṭawri-bni khālī ("my maternal cousin's ox [*ṭawr*]"): with *ṭ*, according to the dialect of the countryside, for they substitute for the *th* in *thawr* ("ox") either *ṭ* or *t* and say *ṭawr* or *tawr*.[280] **5.6.9**

yā man ʿajantī qulaybī fī wuḥaylātik ("You who have kneaded my heart into your daubies"): when this slow-witted, vile-minded dolt found his beloved kneading the daub and the mud after the rain (meaning that she had gathered it and trodden it with her feet, as the country women do when the rain falls on the byre, and mixes with the cow pats, the droppings, and the mud, for they turn the byre into one big kneading trough containing, at a minimum, droppings, cow pats, and mire, the whole lot being called collectively "daub" (*waḥl*), which is a word that may also be applied to a person by the country folk,[281] and then they make that into lumps and coat their houses and ovens with it and sometimes use it to make feeding troughs for the cows and so on, according to their needs)—when, as I say, he saw that, while she was so engaged, she had taken his heart and kneaded it with her feet into the daub, he addressed her with the vocative particle (*yā*) to call her attention to the fact that it is not permitted for the beloved to take possession of the lover's heart and to knead it and stamp it into the mire, dung, droppings, and the rest of it; on the contrary, the beloved should show compassion for it and treat it gently. Subsequently, however, through a process of self-interrogation and working **5.6.10**

ليس له تصرّف في نفسه بل القلب والروح لمحبوبه فلو أنّها ألقتك وقلبك وذقنك في الخراء فضلاً عن الوحل لا تلومها فلهذا تمنّى أن يكون قرصاً من الجلّة بين يديها وإضافة الوحل لها لكونها مالكة له ومتصرّفة فيه ويفهم من هذه العبارة أنّها كانت تعجن الوحل في محلّها حتّى أنّه صار ملكاً لها وأنّ الوحل كان في زريبتها فكانت فيها بيقين والجلّة والزبل فيها أيضاً وقوله

٥،٦،١١ (وُحَيْلاتِكْ) تصغير وحلات وقوله (يا رِيْتَني قَرْص جِلّهْ بَيْنْ أُدَيّاتِكْ) حينئذ تأكيد وبيان أنّ المعجنة التي كانت تعجنها وتدوسها برجليها كان فيها الجلّة والزبل بيقين وقوله

٥،٦،١٢ (يا رَيْتَني قَرْص جِلّهْ) إلى آخره بإبدال اللام راءاً في ريتني من لغة الريّافة وأصلها يا ليتني وقد وُجِدتْ في القاموس الأزرق والناموس الأبلق والمعنى أنّي أتمنّى أن تراني محبوبتي وغيرها وقد مُسِخْتُ قرص جلّة من هذا الوحل الذي عجنته وصرت بين يديها وأكون وحل ابن وحل أي وحلاً بطريق التمنّي وابن وحل بطريق التشبيه فاتّجه الجواب عن هذه اللغة الفشرويّة ونزّل نفسه منزلة قرص جلّة وهو شيء خسيس إشارة على أنّ العاشق ذليل حقير عند محبوبه فشبّه نفسه بهذا التشبيه الحقير والمناسب لحيته التعيسة وتمنّى أن يكون قرص جلّة بين يديها وهذا هو الأنسب لمحبوبته لأنّها دائماً في عمل الجلّة ولزقها وعجنها فهي دائماً في هذا الأمر فأتى لها بما يناسب حالها وما تحبّه وأعزّ ما يكون عندها الجلّة والوحل فما أَخَسَّ هذا العاشق وما أَرْذَلَ هذه المحبوبة وقوله

backwards from a hypothetical response, he became aware of a weakness in his whole argument, as though someone had said to him, "The lover has no rights of disposal with regard to himself; rather, he belongs heart and soul to the beloved: were she to throw you down and shove you, your heart, and your beard into a pile of shit, for example, much less daub, you would have no right to blame her!" This made him want to be a cow pat between her hands. The ascription of the daub to her is because she was the owner of it, with full rights of disposal, and, from the use of this language, we may infer that she was kneading the daub at her own place, which would make it her daub, and that it was in her own byre, for sure, as were the dung and the droppings.

wuḥaylātik ("your daubies"): diminutive of *waḥlāt* ("daubs") and the words 5.6.11
yā raytanī qurṣa jillah bayn ʾudayyātik ("I wish I were a dung cake between your handies") occurring at this point are a confirmation and a declaration that the kneading trough that she was kneading in and treading in with her feet did indeed contain dung cakes and droppings.

yā raytanī qurṣa jillah ("Would I were a dung-cake") etc., with the substi- 5.6.12
tution of *r* for *l* in *raytanī,* contains a rural dialectal form, the origin being *yā laytanī*;[282] it is to be found in *The Blue Ocean and Piebald Canon.* The meaning is: "I would that my beloved and others would behold me transformed into a cow pat taken from that same daub that she has been kneading and that I would find myself between her hands in the form of daub, offspring of daub," that is, "daub" in the first instance by way of aspiration, and "offspring of daub" by way of comparison. Thus the answer concerning this fatuous language is rendered straightforward: he brought himself down to the level of a cake of dung, namely, something vile, in order to indicate that the suitor is himself low and despicable in the eyes of the beloved, and this led him to employ this despicable comparison, of a piece with his miserable beard, and to express the desire to be a dung cake between her hands, that being the thing most appropriate for his beloved, for she was always busy working dung-cakes and sticking them together and kneading them. Since she was always so engaged, he came up with something appropriate to her condition and loved by her, the dearest thing to her being dung cakes and daub. How vile a suitor and how revolting a beloved!

(بَيْن أُديّاتِكْ) هذه لغة أهل الريف والمعنى أنّي إذا كنت قرص جلّة فإنّك تقلّبيني بين يديك من اليمين إلى اليسار مثل ما تفعلي في القرص الجلّة حتّى أنّي ألتذّ بكوني مرفوع في يديك وتمسّ ذاتي أصابعك فيحصل لي الراحة ويزول عنّي ألم المشقّة ولوأنّ صورتي انقلبت قرص جلّة فإنّي لا أبالي من النجاسة ولا أسأم من الخساسة لما فيها من الراحة وبلوغ المنى ونحو ذلك ويقرب من هذا المعنى قولي [طويل] ٥،٦،١٣

وهيفاءَ لمّا خِلْتُها في حُليّها[1] تَمَنَّيْتُ أَنّي مِرْطُها وثيابُها

لكنّ هذا تشبيه طريف في محبوبة لطيفة

(مسئلة هباليّة) لأيّ شيء اقتصر في العبارة بالوحل وكان حقّه أن يضيف إليها أيضاً الجلّة والزبل حتّى يصير فيها مجموع الثلاثة (قلنا الجواب الفشرويّ) أنّه إذا كان الوحل منها ثابتاً بيقين فيكون الزبل والجلّة فيها من باب أولى فلا اعتراض على الكلام فاتّجه الجواب بلا مَلام وقوله ٥،٦،١٤

(هباب) على وزن تُراب أو كِلاب أو سَراب مشتقّ من هُبوب الريح أومن هبهبة الكلاب قال الشاعر [طويل] ٥،٦،١٥

لَقَدْ هَبْهَبَتْ لمّا رأَتْني كِلابُهم فَقُلْتُ مُجيباً قد عَلاني هِبابُها

وهَبْهَبٌ وادٍ في جهنّم (وفي الإحياء للغزاليّ) في كتاب ذمّ الكِبْر والعُجْب عن محمّد ابن واسع قال دخلت على بلال بن أبي بُرْدة فقلت له يا بلال إنّ أباك حدّثني عن أبيه عن النبيّ صلّى الله عليه وسلّم أنّه قال إنّ في جهنّم واد يقال له هبهب حقّ على الله أن يسكنه كلّ جبّار فإيّاك يا بلال أن تكون ممّن يسكنه يقال هب يهب هباباً وسمّى بذلك لكونه يهبّ من الأفران وقوله

---

١ بي: حلبها (كذا في جميع النسخ).

bayn ʾudayyātik ("between your handies"): this is the dialect of the country people.[283] The meaning is: "If I were a cake of dung, you could flip me between your hands from right to left as you do a dung cake, so that I would enjoy the sensation of being lifted up in your hands and so that your fingers would touch my person, bringing me relief and eliminating the pain of my suffering, even though my outward shape should have become that of a dung cake—for I care nothing for uncleanness and feel no aversion to vileness in view of the relief, satisfaction, and so on that they bring." Somewhat in the same vein is a verse of my own, which goes: 5.6.13

Many a slim-bellied lass, when I imagined her in her finery,
I wished I were her tunic and her garments

—though this, of course, is a witty simile referring to a refined beloved.

A Silly Debate: "Why did he limit himself in this phrase to mentioning only daub, when he ought to have added to it the dung cakes and the droppings too, so that all three components would be represented?" We reply: "The facetious response is that if the presence of the daub is established a priori, then the droppings and the dung-cakes are there a fortiori. Thus, the objection to these words is not sustained, the record's straight, the poet not to be blamed." 5.6.14

The word *hibāb* ("soot") is of the measure of *turāb* ("dust") or *kilāb* ("dogs") or *sarāb* ("mirage") and derived from the *hubūb* ("blowing") of the wind or from the *habhabah* ("barking") of dogs. The poet says: 5.6.15

Their dogs barked (*habhabat*) when they saw me,
So I answered, "They have outpaced me and beaten me."

Habhab is also the name of a valley in Hell. The following is found in al-Ghazālī's *Revival* (*Iḥyāʾ*)[284] in the chapter "Against Pride and Self-Admiration," on the authority of Muḥammad ibn Wāsiʿ, who states, "I went in one day to Bilāl ibn Abī Burdah, and I said to him, 'Bilāl, your father told me, on the authority of his father, who had it from the Prophet, God bless him and give him peace, that the latter said, "In Hell is a valley called Habhab, in which God has determined every tyrant should dwell." Beware, Bilāl, lest you be one of those who dwell there!'" The verbal noun is *hibāb*; one says *habba, yahubbu, hibāban*; *hibāb* ("soot") is so called because it gusts up (*yahubbu*) from the ovens.[285]

(ابْنِ عَمّي) العمّ أخو الأب وقد يطلق ويراد به الأب كما في قوله تعالى ﴿وَإِذْ قَالَ إِبْرَاهِيمُ لِأَبِيهِ آزَرَ﴾ أي المراد به عمّه لأنّ العرب تخاطب العم بلفظ الأب وهو مشتقّ من العَمَى أو من العموم ومصدره عمّ يعمّ عمًّا وقوله ١٦،٦،٥

(سودُ) مأخوذ من السواد ضدّ البياض وهو أقبح الألوان (كما اتّفق) أنّ بعض الملوك أرسل إليه بعض الأكابر هديّة لا تليق به وهي عبد أسود فقال له اكتب له بوصول هديّته وأَوْجِزْ فكتب إليه أمّا بعد لو وجدت لونًا أقبح من السواد وعددًا أقلّ من الواحد لأرسلته إلينا والسلام وقيل من السُؤْدُد وهو العُلُوّ والرِفْعة ومصدره سوّد يسوّد سوادًا وسؤددًا وقوله ١٧،٦،٥

(كُحْلاتِكْ) الكحل مشتقّ من المُكْحُلة أو من الكحّال أو من تذكرة الكحّالين والكحل مشتقّ من الكحّال ومثله المتحل من المتحال أو من جبال الكحل قال الشاعر [وافر] ١٨،٦،٥

جِبالُ الكُحْلِ تُفْنيها المَراوِدْ وكَنْزُ المالِ تُفْنيهِ السِّنينْ

ومصدره كحل يكحل كحلًا وكاحل ومكحول (وفي الحديث) اكتحلوا بالإثْمِد المطيَّب فإنّه يُحِدّ البصر والسُنّة الاكتحال به وَتْرًا عند النوم وقوله

(وَحَبْلُ طَوْرِ ابْنِ خالي) الحبل مشتقّ من الحُبْلَى أو من الحبّالين والطور تقدّم معناه وهو مشتقّ من التطوّر أو من الطارة التي يصيدوا بها السمك وأمّا بالثاء المثلّثة وهي اللغة الفصحى مشتقّ من ثَوَران الأرض لأنّه يثيرها بالحرث لأنّه مُعَدّ لذلك وللساقية ١٩،٦،٥

ibn ʿammī ("my paternal cousin")[286]: the *ʿamm* is the father's brother, and the word may be applied to and signify *ab* ("father"), just as *ab* may be applied to and signify *ʿamm,* as in the words of the Almighty, «(Remember) when Ibrāhīm said to his father Āzar,»[287] where the meaning is "his paternal uncle," for the Arabs address their paternal uncles as "father." The word is derived from *ʿamā* ("blindness")[288] or from *ʿumūm* ("commonality"). The verbal noun is *ʿamm,* and the paradigm goes *ʿamma, yaʿummu, ʿamman* ("paternal uncle").[289] 5.6.16

sūdu ("is as black as")[290] is derived from *sawād* ("blackness"), the opposite of *bayāḍ* ("whiteness"), the former being the ugliest of colors. Once an important personage sent an inappropriate gift, in the form of a black slave, to a certain king, who told his secretary, "Write to him that the gift has been received, but keep it short." So the secretary wrote, "Without greetings. If you had found a color uglier than black and a number smaller than one, you would have sent it to us. Sincerely." Others say it is from *suʾdud,* which means "elevatedness" and "highness of rank." The paradigm is *sawwada, yusawwidu, sawādan,* and *suʾdudan* ("to rule"). 5.6.17

kuḥlātik ("your kohl marks"): derives from *mukḥulah* ("kohl pot")[291] or from *kaḥḥāl* ("ophthalmologist") or from *Tadhkirat al-kaḥḥālīn* (*The Ophthalmologists' Memorandum*);[292] and *kuḥl* derives from *kaḥḥāl* ("ophthalmologist")—just as does *muttaḥal* ("bemired") from *mutaḥāl*[293]—or from *jibāl al-kuḥl* ("mountains of kohl"), as in the verse, 5.6.18

Mountains of kohl are consumed by the kohl sticks,
Heaps of money by the years.

The paradigm is *kaḥala, yakḥalu, kaḥlan* and *kāḥilun,* and *makḥūlun* ("to anoint (the eyes) with kohl"). In the Tradition it says, "Anoint (*iktaḥilū*) your eyes with perfumed antimony, for it sharpens the sight!"[294] and the practice of the Prophet was to apply it to his eyes one after the other before he slept.

wa-ḥablu ṭawri-bni khālī ("and my maternal cousin's ox rope"): *ḥabl* ("rope") is derived from *ḥublā* ("pregnant") or from *ḥabbālūn* ("rope makers"). The meaning of *ṭawr* has already been given; it is derived from *taṭawwur* ("metamorphosis") or from the *ṭārah* ("hoop") with which they catch fish. However, when it is spelled with *th,* which is the chaste form, it is derived from the *thawarān* ("stirring up") of the land, because the ox (*thawr*) stirs it up 5.6.19

أيضاً بخلاف البقرة فإنّها معدّة للحلب والولادة قال ابن سُودُون مواليا [بسيط]

التَوْرُ وَالْبَقَرَهْ دا العـامْ وَمِنْ قبـلَهْ   في مِصْرَ والشامِ معْ غزّهْ مَعَ الرَمْلَهْ
هذي ،بتَحْبَلْ وَتُولِدْ عِجْلَ أَو عِجْـلَهْ   والتَوْرُ في السـاقِيَـهْ يأْكُلْ بِفَرْقِـلَّهْ

وقوله (ابْنِ خالي) الخال أخو الأمّ قال الشاعر [وزن غير معروف] ٥،٦،٢٠

يا خالي ياخوامي قالت لك اختك امي   قم كل عسـل
تفـتقت مـا فتحوالك   حككت لك بكيت

فعلى هذا يكون الناظم ابن أخت صاحب الثور والخال مشتقّ من الخُيُلاء أو من الخَيْل أومن الخُلخال أوخَيال الظلّ ومصدره خال يخيل خيلاً ويطلق على الخال الذي يكون على خدّ المحبوب فيزيده حسناً وجمالاً قال أبو نواس [وافر]

يَكُونُ الخـالُ ـفي خَدٍّ قَبِيحٍ   فَيَكْسوهُ المِـلاحَةَ وَالجَمالا

وقوله (كَيْفَ مِدَلّاتِكْ) المدلّات واحدته المدلّة على وزن المبَلّة أو المحَلّة مشتقّة من الدَلّ أو الدَلال قال الشاعر [بسيط] ٥،٦،٢١

لَهُ دَلالٌ وَدَلٌّ زانَـهُ عَجَبًا   سُبْحانَ مَن خَصَّهُ بالحُسْنِ في النّاسِ

أوهي من التدلية لكونها تدلّت على الصدر أو على الحَوْران أو الأكْتاف ونحوذلك ومصدرها تدلّت تتدلّى تدلّيًا فهي مدلّاة وقوله

(عَجْنَتي) العجن مشتقّ من المِعْجَنة أومن العَجين قال الشاعر [رجز] ٥،٦،٢٢

with the plow, because it is made for that, and also for turning the waterwheel, in contrast to the cow, which is made for milking and calving. Ibn Sūdūn[295] says in a *mawāliyā*:

The ox and the cow, year in, year out,
In Egypt and Syria, in Gaza and al-Ramla—
She gets pregnant and bears boy calves and girls,
While he turns the waterwheel and tastes the knout.

ibni khālī ("my maternal cousin"):[296] the *khāl* is the mother's brother. As the poet says: **5.6.20**

O Uncle, mother's brother—your sister, my mother, told you
"Get up, eat honey!"
What they opened for you got ripped.
She scratched it for you and you cried.[297]

According to this passage, then, the poet would be the son of the sister of the owner of the ox. The word *khāl* is derived from *khuyalā'* ("conceitedness") or from *khayl* ("horses") or from *khulkhāl* ("anklets") or from *khayāl al-ẓill* ("the shadow-play"). The paradigm is *khāla, yakhīlu, khaylan.*[298] The same word (*khāl*) is also applied to the mole on the cheek of the beloved, which adds to his comeliness and beauty. As Abū Nuwās[299] says:

If there be a mole on an ugly cheek
It clothes it with beauty and charm.

The words *kayf midallātik* ("like the chains on your lovelocks"): *midallāt* is the plural of *midallah*, of the measure of *maballah* ("soaking pit") or al-Maḥallah, and is derived from *dall* or *dalāl* ("coquetry"). As the poet says: **5.6.21**

He's a coquette and a flirt, which only adds to his charms—
Glory to Him Who has singled him out from the rest in beauty!

Or it may be derived from *tadliyah* ("dangling") because they hang down to the breast, or the anus, or the shoulders, and such like. The paradigm is *tadallat, tatadallā, tadalliyan*, and *midallatan.*[300]

ʿajantī ("have kneaded"): *ʿajn* ("kneading") is derived from *miʿjanah* ("kneading trough") or from *ʿajīn* ("dough"). As the poet says: **5.6.22**

وَالعَجْنُ مُشْتَقٌّ مِنَ العَجِينِ   كَذا مِنَ العِجانِ باليَقِينِ

ومصدره عجن يعجن عجناً

وتقدّم تعريف القلب واشتقاقه وقوله ٥،٦،٢٣

(في وُحَيْلاتِكْ) العبارة من وَحْل وفيها الوحل أيضاً وهو مشتقّ من التوحّل ومصدره وحل يوحل وحلاً وقد يخاطَب به الشخص فيقال يا وحل مثلاً أي من طبعه وخِصاله تشبّه الوحل نجسة خبيثة وقوله ٥،٦،٢٤

(يا رَيْتَنِي قِرْصَ جِلَّهْ) القرص هو الشيء المدوّر مشتق من التقريص أو من القرّاصة أو من القَرْصة ومصدره قرص يقرص قرصاً والجلّة فيها أيضاً ما تقدّم وهي مشتقّة من جلّة البهائم وقوله ٥،٦،٢٥

(بَيْنْ أُدَيّاتِكْ) جمع يد وقد ورد هذا اللفظ في القاموس الأزرق والناموس الأبلق قال الشاعر [بسيط] ٥،٦،٢٦

جاءَتْ لَنا بأُدِيّاتٍ تُشِيرُ لَنا   نَمشي إِلَيْها سُحَيْرًا بالرُجَيْلاتِ

وفي نسخة أخرى (يا ريتني قرص جلّة بين رجيلاتك) والمعنى واحد في النجاسة وعلى القول الثاني تكون الرجيلات جمع رِجْل وهي من الترجّل أو من الرِجْلة قال الشاعر [طويل]

إذا اشْتُقَّتِ الرِجلاتُ فَهْيَ كَرِجْلَةٍ   وإِلّا فَرِجْلٌ كالتَّرَجُّلِ إذ وَرَدْ

ومصدرها رجل يرجل رجلاً والرِجْلان مثنّى رِجْل

ʿajn from *ʿajīn* derives
And no doubt from *ʿijān* ("perineum") likewise.

The paradigm is *ʿajana, yaʿjinu, ʿajnan* ("to knead").

The definition and etymology of *qalb* ("heart") have been given above. **5.6.23**

fī wuḥaylātik ("with your daubies"): the form derives from *waḥl* ("daub, mixed mud and dung") and is full of *waḥl* too. It is derived from *tawaḥḥul* ("to get muddy") and the paradigm is *waḥila, yawḥalu, waḥlan* ("to sink in mire"). Also, an individual may be addressed with the same word. Thus one says, *yā waḥl* ("You daub!"), that is, his nature and his characteristics resemble daub in their filthiness and vileness. **5.6.24**

yā raytanī qurṣa jillah ("I wish I were a dung cake"): *qurṣ* ("cake, disk") is anything that is round, and derives from *taqrīṣ* ("rounding") or from *qarrāṣah* ("pinchers") or from *qarṣah* ("a nip, a pinch"). The paradigm is *qaraṣa, yaqruṣu, qarṣan* ("to pinch"). The word *jillah* ("dung cakes") is as described above and is derived from the *jallah*[301] ("dung") of beasts. **5.6.25**

bayn ʾudayyātik ("between your handies"): *dayyāt* is the plural of *yad* ("hand") and is to be found in *The Blue Ocean and Piebald Canon*. The poet says: **5.6.26**

She came to tell us with her handies
To walk to her at daybreak with our tootsies.

In another copy it says: "I wish I were a dung cake between your tootsies (*rujaylātik*)," the meaning being the same in terms of defilement. In the second reading, *rujaylāt* would be the plural of *rijl* ("foot"),[302] which is from *tarajjul* ("walking on foot") or from *rijlah* ("purslane"). The poet says:

If *rijlāt* be etymologized, it's from *rijlah*,
If not, from *rijl*, like *tarajjul*—supposing it occurs.[303]

The paradigm is *rajila, yarjalu, rijlan,*[304] and *rijlān* is the dual of *rijl.*

وفي الأبيات من أنواع البديع تشبيه شيئين بشيئين لأنّه شبه سواد كلاتها ٥،٦،٢٧
وطول مدلّاتها بهباب الفرن وحبل التور ومن ذلك قول صاحب البديعيّة رحمه الله تعالى [بسيط]

تلاعَبوا تحتَ ظِلِّ السُمْرِ مِن مَرَحٍ كَما تلاعَبَتِ الأَشْبالُ في الأُجُمِ

(الخامس من أشعارهم)

مواليا [بسيط] ٥،٧

سَأَلْتُ عَنِ الحِبِّ قالوا شَتَّ مِنَ التايِهْ مَسَحْتُ دِمْعي بِكِرْسايَهْ وَجِلّايِهْ
وَشِلْتُ وَجْهي لِرَبّي قُلْتُ مَوْلايِهْ جابْ لي رُغَيِّفْ وَعُجُّورَهْ وَقَتّايِهْ

هذا المواليا قليل الأوضاع ركيك المعاني * قليل المباني * خسيس النظام * وهو ٥،٧،١
من بحر زبل الكلام * وطوله باتّفاق * من شُبْره لبولاق * وعرضه المذكور * من الجيزة لبولاق التَكْرُور * وتفاعيله مستثقلن ثاقلن مستثقلن ثقلاً ومعناه الذميم * الذي لا يهواه صاحب الذوق السليم * أن قصد هذا الناظم البليد * من هذا المعنى السقيم الأكيد * أن قوله

(سَأَلْتُ عَنِ الحِبِّ قالوا شَتَّ مِنَ التايِهْ) أي إنّه لمّا عشق هذا المحبوب وزاد به الوجد ٥،٧،٢
والغرام أَكْثَرَ من ذكره وصار خياله لا يفارقه طَرْفَةَ عين فإنّ من أحبّ شيئاً أكثر من ذكره ولو أنّه في أعظم المشقّات وأصعب البليّات قال عَنْتَرة [كامل]

The verse contains a rhetorical device consisting of the comparison of two things with two other things, since he compares the blackness of her kohl and the length of the chains on her lovelocks, on the one hand, with the soot of the oven and the ox-rope, on the other. An example of this is the words of the author of *The Brilliant Poem* (*Al-Badīʿiyyah*),[305] may the Almighty have mercy upon his soul: 5.6.27

They played together beneath the acacias' shade from merriment,
As the lion cubs played in the thicket.

The Fifth of Their Verses: "I asked after the beloved.
They said, 'He skedaddled from the shack!'"[306]

saʾaltu ʿani[307] *l-ḥibbi qālū shatta mina l-tāyih*[308] 5.7
masaḥtu dimʿī bi-kirsāyah wa-jillāyih
wa-shiltu wajhī li-rabbī qultu mawlāyih
jāb lī rughayyif wa-ʿajjūrah wa-qattāyih

I asked after the beloved. They said, "He skedaddled from the shack!"
I wiped away my tears with a dung slab and a dung cake.
And I lofted my face to My Lord, and said "My Master!"
He brought me a loaf, a melon, and a cucumber.

This *mawāliyā* is weakly structured, with insipid senses and restricted constructions; its organization is odious, and it is drawn from the ocean of words malodorous. Its length is, for a fact, from Shubrā to Bulaq, its breadth, for sure, from al-Jīzah to Bulaq al-Takrūr. Its feet are *mustathqilun thāqilun mustathqilun thuqlan*[309] and the debased meaning, which any of sound taste must surely find demeaning, that this dimwitted poet was trying to convey in this definitely queasy way, is as follows: 5.7.1

saʾaltu ʿani l-ḥibbi qālū shatta mina l-tāyih ("I asked after the beloved. They said, 'He skedaddled from the shack!'"): that is, after he had fallen for this beloved and ecstasy and infatuation had carried him away, he started talking about him all the time and the image of him never left his mind for even the batting of an eyelid, for those who are enamored of a thing talk about it constantly, even in the midst of the greatest hardships and the most trying calamities. As ʿAntarah[310] said: 5.7.2

وَلَقَدْ ذَكَرْتُكِ والرِّمَاحُ نَوَاهِلٌ مِنِّي وبِيضُ الهِنْدِ تَقْطُرُ مِن دَمي
فَوَدَدْتُ تَقْبِيلَ السُّيُوفِ لأَنَّهَا لَمَعَتْ كَبَارِقِ ثَغْرِكِ المُتَبَسِّمِ

فالعاشق يلتذّ بذكر محبوبه وإذا ذُكِرَ عنده أيضاً ربّما تختلج أعضاءه عند ذكره شوقاً إليه

٣،٧،٥ (كما اتّفق) أنّ رجلاً زاد به العشق فمرض فأتوه بطبيب فأخذ يجُسّ نبضه ثمّ إنّ الطبيب قال لغلامه هات الفَرَجيّة فتحرّك نبض الرجل فقال الطبيب أنت عاشق ومحبوبتك اسمها فرجية فقال له نعم يا سيّدي فقيل له من أين عرفت ذلك فقال لمّا أمسكت نبضه وذكرت الفرجية فتحرّك فعلمت ذلك بالفراسة أنّه عاشق وأنّ محبوبته اسمها فرجيّة ومن هذا المعنى ما ذكرته في بعض القصائد من قولي [بسيط]

شَكَوْتُ ما بي فَقالَ الصَّحْبُ أَجمَعُهم انظُرْ طَبيباً لَقَدْ أَمْسَيْتَ في وَجَلِ
فَـرُحْتُ نَحوَ طَبيبٍ كُنتُ أَعْرِفُهُ يَدري رُسومَ الهَوى بِالقَوْلِ والعَمَلِ
نَادَيْتُهُ يا رعَاكَ اللهُ خُذْ بِيَدي وانظُرْ لِحالي وَداوِ القَلْبَ مِن عِلَلِ
فَجَسَّ يَدي وقالَ الحُبُّ فارْتَعَدَتْ فَرائِصي وَفُؤادي صارَ في خَجَلِ
فَقَالَ أَنْتَ سَقِيمٌ في هَوى قَمَرٍ بَديعِ حُسْنٍ رَنا بالأَعْيُنِ النُّجُلِ

إلى آخر الأبيات

٤،٧،٥ فلهذا أراد هذا العاشق استفسار الخبر عن محبوبه وأنّه يريد أن يعلم محلّه ومنزله ويسأل عن حاله وفي أي مكان هو لأجل الاجتماع به وبلوغ المطلوب منه فسأل عنه كما تقدّم فقالوا له الجماعة المخاطبون جوابا لسؤاله إنّ محبوبك هذا الّذي تسأل عنه شتّ أي ذهب وراح من التاية وهي محلّ يجعلوه الجمّاسة على شكل دائرة أو نصف دائرة من القُلْقَيل والطين وربّما جعلوا له سقفاً من الغاب والحشيش حكم

As the lances quenched their thirst in me, I said your name,
The silver blades of India dripping with my blood the while,
And then I longed to kiss those swords
For they were flashing with the lightning of your smile!

—for the lover derives pleasure from the very mention of his beloved, and, when his name is mentioned in his presence, his limbs may tremble with longing at the mere sound.

For example, it happened that a man fell deeply in love and became sick. 5.7.3
They took him a doctor, who started to take the man's pulse and then said to his servant, "Hand me my gown (*farajiyyah*)!"[311] at which point the sick man's pulse raced. The doctor said, "You are in love, and the name of your beloved is Farajiyyah." The man replied, "You are right, sir." "How did you know that?" the doctor was asked, and he said, "When I held his pulse and mentioned my *farajiyyah*, it raced, and then I understood, through my skill in interpreting the body's responses to its owner's thoughts, what was going on, namely, that he was in love and that the name of his beloved was Farajiyyah." The following verses from an ode of my composing are on the same theme:

I bewailed my state. My friends said one and all,
"Your condition's dire! A doctor's what you need!"
So off I went to one I knew
Could read the signs of love in word and deed.
"God keep you! Take my hand," to him I called,
"Examine my state, and cure my heart of whatever ill there lies!"
He took my pulse, said, "Love!" and all my muscles
Shook, while chagrin took me by surprise.
"You pine," said he, "for a moon,
One fair beyond compare, who stared with great, wide eyes!"

and so on to the end.

As a result, this suitor wanted to obtain information about his beloved and 5.7.4
to know where he was and where he dwelt, and to inquire concerning his condition and where he might be found, so that he might meet with him and attain what he desired of him. Thus he asked about him, as mentioned, and those addressed replied in answer to his question, "This beloved of yours about whom you ask has 'skedaddled' (*shatta*)," that is, gone and removed himself

بيت صغير فيضعوا فيه أواني اللبن لأجل عملهم الجبن واجتماعهم فيه ويسمّوه التاية فيقال تاية الجمّاسة وتاية الغنّامة ونحو ذلك ممّا هو مشهور بينهم وهذا كلّه في زمن الربيع يمكثوا هذه المدّة على هذه الحالة وربّما لطّخوها بالجلّة والوحل أيضاً لأجل البناء وسمّيت بذلك لأنّها تأوى هؤلاء الجماعة وتقيهم من الحرّ والبرد فعلى هذا أنّ محبوبه كان من أولاد الجمّاسة أو رعيان الجاموس أو الغنم بدليل أنّه سأل عنه من الجمّاسة القاطنين بهذه التاية فلمّا علم أنّه شتّ منها بإخبارهم له تشتّت شمله وحصل له البكاء والنواح عليه بدليل قوله

٥،٧،٥ (مَسَحْتُ دِمْعي بِكِرْسايَهْ وَجِلّايَهْ) أي إنّه لمّا علم أنّ محبوبه سافر وشتّ من التاية ولم يعلم خبره وكان ذهابه من التاية لأحد أمور إمّا أنّه انكسر على أبيه مال السلطان فهرب لئلا يأخذوه عنه رهينة أو أنّه راح في طلب عجلة أو بقرة أو ثور فشتّ في البراري لينظر ما ذهب منه فسأل هذا العاشق الطفس عن هذا المحبوب الغلس فلم يجده فبكى على فراقه كما هو عادة العشّاق وأسلوب المحبّين وسال دمعه وامتدّ سيلانه وربّما اختلط بمخاطه أيضاً (كما اتّفق) أنّ بعض العشّاق المغفّلين يقول لصديق له هذه الأبيات [متقارب]

إذا ما ذَكَرْتُكَ يا مُنْيَتي يَسيلُ المُخاطُ عَلى لِحْيَتي
وَلَيْتَكَ عِندي إذا ما خَرَيْتُ يكونُ لِسانُكَ في ثُقْبَتي
نَسيمُكَ عَطَّلَ ماءَ السَّما وأورَثَني الخامَ في رُكْبَتي
فَإنْ لَمْ تُغِثْني أنا مُذْنِفٌ فَإنَّ الهَوى مُسْهِلٌ مِعْدَتي

"from the shack" (*min al-tāyih*), the latter being a place the buffalo herders make in the form of a circle, or a half circle, of blocks of mud and earth, and sometimes they make it a roof of canes and greenery, like a little house. Here they put the milk vessels for making cheese, and here they meet. They call it a *tāyih*. One speaks of "the *tāyih* of the buffalo herders" and "the *tāyih* of the shepherds" and so on, as is well known among them. All this takes place in the spring, for it is during that season that they live this way. Sometimes they plaster it with dung, and daub too, to make it stronger. It is called a *tāyih* because it "provides refuge for" (*ta'wā*) these people and protects them from the heat and the cold. On this basis, then, his beloved would be a son of buffalo herders or those who look after buffaloes or flocks of sheep and goats, as evidenced by the fact that he asked after him among the buffalo herders who were dwelling in the shack in question. Once he learned from the information that they gave him that he had "skedaddled" (*shatta*) from it, he went all to pieces (*tashattata shamluhu*) and was overcome with weeping and moaning for him, as indicated by the words:

masaḥtu dimʿī bi-kirsāyah wa-jillāyih ("I wiped away my tears with a dung slab and a dung cake"): that is, he did this when he learned that his beloved had departed and skedaddled he knew not where. He might have left the shack for any of several reasons: maybe his father had fallen into arrears on the sultan's taxes, so he had fled lest they take him from him as a hostage,[312] or he had gone in search of a calf or a cow or an ox and had skedaddled into the wide-open spaces to look for what he had lost. In any case, this filthy lover, having asked after his obnoxious beloved and not found him, wept for his bereavement, as is the way of wooers and the fashion of lovers, and his tears flowed copiously, very likely also mixing with his snot, as once described by a certain simple-minded suitor in these verses addressed to a friend: 5.7.5

When I think of you whom I adore
The snot my beard goes running o'er.
Would you were with me when I empty my gut—
You'd push your tongue right up my butt.
The rain in the skies has been stopped by your breeze,
Which also with phlegm has filled my knees.
If you don't save me, I'll throw in the towel,
For love has gone and loosened my bowel!

٥،٧،٦ فلكثرة شوقه وعشقه إلى هذا المحبوب قال مخبرًا عن حاله (مَسَحْتُ دِمْعي) بكسر الدال المهملة جريًا على اللغة الريفيّة أي لمّا حصل لي هذا الأمر مسحت دمعي السائل مع المخاط الّذي هو من لوازمه (بِكِرْسايَهْ) فلم يتيّسر مسح جميعه فمسحت باقيه أيضاً (بِجِلاّيِهْ) أي إنّه استعار له ممسحتين عوضاً عن محرمتين وهذا ممّا يناسب عشقه لهذا المحبوب وأيضاً فيه مناسبة لحال العاشق لأنّه دائماً في قطع الكِرْس وشيل الجلّة وعجنها ولزقها وكذلك المحبوب فالخِسيّة عِلّة الضمّ والأشياء مناسبة لبعضها البعض إذ لو قال مسحت دمعي بمنديل أو محرمة لكان هذا بعيد عن الفلاّح لأنّه لا يُتصوَّر أن يكون له محرمة أو منديل إلّا نادرًا لأنّ الظريف من أهل الريف إذا فرغ من الأكل مسح يده في كمّه أو في لحيته فما بالك بغيره مثل هذا العاشق فإنّه لا يتصوّر منه لبس يليق بهذا المعنى وإذا سلّمنا ذلك وكان نادرًا كما تقدّم فقد لا يتّفق ذلك في وقت سؤاله عن محبوبه لأنّه سأل عنه أهل التاية وهم دائماً في حالة رذلة من الجلّة والطين ونحو ذلك وهو أيضاً على حكمهم ومتخلّق بأخلاقهم ومحبوبه كذلك بل هو واسطة عِقْدهم في الخساسة ورئيسهم في النجاسة ولا يتصوّر أن يكون مع أحدهم منديل ولا محرمة لأنّ مناديل الجماسة في الغيط ومحارمهم ذقونهم وأكمامهم وربّما مسح الشخص منهم يده في القرص الجلّة أو في القلقيل أو الحشيش ونحو ذلك

٥،٧،٧ (فإن قيل) لأيّ شيء مسح دمعه بكرساية وجلاّية وكان الأولى أن يمسحه بكُمّه أو بطرف كُرّه أو بشيء كان عليه من ملبوسه (قلنا) لعلّهلم يكن عليه إلّا ما يستر به عورته فقط أو كان عريانًا كما هو دأب الفلاّحين في غالب أوقاتهم الكبير منهم عليه ما يستر العورة لا غير فربّما كان وقت سؤاله عريانًا من حفر بير أو قناة أو شيل زبل أو جلّة ونحو ذلك ومحبوبه على هذه الحالة ومن هذا القبيل أو أنّه لشدّة بلادته وعدم

In this state of longing and desire for the beloved the poet says, conveying information concerning his condition, *masaḥtu dimʿī* ("I wiped my tears"), with *i* after the *d*, according to the rural dialect;[313] that is, "When this happened, I wiped off my tears, which were streaming down, mixed with snot (a necessary appurtenance of the former), with a *kirsāyih* ('slab of dung mixed with urine used for building'). And since it was not a simple matter to wipe all of them off by this means, I wiped the rest of them off with a dung cake." In other words, he prefers the image of two such wiping cloths to that of two napkins as more appropriate to his love for such a beloved, to his own condition as a suitor—since he spends all his time cutting dung slabs and hauling dung cakes and kneading them and slapping them on walls—and indeed as more appropriate to the beloved himself. It was their common vileness that brought them together, and everything fits together, since it is unlikely that a peasant would say "I wiped my tears with a handkerchief" or "with a napkin," it being inconceivable that a peasant would possess either, except in rare cases, seeing that even the sophisticated peasant, when he is done eating, wipes his hand on his sleeve or on his beard, so what could one expect of a different sort, such as this suitor? It is inconceivable that he would wear the sort of clothes that would go with such an idea; and, even if we admit that possibility, albeit as a rare occurrence as noted above, this would not agree with the timing of his question about his beloved, because the people he asked about him were the shack people, who are always in a filthy state from the dung and the mud and so on, and he too would be in the same condition as them and cast from the same mold, and his beloved likewise. Indeed, the latter would be the very jewel in their crown for vileness and their leader in uncleanness, and it is not to be imagined that any of them would have a handkerchief or a napkin on him, because the handkerchiefs and napkins of the buffalo herders in the field are their beards and their sleeves, and they are quite likely to wipe their hands on a dung cake or a clod of earth or on the weeds or anything of that sort. 5.7.6

If it be said, "Why did he wipe his tears with 'a dung slab and a dung cake' when it would have been more proper to wipe them with his sleeve or the end of his head cloth or any other item of apparel that he was wearing?" we reply, "It may be that he was wearing no more than would cover his privates, or was naked, this being how peasants are on most occasions, the older ones alone wearing just enough to cover their privates, no more. Thus, it may be that he was completely naked at the time he asked the question because he 5.7.7

ذوقه وقوّة جهله لم يتيقّن أنّ الكرساية والجلاّية فيها نجاسة كما هو عادة الفلاّحين أنّهم لا يتحاشوا عن هذه الأمور فمسح دمعهم بهما أو أنّه من باب الخضوع الفشرويّ والتذلّل لمحبوبه وإنّه أراد أن يفهم إذا رجع واجتمع به أنّه مسح جبينه ووجهه ودموعه بكرساية وجلاّية ليتحقّق أنّه محبّ له وأنّه تعاطى لأجله أخسّ الأشياء والأولى أن يقال إنّ هذا من باب المناسبة لحال العاشق وحال المعشوق لأنّ الشخص من أولاد الفلاّحين ينشأ من حين ولادته إلى أن يموت في الجلّة والطين وشيل الزبل ونحوه وإذا جلس لا يجلس إلّا على النجاسة وربّما أكل وشرب على الزبل والجلّة ونحو ذلك فهم خراء أولاد خراء فكان مسحه بالجلاّية والكرساية فيه مناسبة بهذا الاعتبار فلا يؤثّر عنده المسح بذلك كما هو عادة أرباب التايات وأحوال الفلاّحين كما تقدّم فاتّضح الجواب من وجوه شتّى انتهى

٨،٧،٥ ثمّ إنّه لمّا مسح دمعه وصحي لنفسه وتيقّن أنّ محبوبه يطول رجوعه إليه ورأى نفسه جيعان ولم ير أحداً يرسله إلى داره يأتيه بشيء يأكله من الخبز الشعير والجبن القَرِيش والبصل ونحو ذلك كما هو عادة الفلاّحين في أفخر مأكولهم لم يكن له صبر لأنّ الجوع يضرّ بالإنسان خصوصاً مثل هذا الفلاّح لا سيّما إذا كان في حالة حفر بير أو قناة أو شيل وحل وتراكمت عليه الدواهي من عَقِبِ الحفر أو شيل الطين أو العشق الّذي هو فيه وزيادة على ذلك بكاؤه وسيلان دموعه وامتزاجها بمخاطه كما تقدّم وقد أبطأ عليه الغداء فاضطرّ اضطراراً شديداً وساخت عليه نفسه لأنّهم يقولوا الجوع كافر (وسمعت) بعض الفقهاء يقول لمّا خلق الله النفس سلّط عليها أنواع البلايا وقال لها من أنا فقالت أنت أنت وأنا أنا فسلّط عليها الجوع وقال لها من أنا فقالت أنت الله الّذي لا إله إلّا أنت فكان الجوع على النفس أصعب عليها من غيره ولهذا

was digging a well or a canal or hauling droppings and dung cakes or the like; and his beloved would have been in the same state and of the same type. Or the answer may be that given his dimwittedness, obnoxiousness, and ignorance he did not realize that the slab of dung and the dung cake were unclean (since peasants customarily feel no repugnance for such things) and so used them to wipe away his tears. Or it may be that this falls under the rubric of 'facetious submission to and abasement before the beloved' and that he wanted the latter to understand, when he came back and met with him, that he had wiped his brow and his face and his tears with a dung slab and a dung cake in order to prove that he was in love with him and would put up with the most disgusting things for his sake. The best solution, however, is to say that this falls under the heading of appropriateness to the condition of such a lover and such a beloved, for any member of the peasant breed lives from the day of his birth till the day he dies in the midst of dung cakes and mud and the hauling of droppings and so on. When he sits, he has nothing but filth to sit on and he may even eat and drink using droppings and dung cakes and suchlike as a tray, for such people are shit born of shit. Thus his wiping himself with the dung slab and the dung cake would be quite appropriate from this perspective, and wiping with such things would be no reason to get upset so far as he was concerned, these being customary among those who live in the shacks and how peasants are, as previously explained. The answer is now clear from various points of view." End.

Next, after he had wiped away his tears and come to his senses and ascertained that it would be a good while before his beloved returned to him, and finding himself hungry and seeing no one to send home to bring him some barley bread and cottage cheese and onions and so on to eat—as the peasants do with regard to the most sumptuous of their foods[314]—he ran out of patience. Hunger can bring a person to grief, especially one such as this peasant, particularly given that he was engaged in digging a well or hauling mud or excavating a canal or hauling daub and that the grievous consequences of such activities or of the passion that he felt had accumulated, not to mention that he had wept and his tears had flowed and mixed with his snot, as described above. Since, then, he had not yet had any lunch, he found himself in dire straits and felt weak all over, for "hunger makes unbelievers," as they say. I have heard a man of religion say, "When God created the appetitive soul,[315] He gave various afflictions sway over it and then asked it, 'Who am I?' and it replied, 'You are You and I am I.' Then He gave hunger sway over it and asked it, 'Who am I?' and 5.7.8

إنّ الشخص إذا صبر عليه يَصِحُّ جسمه وينشط للعبادة كما ورد في الحديث الشريف جوعوا تصحّوا وإذا أكثر من المآكل والمشارب زيادة عن العادة حال عن العبادة قال بعضهم تأكل كثيرًا فتنام كثيرًا يفوتك خير كثير وقال الشاعر [طويل]

إذا شِئْتَ أنْ تَحْيَى صَحِيحًا مُنَعَّمًا   فَكُلْ من طَعامٍ تَشْتَهِيهِ قَليلَا
كَما قالَ بُقْراطُ الحَكيمُ وغيرُهُ   إذا قَلَّ أَكْلُ المَرْءِ عاشَ طَويلَا

٩،٧،٥ فلما اشتدّ بهذا الفلّاح هذا الأمر أخبر عن نفسه وقال في مناجاته لربّه

١٠،٧،٥ (وَشِلْتُ وَجْهي لِرَبِّي قُلْتُ مَوْلايِهْ) أي لمّا طال عليّ الزمن في حالة بكائي وفي مسحي الدموع وأشرفت نفسي على الهلاك من ألم الجوع وغيره كما تقدّم شلت وجهي أي رفعته وهذه لغة ريفيّة وردت في القاموس الأزرق والناموس الأبلق كما يقال عندهم فلان شال وجهه أي رفعه وقوله

١١،٧،٥ (لِرَبِّي) أي لخالقي ومربّيني ثمّ دعوت

١٢،٧،٥ و(قُلْتُ مَوْلايِهْ) أي يا مولايَ وحُذِفَت ياء النداء لضرورة النظم وألحق الهاء في مولايه لأجل الرَوِيّ ثمّ كان من ضمن دعائه أن قال أطلب منك يا ربّي ومولاي أن تيسّر لي ما آكله والتهي به عن الاستنظار لهذا المحبوب الّذي أذهل عقلي وأجاع نفسي وأسال مخاطي ودمعي فعند ذلك استجاب الله دعاءه كما أشار له بقوله

١٣،٧،٥ (جابْ لي رُغَيِّفْ وَعُجُّورَهْ وَقَتّايِهْ) أي سخّر لي إنسانًا أعطاني مجموع هؤلاء الثلاثة وأكلت وسددت مجاعتي وحصل لي غاية المقصود لأنّ الله تعالى مع المنكسرة قلوبهم

it replied, 'You are God, and other than You there is no god.'" In other words, hunger was harder for the appetitive soul to bear than any other affliction. This is why one may observe that, if he puts up with it patiently, his body becomes fit and energetic in worship, as noted in the Noble Tradition, "Go hungry and keep fit!" If, on the other hand, one eats and drinks more than is usual, he turns away from worship. Someone said, "Eat much and you will sleep much, and much good will pass you by." As the poet says:

> If you want to live healthy and wealthy
> Eat but a little of what food you desire.
> Say Hippocrates the Wise and others:
> If a man eat but little, he'll not quickly expire.

When things became unbearable for the peasant, he spoke of his appetite, saying concerning his supplications to his Lord: 5.7.9

wa-shiltu wajhī li-rabbī qultu mawlāyih ("And I lofted my face to my Lord, and said, 'My Master!'"): that is, after I had spent a long while weeping and wiping my tears and was on the point of expiring from the pangs of hunger and so on, as described above, I "lofted" (*shiltu*) my face, meaning "I raised it," "I lofted" in this sense being a rural usage, attested in *The Blue Ocean and Piebald Canon.* They say, "So and so 'lofted' his face," meaning he "raised" it. 5.7.10

li-rabbī ("to my Lord"): that is, to my Creator and He Who raised me up. Then I prayed to Him and . . . 5.7.11

qultu mawlāyih ("I said, 'My Master!' (*mawlāyih*)"): that is, and I said *yā mawlāyih* ("O My Master!"), the vocative particle being suppressed in the original to preserve the meter, while he adds an *h* to *mawlāya* for the rhyme.[316] His prayer then continued with his saying, "I ask of you, My Lord and My Master, that You bestow on me a little something to eat to distract myself with while waiting for this beloved who has perplexed my mind, made me go hungry, and caused my snot and tears to flow." God then answered his prayer, as the poet indicates when he says: 5.7.12

jāb lī rughayyif wa-ʿajjūrah wa-qattāyih ("He brought me a loaf, a melon, and a cucumber"): that is, He generously provided me with someone who gave me all three of these, and I ate and satisfied my hunger and obtained all that I did seek, for "God Almighty is with the meek."[317] 5.7.13

٥،٧،١٤ (فإن قيل) إنّ استجابة الدعاء لها شروط أن يأكل حلالاً ويشرب ويلبس كذلك وهذا الفلاّح في وقت دعائه كان متضمّخًا بالنجاسة وهي مسح وجهه بالكرساية والجلاّية ووقوفه أيضاً ينتظر هذا المحبوب لأجل ما يقدحه جنب المدود أو الجرن وأيضاً هو لا يعرف الحلال من الحرام ومع هذا عجّل الله له ما ذكر وهو الرغيف وما معه (قلنا) إنّما عجّل الله له هذا من باب الاستدراج أو من باب ما ورد أنّ الرجل الخبيث إذا دعا يسرع الله له بالإجابة بخلاف الرجل الصالح فإنّ الله تعالى يحبّ تكرار دعائه إليه وفي قوله تعالى في حقّ موسى وهارون عليهما الصلاة والسلام ﴿قَدْ أُجِيبَتْ دَعْوَتُكُمَا﴾ أي بعد أربعين عاماً

٥،٧،١٥ (مسألة هباليّة) ما الحكمة في ذكره في الأبيات الكرس والجلّة والرغيف والعجّورة والقتّاية وهذا لا يناسب هذا ولا يجتمع معه فإنّ الشخص لا يمكنه أن يأكل القتّا والعجّورة بالجلّة والكرس نعم يمكن بالخبز وغيره ممّا يناسب فما فائدة ذكره مع أنّ فيها أنواع النجاسة (قلنا) لعلّ هذا من باب تعدّد الأسماء وقد ذكروه نوعاً من البديع فالكرساية واحدة الكرس والجلاّية واحدة الجلّة والعجّورة والقتّاية كذلك وذكر القتّاية بالتاء المثنّاة فوق لغة ريفيّة فيكون بينها وبين اللغة الفصحى الجناس المصحّف فاتّضح الإشكال * عن وجه هذا الهبال *

٥،٧،١٦ وأمّا حلّ الأبيات واشتقاقها فقوله

٥،٧،١٧ (سَأَلْتُ عَنِ الحِبِّ) السؤال هو أن يسأل الشخصُ عن شيء وهذا من باب تحصيل الحاصل وهو مشتقّ من السيل أو من السوليّة أو من السَيالة ومصدره سأل يسأل سؤالاً

If it be said, "There are conditions to be fulfilled before prayers may be answered, namely, that the supplicant should eat only what is permitted by religion, with the same applying to drink and apparel, yet this peasant was, at the time of his prayer, soiled by impurity, the result of his having wiped his face with the dung slab and the dung cake, and also was standing waiting to bang his beloved next to the feeding trough or on the threshing floor, and anyway was incapable of telling what is permitted by religion from what is forbidden, and, despite all this, God hastened to provide him with the aforementioned, namely, the loaf and the rest of the things, so how do you explain that?" we reply, "God only hastened to provide him with these things as a way of tempting him down the slippery slope to his destruction. Or this may fall under the rubric of God being quick to answer the prayers of the vicious, in contrast to those of the righteous, for the Almighty loves to hear the latter praying to Him over and over again. It is said in the words of the Almighty concerning Moses and Aaron, blessings and peace be upon them both, 'He said, «Your prayer is answered»,' meaning that it had been answered after forty years."[318] 5.7.14

A Silly Debate: "What is the sense in his mentioning dung slabs and dung cakes in these verses along with loaves and melons and cucumbers, when they do not go together and have nothing in common, for one cannot eat melons and cucumbers with dung slabs and dung cakes, though one might eat them with bread and other appropriate things, so why mention them, especially given that they contain various forms of impurity?" We reply: "This may fall under the rubric of 'multiplicity of names,' which is mentioned as a type of rhetorical device,[319] for *kirsāyih* is the unit noun of *kirs* and *jillāyih* is the unit noun of *jillah*,[320] and *ʿajjūrah* and *qattāyih* likewise. The use of *qattāyih* with *t* instead of *th* is a rural dialecticism; thus there is 'orthographic paronomasia' between the former and the chaste forms.[321] The problem's now revealed, the silliness no more concealed." 5.7.15

Now for the analysis of the verses and the provision of etymologies: 5.7.16

saʾaltu ʿani l-ḥibbi ("I asked after the beloved"): *suʾāl* ("asking") is when one asks about something, this falling under the rubric of "stating the obvious." It is derived from *sayl* ("flash flood") or *sūliyyah*[322] or *sayālah* ("acacia tree").[323] The paradigm is *saʾala, yasʾalu, suʾālan.* 5.7.17

والحبّ مشتقّ من المحبّة أو من المحبوب والحِبّ بالكسر اسم لزِير الماء (وسمعت من ١٨،٧،٥
أمّي) وأنا صغير لُغز فيه وهو (يا شي من شي بطني على بطنه والمدلّي يعمل شغله)
ولم أفهمه إلّا بعد مراجعة أمّي مراراً أنّه زير الماء والكوز ومصدره حبّ يحبّ
حبّاً وقوله

(شَتَّ) مشتقّ من الشتات أو من الشِتاء أو من الشِيتة التي تستعملها النساء لمحَر ١٩،٧،٥
الكتّان

(والتايِهْ) مشتقّة من التَوهان أو من وادي التِّيه وقوله ٢٠،٧،٥

(مَسَحْتُ) من المسحة على وزن المِروَحة أو من المِسْحة على وزن دَبْحة ومصدره مسح ٢١،٧،٥
يمسح مسحاً

(وَجِلاّيِهْ) كذلك من معناها ٢٢،٧،٥

(وَكِرْسايَهْ) من التكرّس أو من كرس الزريبة وقوله ٢٣،٧،٥

(وَشِلْتُ وَجْهِي) الشيل مشتقّ من الشالِيَة الّتي يوضع فيها اللبن أو من الشليف ٢٤،٧،٥
الذي يُشال فيه التبن ومصدره شال يشيل شيلاً

(وَعُجُّورَهْ) من العَجّ أو من العُجَيْرة وهي حشيشة معروفة ومصدرها عجّ يعجّ عجّاً ٢٥،٧،٥

والقتّاية مشتقّ من القَتّ الّذي يربطوه الفلاّحين أيّام حصاد الأرز وهو معروف ٢٦،٧،٥
عندهم

وفي البيت من أنواع البديع المقابلة لأنّه قابل وجهه بالكرساية وقابل لحيته بالجلاّية ٢٧،٧،٥
وقابل بطنه بالرغيّف والعجّورة والقتّاية وهذا يدلّ على أنّه كان مشغولاً ببطنه أشدّ

ḥibb ("beloved") is derived from *maḥabbah* ("love")[324] or from *ḥubūb* ("grains"). With an *i* after the *ḥ*, it is a name for a water jar (*ḥibb*).[325] When I was young, I heard a riddle about this from my mother, which went "Something from something![326] My belly on its belly and the dangler does its job."[327] I did not understand until I had asked her about it several times, when it turned out that it meant the water jar and its mug. The paradigm is *ḥabba, yaḥibbu, ḥubban* ("to love"). 5.7.18

shatta ("he skedaddled") is derived from *shatāt* ("separation") or from *shitā'* ("winter") or from the *shītah* ("hackle") that women use to comb hemp. 5.7.19

The word *tāyih* ("shack") is derived from *tawahān* ("losing one's way")[328] or from Wādī al-Tīh. 5.7.20

masaḥtu ("I wiped away") is from *mimsaḥa* ("wiper"), of the measure of *mirwaḥa* ("fan"), or from *misḥah* ("mattock"), of the measure of *dabḥah*[329] ("a slaughtering"). The paradigm is *masaḥa, yamsaḥu, masḥan* ("to wipe"). 5.7.21

jillāyih ("dung-cake") is similar in meaning.[330] 5.7.22

kirsāyih ("dung-slab") is from *takarrus* ("lumping things together") or from the *kirs* ("a mixture of dung, mud, and urine, dried, cut into slabs, and used as a building material") of the byre. 5.7.23

wa-shiltu wajhī ("and I lofted my face"): *shayl* ("lifting, hauling") is derived from the *shāliyah* ("medium-sized bowl") in which milk is put, or from the *shalīf* ("net sacks") in which straw is carried.[331] The paradigm is *shāla, yashīlu, shaylan* ("to lift, carry"). 5.7.24

'ajjūrah ("hairy cucumber melon") is from *'ajr* ("unripe, green") or from *'ujayrah* ("little hairy cucumber melon")[332] and is a well-known plant. The paradigm is *'ajara, ya'jiru, 'ajran.*[333] 5.7.25

qattāyih ("long cucumber") is derived from the *qatt* ("sheaves") that the peasants tie in the fields at the time of the rice harvest, and is well known among them. 5.7.26

Among the rhetorical figures employed in the verse is "antithesis,"[334] since he pairs his face with a dung slab and his beard with a dung cake, and he pairs his belly with a loaf, a cucumber melon, and a cucumber, which goes to show that he was more preoccupied with his belly than with his beloved. Also 5.7.27

من اشتغاله بمحبوبه وفيه الطباق المعنويّ أيضاً لكونه ذكر الجوع وشكا ثمّ ذكر ما يأكله فانظر وفّقك الله كم حوى هذا النظم الفشرويّ من غموم وهموم * ومعاني عليها الخراء طُموم * لا يُعرَف إلّا بالذوق * ولا يُدرَك إلّا بالشوق *

(السادس من أشعارهم)

مواليا [بسيط مع كسر عند (ورحينا)] ٨،٥

رَقّاصُ طاحونِنا[1] يُشْبِهْ لِخُلْخالِكْ   وَرُحِيُّنا في الزَّرِيبَهْ قالَتِ ٱشْحالِكْ
إلّا وَكلّافْ يَقولْ لي يا صَبِي مالَكْ   طَوْرُ ٱبْنِ شَيْخِ البَلَدْ حالو مِثالْ حالَكْ

هذا المواليا من بحر التخبيط وهو على أربعة أَضْرُب من التخليط وتفاعيله مستلهطن لاهطن مستلهطن لهطاً وطوله من غير حَصْر * من شُبْرَى لمَصْر * وعرضه مع المصيبه * من باب النصر للصليبه * ومعنى ألفاظه الحويطه * وحلّ معانيه العبيطه * أنّ قوله ١،٨،٥

(رَقّاصُ طاحونِنا يُشْبِهْ لِخُلْخالِكْ) أي إنّ رنّة هذا الخلخال وسماع حِسّه يشبه رنّة خلخال محبوبته وخصوصاً إذا كان خلخالها من النحاس المطليّ بالقَصْدير كما تفعله نساء الأرياف أو من الحديد فعلى هذا يكون المشبَّه به السماع والحسّ لا نفس الرقّاص وسماعه يظهر عند دوران حجر الطاحون فيكون هذا الصوت الّذي شبّه به صوت خلخالها ناشئ من بين الحجر والرقّاص ولهذا عرّفوه بأنّه الهواء المنضغط بين قالع ومقلوع أو قارع ومقروع فاتّضح المعنى واندفع الاعتراض عن الناظم وإلّا لو كان المشبّه به ٢،٨،٥

١ بي: طحونتنا.

represented is "metaphorical contrast," because he refers to his hunger[335] and complains against it, then refers to what he eats. Observe, God reward you, how many sorrows and pains this facetious verse contains, and how many shit-laden senses, such as no one who hasn't tasted them can comprehend and no one who hasn't yearned for them can understand!

The Sixth of Their Verses: "The rattle staff of our mill makes a sound like your anklets"[336]

raqqāṣu ṭāḥūninā yushbih li-khulkhālik 5.8
wa-ruḥiyyunā fī l-zarībah qālat-ishḥālik
illā wa-kallāf yaqūl lī yā ṣabī mālak
ṭawru-bni shaykhi l-balad ḥālū mithāl ḥālak

The rattle staff of our mill makes a sound like your anklets
and our handmills in the pen said, "How are you?"
When suddenly a cowman says to me, "Lad, what's up with you?
The ox of the son of the shaykh of the village—his state is like yours!"

This *mawāliyā* is drawn from the ocean of inanity and comes in four fits of insanity.[337] Its feet are *mustalhiṭun lāhiṭun mustalhiṭun lahṭan.*[338] Its length, near enough, is from Shubrā to Maṣr,[339] its breadth—what a fuss!—from Bāb al-Naṣr to al-Ṣalībah. The meaning of its foxy phrases and the analysis of its silly senses are as follows: 5.8.1

raqqāṣu ṭāḥūninā yushbih li-khulkhālik ("the rattle staff of our mill sounds like your anklets"): that is, the ringing of this anklet[340] and the sound it makes resemble the ringing sound made by his beloved's anklets, especially if her anklets are made of copper plated with tin, as the women of the countryside have them, or of iron; thus the referent of the comparison is the sound and noise made by the rattle staff and not the rattle staff itself. The sound is audible when the millstone turns, and this sound, which he compares to the sound of her anklets, is generated between the stone and the rattle staff, which is why they define sound as "air compressed between what is pulled and what it is pulled out of" or "between what strikes and what is struck."[341] Now the meaning is clear and the objection resolved in favor of the poet.[342] Otherwise, if the referent of the comparison were indeed the rattle staff itself, his words would be meaningless, unless they were to be taken as constituting a suppressed 5.8.2

نفس الرقّاص لم يكن هناك فائدة لكلامه إلّا على تقدير حذف مضاف أي صوت رقّاص طاحوننا الخارج منه ومن الحجر يشبه لصوت خلخالك الخارج من بين الفردتين إذا مشيتي فعلى هذا التقدير أنّها كانت تلبس حَجَلاً كاملاً لأجل ظهور الصوت

٣،٨،٥ فإن قيل إنّ رقّاص الطاحون له حسّ مُرعِب عند دوران الحجر وله فرقعة عظيمة مُنفِرة للقلوب عند سماعها ولهذا يفعله الطاحون لأجل معرفة الناس أنّ هذا محلّ الطحن فيأتوا إليه للطحن أو لأجل دوران الثور والفرس فإنّه ما دام يسمعه يدور فإذا رفعوه وانقطع حسّه عند فراغ القمح من القادوس وقف فهو معدّ لأجل نشاطة البهائم وسرعة دورانها فأين المناسبة بينه وبين الخلخال وأيضاً جَعلُهُ الخلخال مشابه للخشب هذا شيء بعيد الشبه خصوصاً إذا كان الخلخال من الفضّة فإنّ الشيء إنّما يُشَبَّه به شيئاً مثله (قلنا) فالجواب أنّ هذا النَطِع لم ير[١] ولا ملك منذ عمره إلّا رقّاص طاحونه هذا فظنّ بسوء طبعه وعدم ذوقه أنّ سماع هذا الرقّاص لم يكن في الدنيا أحسن منه سماعاً فشبّه سماع خلخال محبوبته به وأيضاً لم يكن من الفضّة وإنّما كان من جنس النحاس أو الحديد فكانت محبوبته إذا مشت يقارب حسّه في السماع حسّ هذا الرقّاص وإلّا لو كان طحّاناً لطيفاً لم يتكلّم بهذا التشبيه الكثيف

٤،٨،٥ وألطف ما سمعته في محبوب طحّان هذين البيتين [بسيط]

طَحّانُكُم قَد زَها[٢] جَمالاً فَما يُطاقُ السُلُوُّ عَنهُ
ودَقّ[٣] خَصرًا فَلَيتَ شَعري بِكَمْ يُباعُ الدقيقُ مِنهُ

٥،٨،٥ وأحسن ما سمعته في محبوب فلّاح قول بعضهم [رمل]

---

١ بي: يره. ٢ بي: طحّانكم زها. ٣ بي: ورَقّ.

genitive construction, that is, "the sound made by the rattle staff of our mill, which emanates from between it and the millstone, resembles the sound made by your anklets, which emanates from between the right and the left anklet when you walk." This implies that she was wearing a full set of foot adornments in order to make a noise.

If it be asked: "A mill's rattle staff makes a terrifying noise when the stone turns, with mighty snapping sounds that make the heart recoil when it hears them (which is why the millers do it; i.e., they do it to make people aware that this is a place for milling so that they will go there to mill, or in order to make the ox and the horse go around, for as long as they hear the sound they keep going around, but if they remove the rattle staff and the sound is interrupted—as when the wheat in the hopper is exhausted—they stop, the whole thing being designed in order to energize the animals and make them move fast),[343] so where is the appropriateness of the comparison between it and the anklets? And his comparison of the anklets to something made of wood is also extremely far-fetched, especially if the anklets happen to be of silver, for things should be compared only to what resembles them," we would say that the response is that this oaf had never as long as he lived seen or possessed anything of any value other than the rattle staff of his mill and so, led by his evil disposition and boorishness, he thought that there could be nothing more beautiful to listen to in the whole world than the sound of it and therefore compared to it the sound of his beloved's anklets—especially since they were not of silver, but of copper or iron, in which case, when his beloved walked with them, the noise they made would indeed be close to that made by the rattle staff. And indeed, had he been a miller of refinement, he never would have uttered such a coarse comparison. 5.8.3

The cleverest thing I have heard about a beloved who was a miller is the following:[344] 5.8.4

Your miller's a radiant beauty—
Can't get him out of my mind!
With waist so slim I wish I knew
How much he charges per grind!

And the best thing I have heard on a peasant beloved is the words of a certain poet: 5.8.5

رُبَّ فلّاحٍ مليح   قالَ يا أَهلَ الفُتوّهْ
كَفَلي أَضْعَفَ خَصْري   فأَعينوني بقُوّهْ

٦،٨،٥ أقول هذا من باب عمى العاشق عن عيوب المحبوب وإلّا فالفلّاح وإن كان جميلاً فإنّ أفعاله بعدم اللطافة مشهورة وغاية الأمر أنّ هذا العاشق نظر إلى الردف الثقيل والخصر النحيل فمدحه فاتّضح الجواب * وبان الصواب *

٧،٨،٥ وأضاف الطاحون لنفسه لكونه كان ملازماً لها وقّافاً فيها أو يحتمل أنّها كانت ملكه وهذا من باب بناء الأمير الجدار

٨،٨،٥ ثمّ ما كفى هذا القائل الخبيث الطبع الرثيث الوضع الذي لا يعرف الحبّ ولا درى وعشقه يشبه الخراء ما ذكره من النظم الركيك والمعنى الديك حتّى خُيِّلَ له أنّ الرُحِيّ تخاطبه بالمقال وأنّها تستفهمه عن شرح الحال فأخبر عنها وقال

٩،٨،٥ (وَرُحِيْنا في الزَّرِيبَهْ قالتِ ٱشْحالِكْ) يُشْعِر هذا الكلام بأنّ الرحيّ خاطبته وأنّها سألت عن حاله وقالت له ما حالك اليوم يا مسكين وقد وصلت إلى العظم السكّين وما حكم صبرك على فراق محبوبتك ومقاساتك التعب والمشقّة من أجلها هذا إذا جعلنا خطاب الرحيّ له وأمّا إذا كان الخطاب لمحبوبته فإنّه من باب سلام الرحيّ عليها واستفهامها منها ما هي فيه في هذا الوقت فإن كانت اللام الّتي قبل حرف الرويّ منصوبة كان الخطاب له وإن كانت مخفوضة يكون لمحبوبته ولعلّ هذا هو الأصوب وسيأتي أنّ فتح اللام وخفضها لا يضرّ في الشعر ويُفْهَم من القرينة الدالّة على أنّ محبوبته كانت مثله طحّانة تطحن على الرحيّ في الزريبة فإنّ هذا العاشق كان يتردّد عليها

Many a cute-looking peasant
Has said, "Good Knight!
My buttocks have tired my waist—
Prop me up with all your might!"

This, I declare, falls under the rubric of "the blindness of the lover to the shortcomings of the beloved," or, if that is not the case, it may be explained by the fact that the actions of a peasant, however beautiful he may be, are well known to be devoid of any refinement, and the long and the short of it is that the lover beheld his ponderous backside and slender waist and praised the peasant on these grounds alone. Thus the answer now's clear, the truth made to appear. 5.8.6

He describes the mill as his own because he was always in attendance there and on duty inside it; or possibly it was indeed his property; or it may be that this falls under the rubric of "the emir built the walls."[345] 5.8.7

Then what this poet of vile disposition and threadbare invention, who knows nothing whatsoever of love and whose wooing resembles shit, has already come up with by way of putrid poetry and mediocre meaning is not enough for him and he has to imagine to himself that the handmills are talking to him and seeking an explanation from him of his state, which he proceeds to provide. Thus he says: 5.8.8

wa-ruḥiyyunā fī l-zarībah qalāt-ishḥālik ("and our handmills in the pen said, 'How are you?'"):[346] these words indicate that the handmills actually spoke to him and asked him about his state and said to him, "What is your state today, you poor thing, now that the knife has cut to the bone? And how are you bearing up under this separation from your beloved and the suffering and hardship you are experiencing for her sake?" This, if we suppose the handmills' speech to be addressed to him. If, however, the speech is addressed to his beloved, it would fall under the rubric of "the millstones' greeting her and interrogating her as to how she was feeling at that moment," since, if the *l* before the rhyme letter is followed by *a*, then the speech is addressed to him, and, if it is followed by *i*, it is addressed to his beloved. It may be that the latter is the more correct; it will be mentioned later that either *a* or *i* is allowable in verse.[347] Contextual clues indicate that his beloved, like him, was a miller, who did her grinding with handmills in the byre. It follows that this suitor would visit her from time to time and observe the situation, and the handmills would see—which is to 5.8.9

ويشاهد هذا الأمر فكانت الرحيّ أي لسان حالها ترى منه هذا الأمر فتخاطب تارة العاشق وتارة المحبوبة خطاباً بلسان الحال لا بلسان المقال فإنّها ليست من أهله ثمّ إنّه لمّا علم من حالها أنّها خضعت له ورثت لحاله حيث خاطبتها الحجارة وعلمت أنّه يريد منها ما يريد الراهب من الحمارة أرادت أن تعرّفه ما يقع لغيره قبل أن تواصله وما يتّفق لبعض أصحابه وإخوانه من الأثوار من نحول جسمه من ضرب الفَرِقلّة وتعب السواقي والحرث ونحو ذلك فأشارت إلى كلّاف البهائم أن يخبره عن ثور ابن شيخ البلد لأجل ما يتأسّى به ويتسلّى بحاله فأتى بأداة الاستثناء فقال

(إلّا وَكَلّافْ يَقولْ لي يا صَبي مالَكْ) وفي نسخة بدل ميم مالك واو يعني والَكْ ١٠،٨،٥
(طَوْرُ ٱبْنِ شَيْخِ البَلَدْ حالو مِثالْ حالَكْ) أي أنّ هذا الكلّاف ويقال له العلّاف بالعين المهملة ويسمّى التوّار أيضاً وهو الذى يكلف البهائم والأثوار ويتعاطى خدمتها لمّا رأى هذا العاشق ومقاساته الأهوال من أجل محبوبته وقد صار في حالة رذلة خصوصاً عند مشاهدة محبوبته لأنّ العاشق إذا شاهد محبوبه اعتراه التغيّر وخالطه الاصفرار وأذبله النحول قال الشاعر [طويل]

عَلامَةُ مَن كانَ الهَوى في فُؤادِهِ   إذا ما رَأى مَحبوبَهُ تَغَيَّرا
ويَصْفَرُّ مِنهُ اللَّونُ عِندَ اجتِماعِهِ   وإنْ طالَبوهُ بِالجَوابِ تَحَيَّرا

وأيضاً في حالة إفلاس وناهيك بالعاشق المفلس كيف يكون حاله فلشدّة خموله وما هو فيه قال له هذا الكلّاف (يا صَبي مالَكْ) أو (والَكْ) على الرواية الثانية لغة في أهل الريف والمعنى واحد أي ما حالك هذا الذى أنت فيه وما سبب مقاساتك الحبّ وخاطبه بلفظ يا صبي لكونه اعترته الصَبْوة أي المحبّة والميل وسيأتي اشتقاقها

say their innate faculties would see[348]—what he was doing. Thus they address at one moment the suitor, at the next the beloved, using "nature's tongues" to speak with and not real tongues, since they don't have any. Subsequently, when he realized from her state that she had submitted to him and taken pity on him, since the stones had spoken to her and let her know that he wanted from her what the monk wants from the donkey, she sought to acquaint him, before granting him union, with what had befallen others and how things had turned out for a friend and brother of his among the oxen in terms of emaciation of body from beatings with the whip and the exhaustion of turning the waterwheel and of plowing; so she called on the man charged with looking after the animals to tell him about the ox of the son of the shaykh of the village so that he might find solace and comfort therein. The poet thus introduces the particle of exception[349] and says:

illā wa-kallāf yaqūl lī yā ṣabī mālak ("When suddenly a cowman says to me, 'Lad, what's up with you?'")—in another copy, instead of the *m* of *mālak* there is a *w*, that is, *wālak*[350]—*ṭawri-bn shaykhi l-balad ḥālu mithāl ḥālak* ("the ox of the son of the shaykh of the village—his state is like yours!"): that is, when this cowman (*kallāf*)—sometimes called *ʿallāf*[351] and also *tawwār*[352]—who is the person in charge of the animals and the oxen and who devotes himself to their care, beheld this suitor and the agonies he was enduring for the sake of his beloved—for he was in a disgusting state, particularly when he caught sight of his beloved, for if a suitor catches sight of the object of his affections, he goes into shock, turns pale, and wastes away; as the poet says: 5.8.10

The sign of a man with love in his heart
  Is how he changes should his sweetheart come his way:
His skin turns pale whenever they meet,
  And, if questioned, he knows not what to say.

—and observed that he was broke (and well you know the state of the penniless suitor), then, as I say, this cowman said to him, in view of the lassitude and extreme emaciation that he was suffering, *yā ṣabī mālak*, or *wālak* according the other reading, the latter being a special usage of the country people though the meaning is the same), that is, "(Lad), what is this state that you're in and what is the reason for your suffering the agonies of love?" He addresses him as a *ṣabī* ("lad") either because he is overcome with *ṣabwah*, that is, love and

أو أنّه كان من صبيان البلد أي من شجعانها وقد أذلّه الحبّ وأنحله الغرام والمعنى إنّك لست مختصّاً بهذه الحالة وحدك بل إنّ بعض إخوانك من الأثوار نابه ما نابك وأصابه ما أصابك وهو ثور ابن شيخ البلد الّذي هو عظيم الأثوار وأجلّها وأكبرها فإنّ حاله الآن كيف حالك قد انتحل جسمه وصفرت ذاته ممّا قاسى من التعب وما كابده من النصب وما أكله من الضرب على أضلاعه وما حصل له من شدّة أوجاعه وهذا من باب التسلية والتأسّي بالغير كما سبق وأراد تسليته بالثور لكونه فلّاحاً ومن شأن الفلّاح أنّه في الغالب لا يضرب الأمثال إلّا بالبهائم ولا يُكْثِر إلّا من ذكرها وذكر آلات الغيط ونحوها فخاطبه من جنس ما يناسبه بمعنى أنّه يقول له تسلّي نفسك وتصبّرها على العشق والغرام فإنّ هذا الأمر ليس مختصّاً بك فإنّ صديقك ورفيقك الّذي هو ثور ابن شيخ البلد يشبه حالك وأتى بهذا التشبيه الخسيس المبنيّ على غير تأسيس ليناسب عشقه وحال محبوبته كما تقدّم بيانه ولكونه لا يخرج تشبيهه عن ماهيّة ما هو فيه لأنّه دائماً في معاشرة البهائم والأثوار وكذلك محبوبته فاتّجه الحال * وظهر الجواب عن هذا الإشكال * إذ هو نظم يشبّه بول الرجال * وقائله أثقل من الجبال *

وأما شرح لغات الأبيات واشتقاقها فقوله ١١،٨،٥

(رَقّاصُ طاحونِنا) الرقّاص آلة يصنعها النجّار من الخشب تشبه الكفّ والأنامل معلّقة في عود من الخشب أو الحديد فإذا دار الحجر فرقعت عليه وسُمِعَ لها حِسّ وسميت الرقّاص لأنّه مشتقّ من الرَقْص على وزن القَمْص أو من قرية في البحر الغربي يقال لها مَرْقَص ومصدره رقص يرقص رقصاً فهو رقّاص والطاحون على وزن المأبون أو المحون مشتقّ من طحن القمح أو من الطحين ومصدره طحن يطحن ١٢،٨،٥

attraction (the etymology will follow), or because he was one of the *ṣibyān* ("young men") of the village, that is, one of its courageous people, though love had afflicted him and passion made him thin. The meaning is:[353] "You are not alone in this state. Indeed, one of your brother oxen has been afflicted as you are afflicted and beset as you are beset, namely, the ox of the son of the shaykh of the village, which is preeminent among the oxen and the most splendid and the largest—for his state now is like yours: his body has grown thin, and his complexion has turned pale from the hardship he has endured and the exhaustion he has borne and the beatings on the ribs that he has tasted and the pains that have afflicted him." This falls under the rubric of "distraction and consolation through the sufferings of another," as previously mentioned.[354] He sought to distract him by mentioning the ox because he was a peasant, and peasants, as a rule, choose only animals as examples and do not talk much about anything other than these and agricultural implements and so on. Bearing this in mind, he addressed him in appropriate terms, as though telling him, "Distract yourself and put up with your love and passion, for such things are not peculiar to you: the condition of your friend and comrade, the ox of the son of the shaykh of the village, resembles yours." He came up with this vile comparison, based on no foundation, to fit the nature of the man's love and the condition of his beloved, as previously demonstrated, and also so that the comparison should not diverge from the essential nature of the man's condition, for he was the constant companion of the beasts and the oxen, and so too was his beloved. Thus everything's now all right, the solution's hove into sight, since the verse to men's piss is tantamount, while its maker's more ponderous than any mount.

Now, turning to the elucidation of the dialectal items in the verse and their etymologies: 5.8.11

raqqāṣu ṭāḥūninā ("the rattle staff of our mill"): the *raqqāṣ* is a device made by the carpenter out of wood and resembling a hand with fingers that is attached to a wooden or iron post; when the millstone turns, it sends out audible reports.[355] It is called *raqqāṣ* because it derives from *raqṣ* ("dancing"), of the measure of *qamṣ* ("galloping"), or from a village on the West River[356] called Marqaṣ. The paradigm is *raqaṣa, yarquṣu, raqṣan*, active participle *raqqāṣ* ("to dance"). The word *ṭāḥūn*, of the measure of *maʾbūn* ("passive sodomite") or *mamḥūn* ("slut"), is derived from the *ṭaḥn* ("grinding") of wheat or from 5.8.12

طحناً فهو طاحن ومطحون

والخُلخال مشتقّ من الخلخلة أو من الخُيَلاء أو من خلخلة الهواء ومصدره خلخل يخلخل ١٣،٨،٥
خلخالاً

(والرحيّ) جمع رَحاً وهي حجرين صغيرين أحدهما مركّب على الآخر الأعلى يدور على ١٤،٨،٥
الأسفل وفي وسط الأسفل عود من حديد يدور عليه الحجر الثاني يقال له القُطب
(قال ابن دُرَيْد) رحمه الله تعالى في مقصورته [رجز]

وإنْ سَمِعْتَ بِرَحًا مَنصوبَةٍ   لِلحَرْبِ فَاعْلَمْ أنّني قُطْبُ الرَحا

والرُحي بضم الراء واحدتها رَحاً كما تقدّم وهي مشتقّة من الراحة أو من الرَوْحاء محلّ ١٥،٨،٥
بأرض الحجاز أو من الرَواح وقيل من المِروَحة ومصدرها رحا يرحو رحاً قال الشاعر
[طويل]

لَهُ راحَةٌ مُشْتَقّةٌ مِنْ رَحائِهِم   تُرَوِّحُني لَمّا أروحُ إلى أَرضي

والزريبة مشتقّة من زَرْب البهائم لأنّهم دائماً يُزْرَبوا فيها ويجلّلوا فيها وربّما بالوا فيها ١٦،٨،٥
أيضاً كما هو معروف بينهم ومصدرها زرب يزرب زرباً

والكلاّف مشتقّ من الكُلْفة أو من الكَلَف وهو النَمَش الّذي يظهر في وجه الأمرد ١٧،٨،٥
أو الجارية بعد بلوغهما ودليله أن هارون الرشيد مرّ يوماً بجارية تباع فقال والله لو
لا كَلَف بوجهها وخَنَس بأنفها لاشتريتها فأنشدت تقول [سريع]

ما سَلِمَ الظَّبيُ على حُسْنِهِ   كَلا ولا البَدْرُ الّذي يُوصَفُ
الظَّبيُ فيه خَنَسٌ بَيِّنٌ   والبَدْرُ فيه كَلَفٌ يُعرَفُ

ṭaḥīn ("flour, meal"). The paradigm is *ṭaḥana, yaṭḥanu, ṭaḥnān,* and *ṭaḥīn* and *maṭḥūn* ("to grind, mill").

khulkhāl ("anklets") is derived from *khalkhalah* ("shaking") or from *khuyalā'* ("fancy, imagination") or from *khalkhalat al-hawā'* ("the rarification of air").[357] The paradigm is *khalkhala, yukhalkhilu, khulkhālan.*[358] 5.8.13

ruḥiyy ("handmills") is the plural of *raḥā,* which is a thing consisting of two small stones, one mounted on the other, with the upper stone turning on the lower. In the middle of the lower is an iron post, called the axle, around which the upper stone revolves. Ibn Durayd, may the Almighty have mercy on him, says in his *Maqṣūrah:*[359] 5.8.14

If you hear that the handmill of war is grinding,
Know that I am its axle!

ruḥiyy with *u* after the *r* is the plural of *raḥā,* as mentioned above, and is derived from *rāḥah* ("rest, comfort"), or from al-Rawḥā', a place in the territory of the Hijaz, or from *rawāḥ* ("evening") or, as some say, from *mirwaḥah* ("fan").[360] The paradigm is *raḥā, yarḥū, raḥan* ("to grind (wheat)"). Says the poet: 5.8.15

He has a hand (derived from their handmill)
That hands off any harm as I hurry home.[361]

zarībah ("animal pen") is derived from the *zarb* ("penning, enclosing") of the animals, because they are always penned up there, and sometimes shit and piss there too, as is well known among them. The paradigm is *zaraba, yazribu, zarban* ("to pen"). 5.8.16

kallāf ("cowman") derives from *kulfah* ("discomfort") or from *kalaf* ("freckles"), which are speckles that appear on the face of a beardless boy or young slave girl at puberty. The evidence for this is that Hārūn al-Rashīd one day passed a young slave girl who was for sale and said, "By God, were it not for a few freckles on her face and a snubness to her nose, I would buy her!" at which the girl recited: 5.8.17

The gazelle for all his beauty is not without,
Nay, nor the moon with whom the poets are besotted:
The gazelle has a snub nose for all to see
And the moon, as all know, is spotted.

فاشتراها هارون الرشيد لفصاحتها وحظيت عنده وإذا كان بمعنى العلّاف كما تقدّم فيكون مشتقّ من العَلَف أو بمعنى الثوّار فيكون من التيران ومصدره علف يعلف علفاً وقوله

(يا صبي مالك) بنصب اللام والبيتين السابقين بكسر اللام فهذا لا يضرّ لأنّه ورد في شعر العرب وتقدّم في غير هذا المحلّ اشتقاق الصبيّ أنّه من الصَبْوة أو من الصابون أو من قناطر الصابونيّ ١٨،٨،٥

وتقدّم تعريف الثور لغةً واصطلاحاً ١٩،٨،٥

(مسألة هباليّة) لأيّ شيء أتى في النظم بالثور فقط وكان من حقّه أن يأتي بالعجلة أيضاً أو بالبقرة حتّى يكون الناظم في مقام الثور والعجلة أو البقرة في مقام المحبوبة حتّى يكون الذكَر للذكَر والأُنثى للأُنثى فيكون هذا من باب المقابلة ويكون أبلغ في النظم (قلنا الجواب الفشرويّ) أنّه يُفهَم من ذِكر الثور ذِكر العجلة أو البقرة كما أن ذِكر عَنتَر يُفهَم منه ذكر عَبْلة فكان الاعتراض على الناظم في غير محلّه وكانت المقابلة معنويّة وهذا من باب قياس فطيس الّذي قاس البحر على التيس ٢٠،٨،٥

(فإن قلت) لأيّ شيء حصر الناظم الرحيّ في الزريبة مع أنّها ليست مُعَدّة لذلك إلّا نادراً لأنّها معدّة لزرب البهائم فيها كما تقدّم أنّهم يبولوا فيها ويخروا أيضاً حتّى يغرقوها فما الحكمة في ذلك (قلنا نعم) وإن قلنا إنّهم يبولوا فيها بيقين فإنّ البول فيها لا يدوم وربّما كان فيها بعض جوانب سالمة من البول فيجعلوا فيها الرحيّ لأجل الطحين أو يقال إنّ نساء الأرياف لا يتحاشوا من الزبل والجلّة فإنّ المرأة منهنّ أثوابها دايماً متضمّخة بالجلّة وغيرها في غالب الأوقات فاتّضح الحال عن وجه هذا الهبال ٢١،٨،٥

So Hārūn al-Rashīd bought her for her quick tongue, and she became his concubine. If we are to read the word as *ʿallāf*, as above, then it would be derived from *ʿalaf* ("fodder"), or if as *tawwār*, then it would be derived from *tīrān* ("oxen"). The paradigm is *ʿalafa, yaʿlifu, ʿalfan* ("to give fodder to").

yā ṣabī mālak ("Lad, what's up with you?"): the *l* is followed by an *a*, while in the two preceding lines[362] it is followed by an *i*; however, this does not matter, since the same is found in the poetry of the Arabs.[363] The derivation of *ṣabī* ("lad") from *ṣabwah* ("love") or from *ṣābūn* ("soap") or from the "the Bridges of al-Ṣābūnī" has already been given above.[364] 5.8.18

The definition of *thawr* ("ox")[365] has also been covered above, both from the general lexical perspective and as a technical term. 5.8.19

A Silly Topic for Debate: "Why does he mention only the ox in his verse, when he should have mentioned the calf too, or the cow, so that the poet could correspond to the ox while the calf or the cow could correspond to his beloved; that way, male would correspond to male and female to female, and it would make an example of 'opposition,' which would have been more forceful as verse?" We respond: "The facetious answer is that mentioning the ox automatically makes one think of the calf or the cow, just as mentioning ʿAntar makes one think of ʿAblah. Thus it would be misplaced to criticize the poet on these grounds, and the contrasts would be figurative, under the rubric of the analogy of Fuṭays, who compared the sea to a billy goat."[366] 5.8.20

If you say, "Why did the poet situate the handmills in the cow barn even though it is not, or is only rarely, designed for such things, being designed rather to hold animals, as explained above when it was pointed out that they piss and shit there too until the whole place is swimming in it, so what is the rationale for this?" we reply, "True. But even though we grant for a fact that they piss there, the piss does not last, and there may be places around the edges that are quite free of piss, and they may therefore put handmills there to grind their flour. Or it may be argued that the women of the countryside feel no repugnance for droppings and dung, for their clothes are always, or at least most of the time, covered with such things. Now the situation's clear, there's no more foolishness to fear." 5.8.21

(السابع من أشعارهم)

٩،٥ مواليا [بسيط]

رايْتْ حَريفي بفَرْقِلَّهْ يَسوقْ تيرانْ   لُوكُرّْ أَصْفَرْ على راسو كما اللَّبْسانْ
يا رَيْتَني كُنْتُ لُوحِدْوهْ مِنَ الحِدْوانْ   أو كانَ لي شَلْقْ على راسي مِنَ الكَتّانْ

١،٩،٥ هذا المواليا من بحر التخريف ومعنى التجريف * وطوله بالتخمين * من الحسينيّة لدَيْر الطين * وعرضه بالتقدير * من سَمَنُّود لأبي صِير * وأمّا معناه الخارج عن الإدراكات * الجارح لقلوب ذوي المُرُوّات * الّذي يمُجّه الطبع * ولا يَسَعُه محلّ ولا ربْع * فإنّ قوله

٢،٩،٥ (رأيْتْ حَريفي بِفَرْقِلَّهْ يَسوقْ تيرانْ) هذه الرؤية بَصَريّة أي شاهدت ببَصَري لا بايدَيَّ ورِجْلَيَّ حريفي أي محبوبي وهذه اللفظة من لغة الرّيافة لأنّهم يخاطبوا محبوبهم بهذا المعنى فيقول الشخص منهم فلان حريفي أي صديقي أو صاحبي أو محبوبي ويقول له يا فلان تعالى حارفني أو لاقشني يا ابو واسعه أو هارشني يا ابو عريضه أو حارفيني يا مليحه أو حارفني يا ابوكاره أو يا ابو كرّ ونحو ذلك من هذه الألفاظ وستأتي كيفيّة لقشهم على المُرْد والنساء في الأُرجوزة الآتية في آخر الجزء إن شاء الله تعالى وقوله

٣،٩،٥ (بِفَرْقِلَّهْ يسوقْ تيرانْ) يريد به التغالي في وصف المحبوب حيث جعله سوّاقاً بفرقلّة لأنّ الشخص إذا عشق إنساناً يصفه بوصف يقتضي الحالة التي هو فيها من لبس أو صنعة أو نحو ذلك ممّا يكون مُغْرَماً به وعاشقاً له (كما اتّفق) أنّ بعضهم كان يهوى غلاماً يهودياً وكان الغلام مُغْرَماً بضرب الناقوس فمرّ به يوماً وهو يضربه فأنشد يقول [بسيط]

The Seventh of Their Verses: "I saw my beloved with a plaited whip driving oxen"[367]

ra'ayt ḥarīfī bi-farqillah yasūq tīrān 5.9
lū karru aṣfar ʿalā rāsū ka-mā l-labsān
yā raytanī kuntu lū ḥidwah mina l-ḥidwān
aw kāna lī shalq ʿalā rāsī mina l-kattān

"I saw my beloved with a plaited whip driving oxen.
He has a cloth on his head yellow as mustard.
Would I were a pair of his sandals
Or he a flaxen cord for me upon my head!"

This *mawāliyā* is taken from the ocean of dredged-up drivel. Its length is from al-Ḥusayniyyah to Dayr al-Ṭīn, at a guess; its breadth from Samannūd to Abū Ṣīr, more or less. Its meaning, which passes all ability to comprehend and wounds the hearts of even stalwart men, and which any constitution would disdain and which no room, or even tenement, could contain, is as follows: 5.9.1

ra'ayt ḥarīfī bi-farqillah yasūq tīrān ("I saw my beloved with a plaited whip driving on"): this refers to ocular sight, that is, "I beheld with my ocular faculties" not with my hands or my feet, "my *ḥarīf*," that is, my beloved, the expression being taken from the dialect of the country people, for they address their beloved in this way. One says, "So-and-so is my *ḥarīf*," that is, my friend or my companion or my beloved. One says to such a person, "You there, come dally with me (*ḥarīfnī*)!" or "You with the wide one, let's fool about!" or "You with the broad one, horse around with me!" or "Make love to me (*ḥarīfnī*), pretty girl!" or "Dally with me (*ḥarīfnī*), you with the ass!" or "You with the headcloth!" and other similar expressions. An account of how they flirt with beardless boys and women will be given in the *urjūzah* at the end of this part, God willing. 5.9.2

bi-farqillah yasūq tīrān ("with a plaited whip driving oxen"): he seeks to exaggerate in describing the beloved by making him a drover with a plaited whip, for when someone is in love with someone else, he describes him in ways that fit his actual condition as far as dress, occupation, and so on are concerned, focusing on what the beloved is passionate about and keen on. For example, it happened that someone fell in love with a Jewish youth who was very keen on bell-ringing.[368] One day he passed him as he was ringing the bells and uttered the following verses: 5.9.3

رَأَيْتُهُ يَضْرِبُ الناقوسَ قُلْتُ لَهُ   مَنْ عَلَّمَ الظَّبْيَ ضَرْبًا بِالنَواقيسِ
وَقُلْتُ يا نَفْسُ أَيُّ الضَرْبِ يُعْجِبُكِي[1]   ضربُ النَواقيسِ أَمْ ضربُ النَوى قيسي

فانظر إلى رقّة الكلام وإلى مصادفة هذا الجناس التامّ فكان هذا مناسباً لحال كلّ منهما لأنّ العاشق فلّاح والمحبوب سوّاق ولا يستغني الفلّاح عن عِشْرة السوّاق ولا السوّاق عن الفرقلّة أيضاً و الفلّاح عنده التيران في مقام الأولاد كما أنّ السوّاق عنده الفرقلّة أعزّ من أخيه وولده ولهذا أنّها دائماً على كتفه لا تفارقه فكان المطلوب من هذا العاشق وصف هذا المحبوب بما يناسب مقامه وما يألفه

٥،٩،٤ ثمّ ما كفى هذا العاشق الماسخ والهمّ الراسخ ما وصف به محبوبه من أمر تعاطيه الفرقلّة واشتغاله بسوق التيران وأنّه من أكابر الرُعيان ومن أعزّ السوّاقين الأعيان حتّى وصف ما على رأسه فقال

٥،٩،٥ (لو كُرُّ أَصْفَرْ على راسو كَما اللَبْسانْ) هذا على حذف مضاف تقديره أنّ لهذا المحبوب كرّ وهو الشَدّ الذي يَلُفّه على رأسه يشبه في لونه نُوّار اللبسان وهذا من قبيل التفاخر بمحبوبه والتعاظم له حيث وصفه بأنّ له كرّا أصفر على رأسه يشبه نوّار اللبسان وأنّه متميّز عن غيره من السوّاقين والرعيان بهذا الكرّ فقلّ أن يلبسه أحد من أبناء جنسه وإذا فرض أنّ أحداً يلبسه لا يكون كلّه أصفر كنوّار اللبسان بل ربما تكون أطرافه فقط مزعفرة أو معصفرة كما تفعله الريّافة لأولادهم (فإن قيل) لأيّ شيء شبّه كرّ محبوبه بنوّار اللبسان ولم يشبّهها بالزعفران أو العُصْفُر أو نحو ذلك (قلنا) الجواب واضح أنّه أوقع التشبيه بهذا الزهر لأنّه لا يعرف الزعفران ولا غيره من المصبغات إلّا ما يظهر من صفرته من أصناف النوّار مثل نوّار اللبسان كونه أصفر لأنّه فلّاح و الفلّاح لا يعرف إلّا ما يظهر من الزرع وكذلك محبوبه سوّاقاً بفرقلّة فكان الأنسب

[1] بي: يُعْجِبُكِ.

I saw him ring the bell and said,
"Who taught this fawn to ring the bell?"
And, "Soul," said I, "Which like you best?
The (w)ringing of the bell, or of your heart? Think well!"

Observe the elegance of the words and how well turned is this example of perfect paronomasia![369] In the case of our verse, the description is perfectly matched to the condition of each, since the suitor is a peasant and the beloved a drover, and the peasant is inseparable from the drover just as the drover is inseparable from the plaited whip, and the peasant holds his oxen as dear as his children, just as the drover holds his whip dearer than his brother or his son, which is why you will notice that it is always on his shoulder and never leaves him. In such a situation it was a requirement that this suitor should describe this beloved in a way appropriate to his station and in terms of things familiar to him.

Next, this grotesque suitor and deep-rooted disaster was not content with what he had achieved by way of describing his beloved in terms of how he waved his whip about and worked with his oxen and how he was one of the mightiest of shepherds and noblest of noted drovers, and he had to go on to describe what he had on his head, saying: 5.9.4

lū karru aṣfar ʿalā rāsū ka-mā l-labsān ("He has a cloth on his head yellow as mustard"): the referent is unspecified but what he means is that *this beloved* has a headcloth (*karr*)—which is the same as the *shadd* ("length of cotton cloth") that they wind around their heads—whose color resembles mustard flowers. This comes under the rubric of "bragging about the beloved and taking pride in him," since he describes him as having on his head a yellow headcloth that resembles mustard flowers and as being distinguished by this headcloth from other drovers and shepherds, for rarely would one of his breed wear such a thing, and if he did it would not be all yellow like mustard flowers; rather, only the edges would be dyed with saffron or safflower, which is what the country people do for their children.[370] If it be said, "Why did he compare his beloved's headcloth to mustard flowers and not to saffron or safflower or the like?" we reply, "The answer is clear, namely, that he chose to compare it to that flower because he was ignorant of saffron or any dyestuff other than the various yellow flowers, such as mustard flowers, that he would actually see, because he is a peasant, and peasants know only those crops that are in front of their eyes. 5.9.5

أن يشبّه كرّه بما يعرفه وإلّا لو فرض أنّه شبّه الكرّ بشيء لطيف أو وصفه بوصف ظريف لخرج عن ماهيّة الرذالة وكان منه تشبيهاً لطيفاً دون الثقالة فاتّضح الحال عن وجه هذا الإشكال

٦،٩،٥ ثمّ لمّا علم أنّ محبوبه دائماً يمشي بحِدْوة في رجله إذا احتاج إلى حرث الأرض أو حصاد الزرع أو الذهاب إلى الساقية إذا كانت بعيدة تمنّى أن يكون حدوة في رجليه من بعض الحدوان فقال

٧،٩،٥ (يا رَيْتَني كُنتُ لو حِدْوَهْ مِنَ الحِدْوانْ) أي ليتني فأبدل اللام راء على لغة الريف كما تقدّم أكون دائماً حدوة في رجليه ولوكان بها النجاسة حتّى أتلذّذ بمسّ رجله الخشنة وكعبه الأقشر فانظر إلى قلّة عقله وسقاعة لحيته حيث عمل نفسه حدوة من الحدوان بل هو جَدْي من الجِدْيان وأرذل من هذا التمنّي في هذه الأبيات قول بعضهم في بعض المُزْدَوِجات [رجز]

يا لَيْتَني كُنتُ لَهُ سِنْداسا أَوْ لَيْتَني في رِجْلِهِ مَداسا

فتمنّيه في الشطر الأوّل أشنع من تمني هذا الفلّاح لأنّ السنداس أشنع من الحدوة لأنّه محلّ الشيء المستقذر نعم الشطر الثاني هو ممّا نحن فيه

٨،٩،٥ ثمّ هذا الفلّاح لمّا أنّه لم يبلغ مناه ولم ينل ما تمنّاه ولم يظفر من محبوبه برضاه تمنّى أن يكون محبوبه مرفوعاً على رأسه فقال

٩،٩،٥ (أو كانَ لي شَلْقْ على راسي مِنَ الكَتّانْ) الشَلْق يطلق على الحبل أو الحزمة من الكتّان حزمة صغيرة يسمّوها أهل الريف شلق وهذا من باب التذلّل لمحبوبه والتواضع له حيث جعل نفسه حدوة من الحدوان في رجل محبوبه وجعل محبوبه شلق كتّان على

Similarly, his beloved was a drover with a plaited whip, so the most appropriate thing was to compare his headcloth to something he knew. Supposing, hypothetically, that he had compared the headcloth to something refined or described it in sophisticated terms, he would have departed from the essence of vileness and it would be a refined, rather than a boorish, comparison. Now the truth's revealed, the problem's true nature no more concealed."

Then, when he learned that his beloved always used to walk shod with a pair of sandals[371] when he had to plow the land or harvest the crops or go to the waterwheel if the latter was far away, he expressed the hope that he might become just such a pair of sandals on his feet, saying: 5.9.6

yā raytanī kuntu lū ḥidwah min al-ḥidwān ("or would I were a pair of sandals"): that is, *yā laytanī* ("would I")—he changes the *l* to *r* according to the language of the countryside, as previously noted[372]—"might be, for ever, a pair of sandals on his feet, even if they were dirty, so that I might luxuriate in the feel of his rough feet and his ill-omened ankles."[373] Observe the brainlessness and brazenness that allow him to describe himself as a pair of sandals—though the reality's yet more remote: he's nothing but a baby goat! Even more disgusting than the wish expressed in the above verses are the words of a certain poet in the couplet: 5.9.7

Would he might use me as his loo,
Or on his foot I might be a shoe!

—for the latter's wish in the first line is even more revolting than that expressed by the peasant, because a latrine, as a place for depositing filth, is more revolting than a sandal; however, the second line is indeed pertinent to the matter in hand.

Having failed to attain his desire or achieve his wish or wrest satisfaction from his beloved, the peasant then expressed the hope that his beloved might be raised and placed on his head, saying: 5.9.8

aw kāna lī shalqa ʿalā rāsī mina l-kattān ("or he a flaxen cord for me upon my head"): *shalq* is applied to a rope or to a bundle of flax; the country people call a small bundle a *shalq*. This verse falls under the rubric of "groveling to and humbling oneself before one's beloved," since he describes himself as "a pair of sandals on his feet" and he describes his beloved as "a flaxen cord" upon his head so that he can bind him around it when his headache or *al-ḍārib*[374] or 5.9.9

رأسه لأجل ما يَعَصِب رأسه به إذا اشتدّ وجعها من ألم الصداع أو الضارب أو الدواهي والمصائب وهذا من عدم ذوقه وقلّة عقله وشدّة جهله

٥،٩،١٠ (فإن قيل) إذا كان هذا العاشق قصده أن يكون محبوبه في صورة شلق من الكتّان يربط به رأسه يكون على هذا التقدير محبوبه دائماً في تعب منه لو فرض ذلك مع أن العاشق لا يريد إلّا راحة محبوبه (قلنا) إنّ هذا من باب التواضع الفشرويّ لمحبوبه وطلب الرفعة له والعلوّ بكونه دائماً فوق رأسه مرفوعاً لأنّ الرأس ما رأس وعلا فلا يكون فوق محبوبه شيء ولا دون هذا العاشق أحد من العشّاق في التواضع أو هو من قبيل الاشتغال بربطه على رأسه فعلى القول الأوّل حصلت هنا المقابلة لرأسه وللحدوة الّتي في رجل محبوبه فكان هذا من باب التدلّي وعكسه فناسب الأمر فاتّضح المعنى وهذا كلّه من تمنّي ما لا طمع فيه على حدّ قولهم [وافر]

ألا ليتَ الشّبابَ يَعودُ يومًا فأُخبِرَهُ بما فَعَلَ المَشيبُ

٥،٩،١١ (مسألة هباليّة) لأيّ شيء تمنّى هذا العاشق أن يكون حدوة ولم يتمنّ أن يكون وطا لأنّه المناسب وربّما يكون ألطف وأظرف من الحدوة وأغلى ثمناً والحدوة فيها النجاسة أكثر من الوطا والوطا يفرح به الفلّاح ويقبله خصوصاً في أيّام الأعياد ونحوها والمحبوب لا يليق به إلّا الشيء النفيس فما الجواب (قلنا الجواب) عن هذا البحث الفشرويّ أنّ هذا المحبوب دائماً مشيه إلى الحرث والحرّاث لا يليق به المشي في حالة الحرث إلّا بالحدوة وأيضاً لكثرة ما يدوس بها في الأرض المحروثة في سروحه ورجوعه وفي شدّة الحرّ وإن كان فيها النجاسة تكون النجاسة فيها أكثر إذ من عادته أنّه لا يسرح ولا يروح إلّا والحدوة خلف قفاه مربوطة بحبل في نَبُّوته والعادة تثبت بمرّة فكان الأَوّلى لهذا العاشق أن يتمنّى أن يكون له حدوة لأنّها لمحبوبه أحسن من الوطا وأيضاً العاشق من شأنه أنّه يحبّ ما يألفه محبوبه ويهواه ومن شأنه التذلّل للمحبوب

other troubles and tribulations get bad—a notion attributable to his want of taste, lack of brains, and extreme ignorance.

If it be said, "If it is this suitor's intention that his beloved take the form of a flaxen cord that he can tie upon his head, he would, supposing such a thing to be possible, become a permanent cause of suffering to him, while the suitor normally wants only his beloved's well-being," we reply, "This falls under the rubric of 'facetious humbling of oneself before his beloved, and the pursuit of high estate and eminence for him by having him placed permanently on top of his head,' for the head is what is 'ahead,' and high up. Thus, there would be nothing higher than the beloved, and the poet would outdo all other suitors in humility. Or, he simply may be obsessed with being tied around his head. If we adopt the first option, what we have here is an example of rhetorical 'antithesis' between his *head* and the *sandals* on his beloved's feet.[375] The statement would then fall under the category of 'self-abasement' and its opposite; thus there is no contradiction and the meaning is clear. All of this boils down to hoping for things that no amount of hankering can bring about; as the poet[376] says: 5.9.10

> Would that youth could return one day
> That I might tell it what gray hairs hath wrought!"

A Silly Topic for Debate: "Why did this suitor express the hope that he might be a sandal and not a slipper, though the latter would be more appropriate, and no doubt also softer and more elegant, than a sandal, and more expensive too, while sandals are stiffer and more uncomfortable than slippers, which in turn are something the peasants delight in and wear readily, especially on feast days and so on, while it is also the case that only something precious is good enough for the beloved? What, pray, is the answer?" We reply, "The answer regarding this facetious inquiry is that this particular beloved does all of his walking while plowing, and the plowman can only walk while plowing if he is wearing sandals. Furthermore, he is always treading the plowed land in sandals, going and coming, and in the midst of the heat, and if there is any filth on the land, the dirt on sandals will be correspondingly greater than on slippers, since the peasant never goes to or returns from work without his sandals slung behind his neck, tied with rope to his stick; and from these general facts we may extrapolate to the specific case of the beloved in question. Thus, it is more appropriate for this suitor to express a hope that he should be a pair of his sandals because these are better than slippers in his beloved's eyes. Note too that 5.9.11

والخضوع له والذلّ في الحبّ لائق بالمقام كما قال بعض الملوك في جاريته وكان مغرماً بها ومشغولاً بحبّها فأنشد [طويل]

أيا ظَبْيَةَ الأتراكِ والخفرِ المَلْكي   على كلّ حالٍ أنتِ لا بدّ لي مِنْكِ
فإمّا بذُلٍّ وَهْوَ أَلْيَقُ بالهوَى   وإمّا بعِزٍّ وَهْوَ أَلْيَقُ بالمُلْكِ

وقال هارون الرشيد في جواره الثلاثة [كامل]

مَلَكَ الثلاثُ الأُنْسَاتُ عِناني   وحَلَلْنَ من قلبي بِكُلِّ مكانِ
ما لي تُطاوِعُني البَرِيّةُ كُلُّها   وأُطيعُهُنَّ وهُنَّ في عِصْياني
ما ذاكَ إلّا أنَّ سُلطانَ الهوَى   وَبِهِ قَوِينَ أعزُّ مِن سُلْطاني

فاتّضح الجواب وبان الصواب

١٢،٩،٥ (مسألة أخرى) فإن قيل كان من حقّ الناظم أن يقول (أو كان شلق في وسطي محزّم به) لأنّ الشلق كما تقدّم حبل من الكتّان أو الخُوص والحبل لا يكون إلّا مُعَدّاً للحزام أو لربط شيء ونحوه ووضعه على الرأس فنادر فما الحكمة في ذلك قلنا الجواب نعم إذا قلنا إنّه معدّاً لما ذكر وسلّمنا ذلك يَشْكُل علينا قصد الناظم إلّا أنّ الغرض للناظم خلاف ذلك وهو أنّه يريد رفع محبوبه على رأسه حتّى يصير في أعلى مكان وأشرف منزل وأيضاً الجواب بأن يقال إنّ من عادة الفلّاحين أنّهم يلفّوا على رؤوسهم الحبال إذا كانوا في شغل دقّ الكتّان أو في فتل الحلفة فيجعلوها مقام الكرّ ويربطوا بها رؤوسهم ويحفظوا بها طواقيهم لئلا تقع من على رؤوسهم وأمّا إذا كان الشلق بمعنى الحزمة الصغيرة كما تقدّم فلا إشكال ولهذا قال (على راسي من الكتّان) فاتّضح الجواب وظهر المعنى والله أعلم

it is typical for the suitor to love and feel affection for things his beloved has regular dealings with, just as it is for him to abase himself to his beloved and act submissively to him, abjection in love befitting the status of the suitor—as a certain king said regarding a slave girl of whom he was enamored and in whose love he was engrossed, when he recited:[377]

> O fawn of the Turks and of the royal guard,
> I cannot live without you whatever else may be—
> Either by abjection, which better sorts with love,
> Or might, which better sorts with majesty.

"And Hārūn al-Rashīd said of his three slave girls:[378]

> These three females have seized my reins
> And everywhere with my heart make free.
> What ails me, pray, that all mankind to me submits
> And I submit to them, while they will not submit to me?
> The truth is this: the power of love,
> With which they're armed, is mightier far than my authority.

"Thus the answer now is clear, the truth made to appear."

Another Topic: If it be said, "The poet ought to have said, '*or he a cord around* 5.9.12
my middle as a belt' because the *shalq*, as mentioned above, is a rope of flax or palm fiber and ropes are made specifically to be belts or to tie things up with and so on but it rarely happens that they are put on people's heads, so where is the wisdom in what he says?" we reply, "The answer is, 'It is indeed a fact that if we grant that it is made for the purposes described, we have a problem in interpreting what the poet meant. However, what the poet has in mind is something quite different, namely, to raise his beloved above his head so that he occupy the highest place and noblest station.'" Or one might equally respond, "It is said that it is a custom of the peasants to wind ropes around their heads when engaged in beating flax or plaiting esparto grass; they use them in place of headcloths, tying them around their heads to keep their skull-caps in place. Equally, were we to take *shalq* in the sense of 'small bunch,' as noted above, there would be no problem either, and this would be behind his words 'a *shalq* of flax upon my head.'" The answer's now clear, the meaning's appeared—but God knows best.

(شرح لغات الأبيات) قوله ١٣،٩،٥

(حَريفي) مشتقّ من الحِرْفة أو من الحَرافة أو من حروف الهجاء أو من حَرْف المَاجُور ١٤،٩،٥
قال الشاعر [طويل]

حَريفٌ إِذا ما اشْتُقَّ كانَ حَرافةً وَقيلَ حروف م الهِجاء[١] وحِرفةِ
وَقَد صَحَّ في القاموسِ الأَزرقِ أَنّه مِنَ الحَرْف لِلماجورِ فاصْغ لِحكمةِ

ومصدره حرف يحرف حرفًا فهو حريف

(والفَرْقِلّة) مشتقّة من الفَرْقَلة على وزن المَزْبَلة أو من الفِرْقال على وزن المِثْقال أو عبيد الزبّال ورأيت في القاموس الأزرق والناموس الأبلق أنّ الأصل في وضعها الطَرّاشة الّتي تلعب بها الخلابيص في السامر وعُمِلت الفرقلة قياساً عليه وكان اسمها في الأصل فرقيعة وأنّ الّذي صنعها صار يضرب بها الناس ويفرقع فكلّ من رآه يضرب آخر يقول فرقع له فحذفوا العين المهملة من آخر الفعل وأضافوا اللام وهاء الضمير إلى بقيّة الحروف وأقاموها الضمير المذكورة مقام هاء التأنيث وجعلوا مجموع ذلك عَلَماً على هذه الحبال المفتولة وقالوا فَرْقِلّة كما قالوا في بَعْلَ بَكّ ومَعْدِي كَرِب ونحو ذلك من التركيب المَزْجي وأمثاله ١٥،٩،٥

(فإن قيل) إذا كان أصل الفرقلة الطرّاشة فلأيّ شيء ترك الناظم الأصل وأتى بالفرع والأصل أشرف من الفرع إلّا في بعض مسائل ذكرها العلماء (قلنا) نعم لو كان محبوبه خلبوصاً كان حقّه أن يأتي بالطرّاشة لكونها من ملازم الخلبوص وإلّا فالمقام لا يناسبه إلّا الفرقلة لكون أنّ هذا المحبوب سوّاقًا للبهائم وهو من أولاد الفلّاحين فكان الأنسب ذكر الفرقلة كما تقدّم ومصدرها فرقل يفرقل فرقلة ١٦،٩،٥

---

١ بي: من الهِجاء.

Elucidation of the dialectal items: 5.9.13

The word *ḥarīfī* ("my boyfriend") is derived from *ḥirfah* ("craft") or from *ḥarāfah* ("acridity") or from the *ḥurūf* ("letters") of the alphabet or from the *ḥarf* ("edge, rim") of the crock. The poet says: 5.9.14

If *ḥarīf* you would derive, say "from *ḥarāfah*
Or maybe *ḥurūf* (of the alphabet), and *ḥirfah* likewise."
And it's true what says *The Ocean Blue*, that it's
From the *ḥarf* (of the crock), so hearken to the wise!

The paradigm is *ḥarafa, yaḥrufu, ḥarfan,* and *ḥarīfan.*[379]

The *farqillah* ("drover's whip") is derived from *farqalah*, of the measure of *mazbalah* ("dunghill"), or from *firqāl*,[380] of the measure of *mithqāl* ("miskal"), or from *ʿabīd al-zabbāl* ("the slaves of the garbageman"). I have read in *The Blue Ocean and Piebald Canon* that the model that led to the coining of the word *farqillah* is the *ṭarrāshah* that buffoons play with at parties and that *farqillah* was invented by analogy to the latter.[381] Originally it was called *farqīʿah* ("a cracking," as of a whip). I read too that the man who created it went around hitting people with it and cracking it, and that anyone who saw him beating another would say, "He gave him a cracking!" Then they dropped the ʿ from the end of the verb and added to the remaining letters an *l* and an *h* for the possessive pronoun, turned the possessive pronoun into the feminine ending,[382] and made the whole the proper name for the thing made of plaited rope, saying *farqillah*, just as they do with Baʿlabakk and Maʿdīkarib and other compound proper names,[383] and so forth. 5.9.15

If it be said, "If the origin of the *farqillah* is the *ṭarrāshah*, how come the poet passes over the original in favor of the derivative, when the original is nobler than the derivative except in a few cases mentioned by scholars?" we reply, "Indeed, had his beloved had been a professional buffoon, it would have been appropriate to use *ṭarrāshah*, for the *ṭarrāshah* is an accessory of such buffoons; in this case, however, the situation permits only the use of *farqillah*, because the beloved was a drover of animals, and of peasant stock. Thus the *farqillah* is the more appropriate for him, as mentioned." The paradigm is *farqala, yufarqilu, farqalatan.*[384] 5.9.16

١٧،٩،٥ وقوله يسوق على وزن قاوق مشتقّ من السوّاق أو من الساقية أو من السواقة ومصدره ساق يسوق سوقًا وسواقة قال الشاعر [طويل]

يَسوقُ إذا ما اشْتُقَّ كانَ سَواقَةً | وساقَ وسوّاقٌ وَسَقيٌ وقد وَرَدْ

١٨،٩،٥ والكرّما يُلَفّ على الرأس من الكتّان والقطن وغيره وهو مشتقّ من الكركرة على وزن الخرخرة أو من الكَراوِيا أو من الكرَب أو من كَرَّ الشيءَ إذا حلّه يقال كرّ عرضي فلان إذا حلّه من على رأسه ومصدره كرّ يكرّ كرًّا وقوله

١٩،٩،٥ (كما اللبْسانْ) اللبسان نبات يطلع في البرسيم له ورق عريض يأخذوه أهل الريف وينزعوا أوراقه ويخرطوا بالسكّين ويضيفوا عليه اللبن والملح ويبقوه زمانًا يسيرًا حتّى يأخذ قوامه ويسمّوا مجموع ذلك كبَرًا وسيأتي ذكره في كلام المتن وزهره يخالف زهر الكتّان لأنّه أصفر وزهر الكتّان أزرق قال ابن سودون [متدارك]

زَهْرُ الكَتّانِ مَعَ اللَبْسا | نِ هما لونانِ ولا كَذِبُ
كَيهودٍ في دَيرٍ خُلِطوا | بِنَصارى حَرّكَهُمْ طَرَبُ

٢٠،٩،٥ وهو مشتقّ من اللَبْس لأنّه ربّما يلتبس على الشخص القليل المعرفة قبل ظهور نُوّاره بنبات آخر غيره يسمّى عند الفلّاحين حُمّاض بضمّ الحاء المهملة وتشديد الميم وربّما اشتبه أيضًا بشجرة تسمّى فِسا الكلاب ورقها أيضًا يشبه ورق اللبسان وفسا الكلاب فيها بيقين منافع مذكورة في منافع النباتات أو من اللبسان وهو بير مشهور بأرض مصر يطلع فيه نبات يدخل في علم الصنعة الإلهيّة ويقال إنّ هذا البير هو باب الكنز الّذي تأتي إليه الحبشة وتأخذه في آخر الزمان ومصدره لبس يلبس لبسانًا

The word *yasūq* ("driving"), of the measure of *fusūq* ("outrage"), derives from *sawwāq* ("drover") or from *sāqiyah* ("waterwheel") or from *siwāqah* ("driving"). The paradigm is *sāqa, yasūqu, sawqan,* and *siwāqatan.* As the poet says: 5.9.17

yasūqu from *siwāqah* comes, if etymologies be invited;
saqa and *sawwaq* and *saqy* are also cited.

The *karr* ("(head)cloth") is anything made of linen or cotton or any other material that is wound around the head. It is derived from *karkarah* ("gurgling"), of the measure of *kharkharah* ("snorting"), or from *karāwiyā* ("caraway") or from *karb* ("grief") or from *karra l-shay'* ("he unwound the thing"), said when one undoes something. One says *karra ʿarḍī fulān* ("he unwound so-and-so's turban") when he undoes it from around his head. The paradigm is *karra, yakurru, karran.*[385] 5.9.18

ka-mā l-labsān ("yellow as mustard"): *labsān*[386] is a plant that grows in the clover, with broad leaves; the country people take it, pluck off the leaves, chop it up with a knife, add milk and salt, and leave it for a little to reach the proper consistency. The dish itself they call "capers," and it will be mentioned in the main text.[387] Its flowers differ from those of flax in that the former are yellow, while the flax flower is blue. As Ibn Sūdūn, may the Almighty have mercy on him, says:[388] 5.9.19

Flowers of mustard and those of flax
Are two different hues, it's true to say—
Like Jews in a monastery with Christians mixed
When both in rapture sway.[389]

The word is derived from *labs* ("confusion") as the ignorant may confuse the plant, before the flowers appear, with another, called by the peasants *ḥummāḍ* ("sorrel"), with *u* after the *ḥ* and double *m*. It also has some resemblance to a plant called *fisā al-kilāb*, whose leaves look like those of *labsān*. This *fisā l-kilāb* has confirmed beneficial properties that are mentioned in the books on the beneficial properties of plants. Or it may be from al-Labsān, which is a celebrated well in the land of Egypt in which grow plants that have a role in the Divine Craft;[390] it is said that this well is the door to the treasure that the Abyssians will come and take at the end of time. The paradigm is *labasa, yalbisu, labsānan.*[391] 5.9.20

(والحِذْوانْ) على وزن الجِرْوان واحدة الحِذْوة وهي جلدة تُعْمَل على قدر القدم لها ٢١،٩،٥
خيوط من الجلد تمسكها يستعملها الحرّاثون وغيرهم لدفع المشقّات وإذهاب الحفاء والعياء عن الرجل ونحو ذلك ومصدره حدا يحدو حدوة وقيل مشتقّة من الحِدّاية وهي طائر معروف من الفواسق الخمس الّتي جوّز الشارع قتلهنّ (فإن قيل) إنّ الحِدّاية من شأنها الخطف والحدوة على خلاف ذلك فكيف أنّها مشتقّة منها (قلنا) هناك أدنى مناسبة وهو أن الحدوة إذا مشى بها الشخص ربّما خطفت بعض الحصى وطرحته إذا أسرع صاحبها في المشي فكان هناك بعض شبه الحدّاية من هذا القبيل

(فائدة) ذكر صاحب القول المعاب في وصف الغراب واقعة عجيبة وهي أنّ بعضهم ٢٢،٩،٥
افتقر فدخل إلى بعض إخوانه من الأغنياء يلتمس منه شيئاً فعبس في وجهه فخرج من عنده منكسر النفس ومضى إلى بعض المقابر فمرّغ وجهه على الأرض ودعا الله تعالى وإذا بحِدَأة ألقت إليه شيئاً فنظر فإذا هو كيس ملآن من الدنانير وفيه جوهرة تساوي مال كثير فأخذه وأتجر فيه وصار في يسرة إلى أن مات فانظر إلى لطف الله تعالى ونعمه ومزيد عطائه وفضله على خلقه

ورأيت في القاموس الأزرق والناموس الأبلق أنّ الحدوة مشتقّ من الحِداد ٢٣،٩،٥
وأتى بشعر فشرويّ فقال [رجز]

وَالحِذْوَةُ المشْهُورَةُ اشْتِقاقُها مِنَ الحَدادي أَوْ مِنَ الحِدادِ

والحدادي على وزن الجنادي جمع حدّاية

(والشَلْق) مشتقّ من الشلوق أو من الشلقة أو من الشاقول الذي يوضع في رُبْع ٢٤،٩،٥
الميقات ومصدره شلق يشلق شلقاً

(والكَتّانْ) معروف وهو مشتقّ من الكَتّانِيّة الذين يتعاطون تعطينه وتشميسه ونحو ذلك ٢٥،٩،٥
ومصدره كتن يكتن كتناً

ḥidwān, of the measure of *jirwān* ("puppies"), is the plural of *ḥidwah*. It is a piece of leather made to the size of the foot with leather thongs that hold it in place. Plowmen and others use it to protect the foot from discomfort and prevent direct contact with the ground, fatigue, and so on. The paradigm is *ḥadā, yaḥdū, ḥadwan* ("to urge on camels by singing"). Some say it is derived from *ḥiddāyah* ("black kite"),[392] which is a well-known bird, one of the five "transgressive" creatures whose killing is sanctioned by the divine law.[393] If it be said, "It is in the nature of the kite to snatch things up, while the sandal does quite the opposite, so how can the one be derived from the other?" we reply, "There is a minimal fit, in that the sandal, when one walks in it, may snatch up some pebbles and then throw them down again if its owner moves fast; thus there is a certain resemblance to the kite along these lines." **5.9.21**

Useful Note: The author of *Reprehensible Lore concerning Birds That Caw* relates an amazing incident. A man became poor, so he went to see one of his richer brethren and beg something from him, but the man scowled in his face, so the poor man left his house broken in spirit and made his way to a tomb, where he rubbed his face in the dust and called on the Almighty. Suddenly a kite appeared and dropped something at his feet. The man looked, and behold, it was a purse full of dinars and contained a gemstone of great price. He took the purse and used it to buy goods to trade and lived a wealthy man until he died. Observe the kindness of the Almighty, His favors, great largesse, and generosity to His creation! **5.9.22**

I have read in *The Blue Ocean and Piebald Canon* that *ḥidwah* is derived from *ḥidād* ("mourning"), the following facetious reference being cited: **5.9.23**

> The well-known *ḥidwah* is said
> To come from *ḥadādī*, or from *ḥidād*.

ḥadādī, of the measure of *janādī* ("troopers"), is the plural of *ḥiddāyah*.

shalq ("cord; small bunch") is derived from *shulūq*,[394] or from *shilqah* ("eel"), or from the *shāqūl* ("plumb line") that is attached to the quadrant for telling time. The paradigm is *shalaqa, yashluqu, shalqan* ("(of a wall) to partially collapse"). **5.9.24**

kattān ("flax, linen") needs no definition. It is derived from the *katātiniyyah* ("flax workers") who handle its retting and sunning and so on. The paradigm is *katana, yaktinu, katnan*.[395] **5.9.25**

(فإن قيل) لأيّ شيء تمنّى أن يكون محبوبه شلق كتّان ولم يقل شلق خوص وحلفة ونحو ذلك قلنا لعلّ شلق الكتّان أقوى من شلق الخوص والحلفة أو لعلّه من باب اشتغال العاشق والمحبوب بزرع الكتّان وقلعه وملازمتهم لهذا الأمر فلا يعرفوا غيره فأتى بما يناسب الحال وما شابهه نعم لوكان محبوبه صعيدي لناسب أن يأتي بشلق الحلفة لكون الصعيديّ يألفها ولهذا يقال صعيديّ مصّاص حلفة أو كان خوّاصاً لناسب أن يأتي بشلق الخوص فاتّضح الإشكال وتمّ المقال ٥،٩،٢٦

وقد أنهينا ما أردناه من شرح بعض أشعارهم * ودشّهم وفُشارهم * وحلّ لغاتهم بلا مِرا * وكشف معناها الّذي يشبه الخرا * ٥،٩،٢٧

If it be said, "How come he wanted his beloved to be a flaxen cord and he does not say 'a cord of palm fronds and esparto grass' or the like?" we reply, "Perhaps a flaxen cord is stronger than one of palm fronds and esparto grass, or perhaps because of the involvement of both the suitor and the beloved in planting and reaping flax and frequent employment in such work, which would mean that that is the only kind they know. Thus, he used the thing that fit the situation best and most resembled him. True, had his beloved been an Upper Egyptian, it would have been appropriate to refer to a cord of esparto grass, because the Upper Egyptians are familiar with that, which is why they call Upper Egyptians 'esparto-grass suckers'; or, if his beloved had been a weaver of palm-frond baskets, he could have referred to 'a cord of palm fronds.' The issue's now exposed, the discussion closed." 5.9.26

This concludes the comments we wished to make on some of their poetry and their blathering and vauntery, and the exposition, for sure, of their words and the revelation of their meanings, which resemble turds. 5.9.27

(ولا بدّ بطرف يسير من شعر من يدّعي النظم وهو جاهل * ويقول الشعر وهو ذاهل) *

فمن ذلك ما اتّفق أنّ هارون الرشيد جلس يوماً عند زوجته زبيدة فجرى ذكر ولدها الأمين وكان بليداً بخلاف أخيه المأمون فإنّه كان حاذقاً فطناً لبيباً بارعاً في النظم والنثر وغيره وكان الخليفة يميل إليه لفصاحته وسرعة جوابه وشدّة حذقه فمدحه عندها فاغتاظت منه لكونه لم يمدح ولدها الأمين فقال لها إنّه بليد لا يدري النظم ولا يعرف النثر فقالت له بل ولدي أشعر من أخيه وأقوى جراءة وأشدّ فكرة ومعرفة في النثر والنظم وإن شاء الله تعالى في غد أقول له ينظم الشعر ويعرضه على أبي نواس فقال لها الخليفة حبّاً وكرامة في غد إن شاء الله نسمع كلامه ونطّلع على شعره قال فلمّا مضى النهار أرسلت خلف ولدها الأمين وقالت له على القصّة وألزمته بنظم الشعر وأن يعمل أبياتاً ويعرضها على أبي نواس فأجابها لذلك واعتزل في محلّ خال عن الناس وقدح فكرته الكاسدة وقريحته الباردة حتّى عمل أبياتاً يأتي ذكرها تشبه رصّ القُلْقَيْل ثمّ إنّه أتى إلى أمّه وأخبرها ففرحت وأرسلت خلف أبي نواس وقالت له اسمع ما قاله ولدي الأمين فقد صار ماهراً في الشعر بارعاً في النظم فقال له أبو نواس أسمعني ما قلت فأنشد [رجز] ١،٦

نحنُ بنو العبّاسِ ونجلسُ على الكراسي ١،١،٦

It Now Behooves Us to Offer a Small Selection of the Verse of Those Who Lay Claim to the Status of Poets but Are in Practice Poltroons, and Who Make Up Rhymes but Are Really Looney Tunes

Verses by al-Amīn

For example, it happened that Hārūn al-Rashīd was sitting one day in the quarters of his wife Zubaydah when the subject of her son al-Amīn came up. Al-Amīn was a dimwit, unlike his brother al-Ma'mūn, who was sagacious, astute, quick-witted, and gifted in several fields, including poetry and prose. The caliph favored al-Ma'mūn because of his mastery of the language, quickness of response, and intelligence, and he sang his praises to Zubaydah, who lost her temper with him because he did not praise her son al-Amīn. On the contrary, he told her that al-Amīn was a dimwit, knew nothing about poetry, and was ignorant of prose. "Not so!" she replied. "My son is a better poet than his brother—more daring, more insightful, and better versed in both poetry and prose. God Almighty willing, tomorrow I'll tell him to compose some verses and show them to Abū Nuwās." "Excellent!" said the caliph. "Tomorrow, God Almighty willing, we shall hear what he has composed and peruse his verses." At the end of the day, then, she sent for her son al-Amīn, informed him of what had occurred, and insisted that he compose some poetry and make up some verses to show Abū Nuwās. He agreed and, taking himself off to a place on his own, he cudgeled his dull wits and sluggish faculties till he had put together some lines—which we will quote below—that resembled clods of mud stacked in courses; then he went to his mother and told her. Delighted, she sent for Abū Nuwās and said to him, "Listen to what my son al-Amīn has made up! He has become a skillful poet and a master of verse!" Abū Nuwās said to him, "Let me hear what you've composed," and al-Amīn recited as follows: 6.1

We are the Banū l-ʿAbbās! 6.1.1
We sit on the thrones!

فقال أبو نواس نعم وأنتم لذلك أَهْلٌ ومَحَلٌّ وأنتم أصحاب الرُتَب العالية كمّل الأبيات فأنشد يقول [رجز]

ونُقـاتِلُ الأَعـادِي   بِالسَّيْفِ وَالمِزْراقِ

فقال له أبو نواس أتلفت ما قلت وغيّرت القافية قال فاغتاظ منه الأمين وأمر بسجنه فسُجِن أياماً فتفقّده الخليفة فقيل له هو في السجن حبسه الأمين لكونه عاب شعره فأحضره وأحضر الأمين وسأله عن السبب فأخبره بالقضيّة كما تقدّم فقال الخليفة للأمين لولا أنّه رأى في شعرك خللاً ما عابه فقال أنا أنظم غيره فقال له افعل قال فمضى وقدح فكرته وأتى إليه بحضرة والده وقد عمل أبياتاً أثقل وأشنع ممّا سبق فقال أبو نواس تكلّمْ بما قلت فأنشد يقول [رجز]

٢،١،٦ يا قـاعِدَهْ فِي الأَرْبُعِ   مـا مِثْلُكِ في الأَبْلَدِ
شَبَّهْتُكِ كُنـافَةً   مَبْسوسَةً بِالخَرْدَلِ
وَالسَّمْنُ فَوْقَكِ سـائِحٌ   مِثْلَ الحِصـانِ الأَبْلَقِ

قال فلمّا سمع أبو نواس هذا الكلام قام يجري فقال له الخليفة إلى أين فقال يا سيّدي إلى السجن ولا أسمع هذا الكلام قال فضحك عليه وعلى شعر ولده الخليفة وأخبر والدته بذلك فتحقّقت والدته زبيدة بلادة ولدها الأمين وسكتت

٢،٦ (وأعرص من هذا النظم) قول مُرجان الحبشيّ وكان أميرًا بثغر إسكندريّة وقد عارض بهذا النظم الشنيع والكلام الوضيع همزيّة الأديب الورع الزاهد العالم الماجد الأبي

"Quite right!" said Abū Nuwās. "You are fit for that and worthy of it, and you are the ones who hold high rank. Proceed with the rest of the verses!" So al-Amīn recited and said:

We fight our enemies
  With sword and lance!

"You've ruined what you said before," said Abū Nuwās, "by changing the rhyme." Al-Amīn lost his temper with him and ordered that he be locked up, and so he was for a few days. Missing him, the caliph enquired after him and was told, "He's in the lock-up. Al-Amīn imprisoned him for criticizing his poetry." So the caliph had him brought, along with al-Amīn, and asked him why, and he told him what had happened, according to what was previously described. The caliph said to al-Amīn, "If he had not detected some shortcomings in your verses, he would not have criticized them." Al-Amīn replied, "I will make up some more." "Do so," said the caliph. So al-Amīn went off and cudgeled his brains, and then he went back to Abū Nuwās, in his father's presence, having composed verses yet more tedious and unpleasant than the preceding. "Say what you have made up," said Abū Nuwās, and he recited as follows:[396]

O woman dwelling in the spring encampments, **6.1.2**
  There's none like you in any burg!
I compare you to *kunāfah*
  Drenched with mustard,
The butter running all over you
  Like a piebald steed!

As soon as Abū Nuwās heard these words, he started to run. "Where are you off to?" said the caliph. "To the lock-up, My Lord!" said Abū Nuwās, "rather than listen to stuff like that!" The caliph dismissed al-Amīn and his poetry with a laugh and informed his mother of what had happened, and even she realized how stupid was her son al-Amīn and said no more.

Verses by Murjān al-Ḥabashī

Even more wretched than the above are the verses composed by Murjān al-Ḥabashī,[397] an emir at the port city of Alexandria, who attempted to outdo[398] with his vile verses and supine stanzas the *hamziyyah* of that glorious, **6.2**

صيريّ رحمه الله تعالى ونفعنا به وخمّسها أيضاً وها أنا أَسْرُدُ لك هذا النظم الخسيس مصحوبًا بالتخميس وهي هذه [وزن غير معروف]

١،٢،٦ يا رسول الله قلّ من الناس المعروفْ
يا رسول الله أصبحت بينهم مثل الطير المنتوفْ
بعد أن كنت مثل الخروف المعلوفْ
يا رسول الله أغثنا استغاثة ملهوفْ قد أضرّت به أشرار من اللُكَعاء

يا رسول الله ما عاد في حدّ خيرْ
يا رسول الله ما بقوا يوقّروا صغير ولا كبيرْ
يا رسول الله كن لي منهم نصيرْ
يا رسول الله أصبحنا بينهم مثل الحميرْ وهم يسوقونا بالعصاء

٢،٢،٦ يا رسول الله إحنا من رعيّتكْ
يا رسول الله إحنا من جملة أُمّتكْ
يا رسول الله أنا في جيرتكْ
يا رسول الله بحقّ صحابتك أَجِرْنا من نار لها سَعْراء

وأنا أمدح نبي ربُّهُ استخاره وعَزَّهْ[1]
ياما غزا الكُفّار بعسكره وغُزّهْ
ومن صلّى عليه ربُّه لم يُخْزِهْ
وقد عرج به ربّنا وعزّه وقد رأى من آيات ربّه الكُبراءِ

٣،٦ إلى أن افتخر بقلّة عقله وكثرة جهله على صاحب الهمزيّة عفى الله عنه وظنّ بأنّ نظمه في غاية البلاغة واستحكام الصناعة فقال

١ بي: وعَزُّهْ.

scholarly, ascetic, and pious man of letters al-Būṣīrī, may the Almighty have mercy on him and benefit us through him. The poet expanded it in pentastich form too, so let me now present to you these vile rhymes, along with the additional lines:

O Apostle of God, kindness has diminished among men! 6.2.1
O Apostle of God, now among them I'm like a plucked hen,
After being like a fat sheep in a pen!
O Apostle of God, aid us as You would one with grief stricken,
Whom the mischiefs of the wicked have harmèd!

O Apostle of God, no one is good anymore!
O Apostle of God, neither small nor great do they show respect for!
O Apostle of God, against them me be a support for!
O Apostle of God, like an ass we have become them for,
Which they to drive with sticks have hittèd!

O Apostle of God, we are Yours in subjugation! 6.2.2
O Apostle of God, we belong to Your Nation!
O Apostle of God, I come to You in supplication!
O Apostle of God, for Your Companions' consideration,
Save us from a Fire that's been kindlèd!

I praise a Prophet, chosen by his Lord and raised to fame—
How often to attack the Infidel with his troops and his Ghuzz was his game!
Who blesses him his Lord will not shame!
Our Lord raised him up and gave him fame
And of his Lord's signs he saw the biggest sizèd![399]

And so on, until he decided, in his stupidity and ignorance, to boast of his superiority to the author of the *Hamziyyah*, God excuse him his sins, imagining that his verse was of the utmost pithiness and most solid craftsmanship. Thus he said: 6.3

ضاهيت بها همزيّة الأبي صيري ٦،٣،١
والفرق بينهما يلوح للنحريري
وانظر للصيّر هو مثل البُوري
والّا جبل مصر مثل الطوري   والّا الصقر الصائد مثل البوماء

أنا انتخبتُ ألفاظها من القاموسا
ومَنْ عارض نظمي في لحيته يلقى موسا
ومن له في الأدب رتبة أو ناموسا
لا بدّ أن يميّز بين الجاموسا والناموسا   وأولاد الحلال ما هي مثل أولاد الزِناء

نظمي هذا ما هو مثل نظم الناس ٦،٣،٢
نظمي هذا مثل دُرّة في كاس
ومن سمع نظمي يقول دوهاس
قد فقت في النظم أبو النواس   أنا مرجان والحُبشان لي آباء

أنا مرجان وفي إسكندريّه
وأدري النظم بالكلّيّه
ومن عارض نظمي يلقى بليّه
أنا أصبحت مثل الشمس المضيّه   ونظمي مثل نظم أبو العلاء

نظمي مثل درّة في حُق ٦،٣،٣
لهفي على فتى عارف مُنْحَق
هو ابن المَخاض مثل بنت الحق
والا النمل السابح مثل البقّ   أنا أصبحت مثل القطّ اصطاد الفاراء

The *Hamziyyah* of al-Būṣīrī, with this I trump it! 6.3.1
The difference is clear to all but a half-wit!
Observe the sprat—is it like the mullet?
Or is Mount Cairo[400] like to, of al-Ṭūr,[401] the summit?
Or can the hunting hawk to the owl be assimilatèd?

I have chosen its phrases from the *Qāmūs*,[402]
And any who tries to beat my verse, may he find a razor on his beard let loose!
And whoever has rank in literature, or say-so,
Should know the difference 'tween a buffalo and a mosquito!
And the children of wedlock are not like those whose mothers fornicatèd!

These verses of mine are not like those of the mass! 6.3.2
These verses of mine are like a pearl in a glass!
Those who hear my verse exclaim, "dūhās"![403]
I have beaten at rhyming Abū l-Nawwās,[404]
And I'm Murjān, by the Ethiopes progeneratèd!

I'm Murjān and I live in Alex!
I know how to versify on all the topics!
May he who tries to beat my verse meet with a hex!
I'm become like the sun at its apex!
And my verse Abū l-ʿAlāʾ[405] has equivalatèd!

My verse is like a pearl in a case! 6.3.3
Alas for a youth discerning, whose right's been effaced!
Does not the daughter of the three-year-old she-camel the two-year-old colt outrace?
Or is the busy ant like the bedbug in pace?
I am become like the mouse that a cat has huntèd!

أنا أصبحت ما لي في نظمي نظير
ولا ضاهى قولي لا كبير ولا صغير
وأنا أعطاني ربّي الخبير
وأنا مرجان الحبشي الأمير أستخرج الدُرّ من البحراء

٤،٣،٦ وأختم قولي بمدح طه الزين
يا سعادة من زاره في حُنَيْن
وقبّل حجرته وشاف بالعين
وقال له يا جدّ الحسن والحسين اشفع لمرجان ينجو من النارِاء

٤،٦ ورأيت له أيضاً نظماً أثقل من الحجاره * وأنجس من ماء الخَرّاره * قد حكى في ترتيبه القُلْقَيْل في الرص * وفي رؤيته ذقن العرص * عارض به لقلّة عقله وسوء جهله خمريّة القطب الربّانيّ والهيكل الصَمَدانيّ سيّدي عمر بن الفارض نفعنا الله ببركاته فقال

[وزن غير معروف]

١،٤،٦ سُقِينا على ذكر الحبيب مُدامة طرِبنا بها
كُمَيْت من الكَرْم ختامها مِسْك
ودارت علينا سقاة في يدها كؤوس
كل ساقي منهم يحكي لنجمة الفُلْك
وياما شُفْنا من خمرتنا ورَيْنا من سَكْرتنا
أمور محتبكات ومرتبكات رَبْك
وشاهدنا العجائب ورأينا الغرائب
واندكّت جبالنا من أطوارنا دكّ
٢،٤،٦ مدامتنا هذي تعلو على مدامة الفارضيّ
وأين الثُريّا من الثرى ولَعَمْري بعيد من الدَرْك

I am become in poetry without peer!
And none, great or small, with my words can compare!
He has granted me much, My Lord, the Seer!
I'm Murjān the Ethiopian, the emir,
Who pearls from the sea has extricatèd!

With praise of Ṭāhā[406] the Beauteous I close my paean! 6.3.4
How lucky is he who visits him at Ḥunayn![407]
And kisses his tomb[408] and sees him plain!
And says to him, "Grandfather of al-Ḥasan and al-Ḥusayn,
Intercede for Murjān, that he not be pyratèd!"

And I have seen some further verses of his more burdensome than boulders and filthier than sewer waters, whose arrangement like courses of muddy clods appeared, and whose shape resembled a pimp's beard. With these, in his stupidity and evil ignorance, he tried to outdo the wine ode of the Divine Axis and Sempiternal Tabernacle, My Master ʿUmar ibn al-Fāriḍ, God benefit us through his blessings. They go:[409] 6.4

We were poured, at mention of the Loved One's name, a wine that sent us into ecstasy— 6.4.1
Bay-red liquor from the vine, whose seal is musk.[410]
And servers passed among us, cup in hand,
Each one of them resembling a starry disk.
What a lot in our cups we've seen and in our stupor beheld—
Things soundly wrought and tightly bound!
We've witnessed marvels and we've seen amazements—
And our mountains did our hillocks pound!
This wine of ours is better than Ibn al-Fāriḍ's:
What hath the Pleiades to do with the Earth?
They are far, I swear, from that hellish murk!
Our wine has no like in the universe at all, 6.4.2
Not with monk nor with priest nor with Turk!
This wine of ours, who tastes it in the cup
Says, of its flavor, "This is like musk!"

مدامتنا ما مثلها في الكون مدامه
ولا عند الرهبان والقُسوس وأبناء التُرك
مدامتنا هذه من ذاقها في كأسها
قال من طعمها هذه مثل المِسْك
ومن أوصاف خمرتنا إذا صُبَّت على حجر
لقام ذلك الحجر من حسن معانيها يبكو
ومن أوصافها كمان إن شربها ضعيف
طاب من وقته ولم يعد قطّ يشكو
ومن أوصافها إن مرّ مزكوم على ديرها
وشمّ رائحتها من بعيد خلَص بلا شكّ
٦،٤،٣ ومن أوصافها إن صُبَّت في قارورة صبًّا
تشاكل الأمراح الطَرف من حسنها يحكو
ومن أوصاف خمرتنا إن غنّت هند
ترجمت بكل لسان مثل سَناء المُلْك
وقد شرب منها مرجان شربة
فأضحى بها هائم في الكون بلا شكّ
فدونك مدامتنا لا تحود عن شربها
ففي شربها يا خالي البال الحكّه والدكّ
وفي شربها في حانها وسط مجلسها
من يد ساقيها السعد والمُلْك
٦،٤،٤ وأختم خمرتي هذه بصلاتي وسلامي
على نبيّ عربيّ جاه الجمل يشكو
وعلى آله وأصحابه كلما حطّوا الحجّاج
عند سيرهم الحمول وفكّوا

To describe our wine: if poured on a stone,
The stone would weep from the beauty of its expression!
To describe it again: if a weak man drank it,
He'd recover at once and no more suffer depression!
And again, if one passed by the monastery where it's made, and he had catarrh,
His nose would clear, for sure, though he sniff it from afar!
Another description: if it were poured into a decanter, 6.4.3
All would be well, and of its beauty the eye would talk!
And another description of our wine: if Hind sang,
She would jabber in every tongue, like Sanā' al-Mulk.[411]
Murjān has drunk a draught of it
That's made him wander through the Universe quite cracked!
So take our wine, turn not aside from drinking it,
For to drink it, happy-go-lucky one, is to get quite crocked!
To drink it in its tavern among those of its school,
From the hand of its cup bearer, is happiness and rule!
And I close this wine ode of mine with my prayers and greetings 6.4.4
To an Arab Prophet, to whom the camel came complaining,[412]
And for his Family and Companions, as long as pilgrims take down
Their bundles, and undo them, on decamping![413]

فانظر إلى عدمِ إصابة ميزان هذه الخمريّة وفرضها * لكون أنّ ناظمها قلب طولها في عرضها *

(واتّفق أنّ بعض القضاة من الأروامِ قال لنائبه) نحن ننظم الشعر ونسمّى بيت النظّامون ونقول الشعر محاظرةً فقال له النائب هذا لا يبعد عليكم فقال له نظمت بيتاً محاظرةً فقال النائب أسمعنا إيّاه فقال [وزن غير معروف] ٥،٦

شين الشرع بالاشاره تقطع مثل المنشارهْ

ما تقول أيّها النائب في هذا الكلام * وحسن هذا النظام * فقال بعد أن ضحك عليه * وأشار بكلامه إليه * وأنا الآخر نظمت محاظرةً عروض كلامك وما يشابه قولك ونظامك فقال القاضي تكلّمْ أيّها النائب ومن هو صاحب الرأي الصائب فقال [مجتثّ مع كسر]

سعيده كانت مزاره * تحبّ طبيخ البيسارهْ

قال فَهام ذلك القاضي طرباً من كلامه * ومن شدّة ما أعجبه من نظامه * وأعطاه جوخة كانت عليه * ومال بقلبه إليه * ولم يزل معه في عزّ وإكرام * وهيبة واحترام * إلى أن عُزِلَ وأموره للسفر قد حضرت وودّعه النائب بقوله فلا رَجَعْتَ

(وكتب بعض البلداء ممّن يدّعي النظم) لرجل من العلماء يسمّى الشيخ محمّد السلسليّ مراسلة يعرّفه فيها عن حال بنت تسمّى هِنْد وعن أخت لها تسمّى عَرَب وكان الشيخ رحمه الله تعالى يحبّهما لأنّ طبعه كان يميل للإناث حتّى أنّه كان لا يأكل إلّا من الزُنْديّة ولا يشرب إلّا من القُلّة ولا يركب إلّا الأنثى من الدوابّ ولا يقبل المذكّر قطّ ٦،٦

Observe how far this wine ode misses the mark in terms of its meter and what it's about, because of the way the author has taken it and turned it inside out!

Verses by a Turkish Judge

6.5 And once a Turkish judge told his deputy, "My family writes poetry and is known as the House of the Versifierers.[414] We can compose verses to shoot any occasion."[415] Said his deputy, "We would expect nothing less of you." Then the judge said to him, "I have composed a verse to shoot the occasion!" "Let's hear it!" said the deputy. So the judge said:

The shin of *shar*ʿ I would shay
Cutsh jusht like a shaw![416]

"What say you, dear Deputy, to this line, and to the beauty of this verse of mine?" Said the deputy, after laughing at it and making some comment, "I too have composed something to 'shoot' the occasion, based on your verse and matching your words and style." "Speak, Dear Deputy and Deliverer of Discerning Decisions!" said the judge. So the deputy said:

Happy was Mizārah—
She loves to cook *bīsārah*!

So pleased was the judge with these verses that he swooned in ecstasy and gave the deputy the coat of broadcloth off his back and took the man to his heart and continued to treat him with honor and veneration, respect and consideration till he ended his tour of duty and his bags were packed for his departure, at which point the deputy bade him farewell with the words, "And may you never come back!"

Verses by Shaykh Muḥammad al-Rāziqī

6.6 And a certain dolt who claimed to be a poet wrote a letter to a scholar named Shaykh Muḥammad al-Silsilī, to give him news of a girl called Hind and a sister of hers called ʿArab. The shaykh, may the Almighty have mercy on him, loved these two because he was by nature attracted to the feminine, to the extent that he would eat only from a *zubdiyyah* ("bowl"), drink only from a *qullah* ("water pitcher"), and ride only female animals, tolerating nothing male.[417]

وكان من الأولياء العارفين غير أنّه كان يغلب عليه الخلاعة والانبساط مع النساء لأجل التستّر على أحواله رحمه الله تعالى ونفعنا به فأرسل إليه يقول [خفيف]

بَعْدَ أَزْكَى السَّلامِ مِنّي نَهاضَهْ لِحَبِيبٍ يُحَبّ مِن غَيرِ بَغاضَهْ
إسمُهُ السَّلْسَلي والشَّيخ محمّدْ زادَكَ اللهُ في الأَنامِ وِعاضَهْ
أَنْتَ في ذا الزَّمانْ قَمْحٌ غزيرٌ وسِواكَ الأَنامِ مِثْلُ النِفاضَهْ
أَنْتَ أَرْسَلتَ في الكِتَابْ بِتَسْأَلْ عن عُرَيْبٍ فإنّها من بِياضَهْ
وهُنَيْدٌ زادت عن الكلِّ عَجَبًا بِسَوادِ العُيونْ لا بِالغِلاضَهْ
مَنْ يُحِبُّ المِلاحَ يَسْلَى الدَراهِمْ عَهْدُنَا بِكْ ما تمتلِكْ شَيْ قُراضَهْ
وأنا إِسْمِي الرازِقي والشيخ محمّد أَلْضُمُ القَوْلْ وَطَرِّزُهْ بِالفِضاضَهْ

قال فلمّا قرأ الشيخ هذه الأبيات ضحك وجعلها معه وصار كلّما حصل له انقباض يعطيها لفقيه يقرأها له لأنه كان بصيرًا فينشرح ويزول عنه انقباضه

٦،٧ (ويقرب من هذا النظم المرثيّة التي رأيتها لبعض البلداء) من الشعراء في رجل مات من الأمراء يقال له ابن الخواجا مصطفى فأحببت أن أثبتها لما فيها من الأبيات المجرفة والمعاني المقلحفة وهي هذه [وزن غير معروف]

٦،٧،١ أحمد الله لطيف اللطفا في ابتدائي بمديح صُنِفا
وعلى أزكى البرايا كلّها صلوات الله جاءت بالوَفا
وعلى الآل جميعا كلّهم وعلى أصحابه الخُلَفا

He was one of the saints who have attained esoteric knowledge, even though licentiousness and enjoyment of women appeared as his predominant characteristics so as to disguise his mystical states, may the Almighty have mercy on him and benefit us through him. So the dolt wrote to him, saying:[418]

After the sweetest of greetings from me very energetically
    To a beloved who's loved without hostility,
Whose name's "al-Silsilī" and "Shaykh Muḥammad,"
    May God provide for you among men exhortatorily[419]—
In these days you're like thick wheat,
    While others resemble what's winnowed chaffily!
In your letter you sent asking
    After ʿUrayb,[420] and she's just hunky-dory,
And after Hunayd,[421] and she's now fairer than them all—
    For the blackness of her eyes, not for being whore-y!
He who loves cute girls can kiss his money good-bye,
    And we all know you're extremely poor-y!
And me, my name's "al-Rāziqī," and "Shaykh Muḥammad,"[422]
    And I stitch together verses with silver embroid-ory!

When the shaykh read these lines he laughed and he kept them with him and whenever he was depressed he would give them to a man of religion to read to him (he was weak-sighted) and would be cheered up, and his depression would leave him.

Elegy by a Certain Dim-Witted Poet to the Emir Ibn al-Khawājā Muṣṭafā

The above verses are similar to an elegy I saw by a certain dim-witted poet in memory of an emir who had died called Ibn al-Khawājā Muṣṭafā. I would like to set it down in writing for the sake of its limping lines and desiccated denotations—and here it is: 6.7

I thank God, most merciful of all, 6.7.1
    At my beginning, with praises composèd,
And on the purest of all mankind
    May God's blessings come unrestricted,
As on his family each and every one
    And on his Companions who succeeded!

بعد هذا أبتدي مرثيّة   في أمير موته قد حَتَفا
جاءه الموت سريعا عاجلا   وعليه عزريل[1] حقا عَكَفا
عندما مات بلغني موته   صحت بأعلى صيحتي يا أسفا   ٢،٧،٦
ودموعي من عيوني قد جرت   مثل ما تجري سواقي مَرْصَفا
قلت لما أن بلغني موته   بعدما دمعي بعيني دلفا
مات من في الناس يذكر اسمه   بالأمير ابن الخواجا مصطفى
يوم مات الأرض كادت أن تغور   والسما صارت سحابا كَسَفا
والأماكن كلّها من بعده   ونبات الأرض حقّا قلْحَفا
كم له وسط المدينة سمعة   كالصناجق بل وأعلى شَرَفا
كان حامي الخيل شُجاعا بطلا   حين تنظره العِدى تَرْتَجِفا   ٣،٧،٦
قد تولّى وانقضت ايّامه   يا نعم يا ابن الخواجه مصطفى
وجميع أمواله قد قُسِّمَتْ   أخذوها أهل الطمع بالجَزَفا
والأعادي فرحوا في موته   لاجل مال ينهبوه جَرَفا
من معادن فضّة مع ذهب   وكنوز أخرجوها قُفَفا
وَرِثوها أعداؤه من بعده   فرّقوها اليوم بِفَرْدَ العَلَفا
من جواهر لامعات كِسَر   لا هطات نورها قد رُصِفا   ٤،٧،٦
ويواقيت زَبَرْجَد لؤلؤا   ودِلاص سابغات رَعَفا
قررت في بيت مال عدّها   ألف ألفي ألف ألفي مِقْطَفا
وعَلِيّ الكاشف منها أخذا   بعد ما أشرع فيها مِقْحَفا

---

١ كذا في جميع النسخ.

And now, an elegy I begin
    For an emir who's now deceasèd.
Death came to him quick and fast
    And ʿAzrīl[423] him seizèd.
I exclaimed aloud when the bad news reached me 6.7.2
    And "Alas!" I shouted,
And tears from my eyes ran down
    Like Marṣafah's waterwheels when rotated![424]
Dead is he who among men
    By the name of the Emir Ibn al-Khawājā Muṣṭafā is commemorated!
The day he died the earth near sank
    And the sky to darkling clouds reverted,
And after him all places
    And all plants went really dessicated!
How great his fame was in the city
    —like the sanjaks, nay, even higher venerated!
He was a protector of horses, brave and heroic, 6.7.3
    When the enemy saw him, they all vibrated!
His days are done and gone forever, Ibn al-Khawājā Muṣṭafā, the highly praisèd!
    All his wealth was then divided,
And the greedy took it off in heaps uncalculated.
    His enemies were very happy at his death
To think of the money in scoops to be despoliated,
    Of metals, silver, and gold,
And treasures that in baskets they expropriated.
    His enemies inherited it after him
    And today by the feed sack all of it have distributed—
Shining gems, individuated, 6.7.4
    Gleaming, whose light has radiated,
And rubies, chrysolites, and pearls,
    And coats of mail trailing like a nose that's bleeded!
In the treasury by count their number was set
    At a thousand thousand thousand thousand baskets completed.
ʿAlī the Inspector kept a portion,
    After he'd waded through them and winnowed out what he wanted.

خزّنوها في بيت مال بعده   أخذ الكاشف منها واكتفى
كم أتى في بيته من مرأة   مع بنات لابسات الغُدَفا   ٦،٧،٥
ثمّ نوّحت عليه حزنا   وعليه الناس صلّت صُفَفا
كم أمير جاء في تربته   ووضع فوق التراب الشُقَفا
كم فقيه جاء في موتته   وتلا ياسين ثمّ الزُخرُفا
يا ترى قد مرض بالبطن   أو بالوبا أو بالرُعاف ارتَعَفا
ليتني شاهدته في كفن   أبيض حين عليه هَفهَفا   ٦،٧،٦
ليته لو عاش قرنا كاملا   لكن الموت عليه زَحَفا
ثمّ أخلى داره من حِسّه   وحِمام الموت منها زَحَفا
يا ترى من عاد يخلف بعده   حين يأتي بعده كي يَخلُفا
فعَسَى يأتي حسين بعده   يفتح البيت ويبقى مُنصِفا
ليت شعري لو تخلّف بعده   ولد مثله كي يُخلَفا   ٦،٧،٧
هكذا الدنيا دواما طبعها   تَقهَر الناس وتأتي بالجفا
كل ما فيها تراه زائل   تنقلب بالغدر مثل المَجرَفا
ليس يعجبني الأمارة كلّهم   كالأمير ابن الخواجا مصطفى
كم غمرنا إحسانه مع جوده   كم عطايا زائدات بالوَفا   ٦،٧،٨
كيف لا أبكي على من جاد لي   بعطايا ما عطاها خُسرَفا
ربِّ ارحمه وخلّي بعده   أمّه والستّ وابنه يوسُفا

They put them in the Treasury later on
  After the Inspector his belly with them had fillèd.
How many a woman came to his house 6.7.5
  With girls in headcloths dressed,[425]
Then wailed for him in sorrow,
  And the people prayed for him in rows arranged!
How many an emir came to his grave
  And potsherds on the earth they placèd!
How many a man of religion to his funeral came
  And Yāsīn, then al-Zukhruf, recited!
I wonder, did a stomach problem finish him off
  Or the plague, or a nose that bleeded?
Would I had seen him in a grave-sheet 6.7.6
  White, all enshrouded!
Would that he had lived a century in full
  But, in fact, death right up to him strided!
Then his house it emptied of his voice
  And from it by inexorable fate 'twas sweepèd.
I wonder who will succeed him later,
  When whoever comes after him comes, that he may be succeeded.
Mayhap a Ḥusayn after him will come
  To open the house and act with fairness unimpeded.
Would that I knew if he would come after him 6.7.7
  And nobly act, that he might be well succeeded!
Such is this world, its nature ever changing—
  It oppresses men and has them harshly treated.
All that's in it is clearly quite ephemeral—
  It turns with treachery like a current that's swirlèd!
With none of the emirs, not one,
  As with the Emir Ibn al-Khawājā Muṣṭafā am I pleasèd!
How often did his charity and generosity envelop us! 6.7.8
  How many were his gifts overflowing, unrestricted!
How not weep for one who on me lavished
  Gifts such as Chosroes never gavèd?
O Lord, have mercy on him, and, after him,
  His mother, the Mistress,[426] and his son Yūsuf keep preservèd!

قــد توفّى في جمــاد اوّلـــــــ　　سادس الشهر خميسا شُرّفا

عام أربع من ثلاثين مـضت　　بعد ألف من سنين تُعـرَفا

بعـد هجـرة من أتانا رحـمة　　بالهـدى أزكى البرايا شـرَفا

يا إلهي اغفر لناظمها اسمـه　　عـابد الرحمن وابنـه يوسُفـا ٦،٧،٩

جده يسمى محمـد مـغوري　　فارض عنه يا لطيفَ اللُّطفا

وارحـم الوالد وأجـداد له　　والأمير ابن الخواجا مصطفى

وصــلاتي وســلامي دائما　　على النبيّ والآل أصحاب الوَفا

ودخـل بعض البلداء من الشعراء على السلطان الملك الظاهر بيبَرس وقد فتح قرية ٦،٨
من قرى الكفّار فقال له أطال الله بقاء الملك أنا فلان بن فلان بن فلانة عاش أبي
من العمر ستّين سنة وعاشت أمّي أربعين سنة وأنا في سنّ الخمسين سنة وقد
عملت لك أبياتًا تتضمّن تأريخ فتح هذه القرية التي ملكتها ثمّ أخرج له رقعة مكتوب فيها

[وزن غير معروف]

قد فـتح السلطان بلده　　وأتى السعـد البـلدهْ

فلمّا فـتحـها أرّختُهـا　　حاكما في شهر ذي القعده

فقال له الملك لم أر أبرد من كلامك إلّا شعرك ولم أر أبرد من شعرك ونترك إلّا لحيتك قال فخجل الرجل ومضى إلى حال سبيله (أقول) قد تقدّم أن هذا كلّه من عدم

He died in the month of Jamād al-Awwal,
The sixth, a Thursday, thus ennoblèd,
In a year dated thirty-four
After a thousand years passèd[427]
After the Hijra of him who came to us in mercy
With guidance, the purest of mankind as rankèd.
O my God, forgive the maker of these verses, 6.7.9
Whose name is ʿĀbid al-Raḥmān, and his son, who Yūsuf is designated,
Whose grandsire's name is Muḥammad Maghūrī[428]—
Please, most Merciful of the Merciful, with him be contented,
And to his father and his forebears
And to the emir Ibn al-Khawājā Muṣṭafā may your mercy be extended!
And my prayers and blessings forever more
For the Prophet and his family, a people perfected!

A Chronogram

And once a certain dim-witted poet presented himself to the sultan al-Malik al-Ẓāhir Baybars, when he had just conquered a town belonging to the unbelievers, and said to him, "God preserve the life of the king! I am So-and-so, son of So-and-so, son of So-and so, son of my great-grandmother So-and-so.[429] My father lived sixty years, my mother lived forty years, and I am fifty years old. I have made some verses for you that incorporate the date of the conquest of this village of which you have taken possession." Then he pulled out a scrap of paper on which was written: 6.8

The sultan conquered a town
And good fortune came to that town.
When he took it, I dated it
Year 70, in the month of Dhū l-Qaʿdah.[430]

The king told him, "I have never come across anything more brazen than your speech, unless it be your verse, or than your prose, unless it be your beard!" The man was abashed, and went his way.

الذكاء والفطنة وكثرة الجهل وقلّة المعرفة وإلّا فصاحب الذوق السليم لا ينطق بمثل هذا الكلام السقيم فقد قال بعضهم لا ينبغي للشاعر أن يَعرِض قصيدته على الرواة حتّى يهذّب ألفاظها ويدقّق معانيها وبعد ذلك يعرضها على من شاء ويعطيها لمن أحبّ وقال الشاعر [كامل]

لا تَعرِضْ على الرُواة قَصيدةً ... ما لَمْ تَكُنْ بالَغْتَ في تَهذيبِها
فإذا رَوَيْتَ الشِعْرَ غَيْرَ مُهذَّبٍ ... جَعَلوهُ مِنْكَ وَساوِساً تَهْذي بِها[1]

١ بي: تهذو بها.

I declare: as has been explained earlier, all this stems from lack of intelligence and perspicacity, an excess of ignorance, and a paucity of education. A man of sound taste, in contrast, would never allow such poor language to pass his lips. Someone has said, “The poet should never show his ode to a transmitter until he has polished its expressions and scrutinized its senses. Thereafter he can show it to whomever he likes and give it to whomever he wishes.” As the poet[431] said on the matter:

Don’t show an ode to the transmitters
Till you’ve polished it time and again!
If you transmit your work unpolished,
They’ll say you suffer delusions that have driven you insane!

(ذِكر فقرائهم الجهّال * وارتكابهم الجهل والضلال) *

١،٧ أمّا فقراؤهم فليس لهم طريقة إلّا هزّ الحوف * وطَرق الكفوف * والنطّ والزعيق * والسِبحة والإبريق * وأخذ الدراويش * وكثرة التشاويش * وعدم معرفة الطريقه * والديك والعليقه * وترك تعليم ما تصحّ به العباده * وقلّة الدين بزياده * والنوم الزائد * والزحف على القُصَع والمتارد * والدردشة باللسان * وقولهم خَبَّرَ الولي فلان * لا يَرْكَنوا لأهل الفضل * ولا يقولوا إلّا بأهل الجهل * لا يعرفوا مسألة في الدين * وليس لهم في الطريق يقين * قد ارتكبوا أشد العظائم * وحُكمهم حُكم البهائم * فهم طائفة تربّوا في أطراف البلدان * ولا يعرفوا الفقرسوى باللسان * والسبحة والانخناس * والخوبشة والانعكاس * وأخذ البدايات * والدوارة في الحارات * وحضور الموالد * والزحف على الموائد * والنخّة الشيطانيّه * والمصائب والبليّه * لا يميّزوا بين حرام وحلال * ولا يألفوا إلّا لأهل الضلال * قد أباحوا الزنا * وشرب المُنْكَر والخَنى * يجتمعوا بالنساء المحرّمات * ويعتقدون أنّ نكاحهنّ من المباحات * قد احتوى عليهم إبليس بكثرة الوساوس * وهم الطائفة الخوامس *

٢،٧ (حكى بعض أهل العلم) أنّه شاف جماعة منهم فرآهم مختلطين بالنساء مثل البهائم ثمّ إنّهم أرادوا أن يَزْنوا فيهن بحضرته فزجرهم ونهاهم فأرادوا قتله فتحايل عليهم حتّى خلص من بين أيديهم ولم يرجع بعد ذلك إليهم

٣،٧ (وحكى رجل من أهل الفضل) أنّه رأى جماعة منهم يأكلون في رمضان من غير عذر يبيح الفِطر فسألهم عن ذلك فقالوا نحن قوم قد سقط عنّا التكليف وليس

An Account of Their Ignorant Dervishes and of Their Ignorant and Misguided Practices[432]

The Practices of the Khawāmis Sect

7.1 As for their dervishes, their only Path[433] is the shaking of their caps and the beating of their palms and jumping and shouting, with their prayer beads and pitcher; they adopt the ways of dervishes and practice many other annoyances; they are ignorant of the true Way, with their cockerel and fodder;[434] they abandon the teaching of the proper practice of worship and are characterized by an excessive lack of religion; they sleep excessively and crowd around the food platter and the crock; they babble in tongues and say, "So-and-so the Holy Man has spoken thus!"; they pay no heed to the people of virtue, while they take their creed from the people of error; they are unacquainted with any issue in religion, and they have nothing of the Path that is certain; they have perpetrated the deadliest of sins and are like dumb animals, for they are a sect that has been raised in the margins of the lands. Of Poverty they know nothing but the name; all they know is prayer beads and devilry, foul deeds and criminality, how to recruit their minions and go around the neighborhoods, attend saints' feasts and crowd around the tables,[435] and their satanically inspired impulses, and disasters and calamities. They do not distinguish between wrong and right, and they are familiar only with the people of error. They have declared fornication lawful, as well as the drinking of what has been declared unlawful and obscene diatribes. They meet with women of illicit degree and believe that intercourse with them is permitted. Iblis has possessed them with his whisperings incorrect; these are the people of the Khawāmis sect.

7.2 A man of religion relates that he noticed a company of them and observed that they were mixing with women, just like beasts. Then they prepared to have sex with the women in his presence, but he rebuked them and forbade them to do so, and they wanted to kill him, but he pulled a trick on them and was able in the end to escape their clutches and never went back to them.

7.3 And a man of virtue relates that he noticed a company of them eating without excuse[436] during Ramadan, so he asked them what they were doing, and

علينا جُناح لأنّنا في مقام الشهود مع الله تعالى وصرنا في حالة الفناء في الله وإذا فنا الشخص سقط عنه التكليف فنحن على حدّ قول القائل [طويل]

وبَعْدَ الفنا في اللهِ كُنْ كَيْفَ ما تَشاءُ فَعِلْمُكَ لا جَهْلٌ وفِعْلُكَ لا وِزْرُ

قال فصاح عليهم هذا الرجل بالويل والثُبور * وعظائم الأمور * فولّوا منه الأدبار * وركنوا إلى الفرار * فانظر كيف دخل الشيطان على عقولهم * وكيف سوّل لهم أموراً جعلها أهلاً لضلالهم *

٤،٧ وإلّا فالعارف بالله تعالى لا يقدر الشيطان أن يدخل عليه من هذا القبيل (كما اتّفق للجُنَيْد) رحمه الله أنّه مرّ في ليلة من بعض الليالي في بادية وخلفه تلميذه فسمع هاتفاً يقول يا جنيد قد أسقطنا عنك التكليف فقال له الشيخ كذبت يا ملعون الأبعد فقال له التلميذ يا سيّدي أليس هو من قِبَل الله تعالى فقال له تأدّب يا ولدي هذا الشيطان يريد أن يدخل على عقولنا بشيء يُضِلّنا به

٥،٧ فهذه الطائفة ينبغي البعد عنهم والتحرّز منهم (وقيل دخل رجل من الملحاء بعض أضرحة الأولياء فرأى رجلاً من الخوامس يَزْني بامرأة) وكلّما ينكحها قالت الله وغابت عن وجودها وكذلك الرجل يفعل مثلها ويهيم ويصير في وجد عظيم وهما على هذه الحالة فقال لهما الرجل يا أشقياء كيف تذكروا الله وأنتم في هذه الحالة الرذلة فقال له يا سيّدي سمعنا قول بعضهم حيث قال [طويل]

ويَلْتَذُّ مِنّي كُلُّ عُضْوٍ ومَفْصِلٍ إذا ذُكِرَ المَحْبُوبُ ثـمّ أَهِيـمُ

فأنا ألذّذ أيري بالذكر وهي تلذّذ فرجها كذلك قال فقام عليهما ذلك الرجل بالضرب والسبّ والصياح حتّى اجتمعت عليه الناس وعرفوا الأمر فأرادوا قتلهما فشفع فيهما البعض من الناس وأخرجوهما من مقام الوليّ على أيشم حال وكلّ هذا ببركة ذلك

they replied, "We are a people who have been relieved of the obligation to obey God's commandments,[437] and it does not matter what we do for we have the status of witnesses with Almighty God and have achieved annihilation in Him, for once a person is annihilated in God, he is relieved of the obligation to obey God's commandments. Thus we are those meant by the poet[438] when he said:

> After annihilation in God, be as you wish,
> For your knowledge is no ignorance, your doings are no sin."

At this the man yelled at them, threatening them with doom and gloom and many disasters, so they turned their backs, making rapid tracks. Observe how Satan had seduced their minds, luring them astray with his evil designs!

Satan cannot, however, seduce in this way any of the Almighty's initiates. 7.4
For example, it happened that al-Junayd, God have mercy upon him, was passing through empty country one night, his disciple behind him, when he heard a voice say, "Junayd! You are relieved of the obligation to obey God's commands!" "You lie, accursed wretch!" said the shaykh. But his pupil said to him, "Master, is this not a voice from the Almighty?" "Be guided, my boy!" said al-Junayd. "This is Satan. He seeks to seduce our minds with what will lead us astray."

This sect is to be shunned and guarded against. It is said that a man of wit 7.5
entered the mausoleum of one of God's Friends and found one of the Khawāmis fornicating with a woman, who with each penetration would say "God!" and swoon; the man would do the same, going into transports of ecstasy and bliss while they were thus engaged. The first man said to them, "You wicked ones, how can you mention the name of God while in this disgusting state?" The other man replied, "Sir, we have listened to the words of the poet who said:

> Each member and joint of mine takes pleasure
> At the mention of the Beloved, and then I swoon.

"So I pleasure my penis by mentioning His name and she pleasures her vagina the same way." At that the man set upon them with blows, insults, and shouts, until people came to him and gathered around and discovered what had happened. The people wanted to kill the two of them, but others interceded and they expelled them from the *walī*'s tomb in the most miserable state. All of this was thanks to the grace of the *walī* in whose mausoleum they had committed

الوليّ الذي ارتكبوا في ضريحه هذه الأمور الشنيعة وتجاوزوا الحدّ نعوذ بالله من ذلك

٦.٧ (ومرّ بعضهم بامرأة من الخوامس كانت تدّعي الزهد والعبادة) وهي نائمة في محلّ منفرد في رمضان وحولها رجال يزنون بها فقال لها الرجل ما هذا يا عابدة وأنتي على العبادة والصلاة والصوم فقالت نعم ولكن كُسّي فطر فيه يوم القَدْر فلا حَرَج عليه قال فأنشد الرجل يقول [وزن غير معروف]

بعيني رأيت عابده وهي نايمه في النوم
وسيقانها مرفوعه ويستعملوها القوم
وانا قلت يا عابده أين الصلاة والصوم
قالت انا صايمه كسّي فطر منه يوم

٧.٧ (وأمّا اصطلاح هؤلاء الطائفة القبيحة قاتلهم الله تعالى) فإنهم إذا اجتمعوا في مجلس وأرادوا الذكر الذي لا يقبله الله تعالى فيجعلوا النساء أمامهم وكذلك الأحداث ويخلعوا وتهيم النساء والأولاد فإذا نظروا إلى تلك الخدود المضرّجات بالخَفَر * والوجوه الحاسرات للنَظَر * والعيون الفاتكات بالحَوَر * وشاهدوا الأحداث بهاتيك الخصور الرقاق * والقدود الرشاق * والخصور النحال * والأرداف الثقال * ماجت أعينهم * وانتصبت أيورهم * فمن أراد منهم الفعل الخسيس * أتى إلى شيخهم إبليس التعيس * فيقول له يا فلان * تريد الحُور أو الوِلْدان * فإن كان من التعساء * وقلبه يميل إلى النساء * فيقول أريد الحور العين * فيقول له خذ ما تريد منهنّ يا مسكين * وإن كان من الفَسَقة العكساء * المفضِّلين البنين على النساء * المائلين لما حسُن من الأمرد ورقّ * القائلين * فيقول أريد الولدان * وأتملّى بالمُرْدان * فيقول له أُذْنُ منهم * ولا تَحَدّ يا مريدي عنهم * فيجعلوا النساء مثل الحور العين والأحداث مثل الولدان ويصيّروا مجلسهم مثل البعث والقيامة وأنّ فيه الجنّة والنار وأنّ قيامهم لذلك مثل قيام الساعة وأنّ الشخص منهم إذا صار في الذكر في عن الدنيا فإذا صحا فكأنّه بُعِثَ

these appalling deeds and overstepped the limits set by God—with whom we take refuge from such things.

And a man came across a woman belonging to the Khawāmis who claimed to be practicing self-denial and devotion while she lay in an isolated spot during Ramadan, with men around her who were fornicating with her. "What is this, good woman," said the man, "and you in a state of worship, prayer, and fasting?" "So I am," she replied, "but my cunt broke its fast for the Day of the Divine Decree,[439] so there can be no objection!" At this the man recited: 7.6

With my own eyes I saw her—a simple soul laid down to sleep;
Legs in the air, all used her as she lay.
"Good woman," said I, "what prayer, what fast is this you keep?"
Said she, "To my fast I'm true—my cunt's just taken off for the day!"

As for the practice of this hideous sect, may the Almighty destroy them, when they gather in an assembly and wish to perform their *dhikr* that the Almighty rejects, they place before them women and also youths and they undress, while the women and boys go into ecstasy. Then, when they look upon those cheeks all blushing and shy, those faces whose beauty exhausts to the eye, those eyes, so black and white, whose glances destroy, and when they observe the youths with their midriffs slim and and figures trim, their slender waists and ponderous nates, their eyes dilate and their penises stand up straight. Any who wants that foul release goes to his shaykh, the vile Iblis, who asks him, "You there, forsooth! Is it a houri you desire, or a youth?"[440] If he be one of those wretches whose hearts incline to wenches, he says, "I desire a dark-eyed girl" and the shaykh tells him, "Take whichever you want, poor soul!" and if he be one of the profligate perverse who prefer the reverse, favoring those beardless boys who are comely and slight, and being one of those who says, «To thy daughters we have no right,»[441] he declares, "I desire a youth of Paradise, and in beardless boys my eyes delight." To him the shaykh will say, "Approach them, my disciple! Do not keep away!"—for they make believe that the women are the houri-eyed maidens of Paradise, and the boys the youths thereof, and they make of their assembly the Resurrection and the Last Day and pretend that contained within it is Heaven and Hell and that their rising up to participate in it is like the rising of the dead at the Last Hour, and that when anyone of them joins the *dhikr*, he is obliterated from this world and, when he wakes, is as one resurrected and is relieved of the obligation to 7.7

وسقط عنه التكليف فإذا وقف بين يدي الشيخ فكأنّه واقف بين يدي الله تعالى في صورة العرض عليه فإذا رضي عنه يقول له مثل ما تقدّم خذ ما شئت من الحور أو الولدان فإنك متّ وبعثت وقد أسقطتُ عنك التكليف وأدخلتُك جنّتي يعني أنّي أبَحتُ ذلك الزناء في النساء واللواط في الأولاد وسائر المحرّمات وإذا غضب على إنسان لكونه باح بالسرّ أو حصل منه هَفوة أو أَطّلَعَ على حالهم أحد ألقاه في بير عميق مظلم وربّما ذبحه وطبخه وأطعمه لأصحابه الأشقياء وينشد عند قتله هذا البيت شعر [بسيط]

مَنْ باحَ بِالسِّرِّ كانَ القَتْلُ سِيمَتَهُ بَينَ الرِّجالِ ولا يُؤْخَذْ لَه ثَأرُ

فنعوذ بالله من أحوالهم ونتبرّأ إلى الله من أفعالهم ونسأل الله تعالى السلامة في الدنيا والموت على الإخلاص واليقين

٨،٧ (ولقد رأيت رجلاً من هذه الطائفة قبّحهم الله تعالى يقول لآخر) يا فلان أنت عينه وهو عينك وأنت هو وهو أنت فأنت الله وأنت الرزّاق وأنت الحيّ وأنت العرش والكرسيّ واللوح والقلم ثمّ ينشد قول ابن العربيّ رضي الله عنه [طويل]

ثَمانِيَةٌ حَمّالَةٌ عَرشَ ذاتِهِ أنا وصِفاتي بَلْ أنا العَرْشُ فَابحَثوا

ثمّ يقول وأنت ناسوته وهو لاهوتك فالناسوت قائم بعين اللاهوت واللاهوت هو شرط في قِدَم الناسوت فكن يا فلان كيف شئت وافعل ما أردت فلا حَرَجَ عليك في عدم الصوم والصلاة فإنّ هذا كلّه منك وفيك أما سمعت قول القائل [متقارب]

شِفاؤُكَ مِنكَ وَتَستَنكِرُ وداؤُكَ مِنكَ ولا تَشعُرُ
أتَزعَمُ أنَّكَ جِرمٌ صَغيرٌ وفيكَ انطَوى العالَمُ الأكبَرُ

في وقول الجبُّلي عينيّته [طويل]

obey God's commands. Thus, when he stands before the shaykh, it is as though he were standing before the Almighty to be judged: if he is pleased with him, he says to him, as above, "Take what you will of the houris or the youths, for you have died and been reborn, and I have relieved you of the obligation to obey God's commands and brought you into my paradise," meaning "I have made fornication with women and sodomy with boys and all other forbidden things permissible to you." If the shaykh is angry with anyone, for revealing their secrets or committing some offense or letting anyone catch sight of what they are about, he throws him into a deep dark well or he may cut his throat and cook him and feed him to his wicked companions, reciting as he kills him these verses:

He who breaks our secrets for murder's marked
Among mankind, and none may take revenge!

We seek refuge with God from their doings, assert before God our innocence of their deeds, and ask the Almighty for safety in this world and a death in faith and certainty!

Once I overheard a member of this sect, may the Almighty disfigure them, 7.8
saying to another, "You, my friend, are His essence and He is your essence, and you are He and He is you. Thus you are God and you are the Provider and you are the Living and you are the Throne and the Seat and the Tablet and the Pen."[442] Then he recited the words of Ibn al-ʿArabī,[443] God be pleased with him:

Eight bear the Throne of His Person—
Me and My Attributes. Nay, I AM the Throne, so seek![444]

Then he said, "And you are His humanity and He is your divinity, for humanity is intrinsic to divinity, and divinity is a condition for the sempiternality of humanity. So, my friend, be as you wish and do what you desire, for you are not obliged to fast or pray—all that is from you and of you. Have you not heard the words of the poet:[445]

Your cure is of yourself, and yet you're unaware.
Your malady's of yourself, and yet you know it not.
The whole world's held within you
And still you claim you're just a jot?

"Or the words of al-Jabbulī[446] in his *ʿAyniyyah*:

وصَومي هُوَ الإمساكُ عَنْ رُؤيَةِ السُّوءِ

وقال بعضهم [طويل]

وما القسُّ والرُهبانُ إلّا إلهُنا   وما اللهُ إلّا راهِبٌ في كَنيسَتي

وأنّ آدم على صورة الرحمن وأنت من آدم وحوّاء فأنت على صورة أبيك وأبيك على صورة المعبود فأنت ترجع لأصلك وأيضاً إذا كانت الخِلقة من التراب ولاصق التراب التراب فلا حُرمة في ذلك فأنت إذا زنيت أو لُطت فإنّما هي تزاحمة أجرام والتصاق تراب ببعضه البعض وقال فلان وقال فلان وصار يخبط خبط عشواء وهو في محلّ منعكف على هذا الرجل وأنا أسمع منه هذا الكلام وكان الرجل المقول له من أعيان الناس غير أنّ هذا القائل الخبيث لم يشعر أنّي من أهل المعرفة لأنّي كنت في حالة اشتغال في صنعة الحياكة وغيرها فلمّا تمّ هلفطته * وفرغ من دردشته * ولقلقة لسانه * وبَغيه وبُهتانه * وضلاله المبين * أقبلتُ عليه وبيدي سِكّين * وأشرت بها ودنوت بها إليه فانقلب إلى الأرض مرعوب * وصار في حالة الكروب * ثمّ إنّ الرجل قال لي ما الخبر * وما الذي بان منه وظهر * فقلت له هذا بان جهله * وحلّ قتله * ثمّ إنّي أظهرت للرجل الأمور * وبيّنت له الصدق من الزور * وقد كان مال إلى ضلاله * وسوء أفعاله * فأنقذه الله وللحق عرف * وذلك الشيطان فرّ هارباً وانصرف * ولم يمكث غير ساعة في القرية ومضى * وعلى لحيته ألف لعنة وخَرْيه *

وأخبروني جماعة أنّه أفسد عقول خلائق كثيرة وهو يدخل عليهم بأمور الحقيقة ٩،٧
بحيث أنّه لا يدري حقيقة ولا شريعة وكان إذا رأى ثوراً أو بقرة يقول أنت الله أنت هو ثمّ ينشد [وزن غير معروف]

My fasting is to abstain from beholding evil?

"Or the words of another, who said:

Priests and monks are our god
And God's but a monk in my church?

"Or that Adam was made after the image of the Merciful? You are of Adam and Eve; thus you are after the image of your father Adam and your father is after the image of the Adored, and so you return to your origin. Likewise, if we are made of dust, and dust clings to dust, then there is no sin in that; and if you fornicate or practice sodomy, it is but a cohering of matter and an adhering of dust unto itself"—and "So-and-so said . . ." and "So-and-so said . . . ." He had drawn the man aside and kept raving on, but I could hear what he was saying. The man to whom he was speaking was one of the eminent, but the wretched speaker had no idea that I was a man of knowledge because, at the time, I was occupied in the craft of weaving and so on. When he came to the end of his claptrap and finished with his prattle and had done letting his tongue flap with his transgressions, patent falsehoods, and lying tittle-tattle, I approached him, knife in hand, and waved it in his face so he fell to the ground in terror, quite unmanned. At this the other asked me, "What's the story, and what did he do to cause all this furore?" I told him, "His ignorance became visible, and his killing's now permissible!" Then I explained to the man how things were and showed him what was truth and what a slur, for he was leaning towards the other's errors and evil acts, but God delivered him and he learned the facts, and that devil fled in disarray, and went his way, and stayed no more than an hour in the village before he quit—on his beard a thousand curses, and shit!

Some people told me that he had corrupted the minds of many of God's 7.9
creatures, gaining their confidence by speaking to them of divine matters, even though he knew neither the Truth nor the Divine Law, and if he saw an ox or a cow would say, "You are God! You are He!" and then recite:

حُـبَيِّبي عـمّ الوجود
وقد ظهر في بيض وسود
وفي نَصـارى مع يهود
وفي كلاب وفي قــطط

ولا يدري معنى هذا الكلام * ولا القصد من هذا النظام *

١٠،٧ ثمّ إنّ هذا الشقيّ غاب عنّي أياما * وأراحني الله منه أعواما * ثمّ ساقته التعاكيس الأزليّه * والدواهي والبليّه * وجمعتني على تعريصه وهو مريض في وُجاق قهوة راقد على الجلّة والرماد وعليه قطعة جبّة لم تستر ما عدا أكتافه لا غير وباقي جسده مكشوف وقد طال شعر رأسه وانقلبت عيناه وطالت أظافيره واسودّ جلده وبان عليه الخزي الأبديّ والمقت من الله تعالى بعد الثياب الفاخرة والهيبة الحسنة ثمّ زاد عليه ذلك المرض فقام إلى بيت الراحة فقُبِض عليه فما أخرج منه إلّا ميتاً وأُخبِرتُ أنّهم لم يروا له قبراً إلّا جانب حائط بجوار تربة خراب فلمّا حفروا رأوا بنياناً ففتحوه فإذا هو مرحاض قديم فدفنوه فيه فعاش خرى ومات في الخرى وقلت فيه [خفيف]

أَهْلَكَ اللهُ مُلحِداً كان نَحْساً على الوَرَى
عـاشَ في القَيْءِ والرَّدَى ماتَ في الخِزْيِ والخَرَى

فانظر رحمك الله بعين الاعتبار * إلى ما حصل لهذا المُضِلّ الغدّار * وهذه الأحوال الذميمة الّتي أوجبت له سوء ختامه

١١،٧ (ودخل عليّ رجل من الفقراء) عليه مَلْبَس حسن وله شعر مرخيّ على أكتافه فأجلسته وأكرمته إلى أن توجّه إلى حال سبيله ثمّ جاءني بعد أيام فقال يا سيّدي عندي الليلة جماعة من الفقراء فأنت تحضر ليحصل لك الثواب ومزيد الإكرام فاعتقدت صلاحه

My beloved encompasses existence,
He's manifest in Whites and in Blacks,
Likewise in Christians and Jews,
And also in dogs and in cats!

—though he did not know the meaning of the words, or the purport of the verse.

After this, the wretch kept away from me for many a day, and God relieved me of him *à longue durée*. Later, one of fate's preordained aggravations, one of its disasters and tribulations, brought him my way again and reunited me with his wretched person when he was ill, in the cookhouse of a café, lying on dung and ashes, dressed in a *jubbah* that concealed nothing but his shoulders, leaving the rest of his body exposed. His hair had grown long and his eyes were turned up; his nails had grown out too and his skin had turned black. In place of the luxurious clothes and fine raiment he had once known were the signs of eternal punishment and God's hatred. Then his sickness took a turn for the worse, and he got up and went to the lavatory, where he expired and whence he emerged a dead man. I was informed that the only grave they could find for him was beside a wall next to a ruined tomb, and that when they dug down they discovered a structure that on being opened turned out to be an old latrine, and that is where they buried him. Thus he lived as shit and died in shit. I composed the following on him: 7.10

God put paid to a heretic
Who to mankind was a blight.
He lived in vomit and foulness
And he died in shame and shite.

Observe, God have mercy on you, and ponder what befell this perfidious deluder and the degraded state that drove him to so evil a fate!

And once a dervish visited me dressed in fine clothes and with hair flowing down to his shoulders. I sat him down and treated him hospitably until he went his way. A few days later he came to me again and said, "Sir, a company of dervishes will be coming to my house this evening. Do come, that you may gain reward in the next world and be done great honor in this!" Not doubting his righteousness, I went with him to his house, where he showed me into a darkened room, closed the door, and absented himself a while. Then he entered 7.11

فحضرت معه إلى منزله فأدخلني بيتاً مُظْلِماً وأغلق عليّ الباب وغاب عنّي ساعة ودخل ومعه جماعة محلّقين الذقون ومعهم القرون فسلّموا عليّ وجلسوا ثمّ غاب وأقبل ومعه امرأة جميلة الذاتّ حسنة الشكل لطيفة القدّ صبيحة الوجه تخطر في الحُلَى والحُلَل فقال لها سلّمي على إخوانك الفقراء وأكرميهم وتلطّفي معهم وأكرمي الشيخ بزيادة فلما نظرتُ إليها ونظرتْ اليّ قالت هو على قَدَمنا وطريقتنا قال نعم ثمّ إنّها صارت تجلس في أحجار القوم وتُظْهِر الغنج والشهيق وأفعال النساء حالة الجماع وتقول الله الله فيقبّلها الرجل منهم ويضمّها إليه إلى أن أقبلت عليّ وجلست على أفخاذي فاعتراني الخجل وسار عليّ العرق من الحياء من هؤلاء فتكلّموا بلسانهم الذي يعرفوه ثمّ نظروا إليّ شذراً وتقلّبت أعينهم فتحقّقت منهم ذلك فقلت للذي عزمني الضيافة ما هذا الحال فقال لي سِراًّ كن معنا وإلّا تموت واحضنها وقبّلها ففعلت ذلك وأنا في حالة لا أشعر بما فعلت ثمّ إنهم قالوا له ما بال هذا الشيخ توقّف أوّلاً واعتراه الخجل الله أعلم أنّه ليس على مذهبنا وهذا يُبِيح بسرّنا فقال لهم لا تقولوا ذلك إنّما هو قادم على أول السلوك فقالوا لا نصدّقك حتّى فعل في هذه قبلنا بحضرتنا وإلّا قتلناه فعند ذلك ألزمني بالزناء فيها فزاد عليّ الخجل وحلّ بي الكرب فتحيّلتُ عليهم بأنّي محصور بالبول وتركت عندهم الفوطة وبعض حوائج وخرجت من البيت فرأيت برّا البيت طاقة واسعة عن يميني إلّا أنّها مسدودة بالطوب لكن رُصّ من غير بنيان وأنها تُطِلّ على خَرّارة زاوية والزاوية على الطريق فألقيت الطوب بيدي فنزل في الخرّارة ونَطّيت من الطاقة في الخرارة وطلعت أجري من جنب الزاوية فرآني مُقَدَّم الدَرَك وكان من نسائبي ويدّعي لي بالقرابة فقال لي ما نابك وما هذا الحال فأخبرته بالقضيّة فهجم عليهم ورأى المرأة عندهم فقبض على الجميع وأسلمهم للحكام وأخذت أنا ما تركته من الحوائج

accompanied by a group of men with shaven beards bearing horns,[447] who greeted me and sat down. Then the shaykh disappeared again and returned with a woman, fair of person and comely of form, elegant of figure and radiant of face, who strutted in jewelry and fine robes. He said to her, "Greet your brethren the dervishes and do them honor and be kind to them. And show special honor to the shaykh." After I had looked at her and she at me, she said, "Is he of our persuasion and Path?" "Indeed," he replied. Then she began sitting on the laps of the people, moaning, sighing, and behaving like a woman having intercourse, and saying, "O God! O God!" and the men kissed her and hugged her to themselves each in turn until she reached me and sat on my thighs. I was overcome with embarrassment and started to sweat with shame before these people, while they began to talk to one another in their tongue that they know[448] and looked at me askance and rolled their eyes. I noticed this and asked the one who had invited me to the party, "What's going on?" Covertly he replied, "Join us or die! Embrace her and kiss her!" I did so, though in a state such that I felt nothing of what I did. The others, however, asked him, "What's the matter with this shaykh that he hesitated at first and was overcome with embarrassment? Could it be that he is not of our school and will reveal our secret?" "Say not so!" the man told them. "It is only that he is taking his first steps on the Path." "We will not believe you," they told him, "unless he does it with this woman before we do, in our presence. Otherwise we shall kill him!" At this, he ordered me to fornicate with her. I became even more embarrassed and was seized with panic. However, I tricked them into thinking that I had to urinate, and leaving my napkin and some of my other things with them, I left the room. Outside the room I noticed a large aperture on my right, and, though it was blocked with bricks, these had been laid without mortar. The aperture looked out over the cesspool belonging to a small mosque and the mosque stood on the street. I pushed the bricks down with my bare hands and they fell into the cesspool, and I jumped from the opening into the cesspool, and set off running around the side of the mosque. The captain of the watch (who was an in-law of mine, and also claimed to be related to me) saw me. "What's happened to you? What is all this?" he said. I told him the story and he rushed in on them and, seeing the woman with them, arrested them all and handed them over to the authorities, and I recovered my belongings. The case made a huge splash, and the woman suffered great harm; had her husband not been an eminent person, they would have put her to death.

وكان لهم ضَجّة عظيمة وحصل للمرأة غاية الضرر ولولا أنّ زوجها من أعيان الناس وإلّا كانوا أهلكوها فنعوذ بالله من أحوالهم ونتبرّأ إليه من أفعالهم ونسأل الله تعالى السلامة من ضلالهم ومكرهم وقد أفتى بعضهم أنّ قتل رجل من هؤلاء الطائفة أفضل عند الله من قتل سبعين كافر حربيّ لأنّ الحربيّ كُفره قاصر عليه وهؤلاء ضلالهم متعدّي فهم ضالّون مُضِلّون

١٢،٧ (وسمعت أنّ رجلاً كان في ثغر إسكندريّة يدّعي علم الغيب وهو في لبس الصوف) ومتخلّق بأخلاق الصالحين وكان كلّ من أتاه وسأله عن شيء ضاع له أو سُرِق يخبره بخبره ويدُلّه على محلّه ومَنْ أخذه فأقبلت إليه الناس واعتقدوه وعظّموه وحاز أموالاً كثيرة إلى أن أماته الله تعالى فدفنوه وعملوا عليه قبّة عظيمة وصار الناس يزوروه ويتبرّكوا به فتخلّف بعده ولد صالح وكان هذا الولد يتعجّب من فعل أبيه وإخباره المغيَّبات ولا يعرف ما السبب إلى أن دخل يوماً إلى القاعة التي كان يجلس فيها والده فرأى في جانبها رخامة كبيرة وفي وسطها حلقة من الحديد فقبض على الحلقة ونزع الرخامة بقوّة فقلعها فرآها على باب طابق نازل في الأرض وفيه سُلّم فنزل من على السلّم إلى أن انتهى إلى محلّ متّسع وفي وسطها سِنْدال من الحديد وبجانبه مِطْرَقة من الحديد أيضاً قال فتعجّب وأخذ المطرقة وطرق بها على السندال وإذا بالقائل يقول نعم يا سيّدي فأرهب الولد وقال له ما تكون فقال يا سيّدي أنا خادم أبوك الذي مات وأنا الذي كنت أخبره المغيّبات فإذا سُرِقَ من أحد شيء فيأتي ويطرق السندال فأحضر إليه وأخبره به وكلّ حاجة أرادها فهذا السندال رَصَدٌ عليّ هو والمطرقة فإن أردت يا سيّدي أن تكون مثل والدك تطيعني وتفعل ما آمرك به في كلّ يوم وأنا أخبرك بكلّ شيء سألوك منه الناس فقال له وما كان والدي يفعل لك قال كان

We seek refuge with God from their affairs, assert our innocence before God of their deeds, and ask the Almighty to be protected from their errors and trickery! One scholar has delivered a legal opinion to the effect that the killing of a member of this sect is better than the killing of seventy infidel warriors, for the warrior's unbelief is limited to himself, whereas the error of these people is contagious, and they are thus both deluded and deluding.

I have heard that a man in the port city of Alexandria used to claim knowledge of the Unseen, wearing the woolen habit and affecting the patched garb of the righteous,[449] and he would tell any who came to him and asked him about things they had lost or that had been stolen from them what had happened to them and instruct them where to find them and who had taken them. People came to him, believed in him, and paid him the greatest respect, and he amassed great wealth, until the day when the Almighty brought his life to an end. They buried him and built a great dome over him, to which people started to make pilgrimage in hopes of his blessing. Then a righteous son of his succeeded him, and this son marveled at his father's deeds and his ability to discover hidden things, and had no idea of how he had done these things until one day he entered the great chamber in which his father used to sit. To one side he noticed a large marble slab, with an iron ring in the middle. He took hold of the ring, tugged strongly on the slab, and pulled it out, finding that it concealed the entrance to a compartment that descended into the earth, with a stairway. He went down the stairs, which brought him to a wide space in the middle of which was an iron anvil with, next to it, a hammer, also of iron. Marveling, he took the hammer and struck the anvil, and lo and behold, a voice said, "Yes, Master?" The boy was terrified and said, "What are you?" "Master," said the voice, "I am the servitor of your father who died, and it is I who would tell him what had happened to things that were lost. If anything was stolen from anyone, he would come and strike the anvil and I would come to him and tell him what had happened to it and anything else he wanted. The anvil is a talisman by which I am bound, that and the hammer. So, Master, if you wish to be like your father, obey me and do as I tell you each day, and I will give you information concerning everything about which people ask you." "What did my father do for you?" asked the boy. "Every day," the voice said, "he would come down to me and strike the anvil, and I would appear, and he would prostrate himself twice—to me, not to Almighty God—and I would provide him with the information." "I seek refuge with God from such things!" said the boy. 7.12

كلّ يوم ينـزل إليّ ويطرق السندال فأحضر فيسجد لي سجدتين من دون الله تعالى وأخبره فقال الولد أعوذ بالله من ذلك ومات أبي على هذه الحالة قال الجنّي نعم فقال لا حول ولا قوّة إلّا بالله العليّ العظيم مات كافرا ثمّ إنّه خرج وتوجّه إلى أفندي المدينة وقال يا مولانا مرادي هدم القبّة التي على قبر أبي وإخراجه من القبر وحرقه بالنار فقال له ولماذا قال لأنّه مات كافرًا وأخبره بالقصّة وأظهره على الرصد واستنطق الجنّي فأخبره كما أخبر الولد فتحقّقوا أهل المدينة أنّه مات كافرًا وهدموا قبّته وأخرجه ولده وحرقه بالنار وكتب على أثر قبره كم من قبر يزار * وصاحبه في النار * فنسأل الله السلامة في الدنيا والعبادة على يقين وأن يجعلنا من الطائفة الذين سلكوا مسالك الحقّ * وساروا على قدم الصدق * وعرفوا الله بخلوص النيّات * وترك المحرّمات * ومنع الشهوات * والقيام على قدم المجاهدات * وترك الفضول * واتّباع ما جاء به الرسول * فهؤلاء الطائفة المتّقون *والجماعة الموحّدون * * فليس الفقر بلبس الثياب والطُرَح * ولا بالصوف والسُبَح * وإنّما الفقر ترك الأسباب * وملازمة المحراب * واجتناب الناس * وموت الحواسّ * قال سيّدي عليّ وفا [وزن غير معروف]

مـا الفـقـرُ بالدرفاسْ   ولا الخنّـاسْ
مـا الفـقـرُ إلا كاسْ   موت الحواسْ
فكـن بـه موصوفْ   والبس صوفْ
لو[١] الصلاح في الصوفْ   طـار الخروفْ

(نادرة) حلف شخص أنّه لا يزوّج ابنته إلّا لحمار فأفتاه رجل من العلماء أنّه يزوّجها لمغنّي فقراء فإنّه في حُكْم الحمار ١٣٫٧

١ بي: لوأن (كذا في ك با م ولا يوجد هذا الجزء من النص في ب).

"And did my father die in this condition?" "Yes," said the genie. Then the boy said, "There is no power and no strength but in God, the Exalted, the Mighty! He died an infidel!" and he left and went to the effendi[450] of the city, and said, "Your Honor, I want the dome that is over my father's grave to be demolished and him removed from the grave and burned." "Why?" asked the judge. "Because he died an infidel," he said, and he told him the story and showed him the talisman and summoned the genie to speak, and the latter told him what he had told the boy. The people of the city then realized that he had died an infidel, and they demolished his dome and his son removed him from the grave and burned him, writing at the spot where the grave had been, "Many a grave is the pilgrims' desire, while its owner is in the Fire!" We ask God for His protection in this world and for true understanding of worship, and that He should make us of the party of those who followed the paths of Truth, and walked the way of sooth, and came to know God through the purity of their intentions, and through the shunning of all that is forbidden and the denial of their passions, while walking in the path of pious exertions, avoiding excesses and following the Apostle's message; for these are the people of piety, and the party of those who in His unity believe—«Lo, verily, the friends of God are those on whom fear cometh not, nor do they grieve,»[451] for true Poverty is not to be had by wearing veils and special weeds nor through wool and rosary beads. Poverty is the abandonment of all earthly ties, and the haunting of the *miḥrāb* that to Mecca our orisons guides; it is the shunning of the human species and the death of the senses. As Master ʿAlī Wafā[452] says:

Poverty is not through banners
  Or the ways of the Devil.[453]
Of the death of the senses
  Poverty's the goblet—
Be known for this
  And take the woolen habit!
Sheep would fly
  If godliness could wool inhabit!

A funny anecdote: Someone once swore that he would marry his daughter only to a donkey, so a scholar delivered a ruling for him[454] that he should marry her to a singing dervish, as that would amount to the same thing. 7.13

وقيل لفقير من فقراء الريف ما مذهبك فقال أنا مذهبي يا نصر يالحرام وكلّ من قال يالسعد يالجدام قتلته ١٤،٧

(وسئل رجل منهم عن الفقر) فقال ما دام الفقير يَفْقُر وسبحته في رقبته وإبريقه في كتفه هو فقير حقّ إن صلّى وإلّا ما صلّى ١٥،٧

(ومرّ رجل من فقراء الريف ومعه تلميذه) فمرّوا على غيط فول أخضر فاشتهى التلميذ أن يأكل من الفول فأخبر شيخه فقال له انتظر لا يأتي أحد من الناس وأنا أدخل إلى الغيط وأجب لك منه ما تريد قال فوقف التلميذ يحرس شيخه ودخل الشيخ وجمع له ما يكفيه من الفول الأخضر وفضل معه بقيّة ليفرّقها الشيخ على أصحابه لمّا وصل إليهم ثمّ إنّهما سارا فرأى التلميذ في طريقه نخلة حاملة من الرُطَب فقال لشيخه قد اشتهيت الأكل من هذا الرطب فقال له اطلع إليها يا ولدي وأنا أقف أحرسك حتّى تأخذ منها ما يكفيك فطلع التلميذ وأكل وأخذ منها جانب ونزل وسار هو وشيخه إلى أن طلعوا قرية فرأوا فيها مولد عظيم وفقراء قائمين فيه بالذكر وضرب الكفوف قال فنزل هذا الشيخ وتلميذه في وسط الجمع وهام ودردش باللسان * وأظهر الزُور والبُهتان * وقال [طويل] ١٦،٧

تجرّدْ لها علّامُ في عَشْوَةِ[1] الدُّجَى جَنَى تَمْرَها والغافلينَ نِيامْ

وكان تلميذه سمّي علّام فأجابه يقول [طويل]

سَعَدَ بها شَيخي وفازَ بما طَلَبْ وَعادَ وفرّقْها وَنالَ المَواهِبْ

قال فلمّا سمع القوم كلام الشيخ والتلميذ صرخوا وهاموا وضربوا بالكفوف وأزبدوا وأرعنوا وترجموا باللسان ولم يعرفوا حقيقة الأمر ولا ما قصد هذا الفقير في كلامه

١ بي: عشو؛ ك با: عشو؛ م: عشوة [؟]

Anecdotes Showing the Ignorance of Country Dervishes

And a country dervish was asked, "Which school of law do you follow?" and he said, "I follow the school of 'Victory to the Clan of Ḥarām!' and any who say, 'Clan of Saʿd! Clan of Judām!' I kill!" 7.14

And one of them, when asked about poverty, said, "So long as the dervish practices poverty and his prayer beads are around his neck and his pitcher's on his shoulder, he's a true dervish, whether he prays or not!" 7.15

And a country dervish and his disciple were going along, and they passed a field of green fava beans. The disciple had a fancy to eat some, and he so informed his shaykh. The latter told him, "Keep watch to see no one comes, and I'll go into the field and bring you as much as you want." So the disciple stood guard for his shaykh, and the shaykh entered and gathered him as many beans as he could eat, with some left over for the shaykh to distribute among his friends when he got to them. As they continued on their way, the disciple came across a palm tree laden with soft ripe dates and said to his shaykh, "I fancy eating some of those dates," and the shaykh told him, "Climb up and get them, my boy, while I stand guard for you, so you can take your fill." So the disciple climbed up, ate some, picked a quantity, and came down again, and he and his shaykh continued on their way until they came to a village, where they found a huge *mawlid* in progress, with dervishes performing a *dhikr* and clapping their hands. The shaykh and his disciple plunged into the middle of the throng, and the shaykh went delirious and started gabbling and uttering lies and slanders, saying: 7.16

> ʿAllām[455] stripped naked for it in the dark of night.
> He plucked its dates while the heedless slept.[456]

Now his disciple was called ʿAllām, so he answered him saying:

> Happy was my shaykh; he won what he desired.
> He returned and passed it all around, and thus God's gifts acquired.[457]

On hearing the words of the shaykh and his disciple, the other dervishes shouted and went delirious, clapping their hands and foaming at the mouth, gibbering and jabbering, even though they had no idea of the truth of the matter or what that dervish and his disciple meant by their words, which, in

هو وتلميذه والحال أنّه أخبر عن السرقة من الفول الأخضر وطلوع تلميذه النخلة وأخذ الرطب منها فلو كان لهؤلاء الطائفة اطّلاع على الحقيقة أو كشف صريح أو قدرة صادقة ما حصل لهم الوجد والهيام *على شيء من السرقة حرام*

١٧،٧ (وأخبرني بعض العلماء أنّ بعض الفقراء كان جالساً في قرية من قرى الريف فحضرت الصلاة) وكان هذا الفقير جالس في القبلة وعليه طيلسان وجبّة من الصوف حسنة وعمامة كبيرة وهو أميّ لا يقرأ ولا يكتب فأقيمت صلاة العشاء فقالوا له أهل القرية صلّي بنا فنفخه الشيطان وتقدّم إلى المحراب وقرأ الفاتحة ثمّ قرأ بعدها هذا الكلام قالوا لها يا مريم دا جاكي منين قالت جاني من عند الله ﴿إِنَّ ٱللَّهَ يَرۡزُقُ مَن يَشَآءُ بِغَيۡرِ حِسَابٍ﴾ يعني بذلك قوله تعالى ﴿كُلَّمَا دَخَلَ عَلَيۡهَا زَكَرِيَّا ٱلۡمِحۡرَابَ﴾ الآية ثمّ إنّه ركع وتمّ الصلاة فانظر إلى جهله وجرأته على القراءة من غير معرفة وتبديل كلام الله تعالى من غير علم

١٨،٧ (وأخبرني بعض العلماء أيضاً أنّه دخل مسجداً فرأى فيه جماعة من الفقراء) قال فجلس هذا العالم يعظ الناس فسمع رجلاً من هؤلاء الفقراء يقول ما بقي في الدنيا علم ولا علماء ما كان إلّا شيخي الّذي علّمني الفقر والطريق كان شيخ مليح يعدّي البحر على السجّاده وعلّمني علوم مليحه قال هذا العالم فلمّا سمعت ما قاله قمت إليه وقبضت على لحيته وقلت له مثلك من يقول ما بقي في الدنيا علماء ولا علم ولكن لا أَفلِتُك من يدي حتّى تقرأ الفاتحة إن كان عندك معرفة مثل ما تقول قال فاعتراه الخجل وانكرب منّي وأراد الانفلات من بين يدي فحلفت لا أطلقه حتّى يقرأ الفاتحة فقال بسم الله الرُحمن الرُحيم برفع راء الرحمن والرحيم الحمد لله مالك العالمين وهادم الصراط يوم الدين الّذين أنعمت عليهم يوم الضالّين آمين هذه القراءة الّتي قالها كما أخبرني بها هذا الرجل الصالح قال فقمتُ عليه بالسبّ والضرب وقلت له من علّمك هذه القراءة فقال شيخي فقلت له أحَيٌّ هو قال لا بل مات قلت وهل علّمك شيئاً غير هذا قال نعم لمّا قرب موته قال لي يا ولدي أنا ما نلت هذه المراتب وصار لي بدايات وسبحة وإبريق

reality, told how he had stolen the green fava beans and how his disciple had climbed the palm tree and taken the ripe dates.[458] Had this sect possessed any real insight into the truth or clear revelation or genuine powers, they would not have gone ecstatic and jinn-ridden over an act of theft quite clearly forbidden!

And a scholar told me that once a dervish was sitting in one of the vil- 7.17
lages of the countryside when the time came for prayer. The dervish was sitting in the prayer niche wearing a Sufi shawl, a fine woolen coat, and a large turban, even though he was illiterate and could neither read nor write. When the evening prayer started, the people of the village said to him, "Lead us in prayer!" and Satan prompted him to go up to the niche and recite the *Fātiḥah*. Then he recited as follows: "They said, 'Hey Mary, where'd ya get that?' and she said, 'I got it from God. «God giveth without stint to whom He will»'"[459]—having in mind the words of the Almighty, «Whenever Zakariyyā went into the sanctuary . . .» etc.[460] Then he prostrated himself and completed the prayer. Observe his ignorance and audacity in reciting without knowing the text and in changing the words of the Almighty, even though he was without learning!

And another scholar told me that he entered a mosque and found a group 7.18
of dervishes there. The scholar sat down and started preaching to the people. Then he heard one of the dervishes say, "There is no learning left, and no learned men. The last one was my shaykh who taught me Poverty and the Path—he was a lovely shaykh who used to cross the river on his prayer rug, and he taught me some lovely sciences." The scholar went on, "When I heard what he said, I went over to him, seized him by the beard, and said to him, 'The likes of you say there's no learning left and no learned men, but I'll not let go of you till you have recited the *Fātiḥah*, since you say you know so much!' The man was embarrassed and scared of me and wanted to escape, but I swore I would not release him until he had recited the *Fātiḥah*. So the man said, 'In the name of God, the Morciful, the Compossionate,[461] praise be to God, Owner of the Worlds and Destroyer of the Straight Path on the Day of Judgment, whom Thou hast favored on the Day of those who go astray! Amen.'" This was his reading of it, according to what that righteous man told me. The scholar continued, "Then I set upon him with abuse and blows and said to him, 'Who taught you to recite it this way?' He said, 'My shaykh.' So I asked him, 'Is he alive?' 'No, dead,' he told me. 'And did he teach you anything else?' I asked him. 'Indeed,' he said: 'When death approached, he said to me,

وديك وعلّيقة إلّا بورْد كنت أقوله عند النوم كلّ ليلة فقلت له يا سيّدي علّمني هذا الورد فقال لي قل كلّ ليلة عند النوم سبحان العتّاب سبحان البوّاب سبحان التوّاب الصبّاب الكتّاب فحفظته من شيخي وأنا أقوله لهذا الوقت قال فقلت له قاتل الله الأبعد ولا تغمّد شيخه برحمته ما كان أقبح صلاته وأشنع تسبيحه قال ثمّ إنّه لاطفني وخضع إليّ وكسر النفس فعلّمته الفاتحة ومنعته من هذا التسبيح الشنيع ومضى إلى حال سبيله

١٩،٧ (ويقرب من هذا المعنى ما أخبرني به بعض الفضلاء أنّه دخل قرية من قرى الريف قبيل الفجر) فسمع رجلاً من الفقراء على رأسه قحف طويل وهو يسبّح ويقول سبحان الله عدد كلاب الأجران سبحان الله عدد فراخ الجيران سبحان الله عدد قوَقَع الغيطان وصار يسبّح من هذا الكلام وأضرابه فحلف هذا الرجل أنّه لا يصلّي الفجر في هذه القرية وصلّى في قرية أخرى

٢٠،٧ (وتشاجر فقير مع تلميذه) وصار يضربه ويشتمه فقال له رجل صالح اخش الله ورسوله وارفق بالتلميذ فقال له من جهله يا رجل الله ورسوله ما لهم شيء في طريق الفقراء طريق الفقراء شيء وطريق الله ورسوله شيء قلت وهو صادق في قوله لأنّ طريقهم طريق الشيطان * وطريق الله ورسوله هي قواعد الإيمان * وسلوك شريعة سيّد ولد عَدْنان *

٢١،٧ (وكان بعض الفقراء يهوى تلميذاً جميلاً) على أنّه لا يقدر على مخالطته خوفاً من شيخه فلمّا مات الشيخ أخذ ذلك الفقير المشيخة وجلس على السجّادة لأجل ذلك التلميذ حتّى يحظى به فلمّا راق له الزمن واختلى به قال له ما كان يفعل معك الشيخ الذي كان قبلي إذا اختلى بك قال كان يبوس ويعنّق ثمّ يلقيني على الأرض ويكشف عن القبّة البيضاء المعلومة ويبوسها وينقر عليها ويقول قَدَرْنا وعَفَوْنا ثمّ يقوم عنّي فكانت هذه

"My boy, I would never have attained these high degrees[462] and acquired novices and prayer beads and pitcher and cockerel and fodder but for a collect I used to recite on going to sleep every night." I said to him, "Teach me that collect, Master!" and he said to me, "Every night on going to sleep, say, 'Glory to the Castigator, glory to the Porter, glory to the Pardoner, the Great Lover, the Reporter!'[463] I memorized it from my shaykh and I say it to this very day."' To this I replied, 'May God strike you dead, wretched man, and not encompass your shaykh with His mercy! What a hideous prayer, and what a revolting magnificat!' At this the man spoke to me in a conciliatory fashion, submitted himself to me, and appeared humbled. So I taught him the *Fātiḥah* and forbade him to say that revolting magnificat, and he went his way."

A similar anecdote was told me by a virtuous man who entered one of the villages of the countryside just before dawn and heard a dervish, with a tall peasant hat on his head, reciting his magnificat and saying, "Glory to God as many times as there are dogs on the threshing floors and chickens by the neighbors' doors! Glory to God as many times as there are snails in the fields!" and he went on uttering magnificats of this type till the man swore that he would not pray the dawn prayer in that village, and he said his prayers in another. 7.19

And once a dervish quarreled with his disciple and fell to beating and cursing him. A righteous man said to him, "Fear God and His Messenger, and have mercy on the boy!" In his ignorance the man replied, "Hey! God and His Messenger have nothing to do with the Path of the dervish! The Path of the dervish is one thing, and that of God and His Messenger is another!" And I say he spoke the truth, for their Path is the path of Satan, and the Path of God and His Messenger is the rules of religion, and adherence to the law of the best of ʿAdnān's children.[464] 7.20

More Anecdotes Showing the Beliefs and Practices of Heretical Dervishes

And once a dervish loved a beautiful novice, but, out of fear of the boy's shaykh, could find no way to associate with him. When the boy's shaykh died, the dervish took over his position and sat on the prayer rug,[465] just so he could win the novice's favor. Then, when the time was ripe and he found himself alone with him, he asked, "What did the shaykh who was before me use to do with you when you were alone together?" The boy replied, "He used to kiss and squeeze and then lay me on the ground and uncover the white dome, as it is known, 7.21

طريقته معي فقال له هذا الشيخ وأنا الآخر أفعل معك مثله وأكون على قدمه انطرح يا ولدي على الأرض قال فرقد التلميذ على وجهه وكشف هذا الشقيّ عن ردف أبيض مربرب سمين * مثل قول المثل حرير في عجين * قد زالت عنه الخشونه * وصار أبا جَهْل في الغِلْظة والنعومه * كما قال فيه بعض واصفيه [طويل]

أبو طـالِبٍ في كَفِّهِ وخُـدودُهُ   أبو لَهَبٍ والقَدُّ منه أبو جَهْلِ

ثمّ إنّ هذا الشقيّ لمّا رأى هذه القبّة العظيمة المشوّبة بالحُمْرة وهذه الوجنات المضرَّجة بالخَفَر نقر عليها بيده وباس وعنّق فانتصب أيره واشتدّ * وقام عليه وامتدّ * وطلب الأنس والصفا * ونيك هذا الجمال بلا خفا * لأنّ بعض الحكماء قال التقبيل زرع والنيك حصاده فالعاشق لا يشفيه بعد التقبيل من المحبوب * إلّا النيك المطلوب * كما قال شريك * لا يشتفي العاشق بالبوس والغنج حتّى ينيك * قال ثمّ مسك هذا الشقيّ التعيس * المفترق من فَيْض إبليس * أيره ونقر به على ردف الغلام * وهو في وجد وهيام * وقرّبه إلى الباب * ودفعه من غير حجاب * فلم يمنعه إلّا الخصيتان * فصاح التلميذ الأمان الأمان * ثمّ ناداه ما كان شيخي يفعل هذا الأمر ولا يجاوز هذا القدر فقال له اسكت يا ولدي كلّ شيخ له طريقه * وكلّ إنسان له حقيقه * وهذا مقام لم يصل إليه شيخك فاصبر فإنّ الطريق صعبة لا تنقطع إلّا بالتحمّل والصبر على المكارِه والشدائد * وترك العَذول المُعانِد * ولم يزل معه على هذا القدم التعيس * والمسلك الخسيس * حتّى انقضى أمره على دين والده إبليس *

(ومرّ بعضهم بامرأة صوفيّة) وهي تصلّي فاستقبلها بالنيك من خلفها لمّا ركعت ٢٢.٧
فصبرت حتّى تمّ أمره وبلغ صفاءه وخرّت إلى الأرض وسجدت وتَحَتَّ وسلّمت والتفتت إليه وقالت له يا بطّال أتظنّ أنّ فعلك هذا يَشْغَلني عن الله وعن إتمام

and kiss it and pat it, saying, 'We had power but forebore!'[466] Then he would get up. Such was his practice with me." The shaykh said to him, "I will do the same with you and proceed in like manner. Lie down, my boy, on the ground!" So the boy laid himself face downward and the rascal removed the veil from a posterior white and fat, with health aglow—as the proverb has it, "like silk mixed with dough." There was not a trace of roughness there—it was like Abū Jahl in stoutness and lack of hair. As someone said describing him:

> Abū Ṭālib in his hands with the cheeks
> Of Abū Lahab, and Abū Jahl in limb.[467]

Then, when the rascal beheld that magnificent dome suffused with pink and those cheeks aflush with rose, he patted them with his hand and kissed and squeezed, until his member stiffened and distended, and rose up and extended, and demanded, quite unashamed, to fuck that beauty and to be funned and gamed. For, as a wise man has put it, "to kiss is to sow, to fuck to reap" and nothing will cure the lover after kissing the beloved but the yearned-for fuck—as says Sharīk,[468] "Kissing and mewing aren't the lover's cure, only screwing." Then this filthy wretch, dollop of Satan's overflow, grasped his prick and whacked it on the young man's butt, to and fro, transported the while into ecstasy and passionate love, and brought it to the portal and thrust it in, without let or hindrance, from above, and the only thing that made him stop was the sac, while the disciple cried, "Alas! Alack!" and called out to him, "My other shaykh didn't used to do such stuff—for him much less was quite enough!" but the shaykh replied, "Silence, boy! To every shaykh his Path and to every man his Truth! This is just a plane[469] your shaykh never quite managed to attain. Be patient, for the Path is rough, to be traveled only with endurance and fortitude against its afflictions and troubles, and by shunning those who insist on obstinate cavils!" Then he went on in the same foul fashion and contemptible course till he was done, according to the rites of his father the Fallen One.

And once one of them passed a Sufi woman while she was performing the 7.22
prayer, and took her as his alignment for prayer by fucking her from behind when she bent over to perform a prostration. She kept her peace until he was done and had taken his pleasure, then went down on her knees, prostrated herself, made her greetings,[470] uttered her concluding salutations,[471] and, turning to him, said, "Evil man! Do you imagine that what you did could distract me from God, or from completing my prayer?" Observe the woman's

الصلاة فانظر إلى جهل هذه المرأة وإلى شقاوة هذا الرجل وجرأتهما على الفعل القبيح

٢٣،٧ (وذكر لي سيّدي عليّ السقّا) المدفون بثغر دمياط نفعنا الله ببركاته يقول أضافني جماعة من الفقراء الخوامس في بعض الليالي فأكرمتهم تلك الليلة وناموا في الزاوية ثمّ قمت أصلّي تباشير في الليل فتيقّظوا فرأوني وأنا أصلّي فقالوا لي يا سيدي بلغت إلى هذه الرتبة وتصلّي وتصوم وأنت قد سقط عنك التكليف قال فقمت عليهم بالسبّ والشتم لمّا تحقّقت أنّهم من الخوامس وقلت لهم يا أشقياء كلّ قولٍ رَدّ * وكلّ طريق سَدّ * ولا وصول * إلّا بما جاء به الرسول * وحلفت أنّهم لا يمكثوا عندي بقيّة الليلة وأخرجتهم من الزاوية وحمدت الله تعالى على خروجهم من عندي

٢٤،٧ (ودخل بعض الفقراء المتلبّسين على العارف بالله تعالى سيّدي عبد الوهّاب الشعرانيّ) نفعنا الله به فصار يترجم بين يديه باللسان ويُرغي ويُزبِد وهو في حالة مكربة فلمّا صحي من السَكْرة الشيطانيّة قال له سيّدي عبد الوهّاب أتعرف فروض الوضوء فقال يا سيّدي هذا كتاب ما قرأت فيه قطّ فقال له قم واخرج من عندي وتعلّم شيئاً في الدين تنفع به غير هذا التلبيس الّذي أنت فيه فخرج من عنده في غاية الخِزْي والخجل والفضيحة

٢٥،٧ (وسئل بعض الفقراء أَهَلْ تعرف الصلوات الخمس) فقال أعرفهنّ بعقدانهنّ وجعدانهنّ وما بقى يغباني فيهنّ إلّا الفاتحة والجبات الّي يقولوا عليها الناس

٢٦،٧ (وسأل بعض الفقراء المتخوشنين أخينا في الله تعالى الشيخ عليّ حبشيّ الشربينيّ) كان الله له عن منام رآه سوّله له الشيطان فقال له رأيت فرساً شهياً وعليها سرج أخضر فما تكون هذه لعلّها النجيبة الّتي تركبها الأولياء فقال له الشيخ عليّ إن صَدَقَتْ رؤياك فإنّها نخلة خضراء تملكها لأنّ النخلة رأسها بيضاء وعروقها خضر فالفرس هي النخلة والعروق السرج والزبل وكان هذا التعبير من لطافة أخينا الشيخ عليّ لأنّ هذا الفقير أراد أن يوافقه على التلبيس والخوبشة فلم يوافقه فجزاه الله خيراً

ignorance, the man's wickedness, and the audacity of both in performing this repulsive deed!

My Master ʿAlī al-Saqqā,[472] God benefit us through his blessings, who is buried in the port city of Dimyāṭ, once told me, "One night a group of dervishes of the Khawāmis sought my hospitality, so I put them up for the night, and they slept in the hostel. During the night I got up and prayed as dawn approached. Awakening and seeing me praying, they said to me, 'Master, you have reached this rank and still you pray and fast? You are no longer under the obligation to follow God's laws!' Realizing, at this, that they were Khawāmis, I set upon them with insults and abuse and told them, 'Wicked ones! All new doctrine resist and from every new path desist, for the only way to be saved is through what the Apostle conveyed!' and I swore that they would not stay under my roof for the rest of the night and expelled them from the hostel and gave thanks to the Almighty that they had left my house." 7.23

And one of these same fraudulent dervishes called on the Initiate of the Almighty, Master ʿAbd al-Wahhāb al-Shaʿrānī, God benefit us through him, and started talking gibberish in front of him, and frothing and foaming in a hideous state. When he had recovered from his satanic intoxication, Master ʿAbd al-Wahhāb asked him, "Are you familiar with the regulations governing ritual ablution?" "That's a book I never read," said the man. "Leave my house," said Master ʿAbd al-Wahhāb, "and learn something about religion that will be of use to you, not this chicanery you're caught up in!" and the man left his house in the greatest ignominy, shame, and disgrace. 7.24

And a dervish was asked, "Do you know the five prayers?" "I know them knots, wrinkles, and all!" he answered. "The only things I know nothing about are the *Fātiḥah* and the *ḥajabāt*[473] that people talk about." 7.25

And one of these reprobate dervishes asked our brother in God Almighty Shaykh ʿAlī Ḥabashī al-Shirbinī,[474] God be with him, about a dream that Satan had put in his mind, saying, "I saw a desirable mare with a green saddle. What might that be? Could it be the steed[475] that God's Friends ride?" Shaykh ʿAlī told him, "If your dream be true, it must be a reference to a radish you possess—for the radish has a white head and its leaves are green. Thus the mare is the radish and the leaves the saddle and the dung!" This interpretation was an example of our brother Shaykh ʿAlī's quick thinking, because the dervish wanted him to go along with him in fraud and infamy, but he would not, may God reward him well! 7.26

٢٧.٧ (وبذكر هذا المنام ذكرتُ ما اتّفق أنّ أبا نواس) دخل يوماً مجلس هارون الرشيد فأقبلت عليه عِنان جارية الناطفيّ وعليها حُلّة خضراء وكان يُضرَب بها المثل في الفصاحة والملاحة فقال لها أبو نواس يريد معها المداعبة والملاعبة رأيت الليلة في منامي كأنّي ركبت فرساً شهياً عليها جُلّ أخضر فقالت له إن صدقت رؤياك فإنّه تدخل في استك نخلة وتصير عروقها خارجة قال فخجل أبو نواس من قولها وانصرف

٢٨.٧ (واتّفق أنّ جماعة من الفقراء عملوا سماعاً) ودخلوا مسجداً يناموا فيه وكان فيه جماعة من الفقهاء يتلون في كتاب الله تعالى فقام رجل من هؤلاء الفقراء وقال لهؤلاء الفقهاء أنتم طول الليلة تقولوا قاقا قاقا خلّوا الفقراء تنام ثمّ بعد ساعة تيقّظ شخص منهم وقال بعلوّ صوته [طويل]

أَلَا يا غُرابَ البَيْنِ غَيَّرْتَ حالتي　　وخَلَّيْتَني بَيْنَ العِبادِ ذَليلُ

فقاموا كلّهم وزعقوا وهاموا ورقصوا وضربوا بالكفوف فقاموا إليهم الجماعة الفقهاء وصاروا يضربوهم ويلعنوهم ويقولون لهم يا أشقياء عملتم كلام الله قاقا قاقا ولمّا زعق الخبيث ألا يا غراب البين هِمتم وزعقتم وصار لكم وجد وهل يا أشقياء الغراب يقول إلّا قاقا قاقا ثمّ إنّهم أخرجوهم من المسجد على أيشم حالة

٢٩.٧ (ونظير ذلك ما أخبرني به بعض السادة الأشراف بالمَحَلّة الكبرى) بمنزل العلّامة الشيخ عبد الحقّ العَبْدِلاّويّ رحمه الله تعالى أنّ بعض الإخوان عزم عليه ليلة وكان عنده جماعة من القُرّاء يتلون في كلام الله تعالى ثمّ حضر جماعة من الفقراء إلى منزل الرجل المذكور وأرادوا الذكر ومال صاحب المنزل إلى إبطال الفقهاء فنهاه حفظه الله وقال له القرآن أفضل وهؤلاء الجهلة لا يعرفوا شيء في الذكر ولا غيره فقال له صاحب المنزل إنّهم عارفون مشهورون بالولاية فقام رجل من أتباع السيّد وقال لصاحب المنزل ولمن حضروا أنا أبيّن لك جهلهم ثمّ إنّه قام يمشي حتّى وقف في وسطهم وغنّى وقال يصف قردًا [رجز]

Apropos of this dream, I am reminded that Abū Nuwās went one day into the audience chamber of Hārūn al-Rashīd and was met by ʿInān, the slave girl of al-Nāṭifī, wearing a green gown; she was known as a model of eloquence and wit. Abū Nuwās said to her, for a joke and a flirt, "Last night I had a dream in which I was mounted on a desirable mare wearing a green cloth." She responded, "If your dream is true, a radish is going to enter your anus, with its leaves sticking out!" Abū Nuwās was abashed at her words and left. 7.27

And it happened that a company of dervishes had been giving a performance of Sufi music[476] and then had gone into a mosque to sleep, where a company of scholars was already ensconced, reciting the book of the Almighty. One of the dervishes went up to the men of religion and said to them, "All night long you keep going, 'Kaa-kaa, kaa-kaa!' Let the dervishes get some sleep!" Then, after a while, one of the dervishes woke up and recited at the top of his voice: 7.28

> Ah, ill-omened crow, you've changed my state,
> And left me among mankind abased!

At this, the dervishes all shouted and raved and danced and clapped their hands. The scholars went over to them and started beating them and cursing them, saying to them, "You miscreants! You called the word of God 'Kaa-kaa, kaa-kaa,' and when this wretch shrieked, 'Ah, ill-omened crow,' you swooned and shrieked and went into ecstasies. But what, you miscreants, does a crow say if not 'Kaa-kaa, kaa-kaa'?" Then they threw them out of the mosque in a pitiful state.

A similar tale was told me by a noble sharif in al-Maḥallah al-Kubrā, at the house of the Learned Shaykh ʿAbd al-Ḥaqq al-ʿAbdillāwī, may the Almighty have mercy on him. It seems that one of the brethren invited him to his house one night when he had a company of reciters there reading from the word of the Almighty. Then a company of dervishes turned up at the house of the aforementioned man and wanted to perform a *dhikr*. The master of the house was inclined to put an end to the recitation of the scholars, but the guest, God preserve him, forbade him to do so, telling him, "The Qur'an is better, and these ignoramuses know nothing about *dhikr* or anything else!" The master of the house replied, "But these are Knowers of God and renowned as God's Friends!" One of the sharif's entourage arose and said to the master of the house and those present, "I will show you how ignorant they are." Then he walked over till he was in their midst and sang the following, describing an ape: 7.29

لُو مَخْظَمَهْ مِنْ جِلْدْ وأَزْرارْ مِنْ وَدَعْ   والطَّبْـلُ دايـَرْ ـفي اِلْلادْ وَراهْ

قال فقاموا وقعدوا وأرغوا وأزبدوا وقالوا اللّهم صلّ وسلّم عليه وفهموا بجهلهم أنّه يصف الرسول فضحكوا عليهم وتبيّن لصاحب المنزل جهلهم فقام عليهم وأخرجهم من منزله وأبقى الفقهاء يتلون في كتاب الله إلى الصباح

٣٠٫٧ (وعشق بعض الفقراء غلاماً) فأراد الخلوة به فلم يتمكّن منه ذلك فدخل إلى طرق الحيل والمكر وصار يترجم باللسان زور وبهتان ويخبر عن أراض بعيدة ويدخل وسط الجمع ويَشْخَصُ بصره إلى السماء ويقول شي لله انظروا يا محجوبين الأولياء طائرين فوق النجائب ثمّ يصيح ويقع على الأرض ويقول يا فقراء النجائب أقبلت من الشرق والغرب فيقبّلون يديه ويلتمسوا الدعاء فلما رآهم الغلام على هذه الحالة اعتقد أنّه وليّ فقال في نفسه أنا لي مدّة أخدم شيخي ما رأيته يقول شفت ولي ولا نبي ولا أوراني لا أولياء ولا نجائب إلّا يقول لي صلّي وصوم على هذه الكيفية والأولى أني أخدم هذا الفقير لعله أن يطلّعني على الأولياء العارفين وأهل النجائب الطيّارين ثمّ إنّه تشاجر مع شيخه وانفصل منه وأقبل على هذا الشقيّ الخبيث وقال له يا سيّدي جئتك طائعاً ولأمرك سامعاً وقد تعبت من شيخي وهو يقول لي صوم صلّي واعبد ربّك الّذي لا إله الّا هو ولا أرى منه بركة وأنا مرادي أنظر إلى الأولياء الطيّارين وأصحاب النجباء العارفين وأرباب النجائب السالكين وأركب على النجائب الخضر فقال له هذا الشقيّ يا ولدي اعلم أنّ الطريق ليست بصوم ولا بصلاة ولا عبادة فأنت تريّح نفسك من هذا التعب وأنا أصبّ لك عمود النور في بطنك فتنظر سائر الأولياء من وقتك وتقبل عليك النجائب الخضر تركب منها ما شئت وتشاهد الملكوت العُلويّ والسُفليّ فقال له يا سيّدي ومتى تصبّ لي عمود النور هذا فقال له حتّى أدبّر لك ماء الحياة فقال له وما يكون ماء الحياة فقال له شيء أبيض يجري في قصبة الذكر عند حصول الوجد للفقير وعند الخَلْوة بالتلميذ قال وكان هذا الغلام مغفّل لا يعرف شيئاً من هذه الأمور فقال له قم بنا إلى الخلوة فأخذه ومضى إلى أن صارا في خلوة

He wears a leather muzzle and seashell buttons,
And wherever he goes, the drums go too!

—at which the dervishes jumped up and down and frothed and foamed and said, "O God, bless him and grant him peace!" for, in their ignorance, they imagined that he was describing the Messenger. Everyone laughed at them, and the master of the house realized their ignorance, set upon them, threw them out, and left the scholars to read from God's book until the morning.

And once a dervish fell in love with a youth. Wanting to be alone with him 7.30
but failing to find an opportunity, he had recourse to cunning and subterfuge, and took to jabbering lies and slanders in every tongue and describing distant lands.[477] He would go into the midst of the throng and train his eyes upon the sky and say, "A sign from God! Behold, ye blind, the Friends of God flying on their steeds!" Then he would cry out and fall to the ground and say, "O dervishes, the steeds approach from the east and the west!" and they would kiss his hands and beg him to pray for them. When the youth saw them behaving so he believed that the man must be one of God's Friends and said to himself, "I have served my shaykh long and never heard him say 'I saw a prophet or one of God's Friends,' or show me God's Friends or their steeds. All he tells me is, 'Pray and fast like this!' I would do better to serve this dervish, in the hope that he will show me the *walī*s who know God and the flying steeds." The youth then picked a quarrel with his shaykh, broke with him, and went to that low wretch[478] and said, "Master, I come to you in submission, your orders to obey! I have grown tired of my shaykh, with his 'Pray!' and 'Fast!' and 'Worship your Lord other than Whom there is no god!' and I have yet to witness in him any signs of grace. I want to watch the flying friends of God and the masters of the steeds who know God and the ones with the steeds that dash through the air, and to ride on the green steeds myself!" Then that miscreant said to him, "Know, my boy, that the Path is not by fasting or praying or worship. Have done with all that fuss and bother, and I will pour into your belly the Column of Light,[479] and then and there you will see all the Friends of God, and the green steeds will come to you to so that you can ride whichever you want, and you will behold the Higher and the Lower Realms!"[480] "When, Master, will you pour into me this Column of Light?" he asked. "As soon," said the man, "as I have prepared for you the Water of Life." "And what," said the youth, "might this Water of Life be?" The man answered, "It is something

العكس والخمول ومحلّ الفسق والفجور فقال له انطرح على بطنك حتّى أصبّ لك عمود النور فانطرح الغلام على بطنه وصار هذا الشقيّ يترجم ويهمهم ويرغي ويزبد ويظهر الزور والبهتان * والنزع الواقع من الشيطان * ثمّ إنّه كشف عن ردف الغلام * فازداد به الوجد والهيام * واشتعلت في قلبه النيران * وقام عليه الأعور الجبّار فحطّه على باب تلك القُبّة المشيّدة الأركان * المرخّمة الألوان * ودكّه فلم يمنعه إلّا الخصيتان * فعند ذلك صاح الغلام الأمان الأمان * فلم يفلته حتّى قضى منه المراد * والغلام معه في همّ ونكاد * فأنشد يقول [طويل]

كَفَى حَزَنًا أنْ لا نَجائبَ خِلْتُها   ولا أَوْلِيـا إلّا القَبـائِحُ والذَّمُّ

ثمّ قام الغلام من تحته وصار يضربه ويشتمه ويلعنه ثمّ تركه واستوفى ما عليه الله قدّر وقضى فانظر إلى هذا الخبيث وشدّة تحيّله على الفعل القبيح قاتلهم الله أجمعين

٣١،٧ (وكان لبعضهم زوجة تدّعي الزهد والعبادة والورع الفشرويّ) وتغطّي وجهها من القمر وتقول هذا ذكر ولا تتوضّأ من الإبريق وتغطّي وجهها من الكلب والحمار والبغل وكلّ مذكّر من جماد وحيوان وتدّعي الورع الفشرويّ وإذا خرج زوجها من عندها تغلق الباب وتسدّ خروقه بمُشاق ودائمًا في صراخ وصياح وكلما قامت أو قعدت تقول الله الله فاتّفق أنّ زوجها حضر في مجلس عند رجل من الأكابر وفيه جماعة من إخوانه فذكروا الرجال الصالحين والنساء الصالحات فقال زوجها بطّلوا هذا الكلام فما من هذا الزمان أصلح من زوجتي ولا أورع منها ولا أكثر عبادة فإنّها تغطّي وجهها من القمر من شدّة ورعها ومن كلّ مذكّر وتفعل كذا وكذا وصار يثني

white that flows in the shaft of the penis when the dervish attains ecstasy and is in retreat[481] with his pupil." The youth was gullible and knew nothing of these matters, so the man said to him, "Off with us to the retreat!" and took him with him until they came to the retreat of perversity and depravity, and the place of corruption and lewdness. There he said to him, "Lie down, my boy, on your belly, that I may pour into you the Column of Light!" So the youth lay down on his belly and that miscreant started gibbering and jabbering and frothing and foaming and spouting lies and slurs, with satanically inspired raptures, while the youth's backside he unveiled, and ecstasy and passion prevailed, and the fires in his heart began to burn, and he took to him the One-Eyed Tyrant and, laying it at the door of that well-buttressed creamy dome, he drove it home, till nothing stopped it but the sac, at which the youth cried out, "Alas! Alack!"—but the man would not let him go till he'd finished what he was about, while the youth endured, in woe and misery throughout. Then the youth recited:

> Grief enough that I saw no steeds
> Or saints, without shame to boot and filthy deeds!

Afterwards, the youth got up from beneath him and started beating, insulting, and cursing him, and eventually left him, having suffered to the full what God had ordained for him. Observe this vile man and the extreme stratagems to which he had recourse to carry out the dirty deed, may God destroy them one and all!

And once a man had a wife who used to put on a show of asceticism, devo- 7.31
tion, and affected modesty. She would cover her face from the moon and say, "The moon is a male!" and refuse to use a pitcher for her ablutions, and cover her face from a dog or a donkey or a mule or anything else of masculine gender,[482] inanimate or animate, out of an affected modesty. When her husband left the house, she would lock the door and block the cracks with tow, weeping and wailing the while and saying, "O God! O God!" every time she stood up or sat down. Now, her husband once happened to attend a salon at the house of an eminent person in company with a number of his brethren. The talk turned to righteous men and women, and the woman's husband said, "Have done with such talk, for there is no one alive today more righteous than my wife nor more modest than she nor more assiduous in her devotions! She is so modest that she covers her face from the moon and from everything else masculine, and she does such-and-such and she does such-and-such," and he

عليها بحسب ما شاهد هو منها قال فقال له صاحب المنزل والله يا فلان ما في هذا الزمان أبدع ولا أقحب ولا أنجس من زوجتك قال فاشتدّ به الغيظ وقال له تَقْذِف زوجتي وأنت لا تعرفها ولا رأيتها فقال له بل والله أعرفها واجتمعت بها مرارًا على الأنس والصفاء أنا وغيري فقال له زوجها تثبت ما تقول بحضرة هؤلاء الأكابر وإلّا ما يقع بيني وبينك خير فقال له تبات عندي هذه الليلة أنت والحاضرين وأنا أبيّن لك قحْبها وشقاوتها قال نعم وأنا أطيعك في ذلك فقال له امضي في هذه الساعة وقل لها أنا مرادي أبات في القرية الفلانية لأمرضروريّ وائتني أخفيك في محلّ عندي في القاعة التي نجلس فيها ويبان لك الحقّ من الباطل قال فمضى زوجها من وقته إليها وقال لها مرادي أبات هذه الليلة في القرية الفلانيّة لمصلحة ضروريّة قال فلمّا سمعت كلامه صرخت وبكت وولولت وقالت له كيف تتركني وأنا أخاف من القطّ إذا نطّ ومن الكلب إذا مشى على الحيط ومن خيال القمر وغيره فقال لها أمر الله ولا بدّ من ذلك وربّما يستر الليلة فقالت لا حول ولا قوّة إلّا بالله العليّ العظيم اقفل الباب وقامت سدّت خروقه وصارت تصيح وتقول الله الله استر يا رب حتّى يعود زوجي ثمّ مضى زوجها إلى الرجل صاحب المنزل وأخبره فقال له اجلس إلى أن يدخل الليل فجلس هو وبقيّة الجماعة إلى أن أقبل الليل وحضر العشاء فأكلوا وشربوا ثمّ إنّه قال لزوجها قم معي حتّى أبيّن لك قحب امرأتك وبَدْعها وشقاوتها فأجلسه في محلّ مظلم بعيد عن من في الحضرة في صدر القاعة وفيه طاقة تطلّ على من في القاعة بحيث من فيه يرى من في المحلّ ولا يرونه لكونه في ظلمة شديدة ثمّ إنّ صاحب المنزل قال لبعض غلمانه تعرف بيت فلانة قال نعم فقال امض إليها وقل لها سيّدي عنده جماعة من الأكابر وبلّغه أنّ زوجكي توجّه إلى القرية الفلانيّة ومراده الاجتماع بك

went on singing her praises, based on what he had seen of her. But the master of the house said to him, "I swear, my dear sir, that there is no one alive today who is more of a godless innovator or more whorish and unclean than your wife!" Furious, the man said to his host, "Would you slander my wife, though you do not know her and have never seen her?" "On the contrary," replied the host, "I swear I know her and have met with her many a time in an atmosphere of intimacy and conviviality, I and others too!" Her husband said, "Prove what you say in the presence of these great men, or it shall not go well between us!" The man replied, "Stay with me this night, you and the others, and I will show you her whorishness and wickedness!" "Very well," said the husband, "I will obey you in this." "Go now," said the host, "and tell her, 'I intend to spend the night at such-and-such a village on important business,' and then come to me and I will hide you in a place I have in this hall in which we are sitting, and then you will see what is truth and what is lies." So the man went straight off to her and said, "I intend to spend the night in such-and-such a village on important business." When she heard this, she screamed and wept and wailed, and she said to him, "How can you leave me when you know that I take fright at the tomcat when it jumps, the dog that walks on the wall, the shadow of the moon, and all the rest?" "It is God's will," he said, "and cannot be avoided, and surely He will provide protection for the night." Said she, "There is no might and no power but with God, the Exalted, the Mighty! Lock the door!" and she went and stuffed its cracks and set to crying, "God! God! Protect us, O Lord, until my husband returns!" Then the husband went to the host, and informed him of what he had done. "Sit till night comes," the latter told him. So he sat, he and the rest of the company, till night approached and dinner was brought, and they ate and drank. Then the host said to the woman's husband, "Come with me so that I can show you your wife's whorishness and her godless innovation and wickedness," and he sat him in a dark place at the front end of the hall far from the rest of the company. There was an opening there that provided a view of everyone in the hall, so that whoever was in it could see whoever was there but they could not see him because it was so dark. Then the master of the house said to one of his servants, "Do you know the house of such-and-such a woman?" "I do," he replied. "Go to her then," the man continued, "and tell her: 'My master is entertaining a group of eminent men and it has reached him that your husband has gone to such-and-such a village. He would like to meet with you for intimacy and conviviality, and the delectation

لأجل الأنس والصفاء والبسط والانشراح لإخوانه قال فمضى الغلام إلى دارها وطرق الباب فقالت له من أنت فقال غلام فلان وأخبرها بما قال له فقالت السمع والطاعة اقف حتّى أمضي معك ثمّ إنها قامت وتعطّرت وتحلّت وتزيّنت ولبست أفخر ما عندها وسارت مع الغلام إلى أن أقبلت على المحلّ فرأته ملآنًا من الأكابر وتلك الشموع موقودة والمدام والشربات والنُقل والمكارم والمآكل وكلّ شيء حاضر فلمّا دخلت من باب القاعة حسرت عن وجهها وخضعت وساقت القحب والبدع وخطرت وقالت السلام عليكم فقال لها صاحب المحلّ سلّمي سلام المحبّين فإنّ لنا مدّة ما رأيناك ونحن مشتاقين إليك فقالت يا سيّدي حتّى يسافر هذا التعيس زوجي لا ردّه الله وزوجها يسمع ما تقول ويرى ما تفعل قال ثمّ إنّها صارت تقعد في أحجار القوم وهم يقبّلونها ويعانقونها وهي تشهق وتغنج وتظهر القحب والسوس إلى أن اشتهوا الفعل منها ففعلوا كلّهم فيها وزوجها يرى ذلك حتّى كاد يموت من الحياء والخجل ثمّ بعد ذلك قال لها صاحب المنزل يا ستّي عندنا رجل من الأكابر غريب إلّا أنّه يستحي أن يفعل شيئًا بحضرتنا وهو في محلّ في صدر القاعة فأنتي تجابريه بحضن وبوسة ولو كان في الظلام فقالت حبًا وكرامة نجبر بخاطره ثمّ إنّه أخذها ودلّها عليه فارتمت في حضنه فامتنع منها وخجل فقالت له ما هذا الحياء وهذا الخجل اخلع الوهم وانحظّ وانبسط كلّ هذا وهو في غاية الغمّ منها ومراده هلاكها لكن لا يقدر على ذلك قال فقام صاحب المنزل وأخذ شمعة من الشموع المسروجة وأقبل عليها وعلى زوجها وقال له ليلة مباركة قال فلمّا تحقّقت أنّه زوجها صاحت وخجلت فقال لها يا قحبه يا خاينه أنتي الّتي تستحي من القمر ومن الكلب والحمار وغير ذلك قاتلك الله يا شقيّه وقام عليها بالضرب فصاحت وخرجت هاربة وقام زوجها يجري وهو في غاية

and relaxation of his brethren.'" So the servant went off to her house and knocked on the door. "Who's there?" she asked. "The servant of so-and-so," he replied, and told her what his master had said. "I hear and obey!" said the woman. "Wait and I will come with you." Then she arose and perfumed herself and applied kohl to her eyes and put on her makeup and dressed in her finest clothes and set off with the servant. When she came to that place, she found it full of eminent men, the candles lit, the wine and sherbets and nuts and other signs of hospitality and food and everything else prepared. When she entered by the door of the hall, she lifted the veil from her face and made obeisance and struck an attitude of whorishness and godless innovation and strutted in with a "Peace be upon you!" The master of the place said to her, "Give us the lovers' greeting, for we have not seen you for a long time and we have missed you!" "Sir," she replied, "I could not come until that wretch my husband went away, may God not bring him back!"—her husband listening all the while to what she said and watching what she did. Then she went and sat on the laps of the company, and they kissed her and embraced her while she sighed and moaned and played the whore, until they desired to perform the act with her, and all of them did it to her, while her husband watched until he was about to die of shame and embarrassment. After this, the master of the house said to her, "My lady, we have an eminent man with us who is a stranger, but he is too shy to do anything in our presence. He is in a place at the front of the hall. Go cheer him up with a hug and a kiss, even if it's in the dark." "It will be a pleasure and an honor to bring him cheer!" said she, and he led her to him and she threw herself into his arms. He, however, pulled away from her in shame. "What is this prudery and diffidence?" she said to him. "Throw aside your cares! Take it easy and enjoy yourself!"—and all this while he was in the depths of chagrin because of her and wanting to destroy her, though he could do nothing. Then the master of the house got up and took one of the candles with a holder and went up to her and her husband and said to him, "A blessed evening!" When the woman realized that he was her husband, she let out a cry and was thrown into confusion. He said to her, "Whore! Traitor! You are the one who is shy of the moon and dog and the donkey and all the rest! God destroy you, you wicked woman!" and he set upon her with blows, and she screamed and fled; and he too ran off, in the greatest embarrassment, saying, "Be my witnesses that I divorce her thrice!"[483] On reaching his house, he found that she had returned to her family, so he sent her her belongings and

الخجل وقال أُشهِدُكم على أنها طالق ثلاثا ثمّ مضى إلى داره فرآها قد مضت إلى أهلها فأرسل لها حوائجها وأعلم أهلها بطلاقها وخرج من القرية هائماً على وجهه لا يدري أين يذهب من شدّة الفضيحة من أهل البلد ومن أصحابه إلى أن طلع مدينة مصر ليلاً فرأى حانوتاً وقدّامه مَسْطَبة واسعة فقام عليها من شدّة التعب وما قاساه من ألم السفر فقدّر الله تعالى أنّ اللصوص أتوا إلى هذا الحانوت الّذي راقد عليه وفتحوه وأخذوا جميع ما فيه وهو نائم عليه لا يدري فجاء صاحب الحانوت فرأى جميع ما في دكّانه سُرِق ورأى هذا الرجل فدقّ فيه وأقام الصياح وقال هذا سرق حانوتي فأقبل صاحب الشرطة ومسكه وقال له أنت أخذت ما في هذا الحانوت قال نعم فقال لا عذر لمن أقرّ فأخذه وأتى به إلى الملك وأخبره بالقضيّة فسأله الملك فأقرّ فقال له الملك وأين الذي أخذته فقال عند أصحابي فقال له الملك وأين أصحابك فقال يا ملك أرسل معي أحداً أفتّش عليهم قال فوكّل الملك به جماعة مرسَّمين عليه ودار في شوارع مصر إلى أخير النهار فرأى مجلس فقراء قائم الذكر ورأى شيخهم عليه ملابس حسنة وفي هيئة الصلحاء وهو قائم في وسط الجمع يرغي ويزبد ويترجم باللسان والحَلْق يقبّلوا يديه ويقولوا شي لله فقال هذا الرجل للموكّلين عليه رأيت أصحابي الّذين سرقت أنا وإيّاهم الحانوت فقالوا من هم فقال هذا الشيخ وجماعته قال فنهروه وشتموه وقالوا له تتّهم الأولياء وتدّعي أنّهم لصوص وهذا كلّ المدينة تعتقده وتعتقد جماعته فقال لهم أنتم ما تعرفوا حاله جميع ما راح من الحانوت وغيره ما أخذه إلّا هذا الشيخ وجماعته وهو رفيقي هو وأصحابه في السرقة خذوه للملك يعاقبه وهو يقرّ وأنا شاهد عليه قال فلم يطيعوه وقالوا حتّى نخبّر الملك فأخذوه وأوقفوه بين يديه فقال لهم أين أصحابه فقالوا أيّد الله الملك إنه ادّعى أنّ شيخ الفقراء فلان وطائفته أصحابه في السرقة وتعرف أن

informed her family of her divorce and, for the disgrace that he had suffered before the people of the town and his friends, left the village and wandered aimlessly he knew not where, until one night he reached the city of Cairo. There he found a shop with a wide stoop in front of it, upon which, tired out from the hardships of the journey, he lay down and slept. Now the Almighty had ordained that thieves should come to the very shop where he was sleeping, break into it, and take everything that was there, while he slept on unawares. Then, when the owner of the shop came, he found that everything that was in his store had been stolen and, seeing the man, he struck him and set up a cry and said, "He has burgled my shop!" The chief of the police came and seized him and asked him, "Did you take what was in this shop?" "I did," he said. "No mercy for those who confess!" said the officer, and he took him off to the king, to whom he described the case. The king questioned the man and he confessed. "And where are the things you took?" asked the king. "With my accomplices," he said. "And where are your accomplices?" asked the king. "Send someone with me, O king," the man said, "and I will look for them." So the king appointed a party of men to keep an eye on him and he roamed the streets of Cairo till the end of the day, when he found a gathering of dervishes performing a *dhikr* and saw that their shaykh was wearing fine clothes and had the appearance of a righteous man. He was standing in the midst of the throng frothing and foaming at the mouth and speaking gibberish, and the people were kissing his hand and saying, "Grant us your blessing!" "That's the man!" said the prisoner to the guards: "I've found my friends with whom I burgled the shop." "Who?" they asked. "That shaykh and his band," he said. But the guards turned on him with angry words and abuse, saying to him, "Would you accuse the Friends of God and pretend that they are thieves? The whole city believes in this man and in his band too!" He said, "You know nothing of his real state. Everything that disappeared from that shop, and others, was taken by this man and his band. He, with his followers, was my partner in the theft. Take him to the king to be put to the torture, and he will confess, and I will bear witness against him before God." They refused, however, to obey him, saying, "Not until we have informed the king!" So they took him and brought him before the king, and the king said to them, "Where are his accomplices?" "God aid the king!" they replied. "He claimed that Shaykh So-and-so of the dervishes and his followers were his accomplices in the theft, but you know that the whole city believes in the shaykh, and that he is a Friend of God!"

الشيخ مُعْتَقَد المدينة ومن الأولياء فقال له الملك أحقّ ما تقول فقال نعم يا ملك هو رفيقي وجميع ما راح من المدينة فعله هو وجماعته فإنّهم فقراء بالنهار ولصوص بالليل وهم مستّرين بالفقر والمشيخة ولله وللرسول تصديق كلامي وتأتي به وتعاقبه فإنّه يقرّ بما أخذه من قديم وجديد قال فالتفت الملك للوزير وقال له ما تقول فقال له يا ملك الناس كثير ولو لا يعلم أنّه رفيقه ما تكلّ عليه فأمر الملك بإحضار الشيخ وطائفته فطلع في ذكر وأعلام على رأسه إلى أن أقبل على الديوان وصار بحضرة الملك فقال له يا شيخ هذا الرجل يخبّر أنّك سرقت أنت وإيّاه الحانوت الفلانيّ فقال الشيخ معاذ الله يا ملك نحن فقراء لا نعرف إلّا الذكر والعبادة قال فصاح الرجل وقال والله يا ملك هو رفيقي في السرقة عاقبه يظهر لك الحقّ فالتفت الملك إلى الوزير فقال له افعل بما قال الرجل فلولا أنّه رفيقه ما قرّ عليه قال فأشار الملك إلى الجلّاد وقال اطرح هذا الشيخ على الأرض وعاقبه قال فعرّاه الجلّاد من ثيابه وشبّحه في أربع سِكَك ونزل عليه بالضرب المبرّح فصاح الشيخ يا ملك الأمان أخذت ما في الحانوت وكلام الرجل صادق وهو عندي في محلّي قال فأمر الملك أن يهجموا داره فهجموها فرأوا ما سرق من الحانوت وما راح من المدينة من قديم وجديد عنده في مطمورة فأتوا به للملك فرآه ونادى كلّ من عرف شيئاً سرق له من قديم أو جديد يأخذه وتعجّب الملك من حاله وحال جماعته وقال لصاحب الشرطة خذه هو وجماعته والرجل الّذي قرّ عليه وأشهر قتلهم في البلد حتّى يعتبر غيرهم قال فصاح الرجل المذكور وقال سألتك بالله يا ملك لا تأخذني ظلماً فإنّي رجل غريب وعمري ما طلعت المدينة إلا ليلة أن بِتُّ على الحانوت ولا عمري رأيت هذا الشيخ إلّا في هذه الأوقات واسأله يا ملك فقال الملك للشيخ تعرف هذا الرجل فقال لا والله يا ملك ولا رأيته قطّ إلّا بين يديك وأنا مقتول أنا وأصحابي

The king said to the man, "Is what you say true?" "Yes, O king," he replied. "He is my partner and everything that has disappeared from the city is his doing, his and his band's. They are dervishes by day and thieves by night, and they use their practice of Poverty and their shaykhly status as a cover. As God and the Messenger are my witnesses, I speak the truth! Just bring him in and torture him, and he will confess to everything he has taken, both now and in the past." The king turned to his minister and asked him, "What do you think?" The minister replied, "O king, the people are many. If he did not know he was his partner, he would not have spoken against him." So the king ordered the shaykh and his followers to be brought, and the latter set off, with the *dhikr* in full swing and banners at its head, and made his way to the audience chamber and entered the king's presence. The latter said to him, "O Shaykh, this man declares that you and he burgled such-and-such a shop." The shaykh replied, "I seek refuge with God, O King! We are dervishes. We know nothing but *dhikr* and worship!" But the man screamed out, "I swear, O King, he is my partner in the burglary! Torture him and he will tell you the truth!" The king turned to his minister, who said, "Do as the man says. If he were not his partner, he would not have incriminated him." So the king nodded to the executioner and said, "Lay this shaykh on the ground and put him to the torture!" So the executioner stripped him of his clothes and made four slashes on his head and beat him severely. "Spare me, O King!" cried the shaykh. "I took what was in the shop and what the man says is true. It is all with me at my dwelling." Then the king ordered them to break into his house, and they did so and found what had been stolen from the shop and everything that had disappeared in the city both then and in the past was there in a vault. They brought it to the king, who saw it and summoned everyone who recognized something of his as having been stolen, recently or in the past, to take it. And the king marveled at the shaykh and his band and said to the chief of the police, "Take him and his band and the man who incriminated him and announce their execution in the city, so that others may take heed!" At this the first man cried out, "I implore you in God's name, O King, do not take me unjustly! I am a stranger and never in my life came to the city till the night I spent at the shop, and I never saw this shaykh before. Ask him, O King!" So the king said to the shaykh, "Do you know this man?" "No, O King," he said, "nor have I seen him except in your presence. I and my accomplices are about to die, and I will not take this stranger on my conscience." "How then, good fellow," the king asked

وما يَحُلّ لي من الله أن آخذ هذا الرجل الغريب في ذِمّتي قال فقال له الملك يا رجل فمن أين عرفت أن هذا الشيخ وأصحابه لصوص فقال يا ملك عرفت بالفراسة والقياس على فعل زوجتي وأحكى للملك على قضيّة زوجته من أوّلها إلى آخرها قال فتعجّب الملك من حسن فراسته وأطلقه وأنعم عليه بجارية حسناء عوض زوجته وجعله من ندمائه وصار يستشيره في بعض الأمور وحصلت له السعادة إلى آخر عمره وكلّ هذا بصدق الكلام وخلوص النيّة مع الله وما يعلم الظاهر والباطن إلّا ربّ العالمين

٣٢،٧ (وقد شاهدت في ثغر دمياط) وأنا ساكن بها سنة ستّة وستّين وألف أنّ جماعة الفقراء المتلبّسين كانوا بالنهار فقراء يظهروا الدين والصلاح وبالليل يتجرّدوا للسرقة وأخذ أموال الناس فيكسروا الحوانيت وينَقُبوا الدور فحصل من فعلهم في دمياط للحكّام وأرباب الدَرَك غاية الكرب الشديد قال فقدّر الله تعالى بهَتْك هؤلاء الأشقياء وكشف الستر عنهم فقبضوا أرباب الدرك على رجل منهم وهو يسرق في دار وأتوا به إلى الحكّام فعاقبوه فأقرّ على جماعة مثله من الفقراء فهجموا عليهم وقبضوا البعض منهم وهرب البقيّة وأخرجوا من عندهم شيئاً كثيرًا من أمتعة وغيرها وشيئاً له عدّة سنين وصار كلّ من عرف شيئاً يأخذه ورأيت بعيني جميع ما أخرجوه من عندهم وكان يوماً مشهوراً قبّح الله أفعالهم وخيّب الله آمالهم

٣٣،٧ (واتّفق أنّ الأمير مُقَلَّد) رحمه الله تعالى كان مارًّا بموكبه يريد قرية من بعض القرى فرأى رجلاً مقتولاً والدمّ يجري من أوداجه وعروقه ونظر فلم ير أحداً فسار قليلاً فرأى رجلاً عليه لبس الصوف متقلّد بالسُبَح وهو واقف يصلّي وقُدّامه عُكّازه والإبريق قال فوقف الأمير مقلّد حتّى فرغ من صلاته وقال لبعض غلمانه اقبضوا على هذا الشقيّ فقبضوا عليه وأوقفوه بين يديه فقال له الأمير مقلّد يا متلبّس على الله وعلى الناس بالفقر والزوكرة هل يُخفى على الله خافية لأيّ شيء قتلت هذا الرجل الّذي مَرّينا عليه

him, "did you know that this shaykh and his accomplices were thieves?" He replied, "O King, I knew from my skill at discerning men's true nature from their outward appearance, and by analogy with my wife's behavior," and he proceeded to tell the king the story of his wife, from beginning to end. The king marveled at his acumen and released him and bestowed on him a beautiful slave girl to make up for his wife and made him one of his boon companions and consulted him on certain matters, and the man was happy to the end of his days, all of which was the outcome of his veracity and his honesty before God, and none but the Lord of the Worlds knows the manifest and the hidden.

I myself, when living in the port city of Dimyāṭ in 1066,[484] witnessed a band 7.32
of fraudulent dervishes who made a show of religion and righteousness as dervishes by day and devoted themselves by night to burglary and the taking of people's property. They would break into shops and make holes in the walls of houses, and great consternation was caused to the authorities and the watch in Dimyāṭ by their doings. However, the Almighty decreed the destruction of those evildoers and their exposure, for the watch caught one of them as he was burgling a house and brought him before the authorities. When they put him to the torture, he incriminated a band of dervishes like himself, so they carried out a raid and arrested some of them, while the rest fled. They recovered from the place where they lived a huge quantity of goods and other things, some of them years old, and everyone who recognized anything took it. I saw with my own eyes what they recovered from the place where they lived. It was a famous occasion, may God deform their deeds and disappoint their hopes!

And the story is told that the Emir Muqallad, may the Almighty have mercy 7.33
upon him, once was on his way to a certain village with his entourage and servants when he saw a dead man, the blood still flowing from his arteries and veins. He looked about but saw no one. Then he went a little farther and saw a man dressed in wool, festooned with prayer beads, standing at prayer, his crutch[485] and pitcher before him. The Emir Muqallad stood by till he had finished his prayer and then said to some of his servants, "Seize that wretch!" They seized him and brought him before him, and the Emir Muqallad said to him, "You who seek to deceive God and man with your 'poverty' and your cozening, is anything hidden from God? Why did you murder the man whom we passed and take what he had on him?" The man set about swearing his innocence and supplicating the Almighty and cursing whoever had murdered the man, and he said to the emir, "Sir, I am a poor man who makes the rounds

وأخذت ما معه فصار يحلف هذا الرجل ويتضرّع إلى الله تعالى ويدعو على من قتله وقال له يا سيّدي أنا رجل فقير دائر على أهل الخير ألتمس منهم الإحسان فقال الأمير مقلّد فتّشوا حوائجه ففتّشوها فرأوا معه السكّين الّتي ذُبِحَ بها الرجل وعليه الدم ورأوا حوائج المقتول معه قال فأمر الأمير بقتله فقطعوا رأسه ووضعوا على صدره الإبريق والعكّاز والسبح وعلّن أنّه لا يدفن فمكث على قارعة الطريق حتّى جاف وأكلته الوحوش والطيور فكان هذا من شدّة معرفة الأمير مقلّد وقوّة فراسته رحمه الله

٣٤،٧ ﴿وسمعت بعض الملحدين من الدراويش المحلّقين الدقون يقول كلاما يخالف الكتاب والسنّة﴾ إنّ البعث والنُشور والجنّة والنار لا حقيقة لهم وإن الشخص جنّته وناره وحسابه في نفسه وإن الدنيا لا تفنى ولا تزول وإنّما هي شمس تطلع وقمر يغيب وينشد قول أبي العلاء المعرّيّ رحمه الله [وافر]

أَتَى عِيسَى فَبَطَّلَ شَرْعَ مُوسَى   وَجاءَ مُحَمَّدٌ بصلاةِ خَمْسِ
وقالوا لا نَبِيٌّ بَعْدَ هذا   فَضَلَّ القومُ بَيْنَ غَدٍ وأمسِ
وَمَهْما عِشْتَ في دُنْياكَ هذي   فما تُخْلِيكَ من قَمَرٍ وشَمْسِ
إذا قُلْتُ المُحالَ رَفَعْتُ صوتي   وإنْ قلتُ الصَحِيحَ أَطَلْتُ هَمْسي

ثمّ يقول إنّ الشخص إذا طلعت روحه ومات دخلت في جسد من الأجساد من آدميّ أو حيوان حتّى يدور عليها الدَوْر فترجع إلى صاحبها الأوّل فيظهر بصورته الّتي كان عليها أوّلا وهكذا سائر العوالم فانظروا إلى شدّة جهلهم وسوء اعتقادهم قاتلهم الله تعالى

٣٥،٧ ﴿وكان بجوارنا رجل فاضل فأضاف جماعة من المتلبّسين﴾ يعتقد أنّهم من الصلحاء فلمّا فرغوا من المأكل والمشرب جلسوا يتحدّثوا فيما بينهم إلى أن تكلّموا في القرآن فقالوا لجارنا أتزعم أنّ القرآن كلام الله فقال نعم ومَنْ شكّ في هذا كفر فقالوا له ليس كذلك

of the more fortunate begging them for charity!" The Emir Muqallad said, "Search his things!" so they searched them and found on him the knife with which the man's throat had been slit with the blood still on it, and they found the dead man's things with him. Then the Emir Muqallad ordered that he be killed, and they cut off his head and put the pitcher and the crutch and the prayer beads on his chest, and the emir had it announced that he was not to be buried, and he remained on the open highway until he dried up and the beasts and the birds ate him. All this was due to the Emir Muqallad's great insight and his acumen in seeing through outward appearances, God grant him mercy!

Once I heard a certain heretical dervish, one of those who shave their beards, making statements that contradicted the Book and the practice of the Prophet Muḥammad, namely, that resurrection and eternal life and Heaven and Hell had no reality and that a person's Heaven, Hell, and Judgment were all within himself, and that this world would not perish and disappear but rather was simply a sun that rose and a moon that set. And he recited the words of Abū l-ʿAlāʾ al-Maʿarrī, God have mercy on him:[486] 7.34

Jesus came and cancelled Moses's law,
  Then Muḥammad brought five prayers a day.
"No prophets after this!" they said,
  And man was lost between tomorrow and yesterday.
However long you live in this world of yours,
  From sun and moon you'll never get away.
I'll raise my voice when speaking lies,
  But whisper long whene'er the truth I say.

Then he said, "If a person's soul leaves his body and he dies, it enters into the body of a human or an animal, and so it continues until it comes full circle and returns to its first owner; then he appears in his previous form as he first was, and the same goes for the rest of the worlds." Observe, my brethren, the depth of their ignorance and misbelief, may the Almighty destroy them!

There used to be a virtuous man living next door to us who once invited a band of charlatans to a meal, believing them to be righteous men. When they had done eating and drinking, they sat talking among themselves until the talk turned to the Qur'an, and they asked our neighbor, "Do you maintain that the Qur'an is the word of God?" "Certainly," he replied, "and whoever doubts that is an unbeliever!" "Not so!" they said. "It is no more than the words of the 7.35

وإنّما هو كلام بَحيرا الراهب علّمه للنبيّ صلّى الله عليه وسلّم فلمّا سمع ما قالوا قام عليهم بالسبّ واللعن وعرف ضلالهم وأخرجهم من منزله على أيشم حال نسأل الله السلامة منهم والبعد عنهم

٣٦،٧ (واجتمعتُ برجل من الفقراء كان يكثر الذكر والعبادة) وكنت أعتقده فجلست معه يوماً نتكلّم في فضل العبادة فقال لي يا سيّدي أنا لي عشرين سنة على هذا القَدَم ثمّ قام فصلّى فلمّا فرغ من صلاته توجّه إلى نحو سيّدي أحمد البدويّ نفعنا الله به وقال كن معي يا أبو الفَرَجات وتقبَّل عبادتي ويسِّر لي رزقي فقلت له ما هذا الكلام لا يتقبّل العبادة إلّا الله تعالى ولا يرزق الخلق إلّا ربّ العالمين وإنّما سيّدي أحمد البدويّ رجل من الأولياء لا يُقْصَد بالعبادة ولا بصوم ولا صلاة فمن فعل ذلك فقد أشرك وجعل لله شريكاً فقال لي يا سيّدي إنّما أفعل ذلك عن شيخي الّذي علّمني ذلك قبل موته وكان يقول لي اقصد بعبادتك وصومك وصلاتك سيّدي أحمد البدويّ فقلت له معاذ الله إنّما هو مخلوق والعبادة لا تكون إلّا للخالق وقد مات شيخك على ضلال وعبادتك كلّها فاسدة باطلة هذه المدة ثمّ إنّه تاب على يدي وأنقذه الله من الضلال إلى الهدى وتوجّه إلى الله تعالى وأخلص في عبادته رحمه الله

٣٧،٧ (وحضرتُ مرّة بعض الموالد) فسمعت رجلاً من الفقراء هام في الجمع وغنّى وقال [رجز]

يا مالِكُ خُذْ مِن لَظَى نارِ مُهْجَتي وعَذِّبْ بِها المُذْنِبينَ حَداكْ

فأجبته أقول [رجز]

يا هايِفًا خُذْ من خراطِيْ كَلْبَتي وٱلْطَخْ لِحاكَ والحاضِرينَ وَراكْ

monk Baḥīrā, who taught them to the Prophet, God praise him and bless him." When he heard this, he heaped abuse and insults upon them, having realized that they were in error, and he threw them out of his house in the most parlous state. We ask the Almighty for preservation from them and distance in this world and the next!

And once I came to know a dervish who spent much of his time in *dhikr* 7.36
and worship, and I had faith in him. One day I sat down with him to speak with him of the virtues of worship, and he said, "Sir, my practice for twenty years has been thus," and then he performed the prayer, and when he had finished, turned in the direction of My Master Aḥmad al-Badawī,[487] God benefit us through him, and said, "Be my support, Abū l-Farajāt,[488] and accept my worship, and help me get my daily bread!" "What words are these?" I asked him. "Worship should be directed to none but the Almighty, and none but the Lord of the Worlds can provide for the needs of His creatures! My Master Aḥmad al-Badawī is just a man chosen by the Almighty to be among His saints and is not to be taken as an object of worship, or of fasting or prayer. Anyone who does such things has denied His unity and attributed a partner to God." The man said to me, "Sir, I do this on the authority of my shaykh, who taught me this before he died and would say to me, 'Dedicate your worship, your fasting, and your prayer to My Master Aḥmad al-Badawī!'" "I seek refuge with God!" I said to him. "He is just a created being, and none but the Creator may be the object of worship. Your shaykh died in error, and all your worship these past years is corrupt and void!" The man then repented at my hand, and the Almighty rescued him from error and brought him to right guidance, and the man turned to the Almighty and worshipped Him with faith and sincerity, God have mercy upon him.

And once I attended a saint's feast and heard a dervish sing as he wandered 7.37
in ecstasy through the crowd:

> Sovereign, take the flame from the fire of my heart's blood
> And with it torment the sinners round about you!

So I answered him by saying:

> Idiot, take the shit from the ass of my bitch
> And wipe it on your beard and on those of the people behind you!

٣٨،٧ (وعشق بعض الفقراء غلاماً جميلاً) فتحيّل إلى الوصول إليه فلم يمكنه ذلك فجاء إلى رجل أشقى منه وأعرض عليه حاله وشدّة حبّه لهذا الغلام فقال له خذ مُصْران غنم واملأه زيتاً ولفّه على بطنك من داخل الثياب وأُقَفْ في وسط الجمع ودردش باللسان وخبّر عن الشام وعن شجر الزيتون وأدخل يدك بلطافة وأنت بجانب الغلام وحلّ المصران وخذ في يدك شيئاً من الزيت وارفع يدك في الهواء فإنّ الزيت يسيل منها وتكون قد وضعت في جيبك زيتونة خضراء فأخرجها بلطافة وأوريها للغلام وللناس فيعتقدوا أنّك من الأولياء ويميل قلب الغلام إليك فإذا أتاك وقال لك علّمني الولاية وهذه الكرامة فقل له الولاية لا تصحّ إلّا بتدبير النقطة الخارقة فإن قال لك ما هي النقطة الخارقة فقل له هي المَنِيّ ولا يصحّ تدبيره إلّا في الخلوة وادخل عليه بهذه الحيلة حتّى تقضي منه المراد قال ففعل ما أمره به هذا الخبيث ونزل الجمع ووقف بجانب الغلام ودردش باللسان وأخبر عن الشام وعن شجر الزيتون ومدّ يده إلى الهواء فسال الزيت من يده وأظهر الزيتونة الخضراء فصاحوا الفقراء كلّهم وقالوا شي لله وقبلوا يديه وجاء الغلام وقبل يده ومال إليه وقال له يا سيّدي أكون معك وعلّمني وأطلعني على الكرامات والولاية فقال له يا ولدي الولاية لا تُنال إلّا بالنقطة الخارقة فقال له يا سيّدي وما النقطة الخارقة قال هي المنيّ فقال يا سيّدي ومتى تفعل معي ذلك فقال له هذا لا يكون إلّا في الخلوة ولا يصح بحضرة أحد فقال له الغلام سر بنا فأخذه ومضى إلى الخلوة وقال له نام على بطنك فنام الغلام وكشف هذا الشقيّ عن ردف ثقيل * وخصر نحيل * وركب فوقه * ودفع أيره * فما مانعه إلّا الخصيتان * فصاح الغلام الأمان * ما هذه ولاية قاتل الله الأبعد ثمّ قام من عليه بعد أن قضى مراده وتحقّق الغلام أنّ هذا كلّه من الحِيَل حتّى وقع له ذلك قال

And once a dervish fell in love with a beautiful youth, but, though he racked his brains for a way to have him, could not come up with an idea. So he went to a man yet more wicked than him and told him his trouble and how much he loved the youth, and the man told him, "Take the intestine of a sheep, fill it with oil, and wrap it around your belly inside your clothes. Then stand in the middle of the throng and speak gibberish and describe Damascus and the Tree of Olives[489] and, standing next to the youth, stealthily insert your hand and untie the intestine and take a little of the oil on your hand and raise your hand in the air. The oil will then run down it. Earlier you will have put a green olive in your pocket; take this out stealthily and show it to the youth and the others. They will believe that you are one of God's Friends and the youth's heart will incline towards you. Then, when he comes to you and says, 'Teach me to be a Friend of God and how to perform this miracle,' tell him, 'You can become a Friend of God only after the readying of the Miraculous Drop.' And if he says to you, 'What is the Miraculous Drop?' tell him, 'It is the Seed, and may be prepared only at the place of retreat.' Work this trick on him until you get what you want." So the dervish did as that vile man had instructed him and went down into the throng and stood next to the youth and spoke gibberish and described Damascus and the Tree of Olives and stretched his hand up into the air and the oil ran down his hand, and he produced the green olive and all the dervishes cried out and said, "Grant us your blessings!" and kissed his hand; and the youth kissed his hand and was drawn to him and said, "Master, let me stay with you, so that you can teach me and show me miracles and how to be a *walī*!" The dervish replied, "My boy, the rank of Friend of God can only be attained by means of the Miraculous Drop." "And what, Master, is the Miraculous Drop?" said he. "It is the Seed," said the dervish. "And when, My Master," asked the youth, "will you do that with me?" "That may be only at a place of retreat," replied the man, "and it cannot work if anyone else is there." Said the youth, "Let's go!" So the wicked man took him with him to the place of retreat and told him, "Lie on your stomach!" and the youth lay down, and that miscreant lifted the veil from a ponderous posterior and a willowy waist, and got on top and thrust in his cock, and only came to a stop when he reached the sac, at which point the youth cried out, "Alack! This is not the work of a Friend of God, God destroy you, you vile rascal!" When he had gotten what he wanted, the dervish got up off him and the youth realized that everything that had brought him to suffer thus had been a trick. Then the two of them set 7.38

ثمّ سار هو وإيّاه فاعترضهما جمع فقراء في مولد فنزل هذا الشقيّ في الجمع وترجم وهمهم فقال [وزن غير معروف]

علونا على قبّه مليحه مرخّمه وصبّينا فيها من النور جانب

قال فأجابه الغلام يقول [وزن غير معروف]

ما عُدْت تنظرها من اليوم يا فتى ما عاد لك إلّا التعب والمصائب

قال فزعقوا الفقراء وهاموا وظنّوا أن هذا الفقير وصل إلى قبّة الفَلَك الأعلى ورقي عليها وأنّ الغلام فات مَرْتَبته وحجبه عنها وفاق على شيخه والحال أنه إنّما رقي على هذا الردف الثقيل * والخصر النحيل * وصبّ في تلك القبّة الدمعة الخارقة * الحارة الحاذقة * وقبّل الخدود * ودفع فيها العمود * فهم في ﴿سَكْرَتِهِمْ يَعْمَهُونَ﴾ * ﴿قَاتَلَهُمُ اللّٰهُ أَنَّىٰ يُؤْفَكُونَ﴾ * ولقد صدق من قال وصرح المقال [طويل مع كسر في الشطر الثاني]

يَضال الوَلَدْ مُنصانَ في حُضْنِ والدِهْ ولمّا يدروش يدور نيّالك

أي لمّا يحتوي عليه جماعة من الفقراء أو من طائفة الملحدين المحلّقين الذقون أو الطائفة الخوامس قاتلهم الله فيفسدوا عقيدته ويشغلوه عن الدنيا والدين ويدور معهم في التعاسة والخزي والنجاسة حتّى تطلع لحيته فيتركوه خراباً يُلَقّع * لا نيك يشبع * ولا مال يجمع *

٣٩.٧ ومنهم طائفة لا يعتقون الأمرد ولو التحى وشاب * ويتمثّلوا بقول من قال ويظنّوا أنّه الصواب [كامل]

أَهْواهُ طِفلاً في القِماطِ وأَمْرَدا وبِلِحْيةٍ وإذا عَلاه مَشيبُ

off together and went their way until they came upon a crowd of dervishes at a saint's feast. The miscreant went down into the midst of the throng and jabbered and gibbered and said:

We climbed atop a pretty dome, all marbled,
Wherein we poured a measure of light!

to which the youth responded by saying:

From today you'll ne'er see it more, good fellow,
And all that's left for you is hardship and afright!

—at which the dervishes shrieked and went into ecstasies, thinking that the dervish had reached the Dome of the Upper Firmament and climbed on top of it and that the youth had exceeded him in rank and interposed himself between him and it, surpassing his shaykh. The truth, of course, was that the only thing he had climbed on top of was that ponderous posterior and willowy waist, pouring into that dome the Miraculous Drop, acrid and hot, and kissing the cheeks and thrusting the Column into the slot—for «in their intoxication they lie . . . God destroy them! How perverse a lot!»[490] How true the words of him who said, and how clear the saying:

A youth is safe in his father's arms,
But once a dervish he goes around getting fucked!

—meaning that when a band of dervishes or of the heretical sect that shaves off their beards or of the Khawāmis sect, God destroy them, get a hold of him, they corrupt his belief and distract him from this world and the next, and he goes around with them in wretchedness, ignominy, and impurity until his beard grows, at which they leave him, an abandoned ruin, ever craving a screwing, incapable of earning a living.

There is even one sect among them that will not let a catamite go his way, 7.39
even if his beard has sprouted and his hair turned gray, taking as proof the words of the poet, which they take for truth:

I love him as a babe in swaddling clothes and as a beardless boy
And with a beard, and covered in gray hairs.

وقول الآخر [طويل]

بِلُوطيٍّ يُدْعَى عاشِقُ المُرْدِ في الوَرَى ويُدْعَى بِزانٍ مَنْ يُحِبُّ الغوانِيا
فَمِلْتُ لِأَصْحابِ اللِّحاءِ تَعَفُّفًا فَما أنا لوطِيًّا وما أنا زانِيا

٤٠،٧ وهذا بخلاف مذهبنا في المحبّة وسلوكنا في العشق فإنّ الأمرد إذا جاوز الثمانية
عشر سنة مجّته النفوس * ولا يرغب فيه إلّا وقت قشل من الفلوس * فإذا بلغ
العشرين * أخشن وجهه بيقين * وظهرت لحيته وتغيّر حاله * وعمّه الغمّ وخفي خاله *
وصار وجهه مثل قفاه * وتُلِيَ عليه لا حول ولا قوّة إلّا بالله * ولله در القائل [خفيف]

اِلْتَحَى الأَمْرَدُ الّذي كانَ في التِّيهِ مُسْرِفا
حَسَنًا كانَ وَجْهُهُ وسَرِيعًا تَصَحَّفا
سُرَّ وللهِ ناظِرِي مُذْ رَأَى ذاكَ واشْتَفَى
شَكَرَ اللهُ لِحْيَةً صَيَّرَتْ وَجْهَهُ قَفَا

وقال آخر [خفيف]

سَلَبَ النّاسَ بالمَحاسِنِ حَتَّى أَذْهَبَ اللهُ حُسْنَهُ والجَمالا
طَلَعَتْ ذَقْنُهُ وراحَتْ عَلَيْهِ وَكَفَى اللهُ المُؤْمِنِينَ القِتالا

ولوالدي عفا الله عنه مع التشبيه البديع والجناس المصحَّف [خفيف]

قارَبَتْ في الطُّلوعِ في الخَدِّ ذَقْنٌ أَثَّرَتْ ظُلْمَةً قُبَيْلَ النباتِ
كانْتِشارِ الظَّلامِ في الشَّرْقِ لمّا تَغْرُبُ الشَّمْسُ عِنْدَ وَقْتِ البَياتِ

وأبلغ من هذا قول بعضهم [بسيط]

And that of another, who says:

A fornicator they call the one who loves cute girls,
While the lover of smooth boys they call a bugger,
So chastely to bearded men I turned,
For I'd rather be neither one nor t'other!

This is the opposite of our school of thought in love and our approach to wooing—for, when a beardless boy passes eighteen, the appetite rebels, and he's only sought during hard-up spells; and when he reaches twenty years of course his face turns coarse; his beard appears and everything about him veers, his whole life turns to woe, and the mole on his pretty cheek disappears; his face ends up like the back of his head, and it's time for "There is no power and no strength but in God!" to be said.[491] On this topic it has been said:[492] 7.40

Bearded now is the lad who
Once with himself was so smitten.
"Comely" once was his face
But soon it got rewritten.[493]
How my sight was gladdened
When it saw him thus and was cured!
Thanks be to God for a beard
That a nape, from a face, procured!

And another said:

He plundered us all with his charms,
Till God put his beauty to sack.
His beard appeared and that was it—
"God spared the Believers attack."[494]

And my father, may God excuse him his sins, wrote in the same vein, with elegant simile and orthographic wordplay:[495]

A beard, soon to grow upon the cheek,
Ere it sprouted began to seep,
Like darkness spreading in the east, when
The sun has set and man's about to sleep.

And another said, more eloquently:

مـا فَعَلَ اللهُ بِاليَـهودِ ولا بِعـادٍ ولا ثَمودِ
ولا بفِرْعَوْنَ مُذْ عَصاهُ ما فَعَلَ الشَّعْرُ بالخُدودِ

فالعشق والغرام * لا يكون إلّا لرشيق القوام * حلو الابتسام * من أبناء العَشْر * وذوي اللطافة في الطَيّ والنَشْر * فإذا بلغ الخمسة عشر سنه * صارت محاسنه لعُشّاقه مَحْسَنه * ولواحظه لعُذّاله مَلْسَنه * وهذا هو الغرض والغرام * والمراد والمرام * ولا اعتبار بعشق هؤلاء الطوائف * فإنّ حبّهم لدين الهوى مخالف * وقبائحهم بادية * وضلالتهم عاديه * واعتقاداتهم فاسده * وتجاراتهم كاسده *

٤١،٧ (وأكبر فعل هؤلاء الطوائف الّذي ابتدعوه * والأمر القبيح الّذي اخترعوه) * مع هذه الأحوال * وارتكابهم الضلال * إذا مات بينهم إنسان غسلوه وكفّنوه * وعلى النعش وضعوه * وتعاطى حمله أربعة أبالسه * كأنّهم من جنس القساقسه * أو من دير الرهبان * أو من جنّ سليمان * فيجرّوا النعش بقوّة باس * وشدّة أنفاس * ويقيموا الصياح والزعيق * ويقولوا طار الشيخ بتحقيق * ويقفوا به في بعض المحلّات يقرّوا فواتح * وتضيع بسببهم المصالح * ويطوفون به حول البلد والمقبره * وهم في * وربما ساروا به من بلد إلى أخرى * وقد يرجعوا به القَهْقَرَى * وهم في خباط وعياط * وصياح وشياط * وطرد وجنان * ويقولوا شي لله يا شيخ فلان * وربّما زلغطوا النسوان * وأرموا عليه الطُرَح بإمكان * وأخبرني بعض الإخوان * ممّن شاهد الأمر عَيان * أنّهم مكثوا دائرين بميّت من أوّل النهار إلى غروب الشمس * حتّى انتفخ من شدّة الحرّ وصار جلده لا يطيق اللمس * فانظر رحمك الله هذه البدعة الذميمه * والطريقة الشنيعه * الّتي ارتكبوها من غير دليل ولا إثبات * وإنّما هي إثم عليهم وأذيّة للأموات * ولم يرد في حديث ولا كتاب * ولا قال به أحد من أهل الصواب * فسبيل العارف أن يقف على قدم الشرع * ليحصل له بذلك مزيد الخير والنفع * قال صاحب الزُبَد رحمه الله تعالى [رجز]

God did not do to the Jews,
Nor to ʿĀd or Thamūd and their race,
Nor yet to Pharaoh when he defied Him,
What hairiness does to the face!

For love and pursuit are meet only for one whose figure is lissome and smile winsome, a boy of ten, full of grace in first slaying and then reviving men. When he reaches fifteen, his charms become a source of joy to the amorous, his glances a source of scandal to the censorious. Such a one is the object of love's fire, the goal and the desire, and no heed should be paid to the passions of those other sects, for their affection with the Law of Love conflicts, their abominations are outrageous, their misguidedness contagious; their beliefs are depraved, and a drug on the market is their trade.

The worst of the acts these sects have introduced and the ugliest of the stuff they have produced, along with the aforementioned things they do and the errors they pursue, is this: if one of them dies, they wash him and shroud him and lay him on a bier, borne by four devils looking like some kind of priest, or monks from a monastery, or jinn from Sulaymān's legion.[496] They run with the bier with hideous strength, breathing hard and shouting and screaming, saying, "The shaykh, in truth, is flying!" They halt to recite the *Fātiḥah* in certain places, and people's interests suffer because of them. They circumambulate the village and graveyard in a cloud of dust and dirt "like frightened asses, fleeing from a lion."[497] Sometimes they take it from one village to the next or walk it backward, bashing around and bawling, shouting and caterwauling, and making commotion and craziness, saying, "Your blessing, Shaykh So-and-so!" and sometimes the women ululate and try to throw their veils on top of it. I was advised by one of my brethren, who had seen it with his own eyes, that they continue to carry the corpse about from dawn to dusk, until it bloats in the heat and becomes too delicate to touch! Observe, God have mercy on you, this blameworthy innovation and hideous procedure they have adopted without authority or proof! It is a sin to be held against them and a desecration of the dead, not to be found in Tradition or Book nor prescribed by any of the righteous.[498] The man of sense will follow the path of the Law and in so doing acquire greater blessing and benefit—as the author of the *The Most Pleasing Portions*,[499] may the Almighty have mercy upon him, says: 7.41

وَزِنْ بِوَزْنِ الشَّرْعِ كُلَّ خاطِرِ   فَإِنْ يَكُنْ مَأْمورَهُ فَبادِرِ

وأن لا يختلط بهؤلاء الطوائف المضلّين * وأرباب البدع الملحدين * بل يكون على حذر منهم * وبمعزل عنهم * وإن رأى منهم ما يخالف الشرع زجرهم إن استطاع * وإلّا تركهم وعاشر من يعود عليه منه الانتفاع * قال بعضهم لا تصحب إلّا من أعجبك حاله * ودلّك على الله مقاله *

Against the Law each impulse weigh—
If it's ordained, then on your way!

Such a man will not mix with these sects that deviate, nor with the heretics who innovate. Indeed, he will be on his guard against them and live in isolation from them, and if he sees them contravene the Law he will rebuke them if he can so contrive, or leave them and associate with those from whom some good he may derive. As someone said, "Befriend only those whose ways please you and whose words to God lead you!"

(ولنختم هذا الجزء بأُرجوزة تتضمّن ما ذكرناه في هذه الأوراق * وما عايناه من أحوالهم باتّفاق) *

كما تقدّم الوعد به عن تحقيق * فنقول وبالله التوفيق [رجز] ١،٨

قالَ الفقيرُ يوسفُ بْنُ خِضْرِ   لله حَمدي دائمًا وشُكري ٢،٨
ثمّ الصلاةُ والسلامُ أبدًا   على النبيّ المصطَفى محمّدا
كَذاكَ على آلٍ لَهُ وصَحبِهْ   ومَن قَفا لِدينِهِمْ وحِزبِهْ
وبَعْدُ إنّي ناظِمٌ أُرجوزهْ   لَطيفةً مُفيدةً وَجيزهْ
تُخبِرُ عَن حالِ ذَوي الرَّذالَهْ   كَذا عَوامِّ الرِّيفِ لا مَحالَهْ
فَخُذْ هَداكَ اللهُ ما أقولُ   في نَظْمِها وَعَنْهُ لا تَحُولُ ٣،٨
إذا أرَدْتَ وَصفَ أهلِ الرِّيفِ   أهلِ الرَّذائِلِ وَذَوي القُحوفِ
وَغَيرِهِم مِن فُقَهاءِ الجَهلِ   كَذا القُضاةِ ناقِصين العَقلِ
والعُلَماءِ مِنهم والخُطبا   وغَيرِهِم ثمّ النِسا والأُدَبا
فاعلَمْ هَداكَ اللهُ للصَّوابِ   لا تَصحبِ الفلاّحَ لاكتِسابِ
ولا لِفَضلٍ مِنهُ حقًّا تَعرِفُهْ   ولا لأمرٍ مِن مُهِمٍّ يَكشِفُهْ ٤،٨
ولا تُرَجِّ مِنهُ نَفعًا يَحصَلُ   ولا تَراهُ للشَّدائِدِ يَحمِلُ

Urjūzah Summarizing Part One

Let us close this part with an *urjūzah* covering what we have mentioned in these pages and what we happen to have observed ourselves of their ways, as we promised earlier for sure, saying (and may God our success ensure): 8.1

The humble Yūsuf, son of Khiḍr, says, 8.2
To God my thanks forever and my praise!
Blessings next and peace forever
Upon the Prophet Muḥammad, His Messenger,
And likewise upon his kin and Companions
And all who became his religion's partisans!
To proceed: an *urjūzah* I've composed—
Brief, useful, and gracefully disposed—
The ways and lives of the base to explain,
And those of the country commons, as is plain.
Accept, God guide you, what I say 8.3
In these verses, and from it never turn away!
If you desire of the country people a description,
And of depraved peasant-hat wearers a depiction,
And of others, such as their pastors, so brainless,
And likewise their judges, so witless,
And of their scholars and preachers,
And others still, as well as their women and men of letters,
Then be advised, God guide you to the truth, again:
Do not befriend the peasant for any gain
Nor for any benefit you may discover in him for real, 8.4
Nor for any important matter he may reveal,
And do not ask him to do you any good,
Or think that of weighty matters he can bear the load.

وليس يُرْجَى لِقضاءِ حاجَهْ   وليسَ تَلْقَى عِنـدهُ لَجاجه
بل إنْ قَضاها ويكونُ نادِرًا   تَلْقَى لَه وَجهًا عَبوسًا كاشِرا
وَيطلُبَ الأجرةَ في قَضاها   أو تَتَّخِـذه سَـيِّدًا وَجاهـا
٥،٨ تَصيرُ في خِدمَتِـهِ والنَّفـعِ   في الحَفْرِ والقَلْعِ وضَمِّ الزَّرعِ
وكُلَّمـا أَرَدْتَ مِـنهُ تَخَـلُّصُ   يَرمِيكَ في هَمٍّ لَه مُنَغِّصُ
فـاسمَعْ لِقولي إنْ تُرِدْ فَلاحا   لِحاجَـةٍ فَمـا تَـرى نَجـاحا
ولا تُسَلِّمْـهُ عـلى مُعامَلَهْ   فَلَيس يُعطيكَ سِوى المُماطَلَهْ
وإنْ تَزِدْ مَعَهُ سَرِيعًا تَختَصِمْ   يقولُ حتّى اسدُّ مالَ المُلتَزِمْ
٦،٨ وإنْ فَضَلْ مِ الزرعِ[1] شيءٌ فهو لك   خـذْهُ وإلّا لا تُطَوِّلْ أَمَلَكْ[2]
وإنْ أطَلتَ مَعَـهُ المخاصَمهْ   أتاكَ بالشَّـرِّ مَـعَ المُلاكَمَـهْ
وَيسحَبُ النَّبُّوتَ والحِزاما   وَيُلْزِمُكَ بِمـا لَهُ إلزامـا
ورُبَّمـا يَقولُ للمُلتـزِمِ   هـذا يُريدُ أنْ يُزيلَ نِعَـمي
ويأخذَ الزَّرعَ ويَذهَبْ جُلَّهْ   والمـالُ يَبـقَى يا أَميرُ كلَّهْ
٧،٨ واخْرَبْ سَرِيعًا وتَبورُ الأرضُ   مِن حَيِّ فلّاحٍ عَليهِ القَرضُ
فَيَمنَعُ الأَميـرُ رَبَّ الدَّينِ   عَنهُ ويُصبِحُ حائرًا في شَيْنِ
فَـليسَ فيهِـم أبـدًا نجاحُ   وليسَ يُرْجَى مِنهـم صَلاحُ
بل مِثلُهُم مِثلُ الكِلابِ الجائِعَهْ   وحالُهم حالُ الوُحوشِ الرّاتِعَهْ
ونَطُّهُم في الوحلِ ثمّ الجِلَّهْ   وضَربُهُم للثَّورِ ثـمّ العِجْلَهْ

١ بي: من الزرع. ٢ بي: خذه ولا تطوّل أَمَلَكْ.

He should not be asked to see through an affair,
For you'll find he doesn't persevere,
And should he see it through—though this is rare—
You'll find he does it frowning, with a glowering air,
Demanding his wage for seeing it through;
Do so, or else take him as your lord, and master too,
And be at his service, to work for his gain,
At plowing and reaping and gathering grain! 8.5
And if you should want to get free of his affairs
He'll drag you into one of his irksome cares.
So heed my words: if you seek out a peasant for some business,
You'll never achieve any success.
Entrust him nothing as a loan to repay,
For all he'll give you will be delay.
And if you press him, he'll quickly pick a fight
And tell you, "Not till I pay the tax farmer his right!
You can have the crop, if there's any left— 8.6
Take it! If not, don't hold your breath!"
If on prolonging the dispute you insist,
He'll do you harm and you'll feel his fist!
He'll pull out his belt and his billy
And make you accept what he has, willy-nilly.
To the tax farmer he may say,
"This man with my assets would do away,
And take the crop, most of which will disappear,
While the tax remains outstanding, O Emir.
I'll soon be done for, and the land'll go unsown, 8.7
All for a poor mortal peasant who owes a loan!"
Then the emir will keep his creditor at bay,
Leaving him disgraced and in dismay.
There's nothing about them that success can bring
Nor should one expect of them to do the right thing.
In fact, they're like hungry dogs
And of browsing beasts they're analogues.
They leap about first in mud and then in dung,
Beat first their oxen and then their young.

٨،٨ تَسبيحُهُم قُمْ رُحْ بِنا للسّاقيهْ   واحْسِبْ لنا مالَ البلدِ في الزاويهْ
غالِبُهُم عُورتُه مَكشوفهْ   وشِعْرتُه من طولِها مَلفوفهْ
وإنْ نزلْ لِحَفرِ بيرٍ أو قَنا   ينزِلُ عَريانًا كَما خلقْتنا
وليسَ فوقَ جِسمِهِ ما يَستُرُ   بل أيرُه مُمطَّطٌ مُطرطِرُ
وفِلْسهُ للحرِّ والبَردِ بَرَزْ   وطيزُه مِن الشّقا بها غُرَزْ
٩،٨ رِجلاه لو تَراهُما من القَشَفْ   مِثلُ جُلودٍ أُخِذَتْ مِن العُطَفْ
وهَمُّهُم وشُغْلُهُم في الطَّرْدِ   في حالَةِ الحَرِّ ووَقْتَ البَرْدِ
ونَطُّهُم في الحَرِّ في الغيطانِ   كمِثلِ نَطِّ الوَحْشِ في الوِدْيانِ
وضَمُّهُم للزَّرعِ وقتَ القيظِ   مِثلُ عَفاريتٍ أتَتْ في غَيْظِ
وإنْ يُريدوا المزحَ والمُلاعَبهْ   مِثلُ كُبوشٍ قد أتَتْ مُحارِبهْ
١٠،٨ تَلْقَى لَهُم زَعْقاتٍ مثلَ الرَّعدِ   وعَفْرَةٍ وغَبْرَةٍ وطَرْدِ
وعِندَما يَجتَمِعوا للكورهْ   كأنّهم في غارةٍ أو غَوْرهْ
مِن كَثرةِ الصِّياحِ والزَّعيقِ   والطَّردِ في الزُّقاقِ والطريقِ
أولادُهم حينَ يِلعبوا للدّارهْ   ويِجلسوا للرّقصِ والزُمّارهْ
أو يَسرَحوا يُجَمّعون الجِلّهْ   أو يَلقُطوا للسَّبَلِ أو رِجْلَهْ
١١،٨ مثلُ عَفاريتٍ أتَتْ في زَوْبعهْ   أو فِرْقَةٍ مِنَ القُرودِ الجائعهْ
صُنانُهم إذ يَلْعبونَ فائحُ   كأنّهُم بَهائِمٌ سَوارِحُ

Their magnificat's "Off with us to the waterwheel, 8.8
And calculate for us the village taxes at the tomb of the shaykh to whom we appeal!"
Most of them their privates expose
And their pubic hair's so long it twists as it grows!
If one of them decides to dig a well or ditch,
He goes down bare, without a stitch,
With naught to hide his flesh from sight;
Nay worse—his member's distended and upright!
In the heat and the cold his bum sticks way out far,
And his ass, from wear and tear, shows many a scar.
His legs have become so chapped, as you may see, 8.9
They look like hides taken from some alley.
Their care and concern is to scurry hither and thither
No matter how hot or cold be the weather.
Their gamboling in the heat in the fields
Is like that of wild beasts in the wealds.
Gathering crops in noontime's fire,
They look like demons come in ire.
When they want to be jolly and indulge in play,
They look like rams coming for the fray.
They set to bawling like the thunder's sound, 8.10
As in dust and dirt they go running round.
When they meet for a game of ball,
It looks like a raid or a free-for-all
Because they shout so loud and bray
And gambol in the alley and highway.
Their children, if playing at *dārah*
And sitting around to dance and blow the *zummārah*,
Or if setting off to gather dung cakes are seen,
Or purslane or grains to glean,
Are like afreets that rode in on a tempest, 8.11
Or a band of monkeys by hunger press'd.
Their stench when playing wafts all around,
As if they were cattle to the pastures bound.

ولو تَراهُمْ إذ أتوا يُعلّلوا تَعليلَةُ الصِّبيانِ تِلكَ العِلَلُ
وفي المَواسِمْ إن أتوا لِلعيدِ يُعَيِّدوا في النَّطّ كالقُرودِ
والمُردُ تَرقُصْ بَينَهم كما النِّسا فَعيدُهُم وحَظُّهُم كما الفُسا
طِباعُهُم مِثلُ طِباعِ البَقَرِ عِشرَتُهُم فيها مَزيدُ الضَّرَرِ ١٢٫٨
ونَطُّهُم كَغارَةٍ إذا أتَتْ مِثلَ قُرودٍ في الفَيافي أقبَلَتْ
وقَتْلُهُم للنَّفسِ عندَ الكِلْمَةْ إن قالَ شَخصٌ يا لَضِدِّ الذِمّةْ
شَخصٌ يميلُ منهُمُ لسَعدِ ويُظهِرُ البَغضاءَ لَهْ ويُبدي
ثمّ يصيحُ يا لَسَعدٍ يا جُدامِ ودونَكم دا من بَني حَرامِ
خذوهُ مِن قَبلِ تَرون باسَهْ ثُمَّ اقتلوهُ وأَخمِدوا أنفاسَهْ ١٣٫٨
فذا يصيحُ يا لَسَعدٍ أَسعِدوا وآخرٌ يا لَحَرامِ أَنجِدوا
كأنّ ذينِ الكلمتينِ عندَهم دِينٌ عليه يقتلون بَعضَهم
ويُخرِبوا البِلادَ بالغاراتِ ويَقفوا للقَتلِ في الطُرقاتِ
وإنْ أتاهُم عَسكرٌ يحارِبُ قاموا إلى روسِ الجِبالِ هَرَبوا
وعندما يَرجِعُ للبِلادِ فَيرجِعوا للشَّرِّ والفَسادِ ١٤٫٨
فلا جَزاهُم غَيرُ قَطعِ الرَّأسِ وشَنقِهِم وضَربِهِم والحَبسِ
فَقَسوةُ القَلبِ لهم طَبيعةْ وقِلّةُ الخَيرِ لَهم ذريعةْ
ومَشيُهم في الحَرِّ مِن غَيرِ وَطا ونومُهم في الغَيطِ من غيرِ غَطا
وطَردُهم في ظُلَمِ اللَّيالي حَولَ الشَّوْنِ والجُرْنِ والتّلالِ

If you see them when they make excuses,
You'll see how childish are their excuses.
And on their holidays, when they come to the Feasts,
They spend them in frisking just like beasts,[500]
And the beardless boys like women among them dance,
So their Feasts, and their lot, are no better than farts.
They're like cattle in temperament— **8.12**
In keeping them company lies great detriment.
Their gamboling's like a raid encroaching,
Or like apes across the plains approaching.
They'll kill a man as soon as he speaks,
If he says, "This of dishonesty reeks!"
One among them against Saʿd may turn,
Showing them hatred and disdain,
Shouting, "Aid me, O Saʿd, O Judām!"
And, "Watch out! He's a son of Ḥarām!
Get him before he can do you a hurt, **8.13**
Then take him and choke the wind in his throat!"
One shouts, "Saʿd, to my aid!"
Another, "Ḥarām, to my side!"
As though these few words to them were a testament of faith
To defend which each will send the other to his death.
They ruin the villages with their forays
And lie in wait to murder on the highways.
If a troop of cavalry come to them to fight,
They set off for the mountain peaks in flight.[501]
And when their villages they regain, **8.14**
To evil and corruption they turn again.
Thus, their only reward is decapitation
And hanging and beating and incarceration,
For cruelty has their hearts in trammel,
And poverty to them is just a stalking camel.
They walk in the heat with no shoes on their feet
And sleep in the fields with no covering sheet.
Under cover of dark they scurry around
Among the barns and threshing floors and from mound to mound.

جُلودُهم تَسَخَّمَت بالحَرِّ   كأنَّهم قد خُلِقَت مِن صَخرِ ١٥٫٨
ونَطُّهم في الطينِ ثمّ الوَحلِ   وضَربُهم للثورِ ثمّ العِجلِ
وحَفرُهم في البيرِ والسَّواقي   وَمَشيُهم أيضًا بلا طَواقي
وقد يَصيرُ الشَّخصُ مِنهم شَهرًا   لا يَحلِقُ الرّأسَ وقيل عُمرا
ولا يَقصُّ شارباً ولحيهْ   ولا يُنَظِّفُ فِلْسَهُ من خَرْيَهْ
وشِدّةُ الشَّخصِ على الخِناقِ   مِنهم وَطولُ الشَّرِّ باتِّفاقِ ١٦٫٨
وضَربُهُ للأب ثمّ الأمّْ   وصَبرُهُ للحبسِ ثمّ اللَّطمِ
وأَكْلُهُ في العَدسِ والبِسِلّهْ   كَمِثْلِ أكلِ كَلبَةٍ أو عِجْلَهْ
ومَن تَراهُ مِنهُمُ يُصَلِّي   تَراهُ لا يَعرِفْ فُروضَ الغُسْلِ
ولا يُمَيِّزْ طاهرًا من نَجِسِ   ولا يُنَظِّفْ ثوبَه من دَنَسِ
وإنْ جلَسْ يوماً على الفِسقيّهْ   يجلسْ وتلقى طيزَهُ مَرْبيّهْ ١٧٫٨
كذاكَ مَنْ بجَنْبِهِ وآخَرْ   وذا يخاصمُ وذا يشاجِرْ
وإنْ سَكَنْ في حيّهم ذو فضلِ   فَهْوَ حقيرٌ عِندَهُم في ذُلِّ
ولا يُطيعوا الشَّرعَ إلّا غَصْباً   أو عِندَما قد يأكُلونَ الضَّربا
وهم عَبيدُ قابِضِ الأموالِ   فعِندَهم كالعَمِّ أوْ الخالِ
ويَجلسونَ عَندَه في أدَبِ   ومَن يَقِفْ مِنهمْ يكونُ كالصَّبي ١٨٫٨
فليسَ فيهمْ رحمةٌ لعالِمِ   إلّا لأهلِ الشَّرِّ والمظالِمِ

Their hides have turned as black in the heat 8.15
As though they were from rock create.
They leap about first in mud and then in mire
And they beat the calf after beating its sire.
They dig pits for waterwheels and wells
And walk about without caps on their skulls.
One of them may go a month at a time
Without shaving his head (some say, a lifetime).
He may well not cut his moustache or beard,
Or clean his asshole to remove the turd.
On quarreling their hearts are set,
And on endless evil without let. 8.16
Their violence they reserve first for their fathers, then for their mothers,
While their patience is kept first for prison, then for beatings by others.
A peasant eats his lentils and peas as though
He were a bitch or a young cow.
If you see one of them saying his prayers,
You'll see he knows nothing of ablution's laws.
He doesn't distinguish between pure and soiled,
Nor clean his clothes when with filth they're spoiled.
If he takes a seat one day at the water spout, 8.17
He'll sit down and you'll see his bottom's puffed out.
The same for the one beside him, and the next,
This one disputing, the other with that one vexed.
If a good man should attempt to dwell in their parts,
They hold scorn and contempt for him in their hearts.
They never obey the Law, unless impelled,
Or on pain of beating are so compelled.
They are the slaves of the tax collector
Who to them's like a father's or mother's brother.
When sitting in his home politely they themselves deploy 8.18
Or stand before him like a little boy.
They have no mercy on a scholar,
Only on those who practice evil and the oppressor.

فالشَّرُّ والعُدوانُ فيهمْ شائِعُ والخيرُ والإحسانُ منهمْ ضائِعُ
أخلاقُهم تُرْوى عن ابنِ جَحْرَ طِباعُهم تُرْوى عن ابنِ بَقَرْ
دَناسَةُ اللِّبْس لهُم مَرْوِيّهْ عن ابن شَلْتوتٍ لَهُ مَعْزِيّهْ ٨،١٩
ذُقونُهم تُرْوى عن ابن وَحْلِ والضِّرط ابو فَسْوٍ وَابنُ زِبْلِ
فلا جَزاهُم ربُّنا خيراً ولا لِقاهُم سِوى الهُمومَ والبَلا
فَقيهُهُم ذو الكُمِّ والعِمامهْ إذا أتَى كأنّه غِمامهْ
والعِلمُ عندَ الله ليسَ يُعْرَفْ سِوى بِذاكَ الإسمِ حينَ يُوصَفْ
وإنْ جلَسْ يوماً على الثَّباتِ كأنَّه ناطورُ في مَقاتِ ٨،٢٠
يَقولُ قالَ الله عِينوا الشّاري ولا تُعِينوا البائِعَ الفَشّارِ
وقَد رَوَيتُ اليومَ لكُمْ رِوايهْ في سيرَةِ الضّاهِرْ لها دِرايهْ
وفي غَدٍ أروي لَكُم قِصّهْ تُسَمّى قِصّةُ عَنترٍ وعَبْلَهْ
والدَلْهَمَهْ أروي عَن البَطّالِ وسيرَةَ الرّاهِبِ والجَمّالِ
واشرَحْ لَكُم واقلْ لَكُم عن شِيحَهْ وأمّ جابرْ بنتِ ابو فُرَيْحَهْ ٨،٢١
واروي لَكُم ما قَدْ أتَى عَن النَّبيّ قالَ كذا قالَ كذا قالَ أبي
وقالَ جدّي ذاكْ أبو غِنْدافِ صَلّوا وَلَو كُنتم على مِقدافِ
وَلَوْ بِلا وُضوءْ بِلا طَهارهْ كما رُوِيتْ عن جدّتي شَرارهْ
قاضِيهمُ إذا أتَى لِشغلِ كأنّه رَئيسِ جَوقِ الطَّبلِ
ينزِلُ عَن البغلهْ أو الحمارهْ كأنّه الرّاهِبْ أبو زَرارهْ ٨،٢٢

Of evil and aggression they have much,
But with virtue and good deeds they're out of touch.
Their morals they derive from Ibn Ḥajar,[502]
Their dispositions they derive from Ibn Baqar.
Filthiness of clothing is a habit they take 8.19
From Son-of-a-Rag, may we hear of his wake!
Their beards from Son-of-Mire
And Fart, Son-of-Gas,[503] and Son-of-Droppings they acquire—
So may Our Lord not reward them with good fortune
And may they meet only with woes and misfortune!
Their pastor, with his sleeves and headgear,
Is like an ox's blinkers, should he appear.
What's knowledge in God's sight is to him unknown—
He has no share of it but the name by which he's known.[504]
And if one day he sits and himself to the ground attaches, 8.20
He looks like a scarecrow of the melon patches.
He says, "God says,[505] 'Aid the buyer,
Aid not the big-talking seller!'
Today I've given you a reading
Of the Ballad of al-Ḍāhir,[506] full of understanding,
And tomorrow you with a story I'll regale
Called "Antar and 'Ablah's Tale'
And the 'Dalhamah' according to al-Baṭṭāl[507] you'll hear,
As well as the 'Ballad of the Monk and the Cameleer.'
And I'll tell you—with commentary—about Shīḥah[508] 8.21
And Umm Jābir, daughter of Abū Furayḥah,
And I'll pass on to you what of the Prophet has been related:
'He said this' and 'He said that' and 'My father narrated'[509]
And my grandfather, old Abū Ghindāf, used to say,
'Even when rowing, pray!
Though without ablution or cultic purity
As it came down to us on Grandma Sharārah's authority.'
Their judge, when to work he comes,
Resembles a band leader with his drums.
When he descends from his mule or donkey
He's Abū Zarārah the Monk, you'd say. 8.22

فعِندما يجلسُ في انتِفاخِ   يُفَرَّشُ له مِن قِطَعِ الأنخاخِ
وبعد ذا يأتي إليه المُشتكي   ثمّ يَقِفْ على عَصاهُ مُتّكي
أو بعضُهم على العَصا يلفُّ   رِجلاً لَهُ وَهوَ ثقيلٌ تَحَفُ
يقولُ يا قاضي بِحرف الجيم   هاتْ لي لِعندي إبنَ ٱبو دُعْمومِ
واحْياةِ دقنكْ جِلّتي سرقْها   وَارْبَعْ قُفَفْ من زِبْلنا فَرَّقْها ٢٣،٨
وقد أخذْ واَحْياتِ راسكْ حِدْوتي   وإشْتواني قد أَخَذْ ولِبْدتي
أُحكمْ بحُكم اللهِ يا قاضي البلدْ   والّا أرصّكْ ألفَ نَبُّوتْ بالعددْ
يقولُ هذا قد لَزِمَهُ الحدُّ   حيثٍ سَرَقْ ومِنْهُ تُقْطَعْ يدُّ
رح يا قِنِفْ يا عَرَصْ يا ابن الزبلهْ   إدْفَعْ لَهُ قيمَةَ هذي[1] العَمَلهْ
وصالحِ الخصْمَ وهاتْ لي فرخهْ   والّا على دقنكْ أشُخُّ شخّهْ ٢٤،٨
وإن عقد عقدا فليس يدري   غيرَ قولِهِ أنكحتُ بنت النِمِر
وليس يَعْرِفْ شاهدًا ولا وَلِي   وليس يَعرِفْ صِحّةً من عِلَلِ
إذا قضى قضيّةً وخِلْتَها   فاقرأ سريعًا عندها يا لَيْتَها
فقيرهمُ ألزُّنْطُ والإبريقُ   والنُطّ والصريخُ والزعيقُ
وذا مريدي ومريدُ جدّي   وذا الولدْ بدايتي وعبدي ٢٥،٨
يصير طول الدهرخلف ظُهري   ولا يصلّي مغربًا ولا ظُهري
إلّا بإذني أو عليهْ تشويشُهْ   ومن رآهُ قالَ ذا درويشُهْ
وعندما قد يحضر الموالدا   من خلفِهِ تلقاهُ حقًا لابدا

---

١ بي: هذه.

Then when he sits, all puffed up and fat,
  They lay down for him a bit of old mat.
Then up comes the plaintiff,
  And stands and leans on his staff,
Or one of them around his stick a leg will wrap,
  A boor, coarse as a peasant cap.
He says, 'O Gāḍī!' with the letter *jīm*,[510]
  Summon me the son of Abū Duʿmūm!
By the life of your beard, my dung by theft he removed 8.23
  And four baskets of our droppings he strewed
And, by the life of your head, he took my shoe
  And my *ishtiwān*[511] and my felt cap too!
Judge of the village, God's law you must impose,
  Or my staff will deal you a thousand blows!"
Says the judge, "We should apply the Qur'anic penalty as stipulated,
  Since he stole, and his hand should be amputated.
Go, you dolt, you pimp, you son of excrement,
  And pay him back for what you did to his detriment
And make up and bring me a fowl for doing this, 8.24
  Or else on your beard I'll piss and piss!"
When he presides over the marriage vows,
  "I hereby wed you the daughter of al-Nimr" is all he knows.
He's ignorant of witnesses and sponsors,[512]
  And cannot tell what's truth, what flaws.
When he delivers a judgment and you've acted upon it,
  Say over it, "Ah, would that it . . ." that very minute![513]
Their dervish is no more than his bonnet and his pitcher;
  His leaping, screaming, and clapping complete the picture
Along with "That's my disciple and was my grandpa's before, 8.25
  And that boy's my minion and abject follower:
He'll walk behind me forever and a day
  And never at sunset or noontime pray
Unless I permit him; or else him I'll punish,
  And all who see him will say, 'That's his dervish!'"
And indeed when to a *mawlid* he goes
  You'll find the boy skulking behind him close.

ويدخلُ الجمع به ينتفشُ وباللِّسان بينَهم يدردشُ
٢٦،٨ فيزعَقوا ويضربوا الكفوفا ثمّ يقوموا كلُّهم صُفوفا
ثمّ يقولوا أخبر الشيخ الولي عن أوليا جاءت مِنَ ٱرْضِ الموْصِلِ
هذا يطيرُ بين السما والأرضِ على النجايبِ ما عليهْ من فَرْضِ
ولا بقى يحتاجْ إلى عبادهْ هذا بقى في رُتبة السيادهْ
هذا فقيرٌ بالقولِ والإشارهْ هذا وَلي وقيد الحمارهْ
٢٧،٨ وإنْ تَسَلْهُ شرطَ في الطّريقِ يقولُ لا أعرفْ سوى الإبريقِ
وهزّ وسطي ثمّ طَرْق اليدّ ومَيلانُ لبدني وشدّي
وقدّم الماجورْ أحُطّ كفّي واطْلَعْ بلُقّمْه مِثْل دَوْر الخُفّ
وبالدّراويشِ بجنبِ الشّطّ أمشي وإبريقي تحتَ إبطي
وٱنزِل على مَن لي عليهْ سيادهْ وٱقول لهُ ألبَيْته وهات العادهْ
٢٨،٨ وهاتْ لِيَ الديك مع العليقهْ ولَيْسَ أعرفْ غيرَ ذي الطريقهْ
ومذهبي يا سعدُ يا حرامُ ولا أقولُ يا فتى[1] حرامُ
أخذتُ عن شيخِيَ هذا[2] الفِعلِ فَهوَ حقيقٌ مُشبهٌ بالعِجْلِ
ومنهمو طائفةٌ خوامِسُ كلُّهمو بجمعهمْ أبالِسُ
لا يعرفوا الصّلاهْ ولا الصّياما ولا حلالاً ولا حَراما
٢٩،٨ الشّخصُ منهم ينكح العمّاتِ وينكح الأخواتِ والخالاتِ
ويستبيح الفعلَ وَهوَ كافرُ وقتله قد حلّ هذا ظاهرُ

١ بي: يا ضِدّ؛ ب: يا ذا؛ ك با: يا ضو؛ م: يا فتى. ٢ بي: هذا.

He takes him into the throng to cut a dash
    And together they babble ecstatic balderdash.
At this the others shriek and clap their hands, 8.26
    And each one takes his place in row and stands.
Next, "The shaykh, God's Friend, brings news," they say,
    "Of Friends of God come from over Mosul way.
This one flies between earth and sky
    Riding his steeds—one to whom no duties apply,
And who no longer to worship is bound—
    Knowledge of the true path within himself is found."
This one's a dervish only in speech and in gesture;
    That one's a Friend of God and "a she-donkey leader."[514]
If you ask him some condition of the Way, 8.27
    "The pitcher's all I know," he'll say,
"And how to shake my waist and clap
    And cock my turban and my cap,
Saying, 'Bring on the crock, so I can stick in my paw
    And pull out a lump big as a camel's foot or more.'
With the dervishes beside
    The shore, pitcher under arm, I stride
And descend on him who's mine to command
    And of him 'Lodging and the usual gift!' demand,"
And "Bring me a chicken, as well as the feed! 8.28
    No other Way than this do I heed,
And my school is[515] either Sa'd or Ḥarām,
    And I never say, 'Good fellow, in religion that's pure harm!'
From my shaykh I got this act!"
    —and thus he resembles a calf, in fact.
Among them is a sect, the Khawāmis,
    All of whom are devilish.
They know not how to fast and pray
    Or what's forbidden and what's okay.
Any of them will wed his aunts paternal 8.29
    And wed his sisters and his aunts maternal.
He claims the deed is lawful, but he's an infidel,
    And his killing's permitted, that's incontrovertible.

فكلُّهم بجمعهم أراذلُ   وليس فيهم رَجُلٌ يماثلُ
لأهل فضلٍ أو ذوي كمالِ   بل كلُّهم في رُتَبِ الجهّالِ
ناظمهم إن قالَ حقًّا شِعْرا   فشعرُهُ يُشْبِهُ طعم العَذْرا
٣٠،٨ أو حشْوَ قولٍ جا بلا روايهْ   أو رَصَّ قُلْقَيلٍ بلا درايهْ
إن لم تكن ذقت الخرا في العُمْرِ   فذق كلامَ نظمهم والنثْرِ
سماعه إذا بدا رزيّهْ   لكنْ له ما بينهم مزيّهْ
لكونهم أجلافُ معْ أوباشِ   مِثْلُ حمير الجُرْنِ والكِباشِ
أسماؤهمْ تُخبِرُ عن أوصافهمْ   ألقابهمْ تُنْبِيكَ عن أشرافهمْ
٣١،٨ وهيْ حُنَيجِلْ وجُلَيجِلْ وقطا   والحاجّ عُنْطوزُ بنِ آبو فَرْدَةْ وطا
وعَفَرْ مَعْ دُعْمومٍ مَعْ زُعَيْطِ   كذا قُسَيْطٌ وأبو مُعَيْطِ
ثمّ قلبيط وشلّاطه قد وردْ   كذا لهاطهْ وزعّاطهْ في العددْ
شُقَلَيْطْ مَعْ مُقَلَيطِ مَعْ خُبَيْطِ   صَفّارُ مَعْ بَهْوارُ مَعْ شُلَيْبِطِ
بُرْبورُ مَعْ عَمّوزٍ مَعْ قرّوشْ   سُمْعوتُ مَعْ بُرْغوتٍ مَعْ غَلّوش
٣٢،٨ كذا النَّبْشُ ثمّ العَفْشُ عنهم ذكروا   ثمّ حُنَيْن بن بُنَيْنٍ أخبروا
كذا سمعنا أنّهم يُكَنّوا   أبو شوالي ومتارِدْ يَعْنوا
كذا أبو عَفْرٍ أبو دعمومِ   وَابو الدواهي معْ أبو الميشومِ
شادوفْ أبو جاروفْ أبو نطّاحْ   مِشْكاحْ أبو رمّاحْ أبو ريّاحْ
من جهلهم ميمَ محمّدْ يكسروا   والحاءُ أيضا قد أتى مكرّرُ

The whole lot of them together are base,
  And for none of them may be made a case
That he's a man of virtue or one of the perfected.
  Indeed, all are from the ranks of the ignorant selected.[516]
Their poet, should he recite any verse, for sure
  That verse would resemble the taste of ordure
Or consist of any old words—not those preserved by transmission— 8.30
  Or clods of mud stacked without precision.
If, in your life, you've never tasted shit,
  Then taste their verse and prose—that's it!
The sound of it, if manifest, is hard to bear,
  Though among themselves they hold it dear—
But then they're oafs and the scum of the masses
  Resembling rams or threshing-floor asses.
Their names give you an idea of each one's particular quality;
  Their nicknames inform you as to their nobility.[517]
These are[518] Junayjil and Julayjil and Qaṭā[519] 8.31
  And al-Ḥājj ʿAnṭūz, son of Abū Fardat Waṭā,[520]
And ʿAfr, with Duʿmūm and Zuʿayṭ,
  And likewise Qusayṭ and Abū Muʿayṭ;
Also Qulbayṭ and Shallāṭah may occur,
  And Lahhāṭah and Zaʿʿāṭah recur;
Shuqlayṭ, plus Muqlayṭ, plus Khubayṭ,[521]
  Ṣaffār plus Bahwār plus Shulbayṭ,
Buzbūz plus ʿAmmūz plus Qarrūsh,[522]
  Sumʿūṭ plus Burghūt plus Ghallūsh.
To al-Nabsh[523] and al-ʿAfsh men say they own, 8.32
  While Ḥunayn,[524] son of Bunayn, is well known.
We hear that their *kunyah*s are varied:
  Abū Shawālī (the last word means *matārid*),[525] Abū ʿAfr, and Abū
    Duʿmūm,
Abū l-Dawāhī[526] plus Abū Mayshūm,[527]
  Abū Shādūf,[528] Abū Jārūf, and Abū Naṭṭāḥ,
Abū Mishkāḥ, Abū Rammāḥ, and Abū Rayyāḥ;[529]
  In their ignorance, the "m" of Muḥammad with an "i" they say,
  And the "ḥ" too may come that way.[530]

مُحَمّدَيْنِ قد سمعتُ منهُمُ   كذا بهايم وترمش عنهُمُ ٣٣.٨
والقَلْطَ والضرّاطَ كما روينا   ويُبدِلون صالحا بسينا
فهذه أسماءُ مِثْل الوحلِ   أو أنها شِبْهُ ضُراط النملِ
وإن ترى الأسماء لا تُعَلَّلُ   فإنّها واللهِ بئسَ العِلَلُ
وإن ينادي الشَّخصُ منهمْ آخرا   يجيبه بلفظ هاه كالخرا
وهَيْهْ وإشمالكْ تعيّطْ قل لِي   نشربْ أجيكْ لما يشُخّْ عِجْلِي ٣٤.٨
قد تُنْسَبُ إليهمُ لغاتِ   كقولهمْ في الإرثِ ذا ميراتِي
وصُبَّ في البوشهْ وهاتْ جوادي   ما ضالَ أيْ ما زالَ هذا الوادي
يعنونَ بالجوادِ مركوب حَضَرْ   كذاكَ هات الكرّ ألِفْو من سَحَرْ
جعبوتي راحت من المرجونهْ   سيري وأسكِنِي حدا الطابونهْ
قومي انحتي لي في الزريبهْ نُقْرَهْ   لأجلِ ما أقومْ وفيها أخْرَهْ[1] ٣٥.٨
غدًا ترى الجدعانْ تنطّ في الفرحْ   يوم الهروبه في الزريبهْ نَنْشَرِحْ
هدهودْ مجمصْ ما يُرى فيهِ بجلّهْ   اليومَ لُهْ عَنْزَيْنْ وعِنْدُهْ عِجْلَهْ
والحاجُّ عنطوزْ بانْظُرُهْ في نَفَشَهْ   أليومَ راحْ هُرَيْطْ وجابْ لُهْ كِرْشَهْ
وحطّها في الدشْتِ عِنْدُهْ فَرْحَهْ   بِنْتُهْ أخذها إبنُ راسِ المِسْحَهْ
أليومْ بلدْنا شيخُها ابو عَوْكَلْ   وابو فُسُوٍّ وسطها يتْخنْجَلْ ٣٦.٨
والحاجُّ قلوّطْ طَرِفْها وهَوْدَجْ   والحاجُّ عُنْطُوزُ بْنُ خَرِق النَوْرَجْ
وإنّما أسماؤهم مناسبهْ   ذواتُهم وافعالُهم مقاربهْ

---

١ بي: أقومُ من سحر فيها؛ ب: اقوم بالليل فيها؛ ك با م: اقوم من سحر فيها.

Muḥammadayn[531] among them I've heard, 8.33
Likewise Bahāyim[532] and Turmush have occurred.
Al-Qalṭ and al-Darrāṭ we have already seen,
And they say Ṣāliḥ as well with *sīn*.[533]
These names put one in mind of mud and mire,
Or thoughts of ant farts inspire.
The "diagnosis" of names, you may think, isn't easy,
But these, I swear, would make anyone feel queasy!
When they call one another,
They respond with a shit-like "Hāh?" to each other
And "Hayh?" and "Say, why're you wailing? 8.34
Let's drink!" "I'll come when my calf's done staling!"
Certain dialectalisms to them are ascribed,
Such as *mīrātī*, which from *irth* is derived,[534]
And "Pour it in the bawshah!" and "Bring my jawād to me!"[535]
And *mā ḍāl* for *mā zāl*, as *in mā ḍāl hādhā l-wādī*.[536]
By *jawād*, they mean a kind of slipper that's worn;
Similarly, "Fetch my *karr*,[537] I'll put it on before dawn.
My *ja'būbah*'s[538] gone from the *marjūnah*![539]
Go sit inside, *ḥidā*[540] ('next to') the *ṭābūnah*.[541]
Get up, woman, and in the barn dig me a pit, 8.35
So I can get up early and have a shit!
Tomorrow you'll see the brave lads at the wedding frolic;
We'll have fun in the barn on the day of the picnic.[542]
Hadhūd[543] is lounging at ease; you won't see on him a speck of dung—
Today two goats and a calf to him belong.
And al-Ḥājj 'Anṭūz all puffed up with pride I spy—
Today he went to Hurbayṭ some tripe to buy,
To put in the kettle: he's got a wedding to celebrate—
His daughter's engaged to the son of Mattock-Pate.[544]
Today our village shaykh is Abū 'Awkal, 8.36
While Abū Fusuww[545] hops about in the middle,[546]
And al-Ḥājj Qallūṭ's on the edge, and Hawdaj,
And al-Ḥājj 'Anṭūz, son of Kharq al-Nawraj."
Their names merely accord with their persons,
And similarly appropriate are their actions.

نساؤهم أيضًا لهنّ أسما   فخذ هُدِيتَ عِدَّها إملا
زعرهْ وبعرهْ مَيْكلهْ خُطَيْطهْ   بلوهْ وعِلْوَهْ شايِعَهْ حُوَيْطهْ
شمّهْ زَرارهْ مَعْ شَبارهْ سمّوا   كذا مُعَيْكهْ ورُكَيْكهْ ضمُّوا ٣٧.٨
ثمّ يسمّوا بينهم شِلْبايهْ   وقد يسمّوا بينهم عطايهْ
كذا شُقَيْره وغاسوله قد وَرَدْ   حمدهْ ولِبْدهْ وعطيّهْ في العددْ
وطالبهْ وهاربهْ حطيبّهْ   كذا فُريجهْ بِنْتْ أبو عريّهْ
وقد سمعتُ رجلاً ينادي   حجّهْ خُريوه إغسلي الزبادي
وإحلبي البَقْرَهْ وهاتي العجلهْ   روحي حدا الجدعانْ وسوقي نجلهْ ٣٨.٨
قومي وحطّي العدسَ في القَفْقولهْ   وأمُّ دَعْبهْ بنْتْ أبو بعبولهْ
يا داهِيَهْ يا داهِيَهْ تعالي   جَتْكي من الحيطْ بنْتْ أبو شوالي
قومي تعالي للعَشا والموضعْ   إبْنَكْ بِيخْرى قوم كُلِ أَنْتَ وَاشْبَعْ
وهاتْ لنا قطعهْ وخذْ علارهْ   وجمّع الجلّهْ وشوفْ عبارهْ
روحي وهاتي يا بوادي البَقْرَهْ   إنتي وجَوْزَةُ وبنتكْ جَزْرَهْ ٣٩.٨
روحي وشوفي يا دعبه النُقْرَهْ   في وسطها جلّهْ طريّهْ خَضْرَهْ
وحولها شوفي الحماره والبَقَرْ   حتّى عليها يُزْرِبوا وقت السَحَرْ
فهذه الأسماءُ للنسا فَخْرا   قد شُبِّهَتْ بالوَحَل في الصحرا
وشتمهم لأمردٍ إذا بَحْ   يا خور اسريحه وبقره شلحْ

Their women have their names too,[547]
So come, God guide you, count, as I dictate to you.
There's Za'rah and Ba'rah, Maykalah, Khuṭayṭah,
Balwah[548] and 'Ilwah,[549] Shāyi'ah[550] and Ḥuwayṭah;
Shammah, Zarārah, and Shabārah are also names with which they're graced, 8.37
Likewise Mu'aykah and Rukaykah are names they've embraced.
Another name they use is Shilbāyah,
And they also use 'Aṭāya.
Likewise Shuqayrah[551] and Ghāsūlah occur,
And Ḥamdah,[552] Libdah, and 'Aṭiyyah[553] recur,
And Ṭālibah[554] and Hāribah[555] and Ḥaṭabiyyah,[556]
Likwise Furayjah,[557] daughter of Abū 'Arabiyyah;
And I've heard a man shout,
"Ḥājjah Khuraywah, wash the pots out
And milk the cow and bring me the calf! 8.38
Go where the brave lads are and . . . ![558]
Get up and put the lentils in the *qafqūlah*,[559]
You and Umm Da'bah, daughter of Abū Bu'būlah![560]
Calamity! Calamity![561] Don't you hear me call?
Abū Shawālī's daughter's a-coming from the wall!
Up with you and come eat dinner and go to bed!"
She says,[562] "Your son's shitting! Go eat your fill instead!
Bring me a piece, and take 'Alārah,
And gather dung cakes and look to 'Abārah!"
"Bawādī,"[563] he may say, "go fetch the cow, 8.39
You, Jawzah,[564] and your daughter Jazarah,[565] right now!
Da'bah, go look in the pit—
In the middle there's some nice wet shit,
And see what donkeys and cows are there,
So that at dawn they may be penned up near."
These names, which their women think are just dandy,
Have been compared to churned-up mud in some place sandy.
Their abuse to a boy, if he offers sass,
Is "Hey, fag, . . . cow, flash us your ass![566]

٤٠٫٨ يا هَـرًا رايحْ فينْ يا ابو كارهْ   يا واسع الصُرمِ افْتَكِرْ في الحارهْ
وانْتـا بِتَنْفِشْ للُمشا في الشونهْ   وكم ينيكوكْ في الدرهْ بالعونـهْ
إسرِح ولاقيني على غيط الجزرْ   وآدّيكَ فَرْقِـلّهْ مليحـهْ للبـقرْ
وآدّيكْ مشمّرْ وأجِبْ لكْ لبدهْ   ويومَ عيد الله طعّمتك كبـدهْ
وإشتوانْ أعطيكَ من سنّ السمكْ   تبقى حدا الجدعانِ ما حدْ يشتمكْ
٤١٫٨ وانشدَّ لي يا عِلقْ أنا أبو جَلَصْ   أنا مَشَدّ الكفْـر آنا مجعْمَـصْ
وعـندنا عـنْزينْ وجـيرْوانـهْ   وآدّيكْ كمانْ سكّينْ أبو شقوانهْ
وآدورُ ويّاكْ في البلد نداورْ   وآنزِّلكْ تلعبْ وَسَطْ ألسامرْ
إن طعتني يا خورُ خلّيتكْ جَدَعْ   وآلاّ أضالْ أهجيكْ أنا ابْنَ آبو بَجَعْ
فيسمع الأمردْ منه ما قد حَصَلْ   يمضي معُهْ فيقدحُهْ جنب البَصَلْ
٤٢٫٨ أو جنبَ مَدْوِدْ أو حدا مِذْرَهْ   إذا ركبْ فوقُهْ عطا لُهْ طيزَهْ
ولقشُهمْ على النسا يا شلْقَهْ   جيتي مِنَيْنْ يا خايِنَهْ يا مِرْقَهْ
افتكري داكْ النهار يا خورهْ   والحاجّ عُنْطُوزْ ماسِكْكْ في الجورهْ
والحاجْ فُسُوّ الدين وآبو دواهي   عمّالْ يجْخُوا فيكِ حدا المواهي
والحاجّ قلّوطْ وَابْنُ ضرّاب البَقَرْ   وَابْنُ ضرّاط النّمَلْ ناكوكِ في السَحَرْ
٤٣٫٨ وإنتي شلكه دايِرَهْ بتضربي   كيف البقرْ ولا تجينا تقربي
تعا لعندي يا مليحة البلدْ   وآدّيكِ للعجْلهْ تِباعَكِ دي الوتدْ
وآدّيكِ شِرْشينْ من بَصَلْ وقُوطهْ   ويومَ عيد اللهْ أجيبْ لكْ فوطهْ

Hey, pansy, where're you off to, you with the fanny? 8.40
Hey, big asshole, remember that time in the alley?
And how you preen yourself for the foot soldiers in the barn?
And how many fuck you at one go in the corn?
Get going and meet me in the carrot field,
And I'll give you a nice drover's whip to wield.
And I'll give you *mishammar,*[567] and I'll bring you a cap,
And on God's Feast[568] I'll give you liver to sup,
And I'll give you an *ishtiwān*[569] from the teeth of a fish
So none of the brave lads will dare call you a swish.
Get hitched up with me, faggot—Abū Jalaṣ is my name, 8.41
I'm bailiff of the hamlet, I've got wealth and fame.
We've got two goats and a besom to sweep,
And I'll give you Abū Shaqwānah's knife too to keep,
And around the village with you I'll ramble
And I'll send you out among the night revelers to gambol.
Obey me, fairy, and I'll make you a tough guy,
Or else, me, son of Abū Baja', your name I'll destroy!"
Then the kid learns what the man's done in the past.[570]
Goes with him and, next to the onions, gets screwed in the ass;
Or by a manger or next to a flail— 8.42
The man gets on top and he gives him his tail.
When flirting with women, they say, "You foul-mouthed witch!
Where'd you come from, you dimwit, you bitch?
Remember the other day, you slut,
When al-Ḥājj 'Anṭūz held you down in the cooking pit,
While Abū Dawāhī and al-Ḥājj Fusuww al-Dīn,[571]
Kept squirting it up you by the panniers of beans,
And al-Ḥājj Qallūṭ and the son of Cow-Beater
Fucked you at dawn, with the son of Ant-Farter,
While you ran circling and kicking out 8.43
Like a cow, and wouldn't come to us or stay near about?
Come over to my place, you belle of the village,
And I'll give you this peg for that calf of yours,
And I'll give you tomatoes and bunches of onions (two),
And on God's Feast a towel I'll bring to you,

وآنامْ ويّاكْ على القَصَلْ شِوَيّهْ   ألْيومْ أنا في الكفرِ شيخْ بَقِيّهْ

فَانْظُرْ هداكَ اللهْ لذي القحافهْ   في وصفهمْ لكنّهم ريّافهْ

فكن سريعاً منهمُ على حذرْ   فعشرة الفلاّحِ تأتي بالضررْ ٤٤٫٨

وعاشرْ أهلَ اللطفِ والصلاحْ   وكنْ مَعَ اهْلِ الخيرِ والفلاحْ

وكلّ هذا في قُرىً قد بعُدتْ   عن نيلِنا وبالجبال اتّصلتْ

وفي بلادٍ ليسَ فيها عالِمْ   يدلّهمْ بل كلّهم بهائمْ

وليس في البلاد مثلُ مِصْرِ   وأهلِها كُفِيتَ شرَّ الحَصْرِ

لأنّها كِنانةُ اللهِ وَرَدْ   ونيلُها يُجْلى برؤياه النَكَدْ ٤٥٫٨

نسيمُها ألطف شيء في الصفا   وأهلُها أهل سرورٍ ووفا

والحمد لله على الإقامهْ   بها وأرجو الله في السلامهْ

مَعْ سعة الرزق وشرح الصدْرْ   وكشف غمٍّ وزَوال الحَصْرْ

ثمّ الصلاة والسلام أبدا   على النبيّ الهاشميِّ أحمدا

وحِزْبِهِ وصَحْبِهِ والآلِ   ما دامت الأيّامُ والليالي

And I'll sleep with you on the straw a bit—
Today I'm the last wise old man left in the hamlet."
Observe, God guide you, the uncouthness in their description—
But what to say? They are of the rural persuasion!
So be quick your guard against them to take— 8.44
For consorting with peasants brings harm in its wake.
Keep the company of men of refinement and integrity,
And be with men of good fortune and prosperity.
All this is in villages far distant
From our Nile, and to the hills adjacent
And in places where no man of learning rests
To guide them—where all, indeed, are beasts.
There is no place like Cairo,
And no people like its people, from the bother of a survey may God save you![572]
For it's God's Quiver[573] as we've been told 8.45
The sight of whose Nile turns dark thoughts to gold.
Its breeze is the height of all pleasure,
Its people, people of delight, who give in full measure.
And praise be to God that here I reside,
And I pray to God to keep danger aside,
With ample provision and peace of mind,
All worries banished, all distress left behind!
Next, blessings and peace forever more I invite
Upon Aḥmad,[574] the prophet Hashimite,
And on his party, companions, and kin,
As long as days shall last and nights draw in!

Notes

1 The book opens with the conventional *khuṭbah* ("preamble"), which weaves references to the book's concerns into a formulaic eulogy of God, the Prophet Muḥammad, his family, and his Companions.

2 I.e., prophetic Traditions (see Glossary).

3 "thick ends of palm fronds" (*quḥūf*, sg. *qaḥf*): the comparison of the lines of the ode to stacked *quḥūf* (and that above to "blocks of mud") contrasts with the conventional likening of verse to "strung pearls." This is the first allusion in the book to the *qaḥf*, which, in addition to denoting the broad, deeply indented, thorny end of the palm frond where it joins the tree, is used by al-Shirbīnī to mean a type of cap worn by peasants (see the author's description in vol. 2, §11.26.1). As such, it is emblematic of people of "evil nature" (*ibid.*) and of the peasant in general, in al-Shirbīnī's eyes.

4 I.e., Aḥmad ibn ʿAlī l-Sandūbī (d. 1097/1686); see Introduction, p. xii and vol. 2, §13.2.

5 These three settlements together constituted Egypt's capital city. Al-Qāhirah (short for Miṣr al-Qāhirah, "Miṣr the Victorious," and the etymon, via Italian, of Cairo) denotes the city founded in the lee of the Muqaṭṭam Hills in 359/969 by the Fatimids. Miṣr (sometimes distinguished as Miṣr al-Qadīmah or "Old Cairo") properly denotes the settlement that preceded it and clustered around the Roman fortress on the bank of the Nile about a mile and a half southwest of al-Qāhirah. Al-Qāhirah and Miṣr al-Qadīmah had become a single conurbation by al-Shirbīnī's time. Bulaq, the port on the Nile west of al-Qāhirah, was separated from it in al-Shirbīnī's day by agricultural land. This "Greater Cairo" of al-Qāhirah, Miṣr, and Bulaq, which is believed by some to have had a population exceeding 300,000, was the largest Ottoman city after Istanbul. The combined population of the remaining cities of Egypt did not exceed 60,000 (Raymond, *Artisans*, 1:243).

6 Unidentified, perhaps merely intended to sound like the title of a typical verse anthology.

7 Here and throughout, al-Shirbīnī invokes and plays with the relationship, fundamental to the literature of the Islamic religious, linguistic, and literary sciences, of word or utterance (*lafẓ*) and meaning (*maʿnā*). This relationship was regarded as being as ordained and immutable in the higher reality as it was argued over in practice. Al-Shirbīnī's point, in this verse and in the following proverb, seems to be that, despite these much-debated distinctions, language is basically speech, and speech is in the end wind, which has the same ambiguity of meaning in Arabic as in English.

8 The "debate" (*mas'alah*) is a device common in Arabic exegetics and literary criticism, by which the author poses and then responds to and dismisses an objection to an argument he has put forward earlier. Al-Shirbīnī usually introduces such passages with the words "a silly debate" (*mas'alah hibāliyyah*), though he sometimes uses the opening "If it be said . . ." (*fa-'in qīla . . .*) or a variant, a wording that led to the technique being named *fanqalah*; *fanqalah* continued to be used at al-Azhar until at least the turn of the twentieth century (Ḥusayn, *Al-Ayyām*, 129); for an entirely serious example of *fanqalah*, see the quotation from al-Munāwī's *Al-Kawākib al-durriyyah* in vol. 2 (§11.32.11).

9 The Pillar of the Columns: Pompey's Pillar (see Glossary).

10 "Silver in bushels brimming" (*qanāṭiran muqanṭaratan min al-lujayn*): cf. Q Āl ʿImrān 3:14.

11 This still-current proverb implies that coyness ill becomes one who has undertaken to perform a public act.

12 "swamps" (*malaq*): "Between each village and the next is a space of ground called a *malaqa*, over which is an earthen dike. When the Nile floods and these valleys separating the villages become filled with water, the people move about by means of these dikes" (Shalabī, *Siyāḥatnāmah*, 431); see Introduction, p. xxvi.

13 Saʿd (also known as Judhām or Judām) and Ḥarām were originally Bedouin federations allied, respectively, with the Fiqāriyyah and Qāsimiyyah military factions whose rivalry dominated Egypt during the latter part of the seventeenth century (Winter, *Egyptian Society*, 21). Saʿd and Ḥarām were still "notorious for . . . petty wars and feuds" in Lower Egypt in the first decades of the nineteenth century (Lane, *Manners*, 196).

14 "what the Law demands . . . what one is free to decide on his own" (*sunnah . . . farḍ*; the elements are reversed in the English for the rhyme): literally, what is obligatory in religion (*farḍ*) from what is simply meritorious, being based on the sayings and practice of the Prophet Muḥammad (*sunnah*).

15 The key to this unexpected criticism may lie in al-Shirbīnī's later accusation (§8.17) that they pay the tax collector before honoring their debts to others (such as, presumably, the money lender who has advanced them money to plant their crop).

16 I.e., the clan elders and largest landholders, numbering (at the beginning of the nineteenth century) between eight and ten in each village, who settled clan disputes, represented the villages before outside authority, and were co-opted by the latter to act as intermediaries in the maintenance of security and collection of taxes (see Cuno, *Peasants*, 85).

17 Winter notes that "Shaʿrānī, himself a migrant to the capital from a small village . . . thanked God for transferring him 'from the village, which was a place of rudeness and

ignorance, to the city, which was the place of gentleness and knowledge'" (Winter, *Egyptian Society*, 153–54).

18 I.e., the two words share, in reverse order, the same basic letter forms, differentiated by dots above or below the line; e.g., ف (f), the last letter of the first word, has one dot above, while ق (*q*), the first letter of the second, has two.

19 "Names, Nicknames, and *Kunyahs*" (*asmāʾ . . . alqāb . . . kunā*): this section covers three forms of personal appellation. The *ism* (sg. of *asmāʾ*) is the most general category, thus the personal name, or the name given at birth. The others represent different types of acquired appellation. Of the *asmāʾ*, al-Shirbīnī notes below that "names can't be diagnosed," i.e., personal names cannot be given clear meanings based on etymologies and thus cannot be related back to ordinary words, with a pun on the two senses of the root *ʿ-l-l*, which includes the ideas of both "root" and "sickness." Despite this contention, many of the names given here (and in the following anecdotes and elsewhere in the book) clearly derive from, or at least are reminiscent of, common nouns, while some are rural forms of more widely used names or have some other peculiarity or association; only a few are completely obscure and do indeed resist analysis. Thus Zuʿayṭ and Muʿayṭ occur today as nonce words in the rhyming phrase *ziʿēṭ wi-mʿēṭ wi-naṭṭāṭil-ḥēṭ*, said of a man who is "fond of company and noisy," the words "expressing merely the sound of a busy crowd" (Burckhardt, *Proverbs*, 100); Miḥimmad is a variant of Muḥammad (though apparently not attested today, the current Egyptian colloquial pronunciation being Miḥammad) and Miḥimmadayn (Miḥammadēn still occurs) adds the dual ending to the name, perhaps by analogy with Ḥasanayn, a form that conflates the names of al-Ḥasan and al-Ḥusayn, the grandchildren of the Prophet. The frequency of diminutives (e.g., Junayjil, Zuʿayṭ) among both the men's and women's names given below is striking. The diminutive occurs rarely in personal names in modern Egypt and is no longer productive for common nouns. However, references in older sources—e.g., to a Zuʿaytar (diminutive of *zaʿtar* "thyme") in 1564 (Hilāl, *Baghāyā*, 28), to a Bizaybaʿ in al-Maghribī's sixteenth-century dictionary (al-Maghribī, *Dafʿ*, 38 (top margin)) and, as late as the late nineteenth century, to Hinēgil and Ziʿēzaʿ (al-Ālātī, *Tarwīḥ*, 43)—support the implication of al-Shirbīnī's highlighting of the diminutive, namely, that it was still productive in his time. The inclusion of ʿImrān, whose name occurs in the Qurʾan (Q Āl ʿImrān 3:33) in the list and again below (§§2.15, 4.10) is puzzling, since it seems out of place among the otherwise eccentric and bizarre names the author attributes to peasants; it may be its Bedouin association that qualifies it for inclusion. Other items in the list are obscure, and the voweling is, in some cases, speculative. Overall, while it is tempting to dismiss the more bizarre names as inventions of the author's, we should bear in mind the practice, probably still current, of giving children names with

unpleasant associations as a way of warding off envy and the Evil Eye: Aḥmad Taymūr noted that "the common people call their children by odious names, that they may live" (Taymūr, *Muʿjam*, 1/137); cf. also the discussion of names in al-Farāfīr by the twentieth-century playwright Yūsuf Idrīs, in which such names as al-Jaḥsh ("The Donkey-Foal"), al-ʿAbīṭ ("The Stupid"), and al-Mughaffal ("The Dimwit") and such *kunyas* (see below) as Abū Kharūf ("Father of Sheep") and Abū Farwah ("Father of a Sheepskin") are cited as commonplace (*al-Farāfīr*, 76–77). Some of the names given by al-Shirbīnī also appear as stereotypically rural names in later sources, that is, Duʿmūm (Nadīm, *al-Aʿdād*, 7/147) and Shuḥaybar (Khayrī and al-Rayḥānī, "Kishkish," 346); in 2004 a comic film entitled *ʿŌkal* (= ʿAwkal, see below), after the lead character, was released in Egypt. On *kunā* and *alqāb*, see §§2.14 and 2.15.

20 Cf. modern Egyptian *lahaṭ* "to guzzle."

21 Cf. modern rural Egyptian *yitmaqliṭ* "to make fun of" (Behndstedt and Woidich, *Glossar*, 454).

22 Cf. modern Egyptian *kusbarah* "coriander."

23 Cf. modern Egyptian *shaḥbar* "to smudge."

24 This is the first example of a comic device used repeatedly hereafter, viz. the facetious analysis of ludicrous, obscene, or otherwise stigmatized words. Though the analysis is in this case correct at the grammatical level (i.e., *zubaylah* is indeed the diminutive of *ziblah*, etc.), correctness is not of the essence, and dubious logic and far-fetched argument abound elsewhere.

25 In Arabic, nouns denoting a single unit or instance are formed from nouns denoting a mass or collectivity by adding *-ah*. Thus *ziblah* "a piece of dung" is formed from *zibl* "dung."

26 It would be more accurate to say that *zibl* and *zubālah* share the same triconsonantal root (*z-b-l*), all of whose derivatives are related semantically. However, al-Shirbīnī's formulation allows him to introduce another comically inappropriate word, a technique used throughout the book.

27 Arabic words with the same pattern of consonants and long vowels are said to be of the same "measure" (*wazn*; literally, "weight"); short vowels, which are not part of the written consonant skeleton but are represented by signs written above or below the line, are irrelevant to the measure.

28 The comicality of the back of the neck (*qafā*), and especially of blows administered to it, is an ancient idea in Arab culture: "Back-of-the-neck-blow-takers" were employed as court comedians as early as the sixth century AD (Moreh, *Theatre*, 10).

29 The point of the story lies partly in the repetition of vulgarisms as proper names, partly in the discrepancy between the bearers' names and their supposed learnedness, and

partly in the incorporation of the second name into the syntax of the punch line, as though its constituent words were meant in their original sense; above all, however, the use of these vulgarisms allows the author to get away, in effect, with insulting the audience relentlessly throughout the narration. Such stories seem to have been a genre; further examples are to be found in the shadow plays of the Egyptian Ibn Dāniyāl (d. 710/1310): "Says Bag-Some-Manure (*Ṣurra Baʿr*), 'Your-Beard-Up-My-Ass (*Daqnak F-istī* [amended]) is a mighty man and he had a herbalist whose name was Suck-Clit (*Muṣṣa Baẓr*), who had two herbs, one called Eat-My-Shit (*Salḥī Kul*), the other Smell-My-Dung (*Rawthī Shumm*) . . . .'" (Ibn Dāniyāl, *Plays*, 20 Arabic).

30 I.e., the Zoroastrians. The reference may be to a secret language of buffoons (see next note), similar to that known to have been used by various groups in the medieval Arab underworld (Bosworth, *Underworld*) and found in modern Egypt among thieves, jewelers, homosexuals, upholsterers, etc. (see ʿĪsā, *Al-Lughāt*; Rowson, "Cant"). Elsewhere, al-Shirbīnī refers later to an argot of counterfeiters (vol. 2, §11.33.6) and to a possible secret language of dervishes (§7.11).

31 "buffoon" (*khalbūṣ*, pl. *khalābīṣ*): Lane describes the *khalbūṣ* as the servant of *ʿawālim* (female singers and musicians) "who often acts the part of a buffoon" and demands money from the audience on behalf of his employers (Lane, *Manners*, 501).

32 "Fire Valley" (*Wādī l-Nār*): a place near Mecca.

33 The point of the story seems to be that the magic of names is so powerful that it influences reality.

34 Cf. modern Egyptian *maʿar* "to brag."

35 See vol. 2, §11.1.6 for al-Shirbīnī's explanation of this name.

36 Cf. modern Egyptian *qashqish* "to scavenge."

37 Cf. modern Egyptian *qaṣālah* "knotty parts of stalks of wheat and barley separated out during winnowing and set aside for fuel."

38 Cf. modern Egyptian *barṭaʿ* "to gallop about (of donkeys)."

39 Cf. modern Egyptian *taʿtaʿ* "to budge, dislodge."

40 See Behnstedt and Woidich, *Glossar*, 239, s.v. *shiʿshaʿ (a)*; cf. modern Egyptian *shaʿshaʿ* "to glow."

41 See, e.g., al-Damīrī, *Ḥayawān*, 216; it also means "catamite, bum-boy" (see Ibn Ḥamdūn, *al-Tadhkirah*, 9:137).

42 Cf. modern Egyptian *khanfar* "to snort, snuffle"; also Behnstedt and Woidich, *Glossar*, 124, s.v. *xanfūra* "Zelle des Schöpfwerks" ("compartment of a water-raising device").

43 Cf. modern Egyptian *ṭarṭar* "to urinate standing up."

44 Cf. modern Egyptian *habal* "silliness, imbecility."

45 Cf. modern Egyptian *zaghab* "down, fuzz."

46 Cf. modern Egyptian *ʿarīsh* "trellis; shaft (for a harness)"; *ʿarīshah* "pen in a field."

47 Or perhaps *futayshah,* as a diminutive of *fattāsh* "peg in the plow-shaft extension" (Behnstedt and Woidich, *Glossar,* 343).

48 Muqallad: again a real given name; see the anecdote about the Emir Muqallad below (§7.33).

49 "Nicknames" (*alqāb,* sg. *laqab*): these items consist of a personal name followed in apposition by a common noun; while the meaning of the second generally is clear, the names themselves consist, as above, of a mixture of the unexceptional (ʿImrān, ʿUmayr, Muḥammad), the bizarre (ʿAnṭūz, Shallāṭah, Kusbur, Barbūr, Lahhāṭ), and the obscure, such as Mashālī. Elsewhere, al-Shirbīnī says "their nicknames inform you as to their nobility" (*alqābuhum tunbīka ʿan ashrāfihim*) (§8.30), implying that such "nicknames" were associated with prominent families. In modern Egypt, only a few families have fixed surnames, most individuals calling themselves by their given names plus that of their father and his father, e.g., al-Sayyid [son of] Ṣalāh [son of] ʿAbduh, so that the full name changes with each generation; this would accord with al-Shirbīnī's assocation of *alqāb* with the "nobility."

50 Cf. modern Egyptian *ʿantaẓah* "arrogance, imperiousness" (Taymūr, *Muʿjam,* 4:449).

51 *Mashālī*: possibly related to the use of the term for Bedouin forward cavalry, whose mission was to encircle the enemy with a pincer movement, from *māshah* ("tongs") + *-lı* (Turkish particle of appurtenance).

52 "gherkin" (*zarārah*): in the dialect of oasis of al-Baḥariyya (Behnstedt and Woidich, *Glossar,* 184).

53 From the same root as *baliyyah* ("calamity") above, but not attested.

54 Cf. modern Egyptian *giʿīṣ* "pompous."

55 Cf. modern Egyptian *ʿamāṣ* "discharge from the eyes."

56 Cf. modern Egypian *shalaḥ* "to remove (a garment)" or "to become short (usually of the skirt of a garment)."

57 Cf. modern Egyptian *ʿurmah* "pile, heap (especially of a harvested crop)."

58 Cf. the modern Upper Egyptian dialectal form *farfūrah* "woman" (Behnstedt and Woidich, *Glossar,* 351).

59 "Calamity" (*dāhiyah*), like "Drat!" (*qaṭīʿah*) below, seems to function here both as an exclamation of exasperation (as in modern Egyptian) and as a comically inappropriate name.

60 The connotation of "from the wall" is not obvious but should perhaps be taken to imply submissiveness; cf. modern expressions such as *yimshi ganb il-hēṭ,* literally "to walk next to the wall," i.e., "to behave in a self-effacing way, to keep out of trouble."

61 *Aḥḥēḥ* is one of the sounds used to represent the panting, gasping, and snorting with which women are conventionally supposed to express sexual excitement, and which, with the accompanying movements of the body, are known as *ghunj*. Many of these expletives, like *aḥḥēḥ*, contain the sound *ḥ* (approximately that made by breathing on a pane of glass to mist it). The nineteenth-century Syrian Mīkhā'īl Ṣabbāgh reports that this sound is so evocative that "if a word occurs in a singing girl's song in which there is a single or a double /*ḥ*/ preceded by a vowel, it sets them in such a turmoil that they ask the girl to repeat the song, in their delight over that word" (Ṣabbāgh, *Al-Risālah*, 48).

62 Sexual intercourse leaves the Muslim in a state of ritual impurity (*janābah*) that can be removed only by ritual ablution. The Muslim cannot, while impure, perform the prayer or various other religious duties.

63 I.e., wearing makeup. Egyptian kohl may be made with smoke-black (Lane, *Manners*, 36).

64 The Showing (*al-jilā'*) is a ceremony at which the bride appears before the groom and other members of the wedding in her finery; it does not seem to be practiced in Egypt today. The author singles it out for condemnation because it violates the prohibition on the appearance of women before strangers (see further Tietze, *Description*, 47–48).

65 The *kunyah* means approximately "Precious One."

66 *Umm Mujbir* also appears in a colloquial play dating to 1064/1654 called *The Umm Mujbir Party Show* (*Misṭarat Khayāl Munādamat Umm Mujbir*) by ʿAbd al-Bāqī al-Isḥāqī (Moreh, *Theatre*, 158, 170–78), where she is depicted as a sort of hell-hag, who, after being buried for ninety years, is resurrected and "travel[s] through the wilderness and the valleys" seeking her former husband.

67 Gifts of money (*nuqūṭ*) are traditionally given to the bride and groom at weddings.

68 I.e., to cover the sounds made by the bridal couple.

69 Either meaning "the author of the work known as *The Drover's Whip Handle*" or being the epithet of the poet, and, in either case, presumably being a figment of al-Shirbīnī's imagination. The verses that follow and that probably parody some contemporary poetic genre are notably obscure in their antic rusticity, even though they follow a classical meter (*ṭawīl*).

70 "Drying grounds" (*masaṭiḥ*): e.g., for sunflower seeds.

71 "bonnet" (*zunṭ*): a fluffy red woolen hat (see Nicolle, *Mamluks*, 40).

72 "And so many" (*wa-ʿiddu*): the Arabic is obscure and the translation tentative.

73 "Flour cloth" (*tifāl al-ʿaysh*): the literary *thifāl* is defined as "a skin that is spread beneath the hand-mill to preserve the flour from the dust" (Lane, *Lexicon*). Possibly the peasant was using it, on this special occasion, as a sheet.

74 Yūsuf al-Maghribī (980–1019/1572–1611) records in his dictionary that tobacco (*al-ṭābighah*) first appeared in Egypt in 1014/1604–5 and immediately became a craze (al-Maghribī, *Dafʿ*, 49 (folio 16b); Zack, *Egyptian Arabic*, 243).

75 Ṣarīʿ al-Dilāʾ ʿAlī (or Muḥammad) ibn ʿAbd al-Wāḥid (d. 412/1021), see Ibn Khallikān, *Wafayāt*, 3/384.

76 See al-Shāfiʿī, *Shiʿr*, 183.

77 Khalīl ibn Aybak al-Ṣafadī (d. 764/1363) (see al-Ṣafadī, *Nuṣrat al-thāʾir*, 153), with differences.

78 "stratagem" (*ḥīlah*, pl. *ḥiyal*): "the use of legal means for extra-legal ends that could not, whether they were themselves legal or illegal, be achieved directly with the means provided by the *shariʿah*" (J. Schacht, "Ḥiyal," in *EI2*). Most schools of law accept such stratagems, provided they are used to maintain the spirit of the law in the face of difficulties posed by the letter; the examples given here and elsewhere (e.g., §4.20) achieve the opposite.

79 Apostasy by either partner automatically nullifies a marriage.

80 "waiting period" (*ʿiddah*): following the dissolution of a marriage, Muslim law prescribes a waiting period for the woman before a new marriage may be contracted, to ensure that she is not pregnant by her former husband.

81 On Arab geomancy—"guessing the future from random marks in the sand"—see Irwin, *Companion*, 189–91; on the use of a divination table "divided into a hundred little squares, in each of which some Arabic letter" (the *zāʾirjah*), see Lane, *Manners*, 259.

82 Q Anbiyāʾ 21:96; thus the peasants are likened, by implication, to the apocalyptic peoples Yājūj and Mājūj (Gog and Magog).

83 "the fine on the landless" (*al-gharāmah*): as al-Shirbīnī explains later (e.g., vol. 2, §§11.3.10, 11.9.2), peasants without land to work (*al-baṭṭālūn*, literally "those without work") were forced instead either to contribute their labor without pay on the tax farmer's private demesne or on public works (*al-ʿawnah*) or to pay a fine (*gharāmat al-baṭṭālīn*).

84 Presumably a village saint.

85 Abū ʿAfr . . . Abū Duʿmūm . . . Abū Zaʿbal: presumably village saints.

86 *ishtiwān*: apparently an item (perhaps a tool or weapon) often possessed by peasants and made of fish or other bone (see also §§8.23 and 8.40); not known today.

87 I.e., his wife.

88 A faux pas that also forms the point of a later anecdote (§4.17).

89 "Heaven on Earth is the bathhouse" (*naʿīm al-dunyā al-ḥammām*): the phrase *naʿīm al-dunyā* (literally, "the comfort of This World") mirrors *naʿīm al-ākhirah* ("the comfort of the Hereafter," i.e., Paradise).

90 As al-Shirbīnī explains later (vol. 2, §11.7.10), "May a disaster consume you!" is a peasant curse.

91 "May He who made you sneeze . . . " (*yarḥamak illī ʿaṭṭasak wa-law shāʾ faṭṭasak wa-akhraj al-ʿaṭsah min qabr Qarāqīr illī khallafak*): similar nonsense rhymes are used today; one says, for example, to a child who sneezes, *ʿaṭasak faṭasak il-ḥumār kassar qafaṣak.*

92 I.e., the peasant is so stupid that he cannot tell gibberish from scripture; variations on this theme appear later (§3.68ff).

93 "God's Big Feast" (*ʿīd Allāh al-kabīr*): i.e., the Feast of the Sacrifice (*al-ʿīd al-kabīr*) celebrated on the tenth day of the month of pilgrimage to Mecca in commemoration of the commuting of the sacrifice of Ismāʿīl by his father Ibrāhīm and marked by the slaughtering of sheep.

94 Presumably his wife, though later he calls her Umm ʿAfr (§3.18).

95 Traditionally, every village had a pond (*birkah*), created by the digging of clay for building, that was used for "washing clothes, drinking, and defecation" (Berque, *Histoire*, 26).

96 "Oven" (*qubbah*): "the roof of [the baking chamber] of a mud oven" (Hinds and Badawi, *Dictionary*, illus. 973); when the *qubbah* is heated, the flat top of the oven above it provides a warm sleeping shelf.

97 "Abū ʿAfr the Bolter" (*Abū ʿAfr Abū Tirbās*): literally "Abū ʿAfr, the one with the bolt," perhaps with a sexual connotation.

98 "Perfume" (*bukhūr*): literally "incense," here implying something scented to smear on clothes, specified below as safflower. Mamluk ceremonies in celebration of the Nile's achievement of its annual optimum flood (*wafāʾ al-Nīl*) included smearing the Nilometer with saffron, and, in 1491, after the ending of a particularly bad drought, "the joy for the plenitude was so great that the commoners smeared saffron on their own bodies" (Shoshan, *Culture*, 73).

99 Perhaps a reference to the pre-Ottoman Mamluks, who were known as "the people" (*al-nās*). Reflections of "a popular nostalgia for the Mamluk past" have been detected in other Ottoman writers, such as the chronicler Ibn Zunbul (Behrens-Abouseif, *Adjustment*, 136).

100 As the language of the Ottoman elite, Turkish was the shibboleth of the military caste.

101 The reference seems out of place, because it has no equivalent in the earlier part of the story. However, jokes about peasants not being able to find a place to relieve themselves in the city are central to other stories that occur later (§§3.40, 3.41) and were apparently a stock element in the mockery of peasants.

102 Umm Duʿmūm: presumably a second wife.

103 *munqār*: i.e., *mangır*, an Anatolian Ottoman copper coin, the equivalent of the Egyptian copper piece (*jadīd*); see further Pamuk, *Monetary History*, 38.

104 Muslims should, whenever possible, perform the noon prayer on Friday communally in a *jāmiʿ* (congregational mosque), the prayer being preceded by a sermon. The description given by the peasant provides an easily recognizable, though distorted, account of the service, for a detailed description of which see Lane, *Manners*, 83–90.

105 *Allāhu akbar* ("God is greater [than all else]") and *lā ilāha illā llāh* ("There is no god but God") are uttered as part of the call to prayer and during the prayer. The first is also used as a battle cry.

106 Presumably a village saint.

107 I.e., between the pillars of the mosque hung chains for lamps, a chain for each arch.

108 I.e., the pulpit (*minbar*), which consists of a flight of stairs entered through a small door at the foot and is surmounted by a small dome on poles covering a platform from which the preacher delivers his sermon.

109 I.e., the *dikkah*—"a platform surrounded by a parapet on which sit the *muballighs*, persons who chant certain portions of the service and also repeat and amplify certain of the portions recited by other officiants" (Lane, *Manners*, 85, 90).

110 The *muballighs* (see preceding note) repeat the call to prayer previously delivered from the minaret. Placing a hand over one ear (or hands over both) is a gesture typical of reciters of the Qur'an and of the call to prayer. Some attribute the gesture purely to custom; others interpret it as helping to "shape" or "focus" the sound (Nelson, *Art*, 112).

111 I.e., the preacher; as described by Lane in the 1830s, men of religion were distinguished by a particularly wide turban, called a *muqlah* (Lane, *Manners*, 35).

112 In countries, such as Egypt, that were taken by the Muslims by force of arms, the preacher formerly carried a wooden sword (cf. Lane, *Manners*, 85 n. 5).

113 The peasant refers to the responses of the *muballighs* (see n. 109, 110) following the sermon (Lane, *Manners*, 90).

114 Of Cairo in the first decades of the nineteenth century, Lane records that "Most of the by-streets are thoroughfares, and have a large wooden gate at each end, closed at night . . ." (Lane, *Manners*, 4).

115 The words are a mixture of Turkish (*şimdi* "now," *bindi* "he mounted") and orotund gibberish.

116 Writing in 1599, the Turkish visitor ʿĀli Muṣṭafā said of the *jundīs* ("troopers") of Cairo that they "are [well] dressed and mounted, they have horse harness of silver, belts and swords, and are archers and fighters, brave and battle-happy ones who for the most part are wearing trousers of Venetian cloth and blouses (*jamé*) of red satin and silk velvet" (Tietze, *Description*, 66).

117 ʿĀlī Muṣṭafā also mentions that the *jundī*s are "conceited, and [their] impudent behavior is beyond comparison. They would never greet an honest person. If he greets them, they never return the salute politely. In their own ill-guided opinion they think: 'He is but an egghead!' By this they mean, not an able-bodied fighter, not a [daring] horse-rider" (Tietze, *Description*, 55).

118 Sanjaks were entitled to have drums in their processions (Crecelius, *Al-Damurdāshī*, 17 n. 1).

119 The woman was acting as a *dallālah,* i.e., a woman who bought goods from merchants and sold them at a markup to women of the upper classes who were confined to their homes (see Lane, *Manners*, 157, 187, 191), the peasant in this case being the pledge for her purchases.

120 The peasant's *kunyah*. *Qurayṭim* is the diminutive of *qurṭum* "safflower."

121 Of these names, only one—Buʿaybir—occurs in the earlier list (§2.9); Dundūf and Zuʿaybir have no clear meaning; Shukhaybir is from the root "to gush (with a gurgling sound)."

122 The peasant may be describing a market stall.

123 "the Boor of Cairo" (*thaqīl Miṣr*): literally, "the heavy one of Cairo"; note the verses at §3.51 below, where the metaphor is taken literally.

124 A Bedouin clan named the Banū Baqar (literally, "the Sons of Cattle") was based in al-Sharqiyyah province.

125 This passage introduces several elements that recur throughout the work: the spurious short poem by a peasant that travesties contemporary taste and is stuffed with inadmissible colloquialisms, invented words, grotesque images, and references to the banalities of everyday life, followed by the author's mock-serious commentary, in which these absurdities are subjected to painstaking analysis, the whole serving to illustrate the coarseness and barbarism of the peasant and his innate attraction toward everything that is inferior. The process parodies the conventional philological technique of *istishhād*, the citing of a verse as evidence for the meaning of a word.

126 "*ʿajājīl* . . . is of the measure of *habābīl*": words of the same vocalic pattern as the word under consideration were used in the dictionaries of the day to disambiguate pronunciation (necessary, given the tendency of copyists to omit or miswrite diacritics); thus the *Qāmūs* states that *k-m-yt* is "like *Zubayr*," i.e., pronounced *kumayt*. The rare form *ʿajājīl* occurs in *Al-Qāmūs al-muḥīṭ*, although as the plural of *ʿijjawl* rather than of *ʿijl*.

127 *The Blue Ocean and Piebald Canon* (*Al-Qāmūs al-azraq wa-l-nāmūs al-ablaq*; also translatable as *The Blue Ocean and Piebald Mosquito*): the title of this fictitious dictionary may be intended to evoke that of the standard dictionary of the time, *The Encompassing Ocean* (*Al-Qāmūs al-muḥīṭ*) of Muḥammad ibn Yaʿqūb al-Fīrūzābādhī

(729–817/1329–1415), though the name is also reminiscent of an abridgment of the latter entitled *Al-Nāmūs al-maʾnūs al-mulakhkhaṣ min al-Qāmūs* (*The Convenient Canon Condensed from the Qāmūs*) by al-Qāriʾ ʿAlī ibn Sulṭān Muḥammad al-Harawī (d. 1014/1605), a work described by Lane as "not . . . held in high estimation" (Lane, *Lexicon*, 1/xvii).

128 On *ʿajājīl*, see n. 126. Other plurals used in this passage (*jafāfīl* "camelings," *habābīl*) imply singulars of the same rare pattern (*jiffawl*, *hibbawl*), though these words are not otherwise attested and may have been invented by al-Shirbīnī to parody the obsession of philologists with unusual forms.

129 *taḥanjul* is the putative literary verbal noun of the colloquial verb *biyitḥanjil*, cited below.

130 "frotters": the peasant says *zalūbyah* for *zalābyah* ("fritters").

131 The second speaker spells out *barbaq* ("to widen the eyes"), which consists of letters that, if provided with different dots and preceded by the letter ا (*alif*), could produce *ibrīq*; the Arabic letter و (*w*) occurs in neither word and has no dot.

132 By "lovers" (*ʿushshāq*), the speaker may mean lovers (i.e., devotees) of the Prophet Muḥammad.

133 "tiddley-pom" (*wa-shin*): the Arabic is distorted beyond recognition.

134 "Whose woids . . . Hārīn al-Rashād . . . al-Ṭaylūn . . . Abū Ṭālūb": the vowels are comically distorted (*kalām mūn . . . Hārīn al-Rashād. . . al-Ṭaylūn . . . Abū Ṭālūb for kalām man . . . Hārūn al-Rashīd . . . ibn Ṭūlūn . . . Abū Ṭālib*). The passage consists of a jumble of names and phrases mostly reminiscent of the Qurʾan, though garbled and colloquialized: "who fell into the pit"— a reference to the story of Yūsuf (Joseph), who was thrown into a pit by his brothers (cf. Q Yūsuf 12:10 «and throw him down to the bottom of the well»); "he was gobbled up by the crocodile"—cf. «then the fish swallowed him up» in the story of Yūnus (Jonah) (Q Ṣāffāt 37:142); "upon whom the mud descended" mimicks the phrase "the divine inspiration descended upon him" (*nazala ʿalayhi l-waḥy*), which is frequently used to describe the Prophet's reception of the divine message; "the mosque of al-Ṭaylūn"—i.e., the mosque of Aḥmad ibn Ṭūlūn, one of the oldest and largest in Cairo (Ṭaylūn was once standard colloquial pronunciation for Ṭūlūn; see Brémond, *Voyage*, 53, and Lane, *Manners*, 581 n. 1); "who made the fire cold and safe" is reminiscent of Anbiyāʾ 21:69 «We said, "O Fire, be cold and safe for Ibrāhīm!"» which refers to God's saving Ibrāhīm (Abraham) from the furnace into which he was cast by King Nimrūd (Nimrod) as punishment for destroying the idols of his people; "ʿĪsā son of Maryam son of Abū Tālūb" conflates ʿĪsā son of Maryam (Jesus son of Mary) with ʿAlī son of Abū Ṭālib, son-in-law of the Prophet and fourth caliph.

135 Several conditions (e.g., ablution), and prescribed elements (e.g., the inaudibly uttered declaration of the intent to perform the prayer proper to the time of day) should be fulfilled or included for the valid performance of Muslim ritual prayer. In each of the

following anecdotes, the peasant invalidates his prayer by violating a condition or prescription.

136 At the start of the prayer, the worshipper "raises his open hands on either side of his face, and touching the lobes of his ears with the ends of his thumbs, says, 'God is most great' (*Allāhu akbar*)" (Lane, *Manners*, 76).

137 The opening words of the prayer ("By the fig and the olive") are those of Q Tīn 95:1. The rest is spurious.

138 Perhaps a local saint, though there is an element of sheer nonsense, because Muʿaykah is a woman's name.

139 The correct form is *wa-lā l-ḍāllīn*.

140 For *Āmīn* ("Amen"), in imitation of the pastor's mistake.

141 The pastor's error is the worse, as *al-ḍāllīn* is revealed scripture, whereas *āmīn* is merely a customary addition.

142 I.e., Bedouin.

143 The words *Shintīr* and *Bintīr* are meaningless, while the remainder is a burlesque of Surah 105 of the Qur'an: "Have you not seen what your Lord did with the Companions of the Elephant? Did He not make their treachery to go astray? He sent against them flights of birds, pelting them with stones of baked clay. Thus He made them like eaten straw," a passage that refers to the miraculous repulse of an Ethiopian army furnished with elephants that tried to take Mecca in the year of the Prophet's birth (ca. AD 570).

144 After the first two sentences, which are indeed from the *Fātiḥah*, the woman launches into a shortened and mangled version of Sūrat al-Naṣr, the words *idhā jāki l-Ḥājj Naṣr al-Dīn iftaḥi lahu l-bāb* ("When al-Ḥājj Naṣr al-Dīn comes to you, open the door to him") mimicking *idhā jāʾa naṣru llāhi wa-l-fatḥ* ("When God's help and victory come to you") (Q Naṣr 110:1) while *innahu kāna ṭawwāban* ("Verily, he was once a maker of bricks") mimics *innahu kāna tawwāban* ("Verily, He is ever ready to accept repentance") (110:3).

145 "I have flung my face towards Him who cracked the Heavens and the Earth, for I am neither a Monotheist nor a Muslim nor an Unbeliever!" (*laqaht wajhī li-llī sharakh al-samāwāt wa-l-arḍ li-annī lā ḥanīfan wa-lā min al-qawm al-kāfirīn*): cf. Q Anʿām 6:80 *innī wajjahtu wajhī li-lladhī faṭara l-samāwāti wa-l-arḍa ḥanīfan wa-mā anā mina l-mushrikīn* "Lo! I have turned my face towards Him who created the heavens and the earth, as one by nature upright, and I am not one of the idolaters."

146 Q Hūd 11:44, referring to the Flood; this verse has often been singled out by critics as particularly eloquent (see, e.g., al-Jurjānī, *Dalāʾil*, 45–46).

147 The *faqīh* confuses two unrelated senses of the root *q-l-ʿ*.

148 The standard formula goes, "I give you in marriage my daughter (name), of legal age, according to the practice of God and His Prophet," to which the fiancé replies, "I agree to marry her according to the practice of God and His Prophet."

149 I.e., to visit his tomb, in Ṭanṭā in the central Delta.

150 The peasant mistakes the scholars for public reciters of romances such as perform at weddings; see §2.24.

151 "He raised the sky without supports" (*rafaʿa l-samāʾa bi-ghayri ʿamad*): cf. Q Raʿd 13:2 *Allāhu lladhī rafaʿa l-samawāti bi-ghayri ʿamadin tarawnahu* ("It was God who raised the heavens with no visible supports").

152 Not a quotation from the Qurʾan but invented for the rhyme.

153 "He 'produces the living from the dead . . . and He produces the dead from the living'": cf. Q Āl ʿImrān 3:27 *wa-tukhriju l-ḥayya mina l-mayyiti wa-tukhriju l-mayyita mina l-ḥayy* "[and] . . . Thou bringest forth the living from the dead and Thou bringest forth the dead from the living" (Arberry, *Koran*, 48).

154 "from next the hole" (*min janb al-nuqrah*): perhaps meaning "while you are defecating."

155 "unprescribed and unpurposed": see n. 135.

156 Possibly a reference to peasants abandoning their land to escape burdensome taxation.

157 I.e., perhaps, by paying attention to him.

158 I.e., the *Ājurrūmiyyah* of Abū ʿAbd Allāh Muḥammad ibn Dāʾūd al-Sanhājī, known as Ibn Ājurrūm (672/1273–74 to 723/1323), "the most widely known and used Arabic grammatical textbook of all time [in which] the whole of Arabic grammar is reduced to about a dozen printed pages of easily memorized rules and stereotypical examples" (M. G. Carter, "Ibn Ājurrūm," in *EAL*). The point of the story is that the country pastor does not know the difference between grammar and jurisprudence.

159 I.e., an abridged version of the famous collection of Prophetic traditions entitled *The Reliable Collection* (*al-Jāmiʿ al-Ṣaḥīḥ*) compiled by Muslim ibn al-Ḥajjāj (d. 261/875).

160 Prayer must not be performed at the precise moment of sunrise, noon, or sunset. Traditions deal with the validity of the dawn prayer if initiated before but completed after sunrise.

161 The occurrence of nearly identical passages in the Qurʾan increases the difficulty of memorizing it. The phrase *la-ʿallahum yatafakkarūn* occurs in three places (Q Aʿrāf 7:176, Naḥl 16:44, Ḥashr 59:21), while *la-ʿallahum yashkurūn* occurs once (Q Ibrāhīm 14:37).

162 *Yatafashkarūn* has no meaning but is reminiscent of *yatafashkalūn* ("they are confused or disordered").

163 "al-Dalhamah and the Worthless One" (*Al-Dalhamah wa-l-Baṭṭāl*): the colloquial name of a traditional popular epic inspired by the feats of Arab warriors during the wars against

Byzantium in the seventh and ninth centuries AD and formally entitled *The Story of Dhāt al-Himmah* (*Sīrat Dhāt al-Himmah*), of which al-Baṭṭāl ("The Worthless One") is a hero.

164 Prophetic traditions are rated as to soundness according to the reliability of the chain of transmitters via which they have been passed down.

165 Utterance of the formula "I divorce thee" three times results in a divorce that is absolute except under the conditions mentioned here.

166 "And He hath created from water a man without fault" (*wa-khalaqa mina l-mā'i basharan sawiyyā*): a conflation of Q Furqān 25:54 (*wa-huwa lladhī khalaqa mina l-mā'i basharan* ("And He it is who hath created men from water")) and Maryam 19:17 (*fa-arsalnā lahā rūḥanā fa-tamaththala lahā basharan sawiyyā* ("then We sent unto her [Maryam, the Virgin Mary] Our spirit that presented himself to her as a man without fault")). It may be that the wily pastor is arguing as follows: water is equated with man and man with God's spirit, which is taken to be an angel; therefore, "water is an angel."

167 Q Hūd 11:44.

168 I.e., the pastor understands the words "and it was said" (*qīla*) in the sense in which they are commonly employed in scholarly usage, i.e., "it was so reported, but the facts cannot be confirmed."

169 *Sūrat al-Kahf* (The Surah of the Cave, Q 18) recounts how some young men, taking refuge in a cave with their dog from persecution for their belief in one God, were miraculously made to sleep for many years. The scholar probably chose it because of verse 19, which contains the passage "Now send one of you with this silver coin unto the city, and let him see what food is purest there and bring you a supply thereof."

170 Q Kahf 18:22.

171 Mukhālif Allāh: literally, "He who disagrees with God."

172 *khunfishār*: the word is not, in fact, simply a nonce word but still exists, in the sense of "something made up of disparate parts."

173 The People of the Cave are mentioned in *al-Kahf*, the eighteenth chapter of the Qur'an (see n. 169).

174 Q Shu'arā' 26:130; the first version uses an apparently nonexistent verb *baṭastum* and substitutes *khabbāzzīn* ("bakers") for *ẓālimīn* ("tyrants"). In this and the following anecdote, the error lies in ignoring or altering the dots written above or below the written consonantal skeleton (for further examples, see n. 18, §4.29, and §4.33).

175 For «*wa-li-llāhi mirāthu l-samāwāti wa-l-arḍ*» ("and God's is the heritage of the heavens and the earth") (Q Āl 'Imrān 3:180); the pastor's misreading of ميزاب ("drainpipe") for ميراث ("heritage") results from his redistribution of the dots over and under the letters (see preceding note).

176 A mishmash of phrases drawn from various chapters of the Qur'an.

177 The forty-fourth chapter of the Qur'an, which contains none of these phrases.

178 The first line occurs twice in the *Book of Songs* (*Kitāb al-aghānī*) (al-Iṣfahānī, *Al-Aghānī*, 4:179–80), where it is described as being recited by drunkards of the Umayyad period as though it were the Qur'an, in one instance in a mosque, in the second in a court room, though in neither of these anecdotes is the audience fooled.

179 "Anthropomorphization" (*al-tashbīh*): i.e., the attribution of human characteristics to God, a topic in theology.

180 The absurdities that follow are all due to the ignorant pastor's misreading of the consonantal skeleton of the key words and of the dots above or below the line by which certain letters are distinguished (see n. 18, §4.29, and §4.33).

181 I.e., Shaʿbān the Gypsy; the opening passage is the chain of transmission, on the credibility of whose constituent authorities the reliability of a Tradition is judged.

182 Ibn Ḥajar lists three transmitters of this name (Ibn Ḥajar, *Tahdhīb*, 11:296ff. (#578–80)).

183 "I bear witness that there is no god but God" and "I bear witness that Muḥammad is the messenger of God."

184 While the pastor's intention is to show who gets what, his telegraphic wording implies that he equates the presents with those for whom they are intended. Baer interprets this as "a serious faux pas while trying to bribe" a judge (Baer, "Significance," 248).

185 On Ibn Sūdūn as a model for al-Shirbīnī, see Introduction, p. xxii. The text as quoted by al-Shirbīnī differs in detail from that to be found in Ibn Sūdūn's *dīwān* (see Vrolijk, *Bringing a Laugh*, 137–39, Arabic).

186 Residential quarters had gates that were closed at night (Lane, *Manners*, 4). The key of a traditional wooden lock is set with small iron pins that fit into holes in the sliding bolt (Lane, *Manners*, 19), and this may explain Funayn's description.

187 The meaning is unclear; perhaps to be understood as diminutive of *qullah* ("water pitcher"), from its shape, and referring to a type of squash.

188 Still a popular dish in the Ottoman period, according to the Turkish visitor ʿĀlī Muṣṭafā, who wrote in 1599, "their dish called *jubn maqlī* . . . which consists of cheese cooked in linseed oil, is their food day and night, and although it has been observed that it causes a weakening of vision and leads to blindness they still stretch out their hands for it in blind greed" (Tietze, *Description*, 44).

189 Jamād is a colloquialized form of Jumādā, the name of the fifth (Jumādā al-Awwal) and sixth (Jumādā al-Thānī) months of the Muslim calendar, but there is no "Middle Jamād"; neither month has more than thirty days; and ʿĀshūrāʾ falls in the month of Muharram while the special (*tarāwīḥ*) prayers for Ramadan are performed, naturally, only in Ramadan.

190 AD 1666–67.

191 The "Tale of the Slave Girl Tawaddud" ("Qiṣṣat al-jāriyah Tawaddud") occurs in *The Thousand and One Nights*. Tawaddud restores her wastrel master's fortunes by answering questions ranging over the religious and secular sciences of the day put to her by a panel of wise men.

192 "The Unblown Rose" ("Al-Ward fī l-akmām"): a story from *The Thousand and One Nights* in which the lovers Uns (or Anas) al-Wujūd ("The Delight of Existence") and al-Ward fī l-Akmām (literally "The Roses in the Calices") overcome adversity.

193 *The Book of the Snare and the Sparrow* (*Kitāb al-Fakhkh wa-l-ʿUṣfūr*): a colloquial verse fable of this name, by one Ibn Yūsuf ʿAbd al-Qādir al-ʿAyyār, appears in Pierre Cachia's collection of modern Egyptian popular narrative ballads (Cachia, *Ballads*, 121–38).

194 "The Tale of the City of Brass" ("Qiṣṣat madīnat al-nuḥās"): a story from *The Thousand and One Nights*.

195 Booksellers probably obtained most of their stock from auctions of libraries for estate purposes.

196 In fact, the verses are by either Abū ʿAlī l-Ḥusayn ibn Saʿd al-Āmidī (d. 499/1105–6) (see Yāqūt, *Udabāʾ*, 9/268–60) or by Abū l-Ḥasan ʿAlī ibn Aḥmad al-Fālī (d. 448/1056–57) (see Yāqūt, *Udabāʾ*, 12:226–27).

197 The original subject of the quotation is a she-camel, which the poet likens to the scholarship that the impoverished scholar is forced to sell cheap.

198 The importance of wide sleeves and large turbans as markers among the religious at this period is also remarked on by Ḥasan al-Badrī al-Ḥijāzī (d. 1131/1718–19), who says, in a poem on dervishes, "they have made their turbans and sleeves large, and vaunt themselves over those learned in the Law" (al-Jabartī, *ʿAjāʾib*, 1:80, line 7) and again, referring to (unworthy) Azharis, "They have made turbans and sleeves large and wide in order to achieve dominance" (ibid. 81, line 2). Al-Shirbīnī mentions wide sleeves again elsewhere, in association with country pastors (§§4.41, 8.19) and also with rural poets (vol. 2, §11.2.16), rural women (*idem*), and peasants in general (*idem* and vol. 2, §11.6.6).

199 This section introduces one of the most frequent, and, for al-Shirbīnī's purposes and methodology, most important comic devices used in this work, namely, a spoof exposition (*sharḥ*) of some lines of verse, of which the prime example—for which these earlier instances may be considered a kind of warm-up—is that of the "Ode of Abū Shādūf" itself. In the immediately following examples, as elsewhere, the author provides a (ridiculous) context for the composition of the verse and designates its meter (using bizarre mnemonics to represent the scansion, which is sometimes misdescribed), then takes each word or phrase and subjects it to a detailed analysis of its morphological structure or "measure," its meanings, and its etymology, using ludicrous paradigms, illustrative but also often wildly digressive anecdotes and philological discussions, pseudo-scholarly

debate in the *fanqalah* mode (see n. 8), and further verse quotations as authority for the commentator's claims (some of which are themselves subjected to the same type of exposition). Predictably, most of the information supplied is erroneous, and red herrings abound; this would, of course, have been obvious to his readers.

200 "the 'abundant' ocean of shite" (*baḥr al-kharā al-wāfir*): al-Shirbīnī puns on the meaning of *baḥr* as both "ocean/large river" and "(poetic) meter" to introduce the term "the abundant" (*al-wāfir*), the name of a meter. However, the latter is a red herring, as the meter is in fact *al-basīṭ* ("the outspread"). The same play on words is repeated several times below (§§5.5.1, 5.8.1, etc.).

201 The root *kh-b-ṭ*, used here, has senses of "striking," "trampling," "dust," "diabolical madness," and "sheep bloat." However, the mnemonic neither mimicks a genuine meter nor fits that of the verse itself; on the use of mnemonics for meter formed from comically inappropriate roots, see Introduction, p. xlii.

202 A literary pre-verbal form with the same meaning. The shift from /z/ to /ḍ/ is anomalous but could be due in this case to the conflation of *mā zāl* with *ẓall*, a literary synonym.

203 Al-Shirbīnī makes a (spurious) distinction between the origin of the word (for which, in this case at least, he gives an plausible explanation) and its derivation or etymology, the latter being, in al-Shirbīnī's hands, merely an excuse to present other forms with comically appropriate, or inappropriate, meanings; while most derive from the same consonantal root (e.g., in this case, *ḍ-l-l*), the author is willing to play fast and loose with even this most basic concept of Arabic linguistic logic by introducing superficially similar but unrelated alternatives, such as, here, *ḍaʾīlah* from the root *ḍ-ʾ-l*.

204 Ziyād ibn Muʿāwiyah al-Nābighah al-Dhubyānī (sixth century AD) (see Ahlwardt, *Divans*, 19).

205 "paradigm" (*maṣdar*, usually "verbal noun"; al-Shirbīnī's use of it in the sense of "paradigm" is idiosyncratic): lexicographers typically use such paradigms to establish the base forms of a verb, i.e., 3rd masc. sg. perfect, 3rd masc. sg. imperfect, active participle, passive participle, and (optionally) verbal noun. The paradigm given here is correct for the verb *ḍalla* ("to go astray"), though this verb's relationship to the word in question is spurious. Similar paradigms often contain made-up, humorous forms.

206 Which is simply the verbal noun of the same and thus provides no further useful information.

207 In fact from the root *sh-ḥ-ṭ*, rather than *sh-ḥ-ṭ-ṭ*, that of the word under discussion.

208 The peasant provides authority for his behavior in the form of a "chain of transmission," as though the words were a prophetic Tradition.

209 The main canals of the irrigation system were maintained by the authorities using forced peasant labor (the corvée), an operation known as "the royal dredging" (*al-jarāfah al-sulṭāniyyah*) (see Michel, "Dafātir," 157–58 and 164).

210 Cf. the modern proverb, said of the mob, "A pipe gathers them, a stick scatters them" (*tigmaʿhum zummārah wi-tfarraqhum ʿaṣāyah*).

211 Al-Sharīf al-Raḍī (359–406/970–1015); see his *Dīwān*, 2:482.

212 Maʿn ibn Zāʾidah: elsewhere ascribed (first line only) to Abū Dulaf (fourth/tenth century) or (both lines) ʿAbd Allāh ibn Ṭāhir (d. 230/845), or others.

213 I.e., he addresses her as Umm Muʿaykah.

214 On the eunuch as doorman, see Marmon, *Eunuchs*, 4 and passim; eunuchs were often black.

215 A twisted double thread is used for depilation.

216 Probably referring to the plowman's custom of choosing two points in front of him as guides to keep his furrow straight.

217 Referring to the habit of burying holy men in a domed sepulchre.

218 Presumably a saying, but the meaning is obscure.

219 Presumably a saying, equivalent to "when you gotta go, you gotta go."

220 *bi-tbāt*, to which al-Shirbīnī devotes most of the following paragraph, represents a different underlying form in each of the two lines. In the first line *bi-tbāt* stands for *bi-tibāt*, i.e., *bi-* (marker of continuous or habitual action in the indicative verb) plus the imperfect verb *tibāt* ("spends the night"), assuming, as seems reasonable, that the colloquial verbal prefix of the time was, as today, with *i* and that modern rules of elision applied. The second *bi-tbāt*, on the other hand, represents *bi-tabāt*, i.e., *bi-* (preposition) followed by the noun *tabāt* ("sureness, certainty," the phrase thus meaning "surely, for sure"). In reality, therefore, the situation is the exact opposite of that claimed by al-Shirbīnī when he says below that the two are "identical in the deep structure" (they are identical on the surface only), and his statement is probably a deliberate red herring. This is not, however, the only problematic feature of these verses. The form *bi-tbāt* in the first line is anomalous in the context, since an indicative verb should not follow a pre-verb such as *rāyiḥah* (marker of the imminent future), while *bi-tbāt* in the second line assumes the elision of *a* in a short unstressed syllable, a phenomenon not typical of modern Egyptian Arabic. These eccentricities may be examples of a conventional characteristic of the *mawwāl*, a colloquial poetic form still in use, according to which all lines in the same quatrain end in the same rhyme word, a phenomenon achieved through complex punning and wordplay that often involves distortions of pronunciation and syntax; much of the audience's enjoyment lies in the unraveling of these puns.

221 The shift from fricatives to dentals, as here from *th* to *t*, is a feature of most non-Bedouin dialects of Arabic, both rural and urban.

222 "using the same verb twice over for the rhyme" (*al-īṭāʾ*): see van Gelder, *Sound and Sense*, 240.

223 This is (deliberate) nonsense, since the *bayāt* of chickens is merely an instance of the use of the word in its general sense, and it is unlikely that the general sense ("to pass the night") is derived from *bayt* (literally, "house") when used as a way of calling chickens in to roost, though the two words do share the same root and may be related semantically.

224 This too appears to be a red herring, since it is in the first line that the verbal form is used, while no verb is involved in this second use of *bi-tbāt* (see n. 220). Taking it at face value, however, one should point out that al-Shirbīnī refers to the verbal prefix *bi-* as a preposition since it is homophonic with the preposition *bi-*. Al-Shirbīnī is compelled to have recourse to this term to describe the prefix because traditional Arabic grammar lacks a term for this purely colloquial feature.

225 I.e., بيات and تبات, when written without dots, have identical consonantal skeletons. Al-Shirbīnī's proviso about the "original forms" is probably yet another red herring, as the ductus remains the same, whether the colloquial form تبات (with initial *t*) or its literary equivalent ثبات (with initial *thāʾ*) is used; بيات is the same in both idioms.

226 The verses are attributed to Abū Dulaf Musʿar ibn Muhalhil al-Khazrajī (fl. fourth/tenth century) (al-Rāghib al-Iṣfahānī, *Muḥāḍarāt*, 2:361).

227 See §5.2.18.

228 The same line of verse, with one difference, occurs in *Risible Rhymes*; the language is classical rather than colloquial.

229 "the 'long' river of shit" (*baḥr kharāʾ al-ṭawīl*): al-Shirbīnī again exploits the pun on *baḥr*, meaning both "ocean/large river" and "(poetic) meter" to introduce the term "the long" (*al-ṭawīl*), the name of the meter employed in these verses.

230 I.e., the meter *al-kāmil*, though, in fact, the meter used here is *al-ṭawīl* (see al-Sanhūrī, *Risible Rhymes*); the mnemonic uses the root *h-b-l*, associated with "raving" and "foolishness."

231 The poet plays with the idea that the day on which the lover is unsure of whether his beloved returns his affections ("the day of doubt") is a "fast." However, to fast on such a day would be forbidden, since the "day of doubt" is also the name given by the jurists to that day of which one doubts "whether it be the last of one [lunar] month or the first of the next" (Lane, *Lexicon*, s.v. *shakk*), especially when that day falls at the end of the fasting month of Ramadan or at the start of the next month of Shaaban, fasting being forbidden under such circumstances.

232 Q Āl ʿImrān 3:92; i.e., "You will never attain God's favor until you've paid alms."

233 Compare today's proverb *in laqēt il-ʿilq ma-tilqā-sh il-kharābah w-in laqēt il-kharābah ma-tilqā-sh il-ʿilq* "If you find the faggot, you can't find the waste ground (to screw him in), and if you find the waste ground, you can't find the faggot" (Hinds and Badawi, *Dictionary*, 593).

234 Cf. Ibn Manẓūr, *Akhbār*, 3/175.

235 I.e., *mizbalah* is a "noun of instrument" derived from the root *z-b-l* (Wright, *Grammar*, 1:130 B).

236 Al-Shirbīnī pretends that *miballah*, "noun of instrument" (see Wright, *Grammar*, 1:130 B) from the root *b-l-l* "to wet," hence, in Egypt, "retting pool" (where flax is soaked to make linen), is of the same root as *mabāl* and *mibwalah*, which are, respectively, "noun of place" and "noun of instrument" from the root *b-w-l* ("to urinate"); the use of such out-of-paradigm lexical items, which are found in numerous other examples of this sort, allows the author to include the word that is the subject of the analysis, thus giving it a spurious grammatical glory as part of the central paradigm, or to introduce further vulgar, obscene, or inappropriate words to bolster the comic impact.

237 Al-Shirbīnī picks up on his earlier idea that "the poet has restrained himself from using anything but *būlī*" (*fa-ktafā al-nāẓim bi-qawlihi būlī*) as a bridge to the technical rhetorical application of the term, on which see the Glossary.

238 Q Naml 27:34.

239 As usual, al-Shirbīnī's suggested etymons have little to do with the word under discussion, only the last two even belonging to the same root (*sh-r-sh-r*).

240 I.e., the headcloth that is formed into a turban.

241 The Janissaries were one of the seven Ottoman regiments stationed in Egypt. The seventeenth-century traveler Jean Coppin describes them as wearing, on solemn occasions, "un long bonnet" (Coppin, *Voyages*, 96).

242 Perfect paronomasia consists of "the use in one context of two words pronounced and written exactly alike" (Cachia, *Rhetorician*, 21) and is "augmentative" when one of the matching terms is longer than the other (Cachia, *Rhetorician*, 28). Thus, there is perfect paronomasia between *waqafā* ("stood") and *wa-qafā* ("a lily-livered dunderhead"). The paronomasia is further characterized as augmentative, presumably because each of these words is preceded by similar, alliterative elements (*al-wafā/baqf, wāqif*); however, the use of the term may be tongue in cheek, since it is usually assumed that such elements should form part of the two words that are compared. A similar play on words is used by al-Sanhūrī in his commentary on the same line of verse (al-Sanhūrī, *Risible Rhymes*).

243 While the verb *nāba* indeed means "to afflict," its verbal noun in that case should be *nawbah*; *niyābah* is a verbal noun of *nāba* only in its other sense of "to represent," in

which meaning the verbal noun developed in Ottoman times the concrete denotation of "the post of a *nā'ib*" or deputy judge. Since *nā'ib*s elsewhere are butts of al-Shirbīnī's satire (§4.35), he may have intended the eccentricity in the paradigm to be understood in this way.

244 "As already mentioned": al-Shirbīnī appears to use the phrase as a link to the reference earlier in the paragraph to *ʿabūr*. The argument that follows in this difficult passage appears to be: if *ʿabūr* and *ʿābir* (both adjectives) may mean the same (see above), then *ʿubūr* (a noun)—here al-Shirbīnī switches forms without comment, on the principle, already well established, that words with the same consonantal skeleton are essentially the same, irrespective of any difference in voweling—and its colloquial derivative *ʿuburāyah* may also be interpreted as adjectives, if the poet is as stupid as the about-to-be-cited Shaykh Barakāt. Thus, in the doggerel cited below, Shaykh Barakāt, when referring to himself as *ʿuburāyah*, thinks he is referring to himself as "passing by" but is, in fact, saying that he is "a crossing place for sheep." *ʿUburāyah* (a voweling supported by the meter) may be interpreted as *ʿubūr* plus the colloquial diminutivizing ending *-āyah* (cf., e.g., *qashshāyah* "(small) piece of straw, bit of chaff" from *qashsh* "straw"), with consequent shortening of the non-prominent vowel, as in modern Egyptian. This solecism is only one of several in Shaykh Barakāt's verse offering; others are the use of colloquial forms (irrespective of their exact nature) in the first hemistich and the mixing of these with hackneyed pseudoclassical imagery in the second, and the fact that the verses do not even rhyme properly.

245 I.e., the East Roman, or Byzantine, Empire; the term denoted Anatolia through the Ottoman period, though the anecdote is probably not contemporary, and the "king" referred to below is probably the Byzantine emperor rather than the Ottoman sultan.

246 Birkat al-Fīl: the Pond of the Elephant (see Glossary).

247 "The etymology of *ʿajūz* has already been given": it has not.

248 The first hemistich is by Abū Firās al-Ḥamdānī (320–57/932–68) (*Dīwān*, 34); the second, which is repeated elsewhere (vol. 2, §11.37.15), appears to have been proverbial, occurring in the work of many poets, and is sometimes attributed, clearly incorrectly, to Bashshār ibn Burd.

249 Abū Nuwās: the attribution is incorrect.

250 Q Naml 27:21. Sulaymān, wishing to perform his ablutions before praying in an unfamiliar place, looked for, but failed to find, the hoopoe, which, according to common lore, could see water that was hidden under the ground and would point it out by pecking at the place.

251 I.e., ʿAlī ibn Abī Ṭālib.

252 I.e., the invasion of the Islamic world by the Mongols under Genghis Khan (ca. 1162–1227), which devastated the lands east of Egypt.

253 This is an abbreviated variant of the episode of the second whore in the story of the three whores of Cairo and the peasant (§3.34).

254 Al-Shirbīnī seeks to explain the usage and origin of the colloquial split negative morpheme *mā . . . shī*, as in the phrase *mā qadar shī* "he could not"—a feature that is standard in modern Egyptian but was probably less well established in his day—versus formal Arabic *mā qadara*. He is probably right in attributing this development to the use of *shī* (reflex of older *shay'* "thing") for emphasis, so that *mā qadar shī* originally would have been understood as "he was not able to at all."

255 These verses also occur in al-Sanhūrī, *Risible Rhymes*.

256 *anqāḍ*: the term is puzzling, given that the verses do not appear to be in any sense a riddle.

257 I.e., the meter *al-kāmil*, with permitted variants; the menemonic uses the root *kh-l-b-ṭ*, which has the senses of "causing trouble maliciously" and "confusing."

258 By the "well-known oath" al-Shirbīnī means *wa-llāhi l-ʿaẓīm* "by God the Mighty," the second word of which the peasant pronounces *ʿaḍīm*, with *ḍ* instead of *ẓ*. This pronunciation reflects a merging of /*ẓ*/ with /*ḍ*/, widespread in the Arabic dialects, in keeping with the general trend toward replacing fricative consonants with their nonfricative counterparts.

259 I.e., the peasant should have said *ʿālimun*; the literary inflections have mostly disappeared from modern dialects, and the peasant poet does not know how to use them correctly or, possibly, uses them according to the special conventions applying to them in certain colloquial verse genres, where they have been frozen in a single form irrespective of the syntactical role of the suffixed word.

260 The phenomenon may be associated with one noted for the modern dialect of al-Sharqiyyah, near Shirbīn, namely, fronting of pre-stress /*a*/ in closed syllables, which may result in a /*u*/, e.g., *ʿuṭshān* for *ʿaṭshān* ("thirsty"), *ṭubbāl* for *ṭabbāl* ("drummer") (see Woidich, *Dialekt*, 84 (3.2)). The author repeats the assertion later (§7.18), implying that he regards it as important evidence of the linguistic crassness of the peasants.

261 Al-Shirbīnī's commentary leaves us little the wiser as to the meaning of *khabāyiṭ*, which, from context, might be understood as "transgressions" or "public acts" or perhaps "public acts of transgression" (hence the translation). His further comments, below, on the word stay within the same circular orbit of definition.

262 "So-and-so 'cut' so-and-so": the Arabic and the English idioms coincide.

263 The verses, and the conceit of an (actually nonexistent) etymological relationship between *ins* ("man (as a species)") and *nisyān* ("forgetfulness") and between *qalb* ("heart") and *taqallub* ("inconstancy"), are well known.

264 Familiar or not, al-Shirbīnī's peasant poet appears to be under the misapprehension that *muhjah* ("heart; lifeblood; soul") means something like "chest," or "breast," or "breastbone." Thus, this line makes no sense, a point that al-Shirbīnī takes up in more detail later (§5.5.13).

265 Using another, still current, colloquial sense of the term; cf. Hinds and Badawi, *Dictionary*: *khabaṭ il-filūs* "he pocketed the money."

266 In the Arabic, the writer switches to the first person before reverting to the third.

267 "with an *a* after the second *k*": the correct form would be *-kumū*; in addition, the meter seems to demand the insertion of an anaptyctic vowel, hence *dhikirkamū*.

268 The poet uses the colloquial form *ṣawābiʿ* rather than the literary *aṣābiʿ* (and, below, *ḍawāfir* instead of *aẓāfir* "fingernails"), whence, given al-Shirbīnī's insistence on the essentially rural and bumpkinish nature of all colloquial forms, the translation "fangers" (and "fangernails").

269 See n. 264 above.

270 According to the rules of classical Arabic prosody, the rhyme should remain the same throughout.

271 An incorrect rendition of Q Nisāʾ 4:78 *fa-mā li-hāʾulāʾi l-qawmi lā yakādūn*.

272 Q Nisāʾ 4:79; i.e., the words that are not italicized immediately follow in the Qurʾan those quoted just before, and, the author believes, can be understood correctly only if the words "this being indicated . . ." etc. are supplied after "said," just as "with my fangers" can only be correctly understood if the words "a knife gripped by" are supplied after "with."

273 "The answer is thus and so and now the truth we know": such rhymed tags are often used by the author to signal the end of a "silly debate" and are carried over from the conventions of *fanqalah*. For a serious use of such tags, see al-Shirbīnī's quotation from al-Munāwī's *Al-Kawākib* below, which ends (vol. 2, §11.31.11) "Thus the discrepancy we repel; the reports agree and hang together well."

274 These verses also occur in al-Sanhūrī, *Risible Rhymes*, with differences.

275 The term refers both to stories based on biblical material and, more broadly, to tales of ancient times drawn from Near Eastern folklore and traditions. While some scholars approved of their use, insofar as they were in conformity with the teachings of Islam, others dismissed them as "idle talk" (see W. M. Brinner, "Isrāʾīliyyāt," in *EAL*).

276 See n. 257.

277 I.e., unless one reads قرن (*qarn*) "horn" with two dots for فرن (*furn*) "oven" with one—a quip on cuckoldry.

278 I.e., a bad thing made worse.

279 "advancement and deferment" (*taqdīm wa-ta'khīr*): i.e., the poet should be comparing the beloved's lovelocks to the rope and not vice versa; however, this phenomenon is usually called "reversed simile" (*tashbīh maqlūb*), while *taqdīm wa-ta'khīr* usually refers to the syntactic phenomenon of placing the object before the verb, as in *Zaydan ḍarabtu* for *ḍarabtu Zaydan* ("I struck Zayd").

280 In other words, nonfricative *t* replaces *th* (which, in this case, further shifts to emphatic *ṭ* under the influence of the emphatic *r*, which behaves, in some respects, like a velarized consonant).

281 I.e., as an insult, see §5.6.10.

282 Al-Shirbīnī is correct in relating the colloquial (but not specifically rural) form with *r* to the classical form with *l*.

283 The form *udayyāt* (plural of **udayyah*, diminutive of *īd* ("hand")) is not attested today and occurs in the manuscripts of *Brains Confounded* both as given here, as *īdīyāt*, and though less commonly, as *dayyāt*, which is the form in which it occurs in the corresponding passage in al-Sanhūrī's *Risible Rhymes*. It may be that *dayyāt* is the more authentic form and *udayyāt* a semi-classicization of the latter, under the influence of the literary *yudayyāt*.

284 I.e., *The Revival of the Religious Sciences* (*Iḥyā' 'ulūm al-dīn*), al-Ghazālī's magnum opus.

285 The meaning of the verb is, as the author says, "to gust"; however, the true verbal noun (in this case *habb* or *habūb* or *habīb*) has been jettisoned in favor of the lexical item under discussion.

286 *ibn 'ammī* ("my paternal cousin"): literally, "the son of my paternal uncle."

287 Q An'ām 6:74.

288 In fact, from the root *'-m-y* rather than *'-m-m* from which *'amm* derives.

289 The meaning of the verb is "to be universal; to include," and the real verbal noun is *'umūm*.

290 *sūdu* ("is as black as"): the form is difficult to interpret but occurs also in al-Sanhūrī's version of this verse.

291 In fact, according to conventional grammatical logic, *mukḥulah* and *kaḥḥāl* derive from *kuḥl*.

292 A standard work on ophthalmology, by Sharaf al-Dīn 'Alī ibn 'Īsā (d. after 400/1010).

293 Possibly a contraction of *mutaḥālī* (cf. the names ʿAbd al-Mutaʿāl for ʿAbd al-Mutaʿālī, al-ʿĀṣ for al-ʿĀṣī, etc.) or to be read *mutaḥāll* from a nonexistent Form VI verb of the root *ḥ-l-l*, but in any case obscure in this context.

294 A medical tradition existed based on sayings of the Prophet (see, e.g., Ibn Qayyim al-Jawziyyah's *Al-Ṭibb al-nabawī*).

295 See Vrolijk, *Bringing a Laugh*, 132, Arabic.

296 *ibni khālī* ("my maternal cousin"): literally, "the son of my maternal uncle."

297 Perhaps a reference to a boy's circumcision. The text is strange: though set as verse, it has neither meter nor rhyme.

298 Meaning "to imagine," with *khayl* ("horses") as the false verbal noun.

299 These verses are probably, in fact, by Bashshār ibn Burd (see, e.g., Ibn Abī ʿAwn, *Tashbīhāt*, 238).

300 The meaning is "to dangle, hang down" (intransitively; the earlier *tadliyah* belongs to the transitive form), with *tadallī* the correct verbal noun, *midallatan* for the sake of the argument.

301 Supposing al-Shirbīnī to be using a literary, and thus "original" and citable, form here, and the colloquial form in the verse.

302 More accurately, *rujaylāt* would be the plural of *rujayl*, diminutive of *rijl*.

303 I.e., *rijlāt*, were it to occur, would be the plural of *rijlah* ("purslane"), but the whole thing is a red herring, as it is not *rijlāt* that is the subject of discussion.

304 The meaning is "to go on foot," and it is moot whether al-Shirbīnī intended the verbal noun to be read as above (as the subject of the discussion) or correctly as *rajalan*.

305 I.e., Ṣafī al-Dīn al-Ḥillī, who describes this device as being what "ties two things to two [other] things, on condition that either of the things compared may take the place of the other" (al-Ḥillī, *Al-Badīʿiyyah*, 231).

306 These verses also occur in al-Sanhūrī, *Risible Rhymes*, with differences.

307 *ʿani l-ḥubbi . . . mina l-tāyih*: to be read *ʿa-l-ḥubbi . . . mi-l-tāyih* as required by the meter and in keeping with colloquial usage; these contractions are made explicit by al-Sanhūrī in *Risible Rhymes*. While al-Shirbīnī interprets *ʿa-l-ḥubbi* as a contraction of *ʿani l-ḥubbi*, al-Sanhūrī interprets it as a contraction of *ʿalā l-ḥubbi*. Both expand the contractions in the presentation forms of the verse, despite the disruption to the meter.

308 *al-tāyih . . . wa-jillāyih . . . mawlāyih . . . qattāyih*: these forms with *-ih* reproduce the vowelling of the items in the corresponding position in al-Sanhūrī, *Risible Rhymes*.

309 A form of the meter *al-basīṭ* with permitted variants; the mnemonic uses the root *th-q-l*, associated with "heaviness" and "obnoxiousness."

310 These lines are taken from his "suspended ode" or *muʿallaqah* (ʿAntarah, *Dīwān*, 150).

311 *farajiyyah*: "a wide open-fronted gown (*jubbah*) with long unslit sleeves" (Amīn, *Qāmūs*, 305).

312 I.e., for the payment of the outstanding taxes.

313 I.e., not *damʿ* ("tears") as in literary Arabic.

314 Meaning perhaps that the peasants treat even the most sumptuous of their foods (among which those listed can hardly count) so crudely as to eat them outdoors, wherever they happen to find themselves.

315 I.e., that aspect of the spirit that comprises the appetitive and sensual faculties, often referred to as "the soul that commands to evil."

316 I.e., the orthography used in the verse (مولايه) reflects the sound, which is homophonic with that of the more correct spelling مولايَ.

317 "God Almighty is with the meek": derived from a saying attributed variously to Moses (see, e.g., Ibn Ḥanbal, *Al-Musnad*, 134) and David (e.g., al-Bayhaqī, *Kitāb al-zuhd*, 367).

318 Q Yūnus 10:89; Moses entered Egypt on God's instruction to preach there and, on being rejected as a prophet by Pharaoh and his people, prayed that their riches should be destroyed, which came to pass when the Israelites left Egypt forty years later.

319 Al-Ḥillī describes *taʿdīd* ("enumeration") as "introducing separate names in one and the same passage" and says that if certain devices, such as punning (*tajnīs*) and pairing opposites in different halves of the line (*muqābalah*), are observed, the result is "extremely beautiful" (al-Ḥillī, *Al-Badīʿiyyah*, 306) Al-Shirbīnī pretends to believe that this banal and mechanical device (i.e., the reduplication of unit nouns) constitutes the elegant rhetorical figure described by al-Ḥillī.

320 Unit nouns are formed from collective or mass nouns by the addition of *-ah*, in the literary idiom, or, in the colloquial, of either *-ah* (realized here as *-ih* (see n. 308 above)), e.g. *bayḍ* ("eggs" (collective)) → *bayḍah* ("an egg" (unit noun)) or, as in this case, of *-āyah/-āyih*.

321 I.e., the two forms differ in the dots above one of the letters, as is self-evident.

322 *sūliyyah*: meaning unknown.

323 In reality, the root of *suʾāl* is *s-ʾ-l*, that of *sayl* and *sayālah* is *s-y-l*, and that of *sūliyyah* is *s-w-l*.

324 Presumably, another example of "stating the obvious."

325 While this may be intended as clarification, *ḥ*bb* is normally pronounced *ḥibb* when it means "beloved" and *ḥubb* when it means "water jar."

326 An introductory formula for riddles (see further vol. 2, §11.2.6).

327 Al-Shirbīnī's mother's explanation was presumably disingenuous, as "its belly" could just as well be understood as "his belly," with an obvious sexual connotation.

328 Pace al-Shirbīnī's earlier etymology (§5.7.4).

329 *Sic*, rather than in the literary form *dhabḥah*.

330 It is not clear in what way *jillāyah* is similar in meaning to *masahtu*.

331 In fact, the root of *shayl* is *sh-y-l*; those of the exemplars are *sh-l-y* and *sh-l-f*, respectively.

332 The reading is speculative, the more obvious *ʿajīrah* being unattested.

333 The verb has several meanings, none of them relevant.

334 The "antithesis" here being face/beard vs. belly and dung-slab/dung cake vs. loaf/hairy cucumber melon, etc.

335 I.e., he refers to it by implication.

336 Similar verses occur in al-Sanhūrī as the seventh in the series; al-Shirbīnī regards the pronominal suffixes at the end of the first line as, on balance, likely to be feminine (*-ik*; see §5.8.18), while in al-Sanhūrī's manuscript it is treated as masculine (*-ak*).

337 In reference to the four rhyming hemistichs.

338 The mnemonic uses the root *l-h-ṭ*, associated with "slapping."

339 Maṣr: the colloquial reflex of Miṣr, required here for the rhyme.

340 Apparently a slip for "rattle staff."

341 By which al-Shirbīnī appears to mean that sound is the result of air either rushing into a space when a vacuum is broken or rushing out of a space when one thing collides with another.

342 Al-Shirbīnī appears to have forgotten that he has not structured this discussion in the form of a debate of the sort that normally opens with the words "if it be said" and closes with a formula of this sort, though the argument is implicit in the contention that the referent of the comparison is not the bearing itself, as the surface structure would indicate, but the sound it makes.

343 On the rattle staff, see n. 355.

344 Epigrammatic verses such as this and the following that celebrate lovers of various professions, or play on the lover's name, became a genre in Mamluk times (see, e.g., al-Ibshīhī, *Al-Mustaṭraf*, 2:228–33; further, Rosenthal, *Male and Female*, 33ff).

345 I.e., it is a figurative usage, since the emir did not build the walls himself, his workers did so, and similarly the mill is only figuratively the poet's.

346 In the absence of voweling, *ishḥālik*, with second person feminine singular pronominal suffix *-ik*, may also be read *ishḥālak*, with second person masculine singular pronominal suffix *-ak*.

347 See n. 363.

348 Literally, the "tongue of (innate) condition" (*lisān al-ḥāl*), i.e., the faculty by which mute creatures, or even inanimate objects, may express themselves.

349 I.e., *illā* . . . , here used to indicate an unexpected event (for more examples, see Wright, *Grammar*, 2:339 Rem.C).

350 *wālak* for *mālak* "what's up?" involves an unusual shift of *m* to *w*, but *wālak* is attested from other contemporary and older colloquial Egyptian texts (Davies, *Profile*, 79–80) and, despite al-Shirbīnī's insistence on the synonymity of the two, may perhaps better be interpreted as deriving from *waylak* "Alas for you!"

351 From *ʿalaf* "fodder."

352 *tawwār*: from *tawr/tōr* "ox" (see n. 280).

353 Al-Shirbīnī omits the repetition of the final hemistich of the verses, to which the following comments apply, namely *ṭawru-bni shaykhi l-balad ḥālū mithāl ḥālak* ("The ox of the son of the shaykh of the village—his state is like yours!").

354 There is in fact no previous mention of this motif.

355 "A small shaft made of wood or iron that is attached to the top of the main shaft that turns the upper millstone. It turns with the stone and is equipped with lugs [which are perhaps al-Shirbīnī's 'fingers'] that bump against the feeder shoe for the stones. The shoe is a wooden container that receives the grain from the hopper above the stones and delivers it into the millstones. In order to feed the grain properly, the shoe has to be agitated or bumped rhythmically by the [rattle staff] . . . . This makes a distinctive noise, which the miller observed to determine whether he was running his stones at the proper speed and feed" (personal communication from John Lovett).

356 I.e., the western branch of the Nile.

357 *khulkhāl* and *khalkhalah* are from the same root (*kh-l-kh-l*) but *khuyalāʾ* is from *kh-y-l*.

358 The meaning is "to shake," with *khalkhalah* the correct verbal noun, *khulkhāl* for the sake of the argument.

359 Cf. Ibn Durayd, *Dīwān*, 124.

360 The root of *ruḥy* is *r-ḥ-y*; that of the other words cited is *r-w-ḥ*.

361 The Arabic combines four words, each of which contains the letters *r* and *ḥ* (and hence are related, according to al-Shirbīnī's deliberately misleading logic) to produce an almost meaningless bit of doggerel.

362 "the two preceding lines" (*al-baytayn al-sābiqayn*): al-Shirbīnī means, in fact, "the two hemistichs of the first line."

363 In Arabic poetry, the changing of the vowel immediately preceding a vowelless rhyme consonant is considered only a minor defect (S. A. Bonebakker, "Ḳāfiyah," in *EI2*); for an example from more conventional poetry, see the verses attributed to al-Shāfiʿī below, in which *Muhalhil* rhymes with *al-awwal* (vol. 2, §11.35.8). The possibility of the different readings *ishḥālak* (with masc. sg. suffix) and *ishḥālik* (with fem. sg. suffix) in the preceding line have been explained by the author at length above (§5.8.9).

364 "has already been given above": in fact is yet to come (vol. 2, §11.2.8).

365 *thawr* is the literary form, as against colloquial *tōr* and *ṭōr*.

366 "the analogy of Fuṭays" (*qiyās Fuṭays*): the meaning of this and the similar *al-qiyās al-fuṭaysī* (vol. 2, §§11.3.4, 11.33.7) is obscure.

367 The same verses appear, with one difference, in al-Sanhūrī, *Risible Rhymes*.

368 In the Arabic, the beating of a plank (*nāqūṣ*) with rods, the functional equivalent of bell-ringing; elsewhere the youth is described as a monk, which fits better (al-Ibshīhī, *Al-Mustaṭraf*, 2:231). In the verse, the poet plays on the homonyms *ḍarb al-nawāqīsi* ("the ringing of the bells") and *ḍarb al-nawā qīsī* ("the wringing of your heart"; literally, the pain of separation).

369 See n. 242.

370 Cf. "[G]et some safflower so that we can stain your son ʿAfr's and his brother Night-Cracker's clothes yellow so they stand out among the village boys and can boss them around" (§3.20 and n. 98).

371 Today's *ḥidwah* are "leather sandals with one thong over the instep and another encircling the big toe" (Hinds and Badawi, *Dictionary*, 1986, 196).

372 "as previously noted": see §5.6.12.

373 On this expression, see vol. 2, §11.31.16.

374 *al-ḍārib*: possibly related to *dammu ḍarab* "(1) he had a (brain) haemorrhage (2) he burst a blood vessel (with anger)" (Hinds and Badawi, *Dictionary*, 520).

375 Here the "antithesis" seems to consist of the contrasts of *feet* (implied through the mention of sandals) and *head* plus *sandals* with *flaxen cord*.

376 Abū l-ʿAtāhiyah, *Ashʿāruhu*, 32.

377 Al-Ṣafadī attributes these verses, with a different first line, to the Naṣrid king of Granada al-Ghālib bi-llāh Muḥammad ibn Muḥammad ibn Yūsuf ibn al-Aḥmar (*Al-Wāfī*, 1:207).

378 The verses are more often ascribed to ʿAbbās al-Aḥnaf (*Dīwān*, 312).

379 The meaning of the verb is "to turn away; to discard," with *ḥarf* the correct verbal noun and *ḥarīfan* "for the argument."

380 Both *farqalah* and *firqāl* seem to be nonce words, inserted to give the impression that *farqillah*—from Greek *phragellion*—conforms to Arabic patterns.

381 *ṭarrāshah*: clearly a kind of whip, though the word does not appear to be attested elsewhere; the root sense appears to be "deafener," from *aṭrash* "deaf." Thus, according to the author's logic, *ṭarrāshah* and *farqillah* are related "etymologically" through their similarity of meaning.

382 I.e., after changing the ʿ to an *l*, they added the letter *h*, which, without superscript dots, may be interpreted as the third person masculine possessive pronoun, so that the meaning of the new word would be "crack him!" With superscript dots, however, the *h* would be read as *tāʾ marbūṭah*, an ending characteristic of feminine nouns.

383 "Compound proper names" (*al-tarkīb al-mazjī*) are made, or conventionally explained as having been made, by joining two or more words; thus *Baʿlabakk* (Baalbek, a town in eastern Lebanon) supposedly derives from Baʿl (name of an idol) plus *bakk* ("to squeeze") and means "Baʿl squeezed (their necks)" (Yāqūt, *Buldān*, 1:538), while *Maʿdīkarib* (a pre-Islamic prince of Hadramawt) supposedly consists of Maʿd (a proper name) plus *yakrubu* ("twists," or "presses hard upon"), though, as Yāqūt hints, such names are not Arabic in origin and the point is moot. On the morphology, see Wright, *Grammar*, 1:108 B.

384 The verb is probably invented.

385 Among the meanings of the verb are "to come back" and (colloquially) "to wind."

386 Any of several plants of the of the family Brassicaceae.

387 I.e., the main ode of Abū Shādūf (§11).

388 Vrolijk, *Bringing a Laugh*, 47 Arabic, lines 19–20.

389 In the fourteenth century, when Ibn Sūdūn wrote, Jews wore yellow turbans, Christians blue; for Jews, see al-Ibshīhī, *Al-Mustaṭraf*, 1:39 ("like the turbans of the Jews—yellow, tall, and thin"), for Christians, see Lane, *Manners*, 531, 550.

390 I.e., alchemy.

391 Among the meanings of the verb is "to confuse," of which the correct verbal noun is *labs*, *labsān* being for the argument.

392 *ḥiddāyah* ("black kite"): *Milvus migrans*, a bird formerly common in Egyptian cities.

393 The rat or mouse, the biting dog, the serpent, the kite, and either the crow or the scorpion; the law permits their killing by those in a state of ritual purity (*iḥrām*) or engaged in prayer (cf. Lane, *Lexicon*, s.v. *ḥayawān*). Their characterization as "transgressive" is explained differently by various authors (ibid. s.v. *fāsiq*).

394 *shulūq*: meaning unknown.

395 The verb means "to be blackened by smoke, to be filthy," etc.

396 None of the lines of the following verses has the same rhyme.

397 I.e., Murjān the Ethiopian, or East African; the name Murjān is stereotypical for blacks (see also Murjānah, for a black slave woman, §3.5), which casts doubt on the authenticity of the verses and implies that they may be a lampoon intended to poke fun at them.

398 "attempted to outdo" (*ʿāraḍa*): "counter-poems" (*muʿāraḍah*), with which a poet either presents a point of view opposing that of an older poem or attempts to outdo it, while retaining the original rhyme and meter, are an established form (see van Gelder, "Muʿāraḍa," in *EAL*). As al-Shirbīnī mentions below, the following verses are in the form of a pentastich (*takhmīs*), i.e., "an expansion of a given poem into a strophic poem of five-line stanzas in which the last two lines consist of one line (two hemistichs) from the original poem, and the three new lines at the beginning rhyme with the first hemistich"

(*idem*). In this case, however, the poet seems to have taken just one verse of the original by al-Būṣīrī ("outdoing" it by introducing changes) and used it as his point of departure for the pentastich, all the rest of which is clearly his own work. In the version found in his published *Dīwān*, al-Būṣīrī's verse reads: *yā nabiyya l-hudā stighāthatu malḥū * fin aḍarrat bi-ḥālihi l-ḥawbāʾū* (al-Būṣīrī, *Dīwān*, 75, line 3) "O Prophet of Guidance, grant aid to one grief- * stricken, whose soul has been afflicted by his state!"

399 "And of His Lord's signs he saw the biggest sizèd" (*wa-qad raʾā min āyāti rabbihi l-kubarāʾī*): cf. Q Najm 53:18 *laqad raʾā min āyāti rabbihi l-kubrā*.

400 I.e., the Muqaṭṭam (a range of hills east of Cairo).

401 I.e., Mount Sinai.

402 I.e., *al-Qāmūs al-muḥīṭ* of al-Fīrūzābādhī, the standard dictionary of the time.

403 *dūhās*: the word is unknown.

404 Abū l-Nawwās: in error for Abū Nuwās.

405 I.e., Abū l-ʿAlāʾ al-Maʿarrī.

406 I.e., the Prophet Muḥammad.

407 The Prophet is buried at Medina and not, as the poet seems to think, at Ḥunayn, which is near Mecca.

408 "tomb" (*ḥujrah*, literally "chamber"): the tomb is called "the chamber" because, according to a tradition, the Prophet was buried under the floor of the chamber of his wife ʿĀʾishah, in his family compound at Medina (Marmon, *Eunuchs*, 46). It was not, in fact, possible to see, let alone kiss, the tomb (ibid., 46ff.).

409 Murjān al-Ḥabashī uses only the first hemistich of Ibn al-Fāriḍ's poem, which is one of his best known, and changes it. Ibn al-Fāriḍ reads *sharibnā ʿalā dhikri l-ḥabībi mudāmatan* ("We drank at mention of the Loved One's name a wine") (Ibn al-Fāriḍ, *Dīwān*, 327), the wine referred to being the intoxicating experience of the divine.

410 Cf. Q Muṭaffifīn 83:25–26 *[yusqawna min raḥīqin makhtūmin] khitāmuhu misk* "[they are given to drink of a pure wine, sealed,] whose seal is musk."

411 Presumably a reference to ʿIzz al-Dīn Hibatallāh ibn Sanāʾ al-Mulk (550–608/1155–1211), whose work *Dār al-Ṭirāz* (*The House of Brocade*) treats of the *muwashshaḥ*, a verse form developed in Andalusia that sometimes contained words and phrases in Romance.

412 In reference to a Tradition that reads in part, "Then he [the Prophet] entered a walled enclosure belonging to one of the Anṣār, where he came across a camel which, when it saw him, moaned and wept. So the Prophet, God bless him and grant him peace, went to it and wiped the back of its ear, and the camel fell silent. Then he said, 'Who is the owner of this camel?' and a young man of the Anṣār came and said, 'It is mine, Messenger of God.' The Prophet said, 'Do you not fear God with regard to this beast that He has made your possession? It complained to me that you starve it and terrorize it.'"

413 "as long as pilgrims . . .": a nonsensical attempt to imitate phrases such as "as long as lightning shall flash" or "as long as doves shall coo" that are sometimes used, in association with praise of the Prophet Muḥammad, at the ends of poems, the sense being "forever."

414 "House of the Versifierers" (*bayt al-naẓẓāmūn*): the Turk makes an elementary mistake in grammar by using the form *naẓẓāmūn* in genitive construct instead of *naẓẓāmīn*.

415 "To shoot any occasion," where *muḥāẓaratan* stands for *muḥāḍaratan*, i.e., "to suit any occasion." This is another jab at the Turk's pronunciation, since the realization of *ḍ* as *ẓ* in modern Egyptian (e.g., *ẓābiṭ* "officer," *ẓaraṭ* "to fart") is believed to have been introduced by Turkish speakers (see Vollers, "Beiträge," 18 §3 (12), and Woidich, *Materialen*).

416 The judge means that the letter *shin* (ش)—first letter of *sharʿ* ("canon law")—cuts like a saw because it has three vertical loops, traditionally known as "teeth." The original depends for its comic effect on the tedious repetition of this letter.

417 Both *zubdiyyah* and *qullah* are grammatically feminine.

418 In addition to being banal in sense, the verses are characterized by the use of colloquialisms (e.g., *arsalt bi-tis'al* ("you sent asking")) and pseudo-high-flown forms rendered with colloquial pronunciations (e.g., *wiʿāḍah* (from *waʿẓ*)).

419 "exhortatorily" (*wiʿāḍah*): implying that the shaykh made his living as a *wāʿiẓ* ("preacher").

420 Diminutive of ʿArab.

421 Diminutive of Hind.

422 I.e., his name was Muḥammad al-Rāziqī.

423 ʿAzrīl: in error for ʿIzrāʾīl (the angel of death).

424 I.e., his tears gushed like water falling from the buckets of a waterwheel.

425 Presumably meaning professional mourning women, who are hired to wail and sing laments, pulling their veils back and forth over the backs of their necks as they do so.

426 "the Mistress": i.e., his wife.

427 I.e., Thursday, 6 Jumādā al-Ūlā (colloquial Jamād al-Awwal) 1034 = 13 February 1625.

428 Assuming that "his grandsire" means "Yūsuf's grandsire," the poet's name was ʿĀbid al-Raḥmān [ibn] Muḥammad Maghūrī.

429 In this last element of his pedigree, the poet switches to the feminine (*fulān ibn fulānah*).

430 Each letter of the Arabic alphabet has a conventionally assigned numerical value under a system known as *ḥisāb al-jummal* (G. S. Colin, "Ḥisāb al-djummal," in *EI2*). Starting in the ninth/fifteenth century, the construction of chronograms capable of being read both as words and as dates became a common feature of congratulatory poetry. Thus, in the line *fa-lammā fataḥahā arrakhtuhā * ḥākiman fī shahri Dhī l-Qaʿdah* ("When he conquered it, I dated it * Year 70 in the month of Dhū l-Qaʿdah"), the word *ḥākiman* (حاكما)

may be understood either as representing the number 70 (ح = 8 + ا = 1 + ك = 20 + م = 40 + ا = 1, i.e., 70 H, referring presumably to the current, seventh, century, i.e., 670), or as meaning "as a ruler." The ineptness of the latter reading ("I dated it as a ruler") is presumably what angered Baybars in the verse (what angered him in the prose is less obvious, unless it was the poet's unusual reference to his grandmother). The month of Dhū l-Qaʿdah 670 H began on May 31, AD 1272. Since the earliest examples of such chronograms are considered to date from the ninth/fifteenth century (*EAL*, 1:173), the whole incident must be spurious.

431 Abū Ḥafṣ ʿUmar ibn ʿAlī l-Muṭṭawwiʿī (see al-Thaʿālibī, *Yatīmah*, 4:436).

432 See Introduction, p. xxx; for a broader discussion of the relations between the contemporary religious establishment and Sufis, see Winter, *Society and Religion*, and al-Ṭawīl, *al-Taṣawwuf*, 1:165–99. The charge of sexual malpractice and charlatanry that al-Shirbīnī levels against rural dervishes in the following pages were by no means new or confined to Egypt: al-Jawbarī, a Syrian of the sixth–seventh/thirteenth century whose *Al-Mukhtār fī Kashf al-Asrār* exposes the tricks of contemporary conmen, devotes a section to "the secrets of those who claim to be shaykhs," in which he refers to the "Permissivists" (*al-mubāḥiyyah*) who permit "obscene acts with women and seclusion with beardless boys" (Höglmeier, *Al-Ǧawbarī*, 99) as well as to several of the tricks referred to by al-Shirbīnī, such as the use of concealed props such as sheep's intestines filled with water (Höglmeier, *Al-Ǧawbarī*, 103–4; see also Irwin, *Companion*, 131–32 and passim). Similarly, "the detractors of the Qalandars and Abdals [antinomian Sufis] of Rum [Anatolia] [whose practices eventually also entered Egypt], in particular accused them of reprehensible forms of sexual libertinism, especially sodomy and zoophilism" (Karamustafa, *Friends*, 20). Nor were religious chicanery and heresy an exclusively Ottoman phenomenon: Shoshan provides examples from the Mamluk period of, inter alia, a man examined by magistrates because he claimed to make heavenly journeys (Shoshan, *Culture*, 9) and of shaykhs who preached idolatry and "abominations and blasphemies directed at the Qur'an" (*idem*, 13). Obviously, neither these nor al-Shirbīnī's accounts should be accepted at face value; as Shoshan points out, "deprived of the oral communication of the past, we can only see the beliefs of the illiterate refracted through the writings of the literate, whose religious understanding was professedly of a different order." On the other hand, as Karamustafa points out with regard to condemned sexual practices (Karamustafa, *Friends*, 20), "while such trite accusations should be taken with a grain of salt, they cannot be discarded altogether . . . . Celibacy [characteristic of antinomian Sufism] . . . meant primarily the refusal to participate in the sexual reproduction of society and did not exclude unproductive forms of sexual activity."

433 In Sufi terminology, the course of instruction and discipline followed to achieve mystical experience, and also, by extension, a specific Sufi "order."

434 A fatwa concerning the Muṭāwiʿah dervishes written in 1197/1782–83 by a certain Shaykh ʿAlī l-Ṣaʿīdī al-ʿAdawī says, "They take the pitcher and fill it with water and carry it in their hands wherever they go so they may perform their ablutions with it from time to time, and [likewise they take] large prayer beads of wood . . ." (al-Ṭawīl, *Al-Taṣawwuf*, 1:85). The first two of these items, and especially the pitcher, are mentioned several times throughout the book as typical of the rural dervish, the list elsewhere being extended to include a crutch (§7.33). The list is thus close to that given by Ḥasan al-Badrī al-Ḥijazī (d. 1131/1718–19) in the first lines of his poem attacking dervishes, where he says, "Beware of those who say magnificats, with prayer beads, wool, crutch, wrap (*shamlah*), woolen cloak (*dilq*), and pitcher . . . ." (al-Jabartī, *ʿAjāʾib*, 1:79). The significance of the cockerel and the fodder is obscure.

435 At saints' feasts (*mawlids*), pious patrons typically provided free food for mendicant Sufis and the poor in general (Winter, *Society and Religion*, 182).

436 Several conditions, e.g., sickness, absolve the believer of his obligation to fast from sunrise to sunset during Ramadan.

437 "We are a people who have been relieved of the obligation to obey God's commandments" (*naḥnu qawmun qad saqaṭa ʿannā l-taklīf*): *taklīf* is "[a] term of the theological and legal vocabulary denoting the fact of an imposition on the part of God of obligations on his creatures" (D. Gimaret, "taklīf," in *EI2*). The belief that the holiest men were exempted from an obligation to follow the rules that bound ordinary believers was widespread during the period and used to explain and justify eccentric and even criminal behavior (al-Ṭawīl, *Al-Taṣawwuf*, 1:116, 155–57), the rationale being that when the spiritual faculties are entirely absorbed in the contemplation of the Divine, the purely material form that remains, without the tutelage of the higher faculty, will follow its instincts without restraint.

438 Muḥammad Wafā ibn Muḥammad al-Shādhilī (d. 765/1364), on whom see Brockelmann, *GAL*, Suppl. 2:4.

439 On "the Day of the Divine Decree" (*yawm al-qadr*), more usually referred to as "the Night of the Divine Decree," see Glossary; despite the implication of the woman's words, there is no authority for breaking fast on that day.

440 In Paradise, the Believers will be waited on by "immortal youths" (Q Wāqiʿah 56:17) and "fair ones with wide, lovely eyes" (56:22).

441 Q Hūd 11:79: said by the men of Sodom to Lot when he offered them his daughters in order to protect the angels who were lodging with him in the form of beautiful youths.

442 "The Provider" (*al-Razzāq*) and "the Living" (*al-Ḥayy*) are among the names of God; the Throne (*al-ʿarsh*) and the Seat (*al-kursī*) of God are described in the Qur'an as embracing the heavens and the earth (Q Aʿrāf 7:254; Baqarah 2:255), and in mysticism are sometimes equated with God's knowledge. The Tablet (*al-lawḥ*) and the Pen (*al-qalam*) are the media with which the decisions of the Divine Will are recorded (Q Burūj 85:22).

443 Ibn al-ʿArabī, *Dīwān*, 207.

444 Cf. Q Ḥāqqah 69:17 "and above them eight will carry the throne of your Lord."

445 These verses are attributed to ʿAlī ibn Abī Ṭālib (al-ʿĀmilī, *Al-Kashkūl*, 470).

446 Perhaps Muḥammad ibn ʿAlī ibn Muḥammad ibn Ibrāhīm Abū al-Khaṭṭāb al-Jabbulī (d. 439/1048), a Baghdadi poet (Yāqūt, *Buldān*, art. "Jabbul"; also al-Ṣafadī, *Al-Wāfī*, 4:124–25).

447 Horns are associated with cuckoldry in Arabic (see, e.g., Hinds and Badawi, *Dictionary*, 696 s.v. *qarn*) as in English, but the appropriateness of the association in this context is dubious.

448 Dervishes are not known to have used an argot (on which, in Egypt, see ʿĪsā, *Al-Lughāt*, and Rowson, "Cant"). Al-Jabartī, writing of the ʿĪsawiyyah order in the late eighteenth century, mentions that they "spoke distorted words in their language," but this may mean only that they used the dialect of their native Morocco (al-Jabartī, *ʿAjā'ib*, 3:39).

449 I.e., dressing as did those Sufis who demonstrated their commitment to "poverty" by wearing conspicuously patched garments, which they sometimes made by taking the fine clothes donated to them by the rich, ripping them to pieces, and reconstituting them, a practice approved of by al-Shaʿrānī (Winter, *Society and Religion*, 191).

450 I.e., the Turkish judge.

451 Q Yūnus 10:63.

452 Al-Khafājī, al-Shirbīnī's older contemporary, mentions an ʿAlī Wafā, chief of the descendants of the Prophet, in his anthology of contemporary poets (al-Khafājī, *Rayḥānat al-alibbā'*, 301), and the resemblance of the colloquial and moralistic verses quoted here to those of Ibn ʿArūs, who may also belong to the Ottoman period, suggests that they were written by him. However, the Wafā (or Wafā') family were preeminent in intellectual Sufi circles in Cairo for five centuries, starting with Muḥammad (d. 765/1363), and the latter's son ʿAlī (d. 807/1405) was also known for his mystical poetry (his *dīwān* remains unpublished).

453 *durfās*: meaning unknown.

454 I.e., to get around the man's hasty oath.

455 ʿAllām is a proper name that means "very knowledgable or learned."

456 The verses exploit the tendency of Sufi terminology to use common words with special, esoteric meanings. Thus "to strip naked" in Sufi terminology is to strip oneself of all that

might impede one's awareness of God; the "it" might be secret knowledge (of God) or the experience of union with Him; and the "heedless" those who are heedless of God (Trimingham, *Sufi Orders*, 145).

457 Here referring to the *aḥwāl* ("states"), or transitory spiritual raptures vouchsafed by God to those who follow the Sufi path (cf. Trimingham, *Sufi Orders*, 140 n. 1).

458 The biographer of the mystic poet Ibn al-Fāriḍ mentions that the latter was also prone to go into ecstasies on overhearing snatches of verse: "One day, on the way to the mosque, Ibn al-Fāriḍ passed a fuller, who was beating and cutting a piece of cloth on the rocks while singing: This piece of cloth / has shattered my heart, / but it's not pure / until it's shredded! Hearing this, Ibn al-Fāriḍ swooned, and he repeated the verse hour after hour, at times falling on the ground, until the state finally subsided" (Homerin, *Ibn al-Fāriḍ*, 50 and, similarly, 45). Al-Shirbīnī, however, approves of Ibn al-Fāriḍ.

459 With the exception of the last sentence ("God giveth . . ." Q Āl ʿImrān 3:37), the words are in colloquial Arabic.

460 Q Āl ʿImrān 3:37: "Whenever Zakariyya went into the sanctuary where she was, he found she had food. He said, 'O Mary! Whence cometh unto thee this (food)?' She answered, 'It is from God. God giveth without stint to whom He will.'"

461 The original reads in translation: "In the name of God the Merciful, the Compassionate, praise be to God, Lord of the Worlds, the Merciful, the Compassionate, Owner of the Day of Judgment, Thee we worship, Thee we ask for help. Show us the straight path; the path of those whom Thou hast favored, not that of those who earn Thy anger nor of those who go astray. Amen."

462 I.e., of mystical knowledge.

463 A mixture of genuine and concocted names of God.

464 I.e., the Prophet Muḥammad.

465 The prayer rug (*sajjādah*) is symbolic of the leadership of a Sufi order.

466 Cf. the modern proverb "How fortunate is he who has power [to do harm] and [yet] is merciful!" (*ya bakht min qidir wi-ʿifi*) (Taymūr, *Al-Amthāl*, 505).

467 These three men were all non-Muslim leaders who played roles in the Prophet's life. Abū Ṭālib was the Prophet's full uncle and protected him as a young man, hence the association of his hands with gentleness. Abū Lahab ("Father of Fire"), the Prophet's half uncle, was so named because of his beauty. Abū Jahl was one of the Prophet's most determined opponents; the evidence for his being stout appears to be the Prophet's comment that when the two were young Abū Jahl was fatter than he was (see, e.g., Ibn Hishām, *Al-Sīrah*, 2:201; Guillaume, *Life*, 304).

468 The Sharīk referred to is Sharīk al-Nakhaʿī (95–177/713–94), a scholar of Traditions and a jurist. However, the attribution is false, the epigram deriving instead from the words

of Abū Nuwās, *ḥaddathanā fī baʿḍi āthārihī | Abū Bilālin ʿan shaykhunā Sharīk: || lā yashtafī l-ʿāshiqu fī ʿishqihī | bi-l-shammi wa-l-taqbīli ḥattā yanīk* ("In one of the sayings he has reported / Our shaykh, Abū Bilāl, on the authority of our shaykh Sharīk, tells us, / The lover will never be cured of his passion / by sniffing and kissing, only by fucking") (*Dīwān*, 5:240).

469 I.e., a stage, attained through the Sufi's efforts, on the Path to the experience of Divine Reality (Trimingham, *Sufi Orders*, 4, 139).

470 After each two cycles of prostration (*rakʿah*), the worshipper offers the greetings or blessings that are collectively known as *al-taḥiyyāt*.

471 "After the last *rakʿah* [prostration] of each of the prayers . . . the worshipper, looking upon his right shoulder, says, 'Peace be upon you, and the mercy of God!' Then looking upon the left, he repeats the same" (Lane, *Manners*, 78).

472 ʿAlī l-Saqqā: unidentified.

473 Literally, "the hip bones"; perhaps a distortion of *al-Ḥujurāt*, the title of Surah 49 of the Qur'an.

474 ʿAlī Ḥabashī al-Shirbīnī: unidentified.

475 "steed" (*najībah*): literally "a camel of good race" but apparently signifying in the iconography of this kind of popular Sufism an animal ridden by Sufi saints, which, in a passage below (§7.30), is described as being green.

476 "Sufi music" (*samāʿ*): literally "audition" or "listening," hence "music (and dance)" in a religious context; despite (or, in part, because of) the association of the latter with Sufism, *samāʿ* was always treated with suspicion by scholars (see Karamustafa, *Friends*, 20).

477 Which he would supposedly have visited, using his supernatural powers.

478 How seriously the breaking by a disciple of his allegiance to his shaykh was viewed is implied by al-Shaʿrānī when he says, "Among the blessings of God, blessed and almighty, that He has bestowed upon me is my not accepting the allegiance of a disciple who has broken his allegiance to his shaykh and come to me to make me his shaykh . . . or showing him a smiling face, out of respect for the pact he made with the shaykh with whom he broke" (al-Shaʿrānī, *Laṭāʾif*, 331).

479 This, and the other similar stories in this section, evoke such legitimate Sufi practices as *tawajjuh*, by which the shaykh transfers knowledge of the divine to his disciple: "In this exercise the shaykh . . . concentrates upon the *murīd* [disciple], picturing the spinning of a linkage between his pineal heart (*al-qalb al-ṣanawbarī*) and the heart of the *murīd* through which power can flow. At the same time, the *murīd* concentrates upon becoming a passive vessel for the overflowing power of the shaykh" (Trimingham, *Sufi Orders*, 148).

480 "the Higher and Lower Realm" (*al-malakūt al-ʿulwī wa-l-suflī*): perhaps a conflation of Sufi theosophy's "World of Sovereignty" (*ʿālam al-malakūt*), which is "the invisible, spiritual, angelic world" (Trimingham, *Sufi Orders*, 160) and the Upper and Lower Worlds (*al-ʿālam al-ʿulwī, al-ʿālam al-suflī*) of the Greek-derived cosmology of the philosophers (see, e.g., al-Tifāshī, *Surūr*, 164).

481 "retreat" (*khalwah*): meaning both the condition of withdrawal from contact with other persons in which the Sufi seeks to draw close to God, and a space designated for that purpose. At the period, a *khalwah* might take the form of a room or cell in a Sufi hostel (*zāwiyah*) or in a private house or cave (al-Ṭawīl, *Al-Taṣawwuf*, 1:67–69). The acquisition of paranormal powers (such as walking on water or flying) was considered to be among the benefits of *khalwah* (ibid., 69).

482 All the words used (*qamar* "moon," *ibrīq* "pitcher," *kalb* "dog," *ḥimār* "donkey," *baghl* "mule") are grammatically masculine.

483 The iteration three times by the husband of the formula "I divorce you" makes the divorce irrevocable.

484 31 October 1655 to 19 October 1656.

485 The Sufi's crutch was short and used not for walking but to support the Sufi when seated and performing lengthy devotions. Examples may be seen at the Gayer-Anderson Museum in Cairo (see Warner, *Guide*, 21, for an illustration).

486 These lines appear in a different form in the published version (al-Maʿarrī, *Al-Luzūmiyyāt*, 2:45).

487 I.e., he turned in the direction of Ṭanṭā, in the middle of the Delta, site of the tomb of Aḥmad al-Badawī.

488 Literally, "father of deliverances."

489 Cf. Q Nūr 24:35: "God is the Light of the heavens and the earth. The similitude of His light is as a niche wherein is a lamp. The lamp is in a glass. The glass is as it were a shining star. [This lamp is] kindled from a blessed tree, an olive . . . ." and Tīn 95:1 "By the Fig and the Olive . . . !"

490 Q Tawbah 9:30 and Zukhruf 43:4.

491 I.e., to exclaim as one might on hearing news of a death.

492 Bahāʾ al-Dīn Zuhayr (581–656/1186–1258) (*Poetical Works*, 157).

493 I.e., the letters of the word حسن "comely, handsome" have been rewritten with the addition of dots above the two first letters, so that the word becomes خشن "coarse."

494 "God spared the Believers attack": Q Aḥzāb 33:25.

495 The last words of each line (النبات and البيات) have the same consonantal skeletons and vary only in the distribution of the dots that distinguish one consonant from another; hence the wordplay is "orthographic."

496 The Qur'an contains several references to the legions of jinn employed to do Sulaymān's bidding, e.g., Q Anbiyā' 21:82, Ṣād 38:37.

497 Q Ṣād 38:50–51.

498 Today, pallbearers at the funerals of holy men, and even of ordinary people, sometimes report that the corpse is directing their movements, forcing them to run or stop.

499 Aḥmad ibn al-Ḥusayn ibn Raslān al-Ramlī, a Shāfiʿī jurisprudent (d. 844/1441) wrote *(Ṣafwat) al-Zubad fīmā ʿalayhi l-muʿtamad*, an unpublished versification of the unpublished *Kitāb al-Zubad* by Sharaf al-Dīn Abū l-Qāsim Hibat Allāh ibn Qāḍī al-Quḍāt Najm al-Dīn al-Juhanī al-Bārizī (645–738/1247–1338), also a Shāfiʿī jurisprudent (*GAL* 1:96, Suppl. 2:113), and is cited as the author in one manuscript (Mingana 1564).

500 "beasts": in the original "apes."

501 Cf. Crecelius, *Al-Damurdāshī*, 84: "They [the Maghāribah Bedouin, when they heard that an expeditionary force had been sent against them from Cairo in 1109/1698] loaded their equipment and their women and sent them to the western mountains."

502 Ibn Ḥajar means "Son of Stone," implying insensitivity or boorishness, but is also the name of the famous Egyptian Traditionist Ibn Ḥajar al-ʿAsqalānī. Ibn Baqar literally means "Son of Cattle"; the name occurs historically.

503 Literally, "the audible fart, father of the silent fart."

504 "He has no share of it but the name by which he's known": i.e., the only connection between true knowledge and a rural pastor (*faqīh*) is that *fiqh*, from which *faqīh* derives, originally means "knowledge."

505 These words do not occur in the Qur'an; al-Shirbīnī implies that the peasant will produce spurious Qur'anic verses in support of his position.

506 Al-Ḍāhir: the Mamluk ruler al-Ẓāhir Baybars (r. 658–76/1260–77), a *sīrah* (epic romance) on whose life was performed publicly in Cairo until at least the twentieth century (Lane, *Manners*, 400ff.).

507 "the Dalhamah according to al-Baṭṭāl": see n. 163.

508 *Shīḥah . . . Umm Jābir . . . Abū Furayḥah*: characters from *The Deeds of the Banū Hilāl* (*Sīrat Banī Hilāl*), a popular romance.

509 I.e., the peasant pastor will credit his father with the authority to relate Traditions, and likewise (see below) his grandfather and great-great-grandmother.

510 This statement is of special importance for the history of Egyptian Arabic, because it implies that, in nonrural speech in the late seventeenth century, the letter *jīm* already was realized like the *g* in "give" (as in modern Cairo and parts of the northern Egyptian countryside) rather than the *j* in "joy" or the *s* in "pleasure" (as in most of the rest of the Arab world).

511 *ishtiwān*: see n. 86.

512 At the conclusion of a marriage contract, the bride typically is represented by a male sponsor or proxy.

513 Cf. Q Ḥāqqah 69:27 "Ah, would that it [sc. Death] . . . (had been the end of me)!" *yā laytahā kānat al-qaḍiyyah*—implying, perhaps, that you should hope that things move to their conclusion before the Judge reverses his decision.

514 "That one's a Friend of God and 'a she-donkey leader'" (*hādhā walīy wa-qayyid al-ḥimārah*): the sense, and even the segmentation, of the words are uncertain. It may be that *qayyid* is to be understood as *qāʾid*, in which case see Ibn Abī l-Ḥadīd, *Sharḥ* 5:497: "They say, idiomatically, of a weak old man that he is 'the she-donkey's leader' (*qāʾid al-ḥimārah*)."

515 Al-Shirbīnī accuses the rural Sufis of substituting allegiance to local feuding groups for membership of one of the four orthodox schools of law.

516 The terms al-Shirbīnī uses in this and the preceding line have specialized Sufi, as well as general, connotations: the "people of virtue" are the Sufis in general; "the perfected" are those who have reach the stage of the "perfect man"; and the "ranks of the ignorant" are the uninitiated masses.

517 See n. 49.

518 The following overlaps with the list given early on in the work (§§2.11, 2.14, 2.15), though some of the personal names appear here in the form of second elements of *kunyah*s; only items not already covered, and to which some meaning may be given, are annotated.

519 Qaṭā: "Sand grouse."

520 Abū Fardat Waṭā: "The Man with One Slipper."

521 Khubayṭ: "Little Blow."

522 Qarrūsh: cf. *qirsh* "shark."

523 al-Nabsh: "Rummaging."

524 Ḥunayn: a genuine name, still in use.

525 On *shawālī* and *matārid*, types of crock, see vol. 2, §11.16.2.

526 Abū l-Dawāhī: "Father of Disasters."

527 Abū Mayshūm: "Father of an Ill-Omened One."

528 [Abū] Shādūf . . . [Abū] Mishkāḥ: since these appear surrounded by *kunyah*s and occur only as such elsewhere, it seems probable that the first element is omitted in the Arabic for the meter.

529 Abū Rayyāḥ: "He of a large irrigation canal."

530 I.e., "Miḥammad" (as today) and "Miḥimmad" (not heard today).

531 Muḥammadayn is the dual of Muḥammad, i.e., literally, "two Muḥammads" or "double Muḥammad"; the name occurs today, as does the similar Ḥasanayn.

532 "Beasts" or "Farm Animals."

533 I.e., they substitute nonemphatic *s* for emphatic *ṣ*. This occurs in modern Egyptian in several roots, e.g., *saddaq* for *ṣaddaqa* ("to believe, credit"), *sandūq* for *ṣundūq* ("box"). However, Sāliḥ for Ṣāliḥ does not occur and is the author's joke, since *sāliḥ* means "shitting."

534 See n. 280; *mīrātī* means "my inheritance" and *irth* "inheritance."

535 The author cites words (*bawshah* ("pot") and *jawād* (a kind of slipper, see two lines below)) that he considers unpleasing to the educated ear.

536 See §5.2.2; the phrase *mā ḍāl hādhā l-wādī* appears to mean "This valley still exists" and may be a quotation, but its significance is not obvious.

537 *karr*: "headcloth."

538 *jaʿbūbah*: meaning unknown.

539 *marjūnah*: a kind of storage basket.

540 *ḥida* occurs in rural modern Egyptian in this sense (Behnstedt and Woidich, *Glossar*, 81).

541 *ṭābūnah*: "baker's oven."

542 "picnic", i.e. "the Day of Escape," see §2.27.

543 Hadhūd: perhaps from *hudhud* ("hoopoe").

544 Son of Mattock-Pate (*Ibn Rās al-Masḥah*): the *masḥah* is a hand implement for scraping and leveling earth, with a broad rectangular iron blade set at right angles to the wooden handle.

545 "He of the Audible Fart."

546 "In the middle" and "on the edge" (below) may indicate that the village was divided among the shaykhs into different zones of responsibility under a primary shaykh, Abū ʿAwkal in this case being the latter, Abū Fusuww the shaykh of the central quarter, and the others shaykhs of the peripheral quarters. According to Shaw, "[i]f the village was held by more than one *Multezim* [tax farmer], each appointed a *Šeyh* [shaykh] to deal with the cultivators in his portion of the village, and the *Šeyh* of the *Multezim* with the greatest interest in the village was made its chief *šeyh*, the *Šeyh ul-beled* [shaykh al-balad]" (Shaw, *Financial*, 54).

547 On women's names see §2.17; only those not occurring in the earlier list are glossed below.

548 Balwah: "Calamity."

549 Cf. *ʿilwah* "hillock" in the modern dialect of Farafra (Behnstedt and Woidich, *Glossar*, 323) and *ʿilw* "heap [rur]" (Hinds and Badawi, *Dictionary*, 597).

550 Shāyiʿah: "Uncontrolled; of loose behavior."

551 Shuqayrah: "Little Blonde."

552 Ḥamdah: "Praise."

553 ʿAṭiyyah: "Gift."

554 Ṭālibah: "Requesting, demanding" (especially of sex, thus approximately "Asking (for it)").

555 Hāribah: "Fleeing, escaping."

556 Ḥaṭabiyyah: "Bit of field trash (e.g., corn stalks) used as kindling."

557 Furayjah: "Little vagina."

558 . . . (*wa-sūqī najlah*): the meaning is unclear; conceivably "drive [home the buffalo or some other animal called] Najlah."

559 *qafqūlah*: "a small pot in which the people of the countryside cook *bīsār*" (§5.3.14).

560 Abū Buʿbūlah: "The Man with the the Glob (or Bobble)."

561 See similarly §2.20.

562 The imperative verbs in this passage are all masculine; the joke is perhaps about henpecked husbands.

563 Presumably a proper name; cf. formal Arabic *bawādī* "plains, prairies."

564 Jawzah: "Coconut."

565 Jazarah: "Carrot."

566 "Hey, fag [?], . . . [?], cow, flash us your ass" (*yā khawr isrīḥah* (اسريحه) *wa-baqarah shalliḥ*): *khawr* (*khawar*?) might be related to *khawal* ("faggot, pansy"); the reading of اسريحه is unclear in some of the manuscripts and yields no obvious sense; بقره ("cow") is described elsewhere (vol. 2, §11.26.8) as a sexually loaded insult used against a boy.

567 *mishammar*: a cake of flaky pastry, to be eaten with cream, honey, aged cheese, etc.

568 I.e., the Feast of the Sacrifice, see n. 93.

569 *ishtiwān*: see n. 86.

570 I.e., presumably, the boy learns of what Abū Bajaʿ has done to other boys by way of implementing his threats and is appropriately intimidated.

571 Fusuww al-Dīn: "Farting of Religion."

572 Or, punningly, "from the evil of the retention of urine God save you."

573 Alluding to the well-known but spurious Tradition "Egypt [or Cairo] is God's quiver on His Earth: no enemy seeks [to take] it but God destroys him" (see, e.g., al-ʿAjlūnī, *Kashf al-khafāʾ*, 2:211).

574 I.e., Muḥammad (from the same consonantal root, *ḥ-m-d*).

Index

ʿAbd al-Malik, xvii

al-ʿAbdillāwī, ʿAbd al-Haqq, xiv, 7.29

ʿAblah, 5.3.13, 5.8.20, 8.20

Abū l-ʿAtāhiyah, 400n376

Abū Nuwās, xvii, 3.8–11, 5.3.8–10, 5.4.7, 5.6.20, 6.1, 7.27, 392n249, 402n404, 407n468

Abū Qurdān, xxii

Abū Shādūf, xi, xvi–xvii, xxiv–xxv, xlviii, l, livn27, lvin37, 1.1, 1.4, 2.14, 8.32, 387n199, 401n387, 411n528

Abū Ṣīr, 5.9.1

adab, xvii, xxi, xlvii, liiin14, livn28, lvn36, lvin43

al-ʿAdawī, Shaykh, 405n434

ahl al-rīf, xvi, xxiii–xxv, xxviii

al-ʿAyyāshī, Abū Salim, xxxix, lviin65

Alexandria, xxxvii, 5.2.1, 6.2, 7.12

ʿAlī (ibn Abī Ṭālib), xxxv, 3.4, 5.4.8, 382n134, 392n251, 406n445

ʿAlī the Kāshif, 6.7.4

ʿālim, ʿulamāʾ, xiii, xviii, xxvi, xxx, xxxix, liin2, lvn37, lviin53, lviiin67

al-Amīn (ibn Hārūn al-Rashīd), viii, 6.1

ʿAmr ibn al-ʿĀṣ, xl

anecdote(s), vii–viii, xii, xiv, xvi, xvii, xviii–xxi, xxviii–xxx, xxxv–xxxix, xlvi, livn25, lvin45, 3.1–3.76, 4.14–4.35, 5.3.7, 7.13, 7.14–7.41, 373n19, 376n48, 378n88, 382n135, 385n174, 386n178, 387n199, 392n245

ʿAntar/ʿAntarah, 5.3.13, 5.7.2, 5.8.20, 8.20, 396n310

al-Aṣmaʿī, xvii, xviii

Awlād Abī Shurayshar Troupe, 5.3.12

al-Azhar, xi, xvii, xviii, xxxix, liin6, lviin53, lviin64, 4.3, 4.5, 372n8,

Azhari(s), xviii, xxx, xxxviii, xl, liin2, 4.5, 387n198

Bab al-Naṣr, 5.8.1

Bab Zuwaylah, 5.6.1

al-Badawī, Ahmad, 4.3, 7.36, 409n487

al-Badiʿiyya (*al-Kāfiyah al-Badīʿiyyah*), 5.6.27, 396n305, 397n319

al-Badrī, 387n198, 405n434

Baer, Gabriel, xiv, xxvi, liin1, liin11, livn25, lvn37, lvin39–42, 45, 386n184

Baḥīrā, 7.35

Bailiff, 3.10, 3.18, 3.21, 3.25, 8.41

balīlah, 2.14

Banū Baqar, 381n124

Banū Hilāl, 410n508

Banū ʿUqbah, 3.76

baṣal. *See* onions

Bashbughāwī, ʿAlī ibn Sūdūn al-, xxii, 1.4, 5.6.19, 5.9.19, 386n185, 401n389

baṭārikh. *See* roe

bathhouse, xxix, lviiin75, 3.11, 3.25–27, 378n89

bawshah, 8.34, 412n535

Baybars, al-Malik al-Ẓāhir, 6.8, 403n430, 410n506
beans (*fūl*), xxvii, 2.5, 2.22, 2.26, 3.11, 3.18.7, 3.18.9, 3.21, 3.23, 3.43, 4.3, 4.13, 4.39, 5.2.11, 5.2.21, 5.6.5, 7.16, 8.42
Binding, House of/Dār al-Shadd, 3.7
Birkat al-Fīl, 5.3.1, 5.4.1, 392n246
bisār/bisārah, xxvii, 2.5, 2.22, 3.8, 3.11, 3.18.9, 3.21, 4.11, 5.2.4, 5.2.11, 5.2.21, 5.3.14, 5.6.5, 6.5, 413n559
The Blue Ocean and Piebald Canon, xliii, 5.2.2, 5.2.21, 5.3.12, 5.6.12, 5.6.26, 5.7.10, 5.9.23, 381n127
The Book of the Snare and the Sparrow, 4.38.1, 387n193
Book to Bring a Smile to the Lips of Devotees of Taste and Proper Style through the Decoding of a Sampling of the Verse of the Rural Rank and File. See Risible Rhymes
book trade, xii
book trader(s), 4.15
bookseller(s), xii, xxx, xl, 387n195
boor/boorishness, vii, xx, xxxiv, xliii, 1.3, 3.49–3.52, 5.2.20, 5.3.8–9, 5.5.13, 5.6.8, 5.8.3, 5.9.5, 8.22, 381n123, 410n502
boys, beardless, 3.21, 5.9.2, 7.7, 8.11, 404n432
Brains Confounded (by the Ode of Abū Shādūf Expounded), xi–xxvi, xxviii, xxxiii, xxviii, xl–xli, xlvi, xlix, l-li, liin11, liiin16, livn25, lvn33, lvn37, lvin38, lvin45, lviin47, lviiin75, 1.4
brave lads/*jid'ān*, 2.23, 2.24, 2.25, 3.17, 3.20, 3.21, 3.22, 3.38, 3.42, 8.35, 8.38, 8.40
bread, 1.4, 2.27, 3.8, 3.11, 4.3, 4.22, 5.6.2, 5.6.5, 5.7.8, 5.7.15, 7.36
buffalo(es), 2.14, 2.24, 3.26, 4.22, 5.7.4, 5.7.6, 6.3.1, 413n558
Būlāq/Būlāq al-Takrūr, xxv, xxx, xlvii, xlix, lviiin74, 1.1, 4.39, 5.6.1, 5.7.1, 371n5
al-Būṣīrī, xiv, xix, 1.4, 6.2, 6.3.1, 401n398

Cairene, xxii
Cairo/al-Qāhirah, vii, xi, xii, xiii, xvii, xviii, xix, xx, xxvi, xxxiii–xxxiv, xxxvii, xxxviii, xlvi, lviin64, 2.6, 3.25–3.28, 3.32–33, 3.36, 3.41–3.42, 3.46, 4.5–6, 4.15, 4.16, 5.4.1, 5.4.7, 6.3.1, 7.3.1, 8.44, 371n5, 380n114, 380n116, 381n123, 382n134, 393n253, 402n400, 406n452, 409n485, 410n501, 410n506, 410n510, 413n574
cap/hat/*qaḥf*, xxviii, xxxi, 2.1, 2.3, 2.5, 2.14, 2.17, 2.26.2, 3.1, 3.8, 3.11, 3.17, 3.23, 3.37, 3.42–43, 4.6–7, 5.5.13, 5.9.12, 7.1, 7.19, 8.3, 8.15, 8.22, 8.23, 8.27, 8.40, 371n3, 377n71
Çelebi, Evliya. *See* Shalabī, Awliyā'
Champion of Discourtesy, xx, 3.46–48
Children, vii, xxix, xxxv, xxxix, 2.7, 2.21, 2.23, 3.4, 3.12, 3.36, 3.67, 4.15, 5.2.7–9, 5.2.19, 5.9.3, 5.9.5, 6.3.1, 7.20, 8.10–11, 373n19
Chosroes, 3.11, 6.7.8
Christian(s), xxviii, 3.19, 3.25, 4.34, 5.9.19, 7.9, 401n389
clothes, xix, 2.6, 2.21, 3.1, 3.20, 3.23, 3.32, 3.34, 3.36, 3.40, 3.47, 3.49, 3.75, 4.17, 4.20, 4.37.3, 4.41, 5.2.8, 5.3.9, 5.4.9, 5.6.5, 5.7.6, 5.8.21, 7.10, 7.11, 7.31, 7.38, 8.16, 8.19, 379n95, 379n98, 400n370, 406n449

colloquial (Egyptian Arabic), xv, xxii–xxiii, xxxvii, xliii, xlviii, li, livn25, lvn33, lviin58, lviiin73, 373n19, 377n66, 381n125, 382n129, 382n134, 384n163, 386n189, 387n193, 389n220, 390n224, 390n225, 390n228, 392n244, 393n254, 393n259, 394n265, 394n268, 395n282, 395n283, 396n301, 396n307, 397n320, 398n339, 399n350, 399n365, 401n385, 403n418, 403n427, 406n452, 407n459
commentary, commentaries, xvi, xvii, xxii–xxiv, xli–xlv, xlix, li, liin6, livn29, 1.1–4, 8.21, 381n125, 391n242, 393n261
Constantinople, 5.3.17
Corvée, xviii, xl, 2.8, 3.28, 4.11, 389n209
country people, vii, xxiii, xxvii, xxxi, xxxvi–xxxvii, 3.7, 3.40–3.45, 3.53–3.76, 5.3.14, 5.6.13, 5.8.10, 5.9.2, 5.9.5, 5.9.9, 5.9.19, 8.3
countryman, countrymen, xxii, xxiii, xxix, l, 2.3, 3.12, 3.13, 3.15, 3.17, 5.1, 5.2.18
countryside, xv–xvii, xix, xx, xxi, xxiii, xxvi–xxxiv, xxxv, xxxvi–xxxviii, xl, xli, 0.1, 1.1, 1.3, 2.1, 2.8, 3.1, 3.4, 4.3, 3.8, 3.9, 3.10, 3.25, 3.32, 3.41, 3.56, 4.3, 4.6, 4.20, 4.21, 5.2.2, 5.2.18, 5.2.20, 5.3.14, 5.5.2, 5.5.3, 5.6.6, 5.6.7, 5.6.9, 5.8.2, 5.8.21, 5.9.7, 7.17, 7.19, 410n510, 413n559

al-Ḍāhir, Ballad of, 8.20, 410n506
al-Dalhamah wa-l-Baṭṭāl, 4.19, 8.20, 384n163, 410n507
al-Damīrī, livn24, 375n41
Dārah, 8.10
Day of Escape, 2.27
Dayr al-Ṭīn, 5.9.1
Delta, xxvi, 384n149, 409n487
demesne, 3.30, 3.42, 378n83
dervish(es), viii, xii, xiv–xv, xix, xxviii, xxx–xxxiii, xxxvi, xxxvii, xlvii, lviin47, lviin54, 1.1, 7.1–7.41, 8.24–8.29, 375n30, 387n198, 405n434, 406n448
dhikr, xxxi, xxxix, 7.7, 7.16, 7.29, 7.31, 7.36
digressions, xvi, xx, xxi, livn27, 387n199
Dimyāṭ, xi, xiii, xix, xxvi, xxxvii, 1.1, 2.6, 5.2.1, 5.5.1, 7.23, 7.32
al-Dirīnī, ʿAbd al-ʿAzīz, 4.41
dress, xxix, xxxv, xxxvi, 3.1, 3.36–37, 4.6–7, 4.17, 5.2.8, 5.3.13, 5.9.3, 6.7.5, 7.10, 7.11, 7.31, 7.33, 380n116, 406n449
Dundayṭ, Kafr, xxvi, 3.58
Dunjayhī, ʿAbd al-ʿAzīz al-, 4.4

Egypt/Egyptian, xi, xii, xv, xvii, xxi, xxii, xxv–xxvi, xxxii, xxxvi, xxxvii, xxxviii, xxxix, xl, xlix-l, liin1, liiin13, liiin14, lvn31, lvn37, lvin38, lvin45, lvin47, lviin55, lviin64, lviin67, 3.52, 4.36, 5.2.1, 5.6.19, 5.9.20, 5.9.26, 371n5, 372n13, 373n19, 374n20, 374n21, 374n22, 374n23, 374n29, 375n30, 375n34, 375n36, 375n37, 375n38, 375n39, 375n40, 375n42, 375n43, 375n44, 375n45, 376n46, 376n49, 376n50, 376n54, 376n55, 376n56, 376n57, 376n58, 376n59, 377n63, 377n64, 378n74, 380n103, 380n112, 387n193, 389n220, 391n236, 391n241, 392n244, 393n252, 393n254, 397n318, 399n350, 401n392, 403n415, 404n432, 406n448, 410n503, 410n510, 412n533, 412n540, 413n574
emir, viii, xxx, 2.6, 3.7, 3.22–24, 3.25, 3.27, 3.29, 3.30, 3.34–35, 3.38, 3.42–43, 3.54–55, 3.59, 3.60, 4.33, 5.8.7, 6.2, 6.3.3, 6.7–6.7.9, 7.33, 8.6–7, 376n48, 398n344

etymology, etymologies, xvi, xxii, xxiii, xxiv, xlii, xliii–xliv, 1.1, 5.4.1, 5.4.4, 5.6.23, 5.6.26, 5.7.16, 5.8.10–5.8.11, 5.9.17, 373n19, 387n199, 388n203, 392n247, 394n263, 397n328, 400n381

fanqalah, xliv, 372n8, 387n199, 394n273
faqīh/fuqahā', xv, xxviii, xxix–xxx, xxxix, xlvii, 4.40, 383n140, 383n147, 410n504
faqīr/fuqarā', xv, xxviii, xxx–xxxiii, xlvii, lviin54, 404n432
farming, xiii, xl–xli
farts/farting, xvi, xxi, xxxvi, 1.1, 2.14, 2.15, 2.17, 3.24, 3.72, 4.9, 5.2.4, 5.5.4, 8.11, 8.19, 8.33, 8.42, 403n415, 410n503, 412n545, 413n571
fava beans, xxvii, 2.5, 2.2, 2.26, 3.11, 4.3, 4.13, 4.39, 5.2.11, 7.16
fine on the landless (*gharāmat al-baṭṭālīn*), xl–xli, 3.7, 378n83
fiqh, xiii, xxix, 410n504
fish, xxi, 1.1, 2.17, 3.42, 3.43, 5.6.19, 8.40, 378n86, 382n134
fisīkh. See fasīkh
flatulence. *See* farts/farting
foot soldiers, 2.23, 2.25, 2.27, 3.21, 3.25, 3.42–43, 8.40
Friend(s) of God (walī), 7.5, 7.12, 7.30, 7.31, 7.38, 8.26, 411n514
Funayn, xii, 4.36, 4.37.1, 4.37.5, 386n186
Funayn's Letter, viii, xii, 4.36–4.37.6
fuqahā'. See pastors
fuqarā'. See dervishes

galleys, 3.32, 3.39, 3.43
al-Gharbiyyah, xi
al-Ghazālī, Abū Ḥāmid, 4.40, 5.6.15, 395n284
Ghuzz, 5.2.10, 6.2.2
grammar/grammarian(s), xv, xvi, xxv, xlii–xliii, xlv, xlvi, xlviii, 5.5.3, 384n158, 390n224, 403n414

al-Ḥabashī, Murjān, viii, xxxviii, 6.2–6.4.4, 402n409
al-Ḥajjāj, 384n159
hamlet(s), xxvii, xxviii, 3.9, 3.10, 3.11, 3.17, 3.18.13, 3.22, 3.23, 3.25, 3.27, 3.28, 3.29, 3.31, 3.34, 3.36, 3.38, 3.39, 3.42, 3.43, 5.6.2, 8.41, 8.43, 372n12
Hamziyyah, 6.2–6.3.1
handmill, 5.8, 5.8.8, 5.8.9, 5.8.14, 5.8.15, 5.8.21, 377n73
Ḥarām, Clan of, xxxii, 2.3, 3.29, 4.10, 7.14, 8.12–8.13, 8.28, 372n13
Hārūn al-Rashīd, xvii, 3.8, 3.10–11, 5.8.17, 5.9.11, 6.1–6.1.2, 7.27, 382n134
al-Ḥasan [ibn ʿAlī ibn Abī Ṭālib], 6.3.4, 373n19
Hazz al-quḥūf bi-sharḥ qaṣīd Abī Shādūf, xi
heretic(s)/heretical, viii, xii, xiv–xv, xix, xxxi, xxxvii, 7.10, 7.21, 7.34, 7.38, 7.41
Hijaz/Hijazi, 5.8.15
al-Ḥillī, al-Ṣafī, 396n305, 397n319
al-Ḥumaydī, Shaykh, 4.15
Hurbayṭ, Kafr, xxvi, 3.17, 3.18.2, 3.58, 5.2.15, 8.35
al-Ḥusayn [ibn ʿAlī ibn Abī Ṭālib], livn27, 6.3.4, 6.7.6, 373n19
al-Ḥusayniyyah, 5.3.1, 5.9.1

Ibn Abī Burdah, Bilāl, 5.6.15
Ibn ʿArūs, 5.5.12, 406n452

Ibn al-ʿĀṣ, ʿAmr, xl
Ibn Baqar, Ḥammār, 3.54
Ibn Durayd, 5.8.14, 399n359
Ibn al-Fāriḍ, 6.4–6.4.1, 402n409, 407n458
Ibn Ḥajar, 8.19, 386n182, 410n503
Ibn Khallikān, xvii, 378n75
Ibn al-Khaṭṭāb, ʿUmar, xvii, 2.13
Ibn al-Khawājā Muṣṭafā, Amīr, viii, 6.7–6.7.9
Ibn al-Rāwandī, 1.4
Ibn Salāmah, Aḥmad Shihāb al-Dīn, xi
Ibn Sūdūn, xxii, 1.4, 5.6.19, 5.9.19, 386n185, 401n389
Ibn Yaḥyā, Yaḥyā, 4.33
ignorance/ignorant, vii, viii, xv, xvi, xx, xxvii, xxix–xxx, xxxiv, xxxv, xxxviii, 1.1, 2.4, 2.14, 3.1, 3.4, 3.7, 3.8, 3.31, 3.43, 3.45, 3.55, 3.71, 4.14, 4.16, 4.17, 4.25, 4.26, 4.28, 4.31, 4.32, 4.33, 4.34, 4.35, 5.2.8, 5.2.9, 5.3.9, 5.3.13, 5.7.7, 5.9.5, 5.9.8, 5.9.20, 6.1, 6.3, 6.4, 6.8, 7.1, 7.3, 7.8, 7.17, 7.20, 7.22, 7.29, 7.34, 8.24, 8.29, 8.32, 372n17, 386n180, 411n516
Ikhtirāʿ al-khurāʿ, xxii–xxiii
ʿInān, 7.27
innovation(s) (in religion), xl, 7.31, 7.41
irrigation, xxvii, lvin44, 389n209, 411n529
Irwin, Robert, xix, liiin21, livn26, 378n81, 404n432
Islam, xxix, xxxii, 3.4, 4.40, 5.4.8, 371n7, 394n275

al-Jabbulī, 7.8, 406n446
jadīd, 380n103
Janissaries, 5.3.14, 391n241
Jesus, 7.34, 382n134
Jew/Jewish/ Jews, 1.4, 5.3.2, 5.9.3, 5.9.19, 7.9, 7.40, 401n389
Jew's mallow (*mulūkhiyyā*), xxii, xxvii
al-Jizah, 5.7.1
joke(s), xii, xviii–xix, xxi, xliii, 4.9, 5.3.7, 7.27, 379n101, 412n533, 413n563
jubbah, xxxiv, 3.8, 3.17, 7.10, 397n311
Judām. *See* Judhām
judge(s), viii, xx, xxix, xxxiii, 3.30, 3.53, 4.16, 4.31, 4.34, 4.35, 6.5, 7.7, 7.12, 8.3, 8.21, 8.23, 386n181, 386n184, 391n243, 403n416, 406n450, 411n513
Judhām/Judām, clan of, 4.10, 7.14, 8.12, 372n13
al-Junayd, 7.4

kafr. *See* hamlet
kāshif(s), lvn37
kathāfah, xx, xxxiii
kathīf, xxxiii, xxxvi
khalwah. *See* retreat
Khalwatiyyah, xxxii
al-Khānkāh, 5.6.1
Khawāmis, viii, xxx–xxxi, 7.1–13, 7.23, 7.38, 8.28–29
al-Khayyāṭ, Shaykh Barakāt, viii, xxxii, 5.3.17–5.4, 392n244
khubbayz, khubbayzah. *See* mallow
khushtanānak, 3.8, 3.11
kirshah. *See* tripes
kishk, xlv
knowledge, xi, xii, xiv, xix, xxx, xxxii, xxxiv, xxxv, xxxviii, xxxix, 0.1, 1.1, 1.6, 2.1, 3.1, 3.4, 4.5, 4.7, 4.25, 4.33, 4.41, 5.5.13, 6.6, 7.3, 7.8, 7.12, 8.19, 8.26, 372n17, 406n442, 407n456, 407n462, 408n479, 410n504

kunyah, vii, 2.14, 2.18, 2.19, 5.2.14, 8.32, 373n19, 377n65, 381n120, 411n518, 411n528
kurrāt , 3.18.14
kuttāb, xxxix, 3.75

al-La'ālī' wa-l-durar, xi
labsān, 5.9, 5.9.5, 5.9.19–20, 401n391
laṭāfah, xx, xxxiii
laṭīf, xxxiii, xxxvi,
latrine(s), xxix, 3.40, 3.41, 3.44, 5.2.18, 5.9.7, 7.10
leeks, 3.18.2
lentils, xxvii, 2.5, 3.8, 3.11, 3.18.9, 4.11, 5.2.4, 5.2.11, 5.2.21, 8.16, 8.38
libbih, xlviii
libdah, 2.14, 2.17, 8.37
literary, xi, xiii, xvi, xvii, xx, xxi, xxii, xxiii, xxv, xxvi, xxxvii, xli–xlvi, liiin14, lvn32, lvn33, 371n7, 372n8, 377n73, 382n129, 388n202, 390n225, 393n259, 394n268, 395n283, 396n301, 397n313, 397n320, 375n30, 399n365
literature, xii, xv, xvi, xvii, xxi, xxii, xxv, xxxiv, liiin14, lvin38, 6.3.1, 371n7,
Luqmān, 4.27
luṭf, xxxiii

al-Maʿarrī, Abū l-ʿAlā', xiv, 7.34, 402n405, 409n486
Maghribis, 5.2.16
Maghūrī, Muḥammad, 6.7.9, 403n428
al-Maḥallah al-Kubrā, xiv, xxxvii, 7.29
Majlis, xiii, xvii, xxi, lii
Malāmatiyyah, xxxi
malaq. *See* swamps
Mālik, Imam, 2.8
mallow(s), xxvii, 3.18.3
Mamluke(s), lviin64
al-Ma'mūn, livn24, 6.1
Maʿn ibn Zā'idah, xliv, 5.2.13, 389n212
al-Maqrīzī, xvii
mas'alah, xliv, 372n8
Maṣbanat al-Ghuzz, 5.2.10
maṣdar. *See* paradigm
al-Matbūlī, Ibrāhīm, xxxii
mawāliyā, xxiii, 1.4, 3.56, 5.1, 5.2.15, 5.3.1, 5.6.8, 5.6.19, 5.7.1, 5.8.1, 5.9.1
mawlid, 7.16, 8.25, 405n435
Mecca, xii, 7.12, 375n32, 379n93, 383n143, 402n407
medicine, xii, xiii
Medina, 402n407, 402n408
meter, xxiii, xxxvii, xlii–xliii, xlvii–xlix, l, livn29, lviiin73, 5.3.10, 5.4.10, 5.5.1, 5.5.14, 5.7.12, 6.4.4, 377n69, 387n199, 388n200, 388n201, 390n229, 390n230, 392n244, 393n257, 394n266, 396n297, 396n307, 396n309, 401n398, 411n528
midallah/*midallāt*, 5.6, 5.6.7–8, 5.6.21, 396n300
miḥlāb, 2.15
milk, xxviii, xxxv, 2.9, 2.15, 2.26, 3.1, 3.2, 3.3, 3.11, 3.15, 3.66, 4.3, 4.24, 5.7.4, 5.7.24, 5.9.19, 8.38
mill, viii, xxvii, xlix, 5.7–8, 5.8.2–3, 5.8.7, 5.8.12, 398n345
mishsh, 2.27, 3.18.12, 4.39
Miṣr, 1.1, 371n5, 381n123, 398n339
mnemonics, xxiii, xxiv, xlii–xliii, 387n199, 388n201, 390n230, 396n309, 398n338
moneychanger, 3.45, 5.3.2
moneylender(s), xiv, liin11, 372n15
Monk and the Cameleer, Ballad of the, 8.20

mosque, xi, xvi, xxvii, xxix, xxxix, liin1, lvin45, 1.6, 2.7, 3.7, 3.29, 3.40, 3.41, 3.48, 3.62, 4.3, 4.19, 4.20, 4.22, 4.26, 4.33, 4.34, 4.37.3, 7.11, 7.18, 7.28, 380n104, 380n107, 382n134, 386n178, 407n458
Mosul, 8.26
muʿāmil, xiv, liin11, 372n15
Muḍḥik dhawī l-dhawq wa-l-niẓām fī ḥall shadharatin min kalām ahl al-rīf al-ʿawāmm, xvi, xxiii, xlvi
Muḥibbī, Muḥammad Amīn b. ʿAbd Allāh al-, xi, xxvi, liin2, liin3, liin6
mullet, 6.3.1
multazim(s), xl, lvn37, 412n546
mulūkhiyyā. *See* Jew's mallow
al-Munāwī, ʿAbd al-Rāʾūf, xvii, 372n8, 394n273
muqābalah, 397n319
Muqallad, Emir, 7.33, 376n48
Murjān al-Ḥabashī, Emir, viii, xxxviii, 6.2, 402n409
Murjānah, xxxv, xxxviii, 3.5, 401n397
Muslim (ibn al-Ḥajjāj), 4.41, 4.15, 384n159
Muslim/Muslims, xxxiii, xxxix, 2.4, 3.11, 3.76, 4.5, 4.15, 377n62, 378n80, 380n104, 380n112, 382n135, 383n145, 384n159, 386n189
al-Muṭāwiʿah, xxxi, 405n434

naked/nakedness, 2.7, 3.3, 3.26, 3.35–36, 3.39, 4.22, 5.2.5, 5.4.9, 5.7.7, 7.16, 407n456
name(s), vii, xv, xvi, xix, xx, xxxi, xxxiii, liin7, 1.4, 2.1, 2.9–20, 2.26.2, 3.5, 3.11, 3.17, 3.43, 4.37.6, 4.38.1–2, 5.2.14, 5.3.10, 5.3.17, 5.4.1, 5.5.2, 5.5.6, 5.6.15, 5.7.2, 5.7.3, 5.7.14, 5.7.15, 5.7.18, 5.9.15, 6.4.1, 6.6, 6.7.2, 6.7.9, 7.1, 7.5, 8.19, 8.30, 8.33, 8.36–39, 8.41, 372n8, 373n19, 374n29, 375n33, 375n35, 376n48, 376n49, 376n59, 381n121, 381n124, 381n127, 382n134, 383n138, 386n182, 396n293, 397n319, 398n344, 401n383, 401n397, 402n409, 403n422, 403n428, 406n442, 406n455, 407n463, 407n467, 410n503, 410n504, 411n518, 411n524, 411n532, 412n547, 413n563
al-Nāṭifī, 7.27
Nile, xi, xiii, xxvi, lii, 2.11, 2.17, 3.29, 3.52, 8.44, 8.45, 371n5, 372n12, 379n98, 399n356
al-Nuʿmān, Abū Ḥanīfah, 4.17
nuptials, xiv, 2.5, 2.25, 2.26.2
nuṣṣ/nuṣṣ fiḍḍah, xxxvii

ode, vii, xi, xvi, xvii, xxiv, xxv, xlviii, l, livn27, lvn37, 1.1, 1.2, 1.4, 2.26, 3.18, 3.18.13, 3.19–20, 5.3.17, 5.4, 5.7.3, 6.4, 6.4.4, 6.8, 371n3, 387n199, 396n310, 401n387
onion(s)/*baṣal*, 2.25
oral material, orality, xvii–xviii, 404n432
Ottoman(s), xi, xvii, xviii, xxi, xxxix, liiin13, lvin37, lvin38, 371n5, 379n99, 379n100, 380n103, 386n188, 391n241, 391n243, 392n245, 404n432, 406n452, 427
ox/oxen, 2.6, 2.21, 3.1, 3.24, 3.30, 3.53, 3.54–55, 5.6, 5.6.7–9, 5.6.19, 5.6.20, 5.6.27, 5.7.5, 5.8, 5.8.3, 5.8.9, 5.8.10, 5.8.19, 5.8.20, 7.9, 399n352, 399n353

palindrome(s), xlv
paradigm(s) (*maṣdar/maṣādir*), xliii, 5.2.2, 5.2.3, 5.2.21, 5.3.10, 5.3.12, 5.3.16, 5.5.4,

paradigm(s) (cont.), 5.6.16, 5.6.17, 5.6.18, 5.6.20, 5.6.21, 5.6.22, 5.6.24, 5.6.25, 5.6.26, 5.7.17, 5.7.18, 5.7.21, 5.7.24, 5.7.25, 5.8.12, 5.8.13, 5.8.15, 5.8.16, 5.8.17, 5.9.14, 5.9.16, 5.9.17, 5.9.18, 5.9.20, 5.9.21, 5.9.24, 5.9.25, 388n205, 391n236, 391n243
parody, xvii, xxiii, xli–xlii, xlvi, 377n68, 382n128
paronomasia, 5.3.12, 5.3.15, 5.7.15, 5.9.3, 391n242
pastors, xxviii, xxix–xxx, xxxix, xlvii, 3.16, 3.70, 4.1–2, 4.10–24, 4.28–31, 4.33, 4.35, 4.38.1, 4.41, 8.19, 384n158, 385n166, 385n168, 410n504, 410n509
pastry, 3.38, 3.58, 3.59, 3.71, 413n567
peasant(s), vii, xiii, xiv, xv, xvi, xviii–xix, xx–xxi, xxii, xxvi, xxvii, xxviii–xxix, xxxi, xxxiii, xxxiv, xxxv, xxxvi, xxxviii, xl–xli, xlvii, liiin14, livn25, lvn37, lviiin75, 2.2, 2.4, 2.14, 2.20, 3.1, 3.6, 3.7–11, 3.16, 3.22–28, 3.29–31, 3.32–39, 3.41, 3.42, 3.44, 3.45, 3.46, 3.53, 3.54–55, 3.56, 3.58, 3.59, 3.60, 3.61, 3.62, 3.63, 3.64, 3.65, 3.67, 3.72, 3.76, 4.3, 4.4, 4.6–9, 4.12, 4.37.2, 4.37.3, 5.2.6, 5.2.11, 5.3.12, 5.7.6, 5.7.7–9, 5.7.14, 5.7.26, 5.8.5, 5.8.6, 5.8.10, 5.9.3, 5.9.5, 5.9.7, 5.9.8, 5.9.11, 5.9.12, 5.9.16, 5.9.20, 7.19, 8.3, 8.5, 8.7, 8.16, 8.22, 8.44, 371n3, 372n16, 373n19, 377n73. 378n82, 378n83, 378n86, 379n90, 379n92, 379n101, 380n104, 380n113, 381n119, 381n120, 381n122, 381n125, 382n130, 382n135, 384n150, 384n156, 387n198, 388n208, 389n209, 393n253, 393n258, 393n259, 393n260, 394n264, 397n314, 410n505, 410n509
perch, 2.14, 2.17
Persian, vii, xviii, livn23, lviiin75, 4.5–9
Pharaoh, 7.40, 397n318
piasters, 4.6
pilgrimage, xii, 7.12, 379n93
Pillar of the Columns, 1.3, 4.22, 372n9
plowman, plowmen, xxviii, xxix, 5.2.5–6, 5.9.11, 5.9.21, 389n216
poetry, xvi, xxi, xxix, xxxiv, xxxviii, xlii, l, liiin14, 1.1, 4.31, 5.2.20, 5.4.7, 5.5, 5.6.8, 5.8.8, 5.8.18, 5.9.27, 6.1, 6.1.2, 6.3.3, 6.5, 399n363, 403n430, 406n452
Pond of the Elephant. *See* Birkat al-Fīl
prayer(s), vii, xii, xv, xxix, xxx, xxxi, 1.6, 2.3, 2.7, 3.1, 3.7, 3.29, 3.31, 3.40, 3.48, 3.63–76, 4.3, 4.10, 4.13, 4.17, 4.33, 4.34, 4.37.6, 5.2.9, 5.3.5, 5.7.12, 5.7.14, 6.4.4, 6.7.9, 7.1, 7.6, 7.15, 7.17, 7.18, 7.19, 7.21, 7.22, 7.25, 7.33, 7.34, 7.36, 8.16, 377n62, 380n103, 380n104, 380n105, 380n110, 382n135, 383n136, 383n137 , 384n160, 386n189, 401n393, 405n434, 407n465, 408n471
preacher(s), xxix, 3.11, 3.29, 4.3, 4.12, 4.33, 4.37.2, 8.3, 380n108, 380n111, 380n112, 403n419

qaḥf. *See* cap
al-Qāhirah. *See* Cairo
al-Qalyūbī, Shihāb al-Dīn, xi, xiii, liin2, liin6, 4.3
al-Qāmus al-Azraq wa-l-Nāmūs al-Ablaq, xliii, 381n127
al-Qāmūs al-Muḥīṭ, xliii, 381n126, 381n127, 402n402
Qiṣṣat al-Miṣrī wa-l-rīfī, xxii
Qulqās. *See* taro

Qur'ān, xvi, xviii, xxix, xxx, xxxix, 2.11, 2.12, 3.1, 3.4, 3.6, 3.16, 3.75, 4.3, 4.15, 4.16, 4.18, 4.21, 4.22, 4.30, 4.31, 4.38.1, 4.41, 5.2.8, 7.29, 7.35, 8.23, 373n19, 380n110, 382n134, 383n143, 384n152, 384n161, 385n173, 385n176, 386n177, 386n178, 394n272, 404n432, 406n442, 408n473, 410n496, 410n505
al-Quṣayr, xii

Rashīd, 5.2.1
al-rayyāfah, xxviii
al-Rāziqī, Muḥammad, viii, 6.6, 403n422
Red Sea, xi
religion/religious, vii, xiv, xx, xxix, xxx, xxxii, xxxiv, xxxvi, xxxviii, xl, lviin54, 2.3, 3.1, 3.4, 3.7, 3.63, 3.64, 3.67, 3.76, 4.5, 4.20, 4.31, 5.7.8, 5.7.14, 6.6, 6.7.5, 7.1, 7.2, 7.20, 7.24, 7.28, 7.32, 8.2, 8.28, 372n14, 380n111, 413n571
retreat (place of) (*khalwah*), xxxi, 7.30, 7.38, 409n481
rhyme(s), viii, l, 4.38.1, 5.2.20, 5.4.10, 5.5.13, 5.7.12, 5.8.9, 6.1.1, 6.2, 372n14, 379n91, 384n152, 389n220, 390n222, 392n244, 394n270, 394n273, 396n297, 398n339, 399n363, 401n396, 401n398
rice pudding (*ruzz bi-l-laban*), xxvii
riddle(s), 5.5, 5.7.18, 393n256, 397n326
Risible Rhymes, xvi, xxiii–xxiv, xlvi, xlix, 390n228, 390n230, 393n255, 394n274, 396n306, 396n307, 396n308, 400n367
Riyāḍ al-uns fī-mā jarā bayn al-zubb wa-l-kuss, xiv
al-Rumaylah, 3.60
rural, xi, xiii, xv–xvi, xviii, xxii, xxiv, xxvi, xxvii–xxviii, xxix–xxxii, xxxiii–xxxiv, xxxvi–xxxviii, xxxix, xlvii, l, liiin14, lviin54, 3.56, 5.2.4, 5.2.20, 5.3.12, 5.5.6, 5.5.9, 5.6.12, 5.7.6, 5.7.10, 5.7.15, 8.43, 373n19, 374n21, 387n198, 390n221, 394n268, 395n282, 404n432. 405n434, 410n504, 411n515, 412n540
rural poetry, xvi, xvii, xxi, xxiii, xxiv, xxvi, xxxiii, xxxviii, xlii, xlviii, 1.1
ruzz bi-l-laban. See rice pudding

al-Ṣābūnī, Bridge of, 3.30, 5.8.18
Sa'd, Clan of, xxxii, 2.3, 3.29, 7.14, 8.12–13, 8.28, 372n13
al-Ṣafadī, Ṣalāḥ al-Dīn Khalīl ibn Aybak, xxii–xxiii, xxiv, 378n77, 400n377, 406n446
safflower, 3.20, 5.9.5, 379n98, 381n120, 400n370
saffron, 5.9.5, 379n98
Ṣa'īd. *See* Upper Egypt
saint(s), xxxii, 6.6, 7.1, 7.30, 7.36, 7.37, 7.38, 378n84, 378n85, 380n106, 383n138, 405n435, 408n475
al-Ṣalibah, 5.8.1
salon(s), xiii–xiv, xvii, xxi, xxiv, 1.1, 4.5, 4.40, 7.31
Samannūd, xxvi, 5.9.1
al-Sandūbī, Aḥmad ibn 'Alī, xii, liin2, liin6, 371n4
al-Sanhūrī, Muḥammad ibn Maḥfūẓ, xvi, xxiii–xxiv, xlvi, liiin15, 390n230, 391n242, 393n255, 394n274, 395n290, 396n306, 396n307, 396n308, 398n336, 400n367
sanjak (*ṣanjaq*), 3.37–3.38, 6.7.2, 381n118
al-Saqqā, 'Alī, 7.23, 408n472

satire, xvi, xvii, xxi, xxiv, xxvi, xxvii, xxxiii, xxxvi, xli–xlii, liiin16, liin17, 391n243
scholar(s), vii, xi, xiii–xv, xvii, xviii, xxii, xxv, xxix, xxx, xxxiv, xxxviii, xxxix, xl, xli–xlii, liin2, livn23, lvn37, 1.6, 2.4, 3.4, 4.3, 4.5–9, 4.14, 4.15, 4.19, 4.20, 4.22, 4.24, 4.25, 4.26, 4.32, 4.33, 4.40, 5.9.16, 6.6, 7.11, 7.13, 7.17, 7.18, 7.28, 7.29, 8.3, 8.18, 384n150, 387n197, 394n275, 407n468, 408n476
schoolmaster(s), 3.75, 5.2.7, 5.2.8
sciences, xi–xii, xiii, xxv, xxx, xlii, 3.4, 3.6, 7.18, 371n7, 387n191, 395n284
sermon, viii, xiv, lviiin75, 4.10–12, 380n104, 380n108, 380n112
al-Shadd, Dār. *See* Binding, House of
al-Shāfiʿī, Imam, xxxv, 1.19, 2.8, 3.4, 4.14, 7.4, 378n76
Shalabī, Awliyāʾ, liin1, 372n12
shāliyah, 5.7.24
Shanashah, xxvi, 3.17
al-Shaʿrānī, ʿAbd al-Wahhāb, xxxii, lviin54, 2.8, 7.24, 372n17, 406n449, 408n478
al-Sharb, market of, 3.38
sharḥ, xi, xli–xlii, xliv, li, livn30, lviiin68, 387n199, 411n514
Sharīk, 7.21, 407n468
shaykh(s), xvii, xxxi, lvii, 2.7, 3.17, 3.23, 3.25, 3.31, 3.43, 4.3, 4.5, 404n432, 412n546; of the hamlet, 3.17, 3.18.13, 3.36; of the village, 2.26.2, 3.11, 3.24, 4.3, 5.8, 5.8.9, 5.8.10, 399n353
Shirbīn, xi, xiii, liin1, 5.5.1, 393n260
al-Shirbīnī, ʿAlī Ḥabashī, 7.26, 408n474
al-Shirbīnī, Yūsuf ibn Muḥammad ibn ʿAbd al-Jawād ibn Khiḍr, xi-l, liin1, liin6, liiin14, livn27, livn29, lvn37, lvin38, lviin53, lviin54, lviiin70, lviiin75, 1.1
The Showing, xxviii, 2.24, 377n64
Shubrā, 5.7.1, 5.8.1
al-Silsilī, Muḥammad, xxxii, 6.6
simile(s), xiii, xxxiii, xxxiv, 5.6.1, 5.6.2, 5.6.4, 5.6.5, 5.6.6, 5.6.8, 5.6.13, 7.40, 395n279
al-Sirw, 5.5.1
The Slavegirl Tawaddud, 4.38.1, 387n191
sleeve(s), 4.41, 5.2.5, 5.7.6–7, 8.19, 387n198, 397n311
slippers, xvi, xix, 3.8, 3.11, 3.17, 3.36–37, 4.35, 4.38.2, 5.2.15, 5.9.11, 8.34, 411n520, 412n535
Solomon. *See* Sulaymān
squabs (*zaghālīl*), 2.14
Sufi(s), xiii, xvii, xix, xxviii, xxxi–xxxiii, xxxvii, xxxix, xl, xlv, livn27, lvin47, lviin53, lviin54, 7.17, 7.22, 7.28, 404n432, 405n433, 405n435, 406n449, 406n452, 407n456, 407n457, 407n465, 408n469, 408n475, 408n476, 408n479, 409n480, 409n481, 409n485, 411n515, 411n516
Sulaymān, 5.4.8, 7.41, 392n250, 410n496
sultan, 3.7, 3.10, 3.32, 3.34, 3.36, 3.43, 3.45, 3.57, 3.58, 4.6, 5.2.6, 5.7.5, 6.8, 392n245
Suwayqat al-Sabbāʿīn, 5.6.1
al-Suyūṭī, Jalāl al-Dīn, xvii, xxv
swamps, swamp lands, xxvii, xxvii, xxviii, 2.3, 372n12

Tadhkirat al-Kaḥḥālīn, 5.6.18
al-Ṭaff, livn27
tafsīr, xiii, xlii, lviiin68, lviiin69
ṭaḥīn, 5.8.12
Ṭalkhah, 3.18.10
al-Ṭanūkhī, Abū ʿAlī al-Muḥassin ibn ʿAlī, liiin22

Ṭarḥ al-madar li-ḥall al-laʾālīʾ wa-l-durar, xi, liiin12
tax collection apparatus, tax collector(s) (*dīwān*), xl–xli, liiin14, 2.4, 8.17, 372n15
tax(es), xxix, xl–xli, 2.7, 3.7, 3.10, 3.17, 3.22, 3.32, 3.34, 3.36, 3.43, 3.45, 3.57, 3.58, 4.6, 4.12, 5.7.5, 8.6, 8.8, 372n16, 384n156, 397n312
teacher(s), xi, xxix–xxx, xxxv, xlvii, liin2, liin6, 1.6, 3.2, 4.24, 4.41, 5.2.7, 5.2.8, 5.2.9
thaqālah, xx
al-Thawrī, Sufyān, 4.33
Thousand and One Nights, xviii, liiin21, 387n191, 387n192, 387n194
tobacco, 2.27, 378n74
tradition(s) (prophetic), xiii, xvii–xviii, xxix, xl, 1.5, 3.1, 3.67, 4.19, 4.24, 4.33, 5.6.18, 5.7.8, 7.41, 371n2, 384n160, 386n181, 388n208, 402n412, 407n468, 410n509, 413n574
tripes/*kirshah*/*kurūsh*, 3.18.14, 3.21, 3.43, 8.35
trooper(s), 3.9–11, 3.23, 3.25, 3.36, 3.38, 3.39, 3.41, 3.43, 3.44, 5.9.23, 380n116
Turkish, viii, xxviii, livn23, lvn37, 3.22, 3.25, 3.27, 3.36, 3.37, 3.39, 6.5, 376n51, 379n100, 380n115, 380n116, 386n188, 403n415, 406n450
Turks, 5.9.11, 6.4.2, 403n414, 403n415

ʿulamāʾ. *See* ʿālim
ʿUmar ibn al-Khaṭṭāb, xvii, 2.13
umm al-khulūl. *See* mussels
Umm Mujbir, 2.24, 377n66
The Unblown Rose, 4.38.1, 387n192
Upper Egypt/the Ṣaʿīd, xxii, xxvi, xxxii, 4.36, 5.2.1, 5.9.26, 376n58
urjūzah, viii, xxxii, 5.9.2, 8.1–45
ūsyah. *See* demesne

village(s), xi, xiii, xviii, xxvi–xxvii, xxviii, xxix, xxx, xl, lvn31, lvn37, lvin45, 2.3, 2.6, 2.8, 2.23, 2.25, 2.26.2, 3.7, 3.9, 3.10, 3.20, 3.22, 3.23, 3.24, 3.28, 3.29, 3.30, 3.31, 3.41, 3.57, 3.59, 3.60, 4.3, 4.10, 4.19, 4.20, 4.22, 4.24, 4.31, 4.33, 4.34, 4.35, 4.37.1, 4.37.5, 4.39, 5.2.5, 5.2.8, 5.2.18, 5.3.10, 5.6.2, 5.6.8, 5.8.10, 5.8.12, 6.8, 7.8, 7.16, 7.17, 7.19, 7.31, 7.33, 7.41, 8.8, 8.13, 8.14, 8.41, 8.43, 8.44, 372n12, 372n16, 372n17, 378n84, 378n85, 379n95, 380n106, 400n370, 412n546
villager(s), xxvii, 3.41, 4.3, 4.11, 4.13, 4.15, 4.22, 4.33, 4.34, 4.37.6
vizier, xxxv, livn24, 2.6, 4.5–7

Wādī al-Tīh, 5.7.20
Wafā, ʿAlī, 7.12, 406n452
Wajbah, xl–xli
walī. *See* Friend(s) of God
wazīr. *See* vizier
weaver(s), weaving, xii, xiv, liin5, 5.9.26, 7.8,
wedding(s), vii, xix, 2.5, 2.23–2.27, 3.29, 3.30, 5.3.6, 8.35, 377n64, 377n67, 384n150
wisiyya. *See* demesne
woman/women, vii, xiii, xix, xxviii–xxix, xxxi, xxxii, xxxiv, xxxiv, lvn30, 1.1, 2.1, 2.17, 2.22, 2.24, 3.4, 3.10, 3.18, 3.22, 3.23, 3.24, 3.34, 3.35, 3.36, 3.38, 3.39, 3.43,

woman/women (cont.), 3.74, 3.75, 5.2.6, 5.2.7, 5.2.10, 5.2.11, 5.2.14, 5.2.18, 5.2.20, 5.3.3, 5.3.7, 5.3.12, 5.3.17, 5.4, 5.4.7, 5.4.8, 5.4.9, 5.6.2, 5.6.5, 5.6.6, 5.6.7, 5.6.10, 5.7.19, 5.8.2, 5.8.21, 5.9.2, 6.1.2, 6.6, 6.7.5, 7.1, 7.2, 7.5, 7.6, 7.7, 7.11, 7.22, 7.31, 7.41, 8.3, 8.11, 8.35, 8.36, 8.39, 8.42, 373n19, 376n58, 377n61, 377n64, 378n80, 381n119, 383n138, 383n143, 387n198, 401n397, 403n425, 404n432, 405n439, 410n502, 412n546

zaghālīl. *See* squabs

Zaydān, Jurji, xxv, lvn36

Zinjiyyah, 5.5.1

al-Zubad, 410n499

Zubaydah, 6.1

About the NYU Abu Dhabi Institute

The Library of Arabic Literature is supported by a grant from the NYU Abu Dhabi Institute, a major hub of intellectual and creative activity and advanced research. The Institute hosts academic conferences, workshops, lectures, film series, performances, and other public programs directed both to audiences within the UAE and to the worldwide academic and research community. It is a center of the scholarly community for Abu Dhabi, bringing together faculty and researchers from institutions of higher learning throughout the region.

NYU Abu Dhabi, through the NYU Abu Dhabi Institute, is a world-class center of cutting-edge research, scholarship, and cultural activity. The Institute creates singular opportunities for leading researchers from across the arts, humanities, social sciences, sciences, engineering, and the professions to carry out creative scholarship and conduct research on issues of major disciplinary, multidisciplinary, and global significance.

About the Typefaces

The Arabic body text is set in DecoType Naskh, designed by Thomas Milo and Mirjam Somers, based on an analysis of five centuries of Ottoman manuscript practice. The exceptionally legible result is the first and only typeface in a style that fully implements the principles of script grammar (*qawāʿid al-khaṭṭ*).

The Arabic footnote text is set in DecoType Emiri, drawn by Mirjam Somers, based on the metal typeface in the naskh style that was cut for the 1924 Cairo edition of the Qur'an.

Both Arabic typefaces in this series are controlled by a dedicated font layout engine. ACE, the Arabic Calligraphic Engine, invented by Peter Somers, Thomas Milo, and Mirjam Somers of DecoType, first operational in 1985, pioneered the principle followed by later smart font layout technologies such as OpenType, which is used for all other typefaces in this series.

The Arabic text was set with WinSoft Tasmeem, a sophisticated user interface for DecoType ACE inside Adobe InDesign. Tasmeem was conceived and created by Thomas Milo (DecoType) and Pascal Rubini (WinSoft) in 2005.

The English text is set in Adobe Text, a new and versatile text typeface family designed by Robert Slimbach for Western (Latin, Greek, Cyrillic) typesetting. Its workhorse qualities make it perfect for a wide variety of applications, especially for longer passages of text where legibility and economy are important. Adobe Text bridges the gap between calligraphic Renaissance types of the 15th and 16th centuries and high-contrast Modern styles of the 18th century, taking many of its design cues from early post-Renaissance Baroque transitional types cut by designers such as Christoffel van Dijck, Nicolaus Kis, and William Caslon. While grounded in classical form, Adobe Text is also a statement of contemporary utilitarian design, well suited to a wide variety of print and on-screen applications.

Titles Published by the Library of Arabic Literature

Classical Arabic Literature
Selected and translated by Geert Jan Van Gelder

A Treasury of Virtues, by al-Qāḍī al-Quḍāʿī
Edited and translated by Tahera Qutbuddin

The Epistle on Legal Theory, by al-Shāfiʿī
Edited and translated by Joseph E. Lowry

Leg Over Leg, by Aḥmad Fāris al-Shidyāq
Edited and translated by Humphrey Davies

Virtues of the Imām Aḥmad ibn Ḥanbal, by Ibn al-Jawzī
Edited and translated by Michael Cooperson

The Epistle of Forgiveness, by Abū l-ʿAlāʾ al-Maʿarrī
Edited and translated by Geert Jan Van Gelder and Gregor Schoeler

The Principles of Sufism, by ʿĀʾishah al-Bāʿūnīyah
Edited and translated by Th. Emil Homerin

The Expeditions, by Maʿmar ibn Rāshid
Edited and translated by Sean W. Anthony

Two Arabic Travel Books

> **Accounts of China and India**, by Abū Zayd al-Sīrāfī
> Edited and translated by Tim Mackintosh-Smith
> **Mission to the Volga**, by Ahmad Ibn Faḍlān
> Edited and translated by James Montgomery

Disagreements of the Jurists, by al-Qāḍī al-Nuʿmān